Praise for
How to Rule the World: Lessons in Conquest for the Modern Prince

"Periodically there comes along a book that captures the complete sentiment of its age. In many ways J.F. Cummings has written such a book with *How to Rule the World: Lessons in Conquest for the Modern Prince*. There has rarely been a book in this age that deals so thoroughly with a critique of domination in the precise terms... Indeed, Cummings proposes in this monumental work to cover every thing from cultural icons to medicine in an effort to uncover the central guiding ideology of conquest. The author has given us new terminology to explain the phenomenon of domination, like 'sustainable exploitation,' and 're-newed subject.'

This book gives the modern prince, those who seek domination, advice about how to use the language of free trade, democracy, human rights, and the rule of law, to control other nations. Indeed, it is possible that the modern prince will have the ability, according to the advice given, to make the dominated believe that their domination is for their own good... *How to Rule the World* will cause all of us to readjust our thinking about the shape and scope of cultural, economic, and psychological domination in the contemporary world. I applaud the author of this brilliant work. This is an outstanding book that I will delightfully recommend to my colleagues and my hundreds of students. The author has satisfied the purposes of the book, met all objectives, and given us a book that is easy to read and follow. "

Molefi Kete Asante, Ph.D.
Editor, Journal of Black Studies
Professor, Department of African Studies
Temple University, Philadelphia, Pennsylvania

In this extraordinary book, Cummings has utilized satire to provide the reader opportunity to participate in a review of the complex problems extant in our times. He has utilized the knowledge bases of the world, has included scholars from many academic fields, and has presented definitions with a remarkable clarity. His decision to involve the reader in a critical thinking, participatory manner, is pedagogy at its best. His candor as the advisor to the Prince includes factual information needed to complete the tasks of ruling the world-or the decision to live well in it. Every adult should read this book to understand and teach the lessons of modern living.

Anita P. DeFrantz, Ph.D.
Emeritus Professor of Education
University of San Francisco, San Francisco, California

"This is a meticulously written thesis. The principal aim of the author in this thesis is to raise awareness in the reader to the fact that the rules of engagement in almost every sphere of life, as dictated by the so-called free world of capitalism and dominance or even establishment of thought and institutions under these episteme, are flawed... ... The author introduces a number of principal premises for his explanation of the Prince and his governed and self-transformed nation-states as the child-like behavior without cumulative maturity. Among these principal premises is the author's arguments centering on Cultural Dissonance. By using Cultural Dissonance the Prince causes Cultural Warfare and isolationism of the otherwise true relational self with the Other. Individualism in this cultural dissonance construct of the Prince then becomes the other groundwork of the author's argument upon which he establishes a social disintegration theory of corruption, governance and subjugation of the Prince's world-system over which he governs with cunning and might."

Masudul Alam Choudhury, Ph.D.
International Chair of the Postgraduate Program in Islamic Economics and Finance
Trisakti University Jakarta, Indonesia.
Professor of Economics in the Department of Economics and Finance,
College of Commerce and Economics, Sultan Qaboos University, Muscat,
Sultanate of Oman

"Writing in the style of Machiavelli's The Prince, J.F. Cummings employs the satire of Swift. In the style of a skilled carpenter, he hits the nails of political satire directly on the head, driving them home. In Book I, "The Art of Cultural Warfare," he explicates the forms of theory and practice required to dominate others through political culture. In Book II, "The Mind of the Conqueror," Cummings applies his wit and satire to expose the shortcomings of domination, and the threat it poses for the future of humanity. In Book III, "The Consequences of Conquest," Cummings explicates the destructive results that will and do arise from employing the tactics of the modern prince. Like Swift, Cummings is an optimist. He does hope for a better future. His work is designed to stimulate the reader's thinking so that the reader will be empowered to create a world quite different from the one that the modern prince has in store for us. I recommend the book to the intelligent reader."

James Sellmann, Ph.D.
Associate Dean of the College of Arts and Sciences
Professor of Philosophy
University of Guam
Mangilao, Guam

How to Rule the World
Lessons in Conquest for the Modern Prince

J.F. Cummings

blue ocean press

tokyo

Published by:

blue ocean press, an Imprint of Aoishima Research Institute (ARI)
#807-36 Lions Plaza Ebisu
3-25-3 Higashi, Shibuya-ku
Tokyo, Japan 150-0011

mail@aoishima-research.com
URL: http://www.blueoceanpublishing.com
         http://www.aoishima-research.com

ISBN: 978-4-902837-00-5

Credits

To the Presidents of the Powerful Countries of the World,

The Captains of Industry,

The Presidents of Finance and Commerce, and

The Custodians of the Natural Resources of the World

The Princes of the Modern World

TABLE OF CONTENTS

III. The Dangers of Using Culture As a Weapon

IV. The Interdependence of Humanity: How the Continued Use of Cultural Warfare Will Lead to the End of "Civilization"

BOOK 3 – The Unintended Consequences of Conquest

I. Your Subject's Nation-State

A Letter to the Prince

Niccolo Machiavelli To The Magnificent Lorenzo dé Medici

Those who wish to win favor with a prince customarily offer him those things which they hold most precious or which they see him most delight in. Very often, therefore, we see princes presented with horses, weapons, cloth of gold, precious gems, or similar ornaments worthy of their greatness. Wishing then, to present myself to Your Highness with some mark of my duty to you, I have been unable to find anything I possess that I hold so dear or esteem so highly as my knowledge of the actions of great men, learned from long experience in modern affairs and from constant reading of ancient ones. Having long examined and reflected upon these matters with great diligence and having now set them down in a small volume, I send it to Your Highness...

The Prince (1513)

My Dear Prince[1],

    I offer You a means of warfare by which You can destroy and exploit nation-states of the world for perpetuity. In this You will attack the very center, its cultural integrity, and replace it with Your own. Because I am Your advisor, I do wish to first provide a disclaimer for this course of action. I do not wish to think of You as weak and undesirous of Empire, but because external campaigns place one at risk, I will offer an alternative in case You decide that You do not wish to take this expansionary approach. I will offer You two roads that You can take: 1. the internal; and 2. the external.

    The methodology of conquest that I offer instructs You on how to attack the very center of a nation-state, its cultural center, how to displace and substitute it with that of Your own, and how to redefine the mandate of government that rules it so that You have a government at Your disposal that is sympathetic and compliant with Your wishes.

The Two Roads

* That concerning the internal road of development begins after this
  letter is the Way of Interconnectedness and Harmony.

* That concerning the external road of conquest follows the Way of
  Interconnectedness and Harmony; it is the Way of Separation and
  Control.

---

[1] The terms "Prince" and "subject" refer to the leaders of modern-nation states. "Prince" refers to You and to Other leaders of nation-states that possess great influence over global modes of resource production, thus having the power to create a universal definition of "modernity" and "civilization". When You are reading these notes on conquest, place Yourself into the perspective of both, so that You can truly understand the power dynamics between "Princes" and "subjects". This will provide You with the ability to hypothesize the actions of Your subject when You attack it.

These roads are essentially two value systems: one is for long-term sustainability; the other is degenerative and will slowly eat through the bonds that hold a society together.

In revealing them I offer You two choices: 1. to not proceed beyond the Way of Interconnectedness and Harmony, concentrating on developing the unique talents of Your nation-state while leaving Yourself vulnerable to the attack of another Prince who is worthy of my advice, if You do not have the proper protections in place; or 2. to continue beyond the Way of Interconnectedness and Harmony becoming enlightened of an effective means to manipulate, weaken, and exploit nation-states. Again, this is not for a weak Prince of faint heart. This is a zero-sum game: win or lose. If You choose the second road and do not follow my exact instructions, these means of manipulation can possess You as well and lead to Your own certain demise.

The Way of Interconnectedness and Harmony

The Way of Trust and Vulnerability

This Way concentrates on developing Your own nation-state's potential while also being in balance with the natural environment, Your neighbors, utilizing and trading in Your own resources, and waging war only when You truly are made to betray Yourself or are disallowed from actualizing Your national potential within Your own boundaries.

Three Statements Representing the Internal Road

I. Constitution of the Federated States of Micronesia
Preamble

WE, the people of Micronesia, exercising our inherent sovereignty, do hereby establish the Constitution of the Federated States of Micronesia.

With this Constitution, we affirm our common wish to live together in peace and harmony, to preserve the heritage of the past, and to protect the promise of the future.

To make one nation of many islands, we respect the diversity of our cultures. Our differences enrich us. The seas bring us together, they do not separate us. Our islands sustain us, our island nation enlarges us and makes us stronger.

Our ancestors, who made their homes on these islands, displaced no other people. We, who remain, wish no other home than this. Having known war, we hope for peace. Having been divided, we wish unity. Having been ruled, we seek freedom.

Micronesia began in the days when man explored seas in rafts and canoes. The Micronesian nation is born in an age when men voyage among stars; our world itself is an island. We extend to all nations what we seek from each: peace, friendship, cooperation and love in our common humanity. With this Constitution we, who have been the wards of other nations, become the proud guardian of our own islands, now and forever.

II. From George Washington's Farewell Address[2]

"It is our true policy to steer clear of permanent alliances with any portion of the foreign world, so far, I mean, as we are now at liberty to do it; for let me not be understood as capable of patronizing infidelity to existing engagements. I hold the maxim no less applicable to public than to private affairs that honesty is always the best policy. I repeat, therefore, let those engagements be observed in their genuine sense. But in my opinion it is unnecessary and would be unwise to extend them.

Taking care always to keep ourselves by suitable establishments on a respectable defensive posture, we may safely trust to temporary alliances for extraordinary emergencies."

III. John Q. Adams[3]

"The true American goes not abroad in search of monsters to destroy . . . [America] well knows that by once enlisting under other banners than her own, were they even the banners of foreign independence, she would involve herself, beyond the power of extrication, in all the wars of interest and intrigue, of individual avarice, envy, and ambition. She might become the dictatress of the world; she would no longer be the ruler of her own spirit."

July 4, 1821

---

[2] (President) George Washington's Farewell Address," in *Documents of American History*, Henry Steele Commanger. Appleton-Century-Crofts, Inc.1958.

[3] (President) "John Quincy Adams. July 4,1821" in William Appleman Williams, *The Contours of American History*. New York: World Publishing Co. 1961.

The Way of Separation and Control
The Way of Strength and Progress

What lies in these pages are the tools to destroy a society through means of cultural warfare. This form of warfare attacks at the very core of a society, the cultural center of its people.

Three Statements Representing the External Road

I. A Prince's Concern on Military Matters

"A Prince must have no other objective, no other thought, nor take up any profession but that of war, its methods and its discipline, for that is the only art expected of a ruler. And it is of such value that it not only keeps hereditary princes in power, but often raises men of lowly condition to that rank. It may be noted, on the other hand, that when princes have given more thought to fine living than to arms, they have lost their states. The first cause of losing them is the neglect of this art, just as the first means of gaining them is proficiency in it..."[4]

II. Charles Darwin

"Living things develop through conflict and races rise to preeminence through war."[5]

---

[4] The Prince, p.53

[5] Darwin, Charles. (1859). *Origin of Species by Means of Natural Selection, or The Preservation of Favoured Races in the Struggle for Life.*

III. William McKinley (1898)[6]

"I walked the floor of the White House night after night until midnight; and I am not ashamed to tell you, gentlemen, that I went down on my knees and prayed to Almighty God for light and guidance more than one night. And one night late it came to me this way--I don't know how it was but it came; first, that we could not give [the Philippines] back to Spain that would be cowardly and dishonorable; second, that we could not turn them over to France or Germany--our commercial rivals in the Orient--that would be bad business and discreditable; third, that we could not leave them to themselves--they were unfit for self-government, and they would soon have anarchy and misrule over there worse than Spain's was; and forth, that there was nothing left for us to do but to take them all, and to educate the Filipinos, and uplift and civilize and Christianize them, as our fellow-men for whom Christ also died And then I went to bed, and went to sleep and slept soundly."

[6.] President William McKinley's explanation in 1899, quoted in Leon Wolff, *Little Brown Brother.* Doubleday and Company. Inc., Garden City, New York. 1961, from his speech in Boston, February 16, 1899. *Boston Herald*, February 17, 1899 pp.2-3

If You choose to read on be deliberate in Your decision, but as a warrior You should accept that Your own death may be the consequence of Your actions so that You are not influenced by fear, empathy or compassion. Thoughts of mortality can cause You to be weak and to empathize with Your subject---You should be deliberate in Your actions of conquest but You must also be aware of the causal reality of Nature, so that You do not take any of Your actions for granted and forget that they are deliberate acts that will result in some corresponding action. This methodology is deeply entrenched in the causal reality of Nature, anyone who disrupts the harmony of Nature must be able to take responsible action or be eliminated by the forces of balance. Your goal is to rationalize as many aspects of the subject's society as possible. Note: abstracted ideas require a point of reference and a point of departure, and that is You.

When using this methodology, You should beware of being intoxicated by feelings of superiority or acceptance caused by their consumption of Your ideals and cultural icons. These are the tools of warfare; if a subject began to praise or covet Your military strength, would You lose sight of it as a target? Of course not. When the subject celebrates the Great Modern You, the Evolved Man, take heed: lavishing in the lights of imitation leads to an arrogance that will blind You to the fact that there is a delicate balance which You must keep to win; You must not allow the utterance and reaction of the subject to confuse You.

The key to conquest through cultural means of warfare, my Prince, is to equate Yourself all that is "Modern and Civilized", using a culture of rationalism to perform this task. You must however, remain aware of the importance of balance in this approach, as this can also be the key to Your destruction. For if You define Yourself as Modern, the Other will see problems in Your nation-state as the inevitable problems of Modernity and take one of two approaches: 1. allow itself to slip into a cycle of social, economic, and environmental collapse that will result from the dislocative and destabilizing nature of Your influence over its society, or 2. have sub-national resistance and fundamentalism grow out of the instability and use any means necessary to eliminate Your influence from its society, or possibly even view Your very ideological presence in the world as a danger to humanity. If You can position Yourself as Prince and as subject, You shall gain insight into the advice that I am affording You.

A Prince must be well aware that there is a difference between the Age of Imperialism, the past, a scramble for resources, and the age of today. The Age of today--Cultural Imperialism through Universal Humanism--is very different due to the creation of mass-media, rapid transportation of goods, and sustained dependency on the exploiting nation-state. Order is domestically maintained by creating a society of consumers with a newfound, continual *need* to have more. The Danger: Consumers (unsustainable consumption), mass media (promotion of pop-culture), and weapons of destructive force (subject states and their internal non-states can now export causes and strike out against enemies that would have been too powerful to fight in the past).

For the success of Your own nation-state, You must, at all costs avoid any behavior You are projecting that may threaten the integrity of Your own state. You must be true to the creed of Your nation. Whether conqueror, artisan, or trader, You cannot deviate from attaining Your true potential: do not allow any difference between the true desire of Your society and the projection of Your ideals. If You perform behavior divergent from Your stated cultural mores and goals, it will eventually come back to You. Take as a warning an illustration of this point by an Antillean thinker of the 1950s:

> And then one fine day the bourgeoisie is awakened by a terrific boomerang effect: the gestapos are busy, the prisons fill up, the torturers standing around the racks invent, refine, discuss. First we must study how colonization works to *decivilize* the colonizer, to *brutalize* him in the true sense of the word, to degrade him, to awaken him to buried instincts, to covetousness, violence, race hatred, and moral relativism; and we must show that each time a head is cut off or an eye put out in Vietnam and in France they accept the fact, each time a little girl is raped and in France they accept the fact, each time a Madagascan is tortured and in France they accept the fact, civilization acquires another dead weight, a universal regression takes place, a gangrene sets in, a center of infection begins to spread; and that at the end of all these treaties that have been violated, all these lies that have been propagated, all these punitive expeditions that have been tolerated, all of these prisoners who have been tied up and 'interrogated,' all these patriots who have been tortured, at the end of all the racial pride that has been encouraged, all the boastfulness that has been displayed, a poison has been distilled into the veins of Europe and, slowly but surely, the continent proceeds toward *savagery*.

> People are surprised, they become indignant. They say 'How strange! But never mind--it's Nazism, it will pass!' And they wait, and they hope; and they hide the truth from themselves, that it is barbarism, the supreme barbarism, the crowning barbarism that sums up all the daily barbarisms, that is Nazism, yes, but that before they were its victims, they were its accomplices; that they were tolerated that Nazism before it was inflicted on them, that they absolved it, shut their eyes to it, legitimized it, because until then, it had only been applied to non-European peoples; that they have cultivated that Nazism, that they are responsible for it, and that before engulfing the whole edifice of

Western, Christian civilization in its reddening waters, it oozes, seeps, and trickles from every crack...[7]

This is only for the Prince who is fearless, strong, intelligent, and introspective. If You are not, I suggest that You enjoy Your prosperity while You can; with the knowledge that another Prince has taken My Blessing and that You will eventually be in sight for His conquest.

Use these strategies only if You are decidedly combative and are willing to endure collateral damage at home due to the relationship that will develop between You and the subject. If You choose the path of a warrior be one, and conquer and rule in Your name; but accept the code of the warrior: "...the Way of the Warrior is resolute acceptance of death."[8] Accepting death eliminates fear and provides You with the fortitude necessary for a successful campaign against Your subject states.

[7] Cesare, Aimee (translated by Joan Pinkham). (2000) *Discourse on Colonization*. New York: New York University Press. pp. 35-6
[8] Miyamoto Musashi.

The Beginning of Conquest

You have made a wise choice. You have decided to take the external course of action. You will be projecting a value system onto a subject nation-state that will erode its solvency. In the following sections I will outline for You the means to destroy using a Culture of Rationalism in governance, and the promotion of a linear thought process. Through this methodology of psycho-cultural warfare You will both individualize and commodify its population, economy, and natural environment. You will in effect destroy the cultural glue that holds its society together. After which, You may do with it what You please.

Book I: an explanation on the Theory of Cultural Warfare followed by a number of examples of the application onto a system of governance.
Book II: the intellectual basis behind the Culture of Rationalism to be projected. In this book is a necessary process of introspection for You to examine those who engage in this type of warfare, as to not become a casualty of Your own conquest.
Book III, some possible negative outcomes of an unsuccessful or irresponsible application of this methodology, and its effect on the long-term viability of Your subject state with Your own nation-state and with the world as a whole.

If You perform this task in the manner that I direct You, paying notice to the precautions that I have also noted, Your influence will last for many generations. The colonial activities of the last 500 years, in particular those since the second half of the 19th century, have shaped the world's thoughts in a way that the present international hierarchy seems to have always been in place and appears to be the natural order of humanity. If You displace the cultural center of Your subject and replace it with Yours it will have no past of its own, only the present and future of You defining its reality. If You can do this effectively, You can place yourself into its remembered residual history and make Yourself an integral part of its ancient civilization; or better yet, replace the historical truth of ancestry with that of a reinvested history resembling You or Your forefathers as the founders of its ancient societies and civilizations. In the past, people thought of age in terms of millennia; You have the power to reshape this.

We now begin our lesson.

Book I
The Art of
Cultural Warfare

Chapter 1:
The Theory

As a means of understanding the process by which nation-states become self-sabotaging and act against the interest of the populations that make them up, I have devised a theory of Cultural Warfare which borrows from Leon Festinger's *A Theory of Cognitive Dissonance*, and from Abraham Maslow's "Humanistic Theory", or "Hierarchy of Needs", to describe the process and its effect on the collective psyche of the nation-state.

The list of applications through which this theory is applied of course, is not complete. The point is to show You the necessity of replacing a consensus value system of "interconnectedness" with others and the environment with Your projected value system of Separation and Control. The user should be able to deduce other applications that are based on this system.

When a foreign culture is introduced, virtually overnight, into a country there is the inevitable danger that the social, cultural, and spiritual unity of that country will be undermined. The more thoughtful and best informed among the leaders of the late Tokugawa period sought to allay this danger by the adoption of various formulas such as 'Eastern moral and Western art' and 'Japanese spirit and Occidental learning.' However, once Japan plunged into the task of modernization such formulas were found to be ineffective, for the simple reason that a civilization or culture is an indivisible whole. It is not possible to embrace only the scientific or technical aspects of it and exclude the rest.[7]

[7] Yoshida, Shigeru. (1967) *Japan's Decisive Century 1867-1967*. New York: Frederic A. Praeger, p. 23

The Objective.

The objective of Cultural Warfare is to create instability by displacing Your subject nation-state's center, its nucleus. Three levels of displacement can be performed simultaneously:

1. Individual : sense of self, sense of purpose, self validatiion
    Replace with a need for external validation and approval

2. Collective Cultural Consciousness : cultural center, point of reference
    Replace with foreign cultural center as point of reference

3. Nation-State's *raison d'etre* : a. to provide for the human security needs of the population
    Weaken the mandate, dissolve the sovereignty of the nation state by using apparatus such as universal rule of law, free trade, individualism, private health care, free press & mass media, aesthetic values, and technology

    b. to perpetuate culture as a binding force for the nation
    Utilize the nation-state's cultural broadcast apparatus to promote Your ideals and cultural icons

Decimating the cultural center of the subject is Your goal; only then can You inflict the prerequisite of psychological discomfort necessary for the successful projection of Your ideals and cultural icons.

NOTE: most newly-independent nations are open for attack because they are "Modern" nation-states, an abstract construction of national boundaries and political systems created to better serve the needs of former colonial masters; these boundaries and political systems are not based on the nation's actual consensus, traditional laws, or cultural mandate of governance.

An individual person's center is 'purpose', life purpose. Within Your subject's nation-state Your goal is to align (redefine) the purposes of the individuals that make up the population with Yours--their point of reference and point of departure should come from You. A person's point of reference and point of departure is based on their connectivity to their culture. The cues of life come from this 'center'; it defines what is 'of the culture' and what is not; what is divergent from the traditional mores and behaviors of members of the society and what is not.

The center of a nation-state is its national purpose, its cultural expression of life. This center is the nation-state's point of reference and departure. Point of Reference determines whether certain behaviors, products, or values are in congruence with the needs and desires of the nation-state and community of people. If the cultural point of reference is well-defined it will be difficult to attack because incongruent values, behaviors, material items, cultural artifacts, will be denied entry into the whole; but if the target is destabilized through Cultural Cognitive Dissonance (CCD), it will be vulnerable to incongruent influences.

AGE :
promote irreverence for elders and the unimportance of tradition.

SEX :
re-establish gender roles in ways that actually limit life choices and disempower.

SKIN COLOR :
quantify human value based on skin hue.

STATUS :
define the poverty of a person based on quantitative consumer value.

COMMUNAL OWNERSHIP :
promote Individualistic Materialism by outlawing collective ownership.

EDUCATION :
individualize and rationalize values in character and career education,
disconnect academia from its host society.

INDIVIDUALISM :
re-assess the value of people in quantified monetary terms;
base worth on the ability to consume.

COMMUNAL RESPONSIBILITY :
promote the 'right' of the Individual and 'free choice' at the expense
of community responsibility.

SOCIETAL TABOOS & MORALITY :
promote the 'rule of law' over culture-based morality, foster perpetual childhood
through legal moralism; nullify the validity of nature and tradition.

BUSINESS :
promote a culture of 'contract' over a culture of trust.

HEALTH :
promote individualized medical care at the expense of public health.

SPIRITUALITY :
replace spirituality with a religion based on Rationalism and Universalism,
with You as the locus of control and source of inspiration for all religious imagery.

AESTHETICS :
dis-empower, de-politicize, and de-culturalize art by making it 'abstract', 'universal'
and 'elite' so that it no longer serves a constructive role in society, relegate indigenous
art to the level of 'handicrafts'.

BEAUTY IMAGE :
encourage body modification to fit extra-cultural ideals of Your projection of
beauty, lower cultural esteem by invalidating indigenous beauty.

SCIENCE & TECHNOLOGY :
justify 'Progress at Any Cost', de-value anecdotal evidence and the wisdom
of an ancestral inheritance.

HUMAN RIGHTS :
protect the right of the Individual while neglecting, and thereby not acknowledging
collective rights and ownership.

On the Application of Cultural Warfare, I have outlined ways in which this methodology of influence and control can be used. I have provided You with thoughts on the application in each of the following: education, individualism, individualistic materialism, free trade, rule of law and democratic governance, science and technology, aesthetics (art forms and beauty image), family, mass media and cultural icons, public health, time and machines, community responsibility, and human rights.[8] With these and other applications of a separationist value system, You will be able to prompt insanity in the subject populace and keep it at a constant state of imbalance.

When You project the dissociative ideology of Rationalism with You as representative of the "Universal Truth" and of "Modern Humanity", the subject will be forced into a state of psychological discomfort. This is because cultural stability which is the subject populace's natural state of calm, was based on an agreed consensus of its validity. Your dissociative projections cause the subject to doubt the significance of its reality, its ideals, its humanity. In this state it is in need of something to relieve this psychological conflict.

Your concurrent projection of SACs (Seemingly Associative Cognitions) acts as a psychotropic panacea: it is delivered to suppress the psychic discomfort of previous cognitions. These projections allow the subject, through embracing Your ideals and assimilation into what it believes is Your way of life, to feel validated as a member of humanity and as an active participant in Modernity. Nothing can truly replace the cultural center of a people but You can keep it so unbalanced that, instead of attempting to alleviate the discomfort of incongruence with Your reality through a re-assertion of itself, it embraces Your center of ideals in an attempt to validate itself in Your eyes and on Your terms.

TOOLS :
Cultural Cognitive Dissonance (CCD), the projection of "civilized"
& "progressive" ideals and cultural icons.
BENEFITS :
Codependent Relationship; the transmittal of Your Seemingly Associative
Cognitions (SACs) for the subject to alleviate feelings of psychological discomfort.
DANGERS :
Involuntary Codependent Relationship; the breakdown of an objective predatory
relationship between You and the subject due to CCD-induced insecurities.

---

[8] Environmentalism can also be included in this list, but it is not in Your interest to prevent the subject from utilizing its resources in the name of "conservation", especially if You or Your predecessors' misuse of the environment and its resources are the reason that they are in scarcity today. If the environment is off-limits to Your subject, it becomes off-limits to You. Making special provisions for You to exploit its environment will be hard for the subject nation-state's government to justify without considerable civil unrest. That is unless You have so successfully projected Yourself as the responsible custodian of Your subject's environment that the people trust You to manage 'it' (the environment) responsibly.

34

Cultural center exists in both the concrete and intuitive worlds of a people; it is the glue that binds a people of a particular culture together through a shared consciousness of the concrete world as well as a connection to the underlying transition of realities and a junction between the concrete and intuitive: a collective conscious, a collective sub-conscious, and a collective unconscious. These are the expressed traits, acknowledged thoughts and unexpressed but centering truth of a people.

The expressed center and acknowledged thought, the conscious and sub-conscious mind, are Your points to target. You cannot disturb the sanctity of the unconscious mind, but You can cause enough confusion at its sub-conscious level so that the subject does not acknowledge what it knows to be true in its unconscious mind. This conflict caused through irreconcilable differences, through non-agreement between the subject's actions, thoughts, and unconscious truth, will bring about a severe psychological distress to which You can placate the sub-conscious mind with Your projections of Seemingly Associative Cognitions (SACs), providing the subject with a temporary and artificial relief from the dissonance that You have caused in its psyche.

Cultural Center as a paradigm refers the point of reference and point of departure that a people rely on to determine the suitability of actions, thoughts, and expressions towards the collective ideal. Through this persons are able to regulate interpersonal as well as inter/extra group relations. To a member of society, the point of reference and departure lends itself to questions such as "Who am I?" and "How does this (particular behavior, thought, or expression) relate to a truthful, harmonious representation of who I am as an individual and as a member of my community?"; "Will this (behavior, thought, or expression) support my community or will it take away from it?"; "Will this sustain my society in a way that is desirable or will it transform it into one that we cannot recognize and manifest an undesirable way of life?" In terms of governance, the most important questions are "Who are we?";"How do we wish to live now, and in the future?"; "How might the implementation of these policies affect the viability and sustainability of our culture?"; "Will this particular influence sustain our society and bring about a harmonious way of life for our people, or will it create dissension and additional hardships amongst us?"; "Will this change fit our collective truths and vision of life?", "Will this particular influence make us a happier people or will it only create artificial needs where before there were none?"

Cultural center defines what is desirable to a society, what is acceptable and what is not. It is a point of reference that works to shape personalities within the group, guiding decision-making and policy formulation of the governing bodies as well. In individuals it internalizes as a sense of right or wrong as an acknowledged feeling of interconnectedness and a desire to contribute to the greater good of society. A person's status within the society, as well as the society's government performance, is evaluated according to standards defined by the center.

Using this methodology of warfare You will be able to disconnect the cultural center and replace it with Yours. Once You have done this, the subject will evaluate its behaviors, thoughts and expressions with You as the point of reference and departure. As long as You are careful not to let the subject's nation-state deteriorate too greatly it will continue to embrace Your projected Center as its own and You will be able to exploit its society, economy, and environment as You so desire.

Cultural Cognitive Dissonance

Cultural Cognitive Dissonance (CCD) is an application of the Theory of Cognitive Dissonance[9], devised in the 1950s by the Stanford researcher Dr. Leon Festinger. Dr. Festinger's field of research was behavioral psychology in the areas of communication and social influence. This theory has been an important contribution to cognitive theory, and is applicable to the processes of Cultural Warfare that are outlined in this book.

According to the theory the quintessence of persuasion is to introduce information into the mind of a subject that, although it is inconsistent with existing attitudes and behaviors becomes difficult to exclude. A person can at least to some extent disregard contradictory ideas, but when faced with dissonant thoughts of ideas about the self in relation to one's actual actions and behaviors, psychological discomfort arises. This self-realization of the contradiction, of how one perceives the self in opposition to one's real actions, and the psychological conflict and discomfort that results, is cognitive dissonance; it is an externally induced psychological conflict of self-perception versus self-reality.

The key to using cognitive dissonance as a method of behavior modification is in allowing the subject to believe that it is coming to its own conclusion when in truth, You have created the conflict in the subject's mind and have offered a solution to the psychological discomfort that You have caused. Before contact with You, the subject was fine and in a stable state of mind. When You begin to influence it through Your projections, You cause it to analyze itself in contradiction to what it believes to be true about its self. In the

---

9. Festinger, Leon. (1957) *A Theory of Cognitive Dissonance.* Stanford University Press. Stanford. pp. 2-31

application of CCD, if You are able to make the subject come to the conclusion that there are Universal standards of 'Culture' and 'Modernity' which in truth are Your projections based on Your own cultural reality, it will compare itself to this "default culture[10]" and "realize" that it is inconsistent with it. Once the subject realizes its inconsistence with these "Universals", it will experience tension and conflict. Your projection of SACs offers a solution to this psychological discomfort: if the subject embraces Your ideals, lives Your way of life, and consumes Your cultural icons and other consumer goods it can then be consistent with the "Universals" that You had initially, and now concurrently, projected onto it. As long as You continue to project the dissonance-causing cognitions along with the SACs, You can manipulate the subject to embrace the very ideals that will disintegrate its society and allow You to exploit it.

Abraham Maslow's 'hierarchy of needs' serves as a good model in describing how You are to use Your projections to induce cognitive dissonance and therefore derange the subject's nation-state for exploitation. Your aim is to disrupt the top three levels through the cognitive dissonance induced by Your projections. As long as You contain these disruptions within the top three levels You can manipulate the subject-population to accommodate Your needs. If You are not careful and also disrupt the lower levels, the subject-population will experience a secondary cognitive dissonance; they will realize their "unfortunate state", reject Your projections, and leave Your weakened subject nation-state vulnerable to those cognizant of the social, economic, and environmentally disruptive policies that the government has been implementing to facilitate its exploitation.

At the base of Maslow's hierarchy are physiological needs, which include food, sex, sleep, and exercise. When these needs are reached, safety concerns come next; the need for security, structure and order, dependency, and freedom from fear and anxiety. After psychological and safety needs comes the need to belong; the need for love and affection. Esteem needs follow; feelings of self-respect, achievement, recognition by others, and a positive evaluation of self. The final need is that of self-actualization; of reaching one's personal potential and actualizing one's self. In terms of my theory on Cultural Cognitive Dissonance (CCD), 'self-actualization' acknowledges the fulfillment of one's true potential in contributing to the greater good of the group, community, or society. The ability to be humble amidst great admiration by the group, community, or society should also be

---

[10]. Professor Lynn Higgins in "Dartmouth Professor Brings Cultural Introspection to the Classroom", Vox of Dartmouth, April 7, 2003 by Tamara Steinart.

considered for the level of 'esteem needs'.[11]

The humanistic theory[12] based on a hierarchy of needs is one of motivation that outlines the steps that an individual must take to reach his or her full potential. According to this theory, once the needs of a preceding level have been met an individual can procede to the next level. If the needs below a certain level are not met however, one must re-focus on those preceding needs (if one's physiological needs have already been met, then next of concern are safety needs; if those are met then belonging and love needs are of concern; if those are met esteem needs are met; and if those are met, one can achieve self actualization). Assuming that this theory on the 'hierarchy of needs' reflects the psychological reality of most persons, one danger that You will face in Your projections which You must watch out for is recognizing that these are psychological, not necessarily tangible states.

Because psychology is not an exact science one can never know every variable in an equation. Therefore, in causing dissonance in the psyche of the subject-population through Your projections, You must be careful only to disrupt the top three levels of their needs. "Being careful" also means that You must prevent the peoples of the subject nation-state from perceiving their 'reality' as divergent from an actual satisfaction of those needs. You can have a population in which people have basic food, shelter, sex and exercise needs met, but if it is a materialistic society in which a person's value is quantified by how much is consumed, they may view themselves as being "worthless". This would technically classify as an esteem need not being met, and because the relational value of the person has now been converted to a quantitative monetary value, their belonging needs are also not being met.

If possessing certain non-essential material goods, exceeding biological needs by incorporating non-essential 'basic goods' into what is considered "poor", is projected as necessary in order to be perceived as being "worth" something then a Culture of Poverty is promoted based on a lack of non-essential material goods thus causing in the subject anxiety and a "realization" that its "basic" physiological needs are in lack. In this scenario it may initially seem like You are only affecting the esteem needs of the population. Later however, it will manifest into the "realization" of "poverty",

---

11. A weak point of this process may be utilizing psychology because it is a method, derived from linear thinking, which analyzes human thought processes and pathologies. Self-actualization is described as an individual achievement of self; however, this might not acknowledge the psycho-logical importance of a "higher" level of relational involvement for a culture of interconnectedness; or it might, if one assumes the perspective of people realizing their collective expression of spirituality in their "individual actualization of self".

12. Maslow, Abraham (1970). *Motivation and Personality*. New York: Harper Collins Publishers.

based on the adjustment of human value from the relational to the quantitative. In this realization of poverty, a seemingly secure person will be open to alternatives that You are projecting as ideal.

Applied psychology is a beautiful study on the abstracted science of psychology combined with its root philosophy of Rationalism. It can be a powerful tool for creating psychosis both in the individual and the collective consciousness of the subject's nation-state.

It is impossible to totally free the subject of its center--this is as unlikely as an atom sustaining its form without a nucleus. There would be no binding energy to hold it together. The crux of the application of Cultural Cognitive Dissonance is to dislodge the Other's nucleus and replace it with the icon of Yours; disarming it so that You can complete Your conquest, but not making it unstable to the point that it falls apart (disintegrates) and seeks stability by embracing an icon of a nucleus that resembles its own (prior to contact with You) and attacks You for causing it so much discomfort.

Be the Invisible Enemy.

If You can cause the subject-population to expend brainpower on externalizing efforts--excessively dieting to conform to a particular beauty image or outdoing peers in materialistic expressions--it cannot at the same time have the energy to be productive, and definitely cannot perceive pervasive attacks on its psyche because it is spending its time reacting to the disrupted mental state that You have put it in.

This is how You should attack Your subject's nation-state. Infest and penetrate every aspect of the society with Your projections, but vehemently deny that there is any grandiose plan to exploit or conquer. Use the Theory of Transnational Corporate Governance[13] as Your shield. If it perceives Your agenda, You can always claim that this is the influence of corporate governance based in a global economy, and not the interests of any particular country.[14]

---

[13] A good representation of this theory is that of the one discussed by Leslie Sklair in *Social Movements and Capitalism*. According to Sklair, "Global system theory" is based on the concept of transnational practices that cross state boundaries but do not necessarily originate with state agencies or actors.

[14] Corporations may appear to be individual actors operating in accordance with perpetuating self-interest, but their ability to operate comes from the lack of, or presence of regulations in the nation-states that they operate in.

Chapter 2:
Applications

Cultural Warfare is practiced through the application and promotion of culture-based "Rational" ideals and cultural icons. Rationalism implies Universalism and Humanism; it brands opposition as parochial and small-minded but requires omnipotence to conduct, necessitating also for a loophole to adjust to mistakes under a banner of "Progress". In order to complete the social transformations that Cultural Warfare causes, a universal governing body is required to manage the resulting social and economic dislocation, environmental mismanagement and scramble for resources, either as open fascism (imperialism) or under the guise of Universal Humanism.

The risk is that the effects of Abstract Rationalism on concrete societies are similar to the effects of a cancer-causing virus on the human body. Because Rationalism is a contrived reality that cannot exist on its own, it requires residence in the minds of the people. It is dependent on the cooperation of the host, whether voluntary or not.

The Culture of Individualistic
Materialism & Linear Separation.

The Culture of Individualistic Materialism and Linear Separation that can be associated with the culture-decimating quest towards global sameness and perpetual economic growth is like a cancer-causing virus. Using a societal analogy, a non-oncogenic virus can be said to be 'conquest-oriented': it seeks and attacks, using resources to multiply and empower itself externally as a group (species) of viruses. The Culture of Individualistic Materialism is like a cancer-causing virus; in addition to conquest, it also has a need to convert its victim into a 'copy' of itself--adopting its characteristics in the form of a malignant tumor, that like itself, seeks to consume resources while forgetting that it is part of an interconnected body.

The strength of this cancer-causing virus lies in its linear thought processes. It can charm its victims with its 'superior' ability to "Progress" because of linear thinking. Being a linear thinker, time is not cyclical, therefore it can go from Point A to Point B independent from the causal reality--the ability to act without consequences. Linear thinking allows the user higher potential for power over non-linear thinkers, because in its mind, it is "free" - free to do whatever it likes at any cost to anyone outside of itself; and it is genuinely surprised if it has to experience negative consequences for a past action. On the other hand, the non-linear thinker is "weighted down" with thoughts of how X action will affect others: 'if X action is in line with established cultural mores'; 'if X action is environmentally-friendly'; 'if X action contributes to a sustainable future', 'how X action affects its family, community, society, economy, and environment', etc.

Those "weighted-down" with thoughts of responsibility or obligation to Others cannot compete on the same playing field as linear thinkers unless they betray themselves and also engage in actions without regard to consequences; and upon this step, the non-linear thinker has to deny its self truth/cultural center and can easily be manipulated by the linear thinker.[16]

When a virus (rational ideas and cultural icons) enters a cell (nation) it incorporates its own genetic code (culture-based ideas of society, family, community, economy, law, education, aesthetics) into the cell's nuclear processes (cultural production and governance). The viral DNA/RNA utilizes the cell's nuclear apparatus (internal information distribution apparatus) to provide for its own replication. This process results in a cellular destruction; either from a disruption in reproductive processes and mutation or disruption

---

[16] Bireda, Martha R. Ph.D., Cummings, Jaha F., Pangelinan, Zita D. (2004) *Preserving Cultural Integrity in the Age of Globalization: An Educational Response.* Tokyo: Aoishima Research Institute. pp.7-8

due to over abundance of itself (culturally incongruent ideals). In this excrescence new viruses burst out of the cell, destroying it and now free to infect more cells.

The objective of Culture Warfare is to operate like an immunodeficiency disorder (like AIDS in humans) that leaves the body open to opportunistic infection - Sustainable Exploitation. The cells that are not destroyed in the process of viral replication but whose genetic material is now modified due to the incorporation of viral genes into its DNA may mutate and become malignant. This malignancy can transform into a "rogue state" in a body (world) made of confederacies of similar cell groups that have found a way to live in relative balance with each other. The "new" cell (developed state) is now out of balance with the homeostasis of the body due to its new genetic code (its new individualistic outlook on life) and concerns itself primarily with individual needs, discounting the fact that it is part of a whole. The disproportionate taking of resources and consumption at a gluttonous rate disrupts the balance of trade of resources at the expense of surrounding cells. The growth and metastasis of its cell colony (tumor), and rate of consumption and use of resources eventually diverts so much energy from the natural distribution system (organs) and localized collectives (regional trade), that the body dies.

Chapter 3: Education

The true objective of education is to teach the people to learn how to think and to understand that their responsibility is in contributing to the collective community and nation. Your job is to reorient the education system of the subject to promote the following:

1. External fulfillment over the productive use of gifts and talents, or self-fulfillment;
2. Reverence of Your icons, other material goods and the personalities that embody these;
3. Individualism and Individualistic Materialism;
4. The continual need for outside assistance as a requirement for keeping up with the Developed World;
5. Reverence of outside advice and dependency on technical assistance;
6. Acceptance of Universal solutions to local realities without the cultivated understanding that there is no 'universal' development model;
7. The idea of higher education as a fulfillment of external status needs rather than for self-improvement and contribution to the good of society;
8. Character education that places the highest value of human worth on consumer potential and the least value on self-actualization and constructive contribution to society;
9. Acceptance of the cultural center of an outside nation as the point of reference for development and nation-building;
10. The branding of non-linear thinking as archaic, parochial, and oppositional to Development and Modernization. Adoption of Rational linear thinking as a primary representation of the attainment of an education.

They must not be taught to think critically or they will analyze the compatibility of all foreign ideas and influences with their point of reference. If a particular concept is not in line with the values and ideals of their society, it will be rejected. You cannot allow this type of critical thinking to develop; You are re-orienting their education system to discourage independent thinking and to promote the uncritical acceptance Your projected model of a Developed and Modern Democratic society. This reorientation must solidify Your superior position so that Your directives are not analyzed and questioned.

Sophisticated people value diversity of purpose as the normal state of being and societies that are psychologically well are inclusive, not exclusive. You want to quantify difference based on external factors at the expense of internal cultivation. This is the beauty of Rational Science: You quantify *everything* to prove the actuality of its existence. Although realties may be as plain as day they should be regarded as "biased", "non-scientific" assumptions--that is, until quantified.

Your goal is to disarm the population from awareness of its subjection to Cultural Warfare. In this condition a nation-state is readily susceptible to the influence of any outside power. With Your influence over the education system, You can gain access into the conscious and sub-conscious of Your subject population's psyche.[17]

[17.] Curriculum should be geared solely towards preparing students to excel at standardized tests. This is because "student achievement" can be quantified so that educational funding as well as teacher and administrator pay can be based on test scores, allowing for personal gain to be an additional factor in promoting this system. If teachers and administrators can be terminated, promoted, or rewarded with bonuses based solely on test scores You can depend on a growing number of educators focusing, especially with the simultaneous effects of other projections on the society, on test preparation rather than cultivating the potential of each student which would ensure proficiency of core education competencies.

When you control a man's thinking you do not have to worry about his actions. You do not have to tell him not to stand here or go yonder. He will find his 'proper place' anc will stay in it. You do not need to send him to the back door, he will go without being told. In fact, if there is no back door, he will cut one for his special benefit. His education makes it necessary.

Dr. Carter G. Woodson, *The Miseducation of the Negro*

The colonial powers sought to destroy the cultural patterns of traditional societies because many of their essential features prevented traditional people from subordinating social, ecological, and spiritual imperatives to the short-term economic ends served by participation in the colonial economy... the young were deprived of that traditional knowledge which alone could make them effective members of their societies.

E. Goldsmith, *The Way: An Ecological World View*[18]

[18.] E. Goldsmith, *The Way: an Ecological World View.* (London: Rider, 1992) p.285 from Legal *Traditions of the World*. H. Patrick Glenn. Oxford University Press. p.76

Teaching Universalism.

Of course, there is no universal means of educating people, especially those of different cultures and backgrounds. To be effective for a particular culture or nation-state, education must correspond to its particular frame of reference. You must use education as a means of promoting Your Universalistic agenda. Reinforcement to the subject's self-esteem will come from mastery of the "educated" model that You provide, and will give the subject a feeling of ownership in this system. The "highly educated" products of the system are to be the protectors of Your way, esteem needs having been met by continued assertions of "Universal Achievement", they will be blind to Your ulterior motives.

Language & Dialect

Make Yourself the point of departure by designating the language as a "dialect", and therefore a variation, of Your language. You shall be the starting point. Language did not exist before contact with You, as with the case of European "languages" and Asian or African "dialects".

Being that the world is aware of some of dynamics of colonization, You have to temper some--only some--of Your projections so that it will appeal to the culture of the subject nation-state. Show just enough interest in the superficials of simple language and cultural nuance that will allow Your subject to feel that You are sensitive to its cultural realities. I must stress that this is only a ploy to have Your subject lay down any guard that it might have to foreign influence. Do not overdo this, because You do not want to legitimize the subject culture as comparable to Yours. You are simply showing superficial respect, not deference.

Orality & Literacy

Know the difference between hearing, which requires active use of the left and right brain, and listening, which is passive. Literate cultures that retain an oral tradition continually reinforced by childhood training and the transmission of knowledge through stories and rote memory do not experience disconnection from the center that literate cultures separated from their historical *clichés* do.[19] Cultures that discourage the use of *clichés* do so because they believe in "Evolution" and linear progress. The Culture of Rationalism that You are projecting upon Your subject's nation-state is one of these cultures.

---

[19] Ong, Walter, J. (1998) *Orality and Literacy.* London: Routledge. (This edition 2003). p.23

Clichés are similar themes that are taught again and again throughout the life of a people. Your goal is to dislodge this center so that Your subject's nation-state will follow Your path of "Evolution" and "Progress", a path unencumbered by thoughts of consequence, responsibility, and sustainability. With collective wisdom denied, Your subject's nation-state can be manipulated to engage in self-destructive actions that its center would never allow. You must separate the society of Your subject nation-state from its collective and cumulative wisdom--its *clichés*--as these are symbolic of non-linear thinking, a cyclical concept of time and spatial reality. These *clichés* are the repetitive voice that judge thoughts, behaviors, and objects as being congruent or incongruent with a people's cultural center; they are its mantra. The recurring themes are to the non-linear thinker a point of reference and departure for all endeavors; to a linear thinker *clichés* are anchor-weights that restrict thought. While these repetitive thought patterns are held by the non-linear thinker as a foundation for wisdom and cultural continuity, and the mark of distinction in intellectual and creative endeavors, they are viewed by Modern Man as an obstacle to "original thought".

By denigrating the oral tradition of Your subject's state, devaluing traditional stories and bringing to an end the culture-based character education which has operated as the primary mode of transmission for collective ancestral wisdom and exchanging it for the teaching of "new" Modern values and ethics based on Legal Moralism and the Culture of Individualism, You will have laid a major blow to the cohesion of its society. This will be easy if present-day culture has become reactionary to Your influence or to prior exposure to Colonial Rule, and if stories and cultural rules taught to the youth have become suffocating rather than nurturing, inactive and unsupportive in the actualization of national potential and fulfillment of individual purpose.

Oral history is living and provides the recipient with a context in which they can apply themselves to the history being passed on, therefore, it must cease to exist: create historical amnesia through a sole reliance on written history. Those grounded in written history are static and are likely as adults to forget the lessons and histories of preceding generations. If oral historical traditions are allowed to exist then there is a high likelihood that history before contact will be remembered and will weaken Your position as point of reference for Modernity.

Without the oral component a language ceases to represent the living culture of a people. You should encourage the eventual extinction of any language that has a strong oral tradition and, most especially, any language that is still oral in nature. Adults in communities where the language is spoken should be made to feel that it will only detract from the chances of the children to succeed in life, that any attention paid to this "minor" language will take away the ability to master Your "major" language, the One spoken throughout Your sphere of influence.

You can "dumb down" a people who still operate through oral retention if You encourage written literacy without the corresponding oral tradition, especially ones with only a small number of letters or ideograms to represent the language. These are good systems for peoples whose languages are based in the oral tradition, as long as oral retention counterbalances it. Those using a written ideographic language require constant memorization to retain the ability to be literate, though most cultures with a scripted language still maintain strong oral traditions. You must watch for this, as failure to do so could allow You to blindly assume that there is no oral tradition to denigrate. Discourage rote memorization and storytelling with the excuse that it is not only unrepresentative of but irrelevant to the Universal values of Civilization and the Modern World, and memory retention will drop dramatically.

Tracking

Contrary to ability theory, IQ does not equal intelligence, and IQ tests measure only a set of cognitive skills functional in Western middle-class culture. The cognitive problems posed by the technoeconomic environment of Western middle-class culture require and promote a distinct set of cognitive skills and strategies involving grasping relations and symbolic thinking. According to Vernon (1969), for some extent these have come to permeate all learning activities at school, at work, and in daily life. But they are not universally valued, nor equally functional; other cultures require and stimulate the development and use of other cognitive skills for coping with their environments. Other cultures possess different intelligences.[20]

The purpose of the Intelligence Quotient is to ascertain learning potential of students in Your subject's nation-state and eliminate the overall productivity and effectiveness of its education system. Your subject's educational authorities should use these sorts of "objective" indicators of student potential to eliminate the focus on all children to excel. In truth, human potential can only be measured if the examiner is aware of all variables that will come into play. Otherwise it is judgment based on inadequate facts, a vain attempt at omniscience. These tests negate true and innate knowledge of self, reflect acquired knowledge while overlooking potential to learn. If the student scores high, ego will encourage superiority over others in the group. Defined as

[20.] "From Cultural Differences to Differences in Cultural Frame of Reference" by John U. Ogbu in Patricia M. Greenfield and Rodney R. Cocking eds. (1994) *Cross-Cultural Roots of Minority Child Development*. Hillsdale, New Jersey: Lawrence Erlbaum Associates, Publishers. p. 367

gifted, above average, average, below average, and hopeless, the children will rise or fall to Your expectations. The safety valve You have n place for potential dissenters is the tracking system, which places those who are not tracked as "academically achieving" at a lower position, and worth less as students.

"Tracking" is key to denying quality education to the majority. As social division can cognitively begin at this stage, focus Your efforts on promoting separation within the society. Differentiations in academic potential must reflect the social divisions that You are exploiting, and students should be developed in relation to ethnicity, social class, and religion. Schools should be run like businesses, and resources should only go to students deemed worthy of instruction. Incorporate the tracking process into administ ation over students in the schools and for greatest efficiency, track children as early as pre-school age. Youth are very malleable at primary school age; they will articulate the cultural values of influential adults in their lives. Whoever acts as the loudest and most consistent voice of "this is right," or "that is wrong," will win. A student's academic path should be mapped out as early as possible for programming and acculturation into a future that has been predetermined. Societal prejudices will repeat in the classroom as counselors, teachers, and administrators take on the task of deciding the future of each student.

Education can be used to prep young citizens to more readily accept projected cognitions: the goal is to have these projections become the template by which additional cognitions can be compared. Give the children Your point of reference so that the subject's centered cognitions of what is good or bad for its culture will be interpreted as dissociative, and will be rejected. This rejection is achieved by the bombardment of You-centric images, ideals, and values into the affected subject-child's life.

Standardized Testing

Goal-based education policies may appear to be a positive endeavor, but in actuality education must be a fluid discipline. There are constants such as literacy, mathematics, hard science, social science, character education, art and culture, but these must be taught in a manner that identifies the individual gifts and talents of students, instilling a shared sense of collective responsibility. In truth, any educational goals *must* be homegrown. They must be devised locally, not by outsiders lacking knowledge of context, alien to the needs of the communities.

In order to turn goal-based education policies into a self-destructive process, emphasis should be placed on standardized tests. If applied effectively, You will have schools and teachers putting every effort in preparing students for these standardized tests, as scores will reflect the productivity and effectiveness of the educators. When successful You will have a system that encourages excellent test-taking and rote memorization abilities at the expense of a true education and the development of critical thinking skills. This trend of academic standardization is a beautiful means of universalizing concepts into Your subject's population.

Concepts in Character Education.[21]

Character education defines and maintains the behaviors, ideals and lifestyles that support a nation while allowing foreign influences that are beneficial to its sustainability and rejecting those that are potentially harmful to it. The most insidious assaults on the society which are also long-lasting are cultural attacks on its integrity, which can destroy the individual psyches of people and therefore damage the collective psyche of an entire nation. Knowing this You should redesign character education to place the highest value of human worth on consumer potential, and the least value on self-actualization and community responsibility.

Individualism

To destroy community responsibility and collective consciousness, promote the cause of "freedom and individualism". Educators must be groomed in the "teacher training" that You provide; they must follow the curriculum that You give them and should not contribute any more than what You dictate. To accelerate into the lives of youth a further decline of community cohesion and collective social responsibility, teach educators to reject their role as perpetuators of the continuity of the native cultural center. Reinforce Your ideology that their role in the child's life is solely that of "teacher" and that almagation with the role of "parent" will only take away from the quality of teaching. The role between parent and teacher needs to be clearly differentiated, as this division will work beautifully in contributing to the erosion of Your subject society. Educators should be implanted with the attitude of "I am here to teach, not to babysit somebody else's child". The educators should be trained to focus their energies on promoting themselves through "star students". In regards to "problem" students, educators should have the attitude that the only future of these children will be as "losers and criminals". In sum, it is important that educators do not realize their importance in translating and transmitting the cultural center to future generations.

[21.] Ibid. "Character Education: Promoting Community Responsibility"

Linguisism

Use linguisism[22] to create problems between the majority group and ethic or religious minorities, so that You may dull the collective brain trust of the population. Children of Other groups are to be looked at as pathological models of the majority children[23]. The minds of "minority" children will be burdened by discrimination, limiting expectation of the self. The "majority" children will never develop their gifts and talents.

You will instill a false sense of inferiority and superiority between the "minority" and "majority" children, and will severely limit the intellectual potential of Your subject nation-state. As a means of maintaining power over the minorities they will learn how to be skilled in organizational discrimination, using rules and semantics to name, define, and objectify simple tasks and truths. It becomes a bog game: the minorities, having to fight discrimination whether apparent or not; having to work twice as hard as the majority just to be considered equally legitimate; and the majority, deconstructing everything---every task, concept, idea, function--so that they can be the ones to re-name, re-define, and re-objectify simple, obvious truths as a Platonic means of "naming to be in control"; all the while, none are able to operate at their full potential. Immigrant labor and brainpower shall be the only hope for fresh intellectual input--that is, until they too are assimilated as "majority" or "minority".

The Education System.

For the education system of a nation-state to be truly effective it must support culture-centered objectives and sustainable development determined by the society; have something to focus on as a point of departure, such as "who are we and where are we going?" and an acknowledged point of reference: "how are we meeting our goal of being who we are in 'X' number of years?; "how does what we are now doing compare to our collectively decided measure of cultural acceptability?" Education should be designed to reach national goals and to promote a desire for lifelong learning in the populace. In this way national objectives will be met in a culturally congruent manner and critical thinking will develop among the populace, generating a sufficient brain trust to carry out the affairs of society.

Non-critical thinkers may be "cultural" according to the standards of the subject's cultural center; because they simply live as members of the

---

[22.] Dr. Anita DeFrantz, Professor emerita, University of San Francisco: presentation at the X Semanario Cientifico Acerca de la Calidad de la Educacion.

[23.] Ibid.

community, cultural tendencies are passive and therefore easier to disrupt through CCD. On the other hand, a decidedly "cultural" person will be a threat to Your influence, having made a conscious decision to resist You and embrace the original cultural center. In the subject nation state's society, this type of person can be a source of resistance to Your influence and instigate the overthrow of Your abstracted collaborative government.

Acculturation through education must be initiated as early as possible, because children grow up using culture as the primary point of reference for connections to the world. The older the child is, the harder it will be to plant permanent seeds of the Culture of Comparison into them. There is only one center that can fit, and if they have already made connections with the native culture You will only be able to influence through Cultural Cognitive Dissonance.

The education system of Your subject nation-state should follow a career-based model. You must hijack the education system from any participation in indigenous culture-based national planning and character education. The youth must be socialized to embrace the Culture of Individualism, seeing Your projected ideals and cultural representations as superior to their own. They are not to become critical thinkers but to be educated solely for employment, so that their value to the social economy is only in skills that You will make "antiquated" through the importing of other processes and technologies from the outside. With a workforce lacking in critical thinking skills, the industries of the subject government will always require Your consultants and executives to provide direction. Regardless of individual differences, gifts, and potential, disregard the fact that children do not all learn the same by teaching a uniform core curriculum. Choose teaching styles that emphasize one type of learning, whether auditory, visual, or tactile, and they will become frustrated, losing interest in education because it will fail to cultivate their individual gifts and potential.

If education is ineffectual in socializing the youth to embrace a culture-based sense of morality, if it simply teaches skills for employment while neglecting to teach critical thought then You will have co-opted the education system into a double-edged sword; "educating" youth without a sense of civic responsibility, with skills that will be obsolete if the nation-state chooses to enter a global knowledge-based economy. This is Your goal.

Schooling should be viewed as a privilege and schools should be encouraged to disavow any obligations to the communities where they are housed. Maintain the ideology of running schools as businesses with efficiency and production being the only factors of importance. "Efficiency" shall equate to the weeding out of obstacles to the quantitative success of the schools, while "production" shall encompass the performance-based education of schools, teachers and administrators through standardized tests. If the subject nation-state's schools can be successfully steered from retaining any influence of culture-based character and moral education, the youth will be extremely vulnerable to Your attacks.

Eliminate any cohesive social-building influence from the school environment so that the youth are devoid of community-bound teaching. With this logic, art, music, and physical education classes will need to be eliminated because they cannot be justified as efficient use of time and resources. These types of classes encourage moderation, creativity, spon- teniety, team building, self-improvement and introspection; with regard to Your long-term social engineering objectives, these are qualities that need to be highly discouraged. Schools are to be the factories that create future compliant workers and consumers in Your exploited society. Rather than teaching Healthy Cohesive Nationalism[24], the schools of Your subject's nation-state should make routine the practice of surface patriotism, with morning anthems, flag worship, and celebrated "historic" events.

Bi-Culturals

Projections work effectively on the masses because of the mystery and allure of Your world. But those raised in a bi-cultural reality see the truths and contradictions of both worlds. A bi-cultural who consciously accepts the indigenous value system as their center will comprise the core of urban and intellectual resistance to Your influence, and could possibly create a unified struggle across the divisions that You have upheld.

Bi-culturals are children who are either the product of mixed parentage, one of the subject's and one of Yours, or of assimilation through processes such as "international schooling". The presence of bi-culturals can be very disadvantageous to You in the future because they are better able than the average citizen to access information about You and Your nation-states. They must be educated with caution. You run the risk of letting Your guard down with the seemingly outward and apparent assimilation of this class, not acknowledging them for what they really are--Your greatest potential enemies in the subject's society. Heed the following story:

[24.] Healthy Cohesive Nationalism: attitudes and behaviors of collective responsibility and collective nation-building.

The alchemist picked up a book that someone in the caravan had brought. Leafing through the pages, he found a story about Narcissus. The alchemist knew the legend of Narcissus, a youth who knelt daily beside a lake to contemplate his own beauty. He was so fascinated by himself that, one morning, he fell into the lake and drowned. At the spot where he fell, a flower was born, which was called the narcissus. But this was not how the author of the book ended the story.

He said that when Narcissus died, the goddesses of the forest appeared and found the lake, which had been fresh water, transformed into a lake of salty tears.

'Why do you weep?' the goddesses asked.

'I weep for Narcissus,' the lake replied.

'Ah, it is no surprise that you weep for Narcissus,' they said, 'for though we always pursued him in the forest, you alone could contemplate his beauty close at hand.'

'But . . . was Narcissus beautiful?' the lake asked.

'Who better than you to know that?' the goddesses said in wonder. 'After all, it was by your banks that he knelt each day to contemplate himself!'

The lake was silent for some time. Finally, it said:

'I weep for Narcissus, but I never noticed that Narcissus was beautiful. I weep because, each time he knelt beside my banks, I could see, in the depths of his eyes, my own beauty reflected.'

'What a lovely story,' the alchemist thought.[25]

Do not suffer from the effects of the bi-culturals having realized their own beauty by looking in Your eyes, at Your projections.

Mass Media

"While basic effects in the educational system have been responsible for the lack of nationalist ideals, mass-media and cultural facilities negate whatever gains are made in some sectors of the educational field."

Renato Constantino, *The Miseducation of the Filipino*

Video games and television sets are the new playmates of coming generations of children in Your subject nation-states. Children raised with electronic media playmates, rather than with other children indoors and outdoors where they create their own games and entertainment, will be far less able to maintain a reasonable attention span in the non-videoscreen-oriented human world. The number of attention deficient disorders and the growing number of associated acronyms--ADD (Attention Deficit Disorder), ADHD (Attention Deficit Hyperactive Disorder)--will continue to grow and these children will be increasingly tracked into classes for students with emotional disabilities, or they will be medicated to mitigate their "hyperactivity". With the assumption that their cognitive abilities are also

[25] Paulo Coelho, from the Prologue of *The Alchemist*

impaired, students with emotional disabilities are to be tracked, allowing for the elimination of another potential group of critical thinkers.

Effective miseducation lies in shaping the world of the youth, limiting what they believe to be possible in life. With the use of media, persons that You deem Modern are to be the only ones portrayed in images of power, responsibility, popularity, and wealth. Conversely, when in the media people of Your subject nation-state should function only as decorative ornaments, tokens allowed entry into Your defined "world of success" because of their conformity to Your projected aesthetics and ideals. In media, the youth of Your subject nation-state are not to see themselves in positive roles; if not in disparaging roles, they should take on the role of enthusiastic emulator of the foreign success model that You have projected.

You will need to have some knowledge of the history and language, the mannerisms and customs of the people in order to approach them intelligently. When designing Your programs, do not use local icons unless it is absolutely necessary, as these will reinforce through cognitive connections, point of reference to the native cultural center.

Critical Thinking Skills.

The true purpose of higher education is to develop critical thinking skills, effectively learning how to make conclusions from information received. One who knows how to think critically can master any discipline without an extensive background on the subject. Academia offers freedom from the concrete so that objective thinking can be utilized to examine problems from the outside. To counter this, teach specific disciplines and avoid interdisciplinary learning, since education that is not holistic will be handicapped by its specialization. You should promote lofty thinking, concepts that have little or no application to the lives of the people. The Académe should be a place where scholars are awarded for the least applicable works, and the greatest minds of the nation-state are to be sent on a wild goose chase to find qualitative and quantitative data in the endless construction and deconstruction of ideas. No academic of worth should sully his or her hands in the dirt of the mundane lives of the people. You should extricate the scholars of their responsibility to serve the community. Academia is to be maintained for this precise reason. You must promote the conceptual world of Academia as reality and eliminate holistic relationships between scholarship, informed governance, and industry.

Any technical or vocational skill taught to promote indigenous business and agriculture should be discouraged and disparaged as lower forms of education. Promote the concept of "blue-collar" and "white-collar". You should strip the skilled laborer and artisan of their esteemed status in society. Those with competencies to be successful at certain skilled trades should be made to feel inferior to those whose gifts lie in the realm of white-collar service professions. When the youth desire to go into one of these fields, parents, motivated through Your projections should say, "you are better than that." A skilled trade, like that of the plumber, mason, automobile mechanic, electronics or industrial engine technician, should be touted as a "less than" profession.

One of the best ways to create unrest in the masses of the subject's state is to promote an education system that fails to encourage the natural development of the students' individual gifts and abilities. Make the people desire higher education to attain a "ticket" to a better future, as opposed to obtaining higher education for the sake of expanding the mind. This delineation of worth should cause a nice rift in the society, as students whose education needs are not met will become incorrigible when they realize that their education is lacking. Higher education should cease to educate; it should instead be used to satisfy esteem needs.

A society of people that live to compare themselves to others is a society of envy, jealousy, insecurity, addiction, and boundary problems. People with unfulfilled potential will still desire the actualization of that potential; they will try to live other people's lives for them and will perpetuate envy and jealousy towards those who seem happy and self-fulfilled. They will participate in destructive behaviors that are non-productive and risky, and suffer from addictions in an attempt to fill the void of self with something external, be it alcohol, drugs, or unhealthy relationships.

Use education to instill Your position of superiority; foster relationship dependency with Your ideals and icons, mis-educate the workforce, create an Académe detached from the lives of real people, and promote a Culture of Comparison with the corresponding denial of true self and potential. For spiritually-minded populations, this will amount to destruction of the sacred (spiritual destruction).

History

When teaching history, disallow the government of Your subject's nation-state from using actual documents, records, and world literature. If possible, eradicate all history and rewrite the curriculum with the aid of educational consultants. Any historical information that could cultivate a healthy sense of nationalism in the youth should be eliminated. Free of this, the youth will feel no need to contribute to society. They should be encouraged to develop from textbook "facts," socialization approved by You. Otherwise, the youth may develop critical thinking skills, through a sense of context of the events studied, and contemplate the contradictions that they see in their government policies, which collaborate with You in its own self-destruction.

Create historical amnesia with sole reliance on written history and ignorance of living oral histories, as those grounded in written h story have static memories and are likely to forget the lessons of the preceding generations. You must convince the government of Your subject nation-state to repress any history of rebellion against Your influence or that of Other Princes, in history curricula.[26] If You eliminate these truths of resistance, the people will readily assume a subordinate position under Your hierarchy, because there is no openly expressed, or realized, collective resistance; thereby giving credibility to subjugation as being in their best interest, however painful[27].

Science

Science is revolution. As a result, those men and women have never lost their concern for the people. Such scientists may be absorbed by the passion for discovery, but they can never betray their sense of the human. Those seeking to enter the field of scientific research are selected on the basis of the moral, ethical and revolutionary values and aren't considered apt if they fail in those aspects.

Carlos Mella Lizama, M.D.[28]

Although a Prince is Himself conscious that, without omnipotence or divine inspiration, it is impossible to be aware of all of the variables in a problem, He should utilize the need for absolute empirical proof that scientific reasoning requires as a means of disabling His subject from seeing realities that are in plain view. In every case a Prince is to teach His subject, that, as long as the procedures are followed the desired outcome will occur.

---

26. As in the case of slavery in the U.S., from written history, one would assume that slaves accepted their lot and worked contently; while in truth, there were constant rebellions. Slaveholders lived in perpetual fear of revolt, hence the creation of the slave codes and subsequent post-slavery Black Codes--any remotely assertive behavior had to be quelled immediately, for it symbolized a threat to the Order. In the same way, sustained African resistance to colonization is not openly noted in history, because it would indicate that the people realized colonial rule was to their detriment.

27. In regards to the situation in Zimbabwe, the media has executed a successful clouding of present-day African realities of "political independence", continued economic exploitation and neccolonization by the "former" Colonial Powers, with criticism on issues of Free Press and New Elections, at a time of on-going war, or social revolution from colonial, to post-colonial independence; all the while negating the real issue of export agriculture on prime arable land that has yet to be returned to the people, as was agreed during political independence in 1980, during which the Colonial Powers acceded, as condition to cessation of hostilities, to the reimbursement of colonial farmers at market prices.

28. Member of the team that produced the Hebermin EGF (Epidermal Growth Factor) ointment for burn victims at the Center for Genetic Engineering and Biotechnology (CIGB).

You must train the subject to believe that there is no reality to a conclusion unless it is proven within the parameters of the scientific method that You give them. In time, the people will stop following common sense and intuition. They will cease to see plain and visible truths. You will destroy their creative spark because they will base experimentation on precedent rather than new ideas that come through intuition and inspiration. Be sure to weed out teachers who still retain this creative spark. Strict conformity with scientific protocols as defined by You must be followed, no matter what proof can be provided as evidence otherwise it is not real science, it is simply "culture-biased anecdotal evidence".

When You reduce a people to left-brained functionality, they no longer function as human beings--they can be replaced by computers and other logical entities that operate solely from the perspective of the programmer. They are not able to intuit. With proper empirical training, You can produce a people whose only use is manual industrial labor.[29]

Language

You must make Your language the *lingua franca*, the language of international communication, or at the very least a language of the sophisticated and learned. De-emphasize the importance of proficiency of the native tongue. If it is an oral (non-scripted) language, have the native language instructed in the script of Your tongue. For English speakers this would be equated to "Romanization" because Roman letters are used to signify the sound of the language. Proficiency in the tongue of Your state is to be paramount to acceptance into "polite" society. Those unable to master Your tongue, or who speak with a strong accent, will be stigmatized for their "intellectual shortcomings". In the Culture of Comparison, You set the standards through language. For example, from the standpoint of caste in the United States, non-Hispanic Western Europeans, including Northern Europeans (such as Scandinavians) can use highly accented speech with a weak command of English and be emulated, while someone with a strong command of English, but with an Asian, African, or Luso-Hispanic accent will be stigmatized.

Switching focus from the native tongue to Your language in elementary education proves to be a greater disadvantage for many students. Changing the process of learning without an adequate bilingual education program will require children to attempt the learning process in a new language, where, previously, they had learned basic concepts through their own language. At

---

[29]. In the 21st century manual labor would include certain professions in the IT industry that are repetitious and non-creative.

these early stages of development learning will be difficult and will contribute to low self-image, making the children prime targets for Your projections.

Spoken language is the vehicle through which cultural knowledge is transmitted, and a number of the world's peoples use languages that are based on oral rather than written retention. The very essence of their lives is bound to their language--knowledge of natural medicines or what foods to eat, how to domesticate plants and animals, or the natural cycle of the physical environment, as well as cultural mores of behavior. If You destroy the continuity of a people's linguistic heritage You cause a major blow to cultural integrity, because for nations of the oral tradition, linguistic survival is a prerequisite to cultural survival. If You force them to use a dominant written language, You will successfully cut them off from their collective past, their ancestral memory, and will easily be able to insert Yourself as the new starting point for definitions of self, society, and environment. You will become the point of reference and departure through successful instruction in a "language that they will need to succeed economically in life."

Educational Expenditures.

One way to initiate the mismanagement of funds is through the "budget". To plant the seeds for further economic problems exploit budget deficits; using reactionary economic proposals, encourage Your subject nation-state to put monies toward defense and investment, creating direct foreign speculation-friendly trade zones while overlooking a comprehensive educational system. The lack quality in national education will lead to high expenditures in the future: juvenile delinquency, criminal activity, adult incarceration, increased welfare costs.

This kind of misallocation will lend itself to social problems that You can say will be alleviated through reactionary "law and order" initiatives, such as an enhanced police force, domestic surveillance programs and of course, more prisons. The prison industry will support Your long-term workforce needs. And if, for some reason, the subject nation-state can develop its economy even with Your interference, enough social breakdown will have occurred that the subject's government, now buying into Your Universalizing influence, will use incarceration as the preferred means of social control.

If You can also convince the government of the benefits of prison privatization, You will from an economic perspective, eliminate potential arguments for preventative social welfare and educational reform as an answer to criminality.

The criminal justice system will be an integral part of the economy; in a "free market" system economics is the precursor for any recognition as a "developed state", which will trust that the "invisible hand" will eventually reconcile its social, economic, and environmental problems.

Higher Education.

Higher education is to be geared to the style of the Academé. In this way, rational thinking can be taught as the way that academics learn. By institutionalizing this method of learning (characterizing, objectifying, and defining) You will breed educators and academics with a scholarship structured in this manner. You will erect Your legacy and projected ideals into procedures of higher learning.

In your ideal, Academia becomes totally obsessed with itself, devoid of any applicability to life and to the service of the community: promoting the Rational Way, to deconstruct, then define, then rename; focusing on endless "de-constructions" and "constructions", creating new paradigms and operating in a variety of different "spaces"--all for the need to control. This is the successful acculturation of Academé into Rationalist culture, a process of control through the redefinition of basic concepts that would easily be understood by a critical thinker.

The educated class should be sought for solutions to all problems. Your job is to miseducate brilliant minds into believing that solutions to problems cannot be found within the society, and that externally-based solutions, training, consultants, and engineers will always be needed.

The voice of the average citizen must not be acknowledged, for it is from the masses that dissatisfaction with the system that You project will be in most abundance. One thoroughly educated on a higher level cannot see because their emotions, or self-esteem, has been invested into Your system. They are most likely to voice outrage at the openly apparent signs of social dislocation caused by Your policies and projections, which include a growing unemployment, income gaps, environmental misuse, resource misallocation, as well as loss of social services, stress on families, increase in crime and incarceration.

Education & A National Development Plan.

All "progressive states" should have a "national development program". Be sure that the youth of the subject's nation-state are inundated with the aims of this plan. The youth need to be given a "mission", of sorts: to be good citizens supportive of their nation's goal and objectives.

Development strategists must always feel that outside consulting and technical advice is necessary; they must "realize" the need for outside consultation to ensure that technology development is in line with Universal standards.You must make them believe that without Your input they will not know even the simplest in human development, such as conducting trade and producing food. Before Your arrival, they existed and prospered because of the benevolent support of aliens--extraterrestrials or some Other external force outside of their collective potential. Make them believe that Your mere presence has brought "Free Trade", conventional scientific agriculture, classical culture, the "arts".

Vocational Education

Emphasize vocational courses of study that serve the needs of production facilities in Your subject nation-state. Workers must be groomed to serve. Supervision and management should be left to foreigners who "always know better" due to the nature of their being from the outside, from the Modern nation-states of You or Other Princes.

You should endorse the teaching of "fundamentals", especially with regard to antiquated skills and technologies that will either soon be obsolete or are perogatives for the components of "dirty industries". For example, emphasize study on combustion engines while neglecting study on photovoltaics. In coastal areas and areas with brackish water, teach techniques of water pumping to the point of exhausting aquifers rather than in using portable desalination plant technologies, and neglecting power solutions based on tidal wave powered generators, instead of those powered by fossil fuels.

The vocational programs that You promote are to ensure that the subject state experiences pains from the mistakes of industrialization, including the misallocation of human resources and the resulting environmental destruction. When problems come up, continue to provide "consultants" so that You many begin the next stage of failure and dependency.

If antiquated infrastructure is already in place, or if infrastructure does not exist at all, in truth, there is no reason for them to build it - the society can "leapfrog"[30] technology. This is not what You want. You must keep dependency on Your "technological know-how" (even though average people might know better not to use it) while having Your "experts" who reside in the

---

[30.] Dr. Mae Jemison mentioned this concept in a paper presented at the 1992 World Space Congress, Washington D.C. "Improving Regional Healthcare in West Africa Using Current Space Systems Technology". Leapfrogging referes to utilizing high-tech, less invasive technologies from the beginning of building infrastructure rather than utilizing more invasive and less effective older generation technologies. For example, in an area with no pre-existing power infrastructure "leapfrogging" would install solar or wind power array to supply the needs of the community instead of building a coal or diesel burning power plant.

subject nation-state require the "comforts of home"--certain foods and products--furthering Your influence over the society. This will cause problems in the society because You are bringing in more products that less people can afford, leaving them with no means of obtaining them. In doing this You will create a chain of unsustainable industries and institutions that are not actually useful to the society.

Workforce Development

It is in Your best interest to export the best minds of Your subject's nation-state to Your nation-state for these reasons: 1. to benefit from its human potential; 2. to cause a brain-drain in the subject's social economy; 3. to encourage entrepreneurship in Your nation-state's social economy.

Encourage the training of workers as consumers as opposed to producers. Promote education as a "means to an end" so that You will have a glut of educated people who will become the cheap labor force for Your operations in the subject's nation-state. Promote the endless pursuit of efficiency: any idle time is time that could be spent working in Your factories or in service jobs in the service industry owned or controlled by You in the subject nation-state. Allow no leisure time for creativity.

Do Not Be Deceived.

A countless number of anthropologists went to "far-off locales" to gather intelligence on populations before the traders as a precursor to formal trade relations being established as the predecessors and contemporaries of missionaries and capitalists. The people lied to them. Believing in their own superiority, the anthropologists assumed that the locals could not see through their motives were and were tricked. Many anthropology dissertations are based on inaccurate fieldwork and narrow-minded culture-based (their own) conclusions. Contemplate this:

> The rapid progress of industrialization as spurred by World War I inevitably brought about a major change in the system of values which until then had been prevalent among the Japanese people. That is, the awakening of 'self-consciousness' among the people under the leadership of the intellectuals, the burgeoning of the sense of personal rights among the increasing number of factory workers, which gave birth to a labor movement and then, a socialist movement, and the advocacy of 'culture' seeking emancipation from parochial nationalism--all this involves the possibility of fundamentally shaking Japan's social system until then predicted upon the selective transplanting of only modern techniques and managerial systems from Western Europe and the rejection of modern Western thought and spirit under the slogan of 'Wakon Yosai' (Japanese spirit and Western learning).

. . . .

Japan's investment in education has all along been in the nature of an advanced investment when viewed in the context of economic growth . . . Looking back on the establishment in the early 1880s of the Tokyo Artisan School, the predecessor of the present Tokyo Institute of Technology, Shin Hamao, who was concerned with the inauguration of the school and later became the president of Tokyo Imperial University, said: 'In our country . . . it was not that industries and factories developed first, followed by the establishment of technical schools, but that technical schools were first established to produce the graduate, whose task was to inaugurate and develop industries and factories.'

. . . .

In the past two educational reforms, Japan sought a model for an educational system to be newly contributed in the advanced Western nations. Nevertheless, Japan in undertaking the third educational reform can no longer seek such a foreign model. For the nation is confronted not merely with unique problems of its own brought about by rapid industrialization, but also, as a highly industrialized society, with common problems facing the Western countries, as well. What course should be chosen for Japan's new educational reform in what may well be called an 'uncharted' ocean? The 1970s will become a decade of groping and experiment for determining the course.[31]

Do not be deceived by apparent emulations of You. The subject may betray its true value through this balancing act, but in the short term it may actually be able to make gains against You, using Your methods, while drawing on its cultural center as a point of reference and departure.

---

[31] Asao, Makoto and Amano, Ikuo (1972). *Education and Japan's Modernization (Kyoiku to Nihon no Kindaika)*. Tokyo: Ministry of Foreign Affairs, pp. 47-87

Chapter 4:
Rule of Law

The current way of looking at Filipino traditional values does not give us a better understanding of the nature of the value system itself. Many interpretations of the system are not consistent with local knowledge and traditionally defined code of conduct that provides Filipino behavior its proper framework, context, and meaning.

Many critics, for example, see Filipino traditional values as something we should not have valued in the first place--an inconsistent but popular view! They say that these values have damaged our culture, brought about the ills in our society, given rise to our undesirable traits, brought about weaknesses in our character as a people, and have caused the moral breakdown of our institutions.

Some critics, particularly foreigners, even see our conformity to traditional norms as passivity, subservience, and lack of initiative. The high premium we place on reciprocal obligations is described by them as scheming; our concern for consensus, lack of leadership; our silence borne out of deference or sensitivity to the feelings of others, concealed dishonesty; our firmness and discipline, authoritarianism; our kinship loyalties, nepotism; our gift giving, bribery; and our *utang-na-loob* (debt of gratitude), a cumbersome system of patronage and the major source of corruption.

There are many other examples. Suffice it to say, at the outset, that these critical views, while intended to enlighten us about ourselves as Filipinos, have not proved helpful in broadening our appreciation of our traditional lifeways. On the other hand, these views have succeeded in confusing us and in producing incongruities in our perception of our society and culture. They have likewise succeeded in creating a perspective that defines our values as negative and our character as weak, this undermining our confidence in our native abilities to excel.

F. Landa Jocano[34]

[34] Jocano, Landa F. (1997). *Filipino Value System: A Cultural Definition*. Metro Manila: PUNLAD Research House, Inc. pp.1-2

Your objective is to replace the cultural center of the subject's nation-state with a center based on the Culture of Individualism. This substitution is important to convert Your subject society of traditional cultural mores with an ever growing system of codified laws and external enforcement. The culture of Individualism that You are promoting requires that any internalized sense of collective responsibility be emptied and exchanged for an internal vacuum that desires to be filled by external possessions, competition, and comparison with Others. Cultural center is collective consciousness, a circle of past, present, and future. To break this: the culture must be made archaic, old-fashioned, outdated, ill-equipped to deal with "modern problems"; it must need You for its survival and perpetuation, happiness and security. Eliminate the mandate which the present governing body has to rule, of meeting the security and social welfare needs of the population, as well as supporting the perpetuation of the culture. You should use Rule of Law in the following manner:

1) to replace the cultural mandate of traditional law and social governance;
2) to protect the abstracted state and its property rights and to sanction any behavior that may impede the desires of the state at any point in time;
3) to create a reactionary legislative body;
4) to uphold law for the sake of legality, regardless of consequence to society, economy, or environment;
5) to create a Culture of Perpetual Childhood in which social order is maintained by the threat of the court systems and incarceration.

All decisions must be based on completing centered objectives. A Prince must accomplish two things: 1. reestablish the center as outside the subject, and based on personal objectives; 2. create a barrage of images, options, icons (during the time that the subject still maintains some semblance of a center), promote desires and reactionary attitudes to effectively dislocate the subject from being able to make productive "life choices". As with each application of Cultural Warfare, Your goal is to create uncertainty in the mind and heart of the subject. Cultural Cognitive Dissonance finds room to grow with this state of insecurity, allowing You to restore psychological comfort through Your projections.

Defining Order

```
X [YOU] = RATIONAL

Y [SUBJECT] = IRRATIONAL
```

You project hierarchy and Order rather than harmony, therefore x's means of conflict resolution is superior. The "state" is the "culture"; You become the culture by merely defining the subject-state.

> The . . . [x][35] . . . state is Plato's Republic. It depends on 'objectification' and abstraction. It is an ongoing attempt to create the perfectly rational; it is both theory and method. It is an ideal based in the mistaken conceptions of the rationalized human: one of moral 'autonomy,' and on the cost error of identification of the good with the scientifically provable. All moral (human) problems are considered to be solved (inherently) in the structure of the state, so there is no basis for a system of morality in the Republic. Morality presupposes ambiguity and fallibility. The issue of morality arises from the need for meaning from emotional responses to other human beings, and from regard for them in relation to self. One continually seeks to answer the ethical questions of 'acting' in the correct manner. To be immoral is not to be concerned with this question. The question of human morality requires spiritual base. The Republic eliminates spirit, emotion, and identification with other, and therefore, it eliminates human meaning . . . [X] . . . culture, at the other end of the chronological spectrum, ends up deficient in moral sensibility; i.e., without a guide for human conduct.[36]

The rational construction of an abstracted nation-state assumes that all problems in society can be solved through the Rule of Law, created and enforced by the government of the nation-state. According to this logic there is no need for internalized morality in the population; hence there is no need for tradition and culture.

Your subject may retain "customs" that have proven to maintain order and sustainability.[37] They are part of what bind the subject society to its center and must be eroded. Your projected argument is that the customs and

---

[35.] The [X] is inserted to represents how Your nation-state is to be projected.

[36.] Ani, p.396

[37.] See "The Law of the Islands," Marshall Islands Journal, pp.18-19; Friday, March 8, 2002.

traditional law of the subject society are not equipped to facilitate the complexities of the Modern world. To quote Francis X. Hezel, S.J.:

> Adoption of a modern legal system is the price of doing business in the world community . . . Laws multiply because development brings about new situations that have to be covered to protect people or government from something or another. Life becomes more complicated as development occurs.

This rationale is one of complicity. You should disparage its customs as "archaic" and project the need to adopt a Modern legal system. By following such logic Your subject nation-state will fail to see that governing philosophies are based in value systems where customs, traditions and laws emanate. This makes the intricacies of its "less sophisticated" society transparent so that You can properly gauge Your conquest and maintain an advantage. A Modern and transparent legal system with proper dislocative features such as "Free Trade" legislation will eliminate barriers to ownership of the land and protect the foreign-based press as well as the right of the Individual, allowing for Foreign Direct Investment to take private ownership at the expense of the maintanence of public resources.

The equation of $x = $ RATIONAL works as long as the subject knows its place in the hierarchy and embraces it. However, if it desires to assert itself in the international community however, it will disturb Your finely ordered hierarchy. You should define its assertions of self-determination as "not respecting" international law; and if the subject expresses displeasure in its position under Your artificially-ordered system, it must be made to feel that it is a pariah to Order. Encourage other Princes of Your caliber to chastise this subject that "does not know its place," as it can potentially upset the order which allows You and Your counterparts to exploit these rich nations.

The Modern State

The Modern State is a Rational construction and is therefore susceptible to the inherent weaknesses of rationally-constructed institutions. The Modern State, dependent on an abstracted locus of control and center to maintain its illusion of concreteness, reveals the essential flow that You can exploit. Because there is no cultural mandate that serves as a binding center for the state, You become the locus of control and therefore the binding center that holds the nation-state together.

On this point I must warn: You become responsible for the social welfare of the state because You are its Center. A Secondary Cognitive Dissonance can recur when basic security and esteem needs are not met, and fundamentalist groups can emerge from the people's desperation to ensure that basic security needs are met. If You do not take this point seriously, it may prove to be an immense problem in the future.

"New" States

During the formal days of Colonialism, traditional structures were severely weakened, if not broken, and replaced by abstracted structures of governance with little experience and subject to colonial policies. Nation-states that were colonized by Western powers are in the position to be most easily manipulated by the application of Cultural Warfare. This is because the very existence of their "nation-state" is an abstraction. Softened up, these newly "independent" nation-states can be seriously disrupted through the vacuum created by Rule of Law.

You are ruling over an illegitimate government with no cultural mandate. As with other bastions of colonial education, "Schools for Democracy" rule through autocracy, raising a nation of leaders in Your methodologies. Force must be used to maintain order and continue the disproportionate allocation of resources, and You can later criticize these "independent" nations for not practicing Democracy.

Rationalism & Governance.

It does not have to be difficult to rule on fairness, especially if those who make up the consensus are thoroughly briefed on the issues at hand. Those who are critical thinkers can wisely rule on any affair, because actions will be judged according to adherence to the accepted value system of consensus. Treating people fairly is a simple concept. The simplicity of the law is respect towards others. It protects those who may lose in the legal system due to ignorance of technical language, imported organizational structures, or foreign concepts of business, family, education, or governance. If the subject were to thoroughly examine the legal system of Your nation-state it would discover that Your attorneys, lawmakers, and judges are not "experts" in the fields over which they litigate, legislate, and judge. If the subject examines this too closely before accepting the "limitations" of its traditional laws and customs it will be able to plainly see that the Modern legal system You are projecting is nothing more than Your own "traditional law" masked as "Modern" through the Universalizing power of the Ideology of Rationalism.

Codification of Law

You should realize that there is no separation between law and morality. For nation-states that are not solely governed through abstracted institutions of "state", tradition is law. For these societies, law is living and adapting to present realities because it is internalized by members of the culture, and is able to have a wider scope of influence than 'Rule of Law', which is codified. It is moral law, a system of socially-accepted behavior mores.

You must eliminate any last vestiges that remain of this "tradition as law"[38] and place all responsibility on the formal abstracted structures of governance. The Rule of Law that You project is based on abstract Universalities. Morality should be separated from the individual who under Rule of Law, will be required to answer to the state. Morality will become obsolete, as the subject government will no longer receive the guidance and support of a cultural mandate. It will have to rely on a limited static code and the people will not know what to do in each situation, having lost trust in the abilities of the community.

Law is interconnected with cultural beliefs, not separate from them. If law is disconnected from cultural values Your subject's nation-state will have many socio-legal problems and potential for a high rate of corruption, as people try to reconcile the incongruent realities of an abstracted legal structure governing a concrete society. Encouraging the adoption of a totally codified legal structure will help the subject into a state of Perpetual Childhood. Once morals and the responsibility to self, family, community, and environment are taken out of the collective and put into the hands of an overseer, You will have created a society of children that are just good enough to get praised and just bad enough not to get caught. When caught they will claim ignorance to the wrong committed, or dance around legalities to avoid responsibility.

The mark of a dying society is one whose center is merely a formal abstraction of Rationalized cultural expression, one in which the people are unable to operate with self-restraint and an internalized sense of morality, thus requiring the court system to handle issues of private or civil law. Legal disputes become prominent when human relations have been compromised and have broken down. For sustainable societies, litigation should be the last resort. However, in the environment of Sustainable Exploitation that You are turning Your subject nation-state into, litigation should be the first choice in resolving disputes. It is impossible to codify every potential behavior of individuals in society. This is the responsibility of the national cultural center, to act as a point of reference and source of societal cohesion. Morality based in codified law will allow amoral behavior to continue as long as there exist

---

[38] See Chapter 3, *A Chtonic Legal Tradition: To Recycle the World* in *Legal Traditions of the World* in Glenn (2000).

loopholes and legislators fail to write new laws. This grants You the power of influence over legislation. You will be aware of all shortcomings of the law, it will serve Your interests.

While You are promoting Rule of Law, Your other socio-economic and environmentally disruptive tactics of Cultural Warfare will be working to break the society down, and skillful semi-transgressions of the law will become an art for those no longer concerned about community or for those placed into precarious situations where they, for their survival or the survival of their family, have to resort to desperate measures to survive. The concern is quantitative: for those who can afford the best counsel, deviant acts can be committed with little to no consequence. For those uninformed of the law who lack sufficient representation in legal counsel, incarceration will be the answer, the only true means of social control in a society of "free" cannibalistic, amoral individuals that will no longer need to conduct themselves with respect, much less have concern for others.

Corruption[39]

The term *kapwa* means 'of the same nature,' 'of equal status,' 'a partnership orientation.' Other writers use it to refer to our consciousness of reciprocally shared identities.

This emphasis on interdependent relationships expresses well the principle of egalitarianism found in the Filipino concept of *kapwa*.

Another expression of *kapwa*, as a relational value, is familism. This concept has to do with our concerns over the well-being of the members of our families or that of our kinsmen. As such, it is said to be another source of the ills plaguing our society, like graft and corruption. We beg to differ. We view familism as one of the sources of our moral strength. Many young Filipinos, in fact are willing to sacrifice personal opportunities, like further studies or early marriage, so that they can find work and help their siblings go to school.

The protective function of familism has been corrupted, however by the current practice of nepotism in modern formal organizations, i.e., the government bureaucracy and private corporations. This practice is not part of familism as a value. It is a *violation* [emphasis added] of its ethical principle. Nepotism is a product of modernization and not of traditional culture. It is used by many of us, however, to cope with unemployment problems or to reward people for their political patronage.[40]

Your subject nation-state's government has "codes" for administrative and

---

39. See pp.76-77, Re: "The State of Middle Ground," H. Patrick Glenn (2000) *Legal Traditions of the World*. New York: Oxford University Press; and pp. 62-70 *Ch. VIII Culture of Corruption: A Problem of Definition and Perception*. Robert A. Underwood, Professor University of Guam in "Government Ethics and Corruption on Guam", Judith Paulette Guthertz, and Daljit Singh, College of Business and Public Administration, University of Guam, Mangilao, Guam 1986; Conversation with Dr. Katherine Aguon, Director, Chamorro Heritage Institute Planning Group, Department of Chamorro Affairs, Re: Issues of Corruption in a clan-based society forcefully assimilated into an abstracted government system based on Rule of Law.

40. Jocano, pp. 61-65

criminal behavior but its private law is that of tradition, which is living. A transgression may be made for instance, but due to mitigating circumstances the act may not be a deliberate act against the community and would not be treated as such. Flexibility and balance thereof depends on the integrity of tradition and definers of it. Corruption in societies with abstracted forms of governance becomes a very real possibility, as the legal structure eliminates the ability of tradition to regulate. Unless the abstracted government can obtain a true mandate to rule, the subject will continue to rely on the system of obligations that gave order and stability to its pre-abstracted reality, without the safeguards intrinsic to a system of tradition-as-law. If You are effective in creating a system of Legal Moralism, the protection mechanisms in Your subject culture will have worn away.

Incarceration

A society is made of communities that are made up of families, which are in turn made up of individual people. If a society is strong, incarceration will be thought as a last resort. Affronts against the community are affronts against oneself; a perpetrator of crimes would be examined according to the scenarios that would generate the impetus for one to commit such crimes, and this person would be viewed as someone who may have been wronged and is striking back at something or someone, therefore the society must face and heal the root problem in the family/community/society. If this person clearly exhibits "negative"/destructive traits, these traits have not been utilized by the society in a constructive manner in which the person can exhibit these traits within balance in the community.

A society that uses incarceration as its primary means of social control is a failed society.[41] Your job is to eliminate any desire within the society to seek and address the root causes as to why its own members would feel the urge to commit crimes. You should promote reactionary attitudes to these crimes and, through the members of the society do away with those who do not conform. Make it so that those who conform are viewed in the highest esteem, and those who participate in lifestyles or policies that Your subject government is promoting as "crazy" and not part of society, are deemed fit only for life-long incarceration and privatized prison labor. You will find in the incarcerated class a good source of cheap labor for industry. [42]

[41.] Gray, John (1998) *False Dawn*. New York: The New Press. p.116

Business Law.

One important aspect that will need to be changed in the subject's society is its business culture. There should exist an unnecessary degree of compliance. Promote the formalization of business under the guise creating a Modern "growth oriented", "streamlined methodology" of "free enterprise". So that You have better access to resources and modes of production, promote the over-bureaucratization of the government as it relates to business law. Trade is a natural human activity, and You must also relegate this to the world of the abstract. People must be required to obtain endless licenses and approvals to conduct even the smallest enterprise. In doing so, You will disengage the average citizen and weaken the domestic economy.

In this way, business clearance can be controlled--granted to those desired, and denied to those despised. With Your persuasion, the institution of trade will lose context of balance nurtured by an interdependent society, bureaucrats although given a directive of objectivity, will be placed in positions of power and bound to the system mutual of obligations. Over-formalization creates these types of dilemmas: a perfect recipe not only for corruption, but also for keeping resources and economy in the hands of a few.

Transparency

Project the adoption of these abstracted rules as a requirement for Development and Modernization and reject any criticism as "attitudes that continue to make the economy and system of governance unattractive to international investors". This application of Rule of Law is a safety measure to allow You to operate freely and with a degree of security (for as long as the subject society stays solvent) because the subject, in an attempt to "keep pace with the Developed World" will do more to promote its image as an "investor-friendly environment" than to protect the interests of its people. Promoting "transparency" will provide You with benefits when operating in the subject nation-state's economy. Unlike local operators, You will have a great advantage over local businesses because You will operate with Your standardized rules. You can forego all cultural knowledge needed.

Culture of Trust versus Culture of Contract[43]

[42.] You will find that in industrialized countries like the U.S., that slavery is legal and can be employed as long as it falls within certain conditions; i.e. Article Thirteen, Section One of the United States Constitution states, "Neither slavery nor involuntary servitude, except as a punishment for crime whereof the party shall have been duly convicted, shall exist within the United States, or any place subject to their jurisdiction."

[43.] See Weidenbaum and Hughes, p.51; and Gray, p.169

A business culture based on trust is one of certainty. Within the business culture of the subject nation-state there is a high likelihood that networks of trust and credit associations based on family, mutual friendship and ethnic affiliation are still active. Trust forms the glue that holds these societies together and breach of trust disallows parties from further participation in the network of associations. The cohesion of the entire business community depends on the reliability of the relationship between different parties.[44] When trust is no longer a part of the local business culture You will have gained substantial influence over commerce. You will be taking over the collective business organizations and mutual aid societies that provide financing, labor, introductions, and business intelligence.

In the Culture of Contracts relationships must be defined concretely-- which does not take into account any natural evolution of a relationship requiring re-negotiation, or the misuse of legal counsel for the benefit of private enterprise--putting financial dealings in the realm of the courts and banking institutions. Agreements are secured with the threat of litigation. Instead of seeking collaboration through mutual agreement in the drafting of the contract, both parties seek to use legal language to individually extract the most out of their relationship. Both parties will insist on loopholes that will allow them to breach agreement under defined circumstances.

You are to push business from the arena of the relational to that of the quantitative. When the business culture of the subject's nation-state becomes quantitative Your firms will have the same access to networks that have, prior to Your arrival, sustained the subject's population and economy. The more paper is required of local businesses to operate, the more You will know of their affairs. With this information You will be able to understand how local businesses operate and You can adjust Your projections, creating holes of disempowerment in the economy through which You will grow Your enterprises.

Once You have placed financing into the hands of banks that rely on credit standards of risk based in world capital markets and on Universal or "generally accepted" financial practices, You can deem any productive financing as "bad loans", especially if they involve (as the means of promoting social welfare with subsidized hiring through loans guaranteed by the government or by the banks, in conjunction with the "national development plan") dealings between the subject government and private industry.[45]

---

[44] An example of a business culture of trust is that of the overseas Chinese in Asia. Generally, no contracts are needed to conduct business. "Losing face" is what is at stake for a breach of trust, and losing face in business due to one's lack of integrity is tantamount to commercial suicide.

The erosion of trust and promotion of the contract is another means of "opening" the subject's economy to Your exploitation. You are able to enter its economic arena and business culture without having to build trust or foster relationships; You have no obligations to the society, and have the same rights as indigenous business interests in legal recourse. With the system of trust, networks keep money in the economy and within a diaspora outside the nation-state. Without the system of trust there are no obligations in place to perpetuate the system. Thus, You can operate in the subject nation-state's economy, create wealth, and export all profit to Your own nation-state.

It makes for humorous irony that, while You promote "Free-Market" as the road to economic development, the subject government will foolishly embrace Your philosophy due to feelings of inferiority, when it should actually be aware that every successful industrial power has ascended with a strong, centralized government that intervened in the economy--tariffs on competitive imports and subsidies on important industries such as agriculture. This is because it is impossible to disengage economy from society without consequence.

Local Resistance.

Political groups that are aware of the destabilizing effects of Your projections, who organize to oppose the regime of Your subject's nation-state must be viewed as 'troublemakers'--traditional, primitive-minded, out-dated, elements in society--that exist solely to bring about the 'continued suffering of the average person' through malicious intent or 'ignorance of Modern political realities'; who promote social discord, resist Development, Modernization and integration into the Global Economy, and at the simplest level, are out for their own personal gain at the expense of the country's future.

Indigenous Peoples

You will find less resistance among "indigenous peoples" who live within the subject's nation state, unless they have had prior experience from an enemy with tactics similar to Yours and have somehow escaped annihilation or forced assimilation; or have had exposure to mass media and have become informed of aggressor tactics in a world armed with Rationalism. If the subject is uninformed in the ways of Rational practices and Cultural Warfare it will give little resistance to Your advances, because it will have a more flexible sense of identity in balance with the environment. The sense of identity for indigenous peoples works in relation to the natural world, not in opposition to an abstracted Other. There is no need for a protected core. Concepts such as

---

[45.] The banking crisis in Japan reflects this concept.

race or a Culture of Poverty are unimaginable. Retaining a collective identity, indignus people fall outside individual property rights and human rights legislation because they are a "community", not individuals. The desire for self-determination can easily be branded as divisive.

A very good way of dispossessing indigenous people from their lands is through the establishment of national parks and conservation areas situated on the lands that they occupy. Under the guise of "protecting nature so that future generations can enjoy it", You will be disinheriting stewards of the land who will oppose any future exploitation. You should be able to easily convince Your subject's government to embrace this ideology, because this of course, is the sort of action that 'Modern states' undertake. Once Your subject's government has established these 'conservation areas', You can proceed with industrial goals in its nation-state and will not have to worry about the higher cost of operating with environmental management in mind. Once the indigenous people have been dispossessed of their lands, You will have effectively decimated the environmental conscience of Your subject's nation-state. You will be able to conduct whatever activities You desire without concern for protest.

To summarize extensive literature and "field studies" on what indigenous peoples commonly experience:

*   Denial of rights to land
*   Denial of use and access to natural resources
*   Denial of political rights and the validity of customary institutions
*   Disrupted kinship systems
*   Disorganized settlement patterns
*   Loss of informal social networks, fundamental to the local economy
*   Undermining of livelihoods, loss of property, no compensation
*   Poverty
*   Disruption of customary systems of environment management
*   Enforced illegality. People become "poachers," "encroachers," and "squatters," on their own land and are subject to petty tyrannies by park guards.
*   Forced resettlement
*   Leadership systems destroyed, for if the community leaders accept the relocation they are accused of betraying their own people, but if they resist they are proved powerless. Forced resettlement presents a no-win situation to community leaders.
*   Symbolic ties to environment broken
*   Cultural identity weakened

* Intensified pressure on natural resources outside the protected areas
* Popular unrest, resistance, incendiarism, social conflict, and ensuing repression[46]

Set up a visible dichotomy between acceptable environmental mis-management and conservation. The existence of these "parks" will justify the need to fully exploit remaining lands for commercial gain, regardless of the environmental consequence, since a large amount of "unusable land" will already be set aside for "conservation". Naysayers in Your subject's populace that call for responsibility in the industry as well as with acquisition of natural resources, can be labeled as anti-industry and anti-capitalist, subsequently deflecting any appeal for "responsible environmental management'. You can even, under the guise of scientific research, actively pursue the acquisition of whichever resources that You so desire without the prying eyes of parties who have a vested interest in the sustainability of these particular geographical areas. You can even have Your subject government make "special exceptions" for commercial projects on these "preserved lands", as has been accomplished with oil drilling, the laying of pipelines, logging, mining, and the biological harvesting of animal and plant materials to be used for commercial enterprises. Using this process of taking collectively-owned private lands and putting them into the public domain, You will have achieved a "politically-correct" win for the environment and "global conservation efforts", while protecting Your resource-rich areas from future exploitation, from peoples who would, in Your words to Your subject government's, "misuse and exhaust the natural resources that belong to all of humanity."

By the time they have been fully dispossessed it is highly likely that, out of the desperation to leave refugee camps and loneliness from living outside ancestral lands, they will engage in behaviors that You can frame in the media is anti-environmental, such as the hunting of animals and harvesting of plants that have been their staple for millennia. And if they can be indoctrinated into the quantitatively valued Culture of Individualistic Materialism they themselves may act as predators and "poach" in excess, as a means to make money; because they have been stripped of their role as stewards of the lands left without the means to survive, and have been made into beings valued only for consumer potential.

---

[46] "Conservation Policy and Indigenous Peoples". Cultural Survival Quarterly: World Report on the Rights, Voices and Visions of Indigenous Peoples, Spring 2004. p.19

Chapter 5: Democratic Governance

Thomas Hobbes in his work *Leviathan*, explained that the stability of a nation-state depends on having a substantial and overwhelming force in its center which is overseen by a monarch. He compares this sovereign to a terrible monster, the Leviathan. Subjects of his nation-state are allowed to pursue their own interests, with the understanding that their interests are restricted and cannot run contrary to the powerful central force. The center must be seen as culture binding energy, a collective reasoning of tradition.

If force is the binding energy, the nation-state will eventually disintegrate because the collective culture of the population will overpower the center. Abstract nation-states are built in the fashion of Leviathan--the postcolonial states were created this way and therefore run the likelihood of having eventual authoritarianism or non-representative "democratic" rule.

A post-colonial state must reconcile its traditional culture with that of the colonialist's before it can reach stability. Authoritarian regimes realize that there is no binding energy to hold their nation-state together. Corruption is common in this stage--traditional obligations still exist as well as a "not-real" system of governance lacking in traditional checks and balances. It is a system run on Rationalist "objectivity" by human beings who, by nature of not being omnipotent are subjective beings.[48] People have to trust an abstract

---

[48.] The concept of "objectivity" is another deception that You feed to Your subject. It is impossible to not be subjective on some level: at no point can one *not* be an observer-participant in their own experience. Within "democratic processes" the ruse of "objectivity" is a means by which people will give up their right to think critically about issues concerning their lives, because they trust that officials will have their best interests at hand simply because they are in a position of power within this "objective" and benevolent system of governance. If an individual in power is not grounded in a sustainable value system, they can become predators empowered by passive complicity in a "democratic" society.

government well enough before they can trust that it acts to protect their interests. They cannot continually be governed by fear. Force can be used to implement laws, however at some point, for a young nation or abstracted nation-state to finally become a mature nation there must be a consensus of acceptance, inclusive of societal mores that define behavior and relationships within the community. Without these, the society is malleable and subject to manipulation by external influence.

The Application of "Good Governance".

The misallocation of resources is a perfect example of "good governance" at work. The subject nation-state's government supports Your agenda, turning its country into a factory to make, produce, or extract whatever Your needs are. To support the agenda true democracy will have to be weakened or support a secretly authoritarian, but deceptively non-representative democratic government.

Democracies threaten Your interests. Electoral democracy is essential to linear-based societies, which is what You are converting Your subject's nation-state into. In non-linear based societies, leaders are easily recognized as "representative" or "not representative" because of the acknowledged need to promote sustainability. This is true democracy, and it is an enemy of the free flow of capital and resources. The non-representative democracy of the subject must be properly constructed and marketed to the populace so that they will be satisfied with what is given to them. Parliamentary democracies are to be discouraged and presidential democracies are to be encouraged because parliaments are ruled through consensus with the "executive" subject to change by a vote of no-confidence, while presidential systems are more easily turned non-representative due to the nature of majority rule. This type of government will often overlook the realities of smaller segments of its population; in the "democratic process" their needs do not come up as "nationally important", and they can be forgotten by officials in the central government. Nonetheless, in the event of mass civil disobedience in Your subject nation-state You can proceed with the implementation of fascist-style "security" measures of social control.

Reason & Democracy

Manipulation of the population becomes easy in a world based on the contrived reality of Reason. The people in this system are taught that their intuition, feelings, and emotions are base elements with little value to Rational people. You, the definer of what is Rational, must create a situation where the population cannot trust its senses. Projection of Rational thinking is of utmost importance when using methods such as Free Trade and Capitalist Materialism to destabilize the subject's society and weaken its sovereignty. No conscious, self-empowered people would allow their society to be dismantled by foreign influence. The population must be made to feel that they could not possibly contemplate and understand the complexity of the affairs of the state and the larger world. They should view themselves as pions and should unwaveringly trust their elected leaders to maintain the state. This process of disarming the public of common sense is important, as it is a very effective tool.

True democracy enables everyone in society, utilizing individual potential to achieve self-fulfillment and to positively contribute to the community as a whole. "New" democracies based on the "availability of free and fair elections" rather than on the former are *weak* democracies that are prone to failure and control by foreign actors. A Prince must project Democracy as a Universal concept, an ideal that supersedes any cultural restraints. The subject must be discouraged from forming its own political institutions that are free from the political procedures that You give them. Discredit any indigenous institutions which are truly democratic. The political doctrines and procedures that You project must be viewed as Absolute and Universal to all people. Democracy is only useful when You define choices for the people. Never allow the populace to come to its own conclusions because there is always the potential for collective consciousness building. Without community responsibility, free choice, free will and Individualism will equate to social breakdown. In a worse-case scenario, if an enlightened collective consciousness seems to be building, support the formation of political parties and policies based on differences that can be exploited.

No people would allow their country to be exploited if they have a vote. It may initially appear that Democracy can provide You with the stability needed to exploit the subject nation-state, but You should realize that Democracy is Your enemy. Although You can initially woo the populace with the allure of popular material culture, it will soon realize what has been lost. So, if You insist on promoting "Democracy", You need to promote a direct non-representative democracy and create political parties based on difference.

You can never allow the following definition of democratic governance to take hold: "workable government with popular legitimacy". This does not fit the model of "Democratic Governance" that You are promoting. A "workable government with popular legitimacy"[49] signifies a critically-thinking population that grants approval for effective policies. This type of society due to an effective educational system and the continuity of traditional wisdom would be aware that its government does not support sustainable development but rather, Sustainable Exploitation. What You are promoting is "Elections". Even better, You are promoting Elections as indicative of an informed representative democracy, no matter how malleable the population is to seductive media campaigns under Your influence. Additionally, the beauty of "majority rule" is that You, with one vote, can make a large percentage of the population voiceless. In the absence of those voices, unbalanced, non-centered policies can be executed.

Progress & Development

In the guise of healthy nationalism You must encourage the subject government to embrace Your influence and promote Your development agenda. Every politician that You crown as being "progressive" should be "Reform" minded, promoting de-regulation through "land reform", "tax reform", "market reform", "regulatory reform". Each reform should be designed to weaken domestic economic capacity to make the subject nation-state a more "favorable investment environment". In the global market scene, "favorable investment" means a race to the bottom. Remember that You are competing with Other Princes to create Your own private "favorable investment environment": a locale with minimal government interference in the economy, low production and material costs, and easy logistics operations--made to sell back to the host nation-state as well as other nations around the world.

Keep up the push for "stability" in governments, as this will continue to support hierarchies designed during the Colonial Period. At some point before there is too much instability You should address the human security needs of the people, otherwise the people may decide to throw off the quantitative value system received during the Colonial Period and may desire to return to a more natural state of being, ultimately realizing that You are the bringer of untruths intended to bring confusion and collapse to the indigenous system for the exploitation of its peoples, lands, and resources. ". . . Instability, a nebulous concept at best, is the normal state of affairs in an international system of sovereign states."[50]

NOTE: As long as You are the most powerful Prince, having no equally powerful rival among Other Princes, this instability will not affect You at all. Remember the mantra: "What's yours is Mine and what's Mine is Mine". Sustainable exploitation requires instability managed on Your terms.

[49] This definition was stated by an Indian journalist during the Q & A session of the EU-UNU Tokyo Global Forum, "From Civil Strife to Civil Society: Post-Conflict Reconstruction, Peace-building and Reconciliation", February 5, 2004, UN House, Tokyo.

[50] Johnson, Chalmers. (2000) *Blowback: The Costs and Consequences of American Empire*. New York: Owl (Henry Holt) p.29

Pre-Softened Nation-States
& Non-Democratic Governance.

Unlike nation-states that are the natural collection of a group of people with shared cultural truths and whose truths operate as a cohesive center, the newly "independent" states do not truly have a center that is solely a *raison d'être* of maintaining cultural continuity and meeting the social welfare and security needs of the populace. Newly "independent" states are most likely to have authoritarian rule or non-representative "democracy". If the subject-nation emulates the hierarchy of its former colonial master, and if there has been no "cultural revolution" of some kind, the "former" master is still dominant over that nation-state.

During the Colonial period, the true center of the nation was dislodged and replaced with a Rational Center, based on the hierarchical system of "natural order" with the colonizer as the locus of control. The center of newly "independent" states has become transfixed on the Leviathan, defining government as an institution with legitimacy to use force against its people, basing "nationality" on geographical boundaries set by former colonial powers. Though the colonies were termed "Schools of Democracy", autocratic regimes ran these states and the indigenous elite were groomed to maintain the regimes using the method of control by force. After political "independence", these nation-states were left standing in their abstracted forms. The government existed to serve itself. Using similar methods of rule through Rationalism, You can easily exert control over these newly "independent" nation-states, because the governing institutions in these states are already set up to receive "guidance" from an external locus of control. Sovereignty-weakening tactics will work. You will be able to influence its/their apparatus of control to serve Your purpose. You will appear as the model for Good Governance.

Non-Representative Democracy

The population may have the vote but due to a higher concentration in the capital, the persons that have financial resources to win urban elections will keep office and will endorse their own representatives in the provincial government. This will help centralize administration over resources of the entire country while perpetuating the myth that votes count. Promote the development of non-representative democracy so that the world community will not interfere with Your actions of autocratic rule required to maintain Order.

Keep in mind that, with ownership of the mass media Your chosen elite will always control the country. A few social programs, immunization campaigns, holiday food giveaways and literacy campaigns will placate the masses. A centralized bureaucratic government will thrive with a major portion of the population living in metropolitan areas, at-large elections that are presidential rather than parliamentary, and major funding for mass media campaigns that support Your chosen candidates. All appointments to the regional offices where resources are located, all decisions involving allocation and privatization of resources, will be handled from the central government. With centralized governance however, You must be aware of the slightest disturbance. If You do not pay attention, small grievances can turn into ammunition for "fundamentalist" groups who realize that the government does not represent them.

People living in the cities are likely to be satisfied with the idea of electoral democracy because they are able to see the mechanisms of governance working around them, even if they do not directly reap the benefits. The mindset is this: the "elected leader" may be flawed, but the system "works" because leadership can be changed if the "majority" votes. But the people in the rural areas and smaller cities may realize that this "Democracy" allows for neglect of these alternate realities. This is because in the "Democratic Process" these needs do not come up as "nationally important"; they can be overlooked by officials in the central government.

If negative sentiment grows in these under-represented areas, it will cause problems for the central government which might have to deal with potential opposition, breakaway separatists, or even revolutionary groups. These reactionary approaches on both sides will keep the general populace from seeing Your influence as the root cause of problems in its "Democratic Process". This distraction is necessary; if You totally disrupt Your subject nation-state's social, economic and environmental realities, its government will have failed in maintaining the human security needs of its population and in order to prevent all-out failure, it will have to switch its mandate of rule to that of "maintaining national security". Remember, Your purpose is Sustainable Exploitation. Fascist measures can be legitimized under the guise of protecting the nation, opposition can be designated as "terrorism" and will be neutralized with popular consent. Your influence over the media can assure that the minds of urban dwellers are embedded with the "right" opinion about those who oppose Your interests in the nation-state. A compliant media source or legislation that allows for foreign-owned media will allow You to confine the thoughts of mainstream population into a spectrum of "political diversity" that stays safely within boundaries that are acceptable to You. With the parameters of mainstream political thought under Your control, You can have Your subject's population believing in a democracy that is really just a continual set of elections and re-elections.

The following is an articulation of the type of democracy that You do not want evolving in Your subject's nation-state.

> Buddhist concepts such as 'established by all causes and conditions', 'oneness and coexistence', 'commonly owned and administered', and 'collective creation', are all democratic principles . . .
>
> The Six Points of Reverent Harmony in the monastic community-- bodily unity by living together, verbal unity by not criticizing others, mental unity through a shared joy, moral unity through upholding the same precepts, doctrinal unity in views, and economic unity through sharing--are the harmonious expression of behavior, words, and thought in the body, speech, and mind of the *Sangha*, and are all democratic. Here, democracy is enacted, for if each individual does not exert his/her own will to participate, then harmony is not realized.[51]

Democracy can only exist in a society of critical thinkers, of persons who have self-cultivated ideas of truth based on holistic views of family, community, society and the world as a whole. It is not made by the opinion of the masses, it is made from the consensus of self-actualized thinkers. Otherwise, it is tyranny disguised by elections. People can be manipulated into believing that voting consensus holds validity by virtue of the fact that they are views held by the majority. That a large number of people believe something does not make it truth. Truth can only be assured through a centered holistic view in each individual, and consensus can only be valid when it is comprised of critical thinkers. True education and the development of individual potential within the collective are paramount to any kind of "expressed" participatory government. Free elections are not a symbol of democracy; a self-critical population is.[52]

Military

The prerequisite for stable governance in a "modern" state is strong military. For the abstracted nation-state, a Hobbesian approach must be realized. Since it does not have the cultural mandate of the people to rule, it rules through "legitimate use of force":

> Another political legacy bequeathed to independent African states was the professional army. In traditional Africa, there were hardly any full-time, standing armies. In the whole of West Africa, it was probably only the kings of Dahomey and Samori Ture who developed real

---

[51]. Venerable Master Hsing Yun trans. John Balcom, Ph.D (2002) *On Buddhist Democracy, Freedom, and Equity.* Hacienda Heights, CA: Buddha's Light Publishing , p.11

[52]. See Metu Neter, p.213

full-time, well-trained armies. However, all the imperial powers developed professional armies, which they used first to occupy and police their colonies, then in the First and Second Wars, and finally in the campaigns against African independence; and these armies were among the most conspicuous legacies apart from physical structures bequeathed to independent African states... In retrospect they have become nothing but a chronic source of instability, confusion, and anarchy as a result of their often unnecessary and unjustifiable interventions in the political processes of African countries. Indeed, African armies are the greatest millstones around the necks of African leaders, and the future of the continent is going to be determined very much on how these armies are dealt with.[53]

It is important that the security forces of Your subject's nation-state are trained in preparation for "uprisings" and people's guerilla struggles. If a popular movement should arise, it could also spill into Other countries. Believing in the struggle, the subjects of these countries will also revolt from the conditions endured. To prevent this, You must do two things at the same time: ensure that Your subject's military and police apparatus are trained in suppression and coercion "in the name of the state", and spearhead "Human Rights" initiatives that criticize oppression by Your subject state's government. Your subject will develop an art in its application of force on ideologically disruptive elements in its society that threaten acceptance of the projected ideals and way of life that You expose its population to.

There is a danger of fusion between the subject's military and society. You should coerce Your subject's government to turn its military into a domestic "security force" tasked with the duty of fighting and protecting against "terrorism". This "new military" should fight intangibles such as the "war on drugs" or the "war on terrorism". Your subject nation-state's role as responsible bastion of international justice will reinforce the needs of Your transnational corporations, even at the expense of its people and environment. In regard to Your own military activities, they should be framed in the same context and this projected onto Your subjects and Other Princes. As long as You remain vague it will not be viewed as a "War on the World".

Right-wing totalitarian governments are to be created and enforced to govern without the burden of popular consensus. To the populace, these governments should appear to be "Democratic", implementing temporary security control and domestic surveillance measures in order to ensure the physical security of the society-at-large. But why make this a "moral issue", why not just do it in the name of conquest? Is Cultural Warfare committed in the name of "Good" or "Democracy" supposed to make You feel better?

---

[53] Boahen, Adu A. (1987) *African Perspectives on Colonialism*. Baltimore: Johns Hopkins University Press, pp. 98-99

Social Divisions

To oppose one class perpetually to another--young against old, manual labour against brain-worker, rich against poor, woman against man--is to split the foundations of the State; and if the cleavage runs too deep, there remains no remedy but force and dictatorship. If you wish to preserve a free democracy, you must base it--not on classes and categories, for this will land you in the totalitarian State, where no one may act or think except as the member of a category.[54]

Your purpose is to create this kind of division in the subject nation-state. Bear in mind that these are not differences but divisions in the vertical, quantitatively-based hierarchy.

The Threat of Communism

Though a large majority of humanity practiced some degree of sustainable living based on philosophies of interconnectedness and maintaining harmony, You should define this trend of thought as having originated in the heads of two gentlemen during the Victorian Age. Any non-laissez-faire economic policy that engages communal, interconnected or nature-oriented long-term, non-linear life or governance philosophy can be attributed to the new intellectual grouping called "Communists". Ironically, Karl Marx and the architects of Communism were actually Rationalist thinkers based in their own social and economic realities. In truth, they were bringing nothing new to peoples who already had cultures based on sustainable life philosophies. What actually happened was that the early European intellectual heirs of this "new philosophy" took ownership of sustainable principles of living by naming them and turning them into the means of incorporating those nation-states into a global hierarchy similar to that of the Capitalists. The same relationships were created, but the intellectual guard of adherent nation-states was down because the philosophy espoused sounded too familiar to what they knew to be true as sustainable and humane. The Prince of Communism used the same methods of Rationality and Universality as the Princes of Capitalism. Like any other Rationalist equation, the Communist nation-state at the top of the "Communist" hierarchy actually made itself the locus of control instead of shifting power to individual collective "cultural centers" that should have been the guiding force for these nation-states. The desire for "the liberation of workers worldwide" was supposedly a founding principle, although world hegemony was the goal. Ultimately, this "named" philosophy of Communism proved unsustainable and was outspent by opposition that, for a long time

[54] Sayers, Dorothy (1971) *Are Women Human?*. Grand Rapids, Michigan: William B. Eerdmans Publishing Co., p.36

already, had been in the business of printing its own money. At the end of World War II the two main proponents of Capitalism and Communism were engaged in a massive worldwide spending war, and Capitalism won--the Communists having insisted on focusing on promoting Ideology, which is temporary, without the concurrent teaching of Culture and National Values, which are long-lasting and sustainable. Because of this victory there is now a strong "intellectual" and "practical" argument against the viability of Communism and Socialism.

Any desire to return to a pre-colonial sustainable lifestyle should be Rationalized as Communist rather than "cultural". If there are any calls for government policies that threaten Your control, such as sustainable development, the nationalization of resources that are still held by "former" colonials, opposition to "Free Trade", community-based development, character education, the prioritizing of domestic economic development over export-based development, land reform, regulation through the increase of export prices for agriculture and natural resources, the elimination of obstacles to self-fulfillment, You can de-legitimize them as "Communist". If You equate any call for sustainable governance policies as Communist, You can discredit detractors of Your policies in the subject's nation-state. This is especially effective if You need to convert the mandate of Your subject nation-state's government to that of a "security" orientation, or fascism. This reiterates the principle of "naming" and "defining" as a means of gaining control over Your subject, and I will elaborate more in Chapter 18, *The Rational Man*.

"Name" any call for sustainable governance or the re-ordering of social hierarchies, land, economic, and social reforms that are not Free-Trade oriented as Communist so that it can be demonized and eradicated. Try not to name them as Socialist, because Socialism and Socialist-oriented policies have proven successful in Western and Northern Europe as well as Japan[55]. You do not want to add any more credibility. But do not fret because efforts are being made to "liberalize" economies so that the "Free Market" can take ownership over these nation-states, converting any relational valuing of society into that of quantification and putting all public goods into private hands, preferably Yours.

---

[55] The success of these policies was sustained, at least until some of these countries began to implement free-market oriented liberalization regimes required for participation in the "Modern Global Economy" that began to eat at the economic and social cohesion of their nation-state under the single-minded linear pursuit of unhindered and perpetual "Economic Growth".

Promotion of Fascist Governance: Rule of Law Governance

In Your means of supporting the subject nation-state's taking on of a new "security-oriented" identity, the end result that You should strive for is to destroy hope.[56] If all forms of opposition to the policies that You project onto Your subject government are brutally and effectively dealt with and branded as subversive, the masses will eventually lose hope for a change in government. When the opposition is afraid to raise its head there will be no "Robin Hood" for the people to place their faith in, to change their current reality. Major social change often requires at least ten percent of the population's support; if there is momentum, if the people believe that change is imminent, more will follow. Democracy can only exist if it is acceptable to Your interests, and the only "democracy" that can be acceptable to Your interests is an un-democracy in which there are elections by an electorate devoid of critical thinkers. The political landscape of "acceptable views and platforms" must be so narrow that no matter which political party wins, You win, because the political parties are each based on the same system of values--ones that promote Your goal of Sustainable Exploitation.

Worldwide Fear, Worldwide Fascism as a Means of Control

Fascism, like a virus--like the AIDS virus--needed a strong host in order to spread. . . The world was too big. Fortunately, the world has changed. Global communications, cable t.v., the internet. Today, the world is smaller. And a virus does not need a strong host in order to survive. This virus . . . is airbourne.

From *The Sum of All Fears* (2002)

"The rise of fascism as the ultimate express of Rationalism"[57] is an efficient process that will cause the desired societal "solutions". You can create a climate of "fear" to solicit a response of domestic crackdown on civil liberties of the population. You can substitute the word "fascism" for "national security interests".

Artificial Peace & True Peace.

Today, people are striving for peace, but because there is not equality, true peace is difficult to attain. Equality is the only proper course to initiate peace; there will be peace only when there is equality. Peace and equality are two sides of the same truth . . . only when there is equality will there be democracy. Only when there is democracy will there be freedom. If there is no equality there can be no democracy or freedom to speak of.[58]

---

56. Chomsky, Noam. *Hegemony or Survival: America's Quest for Global Dominance.* Metropolitan Books, New York. 2003. p.10

57. Ritzer, George (2000) *The McDonaldization of Society.* Thousand Oaks, California: Pine Forge Press. p.28

True Peace is realized in the unconscious. In order to reestablish a natural balance, an unconscious desire for stability and balance may "involuntarily" initiate the destruction of present hierarchies. An "actualizing society" is one that You cannot exploit, because the people derive happiness from inner cultivation and a positive outlook on life, not from the consumption of external icons or a confrontational outlook on life[59].

Oppression as Violence

If the basic needs of a people are not met, and if they have been denied the traditional or formal education needed to develop critical thinking skills, they are living under a system of violence. This can be evidenced in the self-destructive behavior that You see in Your subject nation-state's society.

All people are "co-creators". They will either productively or destructively utilize their personal potential and innate gifts. If these gifts are not nurtured and/or if awareness of them is not cultivated within the person, if the opportunity to actualize them does not exist, the person instead of productively using these talents will instead use them destructively against his or herself and those most resembling themselves, i.e. their own ethnic community, etc. The ones who actually realize the lost opportunity to actualize their personal potential will probably be predisposed to attacking any symbols of the success model that You project onto them because of the inability to achieve their own success and the ensuing envy.

If You manipulate the population to believe in "Peace" by Your definition, You will have a society that cannibalizes itself. If "oppression" (lack of human security needs such as education, healthcare, life options, food, and clean water) are equated with "violence", Your subject will realize that even in "Peace" it is at "war". A people who are living without hope for change will give You the perfect scenario for high rates of criminal behavior because You have sealed the people's fate--life in eternal violence in the name of "Peace".[60] Those who do not submit to Your definition of "Peace", who oppose collaboration with You in creating a perpetual reality of "Sustainable Exploitation" and call for major changes in the society can be written off as "violent persons", "enemies of the civilized world", "terrorists", because they are opposing the culmination of Modern Man's desire for "World Peace".

In order to convince Your subject to accept Your definition of "Peace"--

---

[58.] Ibid. p.37

[59.] "Happy societies" can only be exploited through invasive (or a combination of both invasive and non-invasive) measures.

[60.] This phenomena can be witnessed in Post-Apartheid, "Truth and Reconciled" South Africa.

submission to the structures and systems that best serve You--define "violence" simply as bringing physical harm to another. You must preach the message of "Peace at Any Cost", for Peace is the highest state of evolution for Modern Man. You are the bringer of "Peace"; You are establishing the Modern "social order", the final global order that will last for eternity. Change can only be justified if You dictate its necessity: we are now in the Modern Era, no major social change is to occur except those that comply with Your desired ordering of the Global Community.

Chapter 6:
Individualism

Campaign-style agriculture has given the Japanese one more distinguishing trait: a sense of the unity of all people of the nation. As I said, in the Middle Ages eighty-five percent of the population farmed the land. This meant that at any given period of the year, almost everyone was doing the same kind of work. When the season came to transplant the rice seedlings into the paddies, the entire farming population was engaged in that activity. The exigencies of campaign-style agriculture forbade a going-my-own-way attitude. Since hunger and destitution were the certain outcome of such independence, anyone who insisted on adopting it inevitably became a burden on his neighbors. A Japanese farmer I know well once said: 'I am neither an industrious nor a conscientious farmer; I am merely a neighbor farmer.' Obviously he was being modest, but what he meant by a 'neighbor-farmer' is this: when his neighbor plants seedling, fertilizers the ground, or harvests the rice, my farmer friend must be doing the same thing.[61]

61. Ben-Dasan, Isaiah (1972) *The Japanese and the Jews*. New York: Weatherhill. pp.49-50

As a means of destroying community responsibility and a collective consciousness that might reject Your projections, promote the cause of Freedom and Individualism. You must propagandize the idea that the Individual is most important and therefore is allowed to be "selfish". This freedom to be selfish is what You will name as "freedom"--freedom from responsibility, freedom from familial obligations, freedom from the community and the culture. The Individual's only obligation will be that mandated by law. If this ideal is successfully promoted, social cohesion will be shattered and You will have created a society of Legal Moralism, having replaced its communal sense of ethics into the codified law of Your projection. The type of freedom that You promote lacks purpose. It teaches the subject to sell its soul for self-pleasure. The subject is to be made feel that it has unlimited earning and consuming potential and that its government's role is simply to protect private property.

* *Libertad*: freedom with responsibility
* *Libertinaje*: libertinism--freedom from responsibility[62]

Know the difference between these two freedoms. In languages where they are recognized as two different concepts, they are easily distinguished. Promote the second while using the name and implied meaning of the first. Freedom can mean the ability and opportunity to self-actualize; while the other denotes separation from, without connection to, responsibility for.

The collective-oriented idea of individualism is one in which someone can be an "individual" as long as their behavior does not threaten the sustainability of the society as a whole. In the ideal that You project, "freedom" is an abstraction: freedom equals no commitment; and free time equals time with no commitment. It should be used to coerce the subject population into believing that it has total autonomy, when in actuality, the new societal mores that You project will regulate its behavior.

Freedom.

True freedom acknowledges an unencumbered respect for the causality of nature. The freedom that You project is the "freedom" of irresponsibility, which "frees" the user of any responsibility to the true purpose and potential of self, relinquishing obligations to family, community, society, and humanity as a whole. It is anti-freedom, freeing the user from a "connection to" so that the

---

[62]. Conversation with Tomas Graman, Department of Languages and Literature, Carroll College, Helena

user in order to feel secure, must exert "control over". This kind of freedom is like an opiate: the drug is used to escape from "X" REALITY, and in the process the user becomes enslaved to the drug. The drug owns the user, as a person "freed" of responsibility to the collective becomes "owned by" an addictive relationship of possession in order to alleviate the anxiety of "being alone" in an oppositional world.

Freedom & Time

Your hold over the education system will begin this process of grooming the Individual into what it should be conforming to. You define "good citizenship" by valuing productivity on Your terms. There is no "idle" time; those who are idle can be defined as lazy or "desirous of things without wanting to put in the sacrifice". Also, time should be spent working in order to consume. "Quiet" time is Your enemy, as it allows for contemplation and self-reflection.

If You are effective You will alter the mental development of children. Your goal is to control as many cognitions as possible, so that You transform the population. An exorbitant amount of each day spent watching television and playing video games will decrease the ability of the young subject to "pay attention". These are participatory acts with a tremendous amount of stimulation, and the ability to self-generate "paying attention" atrophies, because it is not needed. With minimal participation, children will be unable to maintain concentration. Children will develop high reaction times and short attention span due to lack of self-cultivated thought. As a side bonus to You, this will probably manifest as some sort of artificial Attention Deficit Disorder in the children and will open another avenue where You can profit by selling pharmaceutical solutions to these socio-development problems.

Remember the following.

1. Quiet is dangerous: Your subject's populace can introspect, plot and scheme when it is not under the influence of Your projected cognitions.
2. All time in Your subject's nation-state should be spent on consuming, working to consume, or transforming people into consumers.
3. Freedom means being free from moral, ethical, cultural constraints. The only restraints are those of Codified Law and adherence to the Culture of Comparison and Individualistic Materialism.

Individualism.

In Individualistic cultures, people become disposable: "we can send some to suffer a fate that we would not desire, to perform jobs that we would not ourselves work, live in situations that we would not like to live through. In this type of society, what role does government play?" It has lost its true *raison d'être* and is left with the single occupation of maintaining law and order. Since the social fabric, the center, has been shattered, the state rules through the threat of incarceration and execution.

> This behavior is, therefore, characterized by hostility and defensiveness. The . . . [Modern] 'personality' is above all a product of a conception of self that isolates the individual. He is alone and vulnerable, surrounded by other alone, vulnerable, and therefore defensive personalities. Once past the level of the primary ideological substratum of the culture, which tends to bind . . . [Modern] individualism together, there is no identification between him and other individuals within the culture. Beyond this there is no commonality. He defines himself and their 'opposites', and his interest as 'opposed to' or 'in conflict with' theirs. 'Meaning' at the level of secondary or derived values, is determined by the needs of survival among hostile beings. The culture into which the individual is born provides him with an individualist and isolating concept of self, while it fails to provide him with a spiritual base of emotional inspiration and support. With these givens he has no choice but to go about the business of surviving as best he can. He is, indeed, in a 'jungle'. An initially defensive posture soon becomes aggressively offensive behavior. The individual perceives that the best way to assure his own survival is to disarm others; to 'beat' them, to 'win', to 'get ahead', to usurp the objects of value before they do, to control them. He must do all of these things before they are done to him (that becomes the Golden Rule). To make matters worse, the culture thrives on violence, and it becoming more intense.[63]

In the Rational mind, the Individual is separate from everything. There is always an opposing side--individual interest vs. group interest. Having a connection with other people implies losing "power" over one's life, because with connectivity comes obligation. Any human interactions are potentially antagonistic. In Rational Thinking, an individual is "opposed to", not "in harmony with".

Individualistic Materialism & the Culture of Comparison

Possessiveness and Materialism result from the separation of a people and their connections. The Individual only has influence over the self. As a means of satisfying power needs and in order to accommodate expansion of self outside the boundaries of self without, possession becomes the objective. The more the Individual owns, the more the Individual has control over life. In becoming an Individual, however, the individual gives up the freedom to

---

[63] Ani, Marimba (1994) *Yurugu*. Lawrenceville, NJ: Africa World Press. p.376

actualize True Self.

This Culture of Comparison that You are promoting is a Culture of Hypocrisy, because it prefaces the espoused ideal and does not acknowledge the True Self. The one who publicly exudes the stated ideals, in the quest to conform with comparison, is celebrated. This causes a great deal of anxiety in members of the culture. When You have effectively promoted this Ideology of the Individual, the primary role of government in the subject nation-state becomes that of protecting private property and subversively projecting a Culture of Conformity.

The "culture" binding the country together is a Culture of Comparison, it is a selfish society where social welfare is self-serving and paternalistic--"non-profit professionals" and "poverty pimps", or is altogether nonexistent. It introduces a psychotic way of thinking into the collective psyche, creating in the subject an addictive personality that alleviates craving for "external-internal satisfaction", for control, power, and expansion through the unbalanced consumption of external material and emotional product. As long as the internal remains void, the Individual will remain in a state of addiction.

The "rat race" becomes a frenzy, a race to "appear to be" with neglect of self-development, without introspection. Insecurity ensures that You have a nation-state of judgmental Individuals unconcerned with personal truths; to feel secure they must project the ideal upon others and attack those who do not embody it, a subconscious means to draw attention away from the dysfunction.

Culture of Comparison & National Self-Actualization
The highest goal of cultural development for a nation-state is to actualize the potential of its collective consciousness, manifesting True Self on its terms. Any nation-state that deviates from its path toward self-actualization is susceptible to influence of oppositeness.

Hypocrisy
You should so establish Yourself as representative of the "Height of Civilization" in the subject's eyes, that it cannot dare question Your actions. In terms of human evolution and the development of the state, You are running and it is just beginning to crawl. If You do not take proper measures to put the subject "in their place", the hypocritical stance that You take will become the root of dissent. A Prince must position Himself as the moral high ground; His actions cannot be judged if this approach is taken. If You do not, it can be Your undoing.

No matter what the reality is, You should portray Your nation-state as the ideal state, the state that all nations desire to be. In this way, when the destructive policies that You project on the subject's society take root, and if these policies also are causing problems in the social stability of Your state, You can call them the problems of the Modern State and the subject will not be able to recognize that these are flawed policies. As it will see them as the "Price of Progress", over time, You will transform its society into one that is very easy to exploit.

The danger of the hypocritical nature of this approach is being unaware of Your own hypocrisy. A Prince's moves must be deliberate. If You wish to attack, attack. If You wish to assist, assist. But do not believe that You are being helpful if You are actually being hurtful. "Humanitarian efforts" grounded in the reality of another cultural perspective may actually be more harmful to the subject than the predicament that You are trying to correct. If You wish to slow down the negative effects of social dislocation caused by Your influence, You cannot expect to assist by attempting to counter it with another method from Your perspective even if in the "correction" You are turning the society into is one based on Your image. To slow down social decline caused by Your projections and icons, You must decrease the frequency of the projections and exposure to the icons. You will have to allow the society to come back into its balance. Otherwise, even helpful measures will continue the destruction of the subject's nation-state.

Using Rationality as a means of attack, hypocrisy is like having a silver bullet tipped with cyanide in Your arsenal. In the system, deceit is key. First of all it is very hard for an Other to win at Your game, as the rules are made to ensure that You win. If a subject wishes to combat You on Your terms, it will have to do as You do--hide its true self and project a desired image. This is something that it cannot afford, for two reasons: 1. there is too much cultural decline already, and without a corresponding domestic nationalistic cultural construction campaign it cannot do this without damaging its inside; 2. Your scholar-anthropologists, students, interns, missionaries, have already infiltrated the society to the point that You know a great deal of the inner workings of its culture, and You therefore know how to temper its attack.

A good example of this is how Christian missionaries in the Colonial Period would often resort to violent and totalitarian means of converting people. They would teach slave owners not only to whip but to treat slaves like animals, violate women, break apart families. Then they would teach the converts and slaves about Universal Brotherhood and Peace; that "the meek shall inherit the earth"; about the ten commandments and Christian ways such as "loving one's enemy". Any opposition to the rule of the missionary and slaver would be an affront to the "Brotherhood of Man" and "Divine Order". These were taught as moral absolutes, but because they were the definers of "Morality" and these rationalizing interpretations, they were allowed more leeway and could be exempt to their own rules.

You should endeavor to make even the most innocuous of thoughts, attitudes, and actions into reflections of an Individualistic nature. People in Your subject nation-state should be moved to verbally support a diverse array of "politically correct" attitudes towards Other people and Nature. They should support an established grouping of "good causes" such as animal welfare, anti-logging, anti-oil drilling, multiculturalism, higher wages for "poor farmers" and factory workers. If You are successful You will have a large number of "liberal-minded" people that are supportive in order to feel good about themselves. In this way, the subject will be sympathetic to the "cause," but will not to take any concrete actions to address these issues or their root causes. They will sit around and possibly even organize to express "outrage" at a variety of causes supporting their self-image of being superior to those that do not hold the views that they express. An example: anti-logging proponents, with their groups of liberal-minded professionals, will meet daily to discuss the evils of logging and deforestation over coffee served in paper cups with paper coffee cup holders, deriding multinational oil companies "abuses of the environment". However, they will drive SUVs to these meetings and wear cosmetics and use hygiene products tested on animals.

Your goal is not necessarily to support or to work against any particular cause in the subject nation-state, but to make the Ideology of Individualism so prevalent and internalized in Your subject that even "well-intentioned" people will act selfishly. The subject should talk incessantly about how bad everything is and how much things need to be changed while putting forth no effort to change, intent on maintaining the appearance of a "superior-minded person", talking of sustainability while living and supporting an unsustainable reality.

NOTE: One way to make this "sustainable" for You is to make the "solutions" to these problems prohibitively expensive, so to even take concrete action against a problem that You are causing, they will have to work to make more money to be able to consume the 'solution'. In this way, even if You eventually lose one venue of exploitation You can gain another through the creation of an exploitative industry, producing "solutions" to the last problem, i.e. the "organic" food industry.

The liberals in Your own nation-state's society although well-intentioned, may be an enemy to You and may actually empower dissent within the subject state, because they will profess to be humanitarian but unapologetically benefit from the realities of Your state. Their hypocrisy will engage dissent, whereas Your more conservative members of society will often be outright antagonistic to the outside and will actually serve as a force appearing to desire reform in the hypocrisy of society. Example: in the US, the mantra about trade is that free trade is good for everybody--for the World, for Growth, for Progress. But conservatives, while nodding to Free Trade as a means of softening up other countries to make them more "transparent and investment friendly", cry for tariffs, agricultural subsidies and other protectionist measures keep the negative effects of Free Trade and Global Capitalism out of domestic economy.

The one thing that will keep You on top is that, if opposition in the subject's state does not desire to outright remove all of Your influence and instead desires to change or "reason" with You, it will lose. This is due to the irony of culture. The subject will view Your actions through the eyes of its culture, assuming that Yours and its thought processes are the same. This is not true, and You always be one step ahead as long as You keep Yourself in the game. In Cultural Warfare, You are powerful as long as You remain important to the state; otherwise, You do not exist.

The Two Different Concepts of
Individualism & Respect for the Individual

"Respect for the individual" and Individualism are very different concepts. One is focused on the the community's group responsibility to its respected personal truths and purpose, the other is self-focused and pays respect only to the Individual's self, desires, truths. Individualism encourages violence as a means of conflict resolution. This is especially true when any shared consciousness about the universe has been removed. Lack of respect for the person as property makes it easy to hurt them; there is no need for conversation, mediation, compromise--if there is enough power over the person, why not crush them.

Competition, winning, individual achievement, and standing apart from others are the ideals. The only thing that holds together a society of detached selves is the unspoken but highly projected system of social conformity based on Materialism, Classism, and nationalistic ideals of conquest, global hegemony, and superiority. The subject's nation-state becomes one big "Me" that desires to "own" all outside of itself to feel powerful and "in control". The boundaries and cultures of others are to be destroyed or submit because of insecurity in the Culture of Hypocrisy.

The teaching of etiquette and refinement is necessary in Individualistic societies, as it creates a social pressure that pulls individuals into conformity, gives hope and motivation to those stuck in monotonous lives, offers externally-based "self-esteem", and promotes snobbery and disdain for nonconformity to the class system. Being "above" Others, sometimes is the impetus for behaving properly. In "traditional societies" every individual has a responsibility to the social unit, be it family, group, or community.

Your goal is to initiate an evolution of the ethic of Modernity by transferring Rationalistic values onto Your subject nation-state's society. Take the following as an illustration:

> . . . [Modern] ethic is the epitome of selfishness. Contrary to the verbal expression of the rhetorical ethic, it is not considered immoral in the ... [Modern culture] to act in one's own interest at the expense of the well being of others; rather, selfishness, competitiveness, exploitation of others are necessary for survival, dictated by the ideology if the culture, indicating, therefore, 'moral' (acceptable, encourage) behavior patterns?. . .
> The truly '. . . [Modern] man' is the most competitive and aggressive person. While the least successful person in the culture, who in no way determines what the West becomes, is characterized by humility and life, i.e. identification with and consequent respect for those around her, resulting in nonaggressiveness (internal peace). This person is trampled upon in and by . . . [Modern] culture. She is considered 'worthless'. What is more, she is 'unethical' in that she attempts to defy the normative behavior sanctioned by the culture as a whole.[64]

There is a difference between individualistic selfishness and selfless selfishness. Promote the former, and define the latter as selfishness: those not wishing to participate in the world defined by You are to be ostracized for their "individualistic behavior". If they stay "outside" to create or even worse, to resist You and attempt to contribute to work divergent from participation in Your commodification of the subject society, they should be made to suffer socially and economically for their non-conformity.

> The distinction between constructive selfishness and just plain selfishness is mostly in intent. Selfishness demands gratification; it is self-centered and self-absorbed. Constructive selfishness demands that a particular yearning be pursued; it is almost impersonal and process-absorbed. Selfishness fills a hole in the self; constructive selfishness seeks to complete, and then share with the whole world.[65]

Providing the Subject with "Free Choice"

Providing the subject with "choices" that it has never contemplated will disguise the Universalism that You are projecting. Standards are derived from a history of action and response, of cause and effect. Over time, the reasons why "this or that" is done or "this way or that way" is thought can be forgotten. Having been time-tested, these mores are embraced because they

---

[64] Ibid p.379
[65] Booth, Eric. (1999) *The Everyday Work of Art*. Sourcebooks, Inc. Naperville, Ill. p.111

encourage the continuity of a shared, desired lifestyle.

If the population of Your subject nation-state has a taboo of a particular food or drink and You are aware of this, in the media You can create a discussion of "why we do not eat or drink x". Initially there may be no response to this at all, but if You co-opt intellectuals and respected media personalities into trying this particular taboo food or drink, they can make the partaking of the tabooed food or beverage a question of "freedom". Opposition to freedom of this choice, even if the effects of its consumption can be readily seen in the society, is seen as restrictive, archaic, and old-fashioned thinking rather than as possibly in response to the undoing of social mores that were established by the forebears of the subject populace because of the very negative effects that are being witnessed with reintroduction of this 'choice' into the society. Calling into question why or providing new "choices" is a way in which You under the guise of innocence can project Your agenda onto the subject and simultaneously cause a rift in its established cultural mores. If You can eliminate widely-held taboos through the manipulation of popular opinion, by devising the appearance of this "new choice" You will be creating the inroads for Other ideals, thoughts, and cultural icons to enter the subject's nation-state under the guise and protection of "Freedom of Choice". The desire for "Freedom" and "Choice without manipulation" will serve dissent in the society, which can then be exploited to further Your agenda of conquest on the subject nation-state.[66]

When Individualism is promoted and the people increasingly turn Individualistic, the state will become more repressive, having to keep order and regulate resource allocation, no matter how uneven. Since there is no emotional or spiritual connection between the selves, a physically manifested overseer must unite the community.

Addictive Behaviors

Self-fulfillment is unlikely when people's natural gifts and talents are not utilized, and You will encourage a growing number of addicts of all kinds in the

[66]. Take for example, an island society in which the people of contemporary times bear high rates of alcohol consumption, but do not have a recent history of this before colonization or "entering the new Global Market". It is likely that sometime in their history, the people made alcohol from coconut milk and drank it as an intoxicant, however, there is no recent evidence of indigenous production of alcohol. Since the forceful entry of this society into the "Modern world", beer (alcohol) is consumed as an intoxicant and the constitution of people, not being that of "regular drinkers", now suffer high rates of alcoholism and associated social problems. Effective disintegration of this society's social fabric is introduced as a product of their "right" to everything that the free market has to offer, even at the expense of society. Restrictions placed on drinking become law enforcement issues rather than issues of cultural-suitability. These are the kinds of "Free Choices" that You need to force on Your subject nation-state.

subject's nation-state. Since there is no basis of unconditionality in human relationships, all relations are formed conditionally and for the sole gain of the individual. The more dissatisfaction there is in the life of the subject and the more Individualistic (therefore isolated) it becomes, the more apt the subject is in becoming an addict.

Expansion & the Individual

In an Individualized society Freedom is to be Universalized, otherwise shunned and destroyed. Thus conformity is the only means for an individual to feel any degree of "security". With the promotion of Individualistic Materialism in Your subject nation-state, You can ensure long-time instability.

> . . . whole attitudes towards prices, sacrifices, import restrictions, new factories, electrification, communications, etc. was governed by his one fundamental principle that no matter how much you change a society, no matter how much you structure it, unless you create a new man, unless you change attitudes, it all ends up in greed, lust, and ambition.[67]

A successful Individual expands self as much as possible. Expansion is the projection and imposition of the cultural ego onto the world.

> The cultural other is a creation of . . . [Modern] culture, constructed, in part, to answer the needs of the . . . [Modern] *utamaroho*. The *utamaroho* is expansionistic. This, as a cultural characteristic, is itself very important to understand. The ego seeks to infinitely expand itself. This kind of self expansion should not be confused with the desire to 'give of oneself'--to 'merge self with other' or to 'become one with the world'. All of these are identified with the spiritual experience of love. Expansionism is the psychological, emotional and ideological opposite of these. Expansionism is the projection and imposition of the cultural ego onto the world. (It is possible to interpret all manifestation of 'universalism' in this way.) It is the expression of arrogance, greed, and an obsession to consume all that is distinguished from self. In this setting, 'discovered' phenomena automatically become areas *to conquer*--to be made *ours*. . . . [Modern] expansionism is the delimitation and redefinition of the world in terms of the . . . [Modern] self; as opposed to the 'losing of self' in the world or in the 'other', which is the obliteration of the isolating boundaries of self.[68]

---

[67] Venceremos! p.48

[68] Ani, p.403. From the glossary: The definition of *utamaroho* is the vital force of a culture, set in motion by the *Asili*. It is the thrust or energy source of a culture; that which gives its emotional tone and motivates the collective behavior of its members. Both the *Utamawazo* and the *Utamaroho* are born out of the the *Asili* and, in turn, affirm it. They should not be thought of as distinct from the *Asili* but as its manifestations. The *Asili* is defined as the logos of a culture, within which its various aspects cohere. It is the developmental germ/seed of a culture. It is the cultural essence, the ideological core, the matrix of a cultural entity which must be identified in order to make sense of the collective creations of its members.

The quest to "Develop" and "utilize the land to its fullest potential" from the perspective of a quantitative value system will follow Your directive of "Progress at Any Cost", and the subject will decide not to respect the sanctity of nature and the complimentary relationship between human and environment. At first this will be a choice, but after the breakdown of natural economy, sustainable agriculture, and the migration from "poor" rural areas to the "opportunity" of the cities, it will relinquish the ability to be self-providing. This will in turn lead to a dependency on the money system; to sustain life, it will become "necessary" to use all land for commercial purposes, especially in urban areas. The Individual will be prone to a sense of loneliness, a result of the destruction of formerly existing communal aspects of the culture[69], and will consume to compensate for the lack of community. The body of the Individual will be deadened by the lack of nourishment of a purpose or center. Surrender of hope to attain self-fulfillment is what kills the person. "And that is the nature of the new hedonism. It is not an obsession with pleasure but a search for stimulation and sensation to overcome the lack of feeling in their deadened bodies."[70]

Elimination of the natural environment in urban settings will contribute to a sense of detachment from others. The presence of nature in one's environment is a constant reminder of the delicate balance that must be maintained between people and the natural environment that sustains them. Living in concrete only adds to feelings of loneliness and separation, moreover, the anxiety of an oppositional life between Others and Nature. If the subject cannot see Nature it will be without Hope; life will exist in a confrontational, competitive race to expand and acquire more and more, as an attempt to reach inner peace. Those who cannot readily access the Hope-giving peace of Nature will be in a state of constant state of anxiety and stress, and a higher likelihood of mental health problems will develop, either as a reaction to or as a means of dealing with this constant state of external agitation. The externally-oriented subject will attempt to reconcile this state of agitation through "winning" and having an edge over the competition which will come from possessing and consumption, or through relationships in which it can dominate the other.

The Detrimental Effects of "Separateness" on Health

The application of this Culture of Individualism and its corresponding Ideology of Rationalism and linear thinking will lead to more treating of symptoms and

---

[69]. Ibid. p.390
[70]. Lowen, Alexander, M.D. (1985) *Narcissism: Denial of True Self.* New York: Touchstone, p.226

less curing of ailments. Health is to be "managed", because it is more profitable to manage than to cure. In addition to this trend in Individualized healthcare, complex medical disorders will arise and the "old killers" will become virulent due to life without balance. People will become so detached from harmonious lives that drastic measures such as major surgery and toxic combinations of pharmaceutical drugs will be needed to reconcile severe symptoms. A quest for "higher" technological solutions to symptoms will ensure that biomedical technologies will focus on "managed care", and will provide a profit motive that will continue this trend of reactionary medicine.

Your subject's nation-state will suffer from plagues of simple pathogens "hitchhiking" on rapid modes of transportation, substandard care due to both the neglect of Public Health and the support of Individualized Care, and changing lifestyles that become consumer-oriented. Exposure to environmental health hazards that result from environmental mismanagement, inadequate infrastructure due to the privatization of public goods and the subsequent allocation of resources based on the population's ability to pay, will lead to a healthcare nightmare in Your subject state and will cause the population to look at its individual life and well-being as preceeding the welfare of the community.

Love

By rationalizing love, separating and defining it in terms of filial and romantic, You will create a state of psychosis in Your subject nation-state's collective consciousness. Non-rationalized people can, conversely, have their love needs met from communal relationships because in actuality, love is a natural state--it is offered freely, simply by existing in the community.

Relationships in Your subject nation-state should become reflections of this Modern value system of quantifying human worth. Relationships are to be made into measures of possession: "x person is *mine*, and *nobody else's*." These relationships are to be based on unrealistic expectations of the Other's compliance to one's own personal truths; not on happiness, connectedness, and collaboration in achieving personal, familial, cultural goals. The following is an illustration of the how Rationalism and its oppositional approach to Nature and Others is expressed:

> While "control" represents "value", "love" does not. In terms of the . . . [Rational/Modern] conception of human emotion they are opposites. In this view one loves to the extent that one gives up control of one' emotions; one controls oneself by not allowing oneself to love. The experience of control is predicated on the rigid separation and distinction between self and other; love is the experiencing of self as being merged with Other. A lack of control is

repugnant to the [Rational/Modern] sense of self; conceived as properly distant from.[71]

> But his is not a universal conception of love. It is romanticized (unrealistic), and it issues out of the inadequacy of the [Rational] self. The . . . [Non-rational/non-Modern] concept of love, while more pervasive (that is, it includes mutually respectful and reciprocal relationships of many kinds), is supported by the structures within the culture and is at the same time not obsessive. *[Non-rational/non-Modern peoples] do not risk the loss of self in love relationships because love is the natural state of being: offered before birth, guaranteed by the kin base natures of the culture, and therefore taken for granted.* It is not anxiety-producing. It is natural.[72]

Codependency and love addiction are the consequence of a Rationalized society and a breakdown of the normal level of connectedness of people in a community. In sustainable human societies, merely existing, or being a member of the community provides one with a sense of worth and belonging. When one is not nurtured and protected by the community or family in this manner (safeguarded against abuse), one can become susceptible to this type of relationship.[73] This is another good illustration of the Rationalist value system that You are to project upon Your subject.

> . . . She will then risk being 'unsuccessful' (as success in . . . [Rationalist/Modern] culture depends on competitiveness and aggression, not love) and she will find herself surrounded by individuals who cannot (do not) return their love.
> When love is translated into the terms of human phenomenal reality for the . . .[Rationalist], its interpretation issues from a bedrock of chronic illness, fear, and aggression. These inherited ancestral emotions (experience) generate an obsessive-possessiveness; a clinging smothering, narcissist, and compulsively unrealistic 'romantic' conception of what love should be.[74]

For a society that is individually isolated and unable to truly depend on or trust any Other, all relationships become competitive and gear towards self-expansion, possession, and control. In the world of Individualists, the most skilled predators become "gods among men" and develop technology for the purpose of achieving the final goal of "Victory Over Death" and ascendance to the top of the hierarchy of Nature and The Universe, thus becoming Creator and Master Over All Things.

[71.] Ani, p.395
[72.] Ibid, p.395. Italicized for emphasis.
[73.] This narrative is also contained in the section "Why Linear Thinking Leads to the Development of Codependent Relationships".
[74.] Ibid, p.397

Individualism puts stress on the concept of love, because in the subject's society love is received from the extended family, community, and social affiliations, and reinforced from all directions. In the world of the Individual a great deal of expectation is placed on "love" relationships between two people. According to Dr. Lowen in *Narcissism: Denial of True Self*:

> Narcissism describes both a psychological and a cultural condition. On the individual level, it denotes a personality disturbance characterized by an exaggerated investment in one's image at the expense of the self. Narcissists are more concerned with how they appear than what they feel. Indeed, they deny feelings that contradict the image they seek. Acting without feeling, they tend to be seductive and manipulative, striving for power and control. They are egotists, focused on their own interest but lacking the true values of the self--namely, self-expression, self-possession, dignity, and integrity. Narcissists lack a sense of self derived from body feelings. Without a solid sense of self, they experience life as empty and meaningless. It is a desolate state.
>
> On the cultural level, narcissism can be seen in a loss of human values--in a lack of concern for the environment, for the quality of life, for one's fellow human beings. A society that sacrifices the natural environment for profit and power betrays its sensitivity to human needs. The proliferation of material things becomes the measure of progress in living, and man is pitted against woman, worker against employer, individual against community. When wealth occupies a higher position than wisdom, when notoriety is admired more than dignity, when success is more important than self-respect, the culture itself overvalues 'image' and must be regarded as narcissistic.[75]

The need to maintain a good self-image becomes paramount because how one is perceived and valued determines one's place in the new hierarchy. Even the so-called "good people" in society that desire change will participate in actions that are self-destructive because they will wish to be seen as having the best "image" as a "good person" or "agent of positive social change". They will neglect sustainable behavior in exchange for reactionary behaviors that are perceived as the better image, not realizing that this is nothing more than vanity. When self-image becomes predominant over self-actualization in Your subject's society, You will have effectively induced a state of narcissism on the population, and the dis-locative effects will be self-perpetuating.

[75.] Lowen (1985), ix Introduction. This quote is also found in Chapter 29, "Why Linear Thinking Leads to the Development of a Codependent Relationship With the Subject". In the section there is more discussion on narcissism, as well as an interpretation of the story of Narcissus that puts this into context.

Chapter 7: Individualistic Materialism

The Prince should promote a Culture of Comparison amongst the populace of the of the subject nation-state. If a people are manipulated into seeking external fulfillment as opposed to seeking internal fulfillment, there will always exist a void needing to be filled by external positive reinforcement. By placing Your cultural icons into the society as symbols of success, You will create a vehicle through which You can foster material-oriented Individualism. Self-actualization is true success, but the opposite can appear to take its place--Conspicuous Consumption. These are the two extremes in the same spectrum of self-fulfillment: one within, the other without. Any sense of community can be destroyed with support of the second extreme. In the Culture of Comparison there is nothing that cannot be bought, and there is always someone to be better than.

As opposed to operating within its personal potential, the subject will base life decisions by comparing itself with Others in the projected success model. Persons living outside the path towards self-actualization are very easy to manipulate, for they have no center or point of reference and departure, and therefore no purpose. They walk blindly through life grasping at any "good opportunity" or "good fortune" that comes, regardless of loss of self, family, community, or society. As the tenet states--one can only love someone as much as they love themselves. Those who walk contrary to their true actualized selves are committing the highest level of self-hate, betraying themselves.

Business & Community Responsibility

Even though businesses are "privately owned" they are still community-owned, because people grow to depend on them to meet their needs, hence creating a social economy. Because businesses are made up of people, they are "living" institutions bound to the same responsibilities and obligations in the subject's society. The projection of Individualism onto businesses will cause a loss in relational value and will advance quantitative monetary value, free from responsibility to anything other than self.

When the Culture of Individualism is promoted, business persons in the subject's nation-state will lose the feeling of community responsibility inherent to those societies which are non-rational. Businesses that are freed of these connections become focused solely on profit. Once business owners realize the monetary gains that come with not acknowledging their responsibility in the social economy they can readily be persuaded to separate themselves further and operate "freely" as "free enterprises". Without the concurrent application of Rule of Law to local business culture, any actions that businesses take, such as disrupting the balance of society and mismanaging the environment, do not have to be considered transgressions against society unless they are judged to break codified law. Even if they are aware of the disruption that they are causing, the dissolution of natural morality and placement into the realm of legality frees them of any responsibility to the community that they would formerly have been liable to.

Spirituality & Materialism

If Your subject's culture is founded in a spiritual tradition You can promote linear thinking as a means of spreading cynicism and cause the questioning of faith. Linear thinking does not acknowledge the interconnectedness of all things, much less causality. To a linear thinker, individual actions can be taken with little to no regard of the corresponding effect. In the desire to expand, the populace will take an oppositional attitude towards all things outside of the self, attempting to control and possess in order to alleviate this new anxiety of living in "chaos". When You have cracked the subject's conscious and sub-conscious sense of spirituality, You can re-assign it a new personal purpose. You can fill the resulting void of purpose with Materialistic desires. In the need for intoxication to escape reality, the subject will attempt to placate discomfort through acquisition and consumption of material representations of Your projected culture, or some other means of temporary self-delusion. In truth, this void cannot be filled by anything other than a connection to spirituality and life purpose. You will have created an "addictive personality". Shopping, eating, drinking, sex, and relationships will become addictive behaviors. You will turn the subject's populace into a nation of "consumers"; the populace will use consumption as a means of acquiring a sense of personal power and alleviating the anxiety of living in a world of disorder.

Individualistic Materialism & Idol Worship

Create a new religion for the subject nation-state: the worship of Mammon, the god of money, and a pantheon of lesser man-gods (hugods). This worship is to be carried out through the conversion of relational value to quantitative monetary value, and through the "idolizing" of other persons who have higher consumer value. When You successfully convert the population of the subject's nation-state into "consumers" and Individuals, You convert the value of the human being from relational and interconnected to that of the quantitative, of separation. In relation to others and to society-at-large, the subject's value becomes determined by its ability to consume. Having been turned into an oppositional society, social relations will be governed by the perceived advantages of dealing with Others.

The worth of the more "valuable" Other is higher than that of the people. The "valuable" Other can be deemed "somebody" while those with less consumer potential can simply be regarded as "nobody". This follows the same thought process as "possession", the coveting of cultural icons as a means of psychological identification with You (see Chapter 13: "Cultural Icons and Mass-Media"). Through contact with or idolization of a "somebody", the "nobody" feels elevated and the anxiety of its relative worthlessness can temporarily be alleviated. One's worth as a spiritual being, a family member, a community member, a society/member of nation-state becomes secondary to that of one's worth as a consumer.

Conflict in the subject nation-state's society, in the quest to obtain worth at the expense of Others and the society-at-large, serves as blood-sacrifice to "the god of money". Every destructive act, every destroyed person, every destroyed life, every drop of blood spilled from conflict over material gain serves to feed the spirit of the god of money. As in the Jungian tradition, imagine the existence of thought-forms as entities that reside in the minds of people. With an understanding of "collective consciousness" You should realize that, if a particular thought form resides in the collective mind of a society, if it receives vitality and sustenance from its host collective mind it will grow to be more and more powerful, actually gaining power over the consciousness of the subject state as well as over individual consciousnesses in the collective.

Every cannibalistic act that the nation-state commits in the name of the entity we can call Mammon, "the god of money", feeds it and provides for its sustenance. With the successful projection of the Ideology of Individualism You can evoke the spirit of the Mammon, elevate members of the society deemed "somebody" to the status of lesser gods and use its own spilt blood, cannibalistic and self-destructive acts as sacrifice at the altar of the "new gods". Remember, With the promotion of Individualistic Materialism in Your subject nation-state, You can ensure long-time instability. "No matter how much You change a society, no matter how much You structure it, unless You create a new man, unless You change attitudes, it all ends up in greed, lust, and ambition."[78]

[78] Venceremos!, p.48

Chapter 8:
Family Structure,
Population Policy,
& Gender Issues

Promote the Nuclear Family to create a mobile labor force. People are to be objectified into units of Quantitative value. Their efficient exploitation is most important, the viability of the family structure is not. Family is the most basic unit of a society, and in the latter days of promoting Individualism the stable family could act as the floodgates that keep society from crashing in on itself. By breaking the extended family down into the construct of a Nuclear Family, You will assist in destroying the cultural continuity that extended families promote. Beware, this is a dangerous game to play. If You break down the family, You will have broken down society.

As long as there is consensus that the Quantitative valuing of humanity outweighs a relational value, monetarily "rich" nation-states will retain influence and "poor" nation-states will generally have less, even if the actual numbers of "votes" may be higher.[79] Power in international affairs must be kept in the hands of the Quantitatively "rich". If not, relative value will prove to overwhelm the power-of-status that quantitatively valued nation-states hold over those that are relationally valued.

When providing foreign aid to the subject You should require the government to show "good faith" that it fully intends to Modernize and Develop. One measure of this commitment will be the nationwide, top-down institution of Population Policy. Besides co-opting the subject's government into essentially committing suicide, You will have made an acceptable practice for the institution of Culturally Incongruent Policies.

[79.] Take for instance, the maintaining of status quo in the UN Security Council and its veto power versus resolutions by the General Assembly.

If Your subject nation-state maintains or develops a large population, a massive collective consciousness may be borne and effective leadership can be moved to commit to the impossible. One method of lessening the probability of the subject in reaching realization of self is to destroy the possibly of it reaching a "critical mass". Provide the subject with "conclusive" data illustrating the benefits of Population Policy and Family Planning programs, show how substantially lowered population growth will assist in meeting national objectives administrated by You. Population Policy and Family Planning are to be pushed as prerequisites to Development and Modernization. Remember the credo of Empire: what is Mine is Mine and what is yours is Mine.

...A people who refuse to express its love and appreciation for its ancestors will die because in traditions, if you are not expressing your own, you are participating in and expressing faith in someone else's ancestors. No person is devoid of an attachment to some cultural fountain. Whose water are we drinking?

Professor Molefi Kete Asante, Temple University[80]

80. From a speech "The Future of African Gods: The Clash of Civilization" Accra--W.E.B. DuBois Center July 10, 1998

Family Structure.

The following is an illustration of the kind of family and community structure that You cannot allow to exist in Your subject state.

Initiation processes vary from culture to culture. For the Dagara, initiation is intended to help young people on the verge of adulthood to 'remember' their purpose on Earth.

Initiation is a six-week long journey into the magical world. It begins when families walk their young ones to the outskirts of the village and surrender them to the wilderness after stripping them of their clothes. The young ones walk into the bush naked and scared, a condition necessary for the ritual remembering. Throughout the ordeal there is no food except that which can be found in the bush.

I was told to sit in front of a tree and to gaze at it. The hot tropical sun broiled me, ants bit me, and I was blinded by sweat. Every so often, an elder would come and check on me. The experience was painful and boring, but it all culminated in a vision in which the tree disappeared and I saw a woman emerge from it. She was familiar as a mother or some sacred caretaker. Whoever she was, the reunion was very emotional, and the experience ended with me hugging that tree and weeping.

I could invoke Western psychology to explain the whole experience away, including the reaction of satisfaction of the elders, but I won't because my respect for trees and nature began after this experience, the first of a series of magical journeys.

What is important is that exercises like this weakened my resistance to the dream world and the supernatural to the point where I was able to consciously journey into an underworld that is only acceptable in the West as a fairy tale. But the experience itself registered in my own consciousness as a disappearance to my own physicality. In other words, in the underworld one has a shape, but that shape is no longer available to the physical sight. By the time one gets back to the world, the body registers things unlike before.

The underworld is the place where one encounter's one's own identity prior to being born into a community of humans. It is the ideal place for remembering one's energetic identity as well as one's life project.

Also, one returns from the underworld with something which serves as the first medicine, a kind of reference book that you return to whenever you feel the need to refresh your memory of what you are doing here on Earth. How it's made accessible to the initiate is part of a tribal secret held tightly by elders. But a cave in a mountain can easily become a gateway.

Coming out of the underworld alive ends the initiation process. You return to where you had been stripped of your clothes six weeks earlier, and your family and the whole village is there waiting for you.

The return to the village is like returning to the human. It's warm, comforting, loving, and relaxing. Everybody knows that you know, and so you dance your knowledge in front of the whole village and celebrate with your loved ones the recovery of your memory.[81]

Work the various projections that I have suggested on multiple levels to break community bonds that tie the people together. You are to be the only constant in the lives of Your subject populace.

For a people still grounded in the relational value of humanity, large families represent "wealth". As long as the extended family is existent You will not be able to dislocate the subject from the type of community-oriented thinking that is at the core of social cohesiveness, especially if there is enough land for cultivation. A decrease in family size is viewed as disempowering, since practical labor force and economic security would also be decreased. In extended family structures the presence of others, most notedly the elders, provides an expectation-free environment by meeting needs communally.

Even if threatened by economic hardship, the subject will not react in the fashion that You see prevalent among nuclear families. But if You change the value system to that of Quantitative monetary value, large families will cease to symbolize wealth and if they lack major purchasing power, they will become a large number of "worthless people". With this You can create the sense of need among the populace for "family planning"--'only if' there was more access to Family Planning, hardships on the community and society-at-large would be alleviated by having fewer children; however, the converse is true:

As far as crime in general is concerned, the evidence suggests that both the predominant types of crime and the increase lawlessness of the last decade are best understood in terms of the long-term changes in British society that have been taking place for almost twenty years . . . the progressive weakening of the traditional social bonds of family and community and the final transformation of the traditional function of the state primary and secondary schools from on of pedagogically oriented social control to one of competitively and socially divisive--oriented acquisition of knowledge and skills. The role of the Victorian Board School, which persisted as a model for primary education well into the present century, has been forgotten . . . It is the virtual control from park keepers to bus conductors and school attendance officers which has left the police overexposed and with inadequate resources to deal with the problem of crime . . . increased resort to carceral solutions for social problems is equally lacking in effect but ruinously expensive . . . crime of the kind that afflicts Britain and much of the post-industrial world reflects an altogether malaise[82].

When You reduce the family down to a "nuclear" unit of parents and children, You will reduce the family to a level of stressful living. Regardless of socioeconomic realities the relationship between parents and children will assuredly be strained; the children expect parents to meet basic security needs and to provide emotional and financial support. Thus, a certain tension

[81.] "Initiation: Remembering One's Purpose," by Malidoma Some. In *Context: A Quarterly of Humane Sustainable Development*, Winter 1993, p.30

[82.] Gray, p.31 from T. Morris, in Kavanaugh and Seldon, eds, *The Major Effect*, op. cit., pp.314-316 can develop between children and parents of the Nuclear Family. In an extended family this "tension" becomes diffused because cultural knowledge is transmitted by the entire family, and lessons can be taught without the strain of a "conditional relationship".[83]

In reference to the argument that "biological factors" were fundamental to the fall of the Roman Empire, Will Durant in *Caesar and Christ, Book III* of his *Story of Civilization* states:

> A serious decline of population appears in the West after Hadrian . . . A law of Septimus Severus speaks of a *penusia hominum*--a shortage of men. In Greece the depopulation had been going on for centuries. In Alexandria, which had boasted of its numbers, Bishop Dionysius calculated that the population had in his time [250 A.D.] been halved. He mourned to see 'the human race diminishing and constantly wasting away.' Only the barbarians and Orientals were increasing, outside the Empire and within.[84]

While You and Other "wealthy" societies suffer from a steady decrease, the hardships endured by the subject empowers its drive to sustain and increase population levels. You must promote Population Policy and the Culture of Comparison at a frequency to which one will reinforce the other. If not, the people will naturally rely on family and community for support and security.

Population Policy.

> . . . The removal of agricultural protection and the establishment of free trade, the reform of the poor laws with the aim of constraining the poor to take work, and the removal of any remaining controls on wages were the three decisive steps in the construction of the free market of mid-Victorian times that is the model from all subsequent neo-liberal policies . . . In Britain, the United States and New Zealand, as well as countries such as Mexico which have had structural adjustment imposed on them by transnational financial institutions, the outcome has been an approximation to a free market in which labour is traded freely as a commodity just like any other.[85]

The growth of nation-states depends on an abundance of labor that can be evidenced in every present-day industrialized economy. Allow skilled workers and intellectuals that can contribute to the brain-trust of Your nation-state to emigrate to Your nation-state; leave those who are less desired in the

---

[83] The primary role in a Nuclear Family is to provide economically for the children. The extended family provides security needs, transmits cultural knowledge, and perpetuates ancestral knowledge.

[84] Buchanan, Pat (2002) *The Death of the West: How Dying Populations and Immigrant Invasions Imperil Our Country and Civilization.* pp.47-48 from Durant, Will. *Caesar and Christ.* New York: Simon Schuster, 1944. p.666

[85] Gray, John. (1998) *False Dawn: The Delusions of Global Capitalism.* New York: The New Press. p.11. Look at Gray p.29 Re: free market and breakdown of traditional social institutions.

subject nation-state, with certain exceptions when allowing seasonal entry visas for the unskilled seasonal work needed to sustain Your economy. This type of emigration will create a brain-drain in Your subject nation-state and contribute to Your efforts to destabilize for exploitation. This is a means by which You can maintain influence over the subject's society, economy, and resources, and alleviate the risk of it developing a "consciousness of nationhood".[86]

Because You have "out-run" the subject government in its race toward Modernity it will do all it can to Industrialize, risking the social welfare needs of the people. Its concern for sustainability will lessen with the introduction of Your biotechnologies. This will foster a dependency on You for its very survival and will prevent the massive exodus of its population to other countries.

It is rare, but the possibility exists that Your subject nation-state is one that already has a very large population and may even face the shortage of food supplies and energy for industry. In this case, You want an opposite in terms of Population Policy. A nation of this size has already realized its "consciousness of nationhood" so You will have to rely on Your projections of social, economic, and environmental dislocation. You should oppose any efforts to decrease population. You can promote the adoption of G-M (genetically modified) agriculture and livestock with production facilities controlled by Your nation-state's biotechnology firms.

[86.] A simple illustration of how beneficial net population growth is to the economic development of a country is the corresponding relocation of Western (Western half of the continent) Africans to the Americas from the 16th to the 19th centuries with the dissemination of the population of Western Africa and at the same time period. The transference of a significant portion of the population of Western Africans to what is now the United States provided a massive labor force, not to mention the benefit of substantially lowered economic costs as compared to wage labor. At the same time Western Africa's population of men and woman who served as its leaders, intellectuals, craftspersons, traders, healers, farmers, laborers, and childbearers was severely reduced, resulting the halting of a substantial amount collective ancestral knowledge due to the long-term absence (300 - 400 years) of people in the critical population ages of 15-35, the laboring and childbearing years. This transfer of population, labor and cultural inheritance, being introduced into a mixed economy of both plantation and industrial capacity unlike its solely plantation- or mine-oriented Latin American and Caribbean cousins, gave the newly-born USA a formidable jumpstart in its economy to the point of surpassing all other countries in the Western Hemisphere, and left Africa in a state of stagnation, open to exploitation by other colonial powers. Every successful Modern industrial power amassed power through high population growth rates (which served as an abundant source for labor and domestic consumption) and access to resources that exceedingly existed outside of its ecological footprint. This is more likely in "pre-softened nation-states" than others.

Methodology

In Your society of Order large families should be seen as "backward", indicative of a "Culture of Poverty and Ignorance". Create an artificial environment of positive reinforcement where people will desire to be "a part of" rather than "in opposition to" the trend of "family planning" and respond to criticisms by stating that the root of poverty reduction is in population reduction. There is a high likelihood that You will encounter resistance from cultural authorities and religious groups. Diffuse the power and influence that these groups have over the populace.

Disguise population control policies with "reproductive freedom" so that those in opposition can be branded as antagonists bent against the "reproductive freedom" of society. Create the appearance of a society that has accepted the validity of Your policies, one that has already made the change.[87] But beware of detractors who may criticize Your efforts they may make the argument that if the resources put towards Your extensive campaign against "excessive fertility" were instead spent on poverty reduction then the people would actually benefit, and would not feel the need to have so many children as a social security measure for old age.

You need to make information about Family Planning available to all who could possibly hear it. Use the mass media and utilize every language spoken and written in the subject's nation-state. Use radio, magazines, newspapers, comic books, traveling theatrical groups, special seminars, endorsement by media celebrities, public service announcements, flyers, bulletin boards, advertising on buses and billboards. Make the message of Family Planning so prevalent that none will be able to escape.

Small communal societies are natural social markets due to the close relationships shared between people, but in cities and industrialized areas that are unnatural and use more resources than are created, a social welfare system must be established to assure stability. With the wide circulation of this projected "need" You can begin to have those Non-Government Organizations (NGOs) that share Your vision offer their services under the guise of general "Development" assistance, and when government fails to address the social welfare needs of the people Your projections will ensure that popular opinion caters to the notion that certain members of society are predisposed to criminal activity. Coercion will be constant at this level of personal contact, and the NGOs will be perceived as experts whose interests are "purely humanitarian". No one of significance will see the increase in crime as a consequence of social dislocation.

---

[87]. In this way the cultural and religious authorities will lose influence over the society.

Non-Governmental Organizations

Because the promotion of Population Policy cannot rely solely on media outlets, it will also require mouth-to-mouth promotion of the ideal of Family Planning. You can use NGOs that are already advancing population decrease programs through the vision of Universal Humanism, or create Your own cover organizations for foreign policy objectives. The NGOs will be involved in a number of "community development" activities and trust in the community will be established through literary programs, economic empowerment programs, health outreach programs, gender empowerment programs. Discuss the benefits first of "child-spacing"[88], then of short-term contraception and finally, long-term. Peer pressure will compel the communities to conform to "widely accepted" family planning practices, which can be reinforced through mass media.

You will be able to conduct a long-term contraception program under the guise of HIV/AIDS programs.[89] To combat any possible resistance from indigenous cultural, family, or religious groups, combine HIV/AIDS programs with long-term contraceptive programs, creating between the two a symbiotic correlation that does not actually exist. From the government level, as a condition of other aid dispersals, mandate the implementation of Family Planning programs and have Your subject government endorse as "partners" the NGOs that are promoting Your agenda. Through the use of NGOs, the subject government will become an active participant in Your Family Planning programs.

To reduce community resistance to programs that are in the same sphere as microenterprise and entrepreneurship development, place Family Planning and the HIV/AIDS effort under the same umbrella. When "clients" are being counseled on how to manage a small enterprise, they can also receive "advice" on the merits of Family Planning, and You can imply that persons who are "responsible" and "progressive" enough to participate in Family Planning have a greater chance at being considered for economic empowerment programs. Making this scheme a formal requirement may provoke opposition, but a "friendly suggestion" from the same people who are helping the subject "make a living" is likely to at least be considered, and the

---

[88]. A family planning method in which children are spaced, such as four or six years between births.

[89]. Use this as a screen to prevent the resolution of root public health problems. Oftentimes, the "deaths" attributed to HIV/AIDS are never tested to confirm whether they are the result of HIV infection; many of these deaths are actually due to common regional communicable diseases and hygiene-related diseases that exist in affected areas due to poor sanitation, unclean drinking water, and ineffective or non-existent bloodbourne pathogens, "Sharps", protocols in hospitals and clinics. You can blame the negative outcome of life in abject poverty on HIV/AIDS and root social, economic, and environmental problems will never have to be resolved.

rumors that those who participate stand a better chance at receiving assistance is a good way to force the "chronically poor" to submit to Your Family Planning objectives.

Maximizing Business Potential

You might desire to utilize and sell contraceptive technologies that have been banned in Your nation-state because of lack of sufficient testing and/or have been proven to be harmful to those who utilize them. To prevent the loss of income to Your firms that manufacture these technologies, simply incorporate these banned technologies into the population policy that You are projecting onto the subject. Utilize Your subject nation-state as both an open market source as well as a site for extensive testing on the population, to observe long-term health effects and reliability.

Emphasize contraception in adolescents, indigenous minorities, and post-partum women. This can be achieved using youth reproductive health out-reach programs for adolescents, general primary care outreach programs for underserved indigenous groups, and tubal litigation immediately following childbirth in post-partum women, as You will find less resistance among these subjects. Vulnerable to coercion, they will submit to other medical schemes and Family Planning workers will have the opportunity to perform procedures without their knowledge.

In the subject's nation-state there may already exist the availability of contraceptives.[90] Your goal in projections and hands-on contact is to create an atmosphere of false "community support" for a much higher availability of contraceptives than would ever naturally occur in the society. Co-opt as many figures of power, trusted government agencies and community development organizations into supporting the availability of long-term contraceptives.

Promote voluntary surgical contraception in both men and women through female sterilization, vasectomies, contraceptive implants, injectable contraceptives and intrauterine devices; promote the continued efficiency and effectiveness of methods of contraception through clinical trials, epidemiologic studies, and methods such as minilap and laparoscopic sterilization, copper IUDs, NORPLANT, low-dose oral contraceptives, post-partum IUDs, and the Filshie Clip for female sterilization, while moving the government to reduce medical barriers to the population as a means furthering the Family Planning agenda.[91]

---

[90] This is most likely in "pre-softened nation-states".

[91] Source: The Agency for International Development, Office of Population Control Contracts (1995-1996).

When combined with Your Population Policy, the advent of AIDS, accompanied by SARS and other "new" cross-species diseases like Avian flu or the Nepa virus and epidemic levels of other communicable diseases such as multiple-drug resistant TB, diphtheria, plague, will result in lowered birth rates--especially if the living conditions of a significant number of the population already lead to compromised immune systems due to malnutrition, unclean drinking water and environmental pollutants.

Population policy aims to reduce the fertility of those aged 15-45 and more specifically, 15-35. If the aforementioned diseases cause mortality in the childbearing population, in addition to lowered birthrates productivity will decline. This decrease in the "economically productive" population will also lead to a loss of a sustainable workforce, severely reducing the viability of the subject's economy. If Your purpose is to maximize the possibility of negative net population growth in the subject nation-state, plan Your programs in conjunction with the spread of public health epidemics.

The Threat of Consciousness of
Nationhood in Your Subject-State

A high population in Your subject's nation-state threatens Your ecological footprint.[92] A smaller population will mean less voices in opposition to Your control over resources. If Your subject nation-state's population grows to the point that it realizes a national collective consciousness, the population will demand that resources be put to the best use of the nation-state rather than for the short-term gains of economic investor relationships with foreigners. You may no longer be able to exert the kind of control that You presently hold over the subject, the land will be "owned" by the nation-state and not by "factions", families, or compliant governments that work in Your interests. You will not be able to continue the claim of "what's yours is Mine" and You will not be able to spread G-M (genetically modified) crops as a "band-aid" solution to the misallocation of land, because arable land and water will be put to use growing food, grazing livestock, preserving fish for domestic consumption.

Abstracted nation-states constructed through legislation but without a

---

[92] An ecological footprint can be described as the actual ecology need to support the level of consumption in a given area. Ecological footprints of some industrialized nations can be many times their actual national land-mass and available resources. William Rees, Professor of Regional and Community Planning at the University of British Columbia offers a more conclusive definition: "The ecological footprint is the corresponding area of productive land and aquatic ecosystems required to produce the resources used, and to assimilate the wastes produced, by a defined population at a specified material standard of living, wherever on Earth that land may be". When determining the ecological footprint of a given nation-state, one must also take into account the actual environmental impact of the its global footprint as well.

cultural mandate can only become "nations" when the populace realizes its national collective consciousness. If the abstracted government still stands when this consciousness is realized, the government will either continue or be replaced by one that is "of the people".[93] You can be assured that a government "willed" into existence by the collective national consciousness will reclaim all lands and resources that had since been held by foreign owners, they will no longer be Yours.

As long as the population level stays below a critical mass You can continue to exploit the resources of the subject because of the lack in collective ownership of land and resources. However, if a "consciousness of nationhood" develops in Your subject it may realize that it is impossible to separate the people from the lands and resources; under duress from the multitude of Your projections, it may move to "nationalize". This can foster the beginnings of a revolution, which You cannot allow.

Do not make the mistake of ignoring the "size" of the collective consciousness of Your subject nation-state, since it can be an easily overlooked aspect of "power". The realization of national consciousness can quickly override the legal mandate that the abstracted government has in place. If there is a "consciousness of nationhood" and the government is not aligned with it, its days are numbered, and so are the days of unencumbered influence over the subject. A considerable population can evoke the unconscious cultural center that You are working so hard to dislocate at the conscious and subconscious levels of collective. Your projection of Individualistic and Universalistic concepts, when combined with social, economic, and environmental breakdowns support the Individualistic mantra: "you can only rely on yourself; you cannot depend on anybody else". But as I have reiterated time and again, psychological manipulation of the collective and individual consciousness of Your subject is not an exact science, as its very process defies the natural order of things: all matter desires stability.

If a large number of the subject population of this type migrates to Your nation-state, the cultural integrity of Your nation-state will be threatened, because these immigrants possess the "consciousness of nationhood" and no matter where they move in the world, they will carry "community" with them. The proliferation of a diaspora of this sort will serve to be a great threat to the Universalistic rhetoric that You are projecting onto the subject, threatening any myth of superiority You may be using to bind together Your own nation-state.

Heed My words on this scenario of "teeming masses" headed to Your shores and the shores of Other nation-states. If this trend is not suppressed,

93. The Common People, the loyal people

125

one of two scenarios can arise. 1. the subject nation-state will export enough of its population to create a worldwide diaspora that can act at its bequest everywhere and simultaneously; or 2. the numbers of persons leaving and transplanting themselves everywhere is so vast that You view this "expansion" as a threat to Your interests at home and abroad and to deal with this, You construct a scenario in which You justify going to war with it. Obviously the second option is invasive and You should not engage it unless it would be beneficial to Your economy and not too detrimental to Your world hegemony.

If You have anxieties about population growth in Your subject nation-state, be aware that it is paranoia arising from Your own projections. You can fall into a state of constant fear for Your safety like slaveowners in the antebellum American (US) South or whites in apartheid South Africa--a perpetual fear of uprising and retribution. In reality, the subjugated will opt for reconciliation instead of a justice that is reasonable, especially with Your concurrent projections about Human Rights and the need for harmony even at the expense of true peace.

The Threat of Too Much Comfort to Your Nation-State

It is harder to get people to have more children once families become smaller because decisions concerning family size are oriented on individual choice rather than on family, community, cultural, or religious needs and expectations. The lack of "resistance" in the lives of Your population combine with trends of the new family being that of a nuclear family, comprising "partnerships of economically compatible units" and DINKS (double-income, no kids)[94].

The perceived "need" for family and community decreases if Your society is physically comfortable and the populace leads a "decadent" lifestyle. This is the same paradigm as when cultures that are originally oriented by collective ownership become influenced and assimilated into cultures of Individualistic Materialism; it is very hard to convince them to "share" again. Individualization risks Your ability to rely not only on the passing of collective ancestral knowledge which serves to bind Your nation-state, but also the collective responsibility in maintaining families and communities as the basic unit of the society.[95]

---

[94]. Buchanan, p.15 from Ellen Hale, "Graying of Europe Has Economies in Jeopardy," USA Today, December 22, 2000 p.A14

[95]. In 1978, Pres. Valery Giscard d'Estaing of France stated that: "a society no longer capable of assuring the replacement of generations is a condemned society".

Genocide & Government Collaboration

If Your population policy is not a balanced campaign the subject will realize that foreign aid is tied to population control. Due to other resulting social, economic, and environmental breakdowns, indigenous and religious groups will receive an audience for opposition and with enough popular support, will erode government legitimacy and open the possibility for one or a number of these organizations to gain the right of leadership.

Be aware that there exist persons who are aware of the motives behind Your domestic population policy. Your population policy can be viewed as genocide because You are deliberately promoting policies that will reduce the population birth rate in the subject nation-state while at the same time, encouraging an increased birth rate in Your own nation-state to support the long-term hegemony. The UN Convention on the Prevention and Punishment of the Crime of Genocide (1945) describes genocide as the following:

a) Killing members of the group;
b) Causing serious bodily or mental harm to members of the group;
c) Deliberately inflicting on the group conditions of life calculated to bring about its physical destruction in whole or in part;
d) Imposing measures intended to prevent births within the group;
e) Forcibly transferring children of the group to another group.

Under this definition civil wars committed in nation-states without a cultural mandate, despite high levels of violence, are not considered genocide, but Your deliberate population decreasing actions can be viewed in concert with what is outlined in the Genocide Convention, because You are purposely imposing measures against the subject group intended to prevent births. You can be charged with hypocrisy in concurrently promoting the growth of the population of Your own nation-state while encouraging the decrease of Your subject's; and showing no indication that You or Your nation-state will be reducing Your consumption of world resources. This would be the basis if charges of genocide against You.

Within Your own state "genocidal policies" may be domestically implemented if the majority culture leads a more decedent lifestyle than the minority population. The higher birth rate in minority populations will support national economic interests, but at some point may threaten the cultural dominance of the majority. Reactionary elements in Your nation-state may direct domestic population policy at the minority populations to lower birth rates through long-term contraception and sterilization.

Gender Issues.

Your work in the matter of gender is to exploit any past and present inequalities and resentments between man and woman to create separate and distinct competitive beings that derive self-definition from the Culture of Comparison. Through Your influence, You will create families and communities in which members are externally competing to meet internal esteem needs. Counteract any practice of mutual respect between the family or community by creating an antagonistic environment of competition for power. The beauty of this methodology is that at some point the people themselves are a party to creating their own social reality, and will reinforce the existence of leadership and social mores that perpetuate these systems. The instigation of antagonism within families, communities, and societies is a beautiful process because if it does this on all three levels, it will sustain itself at least for some time because each level is the microcosm or macrocosm of each other. Support of community antagonism is to be reinforced with projections of Individualism because it preserves Your two methods of control: promoting "separation of" or "separation from"; and, creating through Rationalism the context by which You are the Locus of Control.

Purchasing power becomes paramount to everything else. In the case of the family, whoever "controls the money" controls the house, and thereby "owns" the others. This is in direct opposition to the relational value of being a member of a family, of a community, and of a larger society. Education and career choices will be made to ensure greater economic empowerment, not to develop natural gifts and talents that lead to personal fulfillment and self-actualization. The subject, instead of striving for the betterment of the whole will strive to be "independent", to avoid being put under the control of another who is "economically empowered". This "quantifying of human relationships" causes a great degree of personal confusion in values, desires, needs and self-fulfillment. All efforts are focused on avoiding disadvantage to another, which in actuality will lead to a desire to not have a family. This quest for "empowerment" will place a greater percentage of the subject population in a malleable stage where it can easily be fed, and will devour with delight, any projections of Your cultural icons, because "possession of" and "independence from" will be the only readily available solution to the unhappiness and void of True Self. Most people engaged in this type of reactionary thinking will make life choices, educational choices, and career choices that are totally at odds with who they are.

When You successfully project the idea that acquisition of Your cultural icons and lifestyles is a sure means to happiness, You will have created a Culture of Consumerism, one that leads its subscribers to believe that the consumption of "valued goods" will mean happiness. You will have placed into the external realm that which can only be reconciled at the internal level. The subject will be too busy fighting itself like an autoimmune disorder, unaware of attack by the external aggressor. With enough breakdown, it will no longer be able to resist Your advances, divided to the point that family and community no longer operate to defend the society.

Family-Free Feminism

This type of feminism can counter "womanist" types that support the actualizing potential of all women. If You can separate the personal empowerment of woman from the developmental empowerment of the family You will create a great rift in the subject society. Using the Ideology of Individualism and the mental processes that accompany it, You can separate woman from feeling connected to the family. Encourage a Feminism of Independence--of women freed from family responsibilities. She will be "freed" from family and completely "empowered" because, in the Quantitative sense, she will have eliminated potential drains on her consumer potential as well as any emotional ties that may lessen her earning potential.

The promotion of Family-Free Feminism will not be a reason for social breakdown, but it is an important aspect that You must address if Your psycho-cultural assault on the subject is to be complete. If You can separate both women and men from the family unit You will eliminate the need for people to have families. Weakening the strength of society creates a crack in the integrity of the social whole through which Your other projections can be worked into the center. Emotional relationships will be viewed as disempowering. Only when it is under social, economic, or environmental duress will the society again realize the need for community.

In the extended family, the actions of a particular man or woman will not affect the integrity of the family to the same degree as would the actions of a parent in a nuclear family. You must first focus on breaking down the extended family before attempting to promote 'family-free' feminism. The lack of economic and emotional security in a nuclear family adds a great deal more stress onto the lives of the family members. Those persons raised in an extended family are more likely to be unprepared for a world defined in Quantitative terms. The need for economic and physical control over others becomes a reality, and like all other social phenomena what happens outside also manifests inside. In a nuclear family, abusive tendencies and selfish, non-communal attitudes are more likely to be expressed without the threat of censure.

If You can break down the extended family and perpetuate an Ideology of

Individualistic Materialism onto the subject society, and if the men of the community are not substantially immersed in a culture of community where they realize that transgressions against any part of "the whole" are transgressions against himself as well, he will likely exhibit behaviors indicative of disempowerment. The inability of the disempowered man to realize life in a Quantitative world will suffice; the need to dominate and inflict harm on the family will be an act of self-hate because in the relational sense, the man and his family are one in the same body.

Under the Quantitative valuing system the man, who is the primary wage earner, will "own" the family. If the woman is the major breadwinner, then he will be "owned" by her. In either case the use of physical violence on the woman and the family, viewed as "property", will maintain compliance and obedience. At this point the man has totally embraced the Quantitative value system as the definer of his worth, and he is no longer a "part" of his family or community. If he feels substantially disempowered he may use his greater physical strength to dominate women and other men he believes he holds the "rights of control" over. He becomes one with control needs that are reflective of persons assimilated into a Culture of Individualistic Materialism, of which the natural behavior is to always be at a position of advantage over an other. You should note that this process works best in societies which have already accepted the "nuclear family" as a preferred type of family organization.

Quantify the position of the father, especially if he is the primary "breadwinner". If the single role of father is to financially provide for "his" family, then his worth is measured according to this, and in return he is rewarded with "ownership" of the family. He will no longer feel compelled to be actively involved in the nurturing, raising, and teaching of the children. Having no responsibility to the family beyond financial contribution, his "job" is done. At this point he can view his wife and children as his "possessions". If You promote a reality in which men are estranged from their wives and children due to "fulfillment" of their role as defined by a quantitative value system, You will have successfully broken the family and created 'units of purchased co-habitation and procreation'.

Thirty-odd years ago, when Miss Sayers delivered her lecture "Are Women Human?" she declared prophetically that in the Modern World, the category of personhood is the only one adequate for meeting the needs of women or of a society as a whole. As we cannot afford to squander our natural resources, so we cannot afford to discard any human resources of brains, skills, and initiative, even though it is women who possess them. Inherently, no natural or human resource is good; any can be good or evil depending upon how it is used, and what work it performs.[96]

"The rights of women," says Dr. Peck, "considered in the economic sphere, seem to involve her in competition with men in the struggle for jobs." It does seem so indeed, and this is hardly to be wondered at; for the competition began to appear when men took over the women's jobs, transferring them from the home to the factory. The mediaeval woman had effective power and a measure of real though not political equality, for she held control in many industries--spinning, weaving, baking, brewing, distilling, perfumery, pickling--where she worked with both her head and hands, in command of her own domestic staff. These industries have since gone to the man, and the women have been left not with their "proper" *work* but with *employment* in those occupations. At the same time, the woman is exhorted to be feminine and return to the home from which all intelligent occupation has been steadily removed. If the woman submits, she can be cursed for her exploitation; and if she rebels, she can be cursed for competing with the male. Whatever she does will be wrong, and this is a great satisfaction.[97]

The "family" is the most basic unit of the subject state. It represents the multitude of nuclei that compose the collective cultural consciousness, it is the center. You must practice "separation", and must first break down the family from the molecule (community) of an element (extended family) into an individual atom (nuclear family) and finally, into separate particles (individual family members). Energy released into each subsequent smaller component feeds the disorder that continues the process of "separation" and "disintegration". The subject, instead of introspecting and working to cultivate personal potential, doing purposeful work, and contributing positively to the family, community, and the world-at-large, will covet the dreams and possessions of others. To alleviate pressure, You must continuously support a state of agitation. Dreams, self-motivation, and independent thinking are the products of a proactive mindset. An agitated psychological environment with Your projections will create enough instability and uncertainty to the point where the subject will begin to victimize others in response to Your external influence. You will bewilder the "thinkers" with too much turmoil or incorporate them into the larger anxiety-ridden, reactionary collective consciousness that You have grown in the psyche of Your subject.

If You are suffering from feelings of guilt, You should stop now. Those Princes that desire to be Imperialists are doing so, and those that do not, are not. To effectively use these strategies that I am illustrating, You must be a linear thinker, as You are unlikely to concern Yourself with the consequence of Your actions. A non-linear thinker would likely be terrified of the possible consequences of such manipulation by a nation-state on its people and national psyche. If You "feel bad" about any of Your actions, You should not be

96. "Are Women Human?" Dorothy L. Sayers. William B. Eerdmans Publishing Co. 1971 Grand Rapids, Michigan. Introduced by Mary McDermott Shideler. pp.12-13

97. Ibid. pp.43-44

doing them. If You do, You are betraying Yourself and are not fit to rule. Conquest is not for the faint-hearted. Do not allow Your programs to be motivated by a paranoia that is simply an outward projection of Your feelings of guilt. Either wage war, or do not. If You are waging war for psychologically-demented purposes or reasons, for feelings of inadequacy amongst others and not true conquest, You should desist any further actions. If You wage war for the purpose of alleviating a sense of inferiority, You have no business waging war. Instead of waging a proactive war You will be waging a reactionary campaign, hoping that Your subject realizes its place in the hierarchical order You feel is best.

Chapter 9:
Aesthetics

Art can be a threat to Your influence because it is a physical representation of the collective consciousness; it is living and cannot be taken out of context without it losing its value. Aesthetics call forth an emotional response from the populace; natural, culture-based aesthetics are grounded in this reality. To ascertain what is art, what is beautiful, what is "cultured", use Platonic Rationalizing techniques to objectify, separate, and classify other cultural ideals. Evoke disharmonious dichotomies of good versus bad, rational versus irrational, cultured versus uncultured, beautiful versus ugly; Rational versus emotional, aesthetic versus non-aesthetic.

A Prince should realize that by utilizing aesthetic representations of His past He controls the aesthetic of the subject state.[103] Use images and icons; musical, literary, and oratorical forms that considerably precede formal contact with You. The subject, bombarded with representations of the "ancient" roots of Your own nation-state or "great cultures" that You claim, will no longer be able to speak for itself.[104] Through media influence and formal education You can encourage the development of an "educated aesthetic sense"; use the venue of "popular art" to enter the collective consciousness of the populace and promote Your agenda. Emphasis should be placed in disrupting collective participatory art forms.

[103.] See Ani, Chapter 3: Aesthetic-The Power of Symbols.

[104.] The antiquity of Your past becomes the antiquity of all humanity, whereas Your subject only joined Universal human heritage through contact with You. In this way You and the subject have no shared history.

This durable, active engagement in art in the West carried into the eighteenth and nineteenth centuries, and then things began to change. I will not propose a particular theory to explain this change; there was much going on, and I wasn't there. But by the time we tripped into the twentieth century, the average Western citizen no longer saw art as his or her birthright.

Art was not viewed as a critical tool for connecting to the most important things in life, nor as a means to teach and develop understandings about how a society should be and how we should be in a society. Art became institutionalized, museum-ized, and separated from daily life; it required experts. Art objects became commodified as a currency, and many art events became too expensive for all but the privileged.

Art became what was done by a special talented few. Many romantic notions became attached to the arts: artists became special, hyper-emotional, heroic, not altogether reliable, and a little oversexed; self-expression emerged as an artist end in itself. Art became fused with a particular, educated, abstracted way of looking at things.

Eric Booth, *The Everyday Work of Art* [105]

[105.] Booth, Eric (1999) *The Everyday Work of Art*. Naperville, Ill: Sourcebooks, Inc. p.14

Aesthetics.

Your goal in creating an "educated aesthetic sense" is to Rationalize the experience of aesthetics. You will be able to dissociate the subject from its aesthetic point of reference by turning the experience of art into an analysis of art forms. Natural aesthetics are based in emotional response, and there exists the danger that the collective cultural consciousness represented through indigenous forms may weaken any intellectual aesthetic that You project. "Good" art, music, prose, film, must fall within parameters that You define. Instead of the natural right-brain emotional experience, promote an analytical, intellectual "experiencing" of art. In this way the encounter becomes an intellectual exercise that validates, or invalidates, art for being "experienced".

Since Your objective is to influence the subject so that it discriminates against its own indigenous art forms and instead embraces Your projections, promote self-denial of the emotional and art will become a commercial object rather than a representation of the spirit of a people. At this stage of objectification and separation from the center, the form will increasingly become "not of" the culture it is grounded in and will operate outside moral, cultural, religious, or social guidance. When "experiencing" the forms that You present, the subject will have to engage in the process of first acknowledging the superior "classical" roots of Your aesthetic form--imagining its connection to the art then realizing that there is none. The subject, longing to "experience" Your cultural forms in the same manner as You, will attempt to align its aesthetic taste to those of "sophistication", "class", and "heritage" which Your schemes represent, meanwhile its indigenous art forms become relegated to archaic status or that of "handicraft". Additionally, with what is known as "fusion art" there will be a significant push to "fuse" indigenous forms into parameters based on the aesthetic model projected by You. This process will allow You the opportunity to charge aesthetic forms with representations of Your choice.

A Prince uses His aesthetics to erode physical representations of the subject's collective culture, replacing it with His own. Artists of the subject society must be marginalized through the following methods:

1. suppress the importance of art and music programs in the educational system, construct these into electives, the first courses to be sacrificed during funding shortages;
2. remove art from its relevant utilitarian state in the society and make it in an "elite" form with Your aesthetic models, as the means to criticize it negatively supporting Rationalism's goal do away with differences;

3. for those artisans who insist on continuing in the relevant connected forms, reduce these arts to the status of "handicrafts", trinkets for tourists; and for those musicians who insist on keeping cultural memory alive through music, commercialize and promote only those forms that fit or blend well with Your aesthetic, encourage themes that are incongruent with those of the society. When these commercial art forms are being promoted to the youth, criticize them for socially irresponsible messages and counter-argue with "rights of individual expression".[106]

You should be aware that the living aesthetics of a nation-state, its art and its music, are Your most important targets since they are the physical representation of the consciousness of the people. Corruption of the people's aesthetic is a sure way to break their collective spirit, and will make for a convenient projection of Your cultural agenda into the hearts and minds of the population. In short, Your presence should be seen on every television set, heard on every radio station, in every art show, every market, every store, every billboard, every newspaper, every magazine, every mall, every grocery store. Your images, Your projections of community, nation, self, beauty, morality, family, relationships, vice, all should be vigorously pumped through the cultural distribution apparatus of the subject society. When an object's importance comes to symbolize esteem needs in the Culture of Comparison it loses its true measure of worth, its functionality in the society.

In Your subject society the status of indigenous culture and the non-commercial artist must be disparaged, for it is the artist who holds the key to dissent against the social dislocation and loss of sovereignty that You cause. People are least apprehensive in acknowledging the visual, auditory, and tactile experiences that aesthetics bring to their lives, and although formal ideas may face resistance depending on the sender, aesthetics can seep through the walls of resistance and slowly influence the target audience. The artist deals in the concrete, the emotional, the "irrational". To You, an Individual who does not embrace the artificial order that You project, this is dangerous because the sense of center will be enable the subject to "see" what is happening to society.

Aesthetics & Education

It is very important that You downplay the importance of art and music in the subject culture. There is nothing more important than a society's oral tradition, literature, art, music, and dramatics. These disciplines are the collective

---

[106] From the perspective of Your subject, "socially irresponsible messages" would be those in popular media that promote the conspicuous consumption of the cultures of Individualistic Materialism and Comparison.

culture in action, they make up the aesthetic center from which outside influences can be judged for compatibility.

Local arts and other aesthetics must be absent from the curriculum in schools. If art or music are to be taught in school at all, teach from the perspective of a "classical tradition" that begins with the aesthetic foundations that You are projecting. In this way, indigenous aesthetics, from an academic standpoint, have no relevance to the lives of the children. They will be seen as archaic expressions onto which no serious attention should be paid. Always use Your past as the model of aesthetic ideal. Due to divergent past histories, You can always claim superiority.

You must discourage Your subject nation-state from funding any study of past and present indigenous aesthetics, in particular the artistic represent-ations of culture and religion, because the arts are the living physical presentation of the consciousness and personality of the populace.

"Good Art" & Individualism

To promote the Individualism that You are creating though the Culture of Comparison, You will have to change indigenous art from its form as a living representation of the cultural collective consciousness into an Individualistic, center-opposing expression of ego. In creating separateness and dichotomies in the subject, You must turn art into a divergent discipline that is separated from the populace, into a field raised above the heads of the population and placed on the shelf where only those privy to the intellectual knowledge of how to decipher Your code of artistic criticism can claim ownership over the newly defined aesthetics.

Music & Dance

Again I say unto you, that if two of you shall agree on earth as touching any thing that they shall ask, it shall be done for them of my Father which is in heaven.

Matthew 18:19 KJV

Art is a participatory act, representing the collective consciousness ex-pressed through individual members of the group; there is no separation between artist and audience. You must create separation, because as long as the audience can participate in an art form with the creator there will exist representation that can resist Your projections. Specific attention should be paid to music, because of all art forms music is the most active means of communication due to its participatory nature. Dance and responsive oratory would also fit into this category.

Turn the subject's valued art into abstraction to kill its functionality and resurrect it to be a servant to Your agenda. Art is dead if it is not functional. Once taken out of context and placed on display for analytical criticism it is separated from its life force--its source--and dies, becoming a mere shell of something that used to be alive. This is most certain when You achieve the establishment of "aesthetic truth", having separated the art form from its community and turned it into an abstraction.

When You define what is art You also define what is good, what is the Universally shared aesthetic truth. Any art that inspires emotion is dangerous because messages of the loss of culture and political resistance can easily be threaded into the art form, into the collective consciousness. The artist who is able to evoke this type of connection should be discredited in the Modern world. Place musicians against audience, actor against groundling[107], and exhibition against viewer[108]. Any intercourse that is highly spiritual between performer and audience must be severed and stigmatized as "archaic", "emotional", "unsophisticated" and above all: "primitive".

The forms and rhythms that You represent must be projected onto the subject as suitable for Universal expression, worldwide mass media. The artistic expressions of the subject must be branded as parochial. Only through "fusion" with Your Universal artistic forms can the subject's music and dance become suitable for "international exposure" and critical acclaim in worldwide media circles.

Popular Culture & the Aesthetics of Beauty

Because in applied Rationalism there is an oppositional dichotomy of Nature, the aesthetic value of beauty is quantified as "good" or "bad", "perfect" or "flawed". Remember, to universalize is to eliminate difference; or at the very least, to devalue the difference between the subject and You, the "ideal".[109] Hence, there can only be one Universal representation of "beauty".

Promoting Your beauty aesthetic onto the subject society can have disastrous effects on the psyche of the people. Transforming the beauty image of the subject to Yours will achieve deep, long-lasting effects on the viability of its culture:

---

[107] In Shakespearian England "groundling" was the term used to describe "common" theatergoers who sat on the ground during performances.

[108] See Ani, p.213

[109] An example of this is the Japanese aesthetic. "Imperfection" in art actually denotes the humanity of its creation. A ceremonial tea bowl is valued for imperfection because it is the mark of the artist-- humanity, the real touch. "Perfectly" manufactured bowls may serve a solely utilitarian purpose of holding tea, but they do not serve an artistic and cultural purpose of utility and representation of the cultural center.

In 1970 Pecola, the character in Toni Morrison's debut novel *The Bluest Eye*, prayed for God to grant her blue eyes, like the white girls in her neighborhood. This genetic fantasy became a reality for the 1990s, as the gods of cosmetics came through with proliferation of colored contact-lenses. Post-modern Pecolas could now have not just blue eyes, but any color they wanted. Ads began appearing in the black lifestyle press alongside those for hair strengtheners and skin-lighteners . . .[110]

The image of beauty is something that the subject will carry at all times, which makes it a sure means of supporting Your conversion of peoples' value from that of relational importance to that of quantitative, based on the potential to consume. Those who are more "beautiful" are always to be made most valuable. Conversely, those who do not conform to these standards of beauty are to be of no "worth". Since Individualism is supported by the assumption that every other person is in potential opposition to another, redefining beauty image according to Your definition of aesthetics will support Your concepts of Individualism and will foster a competitive Culture of Comparison where human relationships are formed for the conditionality of perceived usefulness.

Through the preservation of one's body and health is seen as a means of showing devotion to one's parent, because they "received their body" from their parents.

"Cosmetic Surgery for Better Looks in Vogue"
Korea Times, October 7, 2002

The beauty of this "aesthetics of beauty" is that the subject cannot conform without definite harm to health and self-esteem. In order to conform to foreign standards of beauty, the subject will have to resort to chemical, surgical, or severe lifestyle alterations (extreme cosmetic dieting). Body mutilation will be viewed as "stylish cosmetic modifications". With Your projections of unattainable Universal beauty[111], You will create in the subject-state a population of cosmetic and chemical alterations, compulsive dieting, and surgical beauties. [112]

---

[110] Arogundade, p.125

[111] In the case of Your own society You should be aware of the danger of this practice in redefining beauty, if Your own population is exposed to this inundation through the airwaves with its own standard of beauty as the model. It may spurn insecurity in Your own population. "I know that my beauty image is being projected as the model forUniversal beauty, but am I actually more beautiful than the Other?". Your own population may either over-embrace its image as "Universal beauty" and manipulate their bodies to conform; or may attempt to modify their bodies to conform to beauty standards of the Other.

[112] The term "surgical beauties" is from "Surgical Beauty Syndrome". Park Moo-jung. *Korea Times*. May 15, 2001.

If You promote these Universal standards of beauty as "popular culture" the subject populace will be disarmed to the fact that You are assaulting its psyche; it will interpret its actions as "making reasonable sacrifices to be beautiful". These self-inflicted injuries of conformity to Your external beauty standards can include the application of bleaching creams to the skin, of harsh chemicals to drastically change the structure or color of hair; surgery to change the nose shape and make it emblematic of that of an Other racial group, to create double eye folds; enlargement of "small" eyes; shaving of the bones of chins and cheeks; breast augmentation, excessive hair depilation, muscle implants, liposuction; and perpetual diets that exceed genetic body-type predisposition. There is a fine line between regular cosmetic alterations and cosmetic surgical procedures, and those induced by internalization of external projections.

> Most of them wanted double-eyelid operations which is not costly and has become the norm for beauty-conscious women. In particular, many teenagers . . . even expressed to risk operations involving bone-shaving, to alter high cheek bones, to achieve the preferred "Western" looks, the poll said . . .[113]

You will have the subject at a very vulnerable point--it is willing and capable, and more open to embracing all that You project because it has already passed the threshold of performing severe body mutilation to conform to Your standard of beauty. What makes this so powerful is the perspective in which it is carried out.

People over the millennia have performed piercing, cutting, and tattooing as a means of relational traditional conformity; the mindset is rite of passage into the community. The type of body mutilation that You are encouraging is one of quantitative value. It is conformity to an external standard that does not affirm or support existence but instead, constantly attacks the subject's sense of worth.

Residing in both the person's conscious and subconscious mind, this system of conformity to beauty aesthetic sustains itself in the minds of conformants. The unconscious mind, keeping memory of the cultural center alive, causes unalleviated psychological conflict. And since these "ideals" are continually at the mind's forefront, psychosis is passed to the offspring. Raised to value itself quantitatively the subject-child, whose consumer potential is determined by conformity to external aesthetics of beauty, makes a beautiful vessel for Your projections of Individualism and Materialism, and will effectively perpetuate the breakdown of community and social-

[113.] Cosmetic Surgery for Better Looks in Vogue". *Korea Times*, October, 7, 2002.

mindedness within the subject populace.

Your subject's attempts at conforming to the standards that You project will be supported by the business community, and You should ensure that companies from Your nation-state have good market penetration via visual media, such as television and magazines which will consistently remind the population of its nonconformity to Your Universal beauty aesthetics. When celebrities in the subject society embrace these projected beauty standards, resistance will decrease. This is because the populace will be emulating the "style" and "looks" of its own indigenous celebrities. Essentially, indigenous art forms simply held space until You brought unison with the linear progression of the Civilized, Modern Man.

As Your projected Culture of Comparison turns people into consumers, "face value" becomes even more important than it may have ever been; actual "worth" is ascertained through a simple glance. This is true even for cultures with deep-rooted prohibitions against body mutilation: Confucian tenets which condemn damage to any part of the body as a breach of filial piety[114] will be no match for the collective desire to reconcile the psychological conflict of nonconformity with Universal standards of beauty.

A Warning.
A Prince must be careful not to be intoxicated by feelings of control over the aesthetic values of the subject, otherwise He risks fulfillment when the subject strives to fit His projections. Remember that this is a mental exercise against Your subject. Do not have Your esteem needs met through subject identification with Your beauty aesthetic.

[114.] Intentional damage to any part of the body is seen as a breach of Confucian filial piety, because one "receives" their body from their parents. Keeping in good health and taking care of one's body is a sign of showing devotion to one's family, and a fulfillment of one's filial duty.

Chapter 10: Healthcare

Our lives create our disorders, and the more disharmonious lives we live, the harder it becomes to find natural solutions and recognize root causes. We are so detached from harmonious lives and symptoms are so severe that drastic measures such as major surgery and combinations of pharmaceutical drugs are needed to reconcile. The departure from enlightened, proactive healthcare delivery to one that is reactionary makes medical treatment expensive; the combination of other unbalanced aspects of life lead to further complications, necessitating continued reactionary care. Instead of curing ailments, a quest for "higher", more "advanced" technological solutions ensue. Biomedical technologies focus more on "managed care" rather than troubleshooting root causes, which in turn provide a profit motive for continuing this trend of reactionary medicine. Your subject nation-state will suffer both from the plagues of "simple pathogens" hitchhiking on increasingly rapid modes of transportation and substandard care delivered to the masses.

Individualized care, heightening vulnerabilities to "environmental management", inadequate infrastructure and uneven distribution of resources will combine with the race to Progress at Any Cost; together with anxieties and stresses associated with internalized attitudes of Rationalism towards Nature and Others, the overbearing weight of morality in a world set in abstracted time, these will lead to a healthcare nightmare in Your subject state, causing people to become exclusive and treat their own well-being as most important. Mortality will become the fear of all fears, supporting the Fatalistic viewpoint and Individualistic point of reference that You desire to instill in the subject.

Public Health is the Foundation of the Health System for Palau. The definition of Health for Palau: *Health* is the attainment of well-being in optimal environmental conditions that alleviate the effects of the illness agents on the people living in Palau.*

* The definition for health in Palau is based on physical, mental, social, and spiritual well-being in an optimum physical, political, socio-cultural and sacred environment that reduces or alleviates the effects of physical, political and socio-economic agents on people living in Palau.

Ministry of Health, Republic of Palau[117]

117. From the Organizational Chart of the Bureau of Public Health, Ministry of Health, Republic of Palau presented at the Annual Primary Health Care Conference, November 29th - December 3rd, 2004.

Mental Health & Environment

Basing the quest to Develop and "utilize the land to its fullest potential" from the perspective of a Quantitative value system, the people will decide not to respect the sanctity of Nature or the complimentary relationship between human beings and their environment. At first this will be a choice, but after a breakdown in the natural economy and sustainable agriculture, and migration from rural "poor" areas to the "opportunity" of the cities, it will become a necessity to use all land for commercial purposes, most especially in urban areas. In these urban settings, the elimination of natural environments will contribute to a growing sense of detachment and separateness from Others. Seeing only concrete and steel will add to feelings of loneliness and increase anxieties in an oppositional life.

On an unconscious level, Nature fortifies the idea that hope does exist; that one's efforts will lead to something meaningful: peace and balance. Without hope, life becomes a competitive race to expand, to acquire more in the attempt to reach inner peace and consonance of self. Life in a concrete jungle will drive the subject to having endless feelings of tension. Hence, there will be a higher likelihood of developing mental problems either as a reaction, or as a means of dealing with this constant state of externally-inspired agitation.

Traditional Knowledge

In the past, diseases and disorders endemic to a particular geographical area had been managed with traditional means, but the dis-location of society from culture results in a historical and cultural amnesia, the result of knowledge that has failed to pass on. In Your system these traditional treatments are outlawed and disparaged so that the young people will not pay it any regard and do not integrate it into their lives. The beautiful irony is that traditional pharmacology is what makes up the basis, the base ingredients for synthesization, of Modern, "high-tech" commercial pharmacology--at an economic bargain and usually without any intellectual property hassles because You have effectively negated popular support of traditional medicinal knowledge.

Family-Doctor System

The most notable enemy to a successful implementation of Individualized Care is the family-doctor system. Its proponents say that besides providing 100 percent health service coverage to a nation-state it is also intended to "counteract the tendency toward the dehumanization of medicine resulting from super-specialization and the use of high technology"[118]. Each doctor, assisted by a nurse and working in an office oftentimes built by members of the community, bears specific objectives:

1. To promote health through education, changes in lifestyle and improved nutritional, sanitary and hygienic habits.
2. To prevent illness and eliminate environmental conditions that are dangerous to health.
3. To ensure early diagnosis and long term follow-up of each case.
4. To attend to the physical and psychological habilitation of patients.
5. To help integrate families and communities in society.
6. To practice medicine with scientific excellence and a humanitarian spirit.
7. To engage in research related to the needs of the population.[119]

If You allow this type of program to exist it is likely that there will be a drop in infant mortality and mobidity, shorter hospitalization stays, effective vaccination campaigns, improved detection of disease and care for patients with chronic disorders, and more complete and consistent follow-ups.[120]

You cannot allow a system like this to threaten Your apparatus of control, nor can You allow it to deny You the financial gains that come with the implementation of Individualized Care.[121] These betterments in collective healthcare will make Your execution of CCD more formidable, because improvements in the quality of life may be seen as indicative of Modernity and Development. Bear in mind that the population may not be aware of the different functions and levels of medical care: primary, secondary, and tertiary. If You play into this ignorance You can cause the population to devalue primary and secondary care offered in physician offices, so that they only trust hospitals.

Public Health versus Individualized Healthcare.

With regard to individualized screenings and mass screenings: if mass screenings are allowed, there will be considerable long-term costs savings. Mass screenings are an effective safeguard against epidemics because disorders will be recognized sooner than later and the disease will be averted. In cases of rapidly transmitted pathogens or chemical and nuclear agents, presence and prevalence can readily be monitored through an infrastructure set up to perform mass screenings. Individual screening must be encouraged as part of the trend towards a Modern IC delivery system. It is both a Public

---

[118.] Bravo, Ernesto Mario. (1998) *Development Within Underdevelopment?: New Trends in Cuban Medicine*. La Habana: Editorial Elfos Scientiae, p.20

[119.] *Programa de trabajo del médico y enferma de la familia, el policlinico y el hospital* (Havana: MINSAP, 1988) pp.4-5

[120.] Bravo, p.20.

[121.] I will be using the following abbreviations: PH = Public Health; IC = Individualized Care

Health and Civil Defense initiative.

Resources are to be directed exclusively to those who can afford to pay because with an antiquated PH system and a seriously underserved greater population, a health crisis will abound, if it has not already. A brewing PH crisis within the greater population combined with sensationalized media coverage will promote the climate of fear and anxiety required to effectively exploit Your subject nation-state. If Your projections are to be internalized by the subject population, they must be kept in a state of constant agitation, and what better way to keep a population agitated than to maintain a perpetual health threat within the society.

Public Health-Based Medical Care System

An effective Public Health-based Medical system would consist of the following: good public health indicators (see *Individualized Care and Policy*); "an interactive doctor-patient relationship; a national healthcare network of institutions capable of offering efficient primary, secondary and tertiary medical attention; the development of genetic engineering and biotechnology; the production of highly competitive pharmaceuticals and medical equipment; a radical change in common habits, such as smoking, diet, physical activity; as well as the provision of increasing medical and scientific aid to other countries".[122] Do not let a system like this[123] threaten Your apparatus of

---

[122.] Ibid. p.22

[123.] An example from Bravo, p. 168. In reference to efficient methods of field research, this quote illustrates some of the inefficiency in IC-oriented society. A biomedical industry can develop better in a PH-oriented society: " . . . it should be noted that the Ministry of Public Health provides health coverage even in the most isolated places in Cuba, guaranteed follow-up and vigilance when a massive field study is applied, with hundreds of thousands of volunteers-- the Cuban people, who support and have absolute trust in their health-care system and scientific development and who know that development isn't aimed at making anybody rich.

That is, the achievement was the result of the combination of the political decision; the health-care system, which guarantees vigilance; and the 11 million inhabitants, the potential volunteers.

All this means that Cuba has a tremendous advantage over the rest of the world when it comes to developing vaccines and other medicines. A new vaccine is produced once every ten years, on the average, yet, in just ten years--between 1987 and 1997--Cuba obtained three new ones; the vaccines against hepatitis B, meningitis B and meningitis C. Moreover, the field studies for a vaccine against leptospira are being completed. In Cuba, you don't have to pay for life insurance for the volunteer, because they are uninterested voluntaries. In other countries, volunteers demand enormous amounts of life insurance, which makes the field studies very expensive--the field studies can cost between 3 and 7 million dollars. That's why the pharmaceutical consortia do their testing in Third World countries, where they get 'volunteers' who don't even know what's being injected into them. However, that doesn't solve the problem, because those countries' health-care systems don't monitor the massive vaccinations . . . .

Often, Cuba doctors have to explain to would-be volunteers why they weren't selected for the test. This is the result of education for all the people and their confidence in their health-care system."

control over the society; do not allow it to deny You the potential financial gains of Individualized Care (managed care) systems.

Individualized Care & Policy

If You allow the subject nation-state to practice the PH model of healthcare delivery, a "network of administrative, service, and production units responsible for comprehensive healthcare of the entire population"[124], then the other factors that an effective PH system depends on--total and equitable distribution of sanitation services, drinking water, nutrition, medical services, housing, employment and economic growth--will have become its governmental priorities.[125] This reassessment of national priorities will mean difficulties for Your system based on Individualism. Yours is a reactionary system that manages symptoms to a point at which the appearance of near-homeostasis is achieved. And of course, only those with a means to afford managed care will receive it.

Medicine & the Pharmaceutical Industry

In a system where patients are not informed and therefore not empowered to take preventative measures for good health and where primary and secondary care is not easily accessible so that ailments are recognized before they worsen in severity, the government will divide into two systems: one providing just enough indigent care so that the poor will believe that their health concerns are being taken seriously; and one where more affluent persons can pay to have their health managed by profit-centers that accumulate wealth through the alleviation of noticeable symptoms--through pharmacology and major surgical procedures, where patients take no responsibility in proactively maintaining their health.

Besides preventing the spread of epidemics, a major challenge of PH health care is in monitoring patients who take antibiotics and encouraging them to complete the entire course of antibiotics as to lessen the development of antibiotic-resistant strains of bacteria. The difficulty in the former is that public healthcare is often infrequent, inaccessible or unaffordable, even at lowered rates. Consequently, immunization campaigns must always be in place. Since medicines are expensive, patients oftentimes save unneeded antibiotics for the future so that they "will not have to go to the doctor next time". IC patients are accustomed to receiving some "treatment" for every symptom, even if the illness is simply a mild viral infection running its course,

---

[124.] Ibid, p.17
[125.] Ibid, p.17

and will expect some kind of pharmacological solution to their ailment--many feel as if they "did not see the doctor" if they did not receive a prescription for antibiotics. The physicians, playing into these imagined needs, will overprescribe so that they appear to be "good doctors" and also to support the big business of managed care, even at the risk of encouraging the emergence of "superbugs"[126] that are resistant to every pharmaceutical antibiotic in existence.

Concerning biotechnology, You must discount any factual claims to "green medicine"[127] and other holistic methods such as acupuncture, acupressure and sound therapy, unless of course You control the source of the herbal material and can chemically synthesize it. Otherwise You run the risk of allowing a holistic medical science to develop in Your subject's nation-state. If this transpires, You will not be able to force onto the subject nation-state Your managed care system of treatment through synthetic pharmacology and invasive surgical procedures.

Individualized Mental Health.
In regard to the mental health of the nation-state, it is important to recognize that with the stressors that You place on Your subject nation-state, life will become harder and harder to reconcile psychologically in the subject population. With an increase of anxiety caused by the environment of uncertainty and Individualization that You are creating, combined with the erosion of the peace of mind and emotional security that come with intact communities and extended families. The present-day lessening of psychological deterioration of the subject population will be built on Individual and collective trauma suffered by the population under Princes preceding You in the Colonial Era. In this environment, because people will feel increasingly powerless over their own lives, and will not be able to identify You (Your influence) as the main source of discord in their reality, some instead take this frustration out on themselves and their families. With the increasing anxiety, stress, that envelops even the previously "safe" confines of the home, some people will resort to victimizing Others as their reaction to their feelings of victimization under Your influence. Some of these persons will commit

---

126. "Superbugs" are bacteria that have developed resistance to most or all known pharmaceutical antibiotics, rendering them resistant to all antibiotics within category. These antibiotic-resistant strains of bacteria result from swapping genes, some originating from strains such as MRSA (Methicillin-Resistant *Staphylococcus Aureus*), VRE (Vancomycin-Resistant Enterococci), and *Streptococcus pneumoniae*.
127. Ibid, p.17. "Green medicine" is defined as the use of herbs and plants in the treatment of diverse diseases.

heinous abuses (both physical and mental) against Others, including those of their own families. The resulting trauma will leave many victims in a broken psychological state in which the initial trauma will need to be addressed. To increase the further incapacitation of the subject population, take advantage of this growing crisis in the mental health of the subject nation-state.

Because Your power is derived from Naming and Defining reality for Your subject, prevent the resolution of these traumas within the subject population. I suggest this course of action, because an in-depth examination of why abuses, in particular those of a domestic nature, will lead the examiners to the conclusion that they must the examine the state of affairs within the nation-- the growing environment of insecurity, powerlessness, poverty, fear, and anxiety and the population's reaction to the social reality of being a people under a type of a "colonization" and will see the psychological health of individuals and families being tied directly to a sense of collective powerlessless and the lack of ability to articulate discontent with their lives. When they are told that under Your influence they are living increasing within a Perfect System: a system in which, through there may be some pain, that this pain is necessary for Modernization and Progress, and the lack of monetary success within this perfect system is a reflection of personal failure and low worth as a member of society.

To prevent this type of in-depth analysis of the social effects of Your projected system, You should employ the use of the Power of Naming and Defining. Identify psychological disorders of which there are no understood causes, and no cures; disorders that "chemical imbalances" can be blamed on, so no in-depth analysis would be warranted.

Create clinical diagnosis by defining the symptoms of the resulting psychological states and calling them disorders of their own right. For example, Bi-polar and Borderline Personality Disorder, with deep examination have been shown to often arise out of a severe trauma, more than often sexual. In promoting a clinical fixation on the neurochemical "disorders" of Bipolar Disorder and Borderline Personality Disorder, the "starting place" will come with the "disorders" itself rather than the trauma that caused them, and more importantly the social environment that fostered the trauma that was perpetuated onto the sufferers of one of these disorders.

As the society comes apart as a result of Your influence, promote "awareness" in an array of "new" disorders – ADD, ADHD, Bipolar, Borderline, Asperger's syndrome, etc. Instead of an examination of why there was not such as abundance of person's suffering from these newly "discovered" or defined disorders in the past; or if there were, why these traits did not seem to incapacitate their sufferers as they do now (or even variation of incapicitation based on the more or less "interconnected" a culture was, i.e. Victorian England vs. the same period Samoa). The population, including its mental professionals, i.e. psychologists, psychiatrists, therapists, and counselors, will all fixate of "curing" or "mitigating" the individual psychological problems of the patients and cease to see the true connection between individual mental health and community (collective) mental health. Each patient will become an island of its own accord, drifting further and further away from individual mental health supported by collective truth and collective healing. As opposed to sufferers being seen indicative of the collective mental health of the society, they will be only be seen as individual cases. Mental health professionals will be oblivious to the fact that the society itself is mentally ill, because it has forsaken the collective security of a cohesive society, for that of one in which a person becomes more and more alone each day, and who becomes affected more and more by the individualized collective anxiety that they are suffering from. The growing alienation of the population from its True Self will be seen, not as a (collective) Public Health problem, but instead as a problem for Individualized Medicine; and in doing so will negate any chance of the necessary collective treatment that is required to restore the population to a state of 'mental health'.

The sufferer themself will direct all of their own energy towards managing or mitigating their disorder. They will spend their time, possibly even developing an intense research interest in, studying the disorder further in-depth; and will take on an identity as an 'X-sufferer' at the expense of focusing that energy on dealing with the root trauma in a healthy fashion and working to build supportive, sustainable family and community relationships.

The irony is that the sufferer did not become how they are now "alone" (by themself), hence the healthy management of the disorder will not come about "alone", or even with the help of a single mental health professional. Their mental health will arise and be supported with the re-creation of healthy relationships. Your influence in the subject's society works to de-emphasize the importance of healthy, cohesive social relationships, and in doing so creates an environment that nurtures the intensity of the effects of the disorder on the sufferer's life and how they relate to Other people.

The definition of the disorder could be useful it is shared with the sufferer in the following manner: an equal proportion of 'knowledge' (about the disorder) and 'understanding' (about its origins). Knowledge without understanding is the recipe for disaster because one loses context of themselves in the bigger picture, and can come to view themself solely as victim. With a victim mentality, one is both 'alone' and 'powerless'. With this combination the need for necessary help and support systems will not be realized and any self-destructive patterns that the sufferer them self can change will not be, because they will not realize the part that they play in creating their own present life condition.

The anxiety-ridden environment that You nurture in the subject's society breeds and supports a reactionary, rather than proactive, approach to the life in the populace. In doing do, destructive patterns and negative life choices are never introspected on. People are too busy trying to survive. There is a saying that is quite relevant to dynamic that You are to promote among the population. "What is the definition of insanity? Doing the same thing again and again and expecting a different outcome...". In promoting a society in which people feel powerless and only react to the world, rather than contemplate their place within in and then act accordingly, there will be no room for contemplation of one's life patterns, one would be too busy "surviving". In accepting this way of life, the collective mental health of the society can only decline, because the social support system will further breakdown and people will continue to perpetuate behaviors and thought patterns that will serve to disempower them and negatively affect their lives.

Living "alone" in a community of other "alone" people is like living alone in a house with broken mirrors. It is often in one's interactions with others that they see their true selves. In a situation in which one has an antagonistic view of the Others in their live they cease to be "mirrors" that they can reflect off of, they instead become icons that they "compare oneself with" and in such a hyper-intensive state of externalization of self, because of the constant judging of self worth against that of Others, the "quiet" environment that is needed for private contemplation is avoided because the only surface thoughts that will arise are only of one's inadequacy in comparison with Others, and if one is suffering from one of these "personality disorders", the potential for self-loathing is further enhanced.

Vertical Funding & Organizational Structure.

In rationalized medicine, external control increases and shifts to social structures and institutions. Not only is the physician more likely to be controlled by these structures and institutions but also by managers and bureaucrats who are not themselves physicians. The ability of physicians to control their own work lives is declining. As a result, many physicians are experiencing increased job dissatisfaction and alienation .   .   . As a result of the calculability, the patient is more likely to feel like a number in the system rather than a person minimizing time and maximizing profits which may lead to a decline of health care provided to patients.[128]

In order to forge an inefficient system of entrenched bureaucracies in the healthcare delivery systems of Your subject state, promote a top-down organizational structure with one person in charge of each area. In this way inter-agency/inter-divisional cooperation can be discouraged because each "leader" will have a vested interest in "protecting" his or her own territory and the funding that goes into each.

If responsibility for each sector is shared, then responsibility for success and fiscal accountability will emerge from the collaborative work between sectors. You are promoting the development of a vertical society based on Individualism, Consumerism, and the Quantitative valuing of human worth, You should therefore work to create a total IC system. If, for some reason You need to maintain a superficial system of PH, be sure that it does not resemble the organizational chart on the following page. If You allow a horizontal-vertical configuration to develop, as in the following example, You will lose most of the potential territoriality required to keep an inefficient PH system.

128. Ritzer, pp.143-144

Programs

Maternal ------------ Child ------------ Adolescent ------------ Adult ------------ Geriatric

Basic Health Services

Health Information Systems

Emergency Health

Ancillary Support

Health Promotion and Health Education

Behavioral Health

Oral Health

Non-Communicable Disease Services

Disease Surveillance

National Cancer Control and Prevention Program

Extended Immunization (EPI)

Specialized Health Service

Communicable Disease Services

Community Outreach Program

Environmental Health

Spiritual Health

Administrative, Personnel, Procurement, Financial Management, Human Resources

* Health Research, Social Marketing, Advocacy Services[129]

[129.] Ibid, *Organizational Chart of the Bureau of Public Health*, Ministry of Health, Republic of Palau. Presented at the Annual Primary Health Care Conference, November 29th-December 3rd, 2004; and conversation with Division of Public Health Director Dr. Stevenson Kuartei, Director, Division of Public Health, Palau Ministry of Health.

Intellectual Property & Medicine.

In the process of quantifying the value of humanity within Your subject nation-state, make certain that it extends into healthcare delivery. Use the same arguments for IC, include intellectual property and pharmaceuticals, so that the subject will always be a loser in the market economy.

Of course You can make a *few* limited exceptions of "compassionate capitalism", but You must project onto the subject society the hard truth that the protection of private property (in this case intellectual property) is a cornerstone of Capitalist Democracy, and that trust should be placed in the market. If this point is not etched into the minds of those governing Your subject nation-state and its economic community, You will run the risk of resources being allocated towards the development of a local generic pharmaceutical industry that may bring substantial gains to national public health, and no criticism from the "international community" for breech of "international trade laws" will register as important to the government or the population. To properly execute an IC campaign You will have to emphasize both the merits and modernity of managed care medicine and the necessity of protecting intellectual property rights, even at the cost of human lives.

Health Costs.

Progressive rationalization has threatened not only the fantasies but also the health, and perhaps---the lives of people. One example is the danger posed by the content of most fast food; a lot of fat, cholesterol, salt, and sugars. Such meals are the last things many Americans need, suffering as they do from obesity, high cholesterol levels, high blood pressure, and perhaps diabetes.[130]

You can cause a rise in the health expenditures for Your subject nation-state's government. It is likely to already have disproportionately directed funds for the subsidized care of the most affluent in society but with the embracing of the new Modern diets and the race towards Progress, which requires that food be consumed "fast" as to not waste "productive" time, the "new diets" will encourage the flowering of "lifestyle diseases" that can be attributed to Your influence. Food is to be an obstacle to Progress rather than a bonding ritual that strengthens human relationships.

[130.] Ritzer, p.155

Braindrain.

Through the use of Global Capitalism and the Northward flow of capital, You can encourage technical brain drain. Note the advertisement on the following page, from the inside front cover of *Mabuhay Magazine*, dated December, 2002: **Attention nurses seeking employment in the United States!**

(. . .)[131] **offers world class nursing opportunities.**

(. . .) can help make your dreams of living and working in the United States a reality.

(. . .) offers a wide array of opportunities throughout the United States. We recruit only the best from around the world. We want you to be a part of our TEAM. Since 1973, tens of thousands of healthcare professionals have secured employment through (. . .).

(. . .) offers excellent benefits, completely free processing and efficient immigration expertise. And the best benefit of all: Our employees are our family. In order to provide constant service to you, an American (. . .) representative is here 365 days a year to help you.

We guarantee:

• Totally free processing expenses

• Free CGNS/ NCLEX/ TOEFL and FSE reviews

• Free airfare to the USA

• Free accommodation for one month upon arrival

• US$ 6000 bonus over two years

• Minimum starting salary of US $20/hour

• Health insurance

• Malpractice insurance

• 22 days paid leave per year

• Free travel to Guam/Saipan

• Absolutely no fees or hidden costs

Come work in the United States!

Call (. . .) today for more information.
(. . . Address)
If you have friends or relatives working as registered nurses in the United States, give us a call.
We want to talk to you and them about our and "friends and family" bonus program.
In the Philippines, call us at (. . . Phone number), Our U.S. representatives are always in the Philippines and want to hear from you. These are immigrant status positions.

---

131. (. . .) is a substitution for the actual name of the company.

Chapter 11:
Time & Machines

From the perspective of Your subject, You are the possessor of "time" and through its ownership, You dictate the means and context by which Your subject lives. Disrupt the subject society by inducing opposition to the harmonious timing of activities. "Harmony" is not to be achieved through congruence with the natural cycles of life and Nature, but through adherence to Your stated ideals and projected value system. Your goal in redefining time is to create in the subject a neurotic time-obsessed, linear-oriented immoderate predator-consumer that will "consume" Your influence with the passion of one who has been told that they only have 'X' amount of time left to live and is afraid of death. Any indigenous perspectives of time that differ from Yours must be re-defined by You. Your subject population must be excessively oriented to the present, in the context of Individualism.

Separate the subject from its humanity, its connection to a developed intuitive self: a critically thinking intuitive being. Offer a view of life based on You as its "clock". It is to set its watch according to the time and schedule that You provide. It is to become oblivious to any centering introspection; it instead gauges its Modernity, its Progress, its timing according to Your direction, approval, and positive affirmations. By displacing the cultural center of the subject society, You in fact bring cultural death.

When the ruler employs proper timing in public and private endeavors, the officials and governing policy will utilize a timely reform of regulations, promulgate seasonal policy, and perform ritual actions in a seasonal manner. If the ruler, officials, and governing policy are flexible enough to respond to situations in a timely and appropriate fashion, then the state will be well ordered in the spirit of harmony rather than strict "rule of law" or coercive government. This is not to say that there should be "rule of law" at all, but rather that law and the rule of law would always be subordinate to the aesthetic values of proper timing, appropriate seasonal policy, virtue, and ritual action.[133]

Humans constitute time through their *position* and *performance*. Human action is context dependent; it occurs within both environmental and social circumstances. These circumstances provide a ground or given in which actions take on significance and meaning. Ultimately, the function of the action is to bring the circumstances into harmony--a fruitful disposition. The actor and the conditions are mutually dependent and co-determining, so that human action generates the future continuity of both environmental and social circumstances. The ruler or state, which is sensitive to the transformations of history, can enact regulations and reform or abolish outdated statutes, and can be responsible to the role of human life adapting to the environment, performing actions that actually cultivate an environmental climate. The influence on seasonal factors and the ability to articulate time are proportionally correlative with the significance of the actor's position and the quality of one's performance.[134]

[133.] Sellmann, James. D. (2002) *Timing and Rulership in Master Lü's Spring and Autumn Annals (Lushi chunqiu).* Albany: State University of New York Press. p.177
[134.] Ibid. pp.157-8

The clock, moreover, is a piece of power machinery whose 'product' is seconds and minutes: by its essential nature it disassociated time from human events and helped create the belief in an independent world of mathematically measurable sequences: the special world of science. There is relatively little foundation for this belief in common human experience: through the year the days are of uneven duration, and not merely does the relation between day and night steadily change, but a slight journey from East to West alters astronomical time by a certain number of minutes. In terms of the human organism itself, mechanical time is even more foreign: while human life has regularities of its own, the beat of the pulse, the breathing of the lungs, these change from hour to hour with mode and action, and in the longer span of days, time is measured not by the calendar but by the events that occupy it. The Shepherd measures from the time the ewes lambed; the farmer measures back to the day of sowing and forwards to the harvest: if growth has its own duration and regularities, behind it are not simply matter and motion but the facts of development; in short history. And while mechanical time is strung out in a succession of mathematically isolated instants, organic time--what Bergson calls duration--is cumulative in its effects. Though time, not as a sequence of experiences, but as a collection of hours, minutes, and seconds, the habits of adding time and saving time come into existence. Time took on the character of an enclosed space: it could be divided, it could be filled up, it could even be expanded by the invention of labor-saving instruments.

Abstract time became the new medium of existence. Organic functions themselves were regulated by it: one ate, not upon feeling hungry, but when prompted by the clock: one slept, not when one was tired, but when the clock sanctioned it. A generalized time-consciousness accompanied the wider use of clocks: dissociating time from organic sequences.

The modern industrial regime could do without coal and iron and steam easier than it could do without the clock.[135]

[135.] Mumford, Lewis. (1934) *Technics and Civilization*. San Diego: Harcourt Brace & Company. pp.15-16

Time & Linear Thought.

To the Individualistic present-minded person, time is always running out. The future is uncertain because life is an anxiety-ridden reality in which "anything" can happen at "anytime". Every opportunity must be seized, even if at the expense of Others. If the opportunity is not seized, it will be "lost". The Individual will have failed to consume all that was possible, will be without worth. The attitude to "build a foundation for tomorrow", or "build a world for our children" will not exist, as there is simply not enough time. The Individual feels the need to obtain as much as is possible in the shortest amount of time, disregarding future consequences because there is "no time". In an Individualistic context, one becomes excessively consumeristic, highly agitated, and nervous. Conversely, in an interconnected environment, living in the present is ideal. One creates the reality of self as well as the reality of the group with each moment.

Progress is the strongest piece of ideology in Your projections of culturally-based ideals and icons. Your actions can never truly be criticized regardless of how much pain, social dislocation, environmental and economic destruction that You cause because Your influence and "expertise" is Development and Modernization. You can create nation-states that embrace Your cultural ideals, icons, material values, and technology without the means to sustain at the same level as You; encouraging the individual quest to this material ideal and the corresponding community disintegration needed to properly exploit the country's resources, establishing an underclass of low-cost workers from the rural areas to support Your enterprises and government cooperation in providing You with tax incentives, lax environmental standards, lower labor standards and choice land through "reform" at the expense of the people, in order to make an "investment-friendly" environment that will help You to help Yourself to its resources and manpower, all the while leaving the subject state with nothing but a polluted environment, a broken economy, a divided community.

The Prince, through His Platonic devices, must construct the illusion of Progress. In the same fashion that He creates the illusion of Rationality and Reason, He is able to produce Progress. You must create an abstract starting point in the circular continuum of time and define it as the "point"; the point of departure in Your cultural creation of Progress and Development of Humankind. How the subject defines itself "right now" will remain who it is in the future. In the same fashion that You dislocate the cultural point of departure from the collective consciousness of the people and replace it with Your projection, You must also replace its view of time with Yours--with You as the point of departure and You as the representation of Progress, having moved from point A to point B. You, the Developed culture, the Modern Man, can now claim the mandate to rationalize the world in Your image, for You are the evolved representation of what all humanity will become. They will cease to see that You are the "Modern" representation of You based in Your own culture which veritably is not universal, but parochial. Taking possession of the concept of time and combining it with the Universalistic rhetoric that You espouse, You will be able to counter those who oppose You as "enemies of civilization".

Modernity & Progress

One objective in projecting a concept of Modernity centered around Your culture is to establish the point of reference for Progress, on Your terms. This will establish the Universal validity of You, as all aspects of Development and Progress will be based on Your ideology. To reject You, the subject will have to reject the framework of Progress and Modernity, since it was You who brought these concepts in the first place.

Do not become psychologically dependent on the acceptance of Your ideals as acceptance of self. In the case of Modernity, I must forewarn You that, although You may be defining this ideology through Rationalized terms, the subject of Your conquest is also "modern" in its own cultural frame of reference. Meaning this: right now, it is living in the culmination of the experiences of its own group and being that it has existed as least as long as Your group, the subject may in fact be aware of Your objectives without revealing this to You--an illustration that reminds Me of a conversion that once transpired with a member of a royal family in a particular nation-state of the Pacific Islands Region. He told Me of late night discussions about what sorts of lies to tell the resident British anthropologist--and that there are several renowned anthropologists whose fieldwork is nothing but a collection of lies and made-up stories and customs. The people saw no reason why an Outsider would need to know such detailed information on their society if he was not going to join it; they concluded that it had to be for sinister objectives. Since these are a people of oral tradition, to reveal certain truths about spiritual practices would be both highly taboo as well as destructive; orally-revealed secrets would empower the individual with command over vibrational attributes of particular power words. In layman's terms, no one with any good sense would seriously entertain these requests. He said that there were lively social gatherings devoted to making up rituals and such for the resident "colonial".

You will need to project upon the subject's nation-state the need for "Change", "Growth" and "Reform", because this abstract concept of

"Progress" is what will assist in holding the society together long enough for You to exploit it. This is important because in societies whose governments exist through cultural mandate, social rules, or tradition, regulate human relations. Social harmony is maintained through a nonlinear sense of time. A degree of balance is maintained by those living in the constancy of time, the same time as those who have lived before and after them. If the subject continues to live in non-linear time, the loss will be realized.

Because Progress is a perpetual forward motion and because Rationalism supports opposition and antagonism rather than harmony and balance, there is never a possibility of achieving a "state of rest", a perfect state of being. Instead, something must always be wrong with the current state of being, "problems" must exist to sustain the oppositional mindset of reason: there is always a "better way", even, at the expense of a working system. This is so because in the Rational mind, Progress does not cease until perfect order is obtained. So, unless at some point the Rational thinker perceives Himself to be of a god-like omniscience and omnipotence and His "created world" to be of maximum order, the quest towards "Progress" will be perpetual. The "advances" that Progress brings with its ever increasing "efficiency" become so efficient that balance, harmonious life become obsolete. The rush no-where for no-reason becomes the reality, eroding away every semblance of a balanced human life that may have existed.

Man versus Machine.

Make man compete against machine instead of developing personal potential and integrating it with efforts focused on the betterment of community and society at-large. Focus scientific efforts towards the development of Artificial Intelligence instead of maximizing human potential.[136]

---

[136] There is research now, in which living cells are used as "memory chips" with substantially more "storage space" than what current chip technology is able to generate, without the invasive chemical processes required to create silicon or galladium chips. From this kind of research You should contemplate that there is still an unused 90% portion of the human brain that You can ensure is neglected through this sort of "technological advancement". With Your scientific "creations" that are based on "creating new life" rather than expanding upon the capabilities of life, You can misdirect technological developments so that they circumvent "human development". Under the guise of "Progress", place whomever You like under the rule of Your scientific "creations".

Chapter 12:
Science & Technology

The new technologies that You promote will de-value local knowledge and place a premium on outside knowledge. The purpose is to coerce the subject into a mindset of "Progress at Any Cost", to compete in the race to succeed in the global marketplace. The wholesale promotion of Universal technological solutions will achieve this while keeping the subject in a state of unbalance.

The method by which You will keep the subject off-guard is through an attack on all fronts: aesthetics, education, economy, family. Do not allow the government of the subject nation to rule through holistic planning. It must be made to react to Your barrage of projections pulling it to Develop and Modernize each sector of its society and economy. This process is especially important when it comes to the application of technology, which cannot be allowed to serve the *raison d'être* of the subject nation-state's government. Remember, this is an integrated attack with a cumulative outcome. All of Your projections work to embody each other. Use technology to create separation. Your goal is to make the subject's scientific community irrelevant so that it becomes dependent on Your technology transfer. The development of indigenous scientific expertise will not be a priority; educating to compete in a "Global Economy" will take precedence over all other educational prerogatives.

Science is the formal reconstruction or representation of a people's shared set of systematic and cumulative ideas, beliefs, and knowledges (i.e. common sense) stemming from their culture . . . Thus the danger when one adopts uncritically the science and paradigms of another people's reality is that one adopts their consciousness and also limits the arena of one's own awareness.

Wade Nobles[139]

There is no logical path to these laws; only intuition, resting on a sympathetic understanding of experience, can reach them.

Albert Einstein[140]

To acknowledge the limitations imposed by science, to subordinate the wish to the fact, and to look for order as an emergent in observed relations, rather than as an extraneous scheme imposed on these relations--those were the great contributions of the new outlook on life. Expressing regularities and recurrent series, science widened the area of certainty, prediction, and control.

By deliberately cutting off certain phases of man's personality, the warm life of private sensation and private feelings and private perceptions, the sciences assisted in building up a more public world which gained in accessibility what it lost in depth. To measure a weight, a distance, a charge of electricity, by reference to pointer reading established within a mechanical system, deliberately constructed for this purpose, was to limit the possibility of errors of interpretation, and cancel out the difference of individual experience and private history. And the greater the degree of abstraction and limitation, the greater was the accuracy of reference. By isolating simple systems and simple causal sequences the sciences created confidence in the possibility of finding a similar type of order in every aspect of experience; it was, indeed, by the success of science in the realm of the inorganic that we have acquired whatever belief we may legitimately entertain in the possibility of achieving similar understanding and control in the vastly more complex domain of life.[141]

[139.] From Ani, p.67
[140.] Einstein, Albert, "Motiv des Forsens" in *Zu Max Plancks 60 Geburtstag, Ansprachen in der Deutschen Physikalischen* Gesellschaft, Karlsruhe, Muller.
[141.] Mumford, p.326

Science.

'I'm an alchemist because I'm an alchemist,' he said, as he prepared the meal. 'I learned the science from my grandfather, who learned from his father, and so on, back to the creation of the world. In those times, the master work could be written simply on an emerald. But men began to reject simple things, and to write tracts, interpretations, and philosophical studies. They also began to feel that they know a better way than others had. Yet the Emerald Tablet is still alive today.'[142]

Make science an endless array of meaningless experiments, deductions, and divisions in a quest to feel "in control of", under the delusion of "trying to understand something". Understanding comes from "being", not "having" or "possessing". In those quiet troughs present in the waves of realization, You learn nothing but focusing on the wave itself. Emptiness is fullness, realization, truths. Fullness is emptiness, superficiality, reaction.

To share knowledge, publishing in the scientific community is needed on both a national and global scale, but You are to promote this idea out of balance with needs of the subject nation-state. Make publishing the primary focus rather than the development of good science to assist in meeting the needs and aspirations of the nation-state. Convincing the scientists to focus primarily on publishing sets them up for an externalizing act: the seeking of approval and validity from the outside rather than at the expense of meeting internal needs.[143]

Brain Drain & Science

To encourage braindrain You need to create an environment of emulation rather than one of innovation. Create a number of crises within Your subject nation-state so that it becomes bewildered and is not able to solve problems the only way feasible, one at a time. Remember Your goal is to turn a nation-state of proactive thinkers into a band of agitated, anxiety-ridden reactionaries. Under extreme duress of dealing with Your attacks on numerous fronts, some within Your subject government will concede to the pressure of "needing" help from the outside.

[142.] Coelho, pp.127-8

[143.] Adam Smith's "invisible hand" is what is said to bring equilibrium to capitalism. With n a box, a non-imperialistic state, equilibrium will be reached with the threat of social, economy or environmental collapse. It will have to prioritize social, economic, and environmental needs according to stability of the state. However, in economically imperialistic states, recognition of the need for equilibrium will not come under the certain threat of a national social, economic, and environmental collapse; but instead on a global scale at which social, economic, and environmental disintegration can not be reversed because of the finite physical resources at hand. The destruction of the mechanism that caused the unbalance will have to be displaced or destroyed, because there is no room for growth or failure.

When admitted inside the house, the dragon does not allow itself to be used only as a "technical advisor". It directs a myriad short-term solutions that require long-term follow-up, with no technology transfer or inclusion of local talent into the decision making process. Within the subject society a dynamic will form in which any outside advisors, scientists, doctors, are trusted before the experts of its own nation-state. The brilliant minds of Your subject nation-state will desire to leave, or at the very least work for one of Your "iconic" companies in order to bring respectability and affirmation of worth onto self.

"True scientists", those that view their scientific pursuits as the purpose for existence, will only leave the subject state and come to Your nation-state if no support exists for their work. If the subject nation-state supports the efforts of its scientists, as patriotism meant to improve the lives of its citizenry, it is unlikely that these scientists will leave, because their potential will be used constructively, receiving appreciation from those for whom it would mean the most: their communities.[144]

When the scientific research apparatus is weakened by braindrain You can use the subject's nation-state as a testing ground for new scientific discoveries without having to worry about human and environmental costs of the misapplication or development of Your science. You can make the "necessary mistakes for scientific progress" in your subject's nation-state. Any new biotechnology can be tried in the subject society--vaccine trials, agrochemicals and biocrops, human reproductive technologies, radio technologies such as ultra-low frequency and EMF; and any other invasive technologies that have the potential to bring harmful consequences to Your own society before full development. Awareness of Your experiments will be difficult to recognize because the scientific community of the subject state will be minimized via mass brain drain.

Of those who are watchful, there will be few who can or will want to comprehend the fact that You are using the subject society as an enormous testing ground, with the populace functioning not only as scientific "guinea pigs" but also as a market to advance technologies of Your nation-state. Your end goal is to separate the subject society from itself, for maximum exploitation.

[144.] A good number of spies and intelligence officers are created from intellectual-types who are not using their full intellectual potential and do not receive appreciation or recognition for their efforts; motivation is more often psychological than it is financial. Due to the appreciation and recognition factor, it is easier to create these types of spies from citizens of one's own society. There is a high likelihood that if offered an environment in which they could do meaningful work and receive recognition by the society as important contributors to the sustainability and development of their nation-state, they would return to Your subject state.

Science & Development

> What is remarkably new and interesting about Cuba's new research directions are their heavy emphasis on understanding and exploiting the subtle yet powerful abilities of biological organisms to perform many of the tasks previously done by synthetic chemicals, which typically have little subtlety of biological knowledge incorporated in their design. Biologically-based or -derived fertilizers and biological control of pests, as described earlier, are at the heart of this new quest for biologically sophisticated manipulations of agroecosystems.[145]

You must prevent the development of sustainable technologies that require less export input. This will deter the subject nation from gaining access to the raw materials necessary for technology development. Also, if You do not prevent collaboration between the scientific community and the governing bodies it is likely that "science" will coordinate with other efforts and the Modernizing advice that You bring will become irrelevant to specific needs of the subject's nation-state. You must therefore work to ensure that there is a division between scientific research and practice, and the needs of the subject state. The "practice" of science is to consist of "basic science"--the proving and disproving of thesis' that are separate from any particular application to society. Basic research is needed to keep applied science at its best, but it is in Your best interest to do away with the "vulgarity" of applied science and push for the focus on superior abstraction offered by theoretical science. Since Your goal is to disconnect the scientific community from any responsibility to society, objectivity and separateness should be celebrated.

Do not allow the formation of regional scientific information exchanges between local scientists, as subject nation-states that participate in these can bypass the barriers that protect Your control. Any "regional" scientific forums must be monitored and moderated by You in order to control what is disseminated. Forums should specialize in promoting "hi-tech" short-term solutions to the most immediate problems while continuously avoiding the root issues.[146] Preventing the creation of regional scientific exchange forums will discourage effective training of scientists, thus lessening the availability of internships, residences, and joint research projects.

If the subject realizes that it is a dependent state within the hierarchy of Princes, there is a possibility of advancement by cooperative scientific and economic sectors working under the umbrella of developing a biomedical

---

[145.] Ibid, p.74

[146.] Food shortages due to use of the most arable to grow monocultures for export to Your nation-state and the nation-states of Other Princes should be enticed into embracing a "new soil science" of utilizing G-M organisms (GMOs) that can grow on a barren land. The excitement that comes from being able to do the seemingly impossible disengages one's eye from looking at the ball, the root problem.

industry that serves and provides for the nation-state a potential export industry: genetic engineering, production of vaccines, bio-preparations and diagnostic kits and equipment; widespread application of biotechnology to immunochemical diagnosis; production of monoclonal antibodies for diagnosis of therapeutics; prenatal diagnosis of congenital malformations and hereditary diseases; medical microbiology and tropical medicine; neuro-physiological diagnosis; new techniques for research work and the application of their results in production and services; and production of restriction enzymes, tissue cultures, and laboratory animals[147].

If Your subject nation-state coordinates its scientific and economic efforts in such a manner it could truly become a world power in the development, technology transfer, and mass marketing of vaccines and treatments to "developing countries" underserved by multinational pharmaceutical companies such as the ones based, at least ideologically and diplomatically, in Your nation-state.

Science Blinded by Linear Thinking & the Scientific Method

Campa (Dr. Concepcion Campa Huego, President of the Finlay Institute) said that this was the only vaccine to have been developed against meningitis B so far. Therefore, it took audacity, fearlessness in continuing to advance on and on without getting cold feet. In other places where researchers are trying to develop a similar vaccine, they insist on having an exact, strict correlation between the tests results of antibodies and protection before they go to field studies. They are failing because there isn't any exact correlation between the laboratory results and the effectiveness of the vaccine. They've spent years on this, and Campa can't understand why.[148]

Prevent "competitive" science from forming or else Your subject in due time, will overtake You in highly applicable, sustainable, and environmentally non-invasive solutions to improve quality of life conditions. Use abstraction to "step outside of the box" but realize that it is not possible to account for every variable. Scientists must acknowledge that the scientific method does not bestow omniscience upon the researcher; and that anecdotal evidence must also be acknowledged as "proof" because laboratory conditions cannot recreate all of the possible variables that occur outside of it. You have to do Your best to promote effective science, but with the proper understanding and safeguards in place to ensure, as best as You can, that no severe side effects arise, in case the unforeseen emerges. It is said that science is made through

[147]. Bravo, Ernesto. *Ingenieria Genética: Realidades y Perspectives*. Havana: College of Medical Sciences, 1984. p.3
[148]. Bravo, p.169

mistakes, but some mistakes are more detrimental than others and the race to "Progress" can be at the cost of the world. In this present day reality, we have environmental and health problems that are the long-term "side-effects" of various scientific and pharmaceutical applications, treatment and engineering disasters.

Conclusions based on the scientific method are just as subjective as anecdotal evidence, because, without omnipotence, You cannot possibly know of all variables in an experiment, and cannot with certainty make a "control group".[149] In truth, if the scientific method was a perfect universal method there would be no man-made environmental problems, side-effects to pharmaceuticals, or a general "price" for Progress. You do have one major advantage: "traditional medicines" are curative medicines based in a "traditional environment"; made from natural materials, they mitigate "natural" illnesses and it is likely that they will be less effective in the Modern world that You are creating in Your subject's nation-state. Unless the "unnatural" toxins and stresses found in the Modern world are first eliminated from a patient's life, it will be difficult for these "traditional" medicines to work, the body having become poisoned and out of balance. The collaborative ability for these natural medicines to compliment the body's own immune and regenerative abilities are impeded by the poisons and stresses of the "unnatural" Modern world, chemicals present in every aspect of life from food, to water, to hygiene products, to cleaning products, to artificial air, to pesticides, and the state of constant anxiety that comes with living in a world based on a quantitative value system. Because this factor of eliminating unnatural toxins from the body for curative processes to truly work is not acknowledged, even the anecdotal evidence of the reliability of "traditional medicines" will be impacted. The more "unnatural" life becomes for Your subject, the less effective its "traditional medicines" will likely be.

[149.] The following is an example of a study that was conducted in a tropical climate to determine a relationship between weather and the incidence of upper respiratory infections (URI). From the data it is shown that with the extremities of hot and dry weather, incidences of URI consistently rise. From this, one can generalize that there is a possible relationship between extremely hot and dry weather and increased incidences of URIs. Conduct the very same experiment in a temperate location: in this area, one will find that incidences of URIs consistently rise in cold and wet weather. Which test is correct? Both are, but the wrong variable was being studied. The variable that should have been studied was "people gathering in close quarters for extended periods of time". If one person in each group had an URI at the time of the abhorrent weather in each locale, the transmission of the URI could be increased because of the close quarters and extended contact with the sick person. At no point is the scientist not also a participant in his or her experiment--meaning that true objectivity is impossible without the ability to know every possible variable, and the ability for one to separate mentally from one's actions.

"Researchers Use Scientific Methods of the West
to See How Ancient Remedies of the East Really Work"
AP, January 22, 2003

HONG KONG (AP) - Lab rats get stuck consuming everything from morphine to anthrax in the name of medical progress, but some in Hong Kong may be having it a bit easier as they drink a brown liquid made from a yellow-rooted Chinese herb.

Tradition has it that the yellow root, known as huangi, can control swelling and promote regeneration of skin, so researchers at the Chinese University tried it out on rats with diabetic foot ulcers--before testing it on patients in local hospitals.
The tests are part of a growing trend in China, where herbal medicines have been used for centuries with little recognition from the West.

Practitioners and drugmakers are now hoping to win global respect for their products--and potentially big profits--through the same sorts of rigorous testing required in the West for medications, including laboratory, animal and human experiments.

Researchers have used mice to test so-called Bak Foong pils, made of ingredients that include ginseng, deer antlers and more than 20 herbs.

The pills are popular among middle-aged and menopausal Chinese women who believe Bak Foong pills can enhance the immune system, improve digestion, regulate levels of ovarian hormones and reduce the risk of heart problems.

Initial tests showed no effect on young mice. Then the scientists figured out that healthy lab animals didn't make much of a measuring stick.

They tried again with weak, older mice and found that the diminished lymphatic cells--a key component of the body's immune system--returned to a level similar to that in the healthy animals, said physiology professor Chan Hsiao-chang.

In tests that start with animals and, if promising, progress to people, researchers here are working to decode many traditional formulas in 'scientific terms and international language,' Chan said.

They have a long way to go to get their herbal remedies approved as drugs by Western authorities such as the U.S. Food and Drug Administration. The prospects for success are not certain, admit herbal makers and Chinese medicine practitioners, who, however, vow to fight the uphill battle. Western physicians and pharmacists have long been skeptical about whether herbal remedies work at all, and of so, whether they can be scientifically verified as safe and effective.

The FDA has never approved any Chinese--or Western--herbal drugs, said Dr. Shaw Chen, an associate director at the FDA's Center for Drug Evaluation and Research in Rockville, Maryland.

About 40 clinical trials are known to be under way in Hong Kong, mainland China, Taiwan and elsewhere as makers of the herbal remedies race to become first to succeed, Chen said in a telephone interview.

The experiments on patients are being performed with herbal remedies reputed to treat everything from viruses to cancer and skin disease, he said.

Chen wouldn't say whether any of the remedies could get FDA approval for drug registration, though he noted that herbal formulas, which are aimed at curing the body as a whole rather than a specific illness, can't easily match up with the standards set for precise, single-compound Western drugs made from chemicals.

'We have not seen anything close,' Chen said, adding that Western pharmaceutical companies often spend huge amounts of money on new drugs to get them approved for the market, in a process that takes years.

In previous cases involving Chinese herbal remedies, the FDA has cited problems with companies that produce dietary supplements without detecting the presence of contaminants or even listing all the ingredients on the labels.

In 2000, the FDA stopped imports of the Chinese herb family Aristolochia after reports of kidney failure among users in Britain and Belgium.
The Chinese drugs are backed by 'mostly anecdotal experience and don't have good quality data to meet modern standards,' Chen said.
Those in the Chinese drug industry are hoping to change that. They say they're improving their methods and achieving measured success by raising their manufacturing standards.

At the 123-year-old drugmaker Eu Yan Sang, salesman Li Chiu-ming recalls that when he started out 20 years ago, he sifted through herbs by hand, identifying them by shape, color, texture and smell and then heating them over firewood or burning charcoals before letting them dry out in bamboo sieves.

In 2001, the Singapore-listed company invested 20 million Hong Kong dollars (US$2.6 million) in a high-tech, dust-free plant in Hong Kong that executives say is comparable to those operated by Western drugmakers.

'We used to work like a small, traditional family business,' Li said. 'But now we are going high-tech and global.'

A colleague, Poon Hop, wore a surgical cap and lab coat as he greeted a reporter inside a sterile room with tightly controlled temperature and humidity where he chopped Chinese roots on a stainless steel surface. 'I am getting used to the new requirements,' Poon said, beaming with pride.

The Hong Kong plant has been rewarded with a Certificate for Good Manufacturing in conditions that are clean and free of contaminants.

That allows the company to export some products to the United States as dietary supplements, and it hopes soon to enter the Taiwanese and European Union markets. The manufacturing-standards certification would be a necessary step, albeit a small one, toward getting any of the products approved as drugs.

The drugs that Your pharmaceutical companies manufacture are effective because many times they are massive doses of synthesized versions of "traditional medicines", prescribed with the attitude of alleviating symptoms and not treating the body holistically. If healthcare is directed into a holistic practice, it will not be as financially advantageous to You as "Managed Care" is. You need to commit to the following:

1. eliminate the means of Your subject nation-state to export its traditional medicine as Modern "medicine"; it can be exported as "foodstuffs" if You deem it financially advantageous to Your companies, however, I would advise against this, to avoid familiarization of Your own nation-state's population with these medicines, ultimately giving validity to the herbs;
2. cause enough changes in the lifestyle, pathogen exposure, environment, and diet of the subject population to alter its body chemistry, so that traditional methods will not be adequate in maintaining health in Your subject nation-state[150];
3. disparage any "traditional methods" as primitive and "anecdotal" even though these remedies would not have been used continuously for hundreds, if not thousands of years in treating ailments in Your subject nation-state;
4. for those who insist on using their own system of medicine, make them insecure about the viability of their medicine and have them "prove" to You, on Your terms, that their medicine is valid, even though anecdotal evidence exists on its effectiveness;
5. promote the Culture of Consumerism in Your subject's nation-state as to make profit more of a motivation than the honor of treating patients and upholding the professionalism of medical crafts, to the point that pharmacists begin to use cheaper and substituted ingredients in traditional medicines, in order to make greater and faster profits, leading to poisonings and ineffective medications; and lastly,
6. after Your subject population loses confidence in its own traditional medicine and ceases to value the plants and animals used to make traditional medicines, patent them as Your "discoveries" and synthesize the base ingredients into pharmaceutical medicines that You can sell back to the population as "Modern cures". Remember, there is a Universal standard to be measured by. Nothing has national interests. When Your subject buys into this, it is buying into Your game, in turn becoming "subject" to it.

---

[150] Promote the consumption of "fast food" over "slow food". Eating becomes a means of fueling the race towards permanent anxiety, instead of the physical and social nourishment that slower meals provide. Those engaging in sedentary lifestyles that will include spending a great deal of time watching television and playing video games, enter a state of artificial over-stimulation, because interaction with the video medium over time makes the "creating of one's own story" less appealing than having one dictated by the video medium. The subject would rather live the lives of other people on a video screen than be an active participant and co-creator of its own life. Besides the lack of physical activity in a sedentary lifestyle that results in the slow atropy of one's physical strength, health, and agility, constant artificial overstimulation via video media also leads to a lessening ability to maintain focus (attention) on events and tasks in the non-video world, because these events and tasks are far less engaging than that of the video world. It becomes harder to take responsibility for being an active "cognitive protagonist" in one's own life of embarking on real-life encounters with people and nature.

Biotechnology

Cuba's approach to medicine still includes both light technology and traditional medicine, providing a holistic approach to medicine, which views each patient as a physical, mental, emotional, social and economic whole.[151]

As president of NACSEX [North American-Cuban Scientific Exchange Program], I had an unusual opportunity to observe the development of a modern biomedical scientific community and the expansion from the elitist medical school in Havana to a series of medical students in each province and a healthcare delivery system in each community. As this occurred at a difficult time for scientific exchange of information and supplies to Cuba, the accomplishments were all the more impressive, particularly the commitment of the Cuban government to invest in biotechnology at a time of great economic stress.

Dr. Harlyn Halvorson,
Director of the Policy Center for Marine Biosciences and Technology
University of Massachusetts, Dartmouth, Massachusetts USA[152]

If You can implement an agricultural process based on the growing of biocrops, You immediately dispossess the land of its stewards. The laboratory in Your nation-state will determine the viability (in Your interest, of course) of the application of these technologies and there will be no use for the traditional farmer and local knowledge. Even if You were somehow removed from controlling the food production of Your subject nation-state, the use of biocrops would guarantee a severe genetic contamination of indigenous flora and fauna which would not be able to grow again unless an environmental cataclysm literally "cleaned" the land of everything. When You begin the process of growing genetically modified monoculture in Your nation-state, You can ensure within a relatively short span of time that Your subject's nation-state will be unable to convert to organic agriculture because of the genetic contamination that the biocrops will have caused.

Agricultural Models

The Classical Model of agriculture is perfectly designed for use against Your subject nation's government. Its greatest potential and weakness is feeding its population; this is one that can be easily exploited by You to maintain control over life and death in Your subject nation-state.

The Alternative Model is a model that if You are not careful, can be used by Your subject to eliminate Your control over its food production capabilities and export agriculture industry. The prerequisite to the Alternative Model is

---

151. Bravo, p.13
152. Ibid. p.11

"true land reform" because there has to be a total nationwide survey of the land in order to complete a scientific approximation of best uses like optimum crops, locations, and rotation cycles of the land to feed the society. This model also counters the need for the breaking of extended families to have a mobile, urban labor force. If Your subject implements "true land reform" in which the interests of the country as a whole are taken into account rather than the interests of foreign investors or land holders, this can encourage a trend in the subject nation-state of re-evaluating the policies and applicability of Your Universalistic standards of Development and Modernity.

> The Classical Model is based an extensive monoculture of foreign crop species, primarily for export. It is highly mechanized and requires a continuous supply of imported technologies and inputs. It promotes dependence on international markets and, though mechanization, drives migration of people from rural areas to the city. Finally, it rapidly degrades the basis for continued productivity through the erosion, compaction and salinization of soils, and the development of pesticide resistance among insect pests and crop diseases.[153]
>
> . . . .
>
> The Alternative Model, on the other hand, is based on the Low Input Sustainable Agriculture paradigm, known as LISA in the United States. It seeks to promote the ecological sustainability of production by replacing the dependence on heavy farm machinery and chemical inputs with animal traction, crop and pasture rotations, soil conservation, organic soil amendments, biological pest control, and what [are called] *biofertilizers* and *biopesticides*--microbial formulations that are non-toxic to humans. The Alternative Model requires the reincorporation of rural populations into agriculture, through both their labor as well as their knowledge of traditional farming techniques and their active participation in the generation of new, more appropriate technologies. This model is designed to stem the rural-urban flood of migrants, and to provide food security for the nation's population.[154]

Inputs[155]

Yield does not only mean "output", it also includes input. If a large amount or any amount of imported products are needed to produce this "yield", this input must be subtracted from the equation and the vulnerability of this equation to market forces must also be accounted for.

Classic Agricultural Model

This is a good description of the Classical Agricultural Model, the model that You should promote in Your subject's nation-state.

[153.] Rossett, Peter and Benjamin, Medea, eds. (1994) *The Greening of the Revolution: Cuba's Experiment With Organic Agriculture*. Melbourne: Ocean Press, p.4

[154.] Ibid, p.5

[155.] Import coefficients are the percent of value contributed by imports of final product and/or imported inputs used in its production, Rossett and Benjamin, p.19

The Classical Model represents conventional agriculture . . . it relies on an intensive use of chemical fertilizers, pesticides, mechanization, feedlots, petroleum and petroleum by-products, hybrid crop varieties and capital in the form of credit. It is based on crop monocultures planted on large holdings to take advantage of economies of scale. It has led to soil erosion, compaction, salinization and waterlogging, environmental contamination, pest resistance to pesticides and uncontrollable pest outbreaks. It is also a model that has become increasingly expensive as input prices rise and farmers use increasing quantities to compensate for eroding soil fertility and the loss of natural pest controls. For developing countries, it is even worse, because it creates a dependence on imports that use scarce foreign exchange.[156]

The use of conventional agricultural methods leads to environmental problems due to the use of agrochemicals and soil erosion. Countries often discount the cost of their inputs--agrochemical and livestock feed, in their equations for export agriculture. If they did, they would realize how disproportionate the prices that they sell their products for are. For Your own nation-state and those of Other Princes, using conventional agriculture is economically sustainable if You do not mind the environmental issues associated with conventional agriculture, because inputs such as agrochemicals, "cheap" energy sources, and an abundance of water for irrigation, are produced locally.

Once this cost and the emphasis on exporting has been placed on the subject, it will be ripe for the import of G-M (Genetically-Modified) crops just to feed its populace. The only remaining danger then, is that if You, through Your nation-state's corporations make revenue from Your subject nation-state's export agriculture, You may have problems exporting G-M crops to the nation-states of Other Princes and subjects.

Alternative Model

The Alternative Model halts the rapid migration of rural persons to the urban areas because they, as rural persons, maintain an important role in society. This also encourages recognition of traditional knowledge as equally valuable to the society as formal education. But for any Alternative Model or organic farming methodology to work, it would require the in-depth traditional, local knowledge of the people who have always worked the land and are aware of its birth and death cycles as well as other plant and animal life to which it plays a part in the ecology food chain.

To counter Your efforts of creating dependency, the subject's nation-state

---

[156.] Ibid, pp.28-29

may try to adjust its agricultural policy to that of the Alternative Model. If it succeeds it will be able to sell the surplus to meet domestic consumption needs, foster public-private partnerships to give ownership to individual, collective, or private corporations that are in line with national goals, and eventually gain the capacity to sell surplus products on the export market for either hard currency or barter. To really convert its agriculture production from con-ventional to "alternative" it will have to develop non-invasive biotechnology.

Limitations of the Alternate Model

If Your subject nation-state does not attempt to implement an agricultural program based on the Alternative Model to Your advantage is that it could take a few years to convert from "conventional agriculture", which is high input and requires the use of agrochemicals, to organic or semi-organic agriculture. This lag time in conversion is needed to allow for the restoration of lost soil fertility, and to reestablish natural controls of insect and disease population. A hungry population may not be able to afford the time waiting for its nation-state to convert conventional agriculture if it does not have the biotechnology, scientific personnel or foreign assistance to carry out non-controversial techniques such as fermentation, tissue culture, and serological testing to lessen the lag time in reestablishing ecological balance.[157] You can exploit this period of limbo and portray the subject's government as ineffective, beginning an agricultural program that will only increases food shortages and starvation. Exploit the conversion time lag between conventional "Modern" agriculture and organic "traditional" agriculture and if possible, prevent the development of an indigenous knowledge.

Alternative Agricultural Policy & the Free Market

In an organic agriculture program, farmers "rise" to the level of biotech scientists as collaborative contributors to the national food supply and economic development of the nation-state, because of their possession of the local knowledge needed to implement an alternative, organic agricultural program. This would include "programming production [agriculture][158] to take advantage of natural rainfall production[159] with corresponding investment in food storage facilities"--so as to lessen yearlong dependency on irrigation equipment.

---

[157]. Ibid, p.5
[158]. word added
[159]. From footnote in Rossett and Benjamin, p.2

For a commercialized society utilizing conventional or biotech agriculture, rural farmers are some of the lowest ranking members of society being literally, ground-level producers of raw materials destined for export. The implementation of an organic agriculture program will disrupt the re-ordering of society in accordance with consumer value. Do not allow this type of disruption in Your social engineering, because it will unravel Your process of exploitation and diminish Your influence in other aspects of the subject's social economy.

Germ Plasm

The germ plasm--that is, the genetic reserve consisting of plants and animals, the product of millions of years of natural selection--that exists in the underdeveloped countries may be terribly damaged when it is exploited by biotechnological corporations. If their germ plasm ends up in the developed countries, the underdeveloped countries' dependence and commercial competition will be increased.[160]

You should simultaneously project the idea that indigenous scientific, botanical, medical knowledge is nothing but "hocus-pocus" magic, super-stition, and primitive thinking. Do this so that the people lose pride ownership, connectedness, and relevance with local scientific awareness. Invest in expeditions and infrastructure to extract the germ plasm of Your subject nation-state and "own" it--Your pharmaceutical companies with massive research budgets will be able to chemically synthesize substances indigenous to Your subject nation-state and sell them at cheaper prices than what it costs to extract them from nature and take to the worldwide market. Of course, the most desirable scenario is to own the areas that hold this life and control access to it, thereby having complete possession over Your subject nation-state's germ plasm.

Unfortunately, because of their economic limitations and degree of dependence, the developing countries aren't participating in biotechnology and are running the risk of losing control of the genetic wealth (germ plasm) of their flora and fauna.
Meanwhile, the industrialized countries control the world's biotechnological market, especially that of medical products, through their system of patents and, above all, through concealment of the technology by which their products were obtained.[161]

Genetically Modified Crops

The Alternative Method addresses the root problems of Your subject nation-state's agricultural program, not the symptoms. In this way it is proactive

---

[160.] Bravo, p.187
[161.] Ibid, p.189

rather than reactive. Take for example, IPM (Integrated Pest Management) versus imported pesticides or G-M crops to address issues of limited capital. The nation-state spends its resources buying pesticides with hard currency, but due to "world market prices" it will eventually have to resort to using G-M crops modified with a particular pest-resistance gene to maintain its food supply; under IPM it could use intellectual capital to "pay" for this program and could protect its crops from pests without the high inputs that require a constant cycle of hard currency to import items "essential" for survival. Any real nation-state should be able to handle its sustainability needs. Food security is an essential component of a government's mandate, and You will be able to exploit the shortcomings of Your subject nation-state.

Using empathetic language to appear "concerned", You can mask profit motives with the Universal goal of feeding the population. Your insistence on the benefits and safety of biocrops will be viewed as a sincere concern for the welfare of the people, the reoccurring cost of purchases in annual seed stock will seem "fair", and when the monoculture that You have planted in Your subject nation-state becomes a reality, less arable lands will take over and become the primary flora at the expense of other plant and animal life; as well, the "collateral damage" of unpredictable genetic contamination from free traveling plasmid rings[162] to the environment will be accepted as just another "Cost of Progress". In this way, You can still use the subject's lands however You wish and grant its initial desire of monoculture and high-yield agriculture, holding the nation-state's life in Your hands each year before planting time. If it does not pay Your price, whatever that be, for the yearly seed supply, it will die. And You will own the life of a nation-state for the price of a bag of tricks, and an empathetic sigh.

Alternative Model & Genetic Modification

Nearly 150 years ago, Charles Darwin observed in *On the Origin of Species* that wheat fields planted in diverse varieties of the grain were more productive than those planted in single varieties. This is because mixtures check the spread of pathogens and therefore disease. For centuries, farmers have practiced such 'polycropping' to protect their fields against disease...

. . . Single-species fields have become the norm in industrial countries only in the last 50 years, as average farm size has increased, and as operations have become more mechanized. As farms scale up, monocultures become simpler to manage than diverse fields, which require more labor and an intimate knowledge of local ecology. However, crop diversity provided an antidote to the inherent weaknesses of monocultures--the depletion of soil nutrients, for instance, and the vulnerability of such fields to past infestations.[163]

---

[162] A plasmid is a small circular, double-stranded molecule of DNA that exists inside of a host cell. It replicates independently of the host genetic material. Plasmids are used in genetic engineering as vectors to transfer DNA to a host cell.

Your argument to support the adoption of the "conventional" method of agriculture is that monocultures are easier to manage, the price for this being that it requires expensive inputs to be purchased from Your agrochemical companies. Increased output means an increased need for high levels of fertilizers, pesticides, fungicides and herbicides; contamination of ground-water sources by the blend of chemicals; medium and long-term genetic contamination of the environment; and massive crop failures that come with inherent disease susceptibility of monocultures.

Sustainable Farming Methods, Livestock Management & Waste Reduction
Examples of Sustainable Farming Methods:
Ways in which an agricultural policy can be reoriented to that of organic farming is by reintegrating local knowledge into the process--a "re-discovery of sorts"[164] by which it can commit to this through the following four research areas:

1. monitoring techniques which can predict weed pressures and community composition a year in advance;
2. systems of rotations based on the monitoring;
3. a very selective use of herbicides in combination with the above methods;
4. tillage methods, including the design of new farm implements. Include these farmers in the implementation of biological pest control such as the production and distribution of entomophages[165] and entomopathogens[166].

Sustainable Livestock Management:
Voisin Rational Pasture Management, also called rotational or rational grazing: "The basic technique involves using movable electric fencing to confine to small pasture areas, where their manure re-fertilizes the forage plants. The enclosures are moved around the fields on a tight schedule."[167] Environmental pollution is reduced as fewer pesticide and fertilizers are used to produce feed, and manure is distributed to benefit pasture plants and soil rather than concentrated where it can become a pollution problem.

---

163. "Deep Trouble: The Hidden Threat of Groundwater Pollution" by Payal Sampat, Worldwatch Paper 154 December 2000, World Watch Institute, p.41
164. Rossett and Benjamin, p.48
165. Ibid, p.38 Entomophages are insects that eat or parasitize other insects.
166. Ibid, p.39 Entomopathogens are diseases of insects that can be used for biological control.
167. Ibid, p.63 Re: Sustainable Cattle Grazing

Sustainable Waste Recycling:[168]

Converting waste products into energy, "Organic by-products from sugar cane processing, cattle ranches, sheep ranches, poultry and pig farms, coffee harvests, crops and food stuffs are being collected and processed into biofertilizers. Resource recovery programs include waste recycling from the following primary sources:

1. cows, pigs, sheep, and poultry
2. garbage (food waste)
3. crop residue (green manure)
4. sugarcane processing

Processing methods include:

5. vermiculture/vermicomposting
6. static pile (aerobic) composting
7. anaerobic digesters
8. mechanized, on-site recycling of industrial waste
9. reforestation of affected area and reclaiming areas formerly used for mining activities."[169]

Hardship may push countries to "true land reforms", rather than the commercialization to market forces, utilizing the most arable land for domestic agriculture and consumption, and excess for export; utilizing organic farm methods, avoiding the use hard currency and the purchase agrochemicals such as pesticides and fertilizers. You cannot allow the implementation of this type of agricultural "reform" or You will lose control over Your subject nation-state's agricultural sector. Prioritized use of prime arable lands for the production of food for export livestock will put the domestic food supply in jeopardy.

If hardship in Your subject nation-state seems to be approaching a point at which government considers implementing "true land reform" measures, offer G-M crops as a solution. If G-M crops are applied the subject will continue to use land in the same manner that is domestically unstable, and there will be no need for "true" reform".

Science & New Communications Technologies

In regard to all of these new communications technologies such as the internet, it is very important that You host and own the hardware and apparatus through which these communications are routed. This is because

---

[168.] See pp.61-2 Rossett and Benjamin
[169.] See Ibid, p.65 Re: Reforestation and Land Erosion

You need to have the ability to censor and cut off communications between subversive persons within Your subject nation-state as well as between nation-states, because it is through these technologies that peoples can realize that they are living under similar circumstances and may come to the conclusions that these circumstances emanate from the same actor or actors. You should be able to monitor all communication within Your nation-state and between Other nation-states, so that You can anticipate any threat to Your influence over its government.

Technology & the Social Market

With the militarization of the world, technology is developing at an abnormal pace. Because military thinkers of the expansionary order are preoccupied with having the most lethal technologies, development grows under the auspice of "Progress at Any Cost". To an expansionary military mind, there is always an imminent threat, the underlying assumption being that adversaries are of the same expansionary thinking order. Thus, in the attempt to control any possible scenario, there is a continual push to develop. This also leads to environmental mismanagement because imminent military threats outweigh environmental concerns. Ironically, it is this destruction of human security through the reckless application of new technologies that poses a greater "security threat" than any imminent threats. With the progression of military technology, those that cease to be cutting-edge find a way into the commercial realm, subsequently these technologies are integrated into the modes of production for economies worldwide. With the aim of disruption You can apply new Universal technologies to modes of production to the subject state. Many times this will require so much in knowledge and maintenance that, though these technologies will at first appear to be more efficient they will actually be more troublesome, eroding the equilibrium in modes of production. Dependency on You will be furthered, as You will be supplying the "technical know-how", enabling You to control the supervisory, management, and technical spheres of the subject nation-state's corporations.

Apply technologies of which few possess skills to use, to quicken the change to a "technological age" that is so rapid as to cause disruption in the labor market. This will cause a loss of confidence in education because of the inability to address lack of skills in the marketplace. When this happens education also suffers another blow: in the haste to meet the call of technical training, education loses its value in developing the scientific potential of students, instead focusing on meeting "basic competencies needed in today's workplace".

The projection of these "universally applicable technologies" is a means by which You can cause social disruption, replacing laborers with technology in the name of efficiency. If the workers who have been replaced by the new technology are not retrained and placed in positions to supervise and maintain the new technology, they will become unemployable. The only sector that will be able to absorb these dislocated workers is the entrepreneurial sector. With Rule of Law and business law, You should ensure that bureaucracies and startup costs will guaranty significant difficulties in building new businesses.

Rural persons may still be able to "survive", but workers who are landless urban dwellers will be left in a state of insecurity that will allow easier acceptance of Your projections. These workers will seek an understanding of *why* they are in this predicament, the confidence that they once had in the ability of the government and culture to meet security needs will have faded away: the answer, of course, is that their nation-state is not Modern and Developed, and unless it adopts the methodology of Your projections, the subject will be hopelessly mired in the doldrums of existing as an undeveloped, "backwards" society. You will offer a solution to this dissonant psychological state, and with the help of the subject population putting pressure on the subject government to embrace Your rationalizing Modern means of governance, the subject will serve its nation-state to You on a platter. A humorous irony for Your subjugated subject is that technology is thought to improve the standard of living and quality of life; but instead, destroying these by creating efficiency in the modes of production for a socially-dislocated economy.

The Social Cost of Communications Technologies

The telecommunications that You provide should, through its proliferation, eliminate actual communication between people. Make true human contact so tenuous that sense of community breaks down. Instead of talking, people will "text"; instead of going on dates, they will chat; instead of meeting in groups and socializing, they will web conference; instead of having sexual relations, they will have cybersex; instead of cultivating potential and becoming comfortable with self, they will take on cyber alter-egos; instead of playing sports and engaging in other active socializations, they will play multi-player videogames.

I once heard a saying: "the telephone is a symbol of man's inability to communicate". This is the ideal that You should aim for. Sustainable technologies enhance natural phenomena and abilities; in the case of human beings, high-tech communication would work to amplify and transmit brainwaves so that people could communicate telepathically. Instead You should push for the sustained use of technologies that are the antithesis of life, such as the use of combustion engines when less environmentally invasive power technologies exist. With the proliferation of communications technologies that increase distance between people You will create anxiety in society, exploiting these feelings to perpetuate the consumerist value system that You are concurrently projecting on Your subject nation-state.

Your intent is to promote the widespread use of long-distance communication within smaller human circles. Being endlessly "wired" or "wireless" creates a state of permanent agitation where people can never truly relax because they are addicted to receiving messages, texts, or e-mails that temporarily alleviate the anxiety of being perpetually "connected". You will even want children to communicate over electronic media: their games are to be in front of terminals and screens instead of in school yards and in nature; You want them to grow up accustomed to being over-stimulated by electronic visual media, and to feel the anxieties associated with these devices. With the greater scope of things in mind, do not believe that these communications technologies are only for Your malicious use; they can also bring people who live great distances from each other together.

Technology Industry
If You allow the technological and scientific sectors of Your subject state to develop to the point where it is trading on the regional markets and the world market, be aware that it can compete with Your transnational corporations and those of Other Princes. The bartering of finished goods and raw materials can potentially develop into a trade that circumvents the Your economic system and supports Your economy through the artificial valuing of currencies and determinations of worldwide values on commodities and other raw materials.

For most of human history, trade was reciprocal, but this "natural approach to commerce" could usurp the power that You have established and lead to the economic collapse of a system based on world capital market. This could inevitably cause conflict between You and Other Princes, negating the non-invasive intent to conquest over Your subject nation-state.
The peace between Princes is based on the mutual understanding and mutual benefit of the Universalizing of the world and its resources. If at any point, Your subject ceases to be reactionary and takes proactive measures against Your influence in tandem with the other subjects (nation-states), the whole system that You have devised and implemented could fall apart, and You could be one of the main casualties.

Divide & Conquer

Divide and Conquer is best articulated as the weakening of natural relationships combined with external agitation; its intended outcome is the elimination of any prior sense of security and connectedness, through the replacement of what is thought to be a stable relationship. Even if the relationship is "negative" it is a stable one that, for the subject, provides continuity and predictability of a life that You have taken from it.

Look at the narrative below. It is a speech by Willie Lynch, a slaveholder from the West Indies, who during a visit to Virginia is said to have addressed a group of slaveholders, advising them on how to best manage their slaves. Although there is a debate in the U.S. academic community as to whether these truly are the words of Willie Lynch, this is not important. What is important is for You to understand the point that I am making with this illustration about the concept of "Divide and Conquer". Creating anxiety and lessening truthful communication between people will set the stage for effective manipulation of Your subject nation-state's population so that You can achieve Your goal, Sustainable Exploitation of Your subject nation-state.

Gentlemen, I greet you here on the bank of the James River in the year of our Lord one thousand seven hundred and twelve. First, I shall thank you, the gentlemen of the Colony of Virginia, for bringing me here. I am here to help you solve some of your problems with slaves. Your invitation reached me on my modest plantation in the West Indies where I have experimented with some of the newest and still the oldest methods for control of slaves. Ancient Rome would envy us if my program is implemented. As our boat sailed south on the James River, named for our illustrious King, whose version of the Bible we cherish, I saw enough to know that your problem is not unique. While Rome used cords of wood as crosses for standing human bodies along its old highways in great numbers you are here using the tree and the rope on occasion . . .

I caught a whiff of a dead slave hanging from a tree a couple of miles back. You are not only losing valuable stock by hangings, you are having uprisings, slaves are running away, your crops are sometimes left in the fields too long for maximum profit, you suffer occasional fires, your animals are killed. Gentlemen, you know what your problems are; I do not need to elaborate. I am not here to enumerate your problems, I am here to introduce you to a method of solving them . . .

. . . .

In my bag here, I have a fool proof method for controlling your Black slaves. I guarantee everyone of you that if installed correctly it will control the slaves for at least 300 years. My method is simple. Any member of your family or your overseer can use it . . .

I have outlined a number of differences among the slaves; and I take these differences and make them bigger. I use fear, distrust, and envy for control purposes. These methods have worked on my modest plantation in the West Indies and it will work throughout the South. Take this simple little list of differences, and think about them. On top of my list is "Age", the second is "Color" or shade, there is intelligence, size, sex, size of plantations, status on plantation, attitude of owners, whether the slaves live in the valley, on a hill, East, West, North, South, have fine hair or coarse hair, or are tall or short. Now that you have a list of differences, I shall give you an outline of action--but before that I shall assure you that distrust is stronger than adulation; respect or admiration . . .

. . . .

The Black slave after receiving this indoctrination shall carry on and will become self re-fueling and self-generating for hundreds of years, maybe thousands . . .

Don't forget you must pitch the old Black vs. the young Black male, and the young Black male against the old Black male. You must use the dark skin slaves vs. the light skin slaves and the light skin slaves vs. the dark skin slaves. You must use the female vs. the male, and the male vs. the female. You must also have your White servants and overseers distrust all Blacks, but it is necessary that your slaves trust and depend on us. They must love, respect, and trust only us . . .

. . . .

Gentlemen, these Kits are your Keys to control. Use them. Have your wives and children use them, never miss opportunity. If used intensely for one year, the slaves themselves will remain perpetually distrustful . . .

Thank you, gentlemen.[170]

If local traders allow outside firms to both import large quantities of goods and distribute them, the Free Trade argument of "more choices for consumers" is met. However, there is the corresponding loss to a robust local retail economy, because of the inability to compete with the volume buying capabilities of these foreign importers/retailers.[171] You can argue that jobs will be created but now jobs are as "service workers", not as business owners and employees. Wages for these new "service workers" can be excusably depressed because of the number of "new" jobs. There is also less need for people to travel, especially with the breakdown of local relationships as business becomes less relational and more contractual; the need to travel in order to cultivate good trade relationships becomes less of a necessity. This eliminates smaller traders and allows the larger ones to dominate, because with this "sped up" trade they can move ever-large volumes of commodities. The race to grow becomes more important than maintaining local trade and distribution sectors that serve as both a long-term support for large firms and a support for the social economy, from which the larger firms are actually situated. If increased profits come at the expense of a hollowed-out social economy that hosts these firms, the firms acting as a "center" are not of any actual benefit because their place of residence will become uninhabitable and they will lose a local market for their products.

The local economy will convert from one that "produces" and "consumes" to one that only consumes from the "Global Economy". Exporting its surplus industrial capacity will not enforce the backbone of a domestic economy, it will

170. The Freeman Institute, Gambrills, Maryland.
171. An example of these are super retailers or "hypermarkets".

simply express national resources for the gain of a few. Participating in "global trade" while allowing deterioration and neglect of the domestic economy is financially irresponsible for any true businesspersons. It is the fool's errand that You want to encourage.

Land

Food security is a weakness to be exploited in Your subject state. Discourage low-input sustainable agriculture, the alternative to biotech agriculture, as a solution to Your subject nation-state's food production problems. If the subject nation-state insists on maintaining a program of low-input sustainable agriculture and does not buy into Your argument for the use of G-M crops, another alternative is to introduce pathogens and non-endemic species of pests into its natural environment in hopes that an epidemic of diseases or a complete crop die off occurs. In this scenario, You can come to its "rescue", offer food aid to mitigate the immediate shortage, and then plant G-M crops of Your choice either on Your own or with the help of Your NGOs, as an emergency response to the "crisis" that You have created. Resistance to Your influence will be significantly weakened because the population will be forced to consume Your food aid with the very conspicuous markings on bags and cans of food. In a state of panic, Your subject will not have properly monitored the activities of Your aid organizations and NGOs.

Biofuels

A very good way to have total control over the food security of Your subject nation-state, especially if it is already misallocating land resources to export-based economy agricultural schemes as directed by international lending institutions is to use arable land that is used grow food for the purpose of growing crops to be used as fuel. You can promote this trend through the "progressive" sounding phraseology of "alternative fuels" or "reusable fuels". The population of Your subject nation-state will assume because You term these fuels (sugar, corn, wheat, etc.) as "alternatives" that there is a correlation between these "alternatives" and a smaller carbon-output than fossil fuels. In many cases, the carbon produced in the combustion of these "alternatives" will be little, if any, less than that of the fossil fuels; but with certainty, the carbon emissions from the processing of these foods into combustible fuel combined with the carbon emissions from the combustion of these "biofuels" will equal or exceed that of fossil fuels. Initially, You can grow these in Your nation-state or in those of Other Princes, but within a short time it will "prove" to be more efficient and in the "Best Interest of Humanity" to grow these biofuel crops in Your subject nation-state(s).

Within the world of "international public opinion"--the opinion of You and Other Princes--, it will be hard for those subject nation-states to justify their selfish desire to use arable land to grow food for local consumption instead of thinking about the "Best Interest of Humanity" in participating in eco-friendly schemes such as using prime arable land to grow food for fuel instead of for local consumption.

The artificially low prices that You set in the world markets for commodities such as corn, sugar, and wheat can be lifted without hurting Your domestic economy or the domestic economies of Other Princes, because world prices for food commodities such as corn, sugar, wheat will jump considerably from the artificially low prices to protect Your manufacturing industry and to be used as feed for Your livestock production in Your subject nation-state(s) and in Your own nation-state by turning food commodities such as corn, sugar, wheat into fuel commodities to be traded along with petrochemicals in the Energy sector of world and regional financial markets.

Local farmers in Your subject nation-state, hopefully within the control of Your transnational corporations or with complicit major local growers will cease to grow these foods as foods and the prices will skyrocket, because these "foods" are now fuels. In doing so, food shortages will certainly ensure and You can come to their aid with food donations of G-M origin. These G-M seeds can be used to grow food on less than hospitable land. These aid donations will seem to be a blessing to desperate people, but these G-M crops will dominate the indigenous agriculture. Be sure to use sterile G-M seeds in Your aid work. In doing so, Your subject nation-state will be subject to Your will, Your benevolence, and You can demand of it whatever You desire--a particular percentage of the national budget for purchase of sterile seed, land allocations, privatization of local utilities and resource wealth, environmental legislation that favors Your interests and the export of desired labor force from its nation-state to Yours.

Space

In order to ensure dominance, You must maintain "possession" of space as well. Other Princes can be involved in technology development and can feel included in "international" missions but in truth, You must manage ultimate capabilities in launching surprise attacks from space, as well, be able to disable or destroy any Other nation-state's launch vehicles or satellites.

Colonize the orbit surrounding the planet so that no one can oppose Your military front. But in terms of planning for this type of military contingency, You should also take into account the fact the You would likely be launching experimental nuclear-propulsion systems and nuclear warheads into orbit. Your scientists cannot possibly plan for every variable that exists, so You will have to accept the possibility of a major catastrophe, including something as seemingly innocuous as a substantial increase in spacejunk because of a collision or as a result of using a space weapon, which could make the use of that particular orbit unusable essentially forever. But again, if You are serious about conquest You realize that the cost of conquest is the possibility of death[172].

Technology, War, & Idol Worship

In Your perfectly-ordered society, warlike behavior is not a sign of primitiveness, it is rather a sign of "civilization" and growth. Erich Fromm in *Anatomy of Human Destructiveness* states: "The most primitive men are the least warlike and the warlikeness grows in proportion to civilization. If destructiveness were innate in man, the trend would have to be the opposite."[173] Civilization is the "creation" of human society based on the laws of man and the active non-acknowledgement of a natural unconscious connection to harmony, balance, and oneness. "In the mythology of civilization, the life of primitives was nasty, and part of this nastiness was the presumed ceaselessness toil needed to eke out the merest subsistence. But anthropologists have challenged this myth with their discovery that for hunter-gatherers the work of survival leaves considerable time for the simple enjoyment of life."[174]

The spoken word is truly the most powerful weapon; the use of physical force is used by those incapable of verbally battling and bringing conflict to conclusion, thereafter restoring harmony. The spoken word sets in motion changes that cannot be undone through violence. The use of war technologies is an acknowledgement of the inability to outwit Your opponent mentally. Physical violence operates to disrupt the conscious and subconscious levels of consciousness, and although it may give the appearance of results, these are short-lived, as with all destructive behaviors. The word on the other hand, manifests the unconscious.

The reason why Cultural Warfare is superior to physical warfare is because, though it cannot change the unconscious levels of consciousness, it can manipulate targeted conscious and subconscious levels to encourage the

[172]. "The Way of the Warrior is resolute acceptance of death." Miyamoto Musashi.

[173]. from Schmookler, Andrew Bard.*Anatomy of Human Destructiveness* (1973), p.150. *Parable of Tribes: The Problem of Power in Social Evolution.* (1995) Albany: State University of New York Press, p.160.

[174]. Ibid, Schmookler, p.175

subject to utter desires that manifest in an unconsciousness that will call into question these desires, therefore causing dissonance. On the unconscious level, the subject will know that these answers from the unconscious bring about balance and harmony. Instead of acknowledging the causality of the universe, the subject will return to You for answers rather than questioning these processes.

The unconscious will plainly "tell" the subject what behaviors are out of balance and will encourage it to make changes as to live in harmony, but the resulting cognitive dissonance will lead the subject to embrace even more of Your ideals and cultural icons. You will be the "deity" to whom it looks to for direction; You will be its point of reference, and it will discontinue acknowledgement of any true connection to the intuitive knowledge of balance, harmony, interconnectedness, and mutual responsibility. Cultural Warfare replaces a subject's cultural and spiritual connection to the Source, the collective consciousness that binds all into one, with a connection to You as its new point of reference and object of worship.

Chapter 13:
Cultural Icons
& Mass Media

Cultural Icons, in the context the Cultural Warfare, are objects or icons that are constructed to idolize particular cultural ideals that You wish to project. The function of these icons are, in a sense, to transport the subject into Your world, to feel a part of this world as long as it is "touching", or in contact with it. The subject's self-esteem should be in congruence with cultural products or ideals that You project onto it. A successful cultural icon embodies the ideals that You project onto the subject. Do not empower the subject state, though You should profess to. Remember, all of Your methods are Platonic devices, and delineation must be made between Primary and Other, Universal and Parochial or ethnic, Modern and old-fashioned, Sophisticated and small-minded. Bring ideas, products, services, and technologies that will cause social, economic and environmental disruption so that You can exploit the country and eliminate its government mandate to rule. Transform the subject state into one owned and approved of by You and it will derive esteem from Your sanctioning. You are turning its society into one that is comfortable for You to live in, one that suits Your wants and desires.

'Well Lolly Dear, the California Curse strikes you like a disease the minute you set foot in Hollywood, so play close attention.'

'Oh, I am, I am.'

'You see Lolly, this place you've arrived in; this place we call home--it isn't a place at all, but a living creature.'

'A living creature?'

'More precisely an evil wizard, like in the old stories.'

'And you all live on him?'

'Like fleas on the belly of a mutt.'

'Exactly. But unlike the helpless dog; this wizard is able to banish the personalities of those he bewitches, forcing them against their will to carry out his command: to forget the land of their birth; the purpose of their journey; and whatever principles they once held dear.'

'Don't forget about the symptoms, that's my favorite part!'

'The curse is taking hold of you when you experience the following: you see yourself as the most important person in any room; you accept money as the strongest force in Nature; and finally, your morality vanishes without a trace.'

From "The Cat's Meow" (2001)

The Land of Pleasure.

The allure of the lifestyle that You are projecting is that it solely appeals to the physical senses; it is an "escape" from all other realities. You stimulate and are pleasing to the eyes, tongue, nose, skin, sex organs, but without any substance. You project the most entertaining, sexually appealing, richest fantasy-based pleasure. The subject does not have the ability to devise its own concepts of beauty and pleasure; You are to serve all to it, out of balance and of course with no moderation.

Artifacts

In an illustrative sense, when the subject "touches" or "possesses" one of Your cultural icons, it will act as a portal to another world. The physical body remains in the present and concrete world, but through contact with the icon the mental body as well as its consciousness connects with Your world.[179] The purpose of using these devices is to reinforce the transference of the subject's point of reference and cultural center to Your own. Those who are highly materialistic, who possess a considerable number of Your cultural icons, will be in so much "contact" with Your world that they will believe themselves to be a part of it, and the grip of their own concrete indigenous culture-based world will soon slip away, delivering them into a "world" based on Your projected culture. For development of the Culture of Comparison, the use of cultural icons is essential.

The beauty of using cultural icons to dislodge the subject from its center is that it is essentially "chasing a waterfall". Because the cultural icon is based on Your culture and rooted in a history that preceded contact with the subject, it is impossible for the subject to feel a "part" of this world through contact with icons. Cultural icons are ways of thinking that You project--material goods, especially luxury items, fast foods, clothing brands, automobiles, vacation spots, club memberships, art, music, dance, to name just a few.

The "materialization" of the subject culture is a very solid means of separating the populace from the center that unifies it. You can get the subject to switch its entrenched ideas of success, be it harmonious family life, high education, wisdom, humility when wealthy, and exchange these for the material-based values that You project to achieve success, and all connections to a cultural center will cease to exist. Connection will equate to how many projected icons can be possessed and internalized.

Answers to all problems, solutions to everything, will become based on Your success model: an external-based means of achieving, and since what

---

[179.] See Ani, p.232

You are projecting is one that is "seemingly associative", the subject will not be able to achieve fulfillment and will never be able to fill the void of cultural center, which can only be satisfied with a collective creative purpose. More and more, the subject will crave Your projections and icons in the hope that it will find happiness and inner peace in the "success" that You are projecting.

Cultural Icons

When conceptualizing how You will "charge" Your cultural icons, You should make the image of the Superior and Modern so charged that it serves as a symbol of Your "long history of achievement". When in contact with the icon, the subject will experience three simultaneous things: 1. the feeling of sharing a collective identity with You; 2. a feeling of inferiority, desiring to feel the same self-pride as You; and 3. a need to support the co-dependent relationship that You are encouraging through the processes of CCD and the corresponding projections.

This process of supporting codependency and thereby encouraging addictive behaviors serves as a means of opening the subject's collective and individual psyches up as participatory receptacles of Your cultural icons. As a means of trying to resolve the unbalanced relationship, Your encouragement of codependent relationships supports addictive behaviors. The subject will attempt to obtain as many cultural icons as possible in order to feed the "high" that is experienced in sharing a collective identity with You. But like all addictions, feeding the addiction only intensifies the subsequent depression. It is an addiction that can only be cured with the reestablishment of the true Cultural Center, but You have denigrated the indigenous cultural center, so the subject sees it as having no value and tries to erroneously achieve the same "reestablishment of culture" using Yours that are coated in SACs. There is no greater pain than the loss of True Self; without it there is no point of reference, and therefore no means of actually making life choices that are in line with the better interests of the subject. If there is no point of reference, there can be no context through which critical thinking can occur. Rational thinking without its corresponding balance of intuition and emotion leads the user to self-destruction.

Materialism

Locally-produced items and services that mimic the ones that You bring must conform to Your operating practices and be embraced as the model to emulate, otherwise it must be discredited or You will risk the chance that, after the initial stage of copying Your methods, the subject adopts methods that better suit its society's wants and needs.

All material goods and services that You export should be connected to Your system of cultural icons. Your products must be identifiably foreign and divergent from the "parochial, archaic, and ethnic" items; they must be seen as symbols of Modernity, Universal themes of Success and Sophistication.

Mass Media.

Image and power interact on a global scale as well. Postcolonial imagery presents the Third World as spectacle. The exploitation of the non-western world of western sensory gratification, a practice begun in ninetieth-century art, has been extended and refined in the media culture of the twentieth century leading to a kind of 'cannibalism by connoisseurs'. Next to the Barcardi-rum beaches, images of suffering, starvation and bloodshed circulate through the media networks of the World's electronic Coliseum. The abnormal is the norm in the representation of the non-western world. The logic of center and periphery is mirrored in the dual imagery of stability and crisis, life and death, with death, famine, disaster, and upheaval expelled to the margins. The conventional formula, which territorializes poverty, ignores the similarities between North and South, and conceals global economic and political links. The images of aid to the Third World are variations of this formula; fundamentally patronizing, they are ahistorical, preoccupied with symptoms and oblivious to causes, and for all their global scope, parochial. Africa is one of the recipients of aid and targets of this imagery; but the question of how Africa, once a producer of food surpluses, ended up in its present condition is rarely addressed. The role of colonialism, the consequences of export agriculture and the effects of the agricultural and trade policies of western countries are issues that remain outside the framework of the advertisements of western charity. For people living in the best of possible worlds, complacency is nourished by a message that undermines the awareness of common humanity. For all the wealth of information provided in the media age, we are living in a world largely cut from cardboard images. Ours is a planetary age, but we live in a world of false horizons.[180]

When representing images of Yourself or those of Your nation-state in mass media, popular culture, commercial advertising, You must place Yourself above the people in the society. The subject state is to serve as an exotic getaway for Your leisure activities. The local people are to serve as background players in the "primary" activities that You enjoy. Present Yourself as luxuriously partaking in the "beautiful resources, city and its people", all that the subject state has to offer and it will need Your "approval" on how to view itself. If You approve, it has worth; if You do not, it does not. This approach serves other aspects of society. You are the visiting authority; You bestow approval on the society for its "hard work" in living to Your standards.

Because You embody power and sophistication, You must use this to Your advantage in creating a media "beauty image". Your men are the most handsome, powerful and behaved; Your women are the rarest and most

---

[180.] Pieterse, Jan Nederveen (1992) *White on Black: Images of Africa and Blacks in Western Popular Culture*. Yale University Press, in association with Cosmic Illusion Productions, Amsterdam, p.235

beautiful. The men will desire Your women, and the women will desire the men of Your state, no matter how handsome, square; strong, weak; parochial-minded, world-minded; powerful, or powerless they are perceived in their own state. Feelings of inferiority will cause the subject to desire contact with Your world through beauty image; it will feel that it is sharing the experience of Your world when in contact with these symbols.

If You offer rural populations satellite dishes to receive commercial programming in virtually every household, in a relatively short time You will turn a people that were rich in community into one of poverty. In this manner, You can promote labor migration to support wants that You have turned into needs, and at the same time, cause the people to lose focus on communal efforts to improve societal needs such as nutrition, housing, healthcare, stable households, sustainable environment. Focus on bringing the target audience to a "realization of poverty", followed by the encouragement of material desires to high moral stature. The goal, of course, is to transfer the collective consciousness of the subject to one where human value is no longer "relational", but instead quantitative. The "awakening" that You cause through the promotion of mass media will eliminate the binding relationships between people and create a nation-state of individual consumers instilled with the Culture of Comparison.

Mass Media & the Promotion of Sameness.

Those nation-states like Yours, that possess the greatest communicative services, are able to more effectively promote the case that Their "way of life" is the Universal solution to the world's problems. You can promote this idea, because You control the medium of information dissemination and are able to cloud the reality of true social economic and environmental conditions. Take note of the fact that the proliferation of communications technology also allows those upset with the present trends of the governance to easily mobilize.

No-Confidence Media

Instill doubt in people of the institutions run by the people of the subject nation-state, the "locals". Project the need for reform and Modernization of a certain sector. Define the standards by which these can be made, standards of a system that does not match the social reality of the subject nation-state. When problems occur, use Your media to criticize in detail the inefficiencies, possible wrong-doings inside. Promote the new system while destroying consumer confidence in the institutions and products; next, promote the services of Your nation-state as an alternative to the "mismanagement" of local institutions. You need to cause insecurity in the population insecurity to create a market where there was none (or very little market share) before.

Constant economic growth is important to external capital markets, but not necessarily to the host economy. You must promote the idea that economics can operate independent of a host society. But know that economies and societies have a symbiotic parasitic relationship. They both need each other to survive. They are both equally hosts and parasites.

Representations in Media
In the local media You should objectify the indigenous culture as a group and create the feeling that a connection with Your culture is representative of Individuality, more Modern, and better than possessing group identity. Cultural tourism is one means of stimulating the generation of income-earners while instilling a sense of inferiority on the population. Tourists gawk at the "strange": the exotic rituals, customs, and quaint handicrafts of the natives. 'Indigenous' needs to be presented in this fashion--not as equal human beings and actively engaged in travel and trade. Promote conformity to the aesthetic that You establish, and use native-ness to illustrate what is old-fashioned, primitive, and lacking in relevance to this Modern era.

Two Senses: Participatory Media
The use of any two senses produces a participatory act: listening and seeing, listening and touching, seeing and tasting, seeing and touching, touching and smelling. The sixth sense of intuition or "gut feeling" is underdeveloped in many people, so the use of two physical senses is required for participation.

This makes television, movies, video games, and other audio-visual media the most powerful broadcast media (of course, discounting tactile-audio-visual media such as fully-interactive video games and the internet) because the subject is actually "participating" with the media in the experience: its "psychological guard" is down and it becomes open to persuasion. Since one cannot simultaneously participate in and fully protect the self, it is very important that You promote media that utilizes two or more senses for Your projections. There will be far less resistance if You do so.

Mass Media & Television
People *watch* television; they do not "*look*" at it. It is a participatory act. The case is the same for societies whose primary mass media is radio; they *hear* what is said on the radio; they do not "*listen*" to it. People therefore interact with television as "watchers"; their guards down to accept what is being broadcast as "true". The only conflict evoked is when the message opposes

"strongly-held" beliefs, which can be weakened through inducement of CCD and the follow-up of SACs in regular broadcasting and pubic service announcements.

When broadcasting programs onto the population of the subject nation-state, always portray the programs as entertainment, never too heavy. The programs must have content that the target audience can identify with, so that You can change commonly held truths through manipulation; promote the content of groups that the target audience looks down on or despises, so that You can identify these groups with the negative effects occurring in the society under Your influence; or, groups that the target audience idolizes, so that You can promote the acceptance of ideals and thoughts that are in line with consumption of Your cultural icons, or artifacts. This is done to affirm "popular consensus" that You are projecting onto the subject population: the demonization of one or a few despised groups to keep the population from seeing social, economic and environmental breakdown as a consequence of Your influence; the idolatry of those that emulate You and Your projected lifestyle, encouraging the population to accept Your ideals of success and Your political, cultural, social, environmental, religious policies.

Co-opt the media into pushing Your desired agenda. This can be done through pressure applied by the subject government onto broadcasters, the purchasing of advertising on broadcast networks to influence program development, or through the use of Your transnational corporations to control content. This is important, as You do not want too many other messages in the media that will contradict Your projections.

Mass Media & Propaganda

A Christian group that conducted missionary operations in Thailand compiled a book detailing how to utilize mass communications to conduct a successful propaganda campaign in developing nations, *Everything You Need to Know For a Cassette Ministry*. The following are some evaluations of effective communications media. I feel that these should provide You with some sort of direction:

Radio

The most widely used mass media in Christian work is radio . . . In the hands of those with knowledge, means, and courage [it] is a powerful and effective tool . . . Radio can do certain things no other media can. For example, as long as people have a receiver, radio can reach them everywhere--even while they are engaged in doing something else. There is no screen to watch, no reading to do, no records to turn, no other people to rely on . . .

. . . . Christian radio programming should be carefully analyzed to see if it is evangelistic and if it is relevant to the intended audience. Programs produced in London, Detroit, or Houston may mean nothing to the Oriental listener, who has a different understanding and spiritual status, a different education and background, and a different religion and cultural environment.[181]

. . . .

As I mentioned before, radio can do many things for us. Here are a list of advantages and possibilities.

1. *Radio can give knowledge and widen horizons.* Expanding people's knowledge and understanding of Christianity can effectively be done on radio.

2. *Radio can focus attention on the teaching of Christ.* By bringing a certain subject to people's attention over the radio that subject becomes a topic of conversation. In some countries Christianity has been a taboo subject for years. After hearing a Christian program on the air, one villager commented, 'When the government allows it on the radio, it can't be that bad.'

3. *Radio can raise aspirations for change.* If a man listens to another man on the air telling the way God has changed his life, the listener may, by identification with the speaker, aspire to see the same changes in his own life. A positive climate for change may be the result.

4. *Radio can confer status on a weak church.* A ridiculed Christian, or small Christian church in a village or town, will receive recognition and status by the very fact that Christian programs are on local radio stations. If the program carries the testimony of a prince, or well-known filmstar, recognition will be even higher.

5. *Radio can influence social norms.* The social acceptance or rejection of Christians can be greatly affected by Christian radio broadcasting. News of official government recognition can help greatly, too.

6. *Radio can help form tastes.* The matter of music has been a problem in many churches on the mission field. The translation of Western hymns and use of traditional Western tunes by missionaries Christians, has often caused rejection of local, indigenous music, giving the church a foreign face. Radio can help to change such a situation and help form tastes for locally written hymns.

7. *Radio can help to change attitudes.* Though it will be difficult to change strongly held attitudes by radio alone, it can be done over time. By working step by step, the strongly held attitudes may gradually change.

8. *Radio is believed, and in time will give a good understanding of Christian words and concepts.* In countries where radio is primarily used as an information source, it is much more readily believed than in countries where it mainly fulfills an entertainment role. Through daily programming, and using only nationals as speakers, singers, and announcers on Christian programs, a true picture of the Church can be communicated.

9. *Radio gets into closed homes.* In many countries it may be almost impossible for a man with higher education in the community, to come to a Christian meeting. Yet, he is usually interested in finding out what the Christians are really teaching. Radio can solve that problem.

10. *Radio can, for the same outlay reach more people.* The task of bringing the Gospel to all men is so enormous that only through skillful and vigorous use of radio does it seem possible."[182]

[181] Soggard, Vigo. (1975) *Everything You Need to Know For a Cassette Ministry.* Minneapolis: Bethany Fellowship Inc. pp.41-3

Television

Due to its sight, sound, and motion, television has the greatest potential as a communication media . . . There are several points to keep in mind when one is 'encoding' a message for television. Television uses both audio and visual signals, so everything has to be coded into two 'languages' . . . TV brings the communications directly into the living room of millions of people at one time . . .

According to McLuhan, television is a 'cool' media that requires a lot of participation by the viewer . . .

. . . .

It should be mentioned that due to its high cost, television's reception is limited in many countries; however taken all together, television is a most powerful, effective media if its limitations and possibilities are fully understood and utilized by its users. The communicator who understands to talk quietly and intimately with the family who kindly invited him into their home will also be the most persuasive . . .

. . . There is also a great need for educational programs. Dedicated, well-trained Christian television producers could make a tremendous impact on a country by producing good, positive educational programs, There may also be many opportunities for news or feature programs that analyze world events in a truly objective way. Another area of need, especially in developing countries is to provide teachers who are able to train national staffs in television and communications as a whole.

Christian workers in more advanced communities should not forget the possibilities of utilizing Community Antenna Television (CATV) systems . . .[183]

Video Cassettes

Audio cassettes have had immediate acceptance . . . Superficially the use of the video cassette may look like ordinary television, but it is a very different tool. An important stage is introduced, in that there is only one audience at a time. It becomes a 'personal' media, for the video cassette will be used by a person."[184]

Films

Like the video cassette, the use of motion pictures distinguishes itself from the use of television and radio by the fact that only one audience is viewing the film at a given time, and the user of the 'tool' will be there in person. This greatly limits the audience size but, on the other hand, has the advantage of immediate feedback and follow-up.

Potentially, there are few media more persuasive than film. As the viewer sits in a darkened theater or room, all the action is brought to him. Limited effort is needed, for all the action is on the screen. Others have shot the film, edited it, etc., so the viewer is spared all the difficult work. In minutes can travel thousands of miles and span centuries of history.

In many developing countries, films are used in commercial enterprises and in educational projects. This has proven to be most effective as a means of drawing people together and then presenting the message in the context of the film.[185]

[182.] Some points adapted from Schramm, Wilbut. Mass media and National Development, pp.127-144 inside Sogarrd pp.43-4

[183.] Soggard pp.45-7

[184.] Ibid, p.47

[185.] Ibid. p.48

Literature

Many people believe that literature is the most effective, far-reaching media, but it too, has serious limitations . . . for every individual who cannot read at all, many more cannot read at a level that would make persuasive written communication an effective form . . .

. . . .

There does exist a 'climate of learning' between this medium and the individual. The attention must be given to the reading totally, and only one person is reading at a time. Comprehension is helped by the possibility of re-reading. A magazine or book will generally carry high credibility on the subject matter it promotes . . . For those who can read, literature is very important and we cannot live without it . . .

. . . .

Literature has been used in evangelistic outreach, but its effectiveness has often been limited because of the irrelevant text used. Too much has been expected of the reader. During the last decade or so, new unique literature ministries have been developed . . . Another ministry that could be mentioned is the British-based *Soon* ministry that keeps its vocabulary to 1000 words.[186]

Supplementary Media

The preceding media have all been media that could, if necessary, be used for all aspects of our ministry. Their individual strengths and weaknesses must be studied first, though, so that the best 'media-mix' can be selected . . . One further supplementary media that can be used effectively is that billboard and poster. Well made and well-placed billboards can effectively increase the impact of a radio or television campaign . . . Billboards by themselves will probably not be effective in communicating a message, but research studies have shown that they greatly improve the effect of a radio or television campaign.[187]

The Dual Role of Free Press

There is a tendency to accept as universally valid news values that have been developed to meet the needs of individualistic industrial societies. The sensational, the spectacular, the tragic, the sordid and the deviant, tend to get prominence over the orderly, the integrated, the normal and the constructive. These values seem to have evolved as an attempt to gratify the subjective needs of fast-paced, individualistic societies than out of a desire to represent accurately and objectively!

Neville Jayaweera (Third World Communicator)

In the name of "Democracy" promote government policies that support "Freedom of the Press" to disseminate Your propaganda. Until such time that You need to implement Fascist governance measures for the sake of maintaining order and control, the Press will need to be put under the control of press bodies that share the interests of the subject government. During this time, You should promote "true press freedom" allowing "any business interest" to own any portion of any sector of the press without restriction and in

186. Ibid, pp.49-50
187. Ibid. p. 50-1

the name of free enterprise; whether that be broadcast, print, or internet. This will allow You to control the parameters of "acceptable media coverage" via media venues that will exist under the guise and responsibility of free market regulation and "corporate governance".

In this dual role of the Press as integral to the administration of 'security-oriented governance', the Press should not be the divisive agent that You are initially utilizing it as, but instead as a unifying force that defines patriotism as blind faith in the subject government no matter how hopeless life may seem and no matter how many civil rights are repealed in the name of security. In this scenario the Press will define all who support the government as good patriots and citizens, and those who oppose any of its policies will be marked traitors allied with what the "terrorist" enemy that You project onto the population.

In truth, the Press is relational, not divergent from its host society. In Your subject nation-state the Press *should* be divergent from its host society and should also be the agent of dissemination in Your projections to create separation in the population. Questioning the obvious, creating seeds of doubt in things already decided on by consensus, these the are the tools of Your Free Press.

It is said that the role of the Press is to ask questions and newsmakers are to answer them. To serve our needs, the Press both asks questions and answers them. This "small difference" is the difference between news and propaganda. The news that Your Free Press projects *is* propaganda.

The following is representative of the Libertarian model of Free Press Journalism: "Man is no longer conceived of as a dependent being able to discern between truth and falsehood . . . Rather, the right to search for truth is one of the unalienable natural rights of man . . ."[188] This is a nice assumption that You can project onto Your subject, but in actuality this also presupposes the Platonic hierarchy of free men, slaves and women. The enslaved masses are not considered "men" while man (eugenics) is subject to Rule of Law dictated by the Philosopher-kings. Democracy is purported to have evolved from here somewhere.

Because of the monopoly-like powers that the press holds, access to the population's psyche with little resistance and because the assumption of "truth" is being decimated, the press has a natural obligation to promote the sustainability of the society. You must influence this so that the Press neither supports the interest of traditional society nor the abstract nation-state, the subject government. Promote government policies in Your subject nation-

[188]. Maslog, Crispin C. (1994) *Communication, Values and Society.* New Day Publishers, Manila, p. 46

state's government that, in the name of 'Democracy', even though its government is treatened by Your influence in the Press, do not censor the "Freedom of the Press" that is disseminating Your propaganda. Even when civil order is threatended by the invocation of Your Press, "Free Speech" is protected.

Free Press & Morality

Do people deserve a freedom for all mass-media, promoting values of rugged individualism, materialism and greed which inevitably lead to widespread graft and corruption in even the lowest level of public office? Do they deserve a powerful, influential media that systematically negates moral values which teachers diligently inculcate in the classroom? Or would teachers rather have a responsible mass media--promoting, and actually leading by example, such values as social responsibility, public service as public trust, social justice, productivity, industry, and morality?

The journalist Crispin Maslog poses these questions. The kind of press and mass-media that You should promote negates any residual and indigenously constructed education in the system. The media must have no limits and should respect no persons, no hierarchies, no positions, no traditions. It is "free" of any obligations to its host society. You should defend this destructive type of press and mass-media as being a "watchdog for the people" and "representative of the common interest and consensus of the people".

In truth, a "free press" can be free in the sense that it can give, as objective as those who live in an interconnected reality, praise or criticism of the government's policies and programs, the economy, popular culture, or daily life. But this "free press" still recognizes that it has an obligation, while providing constructive criticism, to also promote social cohesiveness and stability in the society. The role for this type of "free press" is to ensure that society is on its stated path; to act as a critic, to reflect popular opinion when the government strays from its acknowledged point of reference and departure.

The variation of the "Free Press" that You promote is not the aforementioned. Its sole purpose is to exacerbate divisions in the society, discourage confidence in the government and any established social mores, through providing an infinite number of "choices" that the society has not contemplated as being culturally-congruent. This form of destructive mass-media uses hyper-morality to discredit every hierarchy in the society while simultaneously providing a number of "Free Choices" that directly conflict with the established morality of the subject's nation-state.

Take for example, the pursuit by the media for the recall of public officials for "alleged" sexual improprieties while broadcasting a wide array of sexually explicit commercials and programming. An "allegation" is enough to discredit a person, a program, a business, a government agency. Proof is not necessary. I preface "alleged" in the example because this type of media derives power from its "objectivity". The claim of objectivity implies impartiality and truthfulness. "Objective" media is media that only "speaks the truth". Your mass-media and Free Press, however, can broadcast anything You desire. Even if a retraction is broadcasted or printed, public perception of the "allegation" from an "objective media" will be drastically altered. If Your mass-media states anything, it becomes truth; even if the stated "truth" can be disproved by others, there will always be a larger number of people in the population that stay loyal to the initial "allegation". At this time when the public's appetite for "allegations" has been created, readership patterns will also increase.

The dual methodology of championing morality and dislocating the population from its collective morality is an effective means separating the society from itself, the cohesiveness that holds it together, its cultural center. If You use this form of mass-media efficiently, the population will cease to look inwards for direction. It instead will look to the media and consequently You for direction, because through Your projections portray Your ideals as that which all societies should embrace in order to become Modern and Developed, and Your Free Press will portray the consumption of Your cultural icons as a physical representation of achieving this status of Sophistication.

Chapter 14:
Free Trade

Over the last twenty years, the emergence of a formalized system of globalization has amplified pricing disparities, in many cases, creating "permanent" North-South, predator-prey relationships based on Free Trade. Examine the dynamic of Colonialism versus Neocolonialism or Free-Trade. Both systems are beneficial to You, but the latter is more cost-effective: maximum profit with least involvement. You can wage non-invasive warfare by sending direction from Your generals, the markets that You control. You can attack using Your corporations and media as soldiers. Free Trade will destroy Your subject's society, ceding national sovereignty to dependence on overseas markets, supplies, and capital for sustainability. The surrender of economic sovereignty will contradict the mandate and responsibility of the subject nation-state's government, the cultural, social, environmental, and security needs of the populace. Create a permanent worldwide poor class by enforcing a standard of prices for goods worldwide.

'Underdeveloped', or distorted development, carries with it a dangerous specialization in raw materials, containing a threat of hunger for all our people. We, 'the underdeveloped', are those of the single crop, the single product, and the single market. This is the great formula of imperial economic domination which is combined with the old and always useful Roman formula, 'divide and conquer'.

Ernesto "Che" Guevara

Slavery was a bad thing, and freedom, of the kind we got, with nothing to live on, was bad. Two snakes full of poison. One lying with his head pointing north, the other with his head pointing south. Their names--slavery and freedom. The snake called slavery lay with his head pointed south, and the snake called freedom lay his head pointed north. Both bit the nigger, and they was both bad.

Patsy Mitcher, Freed Slave[190]

A man does not 'by nature' wish to earn more and more money, but simply to live as he is accustomed to live and to earn as much as is necessary for that purpose. Wherever modern capitalism has begun its work of increasing the productivity of labour by increasing its intensity, it has encountered the immensely stubborn resistance of this loading trait of precapitalist labour.[191]

Max Weber

[190.] Hurmence, Belinda ed. (1996) *My Folks Don't Want Me To Talk About Slavery.* Winston-Salem, N.C.: John F. Blair Publisher, p.80

[191.] Quote in *Parable of Tribes* p.18 from Weber, Max (1958) *The Protestant Ethic and the Spirit of Capitalism.* Charles Scribner's Sons, New York, p.60

Developing countries lost about 55 billion in U.S. dollars from price manipulation. The following chart reveals some striking data:

- in 1960, 6.3 tons of oil could be purchased with the sale of a ton of sugar. In 1982, only 0.7 tons of oil could be bought for a ton of sugar.
- in 1960, for a ton a bananas, 13 tons of oil was purchasable from proceeds.
- in 1982, only 1.6 tons could be bought.
- in 1959 with income from sale of 24 tons sugar, one 60 HP tractor could be purchased. By late 1982, 115 tons of sugar were needed to buy that same tractor.
- in 1959 from the sale of 6 tons of jute fibre, a 7-8 ton truck could be bought. By late 1982, 26 tons of jute fibre exchanged for the same truck.
- in 1959, from the sale value of one ton of copper wire, you could buy 39 X-ray tubes for medical purposes. By late 1982, only 3 such tubes could be bought with that same ton.[192]

To disable the subject's economy, promote the myth of the Free Market and project it as a Universal "truth" of being the most effective means to creating national wealth. Participation in the Free Market is to be synonymous with economic success. Promote abstraction of the Free Market and preach the gospel of the "invisible hand" that is supposed to bring equilibrium to it, while You take the economy out of the subject's social reality and place it into the sphere of Yours, positioning it to serve You rather than its host society. Promote true Materialism: a state in which relationships are Quantitative, and valued as such. In Your regulated Free Market society, people are to be Quantified and given an economic "dollar" value.

Promote the ideology of Progress at Any Cost. You are the Universal representation of Progress, Modernity, and Development, and like the analogy of "limits" in calculus, where one is always approaching but never reaching, You can keep Your subject in the perpetual wild goose chase of attempting to reach Your "level of Development". In the economic realm, You will define this as the necessity for perpetual economic growth. Use the words "underdeveloped" and "developing" to ease the reality that the subject is an economic colony, semi-colony, or dependency.

[192]. Democratic Journalist, April, 1986 pp.4&5. Estimated based on US exports September-December: 1981. from Mendis, L.N.T. (2004) *Descent of Man.* Colombo: Vijitha Yapa Publications, p.46

The Story of Sukus and Tukus[193]

There were once two neighboring islands far away in the oceans. Once was called Aya and the other Baya. A certain people Called the Sukus lived on the island of Aya. It was a fertile island with lush vegetation and tropical fruits. There were numerous waterfalls and rivers that provided the people with clean water and places for family retreats and recreation. The surrounding seas were unpolluted, with abundant fish and other seafood. The island also had gold and the Sukus, particularly the womenfolk, loved gold. They used pieces of gold as money since everyone treasured gold. Their tribal leadership led by a man named Saka, minted the gold coins. They lived a simple cooperative life and there were no interest charges for lending and borrowings among themselves. Occasionally, some tidal waves and strong winds would destroy some property, particularly homes, but the community of people who went about their life gracefully.

The island of Baya, on the other hand, was inhabited by a people called the Tukus. The leader was an elderly man named Taka. The island of Baka was fertile too and the Tukus were mostly farmers who worked rice fiends or kept cows, sheep, and poultry. Some of them were good at handiwork and produced a variety of household items. They too lived a very peaceful and cooperative life, mutually helping each other for survival. The Tukus were, however, not so sophisticated as the Sukus, in that they merely did barter trade. The Tukus realized that the Sukus were much wealthier, healthier and had towns that were much more sophisticated than their own. They had always thought that the Sukus were more gifted and superior beings than themselves. Even though they traded their goods occasionally with the Sukus, they never caught on to the idea of money. However, their women-folk too loved gold, particularly the gold jewelry that the Sukus made.

One day, two smartly dressed men arrived on the shores of the island of Aya. Their names were Gago and Sago. The Sukus being a very hospitable people welcomed their new guests. Gago and Sago impressed the Sukus with the stories of their extensive traveling. They showed them some gold coins from other parts of the world and also some printed papers that were apparently used as money by some far-away people. The Sukus had never seen paper before. The paper money even had pictures of bananas on it--their favorite fruit. The strangers also showed them a machine that prints such money. Wow! That got the Sukus' attention. They were awed because they had never seen anything like that before. The islanders loved Gago and Sago and invited both to live with them on the island.

Gago and Sago convinced the people that an institution called a bank would benefit the people immensely. They explained that a bank would provide a place for keeping their gold money safe while uplifting their economic conditions by making the savings available to others for productive use, which otherwise would remain idle. The Sukus, being a people who loved to help others, though that was a great idea. Gago and Sago then built a small building structure with a vault in it and started operating the first bank on the island of Aya.

They celebrated the occasion by giving the islanders a great feast along with a colorful festival of events. The people thronged to deposit their gold coins with the bank. Depositors were given a piece of printed paper for every gold coin they deposited, with the assurance that they could redeem a gold coin for every paper they turned in. The people were excited with the paper 'money' they got because it even had a picture of their leader Saka beside a banana tree. No doubt Saka was very pleased too!

---

193. Story from Meera, Ahamed Kameel Mydin. (2004) *The Theft of Nations: Returning to Gold.* Selangor Darul Ehsan, Malaysia: Pelanduk Publications (M) Sdn Bhd. pp. 5-9

The people deposited all their gold coins, a total of 100,000 pieces and hence an equivalent number of pieces of paper were given out. Now the people used the paper as money and found that it was much more convenient than the heavier gold coins that they used before. The paper money printed by Gago and Sago, therefore, became the dominant currency of the island. Nobody used the gold coins anymore. The people were pleased with the ease with which they were able to go about doing their businesses. They trusted Gago and Sago very much because each time they brought in a piece of paper for redemption their request was indeed honoured. Gago and Sago became very respected and honoured in their society.

The Tukus who heard about the whole thing became excited and pleaded with Gago and Sago to help them out too. Gago and Sago smiled to each other and told the Tukus that they would indeed be very pleased to do so. They then set up a similar building in Baya, and Sago was placed there as the manager. The difference between Aya and Baya was that in Baya the Tukus had no gold coins to deposit. Sago told them that was alright. He would however give 1,000 paper notes to each family to use as money. Since there were a hundred families in Baya, so 100,000 paper notes were given out.

However, Sago reminded them that at the end of the year each family must return 1,100 paper notes, the 10 per cent extra being a charge for the services he was providing. The Tukus found the paper money truly to be like magic. It made their business dealings so much easier compared to their previous barter trade. People spent much less looking for counterparties to trade with. Now they were able to specialize in jobs they were good at. Their economy began to grow rapidly.

Now Gago and Sago decided that the time was ripe for them to do their "trick" . . . Gago noticed that in Aya, on average only 10 per cent of the gold deposits were redeemed by the Sukus at any particular time. The other 90 per cent remained in the vaults. Noticing that their printed papers were circulating as money, Gago printed an extra 900,000 certificates to be circulated as money too! Gago had calculated that with the extra papers, a total of 1,000,000 pieces of paper would be outstanding and if the people came to redeem their normal 10 per cent, then the 100,000 original deposit of gold would be readily available for redemption. Gago loaned out this extra 900,000 paper money to some 'needy' Sukus at an interest charge of 15 per cent.

The Sukus suddenly found that the price of things were rising. This baffled them and no one could figure out why. Some of them who had borrowed money from Gago were not able to pay back their debt even though they worked very hard trying to earn that extra money. Business became increasingly competitive and the society became less companionate and less caring towards others. The Tukus too found similar things happening to them. Initially, they did not notice any price increase but they noticed some behavioural change in their people. They became very competitive in attitude and less caring towards their fellows.

Even with hard work and such competitive behaviour, some of the Tukus still defaulted on their loans. They were not able to acquire enough money to pay back their total debt. Now Sago began confiscate real wealth from the loan defaulters--like land, cows, sheep, etc. Their elderly leader Taka was among those who defaulted. But Sago gave him and some other Tukus additional paper notes as a rescheduling of their loans. This increased further their indebtedness. Taka defaulted a second time and had his loan rescheduled again. Now Taka began to avoid meetings with Sago. He felt ashamed and found his former power, pride, courage, and dignity falling. On the contrary, he found that Sago was slowly becoming wealthy by acquiring the people's assets. In fact, he found that the power, pride, courage and dignity that he lost were now enthroned on Sago. Gago and Sago did not stop there. They continued to spread their wings to other people and societies, following their ultimate dream of becoming Global Supreme Rulers by establishing a single global bank with single global money.

After a number of years, Gago and Sago who once arrived on the shores of the island of Aya with the only printing machine, were both now the owners of most of the land and property in both Aya and Baya. The people were reduced to mere workers, some of them now living in poverty. Many worked long hours just to make ends meet. They now had less time for family, friends or for religious activities. Social problems were widespread. People cared less for others. It goes without saying that with poverty, other social ills like crime and prostitution began to thrive. Their cultures were gradually replaced because Gago and Sago introduced the new 'superior' culture of a 'superior' people to which they belonged. This meant the end of caring for the people of the two islands of Aya and Baya, who had earlier lived a peaceful yet graceful life before Gago and Sago arrived with a printing machine.

This story serves as a good illustration for the kind of influence that You should hold over Your subject nation-state. Project an abstracted ideal, convince the subject to embrace Your ideal, and through the incorporation of this ideal into its governance and social practices, You will empty its society of monetary and human wealth. But, *do not* under any costs, allow to Your subject nation-state to participate in a true monetary system such as gold or silver currency, much less complementary currencies such as the Thai Bia and Austrian Worgle; or Real Money Units (RMU)[194] because these systems address the weakness of a barter system and negate any argument as to why the subject should participate in a fiat currency system based on Your abstracted currency rather than on real money. These true monetary systems also allow for natural diversification of the economy, specialization, personal and professional fulfillment.

In short, the subject should not be encouraged to follow any natural talents, as happiness derived from internal fulfillment is an affront to Your efforts. You cannot allow the creation of a strong domestic economy based in tangible monetary systems, nor can You allow the population to discard Your externally-based success models and Quantification of human worth.

The Free Market.

The economic sector in Your subject-state is not an "economy" in and of itself, or an economic component of the social market; mechanisms that simultaneously create wealth and promote social cohesion. As in any symbiotic relationship, an economy requires a society to operate in. Your objective in applying the concept of the Free Market on the subject economy is to separate the subject government from its corresponding social component, essentially "freeing" it from obligations and responsibilities to

[194.] See Ibid. p.70

society. The true measure of a good economy is one in which the domestic economy supports a strong export economy, one where the majority of the population retains substantial buying power to circulate money--regardless of outside market forces.[195] [196] You will turn the economy from a contributing aspect of sustainability to that of a malignant tumor operating through homeostasis, seizing all resources at an unbalanced rate, exponentially expanding to the point where its growth disrupts the processes that keep the body alive, killing itself as well as its host environment, the society.

In the same manner that Free Market transforms the value of people from relational to Quantitative, based on how much can be consumed, trade must be kept at a level that is separate from the particular reality of each nation-state. To prevent the true form of free trade, acquire as much of the subject's economy as possible, under the guise of direct foreign investment and privatization. In this way You will possess so much of the subject's resources that, even if it were to withdraw from the world market to participate in "true free trade", this would not affect Your earnings at all. Weaken the subject economy and eliminate any control it retains in pricing its own goods; promote pricing adherance to the "World Market". In this way, trade will be based in the Quantitative value of paper money that has no standard to back it.

Appreciation of Currency

Raise the currency value of Your subject nation so that it focuses economic policies solely on what can be exported. The attention that You pay to this economy will be interpreted as the economy itself growing at a high rate; and within markets it will be rewarded for performance by higher exchange rates. In the near future, You can liquidate Your holdings at a premium, collapse the economy, and then buy out everything that You desire at severely reduced prices, without the headaches of any remaining protectionist legislation, which will have by now been stripped away by Your subject government.

---

[195] Japan's currency did not appreciate until the country was already an industrial power and had successfully created a pseudo social-market economy, in which a majority of the population could be deemed "middle class"; and to the point that Japan could be called a "middle-class country". This was maintained through cooperative relationships between government, banking, and industry. In a "market economy", a nation-state that is governed sustainably should only entertain a "floating currency" when its domestic economy is so solid that non-essential imported goods, such as cultural icons, simply enter as niche items. In this way, with the collaboration of safeguards and cooperatives it can enter a "Global Market Economy" with less risk and greater position of strength, as long as its attitude towards trade is relational.

[196] Look to the Asian Economic Crisis of 1997 as a model for this application.

Special Economic Zones/ Free Trade Zones

Do not be deceived by "free trade zones" or "special economic zones". Yes, You might visualize the subject's labor at a lower cost, but in these areas You will only be creating jobs for excess laborers from the subject-state's "real economy". Use these "special economic zones" for Your stepping stone into the subject-state's "real economy", as they will provide You with a certain degree of familiarity with the business culture of the subject nation-state. Your aim should be to obtain the same "investor-friendly" benefits that You are already receiving at restricted Free Trade "manufacturing zones" in the subject's domestic economy.

The type of Free Trade legislation that created "special economic" and "free trade zones" must be applied to the subject's entire economy. Otherwise, these zones are nothing more than a treaty port, as in the case of Hong Kong. Watch out: the investment capital that You provide and the technology transfer acquired by Your employees can pose a threat to Your longevity in the subject's nation-state. If You have to initially operate in a "treaty-port" type of free trade zone, agree to hire an excessive number of local workers to satisfy the subject government, but at such low wages that it would be difficult for employees to create a duplicate facility inside the "real economy" and outside the "free trade zone". To prevent technology transfer, fill all supervisory and technology sensitive areas with "ex-pat" (expatriate) hires who are only to be involved in venture start-up and the training of local staff. Do not allow Your subject nation-state the ability to use special economic and free trade zones as a means of gaining technology and capital in industries that can compete against Yours.

From the standpoint of government the purpose of private industry is to provide employment for the population, thereby supporting the government's role of meeting the security needs of the populace and administering a tax base for government services. Profit is secondary to these responsibilities. If the social welfare needs of the populace are neglected in the name of profit, the government has no reason to support private industry, for it becomes antagonistic to the interests of the government. Under a natural economy, the value of people in the society is relational, but in a society regulated by the Free Market people are quantified and given an economic "dollar" value. Your projections should create divisions in society and economy, and eliminate cooperation between government and industry.

Price Controls

One method in which the subject may keep social and economic viability is through price controls. The use of price controls (and government subsidies) works to empower local currency, because pricing becomes relative to the average wage earned by the populace, as opposed to being divergent from it. In this way, wage labor pays a living wage. In terms of international trade, those parties who wish to trade with the subject-state must take the wage earnings of the populace into account when determining the price of their goods. Disrupt the equilibrium between trade and domestic consumption. If You do not, the external price controls of the World Market will have no relevance to the subject economy.

Promote the importance of eliminating domestic price controls as a means of "economic liberalization and reform". Once the subject nation-state has dissociated prices from the average wage, Your objective of separating the subject's economy from its society will be furthered. The comfort level of the populace will erode and it will be less inclined to embrace concepts of community and collective responsibility. You will spawn a Culture of Poverty and a class of the "working poor". Community-mindedness will turn into an "every man for himself" mentality. Your projections of Individualism coupled with the availability of Your cultural icons, which will allow temporary relief for esteem needs, will cause a rift in the subject society that You can exploit. The discontent of the population and the concurrent rise of crime due to lack of basic security needs, will pressure the subject government to become open to "solutions" to the "necessary ills" brought on by Modernization and "Market Liberalization".

Hypermarkets

Introduce the superstore. Ideally, the shelves of these superstores will be stocked with products imported from Your nation-state. The advent of the superstore will make smaller businesses become obsolete, unable to compete with the buying power of these hypermarkets. This shrinking of the dispersal of capital within the domestic economy will leave few businesses to survive, putting a sizeable amount of the population out of work. In this setting the only jobs available will be low-wage jobs in the service sector, jobs as workers in the superstores.

> From employees' perspectives McJobs are irrational because they don't offer much in the way of either satisfaction or stability. Employees are seldom allowed to use anything approaching all their skills, are not allowed to be creative on the job. The result is a high level of resentment, job dissatisfaction, alienation, absenteeism, and turnover.[197]

This will also serve to create a severely under-utilized workforce in which even the most skilled and educated minds will have to work in Your low-wage service sector if they wish to have stable employment. Additionally, the more prevalent these jobs become in the society, the lower the expectations that workers will have for fulfilling work. Self-cultivation and fulfillment through work will become increasingly absent, consumerism will fill this void, and will become the prevalent trend.

Your goal is to entrench the subject's economy in the Global Market and disrupt its ideology so that the subject government becomes ineffective in meeting human security needs, giving sovereignty up to You, the "invisible hand". This, all for the perceived benefits of entering into a Free Market; of Modernizing in order to enter into the Global Market and conform to Your Universal culture, to the point that the subject fails to notice the social and environmental costs of its departure from responsible governance. You must commercialize the subject's entire nation, people, land, culture. You must take ownership of these things. You are to destroy the subject's sense of nationality and culture, otherwise You run the risk of some national "enlightenment" in the future, the populace desiring to "join as a nation" to fix its problems.

Heed my words. You must own the subject in its entirety and comm-ercialize it, or You run the risk of future opposition. I use this hypothetical example of a very cut and dry, simple trade of raw materials and low wage manufacturing; whereas a sympathizer to the plight of Your subject may prefer to use the term "sweatshop labor", and turn it into a tool that could potentially disrupt the economic stability of Your nation-state.

Resources.

The subject economy must be "opened" so that You can flood its markets with Your subsidized surplus products and cultural icons, and block exports through tariffs and the bureaucracy of "necessary" approvals such as food safety, environmental compliance, genetically-modified food stuffs. Purchase only *niche* market goods from the subject-state, those which do not have competitors in Your domestic economy, and import raw materials and cheaply manufactured goods made by Your factories (or through contract manufacturing) back to Your home economy. The Free Market means that You can "freely" obtain what You want from the subject state without obligations to its society, and freely decide what goods You want from it at Your desired price. You have influence in the world capital and commodities

197. Ritzer, p.137

markets due to purchasing power and control over the raw materials and subsequent exports from the subject economy. The subject government must be sold on the idea that it can export its way to salvation. When the subject opens its economy to foreign ownership and "invests" in the development of national resources for export, it gives up the power to determine the prices for its raw materials. If it defers pricing to an external commodities market rather than trading directly with buyers in exchange for cash or goods that are needed, the subject defers all powers to the outsider.

If the subject government does not rely on foreign manufactured products and focuses instead on developing, processing, or trading resources with other nation-states that have the manufactured or non-manufactured goods actually needed (such as medicines), then trade becomes a matter between two parties, two nation-states, and not a matter negotiated on the terms of others. In truth, nation-states do not need the "Global Market" to trade, as it is counter to their interests. The "Global Market" is rather the need of nation-states that *do not* have an abundance of their own resources; they consequently must control pricing in other nation-states so that goods can be priced cheaply and traded with products of far less, and largely iconic, value. For the reason that I have just mentioned, You should always project onto the subject that it is in the absolute interest of the subject to be included in the global Free Market; for, as long as the subject remains in the Free Market, it will be open to exploitation by You.

Land

With You, the subject nation-state begins its history on a "clean slate". There is no "history" preceding Your presence and influence over its society. For the subject-state to truly be Modern, it must rid its archaic ideas of collective, citizen-only land ownership and put land on the Free Market, so that it can be openly traded without impediment. Anything other than this would be akin to desiring to remain "un-developed" and not being a true member of the Modern Global community.

What is Yours is Yours, what is theirs is Yours. Do not forget this.Your objective in regard to Your subject nation-state's social economy is to own it., to turn its society into a commodity that can be bought and sold on the world market, on Your terms. Follow the example of the 1885 Berlin Conference, at which the European Colonial Powers divided the African continent up amongst themselves, naming themselves "protectors" and "responsible" stewards of the land who would "act of the best interest" of the people whose resources were being "legally" seized.[198]

Labor

Part of the reasoning behind eliminating wage labor and replacing it with contract and part-time labor is to disrupt the social cohesion of the subject's nation-state. Under the guise of promoting an "efficient workforce" that requires a mobile labor pool that can "meet the demands of today's Global Economy", You can dissemble the system which provides for the social welfare of the populace by avoiding mass employment. In an industrializing or industrial society, unemployment threatens both the security needs as well as the esteem needs of those impacted.

Small private enterprise, which would alleviate these issues caused by employment, is also impacted due to the fact that the resources of the nation-state are sequestered by the government and by powerful business interests. These small enterprises are forced to compete against external competitors that do not have social, economic, and environmental obligations to the society. Further, with the implementation of Rule of Law throughout aspects of the society, opening a small one-person business becomes a bureaucratic nightmare. In the past, one with few means could gather resources and begin an enterprise, not having to worry about "compliance" issues until its size becomes large enough to warrant review by the government to ensure that its actions are not contrary to that of the best interests of the society. By eliminating the means of the masses, through excessive formalities, to compete in enterprises, You gain access to the modes of production and resources of the society while the populace blames the management of companies and the subject nation-state's government as the reasons why they cannot make a living and lead fulfilled lives.

Equality, democracy, and democratic theories of justice depend on a closed economy. This is because in a "closed[199] economy", people are valued relationally; in "open economies" people are quantitatively valued. By weakening the confidence of the subject-state's populace in the fairness and "objectivity" of its legal system, You weaken the sovereignty of the subject government.

Public Goods

The subject government retains its mandate to rule with production and distribution of "public goods", which include the "commodities" of labor regulation, welfare for the needy and infirmed, price supports for agriculture,

---

[198.] See "The Silent Return of Colonialism" Tricontinental, pp.51-2
[199.] "Closed" meaning regulated internally by a sovereign apparatus, rather than by sovereignty-dividing apparatus such as Your capital markets.

commissioning of the arts, law and order, national defense, environmental management, and public utilities; all paid with taxation. One means of disrupting this balance of payments for public goods is through Your corporations, which will consume a disproportionate share of these goods and take advantage of "favorable investment environment" provisions--free or reduced costs for land use, tax abatement, exemption from national labor regulations, loose environmental restrictions. The presence of these corporations will cost the subject nation-state a healthy society, economy and environment; the lack of contribution to the subject-state's tax, resource management, and environmental conversation efforts will lead to an imbalance that will increase difficulties of the subject government in responding to the needs of its population. It will be very difficult for the subject government to disguise the privilege of Your corporations in the domestic business arena. The grassroots will call for an examination of the "true benefits" of development. You can never allow introspective questions such as "who is all of this 'economic growth' actually for?" to spread throughout the populace. Alleviate concerns by projecting that You contribute by employing its populace.

You are to "privatize" life and death. If You control the water, food, and power utilities (especially important in colder regions) of a subject nation-state through the "fairness of the Free Market," You will then have "commodified" the nation-state as a whole and can trade of it as You wish. The distribution of basic needs such as water and electricity become 100% profit-based decisions, leaving those citizens who are most economically vulnerable to be excluded from receiving services once privatization is complete. Once essential services are privatized they are almost impossible to re-nationalize without prohibitive costs or economic upheaval. Privatization counters the raison d'etre of government through the elimination of public goods. When "Market Forces" determine distribution of basic life essentials, the government has turned responsibility and sovereignty over to the "market forces". Therefore, promote the privatization of everything, so that everything in the subject society has an Individualized, Quantitative, non-relational value. Government must be "run like a business", and since business without governmental regulation operates solely to make profit, this trend of privatization will support Your agenda of dissolving the mandate of the subject-state's raison d' etre. With dependency on foreign investment and world capital markets, no government can roll back policies of privatization or act decisively through the tax system to remedy the increase of economic inequalities.

Promotion of Export Economy

How does the position of these cities in the world economy today differ from that which have historically held as centers of banking and trade? When Max Weber analyzed the medieval cities woven together in the Hanseatic League, he conceived their trade as the exchange of surplus production; it was his view that a medieval city could withdraw from external trade and continue to support itself, albeit on a reduced scale.[200]

The focus of Your Free Market efforts should be in converting the subject-state into a strong export economy with a weak domestic economy. Every simply processed product that can be bought in its nation-state should be imported; job creation should be in low-wage industries that You benefit directly from, with motivation to work in these jobs being the ability to consume imported items. Subject nation-states that are located in coastal regions should not even fish for themselves--they should fish to export and consume only canned fish imported from your factories. With a weak domestic economy, the population will be easily manipulated by projections of "how much prosperity the entire population will experience". If so, the Free Market will be operating in its society, allowing You to privatize and commodify everything.

This is a beautiful quote illustrating what You can do with the economy of Your subject nation-state. What is not noted is the fact that monocrop export enterprises are largely under the direction of or actually held by foreign companies either as a continuation of "post-independence" economic colonization, or the result the subject-state's participation in "Free Market" initiatives that opened its economy and resources up to foreign ownership and domination:

. . . colonization saddled most colonies with monocrop economies. During the colonial period, as may be recalled, each colony was made to produce a single cash crop or two, and attempts were made to diversify the agricultural economy. The habit of producing these single cash crops appears to have become so engrained that it has not been changed to any appreciable degree since independence. The other consequences of this concentration on the production of cash crops for export was the neglect of the internal sector of the economy and in particular, of the production of food for internal consumption, so that rice, maize, fish, and other foods had to be imported. Thus, during the colonial period, Africans were encouraged to produce what they did not consume and to consume what they did not produce, a clear proof of the exploitative nature of the colonial political economy. It is lamentable that this legacy has not changed materially in most African countries. To this day, they have to rely on the importation of rice, maize, edible oil, flour, and other foodstuffs to survive.[201]

[200.] Sassen, Sakia (2001) *The Global City.* Princeton: Princeton University Press. p.4

Countries will export their "food" grain to appeal to large export markets due to the newly industrialized countries' improved, more "diversified" diets. If large net importers of grain were to seriously increase the demand for grain, they could because of rise of demand, cause prices to rise beyond the reach of many countries which would in turn lead to food shortages and starvation. This would play right into the hands of Your biocrop manufacturers, who could then promise to make problems go away for a fee of Your choosing and the agreement to buy seeds annually. Your agribusiness firms could then make these poor countries beg for food at any price and, due to the monocrop occupying most arable land they will have nothing but sterile seeds throughout out their nation-state, and will be forced to comply with your directives.

"... President George Bush cited the EU moratorium for exacerbating famine in Africa. 'By widening the use of new high-yield biocrops and unleashing the power of the market, we can dramatically increase agricultural productivity and feed more people across the continent', said Bush."[202] The point: Steer conversation about starvation, famine, food storage from the misallocation (overallocation) of the most productive land for export agriculture (a condition for international loan packages, and a holdover from the Colonial Period, in which political independence was "granted" without economic independence) to one about the non-acceptance of G-M crops and livestock products.

The Creation of a Chronic Underclass
in a Relatively Stable Economy[203]
It is cheaper for the subject government to subsidize full employment than it is to try to alleviate symptoms of high unemployment, rampant poverty, hopelessness, crime and general social breakdown. Therefore, create an underclass by eliminating the social responsibility of corporations. If Your subject-state has instituted policies of full employment to meet the social welfare needs of its people, discourage it from offering compensory "corporate welfare" for its participation in the full employment scheme--tax breaks, subsidies, or bank financing, which, in actuality, are subsidies to cover the cost of employing people.

[201] A. Adu Boahen. (1987) *African Perspectives of Colonialism.* Johns Hopkins University Press. Baltimore. pp.101-2

[202] "EU Ban on G-M Crops". *Environment and Climate News: The Monthly Newspaper for Common-Sense Environmentalists.* Vol. 6, No. 6: July 2003. p.10

[203] See Gray, p.173; pp. 228-9. Re: full employment culture.

Foster an underclass of unemployed persons through the projection of the ideology of corporate value based in financial markets rather than the social economy. First, encourage the subject nation to participate in a scheme of "valuing" itself through sovereign credit ratings, then promote the importance of the stock market and mutual funds as a primary means of finance for corporations. Indigenous financing markets are to be connected with Global capital markets to increase "sovereign" credit ratings. In this process You will establish a situation where an economy that formerly took direction from its own finance ministry will now require approval and affirmation from external financial forces. When the subject-state's domestic economic sovereignty is turned over to Global capital markets, call for "efficiency", "accountability", and "transparency" in the corporate and banking sectors. Upon "examination" of the business practices in the corporate and banking sectors, it will be found that there are scores of "non-performing" or "bad" loans, from the banking to the corporate sector. In actuality these "bad" or "non-performing" loans[204] are not intended to "perform" and not intended to be paid back; they are subsidies for the corporations' over-employment, given with the government's blessing to support national goals of full employment. This "parochial" reality is not to be acknowledged. Instead, collaborations such as these in shared responsibility for the nation's social cohesiveness should be branded branded as financial improprieties and irresponsibility. In the local media You can cause public uproar of the "mis-management" and "corruption" in the banking sector and a loss of confidence in financial procedures. In the corporate sector call for more "efficiency", "transparency", and "streamlining" in order to alleviate the "debt crisis" that these companies are facing.

Before Your influence, the value of local corporations was measured by the number of people employed. Now, it will be valued on share prices. At this time You will have driven the corporations' management into disarray with market pressure and calls for "review of corporate management practices" and "reform of the financial sector" in the media. The media frenzy and confusion generated by the elimination of domestic control over financial and corporate sectors will cause the subject-state to make concerns of responsibility to its social economy and support of social welfare to become secondary. Corporations from Your nation-state can now control these important institutions, recreating management styles to accommodate highest profitability without any burden of obligation to the subject's social

---

[204.] This term is now used to describe Japanese bank loans to industry during the economic "bubble period".

economy. Your corporations can downsize, reorganize, and breakup the subject corporations with impunity.

When You transform a corporation from that of a relational value based on employment of citizens and change it to that of a quantitative value based on shares, the corporation will have to sharply reduce its workforce, the Free Market dictating "over-employment" to be inefficient. The shedding of these "excess employees" in Your corporations will show in the balance sheets with a significant decrease in operating expenses. This "adjustment" will lead to increased "investor confidence", reflected in the rise of share values in the stock market.

The subject should be embarked on the quest to gain an ever-expanding economy at any cost, even if the cost is its own society, economy, and environment. Layoffs across the corporate sector will lead to a severe shrinkage of the labor market and many people will become un-employable, thus creating an underclass. The social costs of this new underclass, for which the society is not prepared for, will far outweigh any perceived gains brought by "greater efficiency", "responsible corporate governance", "transparent banking practices", and increased direct foreign investment. Unless the subject government quickly eliminates any formal barriers to small enterprise and entrepreneurship, instituting protections for small businesses as well as prohibitions on foreign participation in small enterprises, the subject will face extreme levels of poverty and crime which it will have no means of remedying, because it will only be dealing with symptoms of the root problem--Your influence over its economy.

The Redefinition of Poverty.

'Poverty' is redefined and understood within the terms of a [Modern] . . . standard of material wealth. Any living condition outside this standard is regarded as a 'lack' which needs to be resolved by purchasing goods and services provided by the modern production system. People are seen to be poor if they live in self-built housing made from natural materials like bamboo and mud rather than cement houses. They are seen as poor if they wear handmade garments of natural fibre rather than synthetics.[205]

Redefine the condition of poverty as one where people "do not participate overwhelmingly in the market economy, and do not consume commodities produced for and distributed through the market *even though they might be satisfying those needs through self-provisioning mechanisms*".[206]

[205.] Sittirak, Sinith (2000) *The Daughters of Development: Women and the Changing Environment.* London: Zed Books p.27 from Shiva, Vandana. (1989) *Staying Alive: Women, Ecology, and Development.* London: Zed Books. I replaced the original word in the quote [ ] . . . with my own words.

Education

In the education system, Internationalism and Globalism must be promoted at the expense of healthy nationalism. A certain degree of nationalism is needed to give a population pride for its products and services as well as value to national resources. Promote Internationalism with no foundation of nationalism so that the subject population is not conscious of the validity of its personal and natural truths. This will inspire friendship, but also encourage feelings of inferiority in relation to other nation-states.

Without the substantial national pride that brings the people together, the subject populace will view products from the outside as having more value than their own. There will be a preference in importing finished goods and a desire to export raw or non-finished goods to the outside, because the subject populace will believe that it is incapable of producing these finished goods. Promoting Internationalism and Globalism without a healthy level of national esteem will place You in the good position of providing "those things that we cannot do ourselves", encouraging an export-based economy and discouraging the development of a strong domestic economy needed for a sustainable national economy. These tactics will also discourage the subject from creating localized regional trade groups; and if it is contemplating membership in such groups, it will be less outspoken, believing itself to be "not ready" to contribute the group's Modern reality.

Pacify the need for healthy nationalistic expression in the population and promote patriotism instead. Patriotism celebrates the most superficial outward expressions of love of country, as opposed to nationalism, which embraces deep culture and acknowledges those traits and talents that bind and exemplify the nation-state. Patriotism addresses the obvious--love of country, celebration of the natural beauty of the country, respect for the national flag, recognized national monuments and symbols. Patriotism will not threaten Your goal in promoting low national esteem in the international community.[207]

The population must be made to believe that it cannot Modernize and Progress without the "assistance" of foreign capital and foreign business persons, even if this means the exploitation of the indigenous labor force, resources and maintenance of non-productive related industry; even if indigenous "effort" could otherwise have been used to develop local industry for local consumption and eventual export. The irony is that You will be using

---

[206.] Shiva, Vandana. (1989) *Staying Alive: Women, Ecology, and Development.* London: Zed Books.

[207.] Like in human dynamics, persons with high self-esteem usually make the best group members, while those with low self-esteem either take on a docile disposition or take on a tyrannical disposition to compensate for the feelings of inadequacy.

their labor force, materials, and environment to produce finished products to sell back to them and to export at high profit margins for Yourself. You give the subject the right to give You the opportunity to exploit it and to make of its population, consumers of Your product.

Consumerism/The Culture of Comparison

The culture-ideology sphere is, however, entirely different. Here, the aim of global capitalists is total inclusion of all classes, and especially the subordinate classes insofar as the bourgeoisie can be considered already included. The cultural-ideological project of global capitalism is to persuade people to consume above their 'biological needs' in order to perpetuate the accumulation of capital for private profit; in other words, to ensure that the global capitalist system goes on forever. The culture-ideology of consumerism proclaims, literally, that the meaning of life is to be found in the things that we possess. To consume, therefore is to be fully alive, and to remain fully alive we must continuously consume. The notions of men and women as economic or political beings are discarded by global capitalism--quite logically, as the system does not even pretend to satisfy everyone in the economic or political spheres. People are primarily consumers. The point of economic activity for 'ordinary members' of the global capitalist system is to provide the resources for consumption, the point of political activity is to ensure that the conditions for consuming are maintained.[208]

Promote, but do not buy into theories of the Transnational Capitalist Class and Corporate Governance to make it difficult for the subject to see that national agendas are being pushed through transnational (trade) organizations. Companies operate in the interest of their mother countries; mother countries sue the WTO, enforce tariffs, boycott, or take other such actions to push the agendas of their companies.

Corporations only have one duty: to promote their own and their owners' interests. They have no capacity, and their executives no authority, to act out of a genuine sense of responsibility to society, to avoid causing harm to people and the environment, or to work to advance the public good in ways that are unrelated to their own self-interest. Deregulation thus rests upon the suspect premise that corporations will respect social and environmental interests without being compelled to do so.[209]

Transnational Corporations (TNCs) are to be projected as nation-less entities operating in the "Global Market Place". This will disguise the fact that TNCs are almost always singular in their embodiment of the culture of a particular nation-state, the culture of their origin, the interests and protection of the

---

[208.] Jameson, Fredric and Masao, Miyoshi ed. (1998) *The Cultures of Globalization*. Duke University Press, p. 297

[209.] Bakan, Joel (2004) *The Corporation*. New York: Free Press, p.109

"home" nation-state.

According to Leslie Sklair in *Social Movements and Capitalism*[210], "global system theory" is based on the concept of transnational practices, practices that cross state boundaries but do not necessarily originate with state agencies or actors. Although in truth, the ability of corporations to function comes from the lack of, or presence of, regulations in the nation-states in which they operate, perpetuate this global system theory so that the actions of Your corporations to do not appear to correspond with Your dislocative practices in the subject-state.

Social Development.

You must project the idea that the development of economy is a prerequisite to social development, even if independent press points out the flaws in this logic, indicated in the following example.

> WASHINGTON, Apr 30 (IPS) – World Bank President James Wolfensohn Monday extolled the Communist government of President Fidel Castro for doing 'a great job' in providing for the social welfare of the Cuban people. His remarks followed Sunday's publication of the Bank's 2001 edition of 'World Development Indicators' (WDI), which showed Cuba as topping virtually all other poor countries in health and education statistics . . .
>
> 'Cuba has done a great job on education and health,' Wolfensohn told reporters at the conclusion of the annual spring meetings of the Bank and the International Monetary Fund (IMF). 'They have done a good job, and it does not embarrass me to admit it.'
>
> His remarks reflect a growing appreciation in the Bank for Cuba's social record, despite recognition that Havana's economic policies are virtually the antithesis of the 'Washington Consensus', the neoliberal orthodoxy that has dominated the Bank's policy advice and its controversial structural adjustment programmes (SAPs) for most of the last 20 years.
>
> Some senior Bank officers, however, go as far as to suggest that other developing countries should take a very close look at Cuba's performance.
>
> 'It is in some sense almost an anti-model,' according to Eric Swanson, the programme manager for the Bank's Development Data Group, which compiled the WDI, a tome of almost 400 pages covering scores of economic, social, and environmental indicators.
>
> Indeed, Cuba is living proof in many ways that the Bank's dictum that economic growth is a precondition for improving the lives of the poor is over-stated, if not downright wrong. The Bank has insisted for the past decade that improving the lives of the poor was its core mission.

[210]. Leslie Sklair's "Social Movements and Capitalism" is also in *The Cultures of Globalization* eds. Jameson and Masao.

The island's economy, which suffered devastating losses after the Soviet Union withdrew its aid, especially its oil supplies, a decade ago, has yet to fully recover. Annual economic growth, fuelled in part by a growing tourism industry and limited foreign investment, has been halting and, for the most part, anaemic.

It has reduced its infant mortality rate from 11 per 1,000 births in 1990 to seven in 1999, which places it firmly in the ranks of the western industrialised nations. It now stands at six, according to Jo Ritzen, the Bank's Vice President for Development Policy who visited Cuba privately several months ago to see for himself.

'Six for every 1,000 in infant mortality--the level as Spain--is just unbelievable,' according to Ritzen, a former education minister in the Netherlands. 'You observe it, and so you see that Cuba has done exceedingly well in the human development area."'

Indeed, in Ritzen's own field the figures tell much the same story. Net primary enrolment for both girls and boys reached 100 percent in 1997, up from 92 percent in 1990. That was as high as most developed nation, higher even than the US rate and well above 80-90 percent rates achieved by most advanced Latin American countries.

It is no wonder, in some ways, Public spending on education in Cuba amounts to about 6.7 percent of gross national income, twice the proportion in other Latin America and Caribbean countries and even Singapore . . .
. . .'Cuba managed to reduce illiteracy from 40 percent to zero with ten years,' said Ritzen. 'If Cuba shows that it is possible, it shifts the burden of proof to those who say it's not possible.'

Similarly, Cuba devoted 9.1 percent of the gross domestic product (GDP) during the 1990s to health care, roughly equivalent to Canada's rate. Its ration of 5.3 doctors per 1,000 people was the highest in the world.

'What does it is the incredible dedication,' according to Wayne Smith, who was head of the US Interests Section in Havana in the late 1970s and early 1980s and has traveled to the island many time since. 'Doctors in Cuba can make more driving cabs and working in hotel, but they don't. They're just very dedicated,' he said.

'Is the experience of Cuba useful in other countries? The answer is clearly yes. and one is hopeful that political barriers would not prevent the use of the Cuban experience in other countries. "Here, I am pretty hopeful, in that I see many developing countries taking the Cuban experience well into account.' . . .[211]

If You allow an argument that provides evidence against the ideologies of Free Trade and Individualistic Materialism that You are projecting, there may come from within the subject government or population, calls for a re-thinking of economic and social policies, to Your disadvantage.

[211] "Learn from Cuba, says World Bank" by Jim Lobe, InterPress Third World News Agency (IPS), Rome, April 30, 2001.

Free-Market & Socialism

If You are not careful to maintain some semblance of stability in the minds if Your subject populace or at the very least, convince Your subject government to make conciliatory social improvement measures such as vaccination campaigns, literacy drives, and holiday food giveaways, You will potentially face a re-emergence of socialism or communism as a possible solution to alleviate the problems faced by the poor. This is illustrated in the following quote:

> The collapse of the socialist camp has affected him because of what it has meant for Cuba, but it didn't come as a surprise. After living in the German Democratic Republic for six months, he came to the conclusion that that was a case of imposed socialism. He saw the people's unhappiness and found that they were building socialism on the basis of improved form of capitalism. He regrets what happened, because it was a step backward in history; but in the long run, he thinks that what happened may turn out to be good because, the next time around, it will be the real thing.
>
> He is convinced that capitalism doesn't solve man's problems. We know this because Latin America and Africa live under capitalism. This is why he is so sure that people in Cuba will resist--has no doubts about it. He is convinced that scenes such as those Iraqi soldiers kissing the hands of U.S. soldiers, will never take place in Cuba.
>
> Dr. Lopéz Saura
> Former Director of the Biological Research Center
> (CIB) and pioneer of Cuban interferons[212]

If the "consciousness of poverty" expands to the point where the non-satisfaction of self-esteem through the lack of ownership of Your projected cultural icons and success image, this is the least of Your worries. The desires of the "materially poor" can be channeled into the utopian goals of socialism, but for those truly suffering from a consciousness of poverty, their desires can only be quelled through promises of attainment of the same lifestyle of success that You project, and acquisition of the same material goods (cultural icons) that they project which will lead to the possibility of uncontrollable Individualism and Conspicuous Consumption leading to attacks by the "poor" on anything symbolizing wealth and control in the society, with no respect towards authority; but from them, outwardly possessing the lifestyle and artifacts that are held in high esteem.

[212.] Bravo, Ernesto Mario (1998) *Development Within Underdevelopment?* Havana: Editorial Elfos Scientiae. p.65

Free-Market: Later Stages of Development
Influence Your subject nation-state to adjust national budgets to focus on defense rather than domestic security needs (human security) and economic development. Because this is the first of many in the avoidance of root problems and an increasingly militaristic mindset, the subject government will look for "law and order" solutions to social and economic problems. The more society and economy decays, the more there will exist a force of law and order, setting the stage for the eventual move to fascism.

A destabilized government needs order. If You are effective, the business oligarchies will be weakened, making room for Your exploitation of its economy and weakening of its democratic structures. The oligarchies will want to stay in power and will maintain influence over electoral politics. The void left by a deteriorating legitimate economy and representative governance will be filled by crime groups. The threatened oligarchies are likely to proactively seek out relationships with these groups.

In a situation in which the local government increasingly loses its sovereignty, the economic interests of local business powers become threatened by the external influence of Free Trade and the destabilizing affect Foreign Direct Investment. Sectors of the economy, lands, or resources that these oligarchies may have controlled will become available to international investors such as those of Your nation-state and because of international Free Trade legislation, these oligarchies will have no recourse domestically in regard to their claims. Of course, some oligarchies will collaborate with the FDI investors, but those that desire long-term assurance that their business relationships will remain productive, and those who are aware of scenarios like this, will desire to unify with conservative business elements which desire long-term economic gain and control over the nation-state's modes of production.

Chapter 15:
Human Rights

The Modern notion of "Human Rights" implies protection of the individual and not of the collective; the nation-state's culture, minority groups, indigenous groups. This legal designation reinforces the sanctity of the individual but not that of the community. Sell Your subject nation-state societal death under the guise of "rights" so that it receives "rights" but is also converted to an Ideology of Individualistic Materialism which will kill the individual spirit (purpose) of each member of the society, drive families apart, push each person into competitive relationships, and erode the solvency of society--eroding the center that binds it together.

When local law is based on this precedent of "Individual Rights", collective ownership in matters such as land, water, and mineral rights and taxation can be discounted as irrelevant. The only means of recourse through which a collective-oriented people can dispute actions taken against them is through class-action suits, but again this requires the means to secure competent and effective (and in many cases, politically and judicially connected) counsel to maneuver them through a legal system that they have no basis in. They are essentially their own nation-states, but have had to relinquish sovereignty over their collective affairs to an abstracted nation-state that does not recognize the pluralism of its state, believing in and enforcing a mandate based on the legitimate use of force.

Human Rights.

Maintain enough stability to prevent groups of people, political, religious or government, from asking questions of this sort: "What does 'Human Rights' mean to a hungry, disease-ridden, uneducated, inadequately housed person living in a polluted environment? If opposition to a system that benefits the masses threatens the viability of the community, is this actually 'freedom' or could it be just another destructive influence? If Free Press or an unregulated economy means losing the 'rights' of education, healthcare, housing, a clean environment, or occupational safety, is there a need to re-assess the definition of 'human rights'?"

According to such logic, a conclusion would be made, that individual Human Rights and collective human rights are complementary, if not outright collaborative. If collective rights are sacrificed for the appearance of Modernity and the celebration of Individualistic Human Rights, then what is the use of this society? If Your subject society comes to these types of queries, You will need to think about redefining its government mandate to that of a security orientation. Watch for declarations among the subject nation-state that human rights are the "rights" of human security. If these ideas are embraced, it will be harder for You to project ideals of an Individualistic Human Rights. You must be aware of statements such as the following: Health is the right of all citizens and the responsibility of the government"[216].

Human life that becomes Quantified to make a profit and settle debts will cause human beings to lose the relational value of "being", instead adopting the quantitative value of "having". You can promote Human Rights campaigns to "halt the proliferation of human trafficking", but will not have to acknowledge it as a reality of societal quantification.

> Politics is a game of vulnerabilities, and the human rights issue is clearly where the 'socialist' world has proven most vulnerable, just as the economic rights issue is where the 'capitalist' world is most open to criticism. . . The debate on human rights can be conceptualized in part as a struggle between eighteenth century libertarian persuasions [the West] and nineteenth century egalitarian beliefs [China]--that is, from a vision of human rights having to do with the right of individual justice before the law to a recognition of the rights of the individual to social security and equitable conditions of work and standards of living.[217]

Discussions of human nature like the one noted above cannot be acknowledged as valid. Remember that You are the Universalizer, the definer of both

[216]. MINSAP

[217]. Johnson, pp.166-7 from Foreword, in Abdul Aziz Said, ed. *Human Rights and World Order*. New Brunswick, NJ: Transaction Books, 1978) pp.vii – viii.

Modernity and Human Nature. There is only one definition of human rights: the one that You project. The subject of Human Rights has nothing to do with "human rights"; it is something that You use to manipulate the subject government.

Human Rights & Political Repression.
Since the government of Your subject's nation-state has no cultural mandate and is following the directives of Modernization that You have projected, it is an active participant in disintegrating the social cohesion of its own society. At some point, segments of the society will realize this and will use the "free press", the arts, and other means of public discourse to criticize the actions of the state. Because it does not have a true mandate, the people will demand that the subject government be replaced or modified. The subject government of course does not desire to repress its own people, but will come to the realization that its only means of survival as an abstracted institution is the legitimate use of force. To continue to operate, it will have to repress excessive opposition. Through You, through Your influence over the subject society and the notion of "Human Rights", You can keep the subject nation-state in constant flux.

Your Human Rights protests will put pressure on the subject government to be more moderate in dealing with threats while still chipping away at its sovereignty through Your projections. Using non-compliance with Human Rights as Your bargaining chip, You can negotiate even more invasive measures to control resources and influence governance. Feeling the pressure of a united front against it, the subject government may not be able completely do away with the repression of dissidents (it might commit to a few symbolic gestures, freeing some prisoners, ordering house arrest for others) because in order to survive, it has to prevent dissidents from destroying its mandate in the minds of the populace. To keep from bending too much to the weight of Human Rights, the subject makes other concessions in terms of "transparency" that will allow You more access to its resources and modes of production. Of course, these should only placate You temporarily--You must always keep pressure on the subject's government from all sides.

The Re-newed Subject
In the same manner that abstracted governments are manipulated through the rhetoric of Human Rights, You can do the same to governments that are former Colonial *subjects*[218]. You should be able to influence this *re-newed subject* through Cultural Warfare, even if it is indirect, using other subjects of Your nation-state to sanction or manipulate it in other ways. Because it is a *re-*

newed subject, a "new nation", its mandate requires time to solidify. Until this happens, it is still in a state of "revolution". In a "state of revolution", it is imperative that the *re-newed subject* government prevent dissension caused by Your projections---either directly, or through subversive means---from eliminating its mandate before it can really perform to its potential. As long as You can influence other subjects and other Princes to punish the *re-newed subject* for rejecting Your principles, it will be much harder for the subject government to prove to its population that it can meet the true mandate of providing social welfare, security, and cultural needs of the people. But do not take for granted that the government of the *re-newed subject's* nation-state might maintain popular legitimacy with the fact that it has staved off disaster. If the *re-newed* nation-state has a high literacy rate, the populace will not see the nation's hardships simply as failures of its government but as the political result of external pressures, as "punishment" for the nation's rejection of a prescribed post-colonial status based on the former hierarchical ordering of society created by the colonial power.

Until the *re-newed subject* can prove its mandate and prevent its society from being influenced by Your projections, it will stay in a "state of revolution", because the true form of national security is based on the integrity of the society, economy, and environment of a nation-state; and until these aspects of human security can be met without outside disruption, the *re-newed subject* state is still in a state of war. And in war, dissidents are viewed as committing treason. In Your arsenal, You have one very effective weapon against the legitimacy and cohesiveness the government of the *re-newed subject*: Human Rights, based on the Individual, not the collective. Therefore, even if the *re-newed subject* provides for the basic needs of the people as dictated in the Human Rights Convention, but does not make specific overtures towards the Individual, the *re-newed subject* government can be branded as repressive.

Peacemakers

Those calling for "non-violence" at any cost are individuals naive to the reality of Nature and the Law of Cause and Effect, action and consequence. Without changing or eliminating the root, so-called reform will simply be another form of the same state of affairs, because it is grounded in the same base reality and value system that formed it in the first place. Therefore, celebrate, in the

---

[218.] This is in reference to subject nation-states that achieved independence outside Your (and Other Princes) formal process of "independence" during the 1960s, 70s and 80s, and the post-"Independence" period that installed leaders in opposition to Your control over its nation-state. They are still affected by Your cultural contact during the Colonial Period, but they are economically and politically independent of Your continued hegemony.

media and society, those who profess "non-violence" in conflict resolution and social reform; destroy all of those who call for peace. "Peace" brings resolution by examining the root cause of conflict, and stability, or centered-ness. "Peace" can mean Your expulsion from the subject nation-state because You are the cause of instability. True peacemakers will fight for peace at any cost, and can be "violent" personages. However, if the violence (which includes oppression) is continued to a point at which the "peacemaker" comes to believe that the root issue cannot be resolved through non-violent means, the "peacemaker" will then move to use the same means that caused the current state of affairs.

Violence is the state of Nature. The Universe is manifest through the creation and destruction, a constant cycle of building, destroying, and rest. One feels/experiences the negative effects of violence (destruction) when they do not move in unison with the cycles of creation and destruction. Moving against the cycles of creation, one becomes a force of destruction. If there is a need for balance in Nature, social change becomes imminent. The question is, whether the masses will voluntarily deconstruct the old social order, or whether a "peacemaker" (one who feels, through analysis, intuition, or "true" thought, that he or she is an instrument of change) will involuntarily change it. "Peacemakers" like all warriors pray for peace, but will fight a brutal war if forced to. Therefore, You should destroy all who call for peace and do not expressedly claim to believe in non-violence at any cost.

Reconciliation Committees

Create "reconciliation committees" without dealing with the root causes of social problems. This will allow You to create "peace"--people "knowing their place". Your peace promotes a hierarchical order without addressing the root cause, leading to tensions in the society. If anger is not allowed to be legitimately addressed, it will be will be expressed internally. The subject populace, "striking out" at the cause of its anxiety, will strike inward, engaging in self-destructive behaviors that will eat away at the individual, family, and community social structures.

With a properly devised "reconciliation process", You can continue to benefit from the inequities that enrage the populace. When done correctly, You will no longer be a real target where discontent can be focused on. The populace will express discontent with its world through self-hate and other self-destructive behaviors. Through Your projections You will erode the extended family and promote a Culture of Individualistic Materialism, eroding the society's last real source of security, fostering an ideology of predatory cannibalism and a social environment that eats itself alive; lacking an awareness of consciousness that its demise is being orchestrated by You.

A reconciliation that is based on forgiveness without the resolution of root problems is a failed solution to social strife. If "reconciliation" occurs and yet the same hierarchies of ownership over lands, resources, modes of production, or social ordering still exist, anger will be continue to be internally expressed, this time more voracious within the affected group(s) and within individuals of the group. Eliminated through the legislation of "reconciliation", there will no longer exist "hope" for reform, leading to a substantial rise in domestic crime, and self-destructive, high-risk behaviors in individuals.

Chapter 16:
Replacing Spirituality
with Universality

"We are using the Bible like the special constable's handbook, an instrument to keep beasts of burden still while we load them."

Charles Kingsley, Dean of the Church of England

A people grounded in spiritual belief will likely view spirituality as being rooted in the certainty of a singular spiritual power; a formless, omnipresent, omnipotent being or energy force that cannot be divided, whose potential is infinite and inconceivable in the minds of people.

I believe in the religion
Of Love
Whatever directions its caravans may take,
For love is my religion and faith.

Ibn 'Arabi

Universalize spirituality to serve Your purpose and "operate" as a religion within Your sphere of influence, personifying the Higher Being as a Man, more specifically, as a Monarch-God. When You place the Divine Being into a form it becomes an icon through which You can influence the subject populace to perceive 'Godliness' within the nation-state's perceptions of the limitations of man; more specifically, a man-monarch that resembles You. In Your doctrine You can preach against idol worship while concurrently having the population worshipping an idol--You. Replacing spirituality with Universalism under the guise of promoting a Universal Spiritual Truth will mask Your imperialistic motives. With the application of Universality in the evangelical religious teachings that You promote, Your culture becomes the point of reference to this "truth" and opposition to Your influence can be deemed sacrilege.

Personification of God.

The following line from *The Republic* is an illustration of the personification of God: "What would you say again to the tale of Zeus, who, while other gods and men were asleep and he the only *person*[222] awake, lay devising plans...[223]" If You can change the Divine Being, from formless and omnipresent, to having a perceived form resembling a monarch of Your nation-state (or Other nation-states whose primary population phenotypically resembles Yours), You will have a people that will worship You as they do their God. When You change a people's behavior from that of a spiritual nature (one's way of life as a spiritual exercise/practice) to that consisting of only a series of rituals for social and religious compliance, You will create a population that will always admire You (and those of Your nation-state and those resembling them) for being perceived as "closer to God" (on conscious and sub-conscious levels), because You actually "resemble" God more than they do. Your own nation-state's population will always be viewed as higher in status and thus more worthy human beings than the subject population because of the innate "right-ness" perceived, and because You now become a representation of the divine on earth. When You can properly merge this image of a man-monarch-god resembling those in power, You will insulate Yourself from problems in the society; the people will fight themselves before threatening Your interests, in "religious sense" they will, on a sub-conscious level, recognize that You are superior to them because You most closely resemble the 'Supreme Being'.

The Religion of the Individual Self.

Cultural Cognitive Dissonance creates the need for additional "faith", and this "faith" is supported though the projection of Your "civilization" in its "Modernity". As the subject population hopes to achieve Your "level of Civilization", every desire to emulate You will bring it to believe in the actuality of You representing the "Universal Truth". After creating incongruency and discord in the collective centers of Your subject nation-state You will, through Seemingly Associative Cognitions, create a stage through which the subject can meet the need for "faith" in something through believing You.

Oppression Words

Promote the use of "oppression words" in discussing religious imagery. For

[222] I italicized the word "person" for emphasis.
[223] The Republic. Plato. Trans. Benjamin Jowett. Dover Publications, Inc. Mineola, New York. (Book 3) p.61

example: with descendents of a feudal society (serfdom/fiefdom) use words such as Lord, Prince, King, Ruler, prison of... [sin]; with those descendents of the system of chattel slavery should be encouraged words such as chains of... [sin], bondage of..., shackles of..., Master, Lord, King. These are necessary in the process of personifying spirituality and establishing a hierarchy of control.

Proselytizing

Proselytizing is a means of influencing through religious means, under the disguise of Universalism. Proselytizing is a technique by which state and cultural objectives can be achieved through the projection of a "Universal Truth". Truth may be universal, but its expression in human life is cultural.

> Beware: the need for "expansion" indicates the need to control a possible insecurity, requiring the positive reinforcement of others. The subject may realize this after a Secondary Cognitive Dissonance (2nd CD), or even before, and join together the thoughts, n addition to ideals and cultural icons that You are projecting, that proselytization is part of the same process of projecting Your cultural center in order to destabilize and exploit.

Evangelism

If You can 1. simultaneously disrupt the lives of the populace to the point that its basic security needs are not being met; or 2. perpetuate assimilation into a Culture of Poverty or Culture of Comparison to keep the population at a certain level of anxiety in regard to its security needs being met, whether these needs are met or not; the subject population will find in Your evangelism "security" instead of "salvation", guidance in life choices and morality[224], and will only be interested in following religious teachers who provide "certainty": a clear definition of what to do, who or what to blame for difficulties and shortcomings in life or uncertainties about present and future destinies. These religious teachings, instead of promoting self-reflection and personal growth, will provide something to ease the pain and anxiety of living in the oppositional reality of a rationalizing world, a world that You created.

Evangelism works most effectively when there is a constant external force to promote instability in the subject nation-state, such as Your SACs (projections). Failing to meet esteem needs is enough to perpetuate a Culture of Poverty and a Culture of Comparison, and with Your projections of Cognitive Dissonance, the subject populace will feel the anxieties of insecurity; it will embrace Your evangelistic teachings in an attempt to

[224] Lowry, Charles A. (1962) *Communism and Christ*. New York: Collier Books, p.76

alleviate the psychological discomfort of living in a Rational world in which Nature is oppositional, not complimentary.

Religion & Gender

If You take the belief of a formless, all-inclusive, all-expansive, pandemic, omnipresent, omniscient, omnipotent universal creative Source or Being, and compress It into a male (physical) personification, You will then be denying the personal divinity of all females, and instill a sense of lesser importance as human beings, as community and society elements, as members of a family unit. Through this trick, You can eliminate the importance of females in the subject-state in developing individual potential, and the women will instill in the children a lesser sense of importance, especially in the female children.

This act of "revealing the lesser importance" of half of the population will work beautifully to promote an environment of un-fulfilled persons, making a perfect breeding ground for Your projections, to encourage the externalizing of Self through consumption by meeting Your projected success model, consuming Your cultural icons, embracing Your espoused ideals as its own, and adherence to a socially dis-locative competitive nature that views all other members in society as "Others" with whom relationships are to exist only to increase one's competitive advantage over all Others.

Note the following very carefully. Again: *You* are projecting a dis-locative thought process onto Your subject. *You* are not to believe in Your projections. If You do, You place Yourself in danger of developing a serious, potentially self-disastrous, narcissist complex. In particular, when projecting these destructive ideas to manipulate the religious and spiritual beliefs of the subject, You must be careful. I will let Dr. Na'im Akbar, a renowned clinical psychologist, illustrate some of what I am expressing. You must pay heed to this or run the risk of totally losing perspective of Your conquest and falling in love with Your image instead.

> There is a serious psychological problem created for the person portrayed in the form of the Divine image . . . The person who looks up and sees his physical characteristics shared by the deity, begins to develop the idea that he is exactly like God, or that God is like him. This is all right if one sees potential for growth within that idea. The confusion of the physical attributes with the very nature of God, begins to make the person feel that his particular physical features have endowed him with automatic claims to divinity. Such a person can begin to believe in his own mind, that 'I am God, I am the Deity, I am the Creator,' . . . This begins to cultivate an ego maniac. They begin to suffer from ego inflation.
>
> Such thinking is very characteristic of paranoid persons---those people who believe that everybody is out to get them---which they explain as a consequence of their being superior to other people. They seriously misrepresent themselves, over stating their own importance. They then begin to misperceive everybody else. This is a major characteristic of the mind that

begins to believe that it is supposed to rule the world.[225]

In a nutshell, *watch out*! Do not become deceived, do not become attached to or possessed by this image of Divinity that You portray about Yourself. If so, You will mistakenly believe that the Law of Nature, of balance and harmony, do not apply to You.

Universalizing

This is a quote to illustrate the effects of Universalizing the Divine Being into an external culture-based image:

> Black children sit at their dinner tables where a Black daddy and a Black mamma have often overcome racist opposition to provide them with food, and over the table there hangs a picture to which they bow their heads, looking at twelve Caucasians sitting around their table at the 'Last Supper.' There sits 'God's son' and all of his 'closest companions,' and not even the cook, the server, or the busboy is shown to look like them. God's 'mother' (the Madonna) is Caucasian, all of God's 'friends' are portrayed as Caucasians. Michelangelo went all out and portrayed himself (in the ceiling of the Sistine Chapel) with a long white beard to match his long white face, and the heavenly hosts were all portrayed in the same flesh . . .
>
> Perhaps the most disturbing fact is that this Caucasian image of Divinity has become an unconsciously controlling factor in the psychology of African-Americans. Brilliant scholars of the mind, usually so perceptive, were unable to see this influence. Their fear of accepting it even after it was pointed out, demonstrated the presence of a mental barrier to addressing this issue. Some of the most verbal critics of racism and its consequences have been thoroughly incapable of addressing this issue. The evidence of the potency of the effect is in the ability of even the most militant thinkers to openly challenge what they had come to believe unconsciously was actually the image of God.[226]

To better put this analogy of a "white" Jesus into the context that You can truly understand, I will quote a parallel but different example in a statement by Imam Waarith Deen Muhammad:

> What would happen to the minds of Caucasian people if black people would suddenly come into power with their mentality, with their love for religion? What if nappy-headed Black Jesuses were put all over the land and throughout their homes, and in all of their churches? What would happen to their minds over a period of three-hundred years if they were kept coming to churches and seeing our image as their redeemer, seeing our image as their prophets, their apostles, their angels? They would be reduced to inferiority because the image before them of the supreme model of superiority would be 'black' and not 'white'.[227]

---

[225] Ra Un Nefer Amen. (1994) *Metu Neter Vol.2 Anuk Ausar: The Kamitic Initiation System*. New York: Khamit Corp. p.137

[226] Ibid, pp. 56-7

[227] Ibid. p.67 From Muhammad W.D. A Message of Concern to the American People Chicago: *American Muslim Journal*, regular feature, 1980-1983.

Something that You must be watchful for, are movements to eliminate Your influence over the minds of the population, movements that will eliminate Your culture-based Universalistic portrayals of the Divine, based on Your image. A movement such as this was started by the aforementioned religious leader. C.R.A.I.D., the Committee for the Removal of All Images that Portray Divine was created with intent to "remove all images and all racial effects from worship" through rallies, protests, and other political/social action.[228] But even if You are unable to stop movements of this sort from forming, there is always the reality that it will be very difficult for people to remove these images from the psyche.

Liberation Theology

You cannot allow any persons in Your subject nation-state to espouse a collectivist or society-oriented liberation theology, be it Christian, Islamic, Jewish, Ifa, Buddhist, Source, Nature, Universe-oriented. If You allow this to happen, a correlation can be made in the following logic: a relational value system is "good" and constructive; a quantitative value system is "bad" and destructive. An example of this logic can be illustrated through looking at some of Cardenal's[229] interpretations of the Gospels in the New Testament.

Because of world-wide large and small arms (as well as WMD) proliferation, today is a time that effective, asymmetric warfare is possible. If Your subject society views itself as being mortally threatened, even in terms of culture and way of life rather than physically, its people may respond in a manner which to You may seem like a futile act of desperation, but will be a full-on, society-wide, long-term, guerilla assault against Your influence in its society. If it views separation from itself as "death", which You are causing through Your projections, it will see no reason spare You and what You represent.

Here are some passages detailing Cardenal's theology:

Cardenal's key to the Gospels is a depersonalized and collectivist interpretation of the fundamental concepts of Christianity. In adapting the new Christianity and its theology of

---

[228.]Ibid. p.68

[229.]The full discussion of this theology is *The Gospel in Solentiname*. "The discussions belonged to a fishing and peasant community on an island of the Solentiname archipelago at the southern extremity of Lake Nicaragua. Cardenal became an ordained priest in 1965 and, with several friends, moved to the island in January 1966 and founded a Christian grass-roots community. There he practiced conscientization for more than a decade before joining the FSLN (Sandinista Front of National Liberation) with his entire congregation in the middle seventies." From Hodges, Donald C. (1986) *Intellectual Foundations of the Nicaraguan Revolution*. Austin: University of Texas Press, p.280

liberation to Nicaragua, he has altered its fundamental beliefs in God the Father, the Son, the Second Coming, and Resurrection.

Commenting on the passages from Ark 12:28-34, where Jesus says that the most important commandants are to love God and your neighbor as yourself, Cardenal explains why these make up one commandment rather than two; 'God appears before the people of Israel freeing them from the slavery of Egypt . . . he wants the people to be faithful to him and not to recognize other gods of other societies, which do not represent any liberation. So to love him is to love liberation and justice and that's the same thing as to love your neighbor.' In effect, the first commandment tells us there is no other God than love, and the second commandment tells us that love exists only when we show it toward others. The conclusion is inescapable: 'God is love among people . . . God doesn't exist in another way separated from love among people, as God is usually imagined.'

This means that outright atheists who love the poor and oppressed are really obeying the first commandment, whether they like it or not. 'In the Bible the opponent of God isn't atheism, it's the idols.' The idols are the enemies of love. Since God can be loved only in one's neighbor, not through worship, prayer, and ritual, according to Cardenal, God is a collective phenomenon like love and not an individual being or person. Although rot a novel thesis, this explains how atheists can be religious even though they do not believe in a Supreme Being.

As for Christ's Second Coming, when he will judge the world, Cardenal interprets it as the coming of a new society and of a new humanity. 'The Son of Man will not come as an individual, as he did the first time; he will be a collective Christ, he will come as a society, or rather a new species, the New Person [or new man] . . . Christ is the society of the poor, the proletariat, as we say today. And this people is the one that's going to judge.'

Cardenal also interests the Christian doctrine of resurrection in collectivist terms bordering on heresy for the traditional church. Marxism tells us that matter is eternal which suggests to Cardenal that consciousness must also be eternal, since it too, is an essential part of nature. 'And when we die, we can go to form part of that universal consciousness, depending on the degree of evolution that we have reached; or else we can remain eternally separated . . . [In any case] we can understand the resurrection of our bodies this way: that since we're part of the consciousness of the universe, our bodies will be the whole universe.'

This interpretation follows from an earlier discussion that concluded, 'In reality al of us are a single organism, and all together we are a single I. That's why each of us must love the others as part of our own person (that means 'as as oneself'). If we don't, we don't belong to the complete Man, we are cut off from Humanity.' For Cardenal there is no individual soul in need of salvation but only a collective one. And this implies that sin is not personal but structural or collective. It also implies that grace is a collective gift and that the people must be converted en masses to deserve it.

Cardenal did not get his inspiration for these theosophical nostrums from Sandino. Nonetheless, his theology of liberation stresses humanity's collective salvation based on its collective nature as a single organism, as did Sandino's.[230]

If there is severe societal dis-location in Your subject nation-state, fundamentalist groups founded on platforms of liberation theology, such as the preceding, can proliferate or even worse, unify into theocratic political parties that oppose You on the premise that You embody "evil", because of the effects of the value system that You are projecting on its society.[231]

[230.] Ibid, pp.280-282
[231.] See Ibid, pp.200-2

Book II

The Mind of a

Conqueror

I. The Legacy Of Platonic Thought and How Its Misuse Presents A Threat To Humanity

Chapter 17:
Introduction to Section I.
The Legacy of Platonic
Thought and How Its Misuse
Presents a Threat to Humanity

Platonic thought gives You power over Your subject. It is through this concept of Rationalism that You are able to utilize Cultural Warfare in a way that is long-lasting and self-perpetuating.

By objectifying the Universe, and even the nature of Humanity, You are able to own, possess and define both the natural Universe as well as the human ideal. This process of granting Yourself control through the use of abstractions is the basis through which You make Yourself the locus of control and Point of Reference in the "self-definition" of the subject nation-state. Because You are the 'namer' and 'definer' of creation, You become its "god", its model for living and self-actualization.

Plato is the intellectual father of other 'namers' and 'definers' such as Aristotle, Newton, Leibniz, Descartes, and Darwin. In the last century, initially a fellow Rationalist, Einstein broke from this tradition and began a trend in the "Modern World" of questioning the supremacy of the Rationalist world-view. You are returning Rationalism to its supreme status. Plato is the first architect of the "Enlightenment Project", a project that You are completing with the utilization and application of this methodology of Cultural Warfare onto Your subject nation-state and hopefully the world-at-large.

Chapter 18:
The Rational Man - Plato

The Cave.

And now, I said, let me show in a figure how far our nature is enlightened or unenlightened: - Behold! Human beings living in an underground den, which has a mouth open towards the light and reaching all along the den; here they been from their childhood, and have their legs and necks chained so that they can not move, and can only see before them, being prevented buy the chains from turning round their heads. Above and behind then a fire is blazing at a distance, and between the fore and the prisoners there is a raised way; and you will see, if you look, a low wall built along the way, like the screen which marionette players have in from of them, over which they show the puppets.

I see.

And do you see, I said, men passing along the wall carrying all sorts of vessels, and statues and figures of animals made of wood and stone and various materials, which appear over the wall? Some of them are talking, others silent.

You have shown me a strange image, and they are strange prisoners.

Like ourselves, I replied; and they see only their own shadows, or the shadows of one another, which the fire throws on the opposite wall of the cave?

True, he said; how could they see anything but the shadows, if they were never allowed to move their heads?

And of the objects which are carried in like manner they would only see the shadows?

Yes, he said.

And if they were able to converse with one another, would they not suppose that they were naming what was actually before them?

Very true.

And suppose further that the prison had an echo which came from the other side, would they not be sure to fancy when one of the passers-by spoke that the voice which they heard came from the passing shadow?

No question, he replied.

To them, I said, the truth would be literally nothing but the shadows of the images.

That is certain.

And now look again, and see what will naturally follow if the prisoners are released and disabused of their error. At first, when any of them is liberated and compelled suddenly to stand up and turn his neck round and walk and look towards the light, he will suffer sharp pains; the glare will distress him, and he will be unable to see the realities of which in his former state he had seen the shadows; and then conceive some one saying to him, that what he saw before was an illusion, but that now, when is approaching nearer to being and his eye is turned towards more real existence, he has clearer vision, - what will be his reply? And you may further imagine that his instructor is pointing to the objects as they pass and requiring him to name them, - will he not be perplexed? Will he not fancy that the shadows which he formerly saw are truer than the objects which are now shown to him?

Far truer.

And if he is compelled to look straight at the light, will he not have a pain in his eyes which will make him turn away to take refuge in the objects of vision which he can see, and which he will conceive to be in reality clearer than the things which are now being shown to him?

True he said.

And suppose once more, that he is reluctantly dragged up a steep and rugged ascent, and held fast until he is forced into the presence of the sun himself, is he not likely to be pained and irritated? When he approaches the light his eyes will be dazzled, and he will not be able to see anything at all of what are now called realities.

Not all in a moment, he said.

He will require to grow accustomed to the sight of the upper world.

And first he will see the shadows best, next the reflections of men and other objects in the water, and then the objects themselves, then he will gaze upon the light of the moon and the starts and the spangled heaven; and he will see the sky and the stars by night better than the sun or light of the sun by day?

Certainly.

Last of all he will be able to see the sun, and not mere reflections of him in the water, but he will see him in his own proper place, and not in another; and he will contemplate him as he is[232].

The aim of Cultural Cognitive Dissonance is to first put the subject in the "cave" let it realize that it is in the "cave" rather than out of the sun, then through adherence to Your projections it (at least in some intellectual fantasy) will be lifted out of the cave into the land of 'men' and will know, accept, and value its place in it. And it will always be indebted to You and require Your presence as it center to continually reassure it that it is in continual harmony with parameters of being outside and not in the "cave" back with the Others.

"He will then proceed to argue that this is he who gives the season and the year, and in a certain way the cause of all things which he and his fellows have been accustomed to behold?"[233]

But in the relationship that You create with Your subject, it will recognize You as the "cause of all things" – the Point of Reference, the "center".

---

232.   Plato trans. Jowett, Benjamin (2000) *The Republic*. Mineola, New York: Dover Publications, Inc. pp. 177-8. I underlined those lines for emphasis.
233.   Ibid, p.178

Plato & Reason

"Two virtues remain to be discovered in the State – first, temperance, and then justice which is the end of our search.

Very true.

Now, can we find justice without troubling ourselves about temperance?

I do not know how that can be accomplished, he said, nor do I desire that justice should be brought to light and temperance lost sight of, and therefore I wish that you do me the favor of considering temperance first.

Certainly, I replied, I should not be justified in refusing your request.

Then consider, he said.

Yes, I replied; I will; and as far as I can at present see, the virtue of temperance has more of the nature of harmony and symphony than the preceding.

How so? He asked.

Temperance, I replied, is the ordering or controlling of certain pleasures; this is curiously enough implied in the saying of "a man being his own master;" and other traces of the same notion may be found in language.

No doubt, he said.

There is something ridiculous in the expression "master of himself;" for the master is also the servant and the servant the master; and in all these modes of speaking the same person is denoted.

Certainly.

The meaning is, I believe, that in the human soul there is a better and also a worse principle; and when the better has the worse under control, then a man is said to be master of himself; and this is a term of praise: but when, owing to evil education or association, the better principle, which is also the smaller, is overwhelmed by the greater mass of the worse – in this case he is blamed and is called the slave of self and unprincipled.

Yes, there is reason in that.

And now, I said, look at our newly-created State, and there you will find one of these two conditions realized; for the States, as you will acknowledge, may be justly called master of itself, if the words "temperance" and "self-mastery" truly express the rule of the better part over the worse.

Yes, he said, I see that what you say is true.

Let me further note that the manifold and complex pleasures and desires and pains are generally found in children and women and servants, and in the freemen so called who are to the lowest and more numerous class.

Certainly, he said.

Whereas the simple and moderate desires which follow reason, are under the guidance of mind and true opinion, are to be found only in a few, and those the best born and best educated.

Very true.

These two, as you perceive, have a place in our State; and the meaner desires of the many are held down by the virtuous desires and wisdom of the few."[234]

The Prince, as new master of the concrete through exercise of separation also becomes Master of Reason. Reason can be explained as the

---

234.   Ibid, pp.100-1 (Book IV); See Ch.1, Ani, Re: Rationalism pp. 34-48

denial of spirit, or of base urges. With Reason one can "control" the base desires, instincts, - the 'primitive' or 'undeveloped'. Though true mastery comes from being in harmony with one's environment, Reason is used to control the external. I must remind You that Reason is based on separation, which in turn is based on the mental exercise of objectification of the universe. The Prince must project Himself as Possessor of Reason, Champion of Reason, and Protector of Reason, but must not in Himself become so arrogant[235] that He believes that His perception is universal Reason. He must be aware that He is at war and utilize these tactics of manipulation to disarm His enemy, not Himself. The projection of Reason is the projection of the concept of self-mastery. The Prince, and Others whom He desires to publicly acknowledge, as His contemporaries are proficient in the art of self-mastery. "Lower base instincts"/"Human Nature" – do not come into play in Your governance and ideals, for You are Your master over Yourself and possessor of Universal Reason. Those who do not govern with Reason--Your subject--should be made aware that self-mastery, the triumph of Reason, is the final goal of Mankind. Nation-states' desire to become developed nation ought to deny the authority of their experience and put aside their primitive cultural notions of reality – the Modern Man is one governed though Reason. And literally – You are to be the 'Reason' that governs Modern Man.

Man vs. Nature - The Concept of "Good".

"Now, that which imparts truth to the known and the power of knowing to the knower is what I would have you term the idea of good, and this you will deem to be the cause of science, and of truth in so far as the latter becomes the subject of knowledge; beautiful too, as are both truth and knowledge, you will be right in esteeming this other nature as more beautiful than either; and, as in the previous instance, light and sight may be truly said to be like the sun, and yet not to be the sun, so in this other sphere, science and truth may be deemed to be like the good, but not the good; the good has a place of honor yet higher.

What a wonder of beauty that must be, he said, which is the author of science and truth, and yet surpasses then in beauty; for you surely and not mean to say that pleasure is the good?

God forbid, I replied; but may I ask you to consider the image in another point of view?

In what point of view?

You would say, would you not, that the sun is not only the author of visibility in all visible things, but of generation and nourishment and growth, though he himself is not generation?

Certainly.

235.　　　Arrogance to the point where Your narcissism becomes tangibly self-destructive and counterproductive to Your goal of Sustainable Exploitation.

> In like manner the good may be said to be not only the author of knowledge to all things known, but of their being in essence, and yet the good is not essence, but far exceed essence in dignity and power.
>
> Glaucon said, with a ludicrous earnestness: By the light of heaven, how amazing"
>
> Yes, I said, and the exaggeration may be set down to you; for you made me utter my fancies.
>
> And pray continue to utter them; at any rate let us hear if there is anything more to be said about the similitude of the sun.
>
> Yes, I said, there is a great deal more.
>
> Then omit nothing, however slight.
>
> I will do my best, I said; but I should think that a great deal will have to be omitted.
>
> I hope not, he said.
>
> <u>You have to imagine, then, that there are two ruling powers, and that one of them is set over the intellectual world, the other over the visible.</u>"[236]

The oppositional state of being: Man vs. Nature.

Limitations of Platonic Thought (1).

The key contribution that Plato made the abstracted worldview and evolution of "Rational Thought" was the objectification of the universe; it was no longer experienced. This objectification created the concept of separateness. The desire was to "know"; rather than to intuit or experience; or "think critically" using both knowing and intuiting simultaneously to obtain the best 'understanding': real or true thinking. This attempt at "knowledge" or "truth" was an admirable feat of the mental exercise of abstraction, but in his zeal to "know" he may have been the first victim of the shortsightedness of linear thinking. To separate, one requires a point of departure; a fixed point from which one defines or organizes objects. Linear thinking gives the user a feeling of Progress, because there is movement from the "point" to somewhere. Linear thinking can be a valuable tool in creating an abstracted reality, but the use must realize that this is <u>only</u> a mental exercise, and not real thinking.

To 'separate' requires knowledge of the totality. If one is not omniscient they cannot rationalize or separate or objective. If one is not omniscient, they cannot rationalize, separate, or objectify without prejudice unless by chance enlightened through intuition. Without omniscience one must submit to the reality that all of his or her thinking is based on incomplete parameters and no point of reference – therefore one must guess at truth using a combination of his experiences and intuitions. Attempts to understand truth will be from intuition and colored by one's experiences and culture, i.e.

---

236.   Ibid, pp.173-4 (Book VI). Note: The last paragraph is underlined for emphasis.

because one does not really 'know' one cannot judge or classify anything. One only can try our best at living harmoniously. Anything other than this is 'playing God' without admitting to it.--Plato thought that he had found the key to understanding the Universe.[237]

Limitations of Platonic Thought (2).

What You must be wary of is the tendency to view poles of the same as opposites. When defining Reason, the Progress defined that which is Rational, irrational, legitimate, illegitimate, good, bad, modern, primitive, black, white – a tendency to view this defined difference and that of opposing sides, rather than as complimentary parts of a whole. This point is important, because this is the key to the potential break between Yourself and humanity. Rational becomes the opposite of emotional and therefore Reason can separate itself emotionally from the concrete reality of the world. In Your quest to achieve the heights of Reason You will be in danger of denying Yourself the emotional connection to the world that You require. Because of the conscious denial of emotion, You will unconsciously still desire it, because it is necessary to Your existence. But because You have dealt away with the natural tools that You have to have healthy emotional relationships with the world and fellow man, Your subconscious reverts to creating a power need to satisfy their emotional lack. At this point You are susceptible to deviating from Your objectives. Instead of fulfilling Your desire for conquest, You have the additional need of controlling the subject because You will require an emotional relationship with it. Being that You are unable to have balanced harmonious relationships, because You have created a world of opposites in Your mind, You will need to use power to force the creation of the emotional relationship that You desire with the subject. This is a relationship where the subject recognizes Your superiority because of Your grasp of Reason and where You require the constant affirmation of acceptance by it, because You need to feel secure in this relationship. But, alas, the very nature of a control-based relationship will spurn insecurity in You, because subconsciously You know that it is an artificial, forced relationship. And You will project this notion of superiority to Your own population incessantly because of the paranoia that ensues.

Again, heed my warning – The Platonic Man is a delusional and paranoid man. Use Plato's thinking as a means of projecting the concept of Reason

---

237.   Though a Prince uses Platonic thought to forward his endeavors of conquest, he cannot actually need to believe in Platonic thought in order to meet his ego or esteem needs.

over Your subject and to objectify, define, separate, and name its environment. But under no circumstance ever believe that this exercise is reality--It will be Your undoing. You will put as much time into supporting Your addictive relationships with the subject as You put into Your attack and You will not be able to adequately gauge the effectiveness of Your efforts, because You will believe that You are infallible and You will not see any of the wisdom in how Others run their states.

The conclusion of Your conquest will have to act as overseer and master of the subject, any true emotional dependency of the subject will make Your position as master temporary, contingent upon the subject believing that You are its master. At the moment, it decides that You do not matter and that it has the answer to its questions within itself – You cease to exist as master, and become an antagonistic foreign influence--a foreign invader.

Left Brain vs. Right Brain.

Human Brain: Left   (Analytical thinking, Reasoning)
                Right   (Emotional, Intuitive)

Can one live without either side? – one is to intuit and receive sensation while the other is to build thoughts of these receptions. One cuts his or herself off from the world if he or she attempts to "think" everything – but like I said before – that is impossible – he or she just believes that their emotions are Rational thoughts. The seed or origin of thinking comes from our connection to the cosmic (intuition) and physical (perception)--thinking is the sum of right and left brain processing, while solely left brain processing is the origin of irrationality.

An example: Men who feel the need to project the label of 'irrationality' onto women described as their emotional nature; their inability to think with their brains as opposed to their hearts. These men are delusional – they need to feel superior to women, so they make these statements, but that same man is just is prone to "emotional outbursts" and "irrationality" as the woman that he describes, but he erroneously perceives these emotional experiences, as "Rational thoughts", i.e. "I meant to lose my temper at the meeting – that was a strategic tactic to let them know that I meant business" while in truth, he "lost it" and quietly rationalized it. If a woman had become irate in the same scenario, it would be recommended that she not be allowed to participate in such meetings in the future. The "Rational Man" puts himself at a disadvantage on two accounts; he unlike the woman (or balanced man) cannot use his emotions to his advantage in terms of gauging a situation properly, he instead views them as his passion and he is unable to manage them at all; he is a servant to his emotions because of his need to believe that they are his rationally-contrived thoughts.

Objectification.

It is said that power is in the alphabet, the vibration of words. In many traditions, the naming of a child evokes its destiny. Along these same lines, a Prince must realize the power of naming. By objectifying and defining the world, You place Yourself in the position of 'Master'. If You are the 'Namer', no one can debate You, because You have already created the rules of the game. It is very hard to win a battle based on someone else's rules. By creating Your own culture-based analysis and definitions of the 'Modern World', Others who engage in dialogue with You have already lost. An example: the United States generally kept an isolationist foreign policy when the British empire was at its peak; for if it had engaged itself in British games (be it 'Free Trade, international finance, etc.) it would have had to play on England's chess board and had a great possibility of losing everything it had achieved so far, save the shared Anglo-Saxon culture that serves as the center of its culture.

Control.

We control our world by rationalizing it and the objects that we name and define. The control over time was rationalism's greatest victory. Through this, more than any other abstract construction, allows us to believe that we actually have "control over" our world rather than striving for "harmony" within it.

I once watched a television talk show with a psychiatrist talking about Borderline Personality Disorder. He stated that: "We don't know causes, but we know the symptoms" – This is ridiculous. He should just admit that he has no idea what is going on in the human mind, instead of pretending to keep up the pretenses of intelligence that support the mass psychosis of Rationalism. Do not fall into this trap of actualizing and rationalizing shortcomings. It is better to learn and grow from mistakes than to convince Yourself that a particular action was the best simply because it was You that did it.

"Control Over"

The following is the danger of using the logic of: power = control:
Reason is desired, while emotions are not. This is because of their (emotions) intuitive origin which places You in a predicament of seeing Yourself as a "subject" of the cosmos which renders You 'powerless'. Having "control over"

becomes paramount to one's esteem, because no one desires to view themselves as powerless. This is a psychological trap that You set onto Your subject, not onto Yourself.

The world becomes an "us verses them" dichotomy necessary to rationalize our own undesirable traits. Instead of working on improving upon them, we simply project them onto the Other. Then, we disdain the Other for being mirror of our undesirable selves.

There is some usefulness to this illusion of 'power over' the Cosmos. It can give one the prerogative to advance technologically, but technological advances can only be of benefit to the society and the world when one comes back from the illusory land of control and truly attempts to gauge how harmonious this "advance" is with the "reality". Our environmental nightmares and industrial disasters have come from overstaying in the illusionary world of "knowledge and control over Nature".

Control vs. Harmony

Besides creating the position of You as possessor of Reason, therefore 'Modern'; projecting Platonic concepts onto the subject also serves as a magnificent weapon through the concept of order versus disorder. The integrity of a nation-state truly lies in its ability to maintain harmony within its family structure, community structure, environment, and as a nation; and within its harmony with the outside world. Nation-states that desire to propagate themselves for posterity seek balance and avoid policies and decisions that will promote disharmony in their societies. The motives may be to the preserve the state; but the result is a respect for the cyclical reality of the Universe. For example, China and Japan both prevented the proliferation of firearms in their societies to preserve balance. These states had to stifle technological growth in their societies in this decision, but prevented warfare from becoming too brutal via a conversion to mass murder through the use of firearms; and in Japan it was mandated to return to warfare by sword.[238]

Another example is how the Lakes region Central African Haya people stopped the proliferation of their carbon steel smelting technology because of the large amount of timber required for the furnaces.[239]

---

238.   See Parrin, Noel Perrin. (1979) *Giving Up the Gun: Japan's Reversion to the Sword*, 1543-1879. Boston: Nonpareil Books.
In many cultures in the world before the "Modern Era", the death of a few persons was many times enough to signal the end of a conflict. Many "wars" were fought verbally. Resolution was in the form of lost properties or the taking of prisoners. Conflict resulting in death was a symbol of the breakdown of civility. This is why many of the world's peoples until recently did not have highly developed war technologies. Conflict among neighbors never escalated to the point in which further killing technologies were necessary.

To disrupt the society, the Prince must convert the thinking of society from that of reverence to one's environment, and harmony to that of control. It must be made to feel, through Your example, that it can control Nature. This seed of confusion will irreparably change how the subject will see its environment. You will have placed it in a labyrinth with no entrance or exit, just an unsolvable maze. For it is impossible to control the outside, we have no choice but to be in harmony with it. With every technological advance they make, they create a bigger separation and more and more terrible outcomes come about and go farther and farther away from being able to live in harmony. This is a perpetual trap, because we are not privy to all of the variables of the Universe, therefore we cannot truly write a balanced equation. Presenting the subject with the idea that it can <u>control</u> will invalidate its indigenous wisdom, because it is likely based on harmonious living. The invalidation creates the door through which Your ideals and cultural icons can enter.

Control, Harmony, & Reality
Control + Harmony + Reality of the universe: No matter what You do: what will happen, will happen. The outcome will be the same: intent and perspective determine whether an outcome is negative or positive, creative or destructive.This need for control to fulfill emotional needs can also hurt Your administration at home, because this same need for approval for Your subject can also spill in the need for approval in Your society. This "boundary problem" can cause ultraconservatives to awaken and push for strict social conformity in Your society and require You to use extreme means to control and/or repress dissent within your society. Ideas, My Prince, are hard to control once they are let out into the world. Evoking the Idea of Reason and the Culture of Comparison will make Your own society susceptible to it so You must carefully ensure that cultural integrity and national collective goals of Your nation-state are supported and nurtured.

Morals.
Rationality (scientific reasoning) implies morality. A Rational Man is not necessarily a moral man; but due to the method of His reasoning, He is the

---

239.   Journal of African Civilizations Vol. I, No. 2, November 1979; "Ideology and the Archaeological Record in Africa: Interpreting Symbolism in Iron Smelting Technology." Peter Schmidt and Bertram Mapunda, Journal of Anthropological Archaeology, Vol. 16. 1997; Shore, D. "Steel-Making in Ancient Africa." *Blacks in Science, Ancient and Modern* (I. Van Sertima, ed.) New Brunswick: Transaction Books, 1983, pp.157-162; P.R. Schmidt (ed.). (1996) The Culture and Technology of African Iron Production. Gainsville: University Press of Florida.

determiner of what is moral, whether He is or not. The Rational Man grants Himself the right to judge, though in actuality, a part of a whole is unable to judge the whole or any part of it. Judging another part is analogous to two people being in separate rooms with two different realities; and one of the people in the other room, though He does not have the perspective of the other person, decides to assume knowledge about the other and pass judgment on the other, realizing or not realizing that His basis of opinion/ analysis is only based on His own realities and experience.

The Rational Man, in His quest to be "objective", consciously cuts Himself off from the 'past' and starts from "scratch" – but ironically because He is not omnipotent, He sub/unconsciously still has to draw on His 'past' to have a point of departure for His thoughts and analysis.

Morals & The Rational Man

A Prince must realize the position that He holds as the "Rational Man" – He must use this to His advantage when it comes to defining morals. Because You are Rational, Your thought processes will be thought to produce 'good'. This is how You will be able to serve Your subject a dish of poison; with it being fully aware that it is poison and that only a "crazy" or "irrational" person would ingest it. You can bring it Your ideals and icons, like Free Market capitalism, and he or she can predict disaster in their own system and even witness the ill effect on Yours, but because You have taken the "high road" of Rationality – what You say must be right.

Amoral System.

Global Financier George Soros in his treatise on the global economy, *George Soros on Globalization, states*:

> The distinguishing feature of both market fundamentalism and geopolitical realism is that they are amoral – morality does not enter into the calculations. That is one of the reasons why they have been so successful. We have been seduced by their success into thinking that we can do without moral considerations. We have come to worship success. We admire businessmen who make a fortune and politicians who get themselves elected irrespective of how they have done it.

> That is where we have gone wrong. No society can exist without morality. Even our amoral pursuits need a moral justification. Market fundamentalism claims that the untrammeled pursuit serves the common interest; and the exercise of our geopolitical power appeals to our patriotism. The fact remains that these are amoral pursuits. If that is all we have to offer, our view of the world is liable to be rejected by more traditional societies where morality still plays a central role. That is the case in traditional Islamic societies where church and state have not even been separated. In the end, we may not find it satisfactory

ourselves...

But the nation-state still embraces You – Why?, because You bring their central point of self-definition, their reality, to them. If a Prince takes the subject's point of reference, its center, and replaces it with an external point of reference, He, whatever He says will appear to be congruent and in consonance with needs of the nation-state and appear to support its raison d'etre.

Legacy of Plato.

Let us take the view that Descartes is an artifact of the rational methodology of Modernity. He had a desire to use scientific reasoning as a means of solving humanity's problems. This methodology was attractive because of its abstractness and simplicity. The problem is that it has no relevance to anything, because it is totally abstract and grounded in nothing; and it must have a 'starting point'. There is no "abstract" or "objective". One cannot take oneself out of any equation. The only line with no beginning and no ending is a circle. In circles all things are relevant, corresponding, and relational. He desired to build society in the model of the hierarchically-arranged Cosmopolis using Euclidean geometry and the logicality of formal proofs. Let us do the "math" together. If scientific reasoning is used in a static causal environment, possibly Reason could be used without consequence – allowing the user to be his own "Creator" of his own world; but in the concrete reality of an interdependent world/environment, "Rational Thought" without allowance for consequences discouraged responsibility for one's actions, leads to disharmony, and ultimately destruction of the symbiotic reality of Nature.[240]

Platonic thought is a delusional state that with moderation can lead to "Growth" and "Progress", but out of balance leading to direct conflict with Nature, Universe, God--Plato's equation of defined good vs. evil, control vs. harmony, hierarchical rules and competition with Nature as opposed to harmony with Nature.

The Legacy of Plato - Orality vs. Literacy

Homeric Greeks valued clichés because not only the poets but the entire oral noetic world or thought world relied upon the formulaic constitution of thought. In an oral culture, knowledge, once acquired, had to be constantly repeated or it would be lost: fixed, formulaic thought patterns were essential for wisdom and effective administration. But, by Plato's day (427?- 347 BC) a change had set in: the Greeks had at long last effectively interiorized writing –

---

240.   Toulmin, Stephen (1992) *Cosmopolis: The Hidden Agenda of Modernity.* Chicago: The University of Chicago Press, p.177

something which took several centuries after development of the Greek alphabet around 720-700 BC. The new way to store knowledge was not in mnemonic formulas but in the written text... Plato excluded poets from his ideal republic essentially (if not quite consciously) because he found himself in a new chirographically styled poetic world in which the formula or cliché, beloved of all traditional poets, was outmoded and counterproductive...

All these are disturbing conclusions... They show Homeric Greece cultivating as a poetic and noetic virtue what we have regarded as a vice, and they show that the relationship between Homeric Greece and everything that philosophy after Plato stood for was, however superficially cordial and continuous, in fact deeply antagonistic, if often at the unconscious rather than the conscious level. The conflict wrecked Plato's own unconscious. For Plato expresses serious reservations in the *Phaedrus* and his *Seventh Letter* about writing, as a mechanical, inhuman way of processing knowledge, unresponsive to questions and destructive of memory, although, as we now know, the philosophical thinking Plato fought for depended entirely on writing... The importance of ancient Greek civilization to all the world was beginning to show an entirely new light: it marked the point in human history when deeply interiorized alphabetic literacy first clashed head-on with orality.[241]

Literate cultures that retain a concurrent oral tradition that is continually reinforced by childhood training and transmission of ancestral or traditional cultural/religious/spiritual knowledge through stories and rote memory do not experience the separation from 'center' that literate cultures that disconnect from and disparage historical "clichés[242]". Those cultures that discourage the use of clichés do so because they believe in evolution and linear progress. The Culture of Rationalism that You project upon Your Subject's nation-state is one of these cultures. You must separate its society from its collective (and cumulative) wisdom; its "clichés". Clichés are symbolic of non-linear thinking, a circular concept of time and spatial reality. Clichés are similar themes that are taught again and again throughout the life of a people. They are its "mantra". These "clichés" are the repetitive voice that judges thoughts, behaviors, and objects as congruent or incongruent with a people's cultural center. To a non-linear thinker these reoccurring themes are a point of reference/point of departure for all endeavors; while to a linear thinker these "clichés" are anchor-weights that only restrict abstract thinking. For the Rational Man a point of reference/point of departure is seen as an obstacle to "original thought"; while the non-linear thinker sees these repetitively thought patterns as the foundation of wisdom and cultural continuity, and the mark of uniqueness when engaging in any intellectual or creative endeavors. Using Cultural Warfare, Your goal is to dislodge this 'center' so that Your subject's

---

241.   Ong, Walter J. (1988 - This edition 2003). *Orality and Literacy*. London: Routledge. pp.23-24. Some analysis in this source taken from Haverford, Eric A. (1963) Preface to Plato. Cambridge: Belnap Press of Harvard University Press.
242.   Ibid, p.23

nation-state will go in a path to "Evolution" and "Progress", a path unencumbered by thoughts of consequences, responsibility, and sustainability. In this way, with collective wisdom denied, Your subject's nation-state can be manipulated into engaging in self-destructive actions that its 'center' would never allow it to engage it.

My point is that by denigrating the oral tradition in Your subject's nation-state, whether it is defined as a "literate" and "oral" society--devaluing the traditional "stories" and stopping the culture-based character education that have been the primary modes of the transmission of collective ancestral wisdom in the society, and exchanging it for the teaching of "new" Modern values and ethics based on Legal Moralism and the Culture of Individualism--You will have laid a major blow to the cohesiveness of its society. This is especially easy if the present-day culture has been reactionary in response to Your influence (or prior exposure to Colonial Rule) and the "stories"/cultural rules taught to the youth have become suffocating rather than nurturing, instead of proactive and supportive of the actualization of national potential through the support of individual fulfillment of purpose.

Modernity & Plato.

True knowledge comes from experiencing the Universe. Reality is contrary to Your desire to control. If true knowledge comes from the action of experiencing, then all human beings are equally privy to the Truth. This is a reality that You must deny in Your projections. The subjects must be made to believe that Your transformation of the reality of a concrete mutually experienced universe is better defined in an abstract objectified form. The value of experience is to be downplayed and the superior of scientific reasoning is to be celebrated. For, if the subject were to actively realize that what it is experiencing of the Universe was of significance that Your claims to Modernity would thereby be negated--all that exist now are the sums of all their own experiences--therefore are modern in their own perspective. From this perspective of Modernity, all foreign ideals and cultural icons and products would need to be evaluated for their relevance and compatibility to the cultural consensus and sovereignty from their point of reference to determine suitability. In this context, the projections that You sent would be accepted or rejected based on the good to the society, rather than perpetuating Your own goals of conquest. This was Plato's gift to you: **the creation of the object...**

This process allows You to separate Yourself from concrete reality and become a 'subject with the ability to Reason' rather than being a part of the wholeness of the Universe. The creation of the distinct self is now independent of the whole and like Adam in a literal interpretation of the Bible, is given dominion over the Earth; for He was the 'Namer', the definer of reality. But the Prince, at all times must remember that His "independence" from the Whole is a mental exercise used to name, objectify, and control his subject. If a Prince actually believes this, He faces the danger of having the inability to realize cause and effect and the connection between all actions and their effect on the whole.

Plato's intentions were to free 'us' from the 'bondage' of the past – to give us a clean slate. Maybe this was well intentioned, but the illusion of separation prevents from looking at the past as present and leaves us open to making mistakes made in the past because we believe that the past is irrelevant.

This independent self has the ability to be objective, detached, and uninvolved with concrete reality, but also denies the user of this exercise, His point of reference. He becomes an independent self with context, which is impossible when all of our experiences are based from a point of departure, a center. The user, in reality would base His reality of His center – His cultural point of reference, but can be self-deceived into believing that His thoughts and actions are independent and objective. This is how a good-intentioned Universal Humanist can perform the same actions as a Cultural Imperialist and not be aware of it.

The Prince must be aware of what He is doing at all times. A military action, based on manipulating the human mind must be carefully managed so that an imbalance is not created that can get out of Your control and adversely affect You.

This methodology is simply an exercise to control Your external environment through deceiving the subject into believing that Your interests are Universal, free of parochial interest – You should never fall victim to the psychosis that it can create in its users.

The Cosmopolis – "Natural" Universal Hierarchy of Nature

"And if the world perceives that what we are saying about him is the truth, will they be angry with philosophy? Will they disbelieve us, when we tell them that no State can be happy which is not designed by artists who imitate the heavenly pattern?

They will not be angry if they understand, he said. But how will they draw out the plan of which you are speaking?

They will begin by taking the State and the manners of men, from which, as a tablet, they will rub out the picture, and leave a clean surface. This is no easy task. But whether easy or not, herein will lie the difference between them and every other legislator, - they will have nothing to do either with individual or State, and will inscribe no laws, until they have either found, or themselves made, a clean surface...

... Having affected this, they will proceed to trace an outline of the constitution?
No doubt.
And when they are filling in the work, as I conceive, they will often turn their eyes

upwards and downwards: I mean that they will first look at absolute justice and beauty and temperance, and again at the human copy; and will mingle ad temper the various elements of life into the image of a man; and this they will conceive according to that other image, which when existing among men, Homer calls the form and likeness of God.

Very true, he said.

And one feature they will erase, and another they will put in, until they have made the ways of men, as far as possible, agreeable to the ways of God?

Indeed, he said, in no way could they make a fairer picture…

…Why, where can they still find any ground for objection? Will they doubt that the philosopher is a lover of truth and being.

They would not be so unreasonable.

Or that his nature, being such as we have delineated, is akin to the highest good?

Neither can they doubt this."[243]

This is the cosmological order through which Your subject populace must perceive reality. You are to redefine Your subject nation-state by starting with the clean slate: any of its history, traditions, practices, rules of governance, etc. are irrelevant, because they do not follow the natural 'Universal' cosmological order, of which You are the representative, the point of reference and point of departure.[244]

'Hierarchy' is integral to Platonic thought. 'Hierarchy' is representative of a linear thought process that assumes that the opinion regarding the 'ordering of Nature' can be interpolated through Rational Thought. This 'Rational hierarchy' is the model by which You (the locus of control) substantiate the ordering of things in "Your" universe.

Problems (Danger to An Interdependent World).

Rational conquest requires two variables to exist – one superior, one inferior:

If You effectively convert the subject to an Ideology of Rationalism and You continue to be the center of society, the society will eat itself alive from the inside out. This is because You create a society of individuals whose sense of value comes from material wealth and power over "Others", as opposed to a connectedness of simply being. There will be no structure in place to establish morality to keep the population from exploiting itself to its end. Even with codified law, the powerful in the society will use it to subjugate the powerless, because in a codified legal system, sometimes having means can buy reprieves (or at the very least, legal knowledge of loopholes and

---

243.   Plato, P.165-6 Book VI.
244.   See Toulmin (1992) The work is a very good discussion of 'modern' intellectual thought in Europe from the time of great religious wars and the following 'Enlightenment". Re: Cosmology and the Clean Slate pp.177-79

shortcomings of the law). It will require a common nationalistic focus and as place outside of itself to project its negative tendencies onto. To keep them from destroying themselves they will require an external "Other" to use this aggression on, to preserve the integrity of the society. The problem with You maintaining true influence over this society at this stage is that You would have separated the economy from the society, dislocated the people from their cultural center, and dislocated the government's true mandate and sovereignty over its population, through the Rule of Law and extra-national rule - by eliminating its power to provide for the security, social welfare, and cultural sustainability needs of the people. Because there is no "love", no natural connection between the population, and it exists a within judgmental material-oriented value system, an "Other" must exist to maintain the group's collection of individual psyches because the resulting loneliness and feelings of worthlessness can either implode or explode.

If it is Your desire to continue to exploit this nation-state and prevent it from starting a local or regional conflict because of its adopted expansionist ideology, You must decrease the frequency of Your projections on its center and allow some semblance of the national identity to exist in the society. A society of individual global citizens will seek to demonize and destroy its own ethnic minorities and neighboring states as a means to keep itself from falling into a collective depression, along with the corresponding self-destructive or externally destructive tendencies.

The Danger of Taking This Philosophy Seriously.

Those who dangerously embrace Plato as the bringer of light – the father of Rational thinking – must come out of the Darkness and back into The Light (or vise versa) and realize that his contribution was that of a methodology of control. This methodology is one of definition, organization, discourse, and thinking that grants social control to men who deem themselves deserving of rule over others and who possessed the manifest destiny to project their personal truths of wherever they desired.

Plato Conclusion.

The science that Plato created is one of first and foremost Truth, Reasoning, Impartiality, and Universality. He who makes himself the locus from which this scientific reasoning emanates is entitled, through the virtue of Universal Truth and the "Universal Good for Humanity", the right to conquer, enslave, exploit, govern, and destroy any and all who oppose it. For He created the hierarchy of good and evil, civilized and uncivilized--is it not just a small sacrifice that the evil perish for Greater Good, primitive for Modern, old for New, unscientific for Scientific, immoral for Moral, heathen for Evolved, lesser for Greater?

Plato & Creation

When You evoke the spirit of Plato, You can be amoral with a shield of morality, good, and right. As long as You evoke the Name of Reason and Civilization, You can do no wrong. For You have separated Yourself from the law that governs the Universe. You are now the Creator of Your own world. Your challenge is to ensure that Your subjects, Your creation always realize Your sovereignty over them, and their place in the "Natural Hierarchy" that You have created.

Chapter 19:
The Interconnectness of Nature/ Interdependence of Nature (Non-linear Thinking)

In the eyes of the Rational Man, Nature is seen as static, fixed, causal background for the Rational actions of mankind. There is a belief in separateness, more specifically, an oppositional dichotomy between "man" and "Nature", with man working to repress his "natural" emotional tendencies. The Rational Man believes that by suppressing "natural" emotional tendencies in Himself that He is then free to "think" and to conquer Nature for His good, and the good of Other "thinking" men.

The Rational Man does not give Himself enough credit. He believes that He has no effect on the causal reality of Nature. If He has all of His intellectual faculties, He cannot possibly believe this abstracted thought. As man passes through time, He lives in Nature and affects the reality of Nature through his actions. The Rational Man, believes that because of his "separation" from Nature that He has no effect on its supposed constancy. But this is a delusion – He is not in competition with Nature; He is actually part of it. And every one of His actions has a corresponding reaction in/on Nature. This type of "Rational (linear) thinking" allows the user to "Progress" technologically, socially, and economically, because He can rationalize amoral and irresponsible actions and engage in these actions with no regard for their consequences. "Irrational" (non-linear) thinkers are restrained by their cultural inheritance that acknowledges boundaries and safeguards on behaviors that could possibly cause disharmony in Nature (environment, community, economy).

You as the Rationalist have the ultimate power over the majority cultures, because You have no ethical and moral boundaries on Your behavior; except for the codified laws that You create to perpetuate Your power and control over Others.

Interdependence of Non-linear Thinking (Danger).

Linear thinking impedes one's ability to recognize the interconnectedness of actions; therefore encouraging a pattern of alleviating symptoms of a disease, rather than acknowledging the need to deal with the root causes of the disease. For example, using military solutions for social problems. Treating symptoms initiates a cycle of further cause and effect that takes the focus off of the root problems.

Human Beings, Nature, and Consumption.

Nature only "takes" physical life because it requires the materials (matter) to perpetuate future physical life. It does not "take" the non-physical attributes of created things. This process of creation and destruction is what provides the "marketplace" in which spiritual growth can take place.

Hierarchy & the Interconnectedness of Nature.

"Hierarchy" actually equals more or less potential energy; it does not equal higher and lower. The "organization of life" is through the gathering of different amounts of potential energy. "higher and lower" implies a variance in importance and value. All "life" is "valued" relationally; i.e. possessing the potential to affect the 'whole' in some way or another. One illustration of this is the popularly accepted concept of the "food chain". It is said that nature is organized vertically in terms of the apparent power to consume: prey – predator – larger predator, etc... Using this logic microscopic organisms are "lower", at the bottom of the hierarchy, but in actuality the "lowest"--viruses and other microscopic pathogens--"consume" organisms at the "top" of the food chain/hierarchy.

Nature is organized, but it organized relationally through a "system" of potential energy. For example, a lion has the potential to consume less powerful organisms; but it does so in balance with the rest of Nature. If it does not it will be counterbalanced by other aspects of Nature; i.e. if it consumes too much, its population will grow too large while its "prey" slowly repopulates. In the meantime, due to a decrease in the availability of readily consumable "prey" it will become weak and will be susceptible to the ravages of disease by organisms that possess individually less potential energy individually, but in a large group (colony), an immense amount of potential energy (to consume). This is what is called a "relationship". An organism has varying degrees of potential energy directly in relation to its "purpose" in being a created organism. If this potential energy is not utilized in harmony with Nature, Nature will counterbalance it with the collective potential energy of other organisms.

Interconnectedness & Age
(Continuation of Discussion on the Concept of Hierarchy and Interconnectedness).

Children have the desire for 'life' and the least ability to actualize it; while elders have the knowledge and wisdom to actualize, but are lacking in the energy to actualize it. There is no 'hierarchy' in terms of interconnectedness - children, elders, and those in-between must be valued relationally, within a community unit because without the passion of youth and the wisdom and humility of old age a society is inhibited from critical thinking and collective self-actualization and development.

Even Maslow's 'hierarchy of needs' is a psychological abstraction. Thought forms are "real" like physical forms; both are assemblages of energy. The non-fulfillment of the higher levels leaves one to the non-fulfillment of the 'higher' levels of needs leaves no room for the differentiation between greater and lesser stressors. If one is preoccupied with goals of transcendental development and self-actualization, the non-fulfillment of lower levels is "less stressful" because in the mind of this person, it is worse to have "stagnated" one's personal development rather than to suffer from material poverty. While this is true, if physical lack is so prolonged as to not adequately sustain life, the person may not lose hold of the value of the higher ideal, but their body (the vehicle to achieve Self-Actualization) will die and disallow continued "development". But for some even this may be the goal in itself – to expend all possible life energy in the pursuit of achieving "ascendance".

Note: You must promote the 'Culture of Consumption' as to not allow the proliferation of the number of people in Your subject nation-state that essentially live to die, i.e. living for the purpose of actualizing their perceived purpose fully until physical death is achieved/expend all possible life energy in the pursuit of achieving "ascendance". This kind of person is immune to the need to consume solely for the purpose of consumption and possession, and cannot be corrupted by Your external psycho-cultural influence.

Hierarchy & Darwinism.

Social Darwinism has deep roots in the German ultra-right... like Anglo American social Darwinism, German social Darwinism projected human social institutions onto the nonhuman world as 'natural laws,' then invoked these 'laws' to justify the human social arrangements as 'natural.' It also applied the maxim 'survival of the fittest' to society. But where Anglo American social Darwinism conceived the 'fittest' as the individual entrepreneur in a bloody tooth and claw capitalist jungle, German social Darwinism overwhelmingly conceived the 'fittest' in terms of race. Thus, the 'fittest' race not only would but should survive, vanquishing all its competitors in its struggle for existence.[245]

---

245.   Janet Biehl, " 'Ecology' and the Modernization of Fascism in the German Ultra-right", Introduction to Ecofascism, Lessons from the German Experience, by Janet Biehl and Peter Staudenmaier, AK Press, 1995, Scotland.

Chapter 20:
Human Nature

In truth, there is not one 'Universal' Human Nature. There is a range that varies between "extremes" of spiritual and physical states of existence. Those more towards the spiritual pole live with a less invasive approach to Nature, seek more harmonious living, and view physical life as nothing more than a growing period, and physical death as the transition back to the "real" spiritual world (more stable than predatory); while those more towards the physical pole are fixated more on possessing and consuming as much as possible during their lives, have a more antagonistic view and invasive approach towards Nature because they view it as limiting their potential for possession and consumption, and desire to live forever on the physical plane (more predatory than stable). A simple way to view this range is to see one pole as having an understanding of the natural balance between creation and destruction and viewing human life and different from "animal" life because humans can decide to make consumption/participation in this cycle of creation and destruction as secondary (only what is needed for biological/physical plane needs) and actualizing spirituality/purpose as primary; while the other plane, like "animals" views "survival"/consumption and genetic superiority as their prime objective, with the actualization of true self/spirituality as secondary, if important at all.

There is a common human potential energy, but some humans on the physical level orient themselves more towards the physical and others more towards the spiritual. Those humans more oriented towards the spiritual are the easiest to exploit with the Culture of Comparison/Culture of Individualistic Materialism, because they are more consciously fixated on the spiritual plane, so if You displace their 'center', the void of purpose, center, spirituality is more noticeable, as is the psychic discomfort associated with this "loss". Because a more "spiritually" oriented person receives more "energy", inspiration, wisdom and intuition from that plane, if You can convince them (through Cultural Cognitive Dissonance) to deny this, a far larger conscious and sub-conscious vacuum will develop and You can fill this vacuum with this human quantitative value system based in Individualistic Materialism and Conspicuous Consumption, and they will consume with a voracious appetite, never to be satisfied.

Your objective is to pull those who exist more on the "spiritual" pole towards the "physical" by displacing their center and creating an addiction to Your Seemingly Associative Cognitions and cultural icons as a means of them attempting to reconcile the "loss" of self/center. Once You get them to accept the physical plane as the only reality You have then converted them into "animals" that exist only to consume and procreate in Your image. They are sheep and You are the shepherd – You can feed them whenever You desire and they are helpless without Your guidance.

The range of Human Natures: Physical to Spiritual

Physical-Oriented: Survival-focused, physical plane-fixated, consumption fills the void of purpose and the security of interconnectedness, desire to live physically forever - "the true goal of science is to create the fountain of youth and defeat physical death".

Spiritual-Oriented:
No death, eternal life, cycle of physical transformation to spiritual plane, physical plane is an illusion;

"Earth is the market place, Heaven is home" - Yoruba Proverb

actualizing purpose and using ones gifts is the focus of one's life, for personal spiritual development to which excessive attachment is not advised or desirable.

Human Nature & Self Preservation.
Even the concept of self-preservation falls within this range. Physical-oriented humans perceive self-preservation as protecting their body and important interests, while spiritual-oriented humans include spiritual integration, honor, and culture/purpose within this definition of 'body', therefore one leaning toward this side would lose their body to "preserve" their 'self'.

Human Nature & Purpose.

Human beings have forgotten their purpose. Humans exist to create. They should only destroy enough to create with. "Modern man's" sole aim is to destroy (consume). Creation and use (consumption) are to be complementary i.e. creation for destruction and destruction for creation in balance.

Consumption & Physical Plane-Oriented Human Nature (Vampirism).

The process by which You transform Your subject's nation-state into one that serves You through an endless, insatiable desire to consume, even to its own demise, is essentially the same process by which a "vampire" turns its victim.

Through a series of simultaneous dis-locative projections and external influence, You weaken Your subject nation-state to the point of near-death. Then infuse it with some of Your blood (the blood of Individualistic Materialism and Conspicuous Consumption that You project onto it) and it believes that the decision to partake of "Your blood" is a positive one because You promise it "eternal life", on the brink of its physical death. It does not realize that this "eternal life" that You offer is eternal physical life not eternal spiritual life – which it already possessed before You convinced it to deny its center. By consuming of "Your blood" it takes the remaining steps to let its "body" die and is reborn in Your image through the acceptance of a vacuum of the perpetual need to consume for the sake of consumption and possession. Like a vampire, because it has lost its "soul"/center, it must feast on the life energy/ blood of Other less powerful persons and nation-states. If it does not it will truly 'die' because it has denied its conscious and sub-conscious connection to its center – that what exists to bind and sustain it.[246]

Wolves in Sheep's Clothing

"You must be the change that you wish to see in the world" - Mahatma Gandhi

Those who speak of the shortcomings of "Human Nature"--excuse predatory behavior as "Human Nature"--and claim to do or want to do what is best for Humanity are all predators. Conscientious people know that one can only have an impact on the world through their own self-development and actualization. Only the most arrogant of peoples assume to know what is best for the whole of humanity. And only the most chauvinistic of peoples assume

---

246.   For a visual image of this process of vampiric possession/consumption and transference of the addiction to consumption, see Anne Rice's feature film "Interview With a Vampire".

that they are the "default" human beings and that Others are different at best, and pathological versions of them at worst. Interconnected peoples talk of their actions in terms of themselves or those of their ethnic, cultural, religious group--they own their experiences and take responsibility for them--, but those of 'the road of Separation' talk of their actions, in particular their shortcomings, as part of the "Human Experience" to excuse their lack of balance, while their accomplishments are to be attributed to their specific national or ethnic group--they externalize any responsibility for their negative past actions as the "sad reality of Human Nature".

Through Your influence, You are to turn the world into a world of "humans" of the 'physical plane' variety. They are to embody the basest, most selfish and individualistic of traits and be praised for this. In this framework, humanity is to be expected to be only a few steps from the animal kingdom, in which acts of balance and kindness to be celebrated as achievements instead of viewing interconnected and harmonious behavior as representative of "Human Nature". Kindness is weakness and moderation is a lack of resourcefulness in the quantitatively-defined reality.

Chapter 21:
Linear Thinking

If You are the point of departure, You are less likely to be adversely affected by Your cultural attacks on others, because the 'Universalism' that You project upon the others will be designed and engineered to support and benefit Your cultures. The dangers come from the following: 1. the proliferation of Your culture's ideas and thought processes of the Individual like lead to internal than external hording and scarcity of resources; 2. the support of brutal regimes that embrace Your ideals, but have to use brutal governing techniques to hold together societies fractured by the social cohesiveness-eroding consequences of Your projections: these values spreading home or to other regimes, whose eventual fall or emergence of resistance movements spawned out of desperation become mini 'rogue non-states' that use similar brutal means to attack their own fractured society or the society that caused the breakdown in the first place, Yours. People's independent, 'democratic' decisions are not independent and democratic if they are in an environment of (culturally and economically softened up society, projections/Cultural Cognitive Dissonance through mass media and icons); 3. brutal measures practiced outside come home[247]; 4. hypocrisy's adverse effects on codified law at home; 5. a codependent (narcissistic)/ addictive relationship between Your state and subject states.

---

247.   See Cesare

Linear Thinking
(Unencumbered Progress).

You believe that time is not cyclical and that one can go from point A to point B as an actor independent from the causal reality, i.e. the ability to act without consequences. This is the kind of thinking that children utilize; this is why their powers of discovery are so great. They can fully devote themselves to a task or adventure without any worries or the burden of responsibility, and continue to do this until they hurt themselves or break something. They can lose interest in the object that was so intensely focused on in and instead move on to the next item of interest with a mind free of any thoughts of the last object. They can dance through a room playing with everything until either it breaks or they lose interest, and continue to play until an adult brings them back into the causal reality.

Linear thinking allows the user higher potential for power over non-linear thinkers, because in their minds they are "free", free to do whatever they like at any cost to anyone outside of themselves; and they are genuinely surprised if they have to experience negative consequences for a past action. On the other hand, the non-linear thinker is "weighted-down" with thoughts of how X action will affect others – 'if X action is in line with established cultural mores', 'if X action is environmentally friendly', 'if X action contributes to a sustainable future', 'how X action affects their family, community, society, economy, environment, etc..'.

People "weighted-down" with thoughts of responsibility or obligation to others cannot compete on the same playing field as linear thinkers unless they betray themselves and also engage in actions without regard to consequences; and upon this step the non-linear has to deny its truth/center and can be easily manipulated by a linear thinker.

Linear Thinking, Conquest, Violence, & Balance

There is a direct correlation between non-sustainable nation-states and Your definition of "Civilization" and increased violence. The cycle of physical life is balanced by an equal distribution of creative and destructive energies. Societies that consume far beyond their biological needs create the need for a destructive counterbalance; this can either manifest within its population, amongst those it exploits, or even from the natural environment.

Basically, creation requires destruction for fuel: societies that consume large amounts of resources to "Progress" create a vacuum of necessary destruction to balance this. If these societies "destroy" on their own, i.e. contribute constructively to humanity or Nature--making personal creative or environmental "sacrifice" to balance what they have "taken"--involuntary sacrifice is not necessary.

A danger that exists for societies that are governed by linear thinking and are not if they are cognizant of the necessity of maintaining this balance between creative and destructive energies. For them "Progress" is paramount; thoughts of potential consequences are not acknowledged; and when they do come about [the consequences], their origin is either attributed to the victim/"loser" in the equation, or the "loser" is made to suffer the consequences of it. Because the origin of the unbalance is not acknowledged while consumption/"taking" is continuing, the linear thinker is unaware of the reality that whenever something is "taken", that something must be "put back". This, meaning that the intensity of the "violence"/destruction needed to counterbalance what is destroyed/taken to feed their creative endeavors ("Progress") is steadily increasing.

It is possible to "buy time" by expanding their exploitation to more and more places, but at the same time, because more "violence" is used, more "violence" can be expected as its counterbalance. No exploitative (destructive) endeavors go unanswered. An immediate response to "violence" is actually desirable, because it would be low in intensity; but delayed response due to linear thinking only allows the destructive energies to ferment, enabling destruction of greater intensity.

When destructive answers to destructive questions are given, people often see this as "punishment". This is an erroneous thought – Nature has no judgment; it only responds in-kind to what it requires or what is taken from it.

Be aware that in Your conquest that though You may take on a linear thinking process, in order to perform what You believe is a less encumbered conquest, in actuality, the time that You believe that You gain by not paying attention to the details (consequences) of Your action can be lost in recovering from reciprocal violence in Your subject nation-state, Your own nation-state, or throughout the world-at-large. The more effective and expansive Your conquest is, the greater potential energy You are giving to the destructive energies that exist to counterbalance You.

If You do not use all that You have taken to contribute positively to humanity and Nature/The Universe, You will receive an "answer" to the question that You are asking – "Am I God?" This is a timed gamble. You can exploit with a voracious appetite, but at some point You must make a sacrifice of Yourself equal to that which You have taken, or Nature will counterbalance You. The question is when, not if. Remember, the main danger that You face using a war ideology based on Rationalism/linear thinking is that You can actually start to believe that You are the locus of control, that You are the "center". When You cross this line, You are basically making a statement to the Universe – "I am the New God, try to stop me if you can. My science and technology is superior to Your power; and my Rational thought process can predict any possible scenario that you can create. I think therefore, I am."

You, in the midst of hopefully establishing a regime of Sustainable Exploitation upon Your subject nation-state and the world-at-large, need to also contribute a sincere constructive effort towards improving the lives of humanity and the sustainability of the environment at some point, in order to not receive the full brunt of all that You have created for Yourself. You must make a sacrifice: This may sound contradictory because I am instructing You on the subjects of conquest and exploitation--possession and consumption--, but it is not. There is nothing wrong with exploitation/"taking". What is wrong is not putting back in-kind. You must be a benevolent tyrant.

The Rational thinker out-thinks himself. He wishes to be Master of the Universe without taking the responsibility of being the Master of the Universe - He only wishes for the exploitative potential of being at the "top of the hierarchy". In truth if one is a "true thinker" – having highly evolved intuition and critical thinking processes, they could come to be aware of some of the cycles of creation and destruction and in possessing this knowledge, they could live a harmonious life/guide a people/culture in harmonious living because he or she is in alignment with the ebbs and flows of the Universe. If one surrenders to the flow, one can live "freely" because he or she is not moving against the current.

It does not matter whether or not You believe in, or are not cognizant of the Truth. Because You live in a causal reality, ignorance is not an excuse. Ignorant people should not be desirous of things beyond their scope of understanding. But they can be.... There is no crime in that, but like all created things, they are subject to answers to the question that they ask – "Can I have this?" – 'Yes, but what will You give in return'. Not hearing the answer--using only the analytical side of their brain (linear thinking)--does not make the answer away; it only disables the listener from hearing it. If you continue to ask, the answer will be 'Yes', but a corresponding question will always be asked – 'What will you give in return?'. If You prove to be ignorant of the Truth while at the same time asking questions that even a master would be hesitant to ask, the question you are being asked will be answered by itself.

If You approach the Universe with the confidence and attitude that You are capable to rule and to utilize the creative and destructive energies, it will allow You to use them, but if You do not act responsibly with them, to preserve balance, it will counterbalance You.

Creative endeavors on a grand scale are inspired and guided by the Universe. The Universe exists to experience itself: it is all possibilities, creative and destructive. Those who endeavor to be instruments of its song may do so, but they must sit and play for the whole song. Being that creation and destruction are the same, the choice that You face in the path of Conqueror that You have taken is how You will be destroyed. Will You "destroy yourself" voluntarily through self-sacrifice or will You choose to "be destroyed" by the forces of balance. Linear thinking allows You to be the greatest conqueror, but as balance works, it also can make You the greatest fool if You do not acknowledge the choice that You must make. If You "create" by using the physical resources of the causal reality, the choice is whether You "destroy Yourself" or are "destroyed".

Chapter 22:
Non-linear Thinking

In Greek mythology, the Titans (Old gods) were usurped by the New gods; later Prometheus (of the period of the New gods) gives fire to man so that he can "think". But the fire was not to encourage arrogance. Look at the fire as the left-brain - analytical thinking and the gods as right brain--creative thinking. The gods provide framework for conducting oneself in balance (emotion, intuition, tradition) The fire (left brain) is Reason (Rational thinking). But because information is received through the right brain and then interpreted by the left – the two work together, not in opposition to. If man does not use the lessons of both the new and old gods, for they sustained the continuum, and only uses half of its "intelligence, and worse, views its "other half" in oppositional terms, it is doomed to living a totally (supposedly) abstracted (supposed) life based solely on self interest with no checks and balances other than self-annihilation.

Non-Linear Thinking.

Darwin followed the same line of thinking with Evolution. The Rational thinker believes that he is Evolved because He is can think; but in actuality that very thought is a sign of un-evolving. We are the sum of our ancestors. They were sustained through balance, not 'control over'. Those who walked outside of the walls of balance were undone by themselves. The abstracted time that we live in lets us believe that we are separate from our past rather than being in a continuum of it. We are yesterday today. Not realizing the delicate balance that we must live in will be Your undoing. Becoming so specialized that that one loses sight of the interconnectedness of Nature and not realizing that a body runs through homeostasis, not through host-parasite relationships of the cancer-causing viral type. In sustainable host-parasite relationships the successful parasites are aware of how to interact with the host so that they do not actually threaten the sustainability of its life.

Time & Non-Linear Thinking.

Climate and geography, then, influence in many ways, but certainly the most vital and far-reaching of their effects is on agriculture. The Arabs in the vicinity of Palestine, after scattering wheat seeds on the ground, lead their flocks to pasture. When the proper time comes, they return to harvest the grain, then go about other business. Their climate makes wheat raising incidental. In the Philippines, where three rice crops are possible in one year, the people plant and harvest more of less whenever they like. But the Japanese climate and reliance - in the past at any rate – on rice as a staple food combine to create circumstances demanding a much more strictly prescribes, campaign-style agricultural system.

The following passage from an old work on agriculture called *The Farmer's Satchel* shows how the Japanese regard the strict schedule they must maintain if they are to produce enough rice to sustain themselves:

It behooves people to observe heaven's time accurately and to look to local geographical conditions. Farmers must never for a single day fail in these things. The acts of plowing and harvesting depend on heaven's time and on the calendar. The calendar is the official of the court, which must grant it to the people. The calendar is the most important concern of the emperor, and it is the treasure of the people. The astrologers must make the calendar for the coming year and give it to the emperor in the eleventh month. This is called to bestowal of the calendar. It must then be made available to all places as is the custom in both Japan and China. In Japan, recently, priests of the people of the great Ise Shrine come to bestow the calendar on the people of all of the provinces. It is a fortunate custom that this land, the country of the gods, receives the calendar from the Ise Shrine. Above all, the farmer in agricultural work must first observe the calendar with great care. One day's delay means one month's evil fortune. One month's negligence means one hundred days of disaster. The applications of this idea are somewhat different according to local climates and to the signs of divination. Though the time of heaven and of spring, summer, autumn, and winter are the same throughout the provinces of Japan, depending on the location of the region – whether east, west, south, or north – wind, rain, snow, and mist, drought and flood, cold. Heat, warmth, and coolness all differ from region to region. Although the cycle of the seasons is the same for the whole country, the blessings of misfortunes it bestows differ from

282

the sixty-six provinces, each of which has its own peculiar conditions. It is therefore necessary to give profound attention to all local conditions in detail. Not a single plant or tree will flourish if planted without consideration of local variations. We speak of difference among houses, but all things are one body in the truth of heaven and earth, and differences occur because of the four directions and eight positions. Places that are one or two *ri* distant have many dissimilarities. Clearly, then, places forty *ri* apart are not the same in land or climate. One must study with people who know the geography of the land well.[248]

Non-Linear Thinkers & Hierarchy[249]

Non-linear thinking assumes that there are no true 'hierarchies' while Rational thinkers contemplate their existence. Being that Nature, to the non-linear thinker is perfectly ordered and is an interconnected reality that exists as a formless macrocosm as well as a formal microcosm in each physical representation of it, he or she would not assume knowledge of hierarchies, if there are any, without the 'joined' insight of intuition and analytical thought = 'thinking'.

A non-linear thinker would view any person who assumed to 'know' the total awareness of "lesser" and "greater" of any element of Nature as unwise, if not foolish. It through this understanding that a non-linear thinker treats all persons, other beings and objects with respect – for he or she, being unaware of the hierarchies (if there are any), can not be certain of the consequences of excessive action against the "other". The "other" is not "Other"; it is "a part of" them. A non-linear thinker assumes that only at the Source from which all things emanate is the totality of knowledge; and without this "totality of knowledge" all actions must be taken with care, as to not create undesirable consequences, such as events counter to the sustainability of life.

Because the non-linear thinking does not assume the totality of knowledge he or she is at a severe disadvantage in dealing with an aggressive linear thinker. This is because persons often view an antagonist through the perspective of their own reality, rather than looking at it through the antagonist's reality/point-of-view. The naive non-linear thinker will presume that the linear thinker will act with the same degree of self-control, foresight, and conservative actions as his or herself while the linear thinker will have none of these restrictions on their behaviors and will view the non-linear thinker through the same sense that He looks through; He will assume that the non-linear thinker will also use any and all means to protect itself and defeat Him, leading Him to be even more brutal and careless as a precaution.

---

248.   Ben-Dasan, pp. 45-46
249.   In contemporary physics this same discussion exists in the debate between the applicability of particle theory versus wave theory (independent building blocks versus interconnections of energy).

This presumption of possession of the totality of knowledge simply because He is "thinking" (only analytically) allows Him to self-justify His actions and supports the solidification of His will to establish this desired hierarchy. Though this "Rational Thought" may be based on an abstraction" it allows the Rational thinker to focus His energies on conquest rather than dividing them on thoughts of sustainability through harmony or at the very least a better understanding of Nature through true thinking.

An example of this thought process – one might say that a predator in the food chain is "higher" than its prey, but if it excessively hunts the young or breeding-age prey or if for some reason the organisms that its prey feed on were to disappear, the so-called 'higher' order predator would also die. So in the perspective of the linear thinker it may appear that the predator is 'higher' ranking because it is "consuming", but actually it is just as much subject to the forces of Nature as any other being. The fact that it is even called a "predator" takes the presumption that life stops when it consumes, when it actuality something (either through decay that began at physical birth or through the actions of other entities, i.e. other predators, large numbers of its prey, or even microorganisms that cause disease) will be "consumed"/broken down by decay-causing organisms that will put the physical elements that made up its physical body in the food chain (being consumed by the so-called lowest ordered members of the food chain). For the non-linear thinker everything in Nature is "consuming" and "being consumed", created and destroyed, being that this process cancels itself out leading to "0"/stability.

"Life" is a constant contraction and expansion – there is no hierarchy. Using this logic, non-linear thinkers work to live in harmony with Nature as to not "over-consume" because they know that for there to be balance this "over-consumption" must be compensated by further "consumption"--to put the excess taken back into the cycle.

Non-linear thinkers may create hierarchies in their organizations and societies, but this is done through an attempt at true thinking (analytical and intuitive) acknowledging that they do not "possess" the totality. These hierarchies created out of "true" thinking are efforts to better live in harmony with Nature, efforts to better understand the cycles--expansion and contraction, creation and destruction--of the Universe and how to live better in unison with them.

II. Cultural Warfare -
Its Flagbearers:
Cultural Imperialism and
Universal Humanism

Chapter 23: Introduction to Cultural Warfare – Its Flag-Bearers: Cultural Imperialism & Universal Humanism

The Key to Cultural Warfare is disarming Your target through the rhetoric of Universalism. Bathe Your target in the themes of Universalism - "Universal/ International" values; Universally-desired food, Universally-desired clothes, Universally-desired brands, Universally-desired fashions, etc. In the desire to not be "primitive" or "unsophisticated", thoughts of cultural resistance are squelched by the Progressiveness/Modern-ness of Universalism. You project and provide a Culture of Sensory Stimulation and Leisure--appeal to taste, touch, smell, sight, and irresponsibility: The Lights and Glitter of the Big City.

Cultural Imperialism = Universal Humanism.

The cultural other is a creation of ...[Modern] culture, constructed, in part, to answer the needs of the ...[Modern] *utamaroho*. The *utamaroho* is expansionistic. This, as a cultural characteristic, is itself very important to understand. The ego seeks to infinitely expand itself. This kind of self-expansion should not be confused with the desire to "give of oneself" – to "merge self with other" or to "become one with the world." All of these are identified with the spiritual experience of love. Expansionism is the psychological, emotional and ideological opposite of these. Expansionism is the projection and imposition of the cultural ego onto the world. (It is possible to interpret all manifestations of "universalism" in this way.) It is the expression of arrogance, greed, and an obsession to consume all that is distinguished from self. In this setting, "discovered" phenomena automatically become areas *to conquer* – to be made *ours*. ...[Modern] expansionism is the delimitation and redefinition of the world in terms of the ...[Modern] self; as opposed to the "losing of self" in the world or in the "other", which is the obliteration of the isolating boundaries of self.

In ...[Modern] ideology the cultural other is like the land – territory or space into which ...[Modern Princes] expand themselves. The cultural other is there for ...[Modern Princes] to define, to "make over". That is why they can describe their new awareness of objects, peoples, and territories as *their* "discovery". This idea is coherent for them because according to their world-view it is their role to impart definition to the world. People of other cultural traditions and "persuasions" are part of the world to be defined; it is a ...[Modern] world. And in this sense, the conception of the cultural other is that of nonhuman. It is [Modern Princes] who define "humanness" in terms of their own self-image and with such intensity that the ethic and rules of behavior that apply to those who are like them do not apply to those who are not...[250]

Essentially, the linear thinker desires to define Himself as the prototype for all humankind, rather than as the manifestation of a particular cultural group. It is from this self-Universalization of humanity that the flag-bearers of Cultural Warfare, Cultural Imperialism and Universal Humanism come about. Either through malicious intent or the desire for the "Common Good" it is through claiming the right to define humanity on Your cultural terms and through Your worldview that You are empowered to be the Perpetual Leader of Humanity. At all times, no matter the gains, mimicry, collusion, and/or surrender to Your desires, Your targets will never reach truly embody the model of Humanity and Civilization that You project into the world. It is this

---

250.   Ani, p.403. According to Ani's glossary, the word "utamaroho" denotes: The vital force of a culture, set in motion by the Asili. It is the thrust or energy source of a culture; that which gives it its emotional tone and motivates the collective behavior of its members. Both the *Utamawazo* and the *Utamawazo* are born out of the Asili and, in turn, affirm it. They should not be thought of as distinct from the *Asili* but as its manifestations.
Asili is: The logos of a culture, within which its various aspects cohere. It is the developmental germ/seed of a culture. It is the cultural essence, the ideological core, the matrix of a cultural entity which must be identified in order to make sense of the collective creations of its members.
Utamawazo is: Culturally structured thought. It is the way in which cognition is determined by a cultural *Asili*. It is the way in which the thought of members of a culture must be patterned if the *Asili* is to be fulfilled.

endless impossible quest that Your targets will surrender their own "legimate" culture-based perspective on how to live on the planet.

In addition to being the locus of control that defines what is and is not the Human Ideal, You can depend on the fact that no non-linear thinkers would be so arrogant as to be able to claim knowledge of what it is to be "human" and what it is not. For example, a non-linear thinker would talk of the 'Chinese worldview', 'Akan thinking', 'Apache way of life', 'Japanese way', 'Maori thought', 'Cuban point of view', etc.; while the linear thinker would speak of "Human Nature", "the human way of doing things", "human thought patterns", "human behavior", "the shortcomings of human beings", etc. Because You speak for the entire planet, You are entitled to it.

How You take control is up to You, either forcefully through being the living embodiment of the Pinnacle of Civilization, the Heights of Humanity, the Culmination of Truth; or through the setting of a particular 'Humanistic standard' by which all people 'deserve' to live under, alleviation from particular 'economic, social, and environmental evils', or through the "best organization of the natural and human resources of the planet".

Chapter 24:
Universalism & Nationalism

One of Your weapons is the concept of 'brotherhood'/community of the human race. If You mask your efforts under the veil of this ideology, Your efforts can achieve an implied" morality". Where those You oppose You are, according to this logic, opposing the solvency of the brotherhood of Humanity and are therefore "amoral". Morality is 'intellectual', not 'traditional' for the Rational thinker.

Universalism & Humanism.

Universalism represents the ability to realize the universal good of all people – the concept of humanity's source. Nationalism's source is the self as the motivation, which is particular cultural behavior.

Universality

You must make Your nation-state synonymous with Progress and Modernity, even 'post-Modern'. Being that You use the linear as a framework, You must be the point of reference and point of departure. In the continuum of time, where You define different cultures as stages in Human Evolution, Your culture must be projected as the highest stage of Human Development - essentially, the Universal stage in which all human beings will eventually evolve into. Those at home and abroad who question the legitimacy of Your claim to be the highest evolved by listing the social problems that exist in Your society can be rebutted by the claim that those are the problems of the 'Modern Age', rather than admit that those are the problems with how Your society is reconciling itself with the same social cohesiveness-disintegrating institutions of Free Market Capitalism, Rule of Law, technological developments, and family breakdown that You are projecting on subject state.

Those who dissent can be marginalized as 'not-yet-evolved' and incapable of even contemplating the problems of Modern Man. Your inability to solve these problems can be toted as "challenges of the Modern Society". When You require the world community's support of Your foreign policy objectives that are counter to the interests of Others, You must define Your nation-state's interests as being in the best interest of Civilization, Modern World, etc.--use any name that implies Universal benefit and portrays their opposition as parochial, individualistic, and small minded.

Note: some societies in the past that were very materially wealthy, at some point, decided it was in their best interest, to return to, i.e. that of pastoralists and returning to subsistence life. The anthropological term 'subsistence' implies scarcity, but in reality 'subsistence' living is often living in abundance, while being outside of a money economy. The validity of a 'rich' and happy life outside of a money economy that You control must be characterized as primitive and undeveloped. Using anthropological terms You can 're-name' societies like this with names like 'subsistence', 'hunter-gatherer', etc. in order to imply that they are living a precarious existence and need to be "assisted in their life of 'lack' and 'poverty'". Of course we know that every society that exists now is "modern" – it is the sum of the experiences and decisions of its present-day inhabitants and their ancestors it that abstracted point of time. Many of the societies that we now deem "undeveloped" were once "Developed", their present state is due to the cyclical rise and fall of civilization or the conscious decision/drive to return to a more community-oriented organization structures. This must be realized if the attack is to be planned properly. The wisdom of the ages of the Other culture is retained in the minds of the people. What You may think that You are "bringing to them" may be recognized as a flawed philosophy that their ancestors once attempted in antiquity.

This concept of Modern = my present-day culture = the highest level of development must be used in the Cultural Cognitive Dissonance process, otherwise, the wisdom carried in the people will negate the claim that Your culture has any relevance to them at all, being that You are an outsider, have no concept of their reality, and have a different worldview.

Alleviating 'poverty' among peoples that live in areas of abundance that You can exploit for Your own economic gain should be a grand internationally promoted objective. The goal is to bring every 'poor' person on the planet into a money economy in which You can take the vast abundance of the lands which they occupy and in return pay a fraction of what it is worth in the money--money that they can use to buy consumer goods from Your nation-state or from companies that You own or control within their nation-state, and of course a few coins and some vice--alcoholic beverages, etc--for their leaders. You can have access to vast forests, fishing grounds, mineral deposits, biopharmaceuticals, etc... The funny irony of this is that if these peoples were actually "poor", You would not be conquering them, because there would be nothing to exploit.

In addition to these re-namings and re-characterizations of peoples as 'subsistence' farmers, etc. by the very nature of doing so You are implying that those who live in such a manner are very few in number, so in the minds of people who would otherwise oppose You, they will see the exploitation of these peoples still living in abundance outside of money economies as relics of a past era, doomed to extinction, and relegated to monographs in anthropology journals; when in fact, it is from these very peoples that live outside of the money economy from which most of the new resources that You are obtaining from Your subject nation-state are coming in this "post-Colonial" period, the Age of International Development.

Your most powerful tool is the power of definition. If You can re-define something, someone, a situation and it accepts its new name, You possess it and can do whatever You like with it.

Some Thoughts on Universalism.

You should bathe Your subject in the themes of Universalism. You should inundate them with "Universal"/"International" values, and "Universally-desired" food, clothes, brands, fashion, etc.

In the minds of those living Your subject's nation-state, within the desire to not be "primitive" or "unsophisticated", thoughts of cultural resistance are squelched by the "Progressiveness" and "Modern-ness" of universalism.

You need to provide a Culture of Sensory Stimulation and Leisure--appeal to taste, touch, smell, sight, and individualistic pleasure-seeking.

Truth.

The search for truth is an endeavor that many human beings share. The Prince must claim to possess knowledge of an absolute truth – a black and white reality. Though it is actually impossible to know all Truth without omniscience, You can create 'Truth' through the processes of objectification and separation. You, as definer of reality, become its master. Again, this is only a tool for the psychological control of Your subject. Do not believe that You actually are aware of all of the possible variables to extrapolate data; You will be weakened by Your arrogance; will become less self-critical; and become liable to make disastrous errors based on the ignorance of delusional absolute certainty. This again is a means to disavow Your subject of any claim of higher knowledge that can benefit the whole--only You possess the insight to make decisions for the whole of humanity.

The quintessence of this process is very important to realize or You will lose perspective on reality. Being that You are not aware of the totality, all questions, theories, thoughts are derived from an artificially created point of reference--a center. Meaning, when formulating questions, the questioner has to place themselves/their culture into the equation to create a starting point.

To project Your superior intellect and wisdom You must create the view that Your inputs, deductions and conclusions are free of cultural assumptions and ideals. If a subject attempts to counter You – i.e. challenging Your superior knowledge, You will always have the ability to enlighten them to the fact that their perspective is based on parochial interests; not grounded in the 'Universal Interest of Humankind'.

Universal Humanism.

Universal Humanism implies a universal commonality between all peoples, essentially a 'global community'. Being that this is a Rational concept that emanates from linear thinking, "someone" (a locus) must be the point of departure from which the Progress or Success of the ideal can be measured. Being the 'point of departure' denotes hierarchy. In this maintenance of this structure, it is likely that the ideal of a 'global community' becomes more important than nationality. In other words – the universal commonality/shared-ness of all peoples is a community of believers in this concept. It is doubtful that the locus (point of departure) will also have the pandemic knowledge to manage and equally distribute the planet's resources.

Universal Humanistic Rhetoric

The following sentences are from Robert Owens' *Letters to the Human Race on the Coming Universal Revolution*. They are an example of Universal Humanist rhetoric. These appeal to the intellect and the heart with their utopian aims, while masking the universalistic measures needed to bring them to fruition, i.e. success is defined by the definer according to their own cultural lenses.

Any religion that does not produce in practice, universal truth, justice, charity or love, among the whole family of man is spurious – is of no value to the human race...

Happiness can be attained only by the united feelings of charity and love among the entire population of the world...

Charity and love for our race can emanate only from a correct knowledge of the laws of humanity relative to the formation of man...

This is that religion of truth, honesty, and common-sense, which the rational system can and will produce over the world.[251]

The 'Universal' is based on one particular culture, the one of the definer, You. Rationalist endeavors require a locus of control. Though the language that is used appears to be for "Universal Benefit" because it assumes the needs and desires of all in its own image, because of its actual actions on Others they will suffer from the shortsightedness of its own limited knowledge, experiences, and truths.

The 'Universal Good' cannot not be created from an amalgamation of all cultures because of the diversity of complimentary and balancing nature. The "sometimes conflicting", "sometimes cooperating" nature of mankind (humankind) maintains balance within the human race and with the natural environmental that it lives in.

Population, Balanced Management of Resources, & Human Resources.[252]

If the case of one being too aggressive in conquest, the actor will try to conquer the target nation-state to subdue and exploit it, but in the process of allocating thought (mental resources) and physical resources to 'expansion', it neglects its center and the perpetuation of culture and the social, economic, and environmental obligations to the populace and its land; and it will collapse from the inside. This is the natural balance. Attempts to 'legislate' peace are nothing more than means of seizing power over Others (it does depend on whether the motivation is benevolent or malevolent) and re-creating them in Your image and to the benefit of your state. In the oppositional mind of the Rationalist there is no natural balance: Nature must be coerced and manipulated into "acting right". A powerful nation-state that actually desires peace and harmony would redistribute its resources and those of its exploits in its greater ecological footprint to ensure that the basic security and esteem needs of all are met, as well as the cultural freedom for individuals and communities to each their personal/community potential in order to achieve a sense of self and community fulfillment. Because this type of fulfillment is "personal" and "community" -oriented and achieved through discipline guided by the point of reference/departure that cultural center provides, any means to "Universalize" anything will destroy chance at "Peace" because this "Peace" would be destroying the cultural centers that are the root of any fulfillment of potential that lessens the need for expansionary and self-destructive tendencies.

---

251.   Lowry, C.A., p.28
252.   The need for trade in larger nation-states comes from the desire for resources from other nation-states.

295

The peace of the Universal Humanist can be termed in a different way – "know your place". If everyone accepts their place in the social, economic, and cultural hierarchy that the definer names as 'Universal' it is in the best interest of all – and all will be well.

This is the same peace that is achieved through reconciliation processes that do not at the very least reallocate resources and powers in ways to address the root problems of the initial conflict. Without addressing the root problem there is no "fix" and true notion of peace. This is only a peace enforced through the use of force by "peacekeepers".

In Your projection of Rationalist Philosophy You must always remember that for the Rationalist/linear thinker, there is no 'past', only Progress.

Progress is achieved through "making mistakes". Because all that matters is that we progress farther and farther heading no-where, the "mistakes" that brought forth the "Progress" never have to be examined and their ill-effects never have to be rectified. Any casualties are just unlucky victims of the collateral damage of "Progress at All Costs".

Universalism, Humanism & Harmony.

Nation-states desiring to ensure perpetuity cannot engage in excessive expansionary behavior or they will be faced with the forces that maintain balance within the human family and the world-at-large. Like I mentioned before, the conscious and subconscious can be manipulated, harmony can still be maintained if things swing too extreme, but if the extreme is for too long and threatens the 'ability to return to balance' the unconscious that resides in all will have express itself to preserve the cycle of physical life and the balance of Nature.

Compliance with balance can be voluntary or involuntary. Those too relatively "immature" will involuntarily be re-acclimated to balance. But if the "relatively immature" possess a great deal of power, influence, and control of resources, this re-acclimation to balance will be painful for all those they touch and influence as well. The psychology that promotes out-of-balance, living will have to be eradicated or decimated to a point of minority thought again in order to promote thinking to sustain life and 'harmony with'.

Universal Humanism & The Enlightenment Project

Universal Humanism is a seemingly benevolent approach that You should use to weaken Your subject nation-state government's sovereignty and control over its modes of production and resources. To directly profess the tenets of the Universal Humanism--the Enlightenment Project--will be too direct for most nation-states to digest: i.e. a "borderless" world, free of 'divisions' of culture, race, ethnicity, religion all working towards the goal of "Common" Humanity. The direct acknowledgement of a plan for a humanist world government that is structured to guarantee equality for all of humanity would be, for many, a little hard to digest, because it directly threatens the existence of their governments and places them under the rule of a singular power that names itself as the intelligence that is best suited to determine the "commonality" of humanity. Without the simultaneous objectivity and subjectivity that omniscience brings, it is not possible to administer a world government without the influence of culture. This truth can be recognizable to Your subject as well as Other nation-states. You must separate the projections of the "goals" of Universal Humanism into individual ideals of Modernity--Free Trade, Rule of Law, non-proliferation of arms to rogue states, Democratic Governments, Free Press, Human Rights, etc. Being that the administration of these "ideals" is to be made by an abstracted structure, it will have to have a locus of control somewhere. Because a "common culture" will be espoused, but not accepted by all, "true" governments will not have a cultural mandate or consensus to rule; they will have to maintain order through the use of force ("peacekeeping"). The assertion of culture, religion, etc. and the rejection of top-down mandates (rule) will be enforced by peacekeepers who maintain peace through the suppression of diversity rather than allowing national balance to exist. Of course there will always be conflict; one can only hope that conflict is in balance (not the mass killing techniques devised in the 19th and 20th centuries). Conflict brings growth, understanding, and wisdom, but mass murder creates reaction, and negative growth (because too many die).

The lessening the destructiveness of a conflict, has been the reason for diplomacy since time immemorial; the tolerance of difference is that which binds nation-states together into a community capable of consensus or deliberate separation. "Peacekeeping" often ignores the root causes of the conflict: administering first from a top-down perspective that decides in the favor of the side whose strength serves its requirements for perpetuity better.

For Your goal of Sustainable Exploitation, nation-states do not have to "live together peacefully"; but should respect each other's truths as the Other's truth and not infringe on each others ability to exist as long as the overriding 'Universal' truth is based on what You project. You can allow the "respect of diversity" as long as it is grounded in a "Universally Accepted Human Value System" based on what you project as 'Universal'.

Universal Humanism & Rationalism
The appeal of Rationalism to nation-states:

> "It exploited, and exploits, the prestige of science, claiming to be to be a scientific system for a scientific age. It offered, and offers, deliverance from present injustice and misery, promising to all believers a new world of equality and happiness. This gospel of deliverance comes directly to the poor and dispossessed; to the uneasy and idealistic children of privilege it brings vicarious absolution from guilt and participation in righteousness."
> Communism and Christ (1962)

Dangers of Universal Humanism.
The first deception that must be promoted is the illusion of a diverse group working towards a unified goal, rather than a unified group working at the expense and disharmony of the Others.

If You do have problems in Your confederation - export Your problems, i.e. create foreign policy objectives that can be rallied behind as supporting the Universal Good.

Dangers:
As a response to problems in the user's home country, it is likely that politicians will try to convert domestic angst into foreign policy issues – creating an Other as a common enemy – projected either as an actual physical threat to security or an ideological threat to "Our way of life". Domestic issues are neglected and problems are stated originating abroad to draw attention outside. The external party used as a scapegoat may not enjoy its role as pawn and though its fate may be sealed, other countries may realize that they are just as vulnerable to being used as a pawn and may create alliances (possibly in the process unseating the governments friendly to the user) to ensure that they do not become rogue states that can be made into easy targets for the user's domestic problems.

Cultural Imperialism.
In the creation of the "Rational Man" a Prince must first equate Himself and the culture of His nation-state with universal terms such as Mankind, Humankind, Man, Human Being, Humanity, Freedom-Loving People, and Civilization. But He must be careful not to allow these terms to enter his subconscious thinking as terms of self-description. If You do, You are in danger of becoming lost in the intoxication of delusions of the 'reality' of abstraction. Because these terms are intrinsically-connected, You and Your state, no matter what the subject tries to do, i.e., meeting Your ideals, consuming Your cultural icons, etc…. they can never achieve it, because You

are always evolving and You can change the bar at any time.

Rationalism As a Culture.

Most cultures, even in times of conquest and Cultural Imperialism, blend because cultures based on relational value rather than on quantitative value (oppositional, individualist value) will have some semblance of sustainable humanity. Rationalism as a culture cannot coexist with another culture, it or the other survives; but never both at the same time. And it has a much greater likelihood of survival because of its ability to dissolve the relational glue that holds cultures, societies, communities, families, and relational individuals together. This is Your advantage: You are acting like a virus against cells that, because they do not notice your antagonistic motives, do not produce antibodies--alert other "cells" to Your presence.

Cultural Imperialism.

> ... nor when I use the term "imperialism" do I mean the extension of one state's legal dominion over another; nor do I even want to imply that imperialism must have primarily economic causes. The more modern empires I have in mind normally lie concealed beneath some theological or juridical concept – commonwealth, alliance, free world, the West, the Communist bloc – that disguises the actual relationships among its members.[253]

I extend this definition to that of Cultural Imperialism, i.e. projecting a 'cultural thought process' onto an Other in a way that the utilization of this process assists in Your conquest of its society and make its government a collaborator and contributor to its own destruction.

Nationalism.

The Prince must work to make the interests of the hegemony of His state an ideal rather than a concrete reality. The 'interests' of Your own nation-state can cross all national boundaries, deep into the ocean, and into outer space. You must create need in those who are loyal to You to protect the very ideal of Your existence and all potential interests, political, business, cultural, ideological, and resources that Your ideal of a state may possibly require at any time. In this way, the world becomes Yours to partake of, because all that it has cannot potentially benefit the sustainability and perpetuation the ideal of Your nation-state. Your ideal of Your state will supercede the interests of all others, because You project that Your state is what all Others desire to be.

This conversion of the reality of Your state into the projected ideal of Your

---

253.   Johnson, p.19

state is very important to the ease at which You can conduct Your affairs in subject states.

If it appears to be a purely nationalistic campaign--looking to benefit a particular group of persons or nation-state--Your efforts will appear as imperialistic aggression. The protection of Your external interests cannot be recognized as an expression of national interest--it must be in the interest of humankind to sustain Your hegemony.

Nationalistic Imperialism.

Nationalistic Imperialism--the promotion of a particular nation-state's interests outside of its borders--is what You (the user) might realize that You are conducting. You can never be intoxicated by the idea that You are actually the most evolved (Cultural Imperialism) or acting in the best interest of mankind (Universal Humanism), because You will be in danger of ceasing to be objective (as objective as an involved party can be) when evaluating Your plan of attack, sustainability of attack, protection against retaliation, contemplation of potential blowback, and governance of Your home front. You cannot be intoxicated by a sense of superiority. Your attack must be kept in continuous motion - promoting Free-Market trade and all of Your other rationalizing ideas through mass media and the efforts of individual corporations. It can never appear to be a collective effect of transnational corporations on behalf of Your government or a collective effort of cooperative nation-states using individual corporations to promote their interests. This type of Nationalism endows Your corporations with deputy powers of governance. Your job is to promote the merits and individualized responsibility of corporate governance and to use this disarming technique to manipulate and control Your subject's nation-state from all angles.

Chapter 25:
Modernity & Conquest Agenda

A Prince should use the concept of Modernity to establish Himself as the definer of Modernity, as a means of exerting control over the subject's intellectual processes. You should and must project the three pillars of Modernity: 1. certainty, 2. systematicity, and 3. the clean slate[254]. The quest for 1. certainty and 2. establishment of systems free of relationships to the natural environment of whatever it may concern, is easy to project. The third, 3. the clean slate, is more important and will require more of your attention. You must teach the subject that the 'Modern' means of problem solving is to begin from a 'clean slate'--ridding themselves of their 'parochial' traditions and beginning from 'scratch'. You are the subject's scratch line. This scratch line is very important in promoting linear thinking in the subject. Non-linear thinkers view reality in a circle, a continuum tied and held together through cause and effect. You must break the circle and begin a line with You as the point of departure. This process is so important, because the subject must be separated from its own cultural inheritance (this, of course, includes the intellectual and historical inheritance). As You do this, it will cease to view its reality through the lenses of its cultural inheritance. The intellectual processes of all nations are historically conditioned. Nations desire to utilize their inherited conceptions and ideas about the world to fit their present reality. You must, through the doctrine of Modernity, make the subject view its cultural inheritance as irrelevant, and begin with a clean slate with You being the model of its "New", "Modern" self.

---

254.   Lovejoy, Arthur O. (1936) *The Great Chain of Being*. Cambridge: Harvard University Press. p.59. According to Lovejoy, "...the conception of the plan and structure of the world, through the Middle Ages and down to the late eighteenth century, many philosophers, most men of science, and indeed, most educated men, were to accept without question – the conception of the universe as the "Great Chain of Being," composed of an immense, or – by the strict but seldom rigourously applied logic of the principle of continuity – of an infinite, number of links ranging in hierarchical order from the meagerest kind of existence, which barely escape nonexistence, through "every possible" grade up to the *ens perfectissimum* – or, in a somewhat more orthodox version, to the highest possible kind of creature, between which – and the Absolute Being the disparity was assumed to be infinite – everyone of them differing from that immediately below it by the "least possible" degree of difference."

Modernity.
The most important thing to do in order to establish control over the minds in the subject's nation-state is to make the period of contact with You the beginning of their "Modern history". When You define 'Modernity', You essentially wipe away the relevance--and actuality--of a nation-state's past and create a clean slate and new starting line with You as the Point of Departure and Point of Reference.

Chapter 26:
Why The Linear Thinker Is More Likely to Use This Methodology

A Prince must be deliberate in His war-making if He is to conquer, manipulate, disrupt, and plunder. He must do it for these purposes; not as a means of dealing with His own inner demons. I mean to re-visit, once again, the need for caution and introspection when using these tactics that I share with You. The Power of Rationality and Cultural Warfare on the *subject* will be disastrous and leave the subject unable to cope with the disruption that it causes for sometime to come. But my concern is for You – that You do not allow these abstract realities, that You project, to become concrete realities for You. If You view yourself within Rational terms, You will begin to see the need to repress the emotional aspects of Yourself as opposed to accepting Yourself and living in harmony with both. The conversion from "in harmony with" to "in control of" will create instability in Yourself (Your state). In this mindset, Nature--Your surroundings and environment become Your enemy. This lack of inner peace will cause You to desire to leave Your boundaries and Your personal truths, and enter 'an-Others' and through imperialism attempt to remodel Your external environment as an attempt to bring peace to Your inner environment. This will only bring hardship to You. This hardship is concrete not abstract. The brutal means through which You execute imperialist acts based on remodeling the external become Your 'modus operandi' and You will bring it home--and disruption will occur at home. Because You do "like Yourself", You will use more brutal means to subjugate the Other because of the discomfort that You are experiencing.

Internalizing Rationalistic abstractions may cause a cognitive dissonance in You – where You are experiencing psychological discomfort and the only means through which You can reconcile the discomfort and bring consonance back to Your psyche is actually through creating the abstracted rationally, hierarchically-ordered universe that Rationalism requires: most rational to least rational: Divine, Yourself, Lesser Men, Lesser Races, Lesser Sexes, Lesser Species, etc... You have to enact the 'Great Chain of Being'[255] to bring Yourself to an agitated, but less erratic state. This can also happen from internalizing the poison of Reason that You serve to Your subject; so be careful. Conduct warfare for the purposes that You state, (Sustainable Exploitation) not to alleviate internal discomfort that You bring upon Yourself.

Those engaging in Cultural Warfare are likely to be linear thinkers. This method of warfare is very effective, but is also very risky to utilize if it destabilizes social environments. When there is a dis-location of the society, economy, and environment You will need to promote a conversion of Your nation-state's government to one that is more fascist in practice--formed on the strong belief in Rationalism and maintenance of the State, and reestablish the mandate of the government to that of forsaking the maintenance of human security needs for the sole premise of maintaining the physical security of the nation-state, i.e. maintaining 'law and order', protecting private property, and protecting the population from physical threats, real and imagined, from within and without.

... it would be puerile to object to the European colonial enterprises in the name of "an alleged right to possess the land one occupies, and some sort of right to remain in fierce isolation, which would leave unutilized resources to lie forever idle in the hands of incompetents."
And who is roused indignation when a certain Rev. Barde assures us that if the good of this world "remained divided up indefinitely, as they would be without colonization, they would answer neither the purposes of God or the just demands of the human collectivity"?

Since, as his fellow Christian, the Rev. Miller, declares: "Humanity must not, cannot allow the incompetence, negligence, and laziness of the uncivilized people to leave indefinitely the wealth which God has confided to them, charging them to make it serve the good of all."[256]

---

255.   Lovejoy, p.59
According to Lovejoy, "...the conception of the plan and structure of the world, through the Middle Ages and down to the late eighteenth century, many philosophers, most men of science, and indeed, most educated men, were to accept without question – the conception of the universe as the "Great Chain of Being," composed of an immense, or – by the strict but seldom rigorously applied logic of the principle of continuity – of an infinite, number of links ranging in hierarchical order from the meagerest kind of existence, which barely escape nonexistence, through "every possible" grade up to the *ens perfectissimum* – or, in a somewhat more orthodox version, to the highest possible kind of creature, between which and the Absolute Being the disparity was assumed to be infinite – everyone of them differing from that immediately below it by the "least possible" degree of difference."
256.   Cesare, pp.39-40

Age.

If You are the Prince of a "young" nation-state, do not allow the relative youth of Your state blind you to the fact that most Other nation-states, though their "Modern-ness" may be recent, are comprised of cultural groups that held the cultural mandate prior to the establishment of 'Modern Rule' and are aware of history. Those aware of 'history' have more patience than those of "youth". First, through their cultural-historical inheritance, they are usually aware of millennia of historical trends, while those of "youth" may not. "Youthful" Princes that are not careful to be aware of the relative age of their subjects can make major strategic errors in the planning of conquests over the subject. The 'Modern' means and ideologies that You intend on bringing to the subject's nation-state may have, in a different form, been brought to them in their history. They may be initially silent, but cognizant of this.

If You have an emotional need to feel accepted by Your subject as "representative of Modernity", You may possibly be disappointed. The fact that You are using an ideology based on linear thinking may make You, even though You are more powerful than the subject, appear to be unqualified to influence or rule its nation-state. Applied linear thinking is the thinking of a child; only a child performs actions without any concurrent thoughts of the consequences of them.

When there is a response to its (a Prince's) influence that is a negative consequence of past actions, a young Prince may be surprised or even feel persecuted by the subject, even though it is a natural consequence to a series of past actions. Though He may be projecting an ideology based on linear thinking, a "young" Prince must always be prepared to take responsibility for those actions, so that the resultant decay of the society does affect Him adversely.

One means of keeping the subject from doubting the legitimacy of Your influence is to heavily promote the material aspects of Your power--Your cultural icons. If the subject is inundated with the contrast of wealth and Modernity between You and it, it may not acknowledge any thoughts that it may have concerning Your maturity to influence its rule.

III. The Dangers Of Using Culture As A Weapon

Chapter 27:
Introduction to Section III.
The Dangers of Using
Culture as a Weapon

One of the objectives of CCD (Cultural Cognitive Dissonance), besides causing a conflict of values and threatening the integrity of a nation-states' *raison d'être*, is to create a codependent relationship between the user and the subject. With sustained dissonance, the subject will require a "fix"[257]. The danger (which will be addressed in Book II, Section IV, *The Interdependence of Humanity*) is that resulting conflicting values that the subject expresses can initiate or enhance a corresponding codependent (narcissistic)/addictive relationship with the subject due to the satisfaction of the user's emotional needs, because of supposed 'need of the user' (You) that the subject expresses. This relationship can be very disruptive in Your home country when it discourages introspection and perpetuates the building of its own cultural esteem on the need for hierarchical position over 'Others'.

---

257.   A "fix" is the consumption of the "vice" that one is addicted to, providing them with the temporary alleviation of cravings for said vice. It temporarily "fixes" them.

Dangers of Using Culture As a Weapon.

Cultural Cognitive Dissonance creates discord in the reality of the target group. The resulting psychological discomfort is not addressed by the group (the subject nation-state's collective and individual psyches), because its origin is not easily recognized. It, instead, is fed by simultaneously placating the projected solutions. This creates a sort of "codependent" state. A danger to You is that You may also be influenced by this codependent (narcissistic)[258] relationship and develop a need to be "accepted" by the target group; thereby weakening Your ability to wage warfare objectively.

The Danger is that in the process of exercising Cultural Warfare, You initiate the creation of a sanitarium that is out of control: a place where patients administer treatment to the remaining masses of patients.

I will continue along the line of the sanitarium in order to explain this point better: You lure someone into your trap with the song of Sirens (from Greek myth) in order to rob him or her, but in the haste to loot the person's belongings, You forget to put balls of wax in Your own ears and fall into the same trap.

> Why are psychiatric sessions limited to a specified amount of time and frequency of visits? - to protect the therapist from the over inundation of his or her patients' problems. Through the exposure of the problems revealed to You during the session, You, the therapist, are is danger of falling victim to the patient(s)' "projections" of psychosis on to You; causing cognitive dissonance in Your mind, also requiring resolution.

> For example: You project Your image onto the subject and enjoy its expressions of inadequacy[259]. It is initially pleasing to hear these expressions, but the consciously and sub-consciously articulated differences between the target and Yourself put You in danger of developing a complex about Your own attributes, and losing the cemented-ness of Your own point of reference. The following are five examples of this:

---

258.   Narcissism and Narcissistic traits are discussed in Ch. 29.
259.   Two examples: For example, double-eyelid surgery to create "more beautiful" "round eyes", and "bigger eyes" has become so common place among some groups of East Asian women that these surgeries are given as high school graduation presents, and encouragement to undergo this surgery often in the popular media and in the workplace. In some countries where Black women reside in the West, a black woman wearing her hair in a natural state is a very rare phenomenon warranting complements for its 'exoticism' and/or cultural assertiveness; instead of "natural hair", chemically–modified hair is the norm. These examples represent how ingrained an inferiority complex based on a "Universal" beauty aesthetic manifests in the daily thoughts and life decisions of people. These examples more seem flattering, but too much exposure to them, can cause you to doubt the validity of your projections onto them.
See the following Korea Times articles: "Surgical Beauty Syndrome", May 15, 2001 and "Cosmetic Surgery For Better Looks in Vogue" July 31, 2002; and *Black Beauty: A History and Celebration*.

You project stereotypes of the men in the subject's nation-state as 'oversexed', 'strong', 'brutish', and 'aggressive".

The Result: You and Your population can possibly develop feelings of inadequacy -

"Am I sexually powerful?, Am I strong? Am I man?"

You project stereotypes of the men in the subject's nation-state as 'ignorant', 'buffoon-like', and 'incapable of abstract thought'.

The Result: You and Your population can possibly develop feelings of inadequacy -

"Am I actually so intelligent?", "Am I capable of abstract thought?", "What is 'abstract thought' really worth, anyway?"

You project stereotypes of the women in the subject's nation-state as 'too strong', 'over-powering', 'dominating', and 'aggressive'.

The Result: You and Your population can possibly develop feelings of inadequacy -

"Am I weak and insecure", "Am I only pretending to be in control?"

You project stereotypes of the women in the subject's nation-state as 'seductive', 'passive', 'willing to please', and 'docile'.

The Result: You and Your population can possibly develop feelings of inadequacy -

"Am a feminine?", "Am I attractive?", "Am I too aggressive?", "Am I balanced ?"

You project stereotypes of the men and women in the subject's nation-state as 'lazy', 'sloth-like', and 'devoid of seriousness and a strong work ethic'.

The Result: You and Your population may possibly feelings of inadequacy -

"Am I am efficient as I think I am?", "Are my work processes beneficial to the expedient meeting of my professional goals and objectives, or just a series of protocols, formalities, analysis and subsequent characterization and definition in order to fulfill a need for a feeling of control?", "Am I only a slave to a wage farm that lulled me into voluntarily embracing more drudgery?", "Do I enjoy my life?", "How does my actual quality of life compared to theirs?", "Am I self-fulfilled, or am I living the same day over and over again to the benefit of a 'superior'?".

Through the perpetuation of these stereotypes through the projection mechanisms, Your population can develop the same feelings of inadequacy and will require the continual projection of these cognitions in order to reconcile possible cognitive dissonance due to 'dissociative' thoughts resulting from contemplating these possible inadequacies.

Chapter 28:
Why This Methodology of Cultural Warfare is Particularly Dangerous for the Linear Thinker to Engage In

With the opening of 1998, however, came British publication of work by A.P. Pomerantsev and his colleagues at the State Research Center for Applied Microbiology, a Bioprepata Facility in Obolensk. Using sophisticated genetic engineering techniques the Obolensk team inserted virulence genes from the humanly harmless species, *Bacillus cereus*, into *Bacillus anthracis*, the organism that causes anthrax. In addition, the *anthracis* strain upon these feats were performed was bred for complete antibiotic resistance. The result, it appeared, was an entirely new form of anthrax that was, indeed, resistant to penicillin and vaccines, and was capable of residing dangerously inside human cells in ways never previously seen with anthrax.

Lederburg was stunned.

"This as far as I know is the first example of an artificially contrived new pathogen " the elder statesman of biology told his colleagues. "The kind of obvious cat is out of the bag... It's the thought of this kind of work going on sub rosa that is really the black cloud hanging over us."...

Pomerantsev's group had obtained all that they needed from Western sources simply by exploiting the candid atmosphere of basic biology and public health research. The technique that they used to modify *B. anthracis* was borrowed from work published by cell biologist Daniel Portney of the University of California, Nerkley. Portney worked with a different organism – *Bacillus subtilis*. In 1990 he succeeded in forcing *B. subtilis* to express genes from another bacterial species – *Listeria monocytogenes* – resulting in new capabilities for the organism. In particular, Portney crafted *Listeria* genes for destruction of red blood cells in *B. subtilis*, making a new bacterium that could punch holes in red blood cells and survive outside of the soil milieu in which such organisms were usually confined. It was an innocent sort of study, of the type academic researchers in the West were most inclined to perform. Call it "proof of principle," the Portney effort simply showed that the more primitive bacterial organism possessed the necessary machinery for sophisticated activity, provided it got the right genetic blueprints.

Pomerantsev's group paid homage to the Porney work: the cloning of the structural gene for the *L. monocytogenes* hemolysin into an asperogenic mutant of *Bacillus subtilis* resulted in conversion of common soil bacterium into a parasite that can grow in the cytoplasm of a mammalian cell. According to this model an acquisition of hemolytic properties by *B. antracis* strains can allow them to escape host immunity by means of penetrating host cells. The data presented in this study confirm the statement that (the evolutionary lead from an extracellular existence to an intracellular lifestyle may only require the acquisition of a limited number of genes.'"

In other words, a literal garden-variety bug could be transformed into one that could thrive inside the human bloodstream.

Portney was aghast. It had never occurred to him that the work did converting the *B. subtilis* soil bacteria into one that could live inside mouse cells could also apply to other soil organisms – including anthrax. When he first learned of the Rusian experiment Portney tried to throw skeptical water on it, casting doubt on the veracity of Pomerantsev's publication. But as he pored over the paper Portney realized with horror what had been done: his work had been perverted" "Now I'm getting scared." He said.[259]

Dangers of Linear Thinkers Using Cultural Warfare.

Potential Difficulties of Using Cultural Warfare

1.   Those who engage in it will be linear thinkers.

2.   Because of the need to perpetually project associative cognitions, the repetition and presence of the cognitions promotes insecurity and leads to CD which develops into codependency because You will require Your own cognitions to stave off psychological discomfort caused by a realization that Your projected ideals are not working to their full potential or at all in Your own society.

3.   Linear thing denies the interconnectedness of humanity. Linear thinking promotes the idea that actions can exist without any effect on the whole.

Princes that will utilize Cultural Warfare as a method of achieving global hegemony run a high risk of falling into its primary danger--instead of only projecting linear thinking as a preferred thought process onto a subject, they also use linear thinking in governing their own affairs and the execution of Cultural Warfare.

The very fact that You choose to utilize Cultural Warfare puts You at risk, because You have knowingly (or unknowingly) embraced a thought process that presupposes a great command over knowledge and assumes that

---

259.   Garrett, Laurie (2000) *The Betrayal of Trust: The Collapse of Global Public Health.* New York: Hyperion. pp.520-1

meeting Your interests serves to be in the greater interest of Humankind as a whole. This is while taking for granted that omniscience is the only means through which an exact science can be performed: having awareness of all possible variables, and their consequences. This mindset, without the thorough introspection and constant grounding of oneself to the reality of interconnectedness, it is likely that Your decisions will also be that of one who engages in linear thinking and believe that actions are possible without an equal and opposing reaction from the whole.

Why this Methodology is Particularly Dangerous For The Linear Thinker to Engage in.

It is impossible to be "Rational" without knowledge of the totality. Therefore, without omniscience, one requires an Other to act as a point of reference to rationalize, or divide a concrete reality into abstractions. Problems arise when the 'Rationalizer' requires actual control over the "Other" to satisfy his or her power, emotional, and esteem needs.

The Danger to the User is that: 1. He actually believes in and adopts the insanity that He exports to his victim; 2. develops a codependent relationship with the subject; 3. destabilizes the world to become the "ruler" and not take responsibility for the social welfare, economic, and environmental needs of the subject that He attacks and exploits.

Arrogance.

The Prince should not become arrogant when He sees His strategies working. You will likely be amazed at how actively Your subject state accepts Your suggestions of policy and governance; especially if You have had a history of aggression towards the subject nation-state in the past. Following Your lead, the leaders of the subject state have about as much common sense as a state allowing criminals to enact criminal codes and establish the judicial procedure of the courts that they are to be tried in; or following the religious teachings of a colonizing state that used missionaries and these religious teachings from missionaries used by a colonizing state, that are grounded in that state's own cultural woldview and interests as a means of controlling the people and separating them from their land and traditions. In this example, the same culturally-based religious interpretation and foreign traditions were transmitted though missionaries to the subject population, dissociating them from their lands and traditions, the things that had successfully sustained them up until this point, in order to gain control over the physical bodies and psyches of the people.

Time & Linear Thinkers.

One danger of applied linear thinking is the concept of time; it can be Your weakness. If You actually believe that time (Modernity) began with contact with You, this can mislead You into believing that there is such thing as linear time. If Your subject is of the non-linear tradition, it will have a cultural-historical memory that predates You, therefore acting as an additional burden on Your projections--its perspective of time is different than of that You are projecting. You may be projecting a philosophy of 'going nowhere really fast' ("Progress at Any Cost", based on You as a measure of compliance and Success, therefore it can never measure up), but You cannot actually believe in this philosophy or You will be rushing no-where quickly, while the subject has all the time in the world. If it can stabilize itself enough to prevent total social, economic, and environment collapse, it can outlast Your assault.

Non-linear thinking is what wins guerilla wars. A stronger military has far less time than its enemy. It must eradicate all resistance, or every extra day of military readiness will cost it in some way. The conquered nation-state has already "lost" to the conqueror, so it cannot "lose" and subsequently has no fear of "losing". If it wages a well thought-out guerilla war, the conquered initially puts up just enough resistance to cause the conqueror to believe that it has achieved a military victory. In this way, the "conquered" can conserve its military personnel and resources so that it can fight a long-term guerilla war. It can wage a slow, steady attack that eats away at the conqueror's morale on the battlefield (and in its home nation-state) and levies a slow, but constant expenditure of human and monetary costs onto the conqueror. And without the severe loss of life that it would endue in an asymmetric conflict as the weaker military power, it retains a considerable amount of collective cultural energy, from which it can derive the morale to fight a long fight to expel the conqueror.

You should never feel comfortable that Your attack (Cultural Warfare) has fully worked. It is impossible to destroy the third component of the subject's collective and individual psyche, the unconscious mind. Your projections may attempt to replace its consciousness and sub-conscious minds, but only through massive death can the collective unconsciousness of a people be disrupted. Those living can still carry the original center. No degree of psychological manipulation can totally eliminate the chances for resistance to emerge; only in death can there be relative silence.

Chapter 29:
Why Linear Thinking Leads to a Codependent Relationship With the Subject –
(The Need for Power - Consciously Suppressed Emotion - Unconscious Need for an Emotional Connection to the World)

"Dr. Toma Tomov of the Medical University of Sofia, Bulgaria, said that the real question was, "How does the Self gain esteem if the social organism is sick? That requires facilitation - it means coming to terms with reality." A reality that included the knowledge that everything you were taught to believe about the world, and your place in it, was wrong. It was, many psychiatrists argued, a situation that induced regional mass psychosis."[260]

Lauren Garrett, Betrayal of Trust

---

260.   Garrett, p.257

Emotional Needs/Problem.

If You, in the process of using Rationalism to control Your subject, become influenced and infected by it and embrace the ideology of Individualistic Materialism, You place Yourself in danger of creating an emotional and spiritual void in Yourself. The desire to obtain material goods as a function of creating self-value is one that is "not centered". It is influenced by the Culture of Comparison; an external stimulus. Material gain becomes the factor in decision-making; interconnected and emotional expression like love becomes of little importance. But, in truth, because emotional needs are forsaken (out-of-balance) for those not of emotional significance, the true quest becomes that of meeting those 'needs' emotional/spiritual needs. Your search for this inner fulfillment outside of Yourself and You will use power to force your external world to comply to Your emotional needs.

Rationalism and Unhealthy Relationships.

The following quote is an illustration of how rationalism and its oppositional approach to Nature and Others is expressed:

> ... The underlying principle that explains and unites the various aspects of ...[Rational/Modern] life and behavior in the need to control; this is directly related to and easily explains the ...[Rational/Modern] problem with loving. While "control" represents "value", "love" does not. In terms of the ...[Rational/Modern] conception of human emotion they are opposites. In this view one loves to the extent that one gives up control of one' emotions' one controls oneself by not allowing oneself to love. The experience of control is predicated on the rigid separation and distinction between self and other; love is the experiencing of self as being merged with Other. A lack of control is repugnant to the [Rational/Modern] sense of self; conceived as properly distant from.[261]

> But his is not a universal conception of love. It is romanticized (unrealistic), and it issue out of the inadequacy of the [Rational] self. The ... [Non-rational/non-Modern] concept of love, while more pervasive (that is, it includes mutually respectful and reciprocal relationships of many kinds), is supported by the structures within the culture and is at the same time not obsessive. [Non-rational/non-Modern peoples] do not risk the loss of self in love relationships because love is the natural state of being: offered before birth, guaranteed by the kin base natures of the culture, and therefore taken for granted. It is not anxiety-producing. It is natural.[262]

---

261.   Ani, p.395
262.   Ibid, p.395. This quote is also used in the section on Individualism. The underlining is for emphasis.

'Codependency'.

'Codependency' manifested as love addiction is a consequence of a rationalized society and breakdown of normal level of connectedness of people in a community. People can have unhealthy/codependent (narcissistic) relationships because from the onset of the relationship they feel "alone". The "Other" meets their emotional needs. In sustainable human societies, merely existing, i.e. being a member of a community provides one with a sense of worth and belonging. When one is not nurtured and protected by their community or family in this manner--safeguarded against abusive treatment-- they can be susceptible to this type of relationships.

The Myth of Narcissus.

According to the Greek myth, Narcissus was a handsome young Thespian with whom the nymph Echo fell in love. Echo had been deprived of her speech by Hera, the wife of Zeus, and could only repeat the last syllables of words she heard. Unable to express her love for Narcissus, she was spurned by him and died of a broken heart. The gods then punished Narcissus for his callous treatment of Echo by making him fall in love with is own image. It had been predicted by the seer Tiresias that Narcissus would live until he saw himself. One day while he was leaning over the limpid waters of a fountain, Narcissus caught sight of his own reflection in the water. He became passionately enamored of his image and refused to leave the spot. He died of languor and turned into a flower – the narcissus that grows at the edges of springs.[263]

Often those who read this story take the view that Narcissus "loved himself too much". This is an erroneous view. Narcissus did not love himself at all; he was in love with his image at the expense of his actual self. In awe of his self-image he allowed himself to waste away until the point of death. Narcissism is self-destructive pridefulness which is usually manifested through enthusiastic masochism; with whom affected insisting on continuing on a self-destructive path because of the need to adhere to a delusional self-image.

Introduction to Narcissism.

According to Dr. Lowen in *Narcissism: Denial of True Self*:

Narcissism describes both a psychological and a cultural condition. On the individual level, it denotes a personality disturbance characterized by an exaggerated investment in one's image at the expense of the self. Narcissists are more concerned with how they appear than what they feel. Indeed, they deny feelings that contradict the image they seek. Acting without feeling, they tend to be seductive and manipulative, striving for power and control. They are

---

263.   Lowen, p.26

egotists, focused on their own interest but lacking the true values of the self – namely, self-expression, self-possession, dignity, and integrity. Narcissists lack a sense of self-derived from body feelings. Without a solid sense of self derived from body feelings. Without a solid sense of self, they experience life as empty and meaningless. It is a desolate state.

On the cultural level, narcissism can be seen in a loss of human values – in a lack of concern for the environment, for the quality of life, for one's fellow human beings. A society that sacrifices the natural environment for profit and power betrays its insensitivity to human needs. The proliferation of material things becomes the measure of progress in living, and man is pitted against woman, worker against employer, individual against community. When wealth occupies a higher position than wisdom, when notoriety is admired more than dignity, when success is more important than self-respect, the culture itself overvalues "image" and must be regarded as narcissistic.[264]

Narcissism.

Some questions to contemplate:
1.   Should a Prince watch out for developing narcissistic traits?
2.   To engage in such a methodology of conquest (Cultural Warfare) would one already have to be narcissistic?
3.   With the projection and the cultivation of the illusion of the "separate individual" You are cultivating narcissistic traits.
        Is the cultivation of the 'Narcissistic Self' a by-product or a precursor?

Narcissistic Traits.

Watch out for these traits - If You are not aware of any narcissistic traits that You may have and moderate/reconcile them, You, while possessing narcissistic traits are in the perfect psychological state to develop an addictive, 'codependent' relationship with Your subject. If You are engaged in this type of unhealthy relationship with Your subject You will likely perpetuate the destruction and hollowing-out of Your own nation-state's society through practiced hypocrisy and the neglect of Your society because You are more concerned with Your image rather than Your reality. Additionally, You will likely engage in an emotional conquest of Your subject at the expense of Your true (physical) conquest. Instead of exploiting it and responsibly maintaining minimal stability so that You can exploit it for a long period of time, You would be more concerned that they embrace Your 'way of life' and 'values'--the image that You believe that You embody and what You are projecting--rather than providing You with the long-term gains that You can receive through a successful conquest of the subject's nation-state.

The following is a good description of a narcissist, in both psychological

---

264.   Ibid, ix. Introduction.

and cultural terms. You must truly introspect on the following passage. If You in any way can identify with the following traits, and/or notice deficiencies or a decline in Your own nation-state that differs from the ideals and 'image' that You project onto Your subject nation-state, You should seriously stop and evaluate Yourself and then re-evaluate Your relationship with Your subject.

Just because it is 'losing' to Your influence does not mean that You are not also 'losing' because of it. Your need to project a positive image of Yourself onto the subject may cause You to view problems in Your own society in a reactionary manner--treating symptoms, rather than in a proactive, responsible manner--dealing with root issues. If You are "in love with Your image" more than You "love Yourself"--Your own nation-state--You will ensure the decline and destruction of Your own nation-state at the expense of Your subject; and depending on how powerful and intertwined You are into the affairs of other Princes. You will also ensure the decline and destruction of the entire world at-large due to Your need to "convert" all Others in Your "image". If Your society has deep-rooted problems which have been dealt with through the internal projection of Your negative traits onto Your ethnic/religious minorities and the external projections onto Your subject and onto Other enemy states, and if You effectively utilize this methodology of control--Cultural Warfare--and project Your Self onto the rest of the world while neither acknowledging or dealing with Your self-destructive root issues, You will be projecting these onto Your subject and the world. Because You care only about Your image, Your image will be skillfully constructed so that it is so attractive that any Other will, at the very least, see You as 'attractive' and because You have disguised root problems, their defenses will be down, and they will embrace You as the "most beautiful nation". You are the Angel of Light shining so brightly that those in darkness can find their way to You. The danger is that such unencumbered, non-responsible "beauty" is so enticing to Other Princes; or even Your subject, that the moments when their heads are clear and unclouded by the façade that You project are so rare that they will not be able to give You the needed criticism that You need for Your nation-state's society and irresponsible external governance. If You construct Your "image" properly You will be a symbol of instant physical gratification – full physical sensory stimulation – seeing, smelling, tasting, touching, hearing, lack of the need for moderation (excess with no consequences) with freedom from responsibility. This is an "image" that once one comes in contact with it is hard to let go – Also, You will not take criticism as constructive criticism; You will see it as "opposition". Those offering helpful critique of Your policies will be attacked as "embodying" evil and lacking in civilized values.

It is a child's fantasy: consume all You like; an endless supply of goodies, and someone else will clean up after You. The problem is that if the entire world is converted into children, who will clean up, why would they want to clean up; where does the infinite supply of goodies come from?

I am providing You with this little tirade, because I cannot stress the seriousness of the dangers of unchecked narcissism. If You have any of these traits – You must re-evaluate Your entire being as so to even evoke cognitive dissonance in Yourself, so that You can be aware of the differences in Your perceived reality--Your "image" of Your Self--and Your true reality of Self. Otherwise, You will continue to destroy Yourself – if You do have these traits and they are un-moderated, You can externalize Your symptoms for a while, but with certainty, because You are not addressing Your root self-destructive traits, Your nation-state will decline and collapse, and there is a high likelihood that You will take Your subject(s) and the rest of the world with You if You can "convert" them into narcissists, or at least perpetual children, like You.

This is a very delicate psychological state to be in, because You will externalize and project all of Your personal power into possible delusions. Because You entrust Your sense of self to a delusion, Your subconscious will desire some sort of security. This "security" is requiring Others to conform to Your "reality"/Your "image" and "way of life". Though You espouse "freedom", in this state You cannot allow any dissent, because Your subconscious recognizes the fragility of Your condition. Any outside induced cognitive dissonance can cause You to essentially fall apart.

If these narcissist tendencies influence Your domestic and foreign policy, but Your entire nation-state's society does not also embrace these ideals, either 1. because the hypocrisy between what is projected and what is practiced, or 2. because they consist of groups that are demonized by the projections of negative traits onto them, or 3. if they consist of the dominate group and feel separated from humanity because of their participation in perpetuating this hypocrisy, or 4. consist of any persons ostracized or discriminated against in Your nation state's society because they do not embrace their "freedom to involuntarily conform"; the cognitive dissonance-causing projections of Others from the outside onto Your society can cause serious problems for Your nation-state. In which case, it will become apparent that, though You espouse freedom and diversity, the truth is that 1. there is a singular culture, language, and value system that must be adhered to for marginal assimilation, 2. it is impossible for non-dominant cultures to actually assimilate without great personal and cultural costs, and 3. the society-as-a-whole has been maintained by and an artificial center created from the projection of the society's deeply rooted self destructive traits onto its non-dominant culture members, i.e. racial, ethnic, religious, sex, and gender minorities.

The maintenance of a system of domestic oppression ("ism's") is used to maintain this artificial center without reconciling the root problems so that a true center can be created in Your nation-state.

Descriptions of Narcissistic Behavior.

These are quotes reiterating some of basic theory concerning narcissism:

> ... these statements are broad generalization, they bring into focus the central problems of narcissism: the denial of feelings and its relation to a lack of limits. What stands out today is a tendency to regard limits as unnecessary restrictions on the human potential. Business is conducted as if there were no limit to economic growth, and even in science we encounter the idea that we can overcome death, that is, transform nature to our image. Power, performing, and productivity have become the dominate values, displacing such old-fashioned values as dignity, integrity, and self respect.[265]

> "The more narcissistic one is, the less one is identifying with one's feelings."[266]

Linear Thinking and Narcissism

The brain is a "cooperative": its left hemisphere is designed for 'thinking'/analyzing and perceiving and the right hemisphere for intuition and feeling. In linear thinking there is a left brain-right brain split. Instead of being a cooperative organ, it is an oppositional one. Linear thinking only involves analying while non-linear involves both analyzing and intuition.

There is a great danger of developing a psychopathic or paranoid narcissistic personality when engaging in a thought process that requires a split in consciousness--a separation of left and right brain traits. When there is a split in the thinking process, a separation--deliberate or not--between left and right brain, the acceptance of self and its feelings will be lost. This is because the need for control--what drives one to think in a linear fashion--requires You to utilize only the left brain--analyzing--, because You would perceive Nature--where the right brain receives its cues and direction--as oppositional to You rather than complementary. Your focus as a linear thinker becomes conscious separation and control rather than acknowledged interconnectedness and desire to create harmonious relationships. This dislocation of self from its feelings creates a situation in which Your self-image--ego--become 'in control' and You consciously do not acknowledge

---

265.   Ibid, pp.10-11
266.   Ibid, pp.10-11

Your self/self-reality. To put energy into balancing self with self image would be to a linear thinker, submitting to the causal nature of Nature. To a linear thinker Nature must be molded to fit his or her own Self "image". This desire to control and manipulate Nature--which includes all Others outside of its self (image)--takes precedence over any honest introspection to harmonize self-image self reality/self-consciousness even at the expense of his/her self, as well as the outside environment that sustains his or herself. The need to expand, control, and be acknowledged as 'in control' by Others is all that matters to the narcissistic personality that will develop in an unbalanced linear thinker. The fact that You are utilizing the methodology of Cultural Warfare indicates that You are very likely a linear thinker. Most non-linear thinkers would not engage in this type of warfare because of numerous unknown variables that could spell disaster for the maintenance of its subject nation-state so that it can be efficiently exploited and because of the danger of insanity that could befall its user.

You must be aware of this possibility. To a narcissistic personality, self-image is a separate entity from self. It is the 'objective' mind – the "thinker", - I think therefore-I am[267].

Though You are actually in a causal reality, You cannot acknowledge this because You would feel 'out of control' and subject to forces outside of Yourself. To a psychopathic and paranoid narcissist any means necessary to maintain this 'self-image' are justified; and in the case of the paranoid type, You would truly perceive all Others as covetous of what You possess and representative of a true threat to Your existence. All true linear thinkers are paranoid, because of their oppositional relationship with Nature. But in the case of a truly developed narcissist, this paranoia causes one to consider preemptively attacking all who 'differ' from itself image. Because it is so dislocated from its true self it cannot receive any self-love that it requires to stabilize itself. Though it may disavow all need for feelings and love, it requires their existence because it is both a thinking and intuitive organism. This lack of self-love places an inordinate weight on the expression of 'love' from Others. If an Other does not acknowledge the superiority of its self-image and make considerable efforts to emulate it, it must be destroyed, because the pain of rejection is too great. There is no acceptance of self-love, so that is no basis for emotional stability. Its emotional stability must come from external sources. But because it does not actually love itself--it sacrifices itself for the maintenance of its image--it can not truly appreciate the 'love' that an-Other gives to it, so it rejects this love as a constant, requiring endless

---

267.   Descartes, Rene (1637) *Discourse on Method.*

tributes in order for it to prove its allegiance and love to its 'self-image'.

This is a self-destructive trap that You do not want to fall into. You must be very careful in engaging in linear thinking. It may allow it You to "Progress" farther than Others because You are unencumbered by thoughts concerning consequences of actions, but it can also lead You to insanity.

Individualism and Narcissism (Fulfillment).

It is important not to be caught in the narcissism of our culture that identifies personal fulfillment with success in the world of affairs." "There is an ego satisfaction to be obtained from such success, but it does not fulfill the basic needs of the individual not his or her potential for being. The basic needs are body needs and can only be fulfilled on a body level. They are to breathe fully and deeply, to eat with a hearty appetite, to sleep when one is tired, and to make love with a passionate desire. What is the good of being successful, achieving a name, if one is sick and miserable in one's being?..." Fulfillment in the full use of all faculties. It is narcissistic to think that we are only fulfilled through the use of our minds."... " A person finds his true fulfillment in being... in being the kind of person who through his own good feelings can help others to feel good, too." "One's accomplishments are the icing on the cake, the gravy on the meat. Only narcissists confuse the dressing with the meal.[268]

The narcissist image of success, happiness and self-actualization, is neglected instead for congruence with an external image – the one that You project onto Your subject.

---

268.   Ibid, p.188

Chapter 30:
The Development of an Unhealthy Codependent Relationship Between Aggressor & Target
(An Addictive Relationship Between Object & Subject)

One of the objectives of Cultural Cognitive Dissonance (CCD), besides causing a conflict of values and threaten the integrity of a nation-states' *raison d'être*, is to create a codependent relationship between the user and the subject. With sustained dissonance, the subject will require a "fix". The danger is that resulting conflicting values that the subject expresses can initiate or enhance a corresponding codependent (narcissistic)/addictive relationship with the subject due to the satisfaction of emotional needs of user, because of supposed 'need of the user' that the subject expresses. This relationship can be very disruptive in the (Your) home country when it discourages introspection and perpetuates the building of its own cultural esteem on the need for hierarchical position over Others.[269]

This relationship is an emotionally addictive relationship - for example, though Western Europe needs Western Asia's (Middle East) and Africa's resources to thrive and perpetuate itself, it also requires Western Asia and Africa to fulfill its esteem issues and serves as a focal point for pointing all criticism of itself that it can project onto an-Other to feel good about itself and preserve social harmony.

---

269.   This narrative is a reiteration of the introduction for Book 2, Section III.

Dependency.

If the subject sees its nation-state as quickly approaching collapse, and there is an actual representative democracy or an autocracy that is as equally concerned with the sustainability of the nation-state as it is concerned about itself longevity of rule, it may come to the realization that it is because of external advice and influence that the nation-state's society, economy, and environment are at the brink of ruin.

If the subject is especially astute, it will realize that it cannot change its situation by simply addressing symptoms. It will realize that it needs to address the root causes and this will require an indigenous solution, because it will take the collective consciousness and collective will to eliminate the hold You have over its society, economy, resources, and national psyche.

If this situation does arise, Your interests will be threatened, and from THAT point You should work to protect those interests. Do not, instead, get caught up in feeling that because they are ridding themselves of You (rejecting your control), that they are "anti-" you. If You do, You have lost all objectivity over Your conquest. Instead of fighting to protect the spoils that You have gained from Your culture war, You instead will be fighting for a feeling of superiority and fulfillment of a need of acceptance by the population of the subject's nation-state. Beware of this. This methodology is to empower You in a noninvasive conquest of the subject's nation-state, not to create a codependent (narcissistic) emotional relationship between You and the subject, where it gains direction and acceptance as "being" Superior, Modern, and Universal from You and where You gain acceptance and affirmation as Superior, Modern, and Universal from the subject.

Secondary Cognitive Dissonance
and the Development of an Unhealthy Codependent
Relationship Between You and the Subject.

Note: For a full explanation of Secondary Cognitive Dissonance refer to the narrative in Chapter 33 on Secondary Cognitive Dissonance. I will only briefly go over the mechanics of it in this narrative.

I will refer back to the comment that I made when referring to avoiding the pit-falls of linear thinking: believing that actions can be taken without regard (or acknowledgment) of eventual consequences:

> "If You make one of the mistakes of a linear thinker: as a linear thinker You may not realize that "projecting order" without actually establishing it will have dire consequences..."

When dissonance occurs in the subject nation-state's cultural center/ point of reference, You must realize that You become the point of reference and must deal with the responsibility of becoming the "center" of its society. If You do not, Societal Conflict Agents (SCAs) will cause a Secondary Cognitive Dissonance to occur. Societal Conflict Agents are social, economic, and environmental stressors that are trigger points for destabilization.

Feeding the subject projected cultural icons and artifacts will placate a great deal of the collective and individual psychic discomfort, but the social dislocation that will occur if these SCAs are not being addressed will become more of a problem. If it seems (again this is not an exact science) that the SCAs will too adversely threaten the integrity of the nation-state (socially, economically, and/or environmentally), You will have to decrease the frequency of Your projections out of fear that the realization of its true self (true situation) could exacerbate the discord.

When You have this much influence over the subject's nation-state, You have to decrease the frequency of the projections for two reasons: 1. to slow down the disintegration of the social, economy, and environment; and 2. to lessen the danger of You developing a codependent (narcissistic) relationship with the subject.

Because the people and government of Your subject nation-state are in desperate situations, they are prime for CCD (primary) because of the inability to defend themselves and because they are searching for solutions. They will look to You for solutions to these desperate circumstances, because they will "realize" the ineffectiveness of their systems and will desire Yours. You have to decrease the frequency, because if the decline is too great, they will realize a Secondary Cognitive Dissonance (2nd CD) because their basic needs are not being met and then "realize" the "reality" of their situation: that their state of decline is largely due to Your influence in their society and systems of governance. Also, You must decrease the frequency to avert the possibility of You actually believing in the "superiority" of Your projected systems. You will risk the chance of losing Your objectivity in the conquest of the subject's nation-state, and instead desire to continue to influence its society and governance because You "need" the affirmation of the "superiority" of Your systems by "those poor unfortunates". Dealing so closely in the manipulation of the subject puts You and Your society at risk of developing a codependent (narcissistic) relationship with the subject's state.

At the same time You have to be careful to not decrease the frequency of Your projections too much because, they are in "Your world" now. They still need the support of Your projections so that You can rationalize their self-betrayal as necessary for 'Modernization' and 'Development' This is not an exact science; You have to project enough to support Sustainable Exploitation, but not so much as to induce state failure.

You and Your nation-state's populace can be adversely affected by the "projections" of the subject's populace and government in the mass media, stating their desire for Your "benevolent guidance" in leading them to "better, more prosperous" lives. You cannot forget that You are the locus of control in this equation. The purpose of the initial CD (Cognitive Dissonance) is to induce insecurity that allows You to manipulate and exploit the subject's nation-state. 2nd CD is a danger in using Cultural Warfare, because applied psychology is not an exact science. You cannot allow initially hypothesized problems to affect Your ability to continue to focus on Your goal: exploiting the subject nation-state without causing so much instability that it threatens Your own nation-state. If You do not stay objective in Your conquest, the resultant concurrent "projections" from the subject's nation-state when it is experiencing 2nd CD will disrupt Your ability to wage an effective cultural war and cause major problems in Your own nation-state.

Your nation-state's government will have to "need" to "project" its "superiority" in the world. This is because a CD will occur in Your nation-state. Your populace and government will be aware of Your projections onto the subject's nation-state because of its consumption of mass-media. It will be aware of the universalizing "superior" developed ideals, policies, and cultural icons that are projected onto the subject's nation-state. They will be aware of the supposed "superiority" of these ideals, policies, and icons; and will see how these Others desperately embrace them (or at least in the mass-media, Your projections express the idea that everything that represents You is lovingly embraced by the Other as superior to that of its own). If the social, economic, and environmental reality of Your nation-state does not represent the universalistic utopian projections that You are projecting--the existence of social, economic, and environmental problems: high rates of crime and incarceration, wide income disparities, -ism's[270], breakdown of family structure, drug addiction, unemployment, rampant poverty, environmental mismanagement and catastrophes--Your population will experience CD because their "thoughts, actions, and expressions" will not match their actual reality. At this point, to reconcile the psychological discomfort of this dissonant reality, they will embrace the illusion of superiority and project these onto the Other through governmental policies and social attitudes, but will actually "require" the Other and Others to also embrace this "truth" of "superiority" of its ideals, policies, and cultural ideals, as well as the universal applicability of

---

270.   i.e. racism, sexism, classism, etc.

these cultural representations to any other nation-state in the world. If this occurs, You are no longer practicing Cultural Warfare, You instead are the malevolent participant in a destructive codependent relationship. Both You and Your subject are addicted to Your cultural representations and projections of affirmation and acceptance of You as universally superior to all Others.

You do not want to engage in an emotional codependent relationship with Your subject nation-state. Your populace and government will lose the ability to think critically about its policies and ideals, assess the positivity of its popular culture, and accept them as always the "best" and universally applicable. It will assume that regardless of any social, economic, and environmental dislocation that occurs domestically, that these policies, ideals, and popular culture are "the best and only" solutions, valid thoughts, and culture. In dealing with foreign policy, the government will assume the position that its ideals should be universally embraced and implemented by Others, due to their innate "superiority". They will not understand why these are not being accepted by all Others as "Universal Truth". Also, because the belief of "Universal Applicability" is necessary to alleviate the CD suffered by Your nation-state's collective and individual psyches, Your government and populace will not be able to see the shortcomings or mismatches of Your cultural representations, domestically and internationally.

A mindset of "Progress at All Costs" ensues: obvious bad fits and failed efforts become (desperate) mindless quests to "prove" the "Superiority" of Your ideals, policies, and cultural icons and artifacts. If this happens You will be emotionally bound and addicted to a self-destructive inferiority complex that threatens the sustainability of world, because, in order to remain seemingly stable amidst collective CD, You will have to "project" yourself as "Superior", at any cost to Your nation-state and to the outside. At this point, You will have become a linear thinker, and will be oblivious to any consequences of Your actions.

Codependency and Cultural Warfare.

In waging Cultural Warfare, the instigator (You) can never actually believe that They are improving the Other (subject). They must remain objective in their attack and realize the potential gains and the resulting responsibility of maintaining psychological, societal, economic, and environmental stability – otherwise They are in danger of being a codependent counterpart in Their own game. The danger of using culture as weapon is the potential of losing Oneself--Your point of reference--in the battle. Codependent (narcissistic) relationships easily emerge in conflict and under duress.

Carl Jung illustrates the point of not becoming psychologically engaged with Your enemy, or the stability of Your own point of reference is in danger of disruption:

> To know where the other person makes a mistake is of little value. It only becomes interesting when you know where you make the mistake for then you can do something about it. What we can improve in others is of doubtful utility as a rule, if, indeed, it has any effect at all.[271]

---

271.   Noted in "Sustainability: Positioning the Concept As a Global Goal," Global Vision's NGO Position Paper for the International Conference on Environment and Society: Education and Public Awareness for Sustainability. By Michael O' Callaghan. Organized by UNESCO and the Government of Greece, Thessaloniki, Greece, 8-12 December 1997.

IV. The Interdependence Of Humanity: How The Continued Use Of Cultural Warfare Will Lead To The End of "Civilization"

Chapter 31: Introduction to The Interdependence of Humanity: How the Continued Use of Cultural Warfare Will Lead to the End of "Civilization"

Societal Conflict Agents (SCAs) are social, economic, and environmental stressors that are trigger points for destabilization. SCAs can be 'conflict exacerbaters': social and economic inequalities consciously seen as inequities. Individualistic thinking can allow some of the subject's population to view these inequalities as the fault of those suffering from them, i.e. because they are 'lazy', from a stigmatized group, "that's the way it is", etc. Along the same line of thought, 'poverty' is relative to what one perceives those in power possess. Television has shown many "what they do not have and what the Other has", therefore reestablishing the definition of 'poverty'. For example, there are 'poor people' who own their own homes with all of their basic needs met living in Los Angeles. By showing the masses what they do not have; they are encouraged to see these things--Your cultural icons--, though presently unnecessary, so that they will become "future consumers" of these items, but are not given a means to obtain them. This is how You create 'poor people' from people that have their basic needs met. You add additional "needs"--the acquisition of Your cultural icons and the attainment of Your "success" model--to their mental list of what gives them piece of mind, feelings of stability, and self-esteem.

Social Conflict Agents (SCAs).

This like the subject being a stable atom, You make it radioactive by adding additional neutrons to its nucleus--Your dissonance-causing cognitions: the presence of Your cultural center attempts to replace its center on the conscious and sub-conscious levels--and maintains relative 'stability' through the presence of some 'control' medium--Your projections. At this point, it is not stable, but believes that it is 'relatively stable'. But from somewhere additional neutrons are forced and accepted into the nucleus of the subject without adequate accommodation by Your control medium and it (the subject) realizes its radioactivity, and will desperately do anything to return to state of 'stability'. Insecurities (social, economic, and environmental that evoke awareness and action, and can cause a 2nd CD (Secondary Cultural Cognitive Dissonance). The subject is in a state of cognitive dissonance, with severe anxiety suppressed through Your Seemingly Associative Cognitions. These stressors (SCAs) cause the subject (and/or its populace) to go into a secondary state of CD, but this time, there is no pre-planned "projection" that can override these additional dissonance-causing cognitions (solutions). The subject (and/or its populace) makes its own choices as to how to deal with this anxiety. This can be interethnic violence, grabs for power, scramble for resources, etc. The subject (and/or its populace) will make reactionary decisions due to a Realization of Instability.

This may seem like a 'nuclear' question, it is a 'nuclear' question, i.e. nucleus being equated with the cultural center. But it is actually a people question. The reaction is a metaphor for this equation that I am illustrating for You.

If You destabilize the integrity of a nation-state, You must reestablish the (apparent) center somehow or You will create a scenario ripe for resistance – project, project, project. In terms of the minority groups in the nation-state's society - even if they have second-class status, You must encourage the subject nation-state's government to try to make them believe that they belong to the larger group; or at the very least have the potential of integrating with the primary group and sharing in resources, so that if a 2nd CD occurs You do not have problems with the minority group vying for its own portion of the nation-state, because it feels disparaged and neglected by the government, a government that at the time of the 2nd CD proves that it can not provide for the needs of the people, or at the very least, has proven to be a party in assisting outsiders loot the country.

SCAs (Cultural Center)

When dissonance occurs in a nation's cultural center--point of reference--You should realize that You become the point of reference and must deal with the responsibility of becoming the 'center' of the society. If You do not, the SCAs will cause a Secondary Cultural Cognitive Dissonance (2nd CD) to occur.

If these are not addressed You will have to put energy into backpedaling a little bit on some of Your projections; and proceed while supporting (directing) Your subject nation-state's government towards a more fascist direction in order to re-establish its mandate in security terms, so that it can keep its society from deteriorating to a point where it is difficult to maintain Sustainable Exploitation.

Chapter 32:
The Importance of
Responsibility

Why Responsibility is the Most Important Aspect of Utilizing the Methodology of Cultural Warfare (The Dangers of Using Cultural Warfare)

1. As the controlling power (through Cultural Warfare) You cannot allow harmonious relationships to exist, but when projecting "order", You cannot fail to take the responsibility for the destabilizing acts of establishing order over harmony. The natural means of administration will become ineffectual and social welfare must be addressed or societal conflict against could surface and instigate problems.
2. If You make the mistake of assuming the thought processes of a linear thinker, as a linear thinker You may not realize that "projecting order" without actually establishing it will have dire consequences.
3. The Danger to the User is that 1) He actually believes in and adopts the insanity that He exports to His victim; 2) develops a codependent relationship with the subject; 3) destabilizes the word to become the "ruler" and not take responsibility for the social welfare, economic, and environmental needs of the subject that He attacks and explcits.

Taking Responsibility

If You take responsibility for sustaining the subject nation-state's society while You exploit, You can influence it to accept the idea of "knowing your place". When governing a society, especially diverse societies (ethnic/racial/religious, etc.), as long as You promote sustainable development You can preserve this dynamic of Your "superiority". This ideal is relatively acceptable for the long-term as long as the basic material and psychological needs of the populace are met. If the populace has these basic needs met, dissenters (those opposing Your influence) will be discouraged by the average citizen who serves a buffer, much like how a large middle class serves as a buffer between the lower classes and the ruling elite.

Y= irrational   X=rational (Your projections)

X's means of conflict resolution is "superior" – because they are hierarchical and orderly rather than harmonious. 'Harmonious' implies lack of control. Harmonious relationships are ones in which boundaries are respected and control is not being exerted on the other[272].

A controlling power usually cannot allow harmonious relationships to exist, but when projecting "order", the X cannot fail to take the responsibility for the destabilizing act of establishing order over harmony. The natural means of administering affairs will become ineffectual and social welfare must be addressed, because Societal Conflict Agents can surface and instigate problems.

The Problem: the linear thinker may not realize that "projecting order", without actually establishing it, will have dire consequences.

---

272.   For example, mentally disabled persons in non-linear oriented (harmonious) environments are allowed to "be", they are not "dealt with". They are allowed to have their own personal truths/realities. Because they are not overtly stigmatized; they do not feel unnecessarily persecuted (beyond their condition), so any paranoid tendencies are not nurtured, because they are allowed to "be" (who they are). Only when they pose a threat to the safety of other persons in the society are controlling measures required for them.

Chapter 33:
The Emergence of Secondary Cognitive Dissonance and the Resulting Instability (Exacerbation of Societal Conflict Agents)

The Theory of Secondary Cultural Cognitive Dissonance (2nd CD).

I will reiterate the discussion on Maslow's 'hierarchy of needs' and how it serves as a theoretical illustration of this process, as I stated it in the first chapter. After which I will describe the process of 2nd CD in more detail.

"Maslow's Hierarchy of Needs: At the bottom of the 'hierarchy of needs' are physiological needs; these include food, sex, sleep, and exercise. Next are safety needs; these include security, need for structure and order, dependency, and the freedom from fear and anxiety. Next are belonging and love needs; these include love and affection. Next are esteem needs; these include feelings of self-respect, recognition by others, feeling of achievement, and a good evaluation of oneself. Finally, there is self-actualization; this is reaching one's personal potential, actualizing oneself. In terms of my theory of Cultural Cognitive Dissonance, 'self-actualization' also acknowledges reaching one's potential in the context of reaching one's true potential in terms of contributing to the greater good of the group, community, society. Also, the ability to be humble amidst great admiration by the group, community, society is to be acknowledged in the description of the level of 'esteem needs'.

The humanistic theory, based on the hierarchy of needs, is one of motivation that outlines the steps that an individual must take to reach his or her full potential. According to this theory, once the needs of the preceding level have been met, an individual can proceed to the next level. If the needs below a certain are not met, however one must re-focus on the preceding needs--if one's physiological needs have already been met, then next of concern are one's safety needs; if those are met then belonging and love needs are of concern; if those are met esteem needs are met; and if those are met, one can achieve self actualization. Assuming that this theory on the 'hierarchy of needs' reflects the psychological reality of most people; one danger that You will face in Your projections--which You must watch out for is recognizing that these are psychological states, not necessarily tangible states."[273]

This 'hierarchy of needs' serves as a good model in illustrating how 2nd CD can occur. In planning Your projections, Your aim is to disrupt the top three levels through cognitive dissonance. As long as You can contain these disruptions to the top three levels, You are able to manipulate the subject's population to accommodate You needs in its nation-state through Your projections of Seemingly Associative Cognitions. If You are not careful (it is hard to be careful, because this is not an exact science - only knowledge of all of the possible variables and the resulting consequences can make an exact science), and also disrupt the lower levels, the subject's population will experience a Secondary Cognitive Dissonance, because through the non-satisfaction of the first two "needs" in the hierarchy, they will realize the desperate state that they are in. At this point, they will reject Your projections, because they will be of no use helping alleviate the psychological distress of the 2nd CD and the reality of not having those "needs" met. Your projections are tuned to be seemingly associative to the dissonance caused by a conscious and sub-conscious inability to satisfy the "needs" at the top of the 'hierarchy'. Your projections allow the subject to believe that it is able to meet these needs through embracing that which Your project onto it. If the subject experiences 2nd CD, these same projections might exacerbate its collective realization that it is in a desperate state and may actually serve as a target at which it can lay blame for its conditions. It will realize how destructive the ideals and policies are on its society, realize that its government played as a collaborative party to this destruction, and realize that the focus in these external cultural icons and standards promoted an erosion of its traditional values and social cohesiveness. At this point, Your subject's nation-state is ripe for a great change, because its leadership has proven ineffective in providing for the social welfare and security needs of its people.

In simpler terms, when the Societal Conflict Agents (SCAs) reach a

---

273.   This quote is from a narrative in the section on *The Theory of Cultural Warfare*.

critical level of promoting the disintegration and fragmentation of subject's nation-state, an additional level of Cognitive Dissonance occurs based on social realities.

Maslow's Steps of the Levels of Hierarchy
    1 - highest
    2, 3 - middle (psych comfort)
    4, 5 - lowest (basic material needs)

The Initial CD (CCD) is directed at levels 3, 2, and 1. The problems start when social realities cause a secondary CD to occur at levels 4 or 5. CCD is used to disrupt the collective consciousness and then induce a "desire" for "stability".

This is like purposely creating instability in the nucleus of an atom, to make it radioactive, so that it can desire to return to a "stable" state of existence, and in the process perform work for You. In this illustration, the subject's population is like the individual fissionable radioisotopes in a nuclear reactor. Fission is created by allowing extra neutrons to be captured into the nucleus of a fissionable atom for the sole purpose of making it more radioactive so that it can produce energy to do work. This is just like You destabilizing the subject's state so that You can exploit it. Inducing Cultural Cognitive Dissonance can be equated to the fuel rods that are placed in the presence of the fissionable materials to induce a reaction. The control rods in the reactor used to keep a degree of control over the reaction are like the projections of Your Seemingly Associative Cognitions. These rods absorb radiation so that the collective reaction does not get too "hot". If the containment pool were to drain, and the fissionable materials were to begin to get "hot", but You did not stop the deterioration of the conditions of the reactor core from continuing (the total draining of the containment pool and subsequent failure of some of the control rods due to the intense heat) and simply relied on the cooling rods to prevent the source radioisotopes from getting too hot, the reactor would go "critical". This means that radioisotopes would now have their chance to return to a state of rest (stability), but in this process of returning to relative "stability"--for example in the case of uranium, it transitions into its 'daughters' until it reaches "stability" in finally becoming lead--they would cause a great of destruction to their surrounding environment--actually making it radioactive as well--and would take a great deal of time to resolve itself and once again rest. This is the same as You allowing the conditions of the subject's state to deteriorate to the point where projections can no longer help prevent a realization of the "truth'--that it is (made artificially) unstable. "Newly independent states" from the Colonial era are like fissionable materials like uranium at the beginning of the process. They are already radioactive, but in a state of "relative stability" because of the time it will take to return to a state of rest, i.e. lead. (lead is the end product of decay scheme of uranium). However, they are easily agitated by neutrons with enough energy. While nation-states that are not (non-newly "freed" nation-states) would be like the "noble gases", i.e. krypton, xenon - very hard to force into instability because they are so immersed in their culture, they will have a short but very violent change back to themselves if they are forced to "lose center". They would likely (or prefer to) die before "losing center". Going critical can be equated to a coup d'tat/revolution/anarchy that leads to regional conflict and instability because the "failure" of subject's nation-state.

When CCD is used to initiate a process of creating the desire to achieve stability and the original cultural and societal safeguards are not in place, there is a danger of Societal Conflict Agents "going critical". At the initial stages of 2nd CD, large segments of the subject's population can still be influenced by projections, but splinter elements, will emerge to "reestablish order, traditional values, social welfare, prosperity" and will have to either utilize old methods--which may be hard to utilize because too many of the population have new "points of reference"--or still try to use solutions from Your influence and tradition which will likely be technical solutions rather than addressing the root causes of the Societal Conflict Agents.

There is an additional danger: Though the Societal Conflict Agents may not have existed by the initial CCD, they may have been created by the induced psychological discomfort. For example, if a system is not in place to address the new material needs of the people (because of the promotion of materialism via CCD), and the means of obtaining these goods is not established, a secondary CD may emerge as a result. Under non-agitated circumstances this would not cause dissonance, but because of psychological importance given to new material goods, the desire for these goods becomes a "need" and is therefore established in the hierarchy of needs.

Societal Conflict Agents – Truth.

The stressors that "plague" humanity now, are the "plagues" of the Modern Era. If people had not been to effectively grow food, treat disease, acquire water, live with natural disasters, etc., they would not exist today. They would have died out millennia ago. Many of the "problems" that "plague" them are actually "Modern Problems" that exist due to Your influence or are the legacy of other Princes from the Colonial era. You should promote onto the subject that the idea without You--Your influence, advice, cultural icons and artifacts--, it would not survive.

The Danger to You.

The Danger to You is 2nd CCD. If things slip too far, i.e. individual and social, economic, environmental breakdown – they will see You as an active participant in their demise because the preliminary CCD will be replaced by the 2nd CCD.

Societal Conflict Agents and
Secondary Cognitive Dissonance.

The initial Cultural Cognitive Dissonance (CCD) dislocates the subject's 'center' and replaces it with Yours through the projection of Your Seemingly Associative Cognitions (SACs). A Secondary Cognitive Dissonance (2nd CD) is caused by Societal Conflict Agents and/or the re-definition of poverty, success, family, and community resulting from the influence of the CCD and projections of SACs.

This 2nd CD follows Maslow's theory of the hierarchy of needs. The stimulation of psychological discomfort in the subject can cause a "realization" of deficiency on one or more levels of the 'hierarchy of needs'.

Secondary Cognitive Dissonance -
Economics & Family Breakdown

Due to the economic uncertainty brought by the dislocation of economy from society in the subject's nation-state, workers will be under a great deal of stress due to insecurity about the labor market. As long as external forces dictate the subject's economic reality and encourage the subsequent reactionary policies of compliance to the 'Modern Democratic Ideal' and quick fixes to the destruction caused by these policies there will be an insecure future in labor market. This insecurity compounding by the dissolution of the extended family to support the necessity of the mobile labor force, not bound to any locale and relocating upon receiving any news of any better paying "more secure" employment, will be more likely to try to use the democratic process to protest the government's embrace of these destructive policies. Those frustrated with the lack of concern by the government to their issues of insecurity are likely to embrace political solutions that seem to take their needs more into account.

If this insecurity grows to the point that the people feel that their security needs are truly threatened and/or their esteem needs are not met because they have to endure more and more degrading work experiences from employers that exploit their vulnerability, a Secondary Cognitive Dissonance can occur – causing the person to realize that their reality is unstable and is not being served by his or her government.

The Culture of Comparison becomes disempowered because the attainment of basic needs and security becomes the issue. When this realization of instability comes to fruition, there is a great chance that the person will also look at the society, and realize how different it is from "the good old days", "the Golden Age", or any other time of cultural heights that would bring cultural pride to them.

At this point, this realization becomes one of dislocation of cultural center. They realize that under "their old rules, past traditions, and method of governance" that at the very least, their basic needs could be met. This is an illustration of how Societal Conflict Agents can undo Your control over the population.

When the population desires the "past" to correct the present, Your control and influence over the subject's nation-state is threatened. People at this stage of 2nd CD are also primed to at least consider alternatives to the government/ socio-economic system that is failing them.

Secondary Cognitive Dissonance & Family

Family – part of the realization is that of the importance of family. They will realize that in hard times as extended family, the basic unit of a community or society is what shielded them from severe hardship in the past. Larger family units could pull together pool resources, and work collectively to ensure the family's survival, as well as the growth and perpetuation of the family and the greater community or society to which it belongs.

As newly-born Individuals they have been "freed" of their extended family, community, and social obligations, but paradoxically also "freed" from the security of extended family, community, and society.

This realization causes dissonance, but for this 2nd Cognitive Dissonance You have Your projections to be Seemingly Associative Cognitions, they are being used to induce the primary CD. And there is no other projections that You can use--there are two roads, one of separation and one of harmony. You are projecting separation, so if You do think that the Societal Conflict Agents are inducing two much 2nd CD in Your subject's society, You have to reduce the frequency of Your projections to allow some healing of the society. A hybrid culture in which You have influence is at least sustained in the beginning, until they create means of utilized outside goods, and technology, etc. to serve their particular needs and their desired rate of consumption or rejection; and is better than causing the society to fracture and throw You out in a desperate move by the people to set up a present-day "idealized past" "tradition"-oriented regime in hopes that order and security can be brought back into their lives.

Ethnic/Religious Conflict & SCAs.

If Your subject's nation-state was created as an abstract structure rather than through cultural mandate and has minority groups inside, the "national identity" that unites them under one umbrella, problems between these groups may erupt if SCAs (societal conflict agents) (actual or perceived) exacerbate hardships to the point where the abstracted core that binds the nation-state together is pulled apart from pressure within the center. If the ethnic group surrenders, at least partially, the prominence of their individual center as a means of consensus for a common nationality, it will do so as long as it is advantageous for that particular group to belong to this "confederation". If this "confederation" proves to be unable to meet the basic security needs of the group, as a group it may come to the conclusion that a separate identity will serve the needs of their community better. Social economic and environmental dissolution caused by Your influence can exacerbate SCAs that cause the members of particular ethnic groups to realize through a 2nd CD that both life on a path towards Modernity and life as member of a "confederation" does not serve the needs of its people. The presence of these SCAs at the hands of the dis-locative nature of Your 'Universal' ideal that their nation-state's government adheres to a non-representative democracy may push these groups to desire independence from the subject's nation-state. Because these groups have been placed in the 'Modern World', issues such as resource allocation that may not have been important in the past and become important at that time. So, in addition to political separation these groups may also demand a particular territory, mineral rights, water rights, etc. The subject not want to lose sovereignty over any territories and resources will likely try to suppress a movement of this sort because to survive in this 'Global Economy' it seeks every resource that it can obtain. The escalation of political suppression can lead to civil war and/or instability in the society. If You have interests in the subject nation-state they will be threatened, because it is not likely that deals and contracts signed with the subject government will be honored, in the event of a change in government. In addition to this, if Other Princes desire the resources that are in the subject's nation-state and covet Your holdings; they may support the resistance in order gain rights to what is Yours under the present government. The spread of conflict, like disease outbreaks, can be unpredictable. A situation that appears to be easily contained can escalate and spread to other nation-states; especially if neighboring states are composed of the same (or related) ethnic groups. If there is a general feeling of dissatisfaction with the current states of areas (especially in artificially constructed post-colonial nation-states), one small conflict caused by the SCAs that You create in Your subject's state can turn a regional conflict and threaten stability worldwide because of interruption of trade, and other disruptive outcomes.

Ethnic/Religious Conflict - Social and Economic Breakdown

In addition the problems that can be caused by ethnic minorities desiring expression of their cultural center outside of the "confederation" of the subject's nation-state, the same SCAs that cause realizations about the effectiveness of the subject nation-state's government, cause feelings of insecurity in the majority population. Though the most insecure would be initially composed of the lower classes; the presence of ethnic minorities will serve as additional SCAs because of the perception that they are consuming (services, jobs, resources) things that could be going to members of majority. They too will tire of the idea of a "confederation" of diverse peoples within their nation desiring to retain their cultural integrity, but in this case, most likely they make the "interests" of the majority part of the interests of the subject nation-state's government, as a means of desperation to alleviate the feelings of insecurity. After, even if only symbolically, making support of the government synonymous with their cultural assertions, opposition to the policies of the government (though they are disrupting the lives of the whole society) would be taken as a threat to the majority culture's survivability. The majority will make life harder for the minority groups and possibly try to "fundamentally" change the present subject's government into one that asserts the majority's past. A conflict comes from the blind support of government policies as a cultural assertion while its policies cause further social, economic, and environmental dislocation that exacerbate more SCAs that cause more social and economic breakdown, misuse of the environment, and ethnic conflict. As a result of the breakdown of the society, the newly "fundamentalized" subject government will implement more Draconian measures to somehow promote a "present expression" of its past, while embracing the policies of its own destruction. Suppression of the minorities becomes even more important, because at this time they will have no desire to be a part of the subject's nation-state because of the antagonism from the majority and the newly "fundamentalized" group(s) and they will demand whatever territories and resources that they perceive as theirs. Neighbor nation-states with the same or related ethnic groups may assist in their struggle as well as the possible involvement of other Princes that either hope to profit from the conflict or support the subject government to protect their interests. If the majority ethnic group in the society is also pushed to the point of chronic insecurity, the result will be far more terrible than that of just the minority groups desiring autonomy. This type of scenario can easily turn into a regional conflict and/or possibly more, i.e. mass killings of minority groups, especially of there is a history (i.e. during the Colonial Period) or other evidence of preferential treatment or collaboration with Your actors(or those of Other Princes) in the subject nation-state.

Class Conflict.

It is said that as long as the masses have one good meal a day, that class-based social uprisings can be averted. If the actual loss of security or perceived lack of security through a realization of 2nd CD between of SCA causes the lower classes to feel that they have no reason to be compliant, they will likely rebel. If one has nothing, they have nothing to lose. The real danger of this scenario in Your subject's nation-state is if the middle classes feel the same level of insecurity. If all social nets such as government-sponsored social welfare and the extended family are eroded to accommodate an 'Open Society' and 'Free Market Economy' all that they will have left is economic security based on a volatile and unforgiving job market that takes cues from an external source, You and the world markets. If the middle classes are brought to the point of constant insecurity, from among them may arise individuals that through 2nd CD realize the truth about their society: that is government is not operating in the interests of the people and that foreign influence has helped create this reality. It is largely from the middle classes (and of course a small number empathetic persons from the upper classes) that the leaders of the "fundamentalist" and revolutionary movements come who wish to reinvent their society in order to bring security back in the people's lives. The higher the frequency of Your projections, the higher the frequency of the denunciation of Your influence.

If social and economic dislocation gets to the point that the middle classes are in a state of perpetual insecurity, from them will arise the demise of Your subject's nation-state. There are two ways to avoid this scenario if You truly desire to exploit this subject nation-state to its fullest: 1. if the middle classes are small in number You must keep them that way - very small. As long as the poor are not exposed to much, either through actual contact or though the media to how disparate their living conditions are as compared to the wealthy, they can largely be placated through basic food and health programs, and rudimentary education; 2. grow the middle classes through education directed at the poorest citizens and ethnic minorities and employ them in government positions--funded through higher taxes (but with other bureaucratic courtesies granted in return) on the wealthy classes--; and promote small businesses/entrepreneurship through grants from the government and from "community development loans" for Your nation-state's companies operating in the subject's nation-state; and local positions in Your own nation-state's (trans)multinational firms operating in the subject's nation-state.

In this way You create a buffer class that still has roots--eyes and ears--in potential ethnic and social class hot spots in the subject's nation-state. To protect their newfound comfort and inclusiveness in the society they will protect Your and the subject's interests. Though it is a "gamble", and You must be observant and walk a fine line, the latter allows You take from the society and somewhat manage some of the potential threats. But again, this is an imperfect science. Political conflicts, economic instability, public health crisis', or environmental disasters in another location in a region or the world can, in an instant, send world markets into chaos, pulling this fragile scenario down in an instant.

All it takes is one charismatic person who can bring people's attention to the reality that the fragility of the societal, economic, and environmental dislocation that exists, are all a result of participating in someone else's (an outsider's) game. 2nd CD (which is an unconscious manifestation) combined with a viable call for self-determination (including a chance for a fulfilled life) will eliminate the mandate of the subject nation-state's government to rule in the eyes of all those who come to this realization.

The Realization of the Shared State of Instability.

The state of instability that is caused by the utilization of Cultural Warfare, i.e. CCD and sustained and regulated through Your projections should always be monitored to ensure that 2nd CD does not occur. The projections that sustain the instability required for the exploitation of the subject's nation-state can also create the environment for a strong opposition to this approach of warfare. If 2nd CD were to occur and the populace was then aware of external influence on its society, through the networking of intellectuals in other subject nation-states who are also adversely affected by the influence of You (or Other Princes that utilize these methods of Cultural Warfare) it could come to the shared realization of that they are being manipulated by You (or Other like-minded Princes). If this were to occur, it could seem to the populations of these subject nation-states that there is a "conspiracy" of powerful Princes using the projection of the ideals of Modernity and Civilization as a means of controlling and exploiting less powerful nation-states. You cannot allow this to happen. If You do, this "conspiracy" of powerful Princes will be construed as a new age of Colonialism, Neocolonialism. This is why it is important to avoid the limitations of linear thinking, and work to ensure (to the best of Your ability) that Your projections only disrupt the "essential-needs" orientation of the subject's collective and individual psyches. If the social, economic, or environmental conditions of the subject's nation-state deteriorate to a point where there is actual (or perceived) non-satisfaction of these essential needs, it will experience a 2nd CD and You run the risk that through its breakdown, that it develops a collective realization of subjugation by external powers with other subject nation-states.

To maintain Sustainable Exploitation, You then have to resort to working to convert Your subject nation-state's government into a fascist-type regime based on 'the need for security' in order to weaken the focus that the masses have on their own social, economic, and environmental realities and direct it towards the need for 'Security at All Costs'; while granting it--the subject nation-state's government--a public sanction to suppress any opposition that it can portray as anti-security, cowardly, unpatriotic, or in collaboration with or sympathetic to 'terroristic' elements.

Chapter 34:
Progress at All Costs

"There is no inductive method which could lead to the fundamental concepts of physics. Failure to understand this constitutes the basic philosophical error of so many investigators of the 19th century."

Albert Einstein[274]

"Many anti-environmentalists, drunk with the 'hubris' that afflicts scientists, will glibly tell us that whatever changes have been wrought by technology, a new equilibrium will appear. That is absolutely true; but who can assure us that the human animal will survive within the new balance?"

L.M.T. Mendis[275]

"There must be something wrong with a concept of progress that threatens survival itself"

Vandana Shiva, Indian Philosopher

"If human progress follows a law of development, if "Times noblest offspring is the last", our civilization should be the noblest, for we are "The heirs of all of the ages in the foremost files of time.".…[276]

274.   Einstein, Albert (1950) *Out of My Later Years*. Philosophy Library, p.8
275.   Mendis, p.31
276.   Documents on the History of the United States, Part 2. C. Dra. Zenaida Puig Lopez, Lic. Ma. Elena Mateo Palmer. Editorial Pueblo y Educacion (1989) Havana, Cuba from James G. Newbill, et al., op. cit., pp. 337-339 in Newbill, James G., et al., The American Spectrum, Belmont: Wadsworth Publishing Company, Inc. 1971.

The Problem With Progress.

Because 'Progress' is perpetual forward motion and because Rationalism promotes opposition and antagonism, rather than harmony, balance, and consensus, there is never a possibility of achieving a 'state of rest', a comfortable or 'perfect' state of being. Instead, something must always be wrong with the current state of affairs or state of being; 'problems' must exist to sustain the oppositional mindset of Reason. There is always a 'Better Way', even, at the expense of a working system. This is so because in the Rational Mind, Progress does not cease until perfect order is obtained. So, unless at some point, the Rational thinker perceives himself to be of a 'God-like omniscience and omnipotence' and his 'created world' to be of maximum order, the quest towards 'Progress' will be perpetual. The 'advances' that Progress brings with its ever increasing 'efficiency' become so 'efficient' that balanced, harmonious life becomes obsolete – the rush to no-where for no-reason becomes the reality, eroding away every semblance of a balanced human life that may have existed.

Modernity and Progress

One of the objectives of projecting the concept of Modernity centered in Your culture, is to establish the frame of reference for Progress on Your cultural terms. This will establish the Universal validity of Your ideals, cultural icons, and sense of aesthetics. All aspects of Development and Progress will be based on Your ideology. To reject You, they will have to reject the framework of Progress and Modernity, being that it was You that brought these concepts to them in the first place.

Again, I must warn You to not become psychologically dependent on the acceptance of Your ideals as acceptance of Self. In the case of Modernity, I must forewarn You that, though You may be defining Modernity through rationalized terms, the subject of Your conquest is also "Modern" in their own cultural frame of reference. Meaning that, right now, they are living in the culmination of the experiences of their own group; and being that they have existed as least as long as Your group has the subject may be aware of Your objectives and just may not tell You. This case reminds me of a conversion that I had with a member of the royal family of a particular nation-state in the Pacific Islands Region. He told me of the late night discussions about what lies to tell the British anthropologists. There are several renowned anthropologists whose fieldwork is nothing but a collection of lies and made-up stories and customs. The people saw no reason why an Outsider would need to know such detailed information on their society if he was not going to join it; they concluded that it had to be for sinister objectives. Secondly, being that these are a people of oral tradition, to reveal certain truths about their spiritual practices would be both highly taboo as well as destructive; because it is believed that orally revealing the secrets would empower the individual of power of the vibrational attributes of the particular power words – in simple terms meaning no one with any good sense would even entertain these informational requests seriously. He said that there were lively social gatherings devoted to making up rituals, customs, etc, for the resident "colonial".[277]

The Danger of Becoming the "Scientific/Rational Man"

Lost in the illusion of Rationality, the belief that the user possesses the ultimate truth, and a mandate to construct humanity in ways that He desires-- limited by Your own narrow perspective--You dive into a crazed insanity of sorts. In the rush to develop science and promote Progress, You may become lost in Your experiment. You may objectify the Universe and project Your idea of how it should look onto it, ever pleased by Your apparent ability to manipulate the Universe/Nature to Your liking. You may do so, against the cries from the concrete begging You to stop, You pay no mind to dangers, for You are lost in the passion of Progress, destroying the world around You, chasing after the waterfall of divine-like control over Nature.

The following are quotes to illustrate the dangers of possessing the ideology of 'Progress at All Costs'.

...In the typical plot one finds the same person. He (always male) is committed only to his experiments and will not stop them, no matter what danger they imply to the community. What excites him are the implications if his being able to control and manipulate some part of nature that has previously been untouched, perhaps something sacred. This he insists it is "science" and "progress". As he is typically depicted, this man cannot love, has no friends, becomes deaf to the admonitions of those around him. He loses the ability even to understand what they are saying. He is a fanatic in the fullest sense of the term. This is Dr. Frankenstein (depicted in 1920, 1932, and 1941 films), Dr. Jekyll and all other not sufficiently infamous to be known by name, but always there. *The Deadly Mantis* (1977), *Dr. Cyclops* (1940); *Alien* (1979, the more modern vintage) – the theme does not "go out of style" but continues to provide material for the European/American science fiction "thriller".[278]

But unfortunately all "mad scientists" are not as bizarre as these films depict them. There are those who have had deep cultural/philosophical commitments. There is a certain "madness" even in the fanaticism and unidirection of men like Plato, Aristotle, Augustine, and Aquinas.... The reality of the nightmare is that the nature of ... [Modern] culture is such that this monster can and does gain the power to endanger the lives of those not only in his culture but

277.   This story was stated earlier in this Book (2).
278.   Ani, pp.245-6, Re: The Problem with the Mad Scientist

throughout the world.[279]

George Bernard Shaw states in *Man and Superman* that:

> "The reasonable man adapts himself to the world: the unreasonable one persists in trying to adapt the world to himself. Therefore all progress depends on the unreasonable man."[280]

Linear Thinking - A Danger.

A Prince must be aware of the danger of creating linear time, just as He must be aware of the dangers of creating the concept of Reason. Linear thinking, like Rational thinking is a mental exercise used to create a feeling of ownership over Your portion of the universe; and of course can be used to manipulate the subjects You desire to subjugate.

Because You quantify time in the linear exercise, time becomes a measure of length and therefore has finite quantity. When abstracting the journey of point A to point B, point B becomes signified by the concepts of 'Progress' and 'Technology'. Because We are speeding towards B; and because on this linear path, all objectives must be progressive and technological. The faster we head toward 'Technology' We should be able to escape the 'gravity' of causal reality. Consequences of the journey towards point B can be rationalized away as temporary setbacks in the quest to developing or improving 'technology'--"Technology will solve all of Our problems". In reality, this one-dimensional thinking can endanger You in four ways:

1. You can begin to think that You are operating outside of the Law of Cause and Effect. You will cease to be able to contemplate actions before taking them, because they are actions that are "leading" to the 'Progress'. This trend of thought process will also encourage You to not take responsibility for Your actions and will come back to haunt You. You will believe that because You are the bearer of the banner of 'Progress', that nothing "bad" should happen to You. The only problem with the world is that it does not yet realize that You, the sovereign of the world and the Universe are infallible, because You are Progress and Technology;

2. You will make great technological gains, because You are not burdened by the responsibilities of a member of an interdependent

---

279.   Ibid., p.246
280.   Shaw, George Bernard (1951) *Seven Plays*. Mead, New York: Dodd. p.739

world. You can race faster, faster, and faster towards this abstraction of Progress. Progressing becomes paramount at the expense of civil society, quality of life, sustainable environment and the general happiness of the people. The race towards abstraction of Progress can lead to a paranoid anxiety-ridden frenzy, where You are always worried about what will happen if you slow down, You will assume that other states are in the same race with You, and that they are envious and covetous of Your 'Progress', and while in this paranoid state, You are unable to see the damage that You are causing to Yourself, the nation-states around You, and to the very environment that sustains all;

3.   Your own government's funding priorities become increasingly fixed on defense to combat the envious enemies of Your state science; and bringing You close enough to the abstraction of Progress to actually combat that which restricts You to "limitations" - the Universe/Natural Environment;

4.   All efforts lead to the eventual battle with the 'Creator' over the right to rule 'Creation', for You are even approaching technological supremacy over the Universe.

STOP! This delusional state of a battle against time in a race to technological mastery 'against', not 'in conjunction with' the Universe WILL lead to Your destruction. Like in the case of Rationality, You cannot become intoxicated by the illusion of omniscience: using linear thinking You cannot become intoxicated by the illusion of omniscience.

The destruction that You bring onto Yourself will awaken a new dark age of barbarism, if people still inhabit the planet after such transgressions against Nature, and they will be taught the basic law that the early humans (the "primitives") knew and respected, the Law of Cause and Effect.

The great irony of this danger is that it fulfills the Rational/logical Aristotle "final cause" – an object's realization of its purpose; the reason that it exists. The race towards 'Progress' and 'Technology' leads You straight to Your purpose of existence – to manifest Your potential in balance with the Law of Cause and Effect.

If You choose to be a "Progressive" then the question is: will You be destroyed in Your quest towards nothing; or will You destroy Yourself on Your own terms realizing the nothing-ness of the quest?

Progress and Insanity.

"This is the philosophy behind the technological revolution that has produced the so-called Age of Information. Given enough information, the sky is the limit to what we can do. The ultimate goal is to eliminate sickness, overcome aging, and conquer death. We will finally become immortal, gods. Is there a greater megalomania than this?"[281]

Do not lose perspective on reality in a quest to perpetually Progress. This is the greatest manifestation of narcissism--a blind pursuit towards self-delusional perfect self-image with no concern for self and those around You because of the "importance" of Your goal, and because You are entitled to push the limits of Nature, even if humanity is a casualty of Your endeavors.

---

281.   Lowen, p.225

Book III

The Unintended Consequences of Conquest

Chapter 35:
Introduction to the Results of
an Incomplete Conquest

Dear Prince,

I must inform You of the consequences of failure when using this methodology of Cultural Warfare in an interdependent world. Like I mentioned before, the fact that You have decided to use this means of conquest means that there is a great likelihood that You are a linear thinker. The danger of linear thinking is the illusional thought that actions can exist as separate events on their own without corresponding consequences. The reality is that all actions have a corresponding reaction; and ignorance of this fact leads one to not take responsibility of the 'corresponding reactions'.

Linear thinking impedes one's ability to recognize the interconnectedness of actions; therefore encouraging the alleviation of symptoms of a disease (human conflict), rather than acknowledging the need to deal with the root causes of the disease. Treating symptoms initiates cycles of further cause and effect which takes the focus off of the root problem. An illustration of this concept can be in describing a person that eats a terrible diet which leads to high blood pressure. Instead of correcting the diet, the person takes medication to lower their blood pressure. This blood pressure medicine then causes other side-effects which require the person to take additional medications to counter these side-effects, but still does not address the root problem and allows the continuation of self-destructive behaviors.

When promoting Your national interests through the working of transnational corporations, corporate governance also takes on the limitations of linear thinking. Decisions are not made on interdependent realities; they are made based solely of short-term profit motive. I say "short-term", even if planning is "long-term", because the possible long-term effects of the corporate policies are not examined in the analysis of profitability. This is because 'transnational' corporate governance directly influences local decision-making in the nation-states that they operate in, the policies enacted in these locals are based on external markets, international agreements, and corporate movement (i.e. labor migration) rather than local realities. This leads to 'absent' decision-making in the subject nation-state leading to consequences or reactions that are never on the planning or negotiating table, and must be dealt with in that nation-state's reality afterwards.

The effects of the combination of applications of Cultural Warfare on the subject nation-state--promoting individualism, mis-education[282], replacement of aesthetic values, representative governance, family/community/societal breakdown; environmental degradation through Applied Rationalism, Modernity, Universal Humanism, endless Progress, codependent (narcissistic) relationships with Your state, etc. need to be examined. I will provide You with several possible scenarios of mishandled exploitation of Your subject nation-state. I will divide this discussion into three sections: the first concerning Your subject nation-state; the second concerning Your nation-state; and the third concerning the world as a whole.

I will be discussing the long-term effects of SCAs (Societal Conflict Agents) if the resulting economic breakdown, societal inequities, and environmental degradation are not addressed in the Progress of Conquest.

Introduction to 'The End'.

It is becoming clear that humanity is facing a triple security crisis. Societies everywhere have to contend with the effects of environmental declines, the repercussion of social inequities and stress, and the dangers arising out of an unchecked arms proliferation that is a direct legacy of the cold war period....

As the 1994 *Human Development Report* points out, "It will not be possible for the community of nations to achieve any of its major goals – not peace, not environmental protection, not human rights or democratization, not fertility reduction, not social integration – except in the context of sustainable development that is to human security.

Concerns about "human security" are about as old as human history, yet they are now magnified by the unprecedented scale of environmental degradation by the presence of immense poverty in the midst of extraordinary wealth, and by the fact that social, economic, and environmental challenges are no longer limited to particular nations.[283]

---

282.   Mis-education is a term coined by the educator by Dr. Carter G. Woodson. See Woodson.
283.   Renner, Michael (1996) *Fighting for Survival: Environmental Decline, Social Conflict, and the New Age of Insecurity.* New York: W.W. Norton & Company. pp.1-2

Human Security.

If it is not acknowledged by a nation-state whose *raison d'être* is based on meeting the security needs of the population, that does not mean only freedom from civil disorder, crime, and protection of private property, but also freedom from poverty, unemployment, inadequate healthcare, illiteracy, mismanaged, unsustainable environment, and creating a social environment where individuals in the population can achieve a sense of personal fulfillment; it has no true mandate, and definitely will be threatened with replacement by a government that does promise to meet these basic "human security needs".

I. Your Subject's Nation-State

Chapter 36:
Your Subject Nation-state's
Economic Collapse

There is one cause – all else are branches: you have lost the way. You have forgotten the way of our life, the living way. Your ears have stopped themselves to the voice of reciprocity. You yourselves have become a spring blindly flowing, knowing nothing of its imminent exhaustion, ignorant of replenishing reciprocity.

'Reciprocity, that is the way you have forgotten, the giving, the receiving, the living alternation of the way. The offerers, those givers who do not receive, they are mere victims. That is what in the heedless generosity of your blinding abundance you have turned yourself into.

A. K. Armah

Economy.

'Efficient' technologies and economic policies: I preface the word 'efficient', because the question must be asked – efficient in whose interest? If greater productivity threatens the social balance by promoting unemployment, is the result beneficial to the nation-state?

To stay in sync with the trend to "Modernize", develop, enter the "Global Economy", Your subject-states, with no thought to the potential consequences of these trends on their realities, will deregulate, privatize, and do away with social programs. All of these things are done to create an "investor-friendly" environment. These moves are to the benefit of the external "investor" and to the detriment of the internal stakeholder. It is like the slave taking on the interest of the master; though it is not actually in his or her interest. If the master is sick, he or she says "Master, WE sick". If he or she (the slave) does not wake up on their own, his or her family and brethren will wake them up; hence, social conflict instigated by SCAs.

Economy & Protectionism

Watch out for a rise in protectionism in Your subject nation-state as a reaction to the selling of many local business assets, properties, resource rights, and the privatization of public goods, i.e. utilities, etc.

Economy & State Failures

The following quote reflects a delusional attitude in the subject's government that must be tempered by You to avoid state failure. Without some intervention--its government or Your control of the outside economic forces--outside economic forces will act out of tandem with the economic reality of the nation-state and work to devour it. Since Your goal is Sustainable Exploitation, You cannot allow the "Free Market" to operate to the point that You cannot manipulate it in order to provide You with control of Your subject's economy without disintegrating it.

> "The political risks of neo-liberal economic reform cannot be perceived by those who imagine that the institutions of the free market and democratic governance operate in a virtual equilibrium."[284]

---

284.   Gray, p.47

Economy and TNCs.

"The promise of direct inward investment, and the threat of its withdrawal, have significant leverage on the policy options of national governments. Companies can now limit the policies of states."[285]

If You do not coordinate the actions of transnational corporations (TNCs) to create the optimum economic conquest strategy that benefits Your own nation-state's long-term economic hegemony; and instead solely depend on independent "corporate governance" to direct the activities of Your transnationals in Your subject's nation-state, You can have the possibility of these corporations, through the political control that they gain through FDI, acting in opposition to Your goals of Sustainable Exploitation and actually becoming catalysts for the failure of Your subject nation-state, especially when it comes to the acquisition of natural resources which are more cheaply acquired from rebel groups rather than through state agencies.

Banking.

If there is no trust in the local economy by the local population they will also not desire to keep their earnings in local banks. In the short- to medium- term this is good, because You will have the deposits placed into Your banks that have branches in the subject nation-state and from these deposits these banks can make profitable investments abroad. But in the long-term, You would want the local population to have faith in the domestic economy so that they will feel comfortable in re-investing in it as to promote entrepreneurship and the development of a larger middle class. A larger middle class and a population of the poor that have some consumer means creates new markets for Your nation-state's exports. This is not to say that You should not, through stockholders agreements, have controlling interest over these local banks, but "local banks" are more apt to re-invest locally as to have some controlling interest in the local modes of production. Nurturing "faith" in the local economy creates a consumer base for Your exports and maintains a degree of stability for Your investment. If You do allow consumer confidence in the local economy to drop to the point that the population is afraid to invest in local banks You will have a basket case on Your hands – an increasingly more helpless nation-state. Your investments are never meant to become a drain on Your resources, they are meant to be cash cows, not tumors. In regard to the application of 'Free Market' ideology onto Your subject's nation-state; this ideology is to be used to dislodge local control over local resources

---

285.   Ibid, pp.63-4

and control over the economy. It is not to disintegrate the economy. Remember 'Sustainable Exploitation' is Your mantra.

Fundamentalists and Economic Breakdown.

The austerity measures that the 'Free Markets' require of host governments call for reduced government expenditures for social programs. These types of reductions contradict its *raison d'être*. The people will no longer need a government if the government continuously reduces its contribution to satisfying the security needs of the people. 'Fundamentalists' will readily exploit this truth.

Local Business Group, Organized Crime, and Fundamentalist Groups.

A destabilized government needs order: the oligarchies that rule many 'developing nations' are weakened in this process. The oligarchies want to stay in power and crime gangs want to help. Crime gangs are not fickle and the oligarchies, alone, cannot exploit the ensuing chaos to their own advantage, in the race to secure resources and economic sectors of the society.

A democracy is much more fickle than a mafia-controlled economy. These oligarchies are more likely to want to deal with these types of organizations, because there are no illusions in the government. There are certain rules of conduct and a code that must be followed if relations are to be smooth and devoid of violence, as well as shared desire of long-term profitability of the relationship (the Free Market' destabilizes the ordered corruption that maintains some societies). A certain degree of 'instability' or an excessive requirement of background knowledge on local business protocol protects the local economy from the vast financial resources of transnational corporations and offer large investors. Creating an 'investment-friendly' environment threatens the power and sustainability of control over the economic by oligarchies and Mafiosos. Rule of law and 'investor/ Investment-Friendly' business legislation eliminate the advantage that indigenous business owners have in the economy. It eliminates the needs of satisfying obligations in the society to the disadvantage of those living in it.

To prevent the loss of the economy to outside investors, local power brokers may actually be the source of funding for nationalistic fundamentalist groups. In return for guaranteed control over certain sectors of the economy, the fundamentalist group is granted the funding it needs if it can believably overthrow the present government that is being supportive of the dissolution of society.

Reactionary Actions By Your TNCs.

Your companies may react to the new rules of 'resistant' states – responding by having on-site private military to take the "law into their own hands". By taking actions like this, they may feel that they are protecting their interests, but by bringing their own "law and order" they are actually weakening the legitimacy of the subject government. The attackers, may then instead of attacking Your TNC (Transnational Corporation) sites, may actually work to de-stabilize the government itself, because it, in the process of allowing You to operate a militia within its borders, has allowed a foreign power to take territory, therefore negating its mandate to rule--having proven itself a traitor to its nation-state and because of this, can lose its ability to enforce legitimate use of force over its nation-state.

An openly arrogant acting TNC from Your nation-state can potentially cost You the nation-state as a whole, unless You want to involve yourself in an invasive "peacekeeping" mission to re-establish control and give it back to Your chosen government. The problem of course in this scenario, is that 'rule by law' will then be tenuous at best, because, in the process of bringing in "peacekeeping forces" that will inevitably kill civilians in the putting down of any insurrections, will give credibility to the rebel groups, especially if Your corporation is guilty of labor abuses of environmental mismanagement. The rebels, bandits, or terrorists, however You wish to term them, will be viewed as protectors of land and people; and in order to have smooth operations, You may have to keep a ground force or "peacekeeping forces" in Your subject's nation-state for a while until hope for change disappears from the minds of the majority of the people.

Agricultural Trade.

The removal of distortions to agricultural trade and of import restrictions on industrial goods is the trade agenda most directly linked to poverty reduction and economic development. Agriculture is important because poverty in developing countries is in large part rural. Industrial reform is important because many poor people work in the production of basic manufactures.[286]

Though it is important that You continue to subsidize the agricultural sector in Your own nation-state so that the agricultural products produced by

---

286.   ERD Working Paper No.21, The Doha Agenda and Development: A View from the Uruguay Round. Economics and Research Department, Asian Development Bank. J. Michael Finger, September 2002, Manila. p.16

Your subject's nation-state cannot compete in the 'Free Market', You should also realize that at some point, a group of subject nation-states may come together and demand that You eliminate protectionist legislation in Your own nation-state or they will begin to resist embracing the Free Trade ideology that You and Other Princes have been projecting onto them. If the realization of how You have structured 'Free Trade' becomes too widespread among subject nation-states, they may begin to create bi-lateral/multilateral trading relationships among themselves lessening the hold that You have over Your subject nation-state(s) and the hold that Other Princes have over theirs. Their desire to re-order the world according to their own terms may require You to use more invasive means of control of Your subject nation-state.

Economics and Resource Conflicts.

Although some of today's conflicts have their roots in long-standing grievances, there is a self-sustaining vicious cycle at work in which the spoils of resource exploitation fund war, and war provides the means and conditions that allow continued illegitimate access to these resources. The conflict in Sudan provides a telling example: Oil exports have permitted the central government to carry on with the war against southern rebels. To keep paying for the war, the government must expand oil production, but this requires exploiting oil deposits deeper and deeper in rebel-held territory. To control oil-rich areas in southern Sudan, government forces are conducting a scorched earth campaign at terrible human cost. Oil finances the war; the war provides access to oil.[287]

Sustainable Exploitation is Your goal. Your goal is not to start a fire that burns out of control and consumes everything in its path as fuel to keep burning. You are the director of all "chaotic activities" in Your subject nation-state. You are to regulate its brutality against the people as to prevent a chain reaction of violence against an-Other. If this is allowed to happen, the very resources that You desire can be used up in supporting government sponsored conflicts. Remember, I call Your subject a "subject" because it is to be objectified, re-defined (named) and possessed by You. It is not to be able to exhibit any expressions of self-determination, even if these actions are self-destructive. Its self-destructive actions are to weaken its government's hold over its society, lands, economy, and resources; and weaken the binding force of a collective culture. Manipulating resource wars is a dangerous game which I suggest You not engage in. You must always keep your eyes on the prize. The prize is a sustainable colony that serves the material desires of Your nation-state.

---

287.   "The Anatomy of Resource Wars," World Watch Paper 162, October 2002, Michael Renner, p.11 from International Crisis Group, *Dialogue or Destruction? Organizing Peace as the War in Sudan Escalates*, ICGF Africa Report No.48, Nairobi and Brussels, 27 June 2002.

I know that You may believe that funding internal and regional wars may serve Your purposes. In truth, they do, but only in the short-term. For example, relegating resource-rich areas to rebels may bring about lesser materials costs, but the source is not stable and if the rebels were to utilize these resources themselves (i.e. creating a trade with others or diverting these for processing) You may have a larger problem than You will have anticipated. A rebel group with resources and an ideology that attempts (even if only in name) to address the needs of the majority of Your subject nation-state's populace that is neglected, may be able to obtain a mandate to rule and will threaten the "friendly" government that You have in place. Because this is a "rebel group", it is far less likely that You will be able to co-opt them into serving Your purposes in the medium-long term. And because they so intimately understand the importance of lands and resources in this present-day Global Economy, they are more likely to nationalize or appropriate lands and resources, and make them property of their new state.

It is very easy to feel like a chess master at the beginning of a conflict like this. But further into it,You will either have to seriously assist Your subject nation-state's government in maintaining control through counterinsurgency technical assistance and arms and/or utilizing Your own military or private military companies (mercenaries) to retake control of nation-states for Your "friendly government". Remember "Free Trade" includes the arms trade; and those non-state militants have access to these just like formal states do. Heed my advice and work towards Sustainable Exploitation, not some ego-maniac fantasy of being the chess-master of the world. If You choose the latter, You are exchanging the objective of conquest for an unhealthy codependent (narcissistic) relationship with Your subject in which You derive Your esteem needs through feeling like a god.

Rebels and Resource Wars.

Rebel groups infused with the predatory 'separatist' value system that You have projected onto Your subject's nation-state may wage full-scale wars against their own nation-state and neighboring nation-states in order to "own" resources so that they may too participate in this new Global Economy. If they are aware of the status of their nation-state in Your hierarchy--or even the overall hierarchy of Princes and subjects--they may assume that there is no chance of ever achieving parity with other "Developed" nation-states in the world, especially if they do not have the benefit of availability of access to Your and Other Princes' markets in exchange for regional military security alliances. If they are simply "food"--existing for the purpose of future consumption by You--they may act accordingly if they give up the hope of ever winning in Your "game"; thereby also becoming predators like You, deciding to exploit their nation-state as effectively as they can before You do. The lack of any "hope for change" in the minds of Your subject nation-state's population does not serve you well. Again, the populace must be made to believe in "Democratic Values" and the eventual hope that through adherence to "Democratic"/"Market" values and through a series of reforms based on the liberalization of their economy and government that they too will achieve prosperity and a level of consumption equal to Yours. If the population does not possess this "hope" of being able to mimic You, some of its population may accept their "fate", but because they have embraced (internalized) the Individualistic Materialist value system that You project onto them, they become conquistadors in Your subject nation-state just like You.

Foreign Aid and Resource Wars.

If Your subject nation-state is debt-ridden and has to pay to keep from defaulting on these loans, its government will do whatever means are necessary to continue receiving loans for the elusive "goal" of "economic development". I say elusive because no matter what economic gains it makes, in order to satisfy You and Your markets, it will have to continuously "grow". It can plateau, maintain stability and improve the quality of life of its people it has to stay in course and keep created record economic growth rates that will result either in a "bubble" scenario in which the economy collapses into recession or depression--a scenario in which You can then obtain its 'Developed' economy at a discount rate--or if it is resource rich, to the total exploitation and exhausting of its natural resources in order to keep "growing".

Land and Economy.

A major threat to the economic wellbeing of many countries is land degradation – principally through the plowing of highly erodible land, the drawing down of water tables through overpumping for irrigation, the salinization of irrigated land, the overgrazing of rangelands, and loss of arable land, rangeland, and forests the expanding urban and industrial need. Although the immediate reasons may be found in inappropriate practices or inefficient technologies, land degradation often is the result of social and economic inequities.[288]

Land degradation, if not checked, can lead to the development of SCAs (Social Conflict Agents) that may threaten the stability of Your subject nation-state government's ability to rule. Land degradation, though it may come about because of 'market pressures' that You place on the people in Your

---

288.   Renner, p.36

subject's society, especially in areas highly susceptible to loss, can lead to conditions in which the actual survivability of those inhabiting or depending on it for survival is threatened. If the basic needs of the people are threatened by land degradation, Your subject nation-state's government will have lost its mandate to rule and the people will decide to do whatever they need to do to fend for themselves. Reactionary responses to scarcity will probably lead to further degradation can set conditions for state failure, and unless You or Your subject nation-state's government can mitigate this situation, You will have to deal with the consequences of a failed or failing state and any local, regional, or global ramifications that this brings.

Chapter 37:
Your Subject Nation-State's Environmental Collapse

When the Western concept of a unified, law-abiding nature came in and wiped out the particularized, local relationships Thais had had with their environment, it also removed the fears, contentment and inclination to sit still and do nothing that had been the foundations of the previous Thai 'balance'. Westerners showed Thais how to wind up the machinery of exploitation, development and economies of scale, but neglected to explain how and when the equipment should be turned off or allowed to run idle. Thais could go to work with a vengeance, cutting down forests and polluting rivers in accordance with the best capitalist growth models of the time for two reasons: first, they were operating with the frenzy that always accompanies a shedding of old values, and second, they had never experienced the measuring of strength that come with the taste of victory and defeat, the taste Western man has had again and again in his struggles with nature.[289]

Mont Redmond

---

289.   Mont Redmond, "Nature: Human Outcry and Natural Outcome," *Nation* (Bangkok), August 29, 1993 from Fahn, James David (2004). *A Land on Fire: The Environment Consequences of the Southeast Asian Boom*. Bangkok: Silkworm Books, p.144

Introduction - Environment.

If economies grow as a result of trade agreements, politicians in developing countries are actually likely to be rewarded politically, not chastised for the resulting environmental degradation. In a corresponding way, those politicians can normally assume that they can negotiate trade openings without need to take steps to appease an environmentally based opposition coalition.... To developing countries, the effort to use trade agreements to promote higher common environmental standards often appears as a kind of protectionism in disguise. Because the higher environmental standards usually require them to make changes in production processes, inputs, or equipment, developing countries worry that the resulting increased costs will hurt their ability to compete with countries that already meet the new standards.... A corollary is the expectation that countries facing the increased economic competition of a free trade area will be unlikely to strengthen their environmental protections, especially at the national level, because new environmental protections would make them less competitive.[290]

There is great potential for environmental disaster in Your subject nation state, because of the global race to attract the most FDI (Foreign Direct Investment) and develop a strong export-based economy, there is the need to be more and more competitive. There is less concern about environmental sustainability and more and more about profitability. There is the belief that "if we can get rich today, we can worry about cleaning up the environment tomorrow."

From the standpoint of Public Health, the presence of environmental pollutants increases the development and incidences of allergies and asthma. Preventable illnesses drain public health budgets and adversely effects productivity in the workplace. In these days of the misuse of antibiotics leading to a "post-antibiotic age"[291], additional weakness of the population's immune systems is not a positive reality; weaker people make good hosts for these new generations of stronger, more-resistant pathogens.

Environmental Danger.

A Prince must be careful in the process of acquiring resources from the subject and using the subject nation-state as a base from industrial development, that He realizes that the subject nation-state is not only a independent source of resources and production, but also connected environmentally, socially, and economically to Himself. If You are not cognizant of this fact, You run the great risk of continuing the process of

---

290.   "Fading Green? Environmental Politics in the Mercosur Free Trade Agreement" by Kathryn Hochstetler. Latin American Politics and Society, University of Miami, Winter 2003, Vol. 45, Number 4, pp. 2-3
291.   See Garrett.

ecological, social, and economic disasters that were common in the 20th century. You must argue that Your motives are for the Human Good in order to neutralize any popular sentiment that may brand Your efforts as parochial or hegemonic; but because You live on the same planet, You must gauge Your actions based on the best analysis of potential consequences that You can ascertain.

Environment.

Your subject nation-state, if serious about being an "attractive investment site", will make the decision to become as "Investor-Friendly" as possible, i.e. having the least restrictions on pollution, most lenient health and safety standards, and highest level of embrace of the cheapest and dirtiest manufacturing and production technologies.

Environmental Conflict.

The following is indicative of the increasing number of environmental conflicts:

> "Our land is being polluted, our water is being polluted, the air we breathe is being polluted with dangerous chemicals that are slowly killing us and destroying our land for future generations.
> Better that we die fighting than to be slowly poisoned.
> Bougainville Revolutionary Army, 1990"[292]

"Sustainable" Environmental Conflict

Environmental-based conflicts may arise from some of the following conditions:

High population density in slums populated by displaced rural peoples; the creation of conservation parks out of indigenous lands, the commercial encroaching on wildlife (plant and animal habitats) that is utilized by rural peoples; mining and drilling on lands utilized by rural and indigenous people; environmental pollution from mining, drilling, and industrial activities, etc.

If these environment conflicts are "sustainable"--in existence, but not threatening to the actual procuring of natural resources that are needed for Your purposes--You can continue to exploit what You need to, using private armies to guard whatever assets are integral to Your operation and with increasingly advanced extraction methods without having to be concerned about any environment impact. The combantants that oppose You will have

---

292.   Fighting for Survival from Volker Boge, "Bougainville: A 'Classical' Environmental Conflict?" Occasional Paper No.3, Environment and Conflicts Project (ENCOP), Bern, Switzerland, October 1992. p.52. In 2002 a cease fire was reached.

already exposed You, so You simply need to manage them: 1. through drawing Your subject nation-state's government into conflict with them, because they are "opposing the economic development of the nation-state", 2. through gifts of vices and money to the leaders of the community from which they come from in order to erode their base of support among the people; 3. extract as many resources as You can as fast as you can, while You still can maintain the "sustainability" of the exploitation of Your subject nation-state's resources.

Consumerism-Driven Non-sustainable Environmental Policies.

The following quote is an illustration of how a nation-state such as Your subject can, under the influence of Your projections of Individualistic Materialism and Modernity, participate in behavior that while it does affirm what You have taught it in regard to the need to separate themselves from the consequences of their actions through linear-thinking in order to achieve unencumbered Progress, can promote non-sustainable environmental policy that can make life very hard for its people in the future; and make it a less attractive target of conquest for You, because You have to somehow abate these future problems in order to continue to exploit it.

At the rate that Pohnpei's famed rainforests are being destroyed, its self-proclaimed title as the "Garden State" of the Federated States of Micronesia may become a misnomer. The native tropical rainforests, which control the flow and purity of water that is the lifeline for countless villages, are the linchpin to Pohnpei's natural heritage. But today, what many families see in the finite forests is a fistful of dollars from clear-cutting sakau plantations. Sakau – known popularly as kava – is the cultural cornerstone of Pohnpeian society. Now it's become a prized cash crop that is caused a virtual strip mining of the forests.

Sakau generates approximately $5 million a year for 5,000 farmers. "People know that sakau is really good if you cut all the trees down," said Nett area Sakau grower Sonsper Helgenberger. "If you leave the big trees Sakau doesn't grow good.[293]

Development and Environment.

Environmentally sound indigenous technologies are regarded as 'backward' or 'unproductive' and 'regeneration of life' is referred to as 'passivity'. Above all, 'destruction' is viewed as 'production' or the assumption that:

Production' takes place only when mediated by technologies for commodity production, even when such technologies destroy life. A stable and clean river is not a productive resource in this view: it needs to be 'developed' with dams in order to become so. Women sharing the river as a commons to satisfy the water needs of their families and

---

293.   "Cash for Kava, But A What Cost?" Olivier Wortel. Pacific Magazine. April 2004. p.10

society are not involved in productive labour: when substituted by the engineering man, water management and water use become productive activities (Shiva, 1990:4).[294]

Though 'Development' is a means through which You can co-opt Your subject nation-state into its own 'commodification' and exploitation, You must be aware of the limits to which You push this development. If 'Development' comes at the expense of Your purpose--Sustainable Exploitation, You have been deceived by Your own self into perpetuating conditions contrary to Your own interests.

_____

294.   Sittirak, p.28

Chapter 38:
Your Subject Nation-State's Social Collapse

Not so long ago people in the Western world knew little about the nature of baboons or, indeed, of other species of monkeys and apes that are the closest relatives to man among the animals.

About half a century ago, a man named Zuckerman undertook to study baboons, specially a large colony of hamadryas baboons living in the London Zoo.

What he saw when he began to observe them was most disturbing. The colony was beset by violence. The fighting was chronic and brutal, the carnage ultimately claiming the lives of a third of the original members. Adult males were the main offenders, and their victims included not only one another, but females and young as well.

When Zuckermen told the world what he had seen, many drew the obvious conclusions: baboons are unrestrainedly violent by nature, and baboon society is a bloody battleground. To many the mystery of a baboon nature seemed solved.

Some years later, a different picture of baboon nature began to emerge. Other investigators had gone off to observe baboon behavior not in the zoo but in the savannas of Africa, the animals' natural home. Under the conditions where the baboon had evolved and lived for millions of years, the baboon still showed a pugnacity of character.

But aggression was a game primarily of threat and retreat. Its occurrence was quite occasional and its injurious effects almost nonexistent. The elements of conflict and dominance that had proven so disruptive and destructive in the zoo were, in the savanna, part of the means of maintaining the tight social order that protected baboon survival.

What was seen in the wild cast the murders in the zoo in an entirely new light. In nature, baboons establish a hierarchy as they grow up; by the time they are fully armed with formidable teeth of adulthood; it has already been established who has priority and who has priority and who will back down. In the zoo colony, dozens of adults from different baboon troops were suddenly thrown together; the baboons' natural repertoire of behavior gave them no way of establishing order peaceably. In nature, the baboon who loses a confrontation can signal his defeat and escape the victor by retreating from the fray. The zoo society was enclosed, preventing the retreat that would end the fight without bloodshed. What Zuckerman saw were baboons in a state of high agitation and confusion, encountering problems that baboons had never faced before and for which their natural responses were wholly unsuitable.[295]

Asymmetric Warfare.

Machemba, King of Yao in modern Tanzania, told the German commander, Hermann von Wissman, in 1890: "I have listened to your words but can find no reason why I should obey you – I would die first... If it should be friendship that you desire, then I am ready for it, today and always; but to be your subject, that I cannot be... If it should be war you desire, then I am ready, but never to be your subject... I do not fall at your feet, for you are God's creature just as I am... I am Sultan here in my land. You are Sultan there in yours. Yet listen, I do not say that you should obey me; for I know that you are a free man... As for me, I will not come to you, and if you are strong enough, then come and fetch me."[296]

In 1895, Wobogo, the Moro Naba (King of the Mossi) to the French Captain Restenave: "I know the whites wish to kill me in order to take my country, and yet you claim that they will help me to organize my country. But I find my country good just as it is. I have no need of them. I know what is necessary for me and what I want: I have my own merchants; also, consider yourself fortunate that I do not order your head to be cut off. Go away now, and above all, never come back."[297]

The world is full of cultures of oral tradition who do not forget – they may appear to be peaceful today, but that day when they have to means to "set wrongs right", they will be back, even if it is the next generation, or the next, next, next generation. Ironically the more 'Rational' a society is the more likely that it has a need for vengeance, whereas more 'nature-oriented' non-linear societies are more likely to view said past offenses as simply a passing period in the cycle of life; as long as harmony is restored there is no need for retribution. Asymmetric warfare brings these "righting of wrongs" to fruition in a much shorter time period. The internalization of linear/rational thinking by Your subject works to eliminate the chances that Your subject culture exhibits cultural traits that, in a non-linear thought process, would more likely lean towards reconciliation rather than fostering the need for vengeance.

"... the acts of empire are seldom forgotten by those who have suffered them."[298]

---

295.   Schmookler, p.135
296.   Boahen, p.23 from Davidson, Basil (1964) *The African Past*. London:Longman. pp.357-8
297.   Ibid. p.25 from Crowder, M. (1968) *West Africa Under Colonial Rule*. London: Hutchinson. p.97
298.   Johnson, p.58

Asymmetric Warfare - Now & Then

In the Colonial Era in which invasive means were used to rule over the colonies, the following poem was inspired by the attitude that succeeded at that time.[299] This poem was inspired by the events at Omdurman (Sudan) where the British military retaliated for the Mahdi's massacre of General "Chinese" Gordon's command in Khartoum. In this battle 11,000 dervishes perished before the Maxim Guns of Kitchener.[300]

> "When asked in 1884 why Western nations had colonized almost the entire known world, the English writer Hilaire Belloc said that it was not because of their advanced civilization, greater universities or cultural advances. No, he quipped, 'Whatever happens, we have the Maxim gun, and they have not.' Of course, the technology for this early machine gun and other technological information was routinely shared and sold in open contracts between 'civilized nations'."[301]

The Modern Traveller

Blood thought he knew the native mind;
He said you must be firm, but kind.
A mutiny resulted.
I shall never forget the way
That Blood stood upon this awful day
Preserved us all from death.
He stood upon a little mound
Cast his lethargic eyes around,
And said beneath his breath:
'Whatever happens, we have got
The Maxim Gun, and they have not.'

Hilaire Belloc

The difference is now that <u>they</u> also have access to the maxim-gun and its successors due to the widespread proliferation of large and small arms to feed the multitude of civil wars and ethnic conflicts perceived as needed by the stronger Princes to make massive profits through arms sales and to achieve and maintain regional and global hegemony. Unless You want to cross the threshold of using nuclear weapons, You should recognize that the game is becoming more even, even through it as an asymmetric "even-ness". Using this logic, though Your soldiers may kill numbers of Your subject's people many times the numbers that die on Your side; because Your

---

299.   Ibid. p.20 from Perham, M. (1961) *The Colonial Reckoning*.London: Collins. p.32
300.   "Who Gave Mankind the Gift of WMD?" Pat Buchanan. WorldNetDaily August 23, 2002. Creator's Syndicate 2002.
301.   "Open Source Information". Army Magazine, July 1997.

expeditionary force is essentially fighting the entire nation-state, the numbers of these deaths are comparable. The question is: "As combat becomes more intense they have years to send waves upon waves of fighters, and while You will have to decide how many deaths of Your own nation-state's soldiers are You willing to accept investing blood essentially into an idea?" I say an "idea" because if combat comes to this point, Your exploitation is no longer sustainable and in the case that You are victorious militarily, You will have to still rebuild the country and somehow win the hearts of the people before it can become useful to You again.

Rebellion

For persons desirous of rebelling against systems of oppression in Your subject nation-state, other means such as passive resistance can be used. For example, for forced laborers--or desperately poor people who basically **have** to accept whatever work conditions of factories or farms--insubordination, "absenteeism, feigned illness, loafing and work slowdowns, refusing to grow compulsory crops, and rejecting all the "civilized" innovations introduced or connected with the colonial system or the foreign presence, whether schools, churches, or the colonial languages."[302]

Military.

There may be a problem of supporting the application of fascist-style "security"-oriented governance to maintain social order amidst governmental adherence to socially, economically, and environmentally dis-locating policies that serve Your need for Sustainable Exploitation.

> ... and these armies among the most conspicuous legacies apart from physical structures bequesthed to independent African states. And what a legacy these armies have turned out to be! In retrospect, they have become nothing but a chronic source of instability, confusion, and anarchy as a result of their often unnecessary and unjustifiable interventions in the political process of African countries. Indeed, African armies are the greatest millstones around the neck of African leaders, and the future of the continent is going to be determined very much on how these armies are dealt with.[303]

Fundamentalists and Coups d'etat.

The reality of the deteriorating state is that people will form back into the 'tribes' (ethnic, religious, or cultural groups) that existed before the establishment of abstracted nation-states, but not on their terms, and in a very

---

302.   Boahen, p.67
303.   Boahen. p.99

reactionary fashion. The situation basically creates antagonism between the 'traditional' non-state and nation-state. The abstract nation-state derives its power from the legitimated use of power over the society. When it is weakened it loses its monopoly on the legitimated (in the eyes of the people) use of force, and 'alternative' non-states gain legitimacy of the use of force. The nation-state's ownership of the right to wage war becomes lost to the opposition representative of 'traditional' non-state within its borders. When nation-states lose their mandate to rule, coup d'etat or revolution is no longer treason in the eyes of the people. It becomes the assumption (commandeering) of leadership from those "incapable of responsible leadership". In the Age of Cultural Warfare, this can be expressed as the coming of the "free wars"; wars between nation-states and non-states.

Healthcare.

This is quote is an illustration of the potential dangers that nation-states face in 'entering a Globalized World':

> The collapse of the Soviet Union foisted its former socialist states into the world community, which had three impacts. First, long-sealed exit doors were opened, allowing for record-breaking brain drain that stripped the region of most of its brightest scientific and medical minds. Second, doors also opened inward, allowing both the aspirations and sins of the external world entry into long-sequestered societies: the populations for the first time realized their comparative material poverty, experienced resentment and avarice, and discovered drugs and other ways to dull the pain of that awakening. Third, the legacy of Soviet-era science, psychology, public health, and human rights left the professionals, their infrastructures, and individual citizens without the tools to cope with the New reality: narcology, TB sanitariums, SanEp, venereology, KGB-affiliated psychiatry, and Lysenko-devastated biology could not protect the health of a free public.
>
> The Soviet public health-infrastructure, in short, required authoritarianism. In the absence of centralized despotism and the intrusive power extended to public health authorities, the fundamental flaws in the system were frightfully exposed.[304]

Healthcare & Braindrain

In conjunction with following the flight of capital out of Your subject's nation-state in the hope of receiving foreign currency remittances, it will also export its healthcare professionals, especially nurses to industrialized nation-states while neglecting its own domestic healthcare needs.

---

304.   Garrett, p.284

Healthcare & AIDS

Diseases in which immunodeficiency is a common complicating element include malnutrition, neoplasias, and infections. Protein-calorie nutrition is extremely common in developing countries and is associated with impaired cellular and humoral immunity to microorganisms. Much of the morbidity and mortality that afflicts malnourished people is due to infections. The basis for the immunodeficiency is not well defined, but it is reasonable to assume that the global metabolic disturbances in these individuals, caused by deficient intake of protein, fat, vitamins, and minerals, will adversely affect the maturation and function of the cells of the immune system.[305]

The socially dislocative results of Your conquest can work against You. If there is substandard nutrition intake in Your subject's population, it can be at increased risk for the development of the aggressive infections that are often associated with HIV/AIDS. If this is the case, You must work to address the spread and deterioration of affected persons through better nutrition, the use of anti-retrovirals, and research in using natural and synthesized interferons to arrest replication of the virus.

You cannot let the free-market directive of unencumbered international intellectual property laws create an unsustainable health situation in Your subject's nation-state. Remember, 'Free-Trade' is a means through which You dominate Your subject nation-state, but it is not to so disable it that it ceases to be a viable area of conquest for You. The goal of conquest is Sustainable Exploitation, not the decimation of population by means that can easily spread to Your own nation-state.

In addition to the danger that HIV/AIDS I wish to include a short tangent in this conversation concerning the shared reality of global public health. From the standpoint of the development proliferation of genetically targeted biological agents[306] to eliminate target populations, the spread of this type of disease, may seem like a blessing in disguise, but in actuality, because it cannot be contained, it is also a danger to those who would gain from a decrease in the target population. The development of agents of this type is to be viewed from the same perspective: because genetic science has not been perfected and because scientists are not privy to the omniscience needed to incorporate all possible variables into the scientific method, there is a great chance for unforeseen errors in the development of these agents that could lead to the demise of the group whom is perceived to gain from the elimination of the other, as well as humanity as a whole.

---

305.   Abbas, Lichtman, and Pober. (1994) *Cellular and Molecular Immunology.* Philidelphia: W.B. Saunders Company. p.428
306.   With the completion of the Human Genome Project, work on genetically-targeted biological agents can be done with more confidence.

Thinking short-term, less people means less obstacles to "Your" resources in its nation-state. You can have a self-perpetuating genocide that will eliminate claims to the resources of Your subject nation-state; but thinking long-term: 1. You will have no viable domestic economy, meaning that You will lose a market for the consumption of Your exported goods; and 2. You cannot control the spread of pathogens in this age of mass transportation. One nation-state's plague is the plague of all. The more "Globalized" the world becomes, the faster, microscopic killers can reach greater numbers of potential victims.

With the emergence of many "new" cross-species pathogens, rapid transport and transoceanic travel even allows the spread of pathogens that would otherwise kill its victims so quickly that they cannot be spread outside of a limited geographic area.

Population Control

If they have "more", they do not have to produce children. "Population control" is often proportional to the 'economic need' and social need (mortality rate) to have many children – if they are not needed as labor and the infant mortality rate is low, so many children are not needed.

Otherwise, to survive economically and preserve the continuity of family lines, high birthrates are needed to perpetuate existence. Families cannot take "proactive" limitations on family size if it does not truly serve their reality. Only short-sighted parents would have less children if their economic situation could be improved with more children; and the continuity of family line, perpetuation of family values and culture can be sustained, and care in old age can be "guaranteed" through having many children. This is like expecting hungry people who did not contribute to the decline of a population of certain animal and plant species (that are now deemed endangered by the same people (Outsiders) who consumed them to the brink of endangerment or extinction) not to "poach" them because of some foreign "conservation" directive.

The hard realities of life make people gamble with having children – "maybe one can live my dreams for me", "maybe one will make it and we'll all be rich", etc.

The Corruption of Society.

If corruption goes on too long in a society, where the government cannot effectively meet the social welfare needs of the people, and the resulting lack in confidence of the legitimacy of government promotes the idea that corruption is the only way to meet traditional obligations; over time a 'Culture of Crime' will develop to ensure the satisfaction of these obligations and because traditional safeguards have been weakened, it will be hard to rid it of the new system unless the government can somehow, while being cannibalized, address the social welfare needs of people at least as effectively as are being done through the system of corruption.

In this case, unless there is an external body overseeing the administration of the subject's nation-state it will be very hard to rid the 'system' of corruption, because of the (truly) subjective reality of legislation being that which those in power are able to exert influence to promote their special interests.

Without an internalized system of morality, only those directly involved in the creation of legislation can truly be said to be served by justice. It is impossible to be objective in making codified laws because the persons or groups creating legislation will be the locus, a definition of what is right and wrong and will have to deal with the influence of their particular affiliations to ensure that legislation does not censure their particular interests.

Social Breakdown.

The elimination of full-employment policies in the process of labor de-regulation will lead to the inability of many persons to obtain work at a livable wage. This coupled with reductions in social spending, compounding inequalities in healthcare and educational opportunities, the self-esteem afforded to every member of community in a society regulated by tradition and the relational value of people, will lead to feelings of desperation that of course for some, will lead them to commit transgressions of law; be motivated by either desperation, or have a desire to operate in opposition to the status quo and will lead to an increasing rate of incarceration. Mass incarceration will be the means of controlling the social breakdown that ensues when the subject's government divorces itself from addressing the social welfare and security needs of the populace in exchange for acceptance in the world of the 'Developed' that You have projected onto it.

Social Breakdown & Chaos

If we deny or ignore limits, we destroy structure. Without structure, a situation becomes chaotic in that anything goes. In the absence of structure, there is no meaning.

When structure breaks down in a society, chaos develops, creating an atmosphere of unreality... Unreality threatens a person's sanity, unless the person cuts off feelings and operates from thinking alone... That is narcissism...

Yet an old structure must break down if a new one is to emerge. That is the natural process of growth. We should not, however delude ourselves it thinking that the breakdown, in itself, represents progress. It holds out the possibility of growth, but there is no guarantee that the new will be better than the old. Historically, the breakdown of a society has sometimes led to a period of darkness before a new light dawns. We may be in for such a time, a new Dark Ages, if we cannot distinguish between order and chaos.[307]

There is nothing new, though the Ideology of Progress may state it as so. Such thoughts of "new-ness", 'change', and 'Progress' are based in myopic linear thought processes. Real time is cyclical/non-linear, meaning: what is, has come before; but is now wearing different clothes.

Social/Economic Breakdown

In the quest to 'Develop', the subject nation-state's government will implement policies that weaken the domestic economy and weaken its ability to provide for the security needs of the people. Out of the desperation to generate more income, it will likely move to acquire more the natural resources of the nation-state, even if it has to be through improper means such as imminent domain, or through control through non-representative democracy. The struggle for resources will likely result in the government siding with external "investors" against a population that feels that it should be properly compensated for resources in their particular locale. The conflicts that ensue can be simultaneous internal conflicts, as well as external conflicts with other nation-states that may also lay claim to said resources.

This reality creates a paradox for a subject nation-state. It assumes a new *raison d'être*, through its own volition, to protect its citizens from the anarchy of global capitalism; seizing control, and the ensuing 'scramble for resources' as a means of buying time to stay afloat and stay 'viable' in the Global Economy. This will prove to be a vain effort if the people's needs are not met. Its acts of desperation will only hasten the dissolution of its mandate to rule.

Fundamentalists.

The Danger of Fundamentalism, as a reaction to the rationalization of the subject nation-state's society, is that those of that mindset will attempt to address the problems in the society by using methods that were used in the past and may not actually deal with root issues at hand. If the fundamentalist approach is as reactionary to the actions of the government as the government was to Your projections, chaos will ensue. To achieve order and stability, there will have to be a very harsh middle period, because simply reacting to the government's misactions will only cause a division in the society between those who embrace those "new-ideas" of the fundamentalists

---

307.   Lowen, p.208

and those who embrace that of the government. If the fundamentalists truly desire to "cleanse" their society of the influence that has crippled it, they will have to become the new locus of control and either become the point of reference, this attempted through some hybrid ideology desirous of utilizing the abstract structures (that You provided) through the guidance of the consensus of cultural or religious principles, or through totally creating a society based on tradition (culture and religion). The only way that this transition can be done 'in moderation' is if somehow the new architects of the society are able to, as best as they can, apply the methodology of the "past" into 'today' as an 'action'/construction, and not as a "reaction".

Fundamentalists & War Orphans

"Indeed, the most dangerous movements are composed of war orphans, who, being unsocialized, are exceptionally brutal ... Of course, the longer wars go on, the more orphans are created."[308]

There is a cause and effect to every action. The resource wars that You have been in and are presently involved in and the conflicts that are and have ensued because of Your influence on Your subject nation-state(s), have the consequence of creating casualties of war. Many of these casualties are children; and these children grow up. Moreover, they grow up in reactionary social environments in which a predatory outlook on life becomes necessary for survival. Without the normal socialization and relational valuing of human life that children require in order to become healthy, productive adults, these human 'casualities' have the potential of perpetuating the only reality that they know.

Fundamentalists & Stability

Fundamentalist movements will garner an audience because of the dis-locative effects of Your influence on the subject's society. The only "effective" alternative to the standing by and watching their society collapse is to take a 'hard-line' and 'fix' these problems. The populace may at least initially welcome the extreme nature of the fundamentalists because the social disarray and chaos that envelops the society.

If not responsibility regulated, Your influence (projections) will create an environment where fundamentalism is welcomed, because the people will have no other apparent choice to bring stability and 'security' back into their lives.

---

308.   Kaplan, p.237

WMD (Weapons of Mass Destruction)
Persons in Your subject nation-state, after the conquest of its state, may come to the realization that in order to protect themselves from You, and might secretly work to develop "Weapons of Mass Destruction" as a means of asymmetric warfare to protect themselves from Your reach. They may realize that neither diplomacy nor conventional war can deter or restrain You, so they might undertake this course of action as a reactionary means of self-preservation.

Revolution.
The populace of your subject nation-state may view Your intentions in the manner mentioned below if too much instability results in a decrease in the human security of their nation-state. They could make statements like the following made by Thomas Jefferson to describe the geopolitical realities of his time:

> We believe no more in Bonaparte's fighting merely for the liberties of the seas, than in Great Britain's fighting for the liberties of mankind. The object is the same, to draw tc themselves the power, the wealth, and the resources of other nations.[309]

Or those made by U.S. President Woodrow Wilson's secretary of state, Robert Lansing about his world:

> How willing the British, French or Italian are to accept a mandate [from the League of Nations] as long as there are mines, oil fiends, rich grain fields or railroads [that will] make it a profitable undertaking". And they as "unselfish governments" state that their mandates "must be accepted" "for the good of mankind": "they will do their share by administering the rich regions of Mesopotamia, Syria...[310]

Revolution & Crime Gangs
Without Your knowledge, "revolutions" can occur within Your subject's government through the proliferation of corruption to the point that criminal gangs integrate into the government structure.

309.　　Chomsky, Noam (2003) *Hegemony or Survival: America's Quest for Global Dominance*. New York: Metropolitan Books. p.48 from Mexican historian Jose Fuentes Mares in Robinson, Cecil ed. (1989) *The View from Chapultepec*. Arizona. p.160
310.　　Ibid, p.48 from Stivers, William (1982) *Supremacy and Oil*. Ithaca: Cornell.

Fascism.

Fascism is the final page on the road to Rational Enlightenment – A rationally organized society governed by an elite group deemed to be higher in order in Nature.

The Rise of Non-state Organizations

Criminal organizations, legitimized criminal organizations, groups that oppose You (or even the poor masses in Your subject's nation-state); they will destroy and take from whatever represents the power that they do not have etc...

In reference to asymmetric warfare, they learn the same lesson of linear thinking: "you can win if you are unencumbered by thoughts of consequences".

States will have to turn their security forces into "counterinsurgency militias" and also look at the possibility of hiring private armies to supplement the strength of their own forces.

Asymmetric Warfare and Organizational Structuring

You should not allow arrogance in Your perception of the hierarchical linear organizational structuring that You promote in Your subject's nation-state to blind You to the reality that Your subject nation-state may be inhabited by non-linear thinkers, especially the armed, political non-state actors within it. In terms of asymmetric warfare, if You assume that 'top-down' hierarchies are the universal organizational structure that all human beings employ, You will not be cognizant of the reality that Your "enemy" may be operating in a non-hierarchical organizational structure (i.e. cells in which one person only knows two other people in the organization); and fighting an internal-based war: one based on a common long-term purpose, not simply on externalized objectives to be achieved within a particular time frame.

Self-Cannibalizing Nation-States

In Chapter 2, Application, I discussed the concept of "The Culture of Individualistic Materialism & Linear Separation". In the last paragraph on this topic I state:

> The objective of Culture Warfare is to operate like an immunodeficiency disorder (like AIDS in humans) that leaves the body open to opportunistic infection - Sustainable Exploitation. The cells that are not destroyed in the process of viral replication but whose genetic material is now modified due to the incorporation of viral genes into its DNA may mutate and become malignant. This malignancy can transform into a "rogue state" in a body (world) made of confederacies of similar cell groups that have found a way to live in relative balance with each other. The "new" cell (developed state) is now out of balance with the homeostasis of

the body due to its new genetic code (its new individualistic outlook on life) and concerns itself primarily with individual needs, discounting its relation to the whole. The disproportionate taking of resources and consumption at a gluttonous rate disrupts the balance of trade of resources at the expense of surrounding cells. The growth and metastasis of its cell colony, of its tumor and rate of consumption and use of resources eventually diverts so much energy from the natural distribution system (organs) and localized collectives (regional trade), that the body dies.

A consequence of successfully mutating the culture of Your subject nation-state, whether You deem it positive or negative, is that it will be unable to distinguish between this mutated culture and its "true culture" in the same way that the immune system of a body cannot tell the difference between benign and malignant cells. Because You keep the subject under considerable stress from all sides and it has to deal with the subsequent social, economic, and environmental problems that You have initiated within its state, in its desire to maintain a degreee of stability, it will turn to its "culture" for direction. It is this very "culture" that will ensure its destruction. By re-valuing the mores of Your subject's culture to that of Individualistic Materialism, Separation, Control, and Linear Thinking, its own culture will be the vehicle of its demise. At some point, as stated earlier, the society may realize through the emergence of SCAs that there is some external interference with its affairs. For most, this "external interference" will not be viewed with disdain, but rather with awe if You have been successful in Your projections of the universality of Modernity & Development. To make sense of why the society is falling apart, the subject will turn to "traditional culture" to mitigate the collapse of society, economy, and environment. Since this "traditional culture" now embodies Your projected mores, the subject will not critically analyze itself for self-destructive traits, because, of course, it is this "traditional culture" which maintained the integrity of the population since antiquity. If the subject is unable to see that even more than the expressions of "traditional culture", that a sustainable value system was that which grounded and directed those cultural expressions and worldview so it could be a viable culture, the re-invigoration and "preservation" of "traditional culture" will, in truth, be giving life to a self-cannibalizing nature which will reke even more havoc on its society that Your influence, because the subject will not view its "own culture" with critical eyes; it will let down the gates and welcome in the Trojan horse disguised as its former sustainable self.

This lack of critical analysis of its own "Modern Culture" will be what pushes the society to its end, and if You do not carefully monitor and balance it; it will lead to the total collapse of Your subject nation-state. The problems caused by Your projections will be inconsequential as compared to the vigor and voracity in which Your subject eats itself alive. In the name of "family", "cultural preservation", and "tradition", it will prey on itself with a passion that even You lack, because it is now a totally reactionary population who grasps for anything to stay afloat.

II. Your Own Nation-State

Chapter 39:
Your Own Nation-State's Economic Collapse

With the increasing rationalization of industry, i.e. the continuous process of naming, objectifying, and defining as a means of control, the number of superfluous "service industries" will grow as a means of gaining ownership over the industrial and financial processes. These new "service industries" may appear to be "service" but they are actually modes of production that replace the need to manufacture (produce) domestically. Because they are the "facilitators" of commerce they can act as localized islands of control while the actual "productive" industries such as manufacturing, move offshore. The problem is that with the erosion of the manufacturing sector in Your nation-state, disguised by the appearance of "production" through these "facilitative" industries, the natural economy can appear to be doing well because of the capital that flows through the hands of these "facilitative" industries, but the actual domestic economy will suffer because of increasing job loss to offshore locales, all in the name of national competitiveness. This erosion of the domestic consumer base/middle class combined with flows of capital outside of the nation-state to reinvest in offshore ventures, debt financing in emerging markets, and investment in offshore locales to avoid taxation can actually lead to domestic economic collapse. This is while maintaining having the appearance of a strong economy because of movement of capital through this "service" industry. If this "service" economy operates against the mandate of Your nation-state to provide for the human security needs of the populace, it will become a collaborator in its own dissolution. The more the domestic economy is allowed to erode in the name of "national competitiveness", the greater the disparity of wealth in the population will be of harm to the domestic business sector through the loss of consumer base. This will make the government appear to be ineffective in meeting its obligations to its population. If this situation is allowed to fester, Your government will have to make a decision; 1. pay heed to the growing divisions in the population based on race, class, religion, sexual preference, etc. as scapegoating to rationalize the growing hardships--because those believing in the integrity of the government will not believe that their government is a partner in the dissolution of the social economy of the nation-state--and pay heed to calls from Your domestic business sector that depends on strong domestic commerce to restrict outward job movement and cheap imports; or 2. allow things to become so bad that You have to lose Your "national soul" by implementing fascist-oriented security measures of control and governance to re-define the government mandate as solely to "protect private property and security", while also suppressing any democratic calls for reform of the measures that lead to the erosion of the middle class and domestic consumer base.

Again, these Rationalist measures are for "export only". If You allow them to too strongly take root in Your (own) nation-state, You will run the risk losing Your own cultural center and point of reference to the very ideology of Separation and Control that You are projecting onto Your subject nation-state.

Economy.

The free flow of capital will hollow out Your economy--this leads to lower domestic spending capability. The wealth centers. (i.e. tax base) no longer exist because they operate largely outside and through the ability to buy and sell via off-shore subsidiaries and are not liable for taxes in their home countries. The wealth sectors (as long as they still exist and not threatened by excessive foreign ownership of the economy) can exist, but the middle and lower classes which consume most of the products and make the true tax base will lessen because of the loss of jobs. You will have to depend on foreign sales--To what end is this?--why not have a prosperous domestic economy?

Migration

"The growing diversity of the region's population may be seen as a harbinger of the direction the nation and, eventually, other developed nations are headed under globalization."[311]

As long as capital, goods, and services can "freely" travel between borders, people will follow the available resources. People follow money and resources in the same manner that people have followed the movements of animal herds, and planted and havested according to location and season. The

---

311.   "The New Melting Pot: Changing Faces of International Migration and Policy Implications for Southern California". Georges Vernez. October 2003. Pacific Council on International Policy. Los Angeles, California.

consequences of this "free" flow of capital, goods, and services are the "free" flow of people to the final destination of the capital, goods, and services: Your nation-state. You should be willing to deal with whatever consequences come about from increased emigration of persons from Your subject's nation-states due to Your extraction of their wealth.

Finance-Driven Democracy
Like I mentioned before – if You project *X behavior/value system/ideal* outside, *X behavior/value system/ideal* will appear inside, because You cannot separate Yourself from Yourself.

The greater and greater internalization of a consumerist culture and quantitative valuing of the population will lead to less and less substantive evaluation and critical analysis of government and elected officials. The "quantitative worth" and media appeal (idolization by the population of bureaucrats and elected officials will also lead to less and less substantive evaluation and critical analysis of these government officials). The "quantitative worth" and media appeal of persons will outweigh the intelligence needed for a democratic process to work. Like in Your subject nation-state, elections will become primary; and democracy secondary, if important at all. In this climate, because the "valuing" of people is based upon a materialistic/iconoclastic ideal, any opposition to the status quo can be viewed then as "anti-democratic" or "anti-patriotic" because it opposes the widely-held and embraced parameters of acceptability and aesthetic/ iconoclastic valuing of the society.

In a political reality such as this, any decisions by the government and politician that embody the status quo ideal of acceptability can be rationalized away as in the "best interest of the country". The democratic process is then determined by aesthetic value and politically correct sound bytes rather than by a critically-thinking populace.

In addition to this, any "checks and balances" in government can be eroded by this dollar democracy, through two primary means: 1. because political campaigns become more and more focused on aesthetic value and congruence with images that reflect this quantitative valuing, money becomes very important in the campaign process. A candidate must purchase a particular electable "image", and the capital that these candidates need is held by those with particular political agendas – 'my money for your influence/ consideration'. The more this game grows, the more indebted politicians are to these special interest groups, especially if staying in office is an objective. Even good-intentioned candidates must succumb to this unless they are truly 'independently wealthy', because as a politician one must have enough seniority or influence over those with seniority to push a particular issue and cause. Otherwise, it is a wasted effort. A non-'independent' politician does have to put some thought into where he or she will get his or her money to stay in office; 2. with an increase in political improprieties due to the need to honor financial obligations to donors, the public may call for the conversion of positions that are traditionally appointed or bureaucratic positions--judges, district attorneys, attorney generals, insurance commissioners, etc.--; believing that by making these positions elected, that they somehow will become "objective" and "independent" of political interference." Of course, this is a naïve presumption: all elected officials must be elected, therefore are subject to the "aesthetics of electability".

Any true calls for "election reform" in regulating political contributions will be dealt with loophole-filled legislation; this would still allow for the continuation of finance-driven democracy, because the value system held by the populace will not allow for the changing of the political landscape to one in which the accepted aesthetics of electability are no longer embraced. The populace will require their "heroes" and "icons" to be worshipped and held in high office because this is necessary for their own sanity. By converting to a life of insecurity based on the quantitative valuing of Others and the quest to consume material icons to obtain happiness, the high placement and worship of human icons are needed as compasses to which one's own success can be compared and to be models to which one aspires to emulate.

Economy & Market Forces
Capitalism = competition
Trading = relationships

Business is best for all when there are long-term collaborative relationships. It is harder for new, possibly disruptive, players to come in this way. Also, if one does wish to admit a new player they will have to fit into the supply or distribution scheme as to not put other members at a disadvantage. New players are let in when there is possibility for sustainable growth.

Opening up Your economy to 'Market Forces' that are out of Your control is a dangerous road to go down. From the standpoint of "eliminating domestic barriers to trade", You need to evaluate which barriers are a benefit and which are a detriment to the sustainability of the economy of Your nation-state. It is possible, because of the pervasiveness Your projections of the merits of 'Free Trade' onto Your subject nation-state without the cultivation of a conscious identity of cultural center in Your own nation-state, that Your own population will likely embrace this ideal because it will not be cognizant of the intent of its creation. With no evaluation as to whether or not there is a full embrace of 'Free Market' ideology, the following scenarios could manifest: 1. Your own domestic economy 'flooded' with foreign versions of products that You already produce and that makeup crucial industries in terms of employment and supporting related sub-industries in Your domestic economy; and 2. in this 'Free Trade' arena, Your transnationals can profit handsomely, but if they wish to be "the most competitive" they will need to dismantle the domestic manufacturing base and move it to locales where operations are cheaper and there is a more productive workforce--or have cost savings that are so substantial that allowances can be made for the development of the workforce--and where there are more "relaxed" environmental standards; and to transition to this hyper-competitive business model, environmental regulations must also be relaxed at home, because every bit of profit that can be extracted from Your domestic economy will need to be re-invested as FDI in other nation-states, simultaneously eroding the manufacturing and wage base of Your nation-state's domestic economy.

Domestic Economic,
Environmental, & Social Breakdown
Due to an Embrace of 'Free Market' Values

If the ideology of 'Free Trade' is also embraced by those of Your nation-state, You can also experience the same dislocating effects. It will not be as severe from the standpoint of You controlling the global capital markets, interest rates, etc, but from the standpoint of free moving capital - "the race to the bottom" brand of business competitiveness, and eliminating protective tariffs, Your nation-state can be opened up for serious deterioration of its middle class, leading to the development of a service-based economy with those controlling the modes of production and the associated intangible businesses, i.e. finance, consulting, etc. and entry-level service workers that literally "support" the new governing apparatus.

The actual "work" and production will be done off-shore in the cheapest locales with the most lenient labor, environmental, and trade laws. This trend can be profitable for transnationals, but not necessarily for Your nation-state, because the value of companies to Your nation-state is in the fact that they create jobs and support a tax base for the government to ensure that basic human security needs are met. The government responds in kind by protecting this optimum sustainable business environment. A large middle class is needed to sustain a strong domestic economy. A strong domestic economy is the most important factor in providing for the economic security of Your nation-state, otherwise it is subject to the waxing and waning of the external financial and commodities markets. Strong nation-states have equally vibrant domestic and export economies, with the former being of greater importance. Also, a "race to the bottom" will, with certainly, dissolve Your domestic manufacturing base, leaving another even larger whole in your economy. Remember the logic of Henry Ford: he paid his workers $5 a day so that they could afford to buy his cars. If You allow for the dissolution of Your manufacturing base in the name of participating in a game that this not in the interest of Your nation-state, but only is to be used as a tool against an-Other, You will be essentially destroying Your middle class. One could say that the loss of manufacturing jobs locally to offshore locations saves companies money, essentially "opening up" the job market for these former workers to enter higher-wage jobs, with additional training, but You should not think this way. Why in this age of high-speed information technology would any business that has already moved its production to a low cost location, decide to re-invest its cost savings in additional white-collar workers at home? This makes no business sense, in a 'quantitative' (valued) sense of viewing things. If production is moved abroad there is no reason to not also have Research and Development and middle management move abroad as well. A company can more effectively and more inexpensively train more people to actually run its operations abroad if the condition of the domestic economy of its home nation-state is of no concern. Information technology allows for real-time communication and data transfer from most places on Earth. There is no short to medium-term rationale for being located "locally" if there is no concern for the sustainability of the local economy. Shareholders that possess this quantitatively-valued 'Free Market' ideology have no concern for the short to medium term. They believe that they can safety and separately live in gated communities or just move to another country if things deteriorate too greatly at home.

The domino effects of the loss of the manufacturing sector will appear throughout the economy, because decently-paid workers make good consumers. Having a larger underclass and/or population of working poor is a destabilizing factor where there was once a larger middle class. Issues of social class that will have been long been neglected by the use of distraction such as racism, sexism, religious/ethnic discrimination can come to a head because of more a desperate economic reality. The disintegration may be along those former or present fault lines, but the effect is the same: You will have a fractured society due to the embrace of 'Free Trade' by those in power in Your nation-state.

In addition to this, if the local population (or dominant segment of the population) is a racialized group that believes that it deserves privilege over others in its society simply by virtue of its racial, ethnic, or religious background, it may actually even work to increase immigration of foreigners that are of its racial, ethnic, or religious background in order to ensure the genetic dominance of its group within the population, leading to the creation of another level of social fracturing, where on one hand the population is highly xenophobic against particular Others, while it is embracing of a group of New Others.[312] Your nation-state will also experience immigration of national groups from locales from which Your transnationals transact their business. This can be expected as a result of capital flows from their nation-state to Yours. You can take advantage of the braindrain. If You have marketshare in their nation-state You can also benefit from the purchases made by recipients of foreign remittances that purchase Your exported items that are available in their nation-state. A danger of increased immigration can come from the badly timed effects of 'Globalization': if the middle class is hollowed out by the export of jobs and there is a desperate need for cheaper and cheaper local production of goods, these immigrants can provide for the cheap labor needed to accommodate these cheaper production costs. Problems can arise when these immigrants are seen as "taking the jobs" of locals, even through these are jobs that no national would take because of low wages and status attached to them, by individuals who themselves are experiencing the effects of joblessness and lessening opportunities. Besides "taking" these jobs, immigrants, often due to their more precarious situation and lack of safety net, have a more disciplined work ethic than locals, over time making them preferable hires with the added bonus of being willing to accept lower wages and fewer benefits than locals. New or existing ethnic, racial, or religious strife between locals and the new immigrants can arise because of the "unfairness" that locals believe that they are enduring, leading to less social cohesiveness.

If You actually implement the same "anti-protectionist" legislation that You are promoting in Your subject's nation-state within in Your own nation-state, You are only setting Yourself up for the elimination of the competitive advantage of Your own locally produced and traded products and services. It is in the best interest of a nation-state to preserve its own economy, as to support the livelihoods of its populace. Like in any relationship, if an "Outsider" desires to participate in an 'in-groups' affairs it is admitted if his or her presence is not detrimental to the already existing relationship. He or she is welcomed "inside" it if there is valued-added (the in-group is enhanced) by his or her presence. The point is that the presence of foreign goods in Your

---

312.   For example in the United States, Mexican immigrants are constant source of ' concern", while Eastern European immigrants are welcomed.

economy is to benefit the populace of Your nation-state, not just a small percentage of the population of Your nation-state. The long-term economic viability of your nation-state is assured through the participation of your whole population in the economy. Enriching a few, using the argument of performing a civic duty by providing "greater variety" for consumers is not enough. A nation-state's interest in cultivating trade and trading relationships is for the purpose of empowering the nation-state, ensuring that its population has all its essentials provided for, and affording its importers and exporters with business opportunities. This whole push for 'Free Trade' comes from individuals that do not desire to pay a fair price for a product.[313] The essence of a good trade relationship is to cultivate long-term mutually beneficial trading relationships that provide good incomes for the traders as well as good income for their home nation-states, provide a diversity of goods for consumers, and support the domestic and export economies by supplying raw material to be used for manufacturers and processed goods for re-sale.

Due to an excessively competitive domestic business environment and to direct competition with low-wage, environmentally irresponsible locales; sentiment to dismantle domestic environmental safeguards is likely to arise. In the quest to "Compete Globally", Your nation-state can lose all perspective of its present and future reality and live within the "center" of an Outside entity that has escaped Your control and is now out of hand. If Your own nation-state participates in the same environmentally destructive behaviors that You encourage in Your subject(s) You will have become a 'subject' as well--to a force that simply used You to put it into play. You will in a sense, have given life to the "Invisible Hand"; and as You well know, it does not operate in equilibrium with anything.

Imperialism as a Means of Averting Internal Social Upheaval
Decide whether or not you want to take this road or not...

The advent of a global depression further deepened such a sense of crisis. A rise in the unemployment ratio of factory workers was followed by the growing frequency of labor disputes cropped up between landlords and tenant farmers. Unemployment among the

---

313.   An example of this was in the Chinese Opium Trade. British traders desired to purchase tea from China, but the Chinese only sold tea for silver. The British traders, rather than gradually developing this trade with the capital that was available to them, instead decided that they would not pay the price offered. They instead grew opium in Colonial India to be sold to the Chinese for silver, and then used this silver to purchase tea. When the Chinese protested this narcotics trade, Britain then waged a war to obtain "free treaty ports" in order to support their right to 'free trade'.
For a more in-depth look at the tea-opium trade and its concurrent complimentary trade in natural resources from the Sulu Zone see: James Francis Warren's *The Global Economy and the Sulu Zone: Connections, Commodities, and Culture* (2002).

"intellectual class" produced by the sharply expanded opportunities for higher education during the Taisho period developed into a social problem of serious proportion, further fermenting social unrest. Against the background of such a heightening of economic crisis, political leaders were seized with the fear that the enhanced socialist movement might uproot and overthrow the Establishment. And they sought an imperialist advance into Asia as a means of overcoming this internal social unrest and the structural contradictions lying at its root...[314]

Military "expansion" is an indicator of instability at home. Military expansion may alleviate some social or economic pressure for a while, but the root human security issues are still not being met. Additionally two other dangers exist: 1. the tactics that You use abroad may appear at home; 2. You may lose the war(s) that You initiate and You may be subject to the Cultural Imperialism of another nation-state, leaving You open at the very least in a final state that necessitates cooperation in practices that may violate Your own social code.

Loss of Hegemony

What were the features of colonialism? Basically, the colonists were the true rulers of the countries they colonized. They set the laws, rules, resources and policies. They basically decided on the use of national resources, the education policies, social structure and even culture. Colonialism is nothing new.

Many developing nations including Malaysia hence fought to regain their sovereignty and independence. But when the colonists left, they left behind an education system that effectively separated religion from science (i.e. secular) and a financial system that is basically a fiat money interest-based one.

In Malaysia, long before the era of colonialism, the historical rulers of the northern states of the peninsula paid *ufti* (flower ornaments made of gold) to the Kings of Siam as "protection money". The Kings of Siam did not interfere with the local rulings and policies though. They merely took the gold "gifts".

What we intend to highlight here is that the financial liberalization that is being championed in the West in the name of globalization in effect can be a tool to re-colonize the developing nations. To see this, one needs to understand how the fiat money interest-based system works. If globalization succeeds in bringing in foreign banks to operate in the land, then it is merely a matter of time before the national wealth and sovereignty will fall into the hands of foreign financial institutions. With sovereignty lost, developing nations will be back to the olden days of colonialism, but this time the colonialists will be much more powerful. Every citizen will be basically transformed into a "slave". The interest rate will determine the "*ufti*" rate. This is necessarily a huge *ufti* because even a small interest rate of 5 per cent represents a large amount of the real economy! Not only will the developing nations be paying the *ufti*, but vital decisions will be made by the colonists including the law of the nation, the education system and even the culture. Colonialists of the past were able to obtain such power only after some serious confrontations like battles, wars, etc. However, today the financial system provides an easy and convenient tool.

---

314.   Asao, Makoto and Amano Ikuo (1972) *Education and Japan's Modernization (Kyoiku to Nihon no Kindaika)*. Japan: Ministry of Foreign Affairs. p.48

The impending financial liberalization will effectively transfer such colonial power to the financial institutions "peacefully". The people will be basically transformed into "slaves" who have to give to the colonists a portion of their produce and take orders from them with respect to laws, education, etc.
Financial liberalization within the fiat money framework is, therefore, a tool for global colonization.
Nothing of the past can match it... If, in the past,, such powers were basically acquired through battles and wars, by analogy, financial liberalization is war. The gold dinar breaks the very foundation of the tool for colonization, i.e. the fiat money. It significantly reduces the reliance on foreign reserve currencies for trade. Gold places strong resistance against economic colonization. The developing world may thus unite on the gold dinar and reap all the benefit of a common global currency that has intrinsic value on its own.
Gold money and trade settlement mechanisms using gold are means by which this new economic colonialism can be prevented.[315]

You can lose the basis of Your economic hegemony, the fiat monetary system, if the subject nation-states come to the realization that it is only through belief in Your projected abstractions that You have power (non-invasive power) over them. If so, to protect Your influence over the world economy, and to prevent a domestic economic meltdown due to the push for You to match the fiat money with true, tangible money, such as gold, silver, other commodity monies, etc.; You will have to go to war and utilize Your now severely depreciated assets to finance this war to maintain Your currency as an internationally accepted fiat currency. And in this day of asymmetric warfare, with certainty, though You may possess a greater share of high-tech weaponry, well-trained troops, and WMDs; Your subject and its alliances of like-minded subject nation-states may bring this war to Your doorstep as in the form of soft-targets--that represent Your interests--in Your subject nation-state, or in the subject nation-states of Other Princes; or even worse of all, on Your soil in the form of attacks on financial centers, crowded areas, utilities installations, modes of mass transportation, ports, etc.

---

315.   Meera,pp. 83-4

Chapter 40:
Your Own Nation-State's
Environmental Collapse

This quote is an illustration of the effects of applied linear thinking on the natural environment:

The menace of salt is also evident in specific localities of irrigated areas, with a thin white crust appearing on the soil surface, leading to falling crop yields, and trees have died in water-logged tracts. These are the after-effect of irrigation projects built without drainage to remove excess water from the soil, thereby raising the ground water table, and with it the salt under the ground rises to the surface, creating the white crust. The Kampangsaen area witnessed these phenomena not long after the irrigation feeding canals came. The Sumerians invented irrigation but never mastered drainage, and by ruining the soil they destroyed the ancient Mesopotamian civilization man had built. Mesopotamia across the plain between the Euphrates and Tigris rivers still remains to be seen after four thousand years as vast areas glistening with salt crystals when we fly over southern Iraq today. We now know all of this, but decision makers are obsessed with expediency and short-term considerations without regard for the after-effects on the environment. Such is the stance of men belonging to a subculture of modern civilization.[316]

---

316.   "The Environmental and Culture of Thailand" Adul Wichiencharoen. Paper Submitted to the Symposium on Environment and Culture with Emphasis on Urban Issues, The Siam Society Under Royal Patronage, Bangkok, 1993. p.19

Conventional Agriculture and the Utilization of Biocrops.

Once the ever increasing cost of conventional agriculture and the emphasis on exporting its agriculture to Your (and Other Princes') markets has been placed on the subject; it will be ripe for import of genetically-modified (G-M) crops just to feed its population. The one negative is that though Your biotech industry will benefit from this new reliance on biotech agriculture and the usage of related technologies, these will also proliferate in the agricultural sector of Your own nation-state. Being that You are promoting 'corporate governance without a sense of responsibility' to either or both Your subject nation-state(s) or to Your own domestic market as a component of the "Free Trade" philosophy that You promote; these companies will likely desire to enjoy the increased profits and actual ownership over food security that G-M technology provides. In doing so, You might control food production in Your subject states, but this focus on G-M technology may exclude You from continued exports to the nations of Other Princes, and even possibly to those of Other subjects who are aware of the dangers of G-M crops to Your indigenous agriculture (that is unless, of course, You have established Free Trade agreements with them).

Environment and Health.

We know that the number of diseases associated with environmental risk factors is growing. WHO estimates suggest they account for almost a third of global disease.

The new strategy on environment and health seeks to generate and pool knowledge about the interaction between the environment and health, focusing on children's health. We must strengthen EU policy-making in this arena.

Children are the most directly and acutely affected. At the global level, over 40% of the burden of environmentally induced diseases falls on children under five, even though they make up only about 10% of the population. And the number of the diseases is rising rapidly.

In Europe, one child in seven suffers from asthma – three times more than 30 years ago. In some European countries, every fourth child suffers from an allergy. In certain regions, up to 10% of infants develop physical or mental disabilities associated with exposure to lead, mercury and PCBs. These chemicals were widely used in the past, and are still present and persistent. Incidents of leukaemia have also become more frequent.[317]

For Your own nation-state, the cost of a sickly population in a medical environment based on Managed Care, with less emphasis on preventative medicine, will become prohibitive because of the dual strain on the health care system and lessening productivity in the industrial and service sectors. If there is a public pension system for the elderly, it will be taxed heavily by the massive number of pensioners that will be collecting benefits. The entire post

---

317.   "Defending REACH". Environment Business. December 2003. Surrey, UK. p.18

World War II generation will be soon at retirement age, putting a severe drain on the social security, pension, and health services for the elderly, disabled, and indigent. Their taxable incomes paid for the services of the present generation of pensioners, while they will have to depend on the taxes of the present working generations that are smaller in number and who are increasing becoming less productive because of illnesses. Due to dietary changes over the last fifty years, people are already at far greater chance for developing chronic "lifestyle illnesses" such as diabetes, heart disease, hypertension, obesity, etc. making them more apt to miss work. The hypersterile environment that children are now growing up in, with the proliferation of OTC[318] antibacterials such as triclosan and the over-prescription of antibiotics, and shorter breastfeeding periods, children grow up without fully developed immune systems. The combination of a compromised immune system due to lack of stimulation and fewer antibodies, with the presence of more and more environmental irritants, promotes the development of "weaker" children that are more illness-prone than any other generations. The only saving grace for these new generations of children is if they are immunized, at least they will be protected from regular gamut of communicable diseases. But nevertheless, these new generations of youth are disproportionately afflicted by allergies starting at youth and the older they become, with the combination of bad diet, stress (including the stresses of living according to a quantitatively-based value system), environmental irritants, and a reactionary approach to health maintenance; they will become less and less productive people. From the standpoint of industrial output and taxable income, they will become less and less reliable to the society, leaving the coming generations of pensioners at risk for non-viability of the social security system; and providing justification to businesses that desire to go offshore in order to stay competitive.

Environment and Business.

To excel in this Global Economy, of which You are one of the major architects, businesspersons of Your nation-state may perceive it as necessary to participate in a hyper-competitive mode, regardless of the consequences. In terms of the environment, they may opt for the same environmental philosophy that Your subject subscribes to: "If we can get rich today, we can worry about cleaning up the environment tomorrow". Those who do follow this modus operandi will call for the elimination of all barriers to business competitiveness and technological development--the omission of costly

---

318.   Over the Counter (Non-prescription) Drugs

environmental compliance directives and a "green light" for scientific and industrial development at any ecological cost.

Business - Environmental Legislation

To compete in the "Global Economy" that You have worked to create, Your own businesses will feel the pressure to cut-costs as much as possible as to stay competitive with low-cost centers in subject nation-states. Even though they may benefit substantially from outsourcing and/or direct off-shore investment in low-cost locales, the desire to amass as much capital as possible and subsequently consume as much as possible will prevail if You successfully export this ideal of Individualistic Materialism as a virtue, because it will, in turn, be internalized by Your own populace. Businesspersons, rather than calling for protective measures for the domestic economy against non-beneficial external trade, will instead request legislation for the total repeal of domestic environmental protection laws that can be viewed to impede business and, at the very least reduce the competitiveness of Your nation-state's businesses. They may call for unrestricted logging, offshore drilling, mining, biotechnical, chemical, and nuclear research, clearing of land, grazing, dredging, cutting of coral, the elimination of air emissions and water standards and of environmental regulations of activities such as dumping, logging, mining, offshore drilling, fossil fuel burning, land clearing and development, hydroelectric and waterways projects, dredging, desalinization, coral cutting, fishing, grazing, conventional agriculture, and the creation of genetically-modified organisms.

If this sort of thinking is allowed to prevail and legislators in Your nation-state make these provisions, it is indicative of a true adaptation of a linear thought process. Both the business leaders and the politicians will have failed to include the long-term costs of environmental collapse in their profit-cost analysis concerning the elimination of sustainable environmental management policies.

Environment and Business - Local Agriculture

Rooftops continue to sprout on more and more farmland in the Kansas City area.

That's not good; it makes area residents more dependent on food from states such as California and California and Florida and countries such as Mexico, Australia and Argentina. Ted Carey is working against that trend...

"There are precious few vegetable producers around right now," said Carey, a vegetable crops specialist with the Kansas State University Extension Center in Olathe.

Carey has a doctorate in horticulture form the University of Illinois. His experience included years at International Agriculture Research Centers working with farmers in Colombia, Peru, and Kenya...

"One of the keys to success for the current vegetable grower is direct marketing so they can command a very high price," Carey said. "It has to do with what people are willing to pay for food."

Right now folks don't pay much, and that's the problem. Cheap labor and fuel enable produce to be shipped from other states and countries to area stores and sold at low prices. Meanwhile, area growers struggle against the urbanization of farmland and what Ben Kjelshus called "the corporate-dominated, industrialized and heavily centralized food system." Area residents' dependence on cheap foreign oil and labor is what troubles Kjelshus, founder of the Kansas City Food Circle Project.

He said, "The ultimate control over people is control over the food supply."

The globalization of food production creates a dependency at home, said Craig Volland, a Kansas City Food Circle coordinating committee member.

The group connects area growers and consumers to promote healthy eating habits and the survival of small family farms.

Consumers think they're getting low-priced food, but the hidden costs include social and economic instability in other nations. So locally produced food is a major world peace issue, too.

"I think peace is related to feeling secure and not feeling fearful," Volland said. "You cannot be fearful about your food supply"[319]

Besides the economic impact of a 'Globalized' food supply on Your own nation-state, there are cultural concerns that You should also be aware of, in terms of the sustainability and perpetuation of Your own nation-state. Small farms and farming rural people are the custodians of Your nation-state's purest form of 'cultural-center' because they believe in Your espoused national ideals, and because they are not in the cities they cannot experience it in an accommodated, corrupted, or 'Globalized' form. The 'geographical center' of Your nation-state must not be placed under too much duress because of the forces of Globalization or You will lose the core believers in Your system of governance. It is important for the integrity of Your own nation-state to not have the 'center' rural people endure too much hardship or You will risk losing Your truest, most faithful, and most unquestioning citizens.

Unnatural Disasters.

Around the world, a growing share of the devastation triggered by "natural" disasters stems from ecologically destructive practices and from putting ourselves in harm's way. Many ecosystems have been frayed to the point where they are no longer resilient and able to withstand natural disturbances, setting the stage for "unnatural" – those made more frequent or more severe due to human actions. By degrading forests, engineering rivers, filling in wetlands, and destabilizing the climate, we are unraveling the strands cf a complex ecological safety net...[320]

---

319.   "Local Crops Help the Whole World". Lewis W. Diuguid, The Kansas City Star, August 20, 2003.

Just as not every natural disturbance is a disaster, not every disaster is completely natural. We have altered so many natural systems so drastically that their ability to bounce back from disturbances has been greatly diminished. Deforestation impairs watersheds, raises the risk of fires, and contributes to climate change. Destruction of coastal wetlands, dunes, and mangroves eliminates nature's shock absorbers for coastal storms. Such human-made changes end up making naturally vulnerable areas – such as hillsides, rivers, coastal zones, and low-lying islands – even more vulnerable to extreme weather events.

Droughts, and the famines that often follow; may be the most widely misunderstood – if underreported – example of an unnatural disaster. They are triggered partly by global climate variability (both natural and human-induced) and partly by resource mismanagement such as deforestation, overgrazing, and the overtapping of rivers and wells for irrigation.[321]

In the quest to develop and maintain its place as the pinnacle of Modernity and Civilization, Your own nation-state will have to engage in behavior and have to make decisions that are contrary to its own existence. The environment is not a "sector"; it is a large part of the body of a nation-state. In the same manner that, if Public Health were to be neglected, the whole society (population) will become sick; neglect and misuse of the environment will also literally make the nation-state sick - physiologically, mentally, and economically. Neglect and mistreatment of the environment to the point where it begins to counterbalance that which is assaulting it, leads to unnatural disasters. The danger of unnatural disasters is that they could, 1. be an indicator of an entire ecological change due to abuse exceeding a threshold of sustainability of its current state; and 2. because linear-based thinking having pushed the environment to this threshold, the intensity of its counterbalance can reach unimaginable parameters because the same behaviors that cause this imbalance will continue because a linear mind does not contemplate consequences; and with the ever increasing speed of the commodification of Nature to feed the consumerism of a Globalized World, Nature's response to this trend could reach nightmarish proportions. Additionally, with the massive migrations to urban centers, environmental disasters will bring a tremendous number of casualties because of the population density, the ensuing panic caused by a major unmitigatable disaster, the massive food shortages; and for those fully urbanized, they will be without the basic knowledge of how to survive in nature, i.e. growing food, catching fish, skinning animals, picking edible plants, etc. There is no malicious response in Nature to what is done to it, It will only respond in-kind to take back what is being taken from it.

---

320.   "Unnatural Disasters" by Janet Abramovitz. Worldwatch Paper 158, Worldwatch Institute. Oct. 2001. p.6
321.   Ibid. p.15

Chapter 41: Your Own Nation-State's Social Collapse

"Those who desire to give up freedom in order to gain security, will not have, nor do they deserve, either one." - Benjamin Franklin

Asymmetric Warfare.

If You have to engage in asymmetric warfare to protect Your economic and ideological interests, remember one thing – You will be viewed as a bully because of Your size. But remember, bullies also have eyes, throats, groins, and knees (and psyches). Yours may not be as easy to get at, but all bodies have "soft spots" that cannot withstand too much pain.

Asymmetric Warfare and Information Technology

The networked global economy will be driven by rapid and largely unrestricted flows of information, ideas, cultural values, capital, goods and services, and people: that is, globalization. This globalized economy will be a net contributor to increased political stability in the world in 2015, although its reach and benefits will not be universal. In contrast to the Industrial Revolution, the process of globalization will be more compressed. Its evolution will be rocky, marked by chronic financial volatility and a widening economic divide…

…computer-based information operations could provide our adversaries with an asymmetric response to … military superiority by giving them the potential to degrade to circumvent our advantage in conventional military power…

…attacks on our military, economic, or telecommunications infrastructure can be launched from anywhere in the world. And they can be used to transport the problems of a distant conflict directly to… heartland…[322]

In addition to the obvious military disadvantages brought about by the "democratization" of IT (Information Technology): the global proliferation of these technologies through Globalization and "Free Trade"; a major danger comes from the offshore housing and outsourcing of Your nation-state's technology industries, in particular those of the IT sector.

IT essentially becomes "open source technology" and what "open source technology" means to You, means something very different to those disgruntled with Your control and influence over Your subject nation-state(s) and in the world-at-large.

This example is in reference to the defense industry information that is openly available on the market:

Through the eyes of a western analyst the publications are what they seem military trade journals that cover market phase, sales opportunities, competitive and joint venture, and national acquisition goals…

… graphs and computer-generated art enhance the stories and illustrate the concepts. In the photographs use, sleek missiles fly, spotless armored vehicles roll and wholesome, clean

---

322.   Statement of the Record for the Joint Economic Committee "Cyber Threat Trends and US Network Security". Lawrence K. Gershwin, National Intelligence Officer for Science and Technology. June 21, 2001. pp.1-2

soldiers pose with the latest weaponry in pleasant pastures. There is no blood.

Consider now the reader of this same information from poorer, less industrialized, embargoed or other-wise ostracized nations. Consider also the people of para-nations, the ethnic clans, narcotics traffickers and terrorists. They see the same information in terms of life or death choices. They cannot afford technical research or development, and they cannot "comparison shop". They know they must choose wisely the first time because there may not be what they can learn from open publications. The more sophisticated groups can build on information from open sources and confirm their conclusions with traditional collection methods. Their interest is far from abstract...

... These poorer countries want to know, simply put, how to beat... in battle. To be able to surprise the ... military, they will try to learn more about it than the military knows about itself. They do not have the wherewithal to conduct massive technical research, so they will take any shortcut. All open sources will be exploited. Why spend the money on research and development if the final product is going to be for sale or is explained on the Internet? Why test weapons if the answers nations seek are printed in publications that cost only a few dollars each? Comparison tests will be done by these governments that see weaponry more as a commodity to be marketed than as a means of killing people.[323]

Even if Your industries produce proprietary technologies--software, hardware--You will have given them the building blocks of these technologies. Also, in the Individualist-Materialistic environment that You have created and continue to promote, marketable intelligence goes to the highest bidder. Those working on Your technologies abroad can be approached by those desirous of asymmetric warfare against You and may offer better compensation for their knowledge, leaving You with one safeguard: the hope of being affirmed as an employee of Your nation-state's industries' companies with whom the sense of approval and affirmation be that which symbolizes Universal Success, Progress, and Status will outweigh that of higher compensation.

I mention this because if You outsource the maintenance and Research & Development of Your nation-state's IT sector offshore because of the motive of cost-savings, You should be aware that while You might have "cost" savings initially; that this also opens up opportunities for Your nation-state's cyber networks and technological apparatus that control its national infrastructure--communications, banking, utilities, healthcare (HIS/PACS), logistics, and military--to be open to attack. You could already be training the army that attacks Your national IT infrastructure.

Though You may be projecting an ideology based on linear-time and You claim that Your hegemony and influence are the culmination of the Human Experience; You cannot ever actually forget that time is cyclical, that all empires rise and fall, and that the overexpansion of empire is often one of the

---

323.   "Open Source Information" Army Magazine, July 97 Issue.

root causes of its own demise. If You have not totally decimated Your subject nation-state populace's memory (knowledge) of cyclical time through Your assaults of Cultural Warfare, it could just be waiting for the opportune time to attack. And IT (Information Technology) is perfect weapon for asymmetric warfare.

Being that access to the most computer technology and access to the Internet is relatively inexpensive--for many nation-states, cheap--this method of warfare is particularly cost-effective in comparison with other forms of warfare. The major costs that an enemy may incur is in the acquisition of a particular piece of hardware or software or through the payment for the intellectual services of an expert who knows how to create or access these proprietary systems; and even these expensive tools are likely not needed because of the growing number of skilled hackers that reside throughout the world.

Attacks will not have to actually be debilitating (though if they were this could be very disruptive to national infrastructures based on IT) they only have to cause public--and even greater danger--global doubt in the reliability and security of these systems, especially if the effected infrastructure are financial networks. Successful attacks could strangle national and global financial systems, communications, utilities operations, logistics and transportation (i.e. air traffic control, and ship traffic), military operations, etc.

IT is an avenue through which both state and non-state actors can operate against You with the greater success ratio, in comparison to the cost of lives and equipment that other forms of asymmetric war would require.

You should think carefully about integrating the actions of Your transnationals with the security needs of Your nation-state. Your projection of "Free Trade" onto Your subject nation-state can create a situation in which the actions of Your own populace and businesses play as integral part in making Your nation-state vulnerable to asymmetrical attack.

What You Call 'Terrorism'
If You make a blanket designation of "terrorist" and fight a war on "terrorism", You lose the ability to fight an effective war, because there is no focus to Your military campaigns. Terrorism is not a term to describe people, it is a term to describe particular tactics of warfare, primarily the killing of civilians to directly achieve objectives or indirectly through causing fear and panic. Not all "terrorist" groups pose an imminent threat to You or Your interests. Who is defined as a 'terrorist', 'freedom fighter', 'legitimate government' is defined by those actually affected by these groups. A worldwide campaign against 'terrorism' is only an invitation to fascism and security-oriented governance. Though You may have concern for those affected, a 'terrorist' group in 'X'

nation-state 10,000 miles away that states (and acts in) no opposition to You and poses only a 'threat' to those it involves is not a 'terrorist group' to You, because if You do not operate/'live' (have Your resident citizens effected) in that nation-state' or region's reality You are not aware of all of the dynamics involved and cannot as an outsider make an intelligent assessment of the actors in the conflict. In actuality this does affect You, but in a greater interconnected human-environment sense, not in terms of You promoting and maintaining Sustainable Exploitation.

Even Your calls for "peace" and non-violence are still without context. The use of violence may be a cry of desperation for those severely negatively affected by a particular hierarchy. Open dialogue--listening to those affected and those 'affecting' and the true intent to resolve root issues--is a way to address of 'terrorism', but blanket calls for solidarity against [terrorism] is only a deliberate or subconscious call for security-oriented governance instead of Democratic Governance and possible retaliatory asymmetric attacks on Your nation-state and/or its citizens and interests in Other nation-states.

Social Breakdown and Human Rights.

In Your quest to conquer and exploit Your subject nation-state, You cannot lose sight of the social reality of Your own nation-state including watching the signs of the domestic internalization and proliferation and application of the disintegrative value-system that You are projecting onto Your subject's nation-state. Let me reiterate a quote that I used in the beginning of our dialogue to illustrate the domestic internalization, proliferation, and application of a separationist process and a value system used on Others.

First we must study how colonization works to *decivilize* the colonizer, to *brutalize* him in the true sense of the word, to degrade him, to awaken him to buried instincts, to covetousness, violence, race hatred, and moral relativism; and we must show that each time a head is cut off or an eye put out in Vietnam and in France they accept the fact, each time a little girl is raped and in France they accept the fact, each time a Madagascan is tortured and in France they accept the fact, civilization acquires another dead weight, a universal regression takes place, a gangrene sets in, a center of infection begins to spread; and that at the end of all these treaties that have been violated, all these lies that have been propagated, all these punitive expeditions that have been tolerated, all of these prisoners who have been tied up and "interrogated," all these patriots who have been tortured, at the end of all the racial pride that has been encouraged, all the boastfulness that has been displayed, a poison has been distilled into the veins of Europe and, slowly but surely, the continent proceeds toward *savagery*.

And then one fine day the bourgeoisie is awakened by a terrific boomerang effect: the gestapos are busy, the prisons fill up, the torturers standing around the racks invent, refine, discuss.

People are surprised, they become indignant. They say "How strange! But never mind – it's Nazism, it will pass!" And they wait, and they hope; and they hide the truth from

419

themselves, that it is barbarism, the supreme barbarism, the crowning barbarism that sums up all the daily barbarisms, that is Nazism, yes, but that before they were its victims, they were its accomplices; that they were tolerated that Nazism before it was inflicted on them, that they absolved it, shut their eyes to it, legitimized it, because until then, it had only been applied to non-European peoples; that they have cultivated that Nazism, that they are responsible for it, and that before engulfing the whole edifice of Western, Christian civilization in its reddening waters, it oozes, seeps, and trickles from every crack...[324]

Social Breakdown

The following social trends indicate, internal social decay and unsustainable value systems:

1. Ineffective protection of life and security of persons; and excessive violence in Your nation-state's society and incarceration used as a primary means of social control--"law and order" solutions to all social problems--while avoiding any attention to root problems;
2. Serious human rights violations by law enforcement officials - legislation of domestic intelligence: gathering, and counterinsurgency or terrorism laws that violate civil liberties of the citizenry and the social acceptability of police brutality on some or all sectors of the society;
3. Finance-driven democracy - elections won through massive media campaign, and decisions made through personal deals rather than elections by a critically-minded population and governance decisions based on attaining collective community and national interests;
4. Poverty, Hunger, and Homelessness - poverty, hunger, and homelessness amongst members and sectors of Your nation-state's society actually becoming so acceptable that there is a basic consensus that they deserve their plight and/or created this themselves and that it is not the responsibility of the society to look after its fellow citizens – with an increasing gap between rich and poor that is acceptable to the majority of Your populace and natural hierarchy even though Your nation-state has the means to ensure the sustainability of its entire citizenry; Your production of surplus food being so great that Your government subsidizes farmers not to grow food and You have hungry people living in Your nation-state; and the allowing of fellow citizens to go hungry as an acceptable reality for Your nation-state's society;
5. Women and children are in state of violence - sexual discrimination, sexual violence, domestic violence, "obliviousness" to the needs of families (i.e. maternity and paternity leave), and the lack of quality educational opportunities for all children though there may be occasional emotional outcry

---

324.   Cesare, pp.35-6

from the public against these and attention paid to these by politicians around election time; the perpetuation of the status quo is acceptable in the society;
6. Deep-rooted Racial Discrimination - severe disparities in application law enforcement, education, healthcare, housing, financing;
7. Double standards in International Human Rights – not ratifying international human rights treaties because of Your support of policies in Your subject nation-state in other nation-states that support Your interests, but violate the human rights ideals that You project onto Your subject nation-state(s). This hypocrisy can have negative effects in Your own nation-state, especially if highlighted as a pattern of behavior or value system of oppression that is used on individuals in Your own nation-state.[325]

Individualism.

If the Individualism that You project onto Your subject also is internalized by Your own nation-state, You will need to ensure that it is molded into a more manageable type. This type being one in which there is a social contract of a Culture of Individualism; this being one where one is encouraged to act as an individual without concern for other, except in the case where such actions are counter to the interests of the nation-state as a whole.

This can be created by encouraging conformity in family life, corporate culture, etc. Those who are different are to be chastised for their differences, while at the same time You are projecting legislated 'Freedoms of the Individual'. Promote countless 'citizen's groups' that can govern the behaviors and social mores, even to the extent of having neighborhood groups that determine the suitability of potential tenants and homeowners based on their conformity to a particular cultural form. Any shortcomings in Your nation-state or in the 'system' are to be blamed on minority groups (ethnic, religious, sexual, etc.). The only danger in this is that domestic racism, xenophobia, etc, can get out of control; and the public may call for foreign military expeditions (or domestic internment or segregation of these groups) to eliminate those who embody this difference or "evil" that threatens the sustainability or "way of life" of Your nation-state.

If things do become difficult for many of Your own nation-state's citizens because of social, economic, and environmental consequences of a full embrace of 'Free Trade'--outsourcing and subsequent job losses, wage and benefit cuts to compete with offshore locales--and 'Individual Responsibility'--

---

325.   List of trends from "Human Rights Record of the United States in 2002" by the Information Office of the State Council of the People's Republic of China. April 3, 2003. From *Human Rights*, China Society for Human Rights, Beijing. Vol. 2, No.4, July 2003, pp.12-19

loss of 'community'/collective responsibility for community life, breakdown of 'family' from extended to nuclear to civil unions--there might be calls for serious social reform which could lessen Your grip over Your own nation and lessen its 'Progress' because it will be encumbered with thoughts about how its domestic and foreign policy affects its domestic reality. To stay in control, and to continue Your external policies of conquest You will probably have to initiate a fascist-oriented style of governance based on 'security threats' in order to call attention away from domestic realities and focus on creating fear and paranoia in order to redefine Your government's mandate as that of focusing primarily on providing for physical security of the state, while neglecting the human security of the state - of which demise spells a greater threat to the solvency of Your nation-state than that of imaginary, exaggerated, or encouraged external security threats. This change into a more fascist-oriented style of governance will allow You to coordinate Your industrial sector with Your goals for the nation-state, but this will require You to maintain an almost martial law or heightened state of security in order to occupy the minds of the populace. Problems may occur when You have to fight these "monsters" or embodiments of "evil" abroad in order to appease the public; and/or if these excursions or those for other reasons, such as profit or control over resources, get out of control and You provoke the targets of Your conquest to engage in asymmetric warfare within both their own nation-state and within Yours, in order to maintain their self-determination and protect their cultural integrity and resources from Your attacks.

Health.

The nineteenth-century and early twentieth-century creators of America's public health systems would have found this emphasis on individualism amid such grand prosperity shocking. For them, the health of a community was the key measure of its success, and if pestilence and death stalked even one small segment of the population it was a stark indication of the community's political and social failure.[326]

A few things that You should think about regarding health:

Watch for the re-emergence of former killers in new multidrug-resistant forms. Because these are "former killers" for Your nation-state and "present killers" for the developing world, the presence of these diseases may not evoke a strong reaction. There can also be a re-emergence of childhood epidemics because of an increasing division of wealth that leads to less oversight over immunization, school attendance, and other public health

---

326.   Garrett, p.269

basics such as clean water, good nutrition, and community hygiene.

Do not underestimate the human and economic costs, especially in an individualized medical care system, the cost of "lifestyle diseases" such heart disease, hypertension, obesity, and diabetes. These "lifestyle diseases" develop with the lifestyle changes that a consumeristic society brings, as well as from changes in the natural environment (including stresses) that contribute directly to human health.

Being that Your nation-state is also in the world, and that there is a combination of inadequate individualized care systems and inadequate public health systems stirring the pot of the increasing number of antibiotic resistant pathogens, Your nation-state will also be subject to the reality of a post-antibiotic age, one that is coming soon because of the trend of over-prescribing antibiotics to the rich and underutilization of antibiotics[327] by the poor.

Watch for the continued emergence of cross-species diseases especially with the trend of deforestation and development of formerly untouched wildlife areas, the migration of rural people to urban areas and the cramped living quarters that different species of animals are now bred in, the proliferation of xenotransplantation and genetic engineering based in linear thought processes, and the modes of mass transportation that will bring these "new" diseases to You.

Free Trade, Urbanization, and the Spread of Disease.

New exotic and cross-species diseases can make an easy entry into Your nation-state because of the global economic 'race to the bottom' that forces those in low-cost locales to quickly urbanize leading to three major Public Health stressors. Due to Your nation-state's participation in this 'Free Trade' with the present-day rapid modes of transportation and enormous volume of shipping, it will be susceptible to whatever Public Health dangers that brew in the locales from which You and Your nation-state's businesses extract resources, products, and services from. These stressors are:

1. High population density in small cramped unsanitary urban spaces - the spread of communicable diseases, and if antibiotics are being misused, also being a breeding ground for resistant strains;

2. High population density in areas susceptible to disasters[328] such as flooding, mudslides, etc. a breeding ground for water-bourne human

---

327.   Not completing full courses of antibodies because of the desire to "save" some of them for future illnesses.

diseases.

3.The aforementioned (Number 2) is likely to occur more and more because of the need to acquire land to build new urban dwellings.

Clearing land, hills, forests to do so, make very unstable environmental and ecological systems that will still have to contend with the normal cycle of natural disasters of which there will possibly be a lot more of because of an increase in erratic weather that stems from natural and human-induced climate change;

4.The close dwellings of rural people in urban settings allows for the spread of disease that would not normally (or at least frequently) occur in rural environments, i.e. the raising of many species of animals in close quarters and in contact with each other leading to cross-species disease outbreaks due to natural vectors such as pigs that can host both, for example, avian and human disease, and the contact of such disease within this host vector can lead to genetic exchanges with disastrous outcomes for human and other animal populations;

5.The paradigm of the former (Number 4) combined with the encroachment of lands that have only been occupied by wildlife since time immemorial placing human beings and animals in contact with other organisms such as previously unknown plant, animal, and human-affecting viruses, bacteria, and fungi. This can reek havoc on these previously unacquainted populations;

6.With this dynamic of rapid, unplanned urbanization in the low-cost locals which Your nation-state outsources services, manufactures and imports raw materials and/or finished products, in order to join Your 'Global Economy', You in a sense, may be creating a series of Petri dishes that are growing pathogens that You cannot yet conceive of. And on every airplane or container ship there could be a potential microbial hijacker that could overwhelm Your Public Health system, and lead to a substantial loss of human, animal, or plant life in Your nation-state, this having another series of unknown domino effects such as quarantines, shipping stoppages, crop failures, animal die-offs, financial crisis, etc...

328.	I did not use the term 'natural disasters' because a number of contemporary 'natural disasters' are the direct result of past environmentally-invasive actions such as excessive cutting and clearing of wetlands followed by the settlement of adjacent hillsides. The resulting mudslides and flooding are not 'natural disasters'.

Society.

The historian Paul Kennedy has dubbed this condition "imperial overstretch". In an analysis of the United States in his book *The Rise and Fall of the Great Powers*, he wrote that – it cannot avoid confronting the two great tests which challenge the *longevity* of every major power that occupies the "number one" position in world affairs: Whether, in the military/ strategy realm, it can preserve a reasonable balance between the nation's perce ved defense requirement and the means it possessed to maintain these commitments; and whether , as an intimately related point, it can preserve the technological and economic bases of its power from relative erosion in the face of the ever-shifting of global population. This test of American abilities will be the greater because it, unlike Imperial Spain around 1600 or the British Empire around 1900, is the inheritor of a vast array of strategical commitments which had been made decades earlier, when the nation's political, economic, and military capacity to influence world affairs seemed so much more assured.[329]

You, as Prince, have to evaluate Your decisions based on Your purpose of conquest as well as these two "great tests". If You do not acknowledge that You are an Empire, and if You in actuality act as one, You will certainly lose Your Empire. Imperialists/Emperors who view themselves as anything other than this are destined to lose because of a lack of introspection and honest evaluations of their decisions in conquest, expansion, and sustainability.

Military Assistance.

In other words, most of the training exercises are meant to prepare foreign militaries for actions against their own populaces or rebel forces in their countries. The manual defines FID as organizing, training, advising, and assisting a foreign military establishment in order to protect its society from "subversion, lawlessness, and insurgency".

Stripped of its euphemistic language, FID amounts to little more than state terrorism.[330]

This is the danger – You training the subject's armed forces (including police) can be construed by the populace as well as by Other subjects as state terrorism. It is unlikely that Other Princes would join in this chorus of criticism, but their support of the policies that You project onto Your subject as well as Your other influences can be perceived as co-conspiring actions-- belonging to a group of powerful and dominating nation-states--and they can face problems in their subject nation-states as well as amongst the voices of the transnational organizations that are supposed to be supporting the national interests of Your nation-state and those of Other Princes.

---

329.   Johnson, p.30 from Kennedy, Paul (1988) *The Rise and Fall of the Great Powers: Economic Change and Military Conflict from 1500 to 2000.* (London: Unwin Hymin) P. 514-5
330.   Ibid, p.73. Re: FID "Foreign Internal Defense"

Blowback.

Chalmers Johnson describes a concept that You should pay close attention to because those engaging in linear thought usually are oblivious to it, and those non-linear thinkers that would take the risk of participating in unsustainable conquest take this seriously.

> "Blowback" is shorthand for saying that a nation reaps what it sows, even if it does not fully know or understand what it has sown...But it is blowback in its larger aspect – the tangible costs of empire – that truly threatens it. Empires are costly operations, and they become most costly by the year. The hollowing of... industry, for instance is a form of blowback – an unintended negative consequence of ... policy – even though it is seldom recognized as such. The growth of militarism in a once democratic society is another example of blowback. Empire is the problem. Even though the... has a strong sense of invulnerability and substantial military and economic tools to make such a feeling credible, the fact of its imperial pretensions means that a crisis is inevitable. More imperialist projects simply generate more blowback. If we do not begin to solve problems in more prudent and modest ways, blowback will only become more intense.[331]

Society (War).

Inside of Your own nation-state, opposition to increased entanglement in foreign disputes when domestic issues are not being addressed, i.e. "Is... not suffering a serious internal crisis of a social, political, and economic nature that deserves to be resolved? Do they perhaps want our forces to be used to 'solve conflicts throughout the world' when we have our own serious economic, social, and political problems to solve? I think our priority is to look out for the security and development of our own country."[332] These questions can be the rationale for the weakening of Your mandate to govern.

Society (Law)

You have to be careful to every control transnational governing body. If they are not under Your control, or at the very least under substantive influence You should then proclaim them as illegitimate and ineffective. One example is a transnational organization gone wrong is the World Court when in the case – it made a precedent stating that intervention is "prohibited" if it interferes with the sovereign right of "choice of a political, economic, social, and cultural system, and the formulation of policy": intervention is "wrongful when it uses methods of coercion in regard to such choices"[333]. If Your methods of Cultural

---

331.   Ibid, pp.232-4
332.   "Plan Colombia" TRIcontinental, Year 36, Number 151, 2002.
333.   Chomsky, p.99 in reference to *Military and Paramilitary Activities in and against Nicaragua*, International Court of Justice, 27 June 1986. Security Council S/18221, 11 July 1986.

Warfare are discovered, You can face sanction in the eyes of the world through the International Criminal Court for violating this precedent. The ICC cannot hurt You, but it would call attention to Your methods and if You were to desire to continue Your exploitation of Your subject nation-states and/or Other subject nation-states, You might have to resort to more invasive measures to do so.

Development of Fascism in Your Own Nation-state

Over time, if Your own nation-state begins to assimilate Your projections as its own primary value system, You may have to develop a form of fascism to have direct hold over Your foreign policy--the use of state-military-centered thinking can lead to the inability to see domestic problems: in regard to the societal breakdown in Your nation-state, instead of dealing with root problems You would use a linear thought process which would lead to the utilization of further fascist measures to solidify state control, discourage detractors, and create a climate of fear which will be used to govern.

The problem comes with You neglecting root issues in Your nation-state and taking on a linear approach. You will implement further fascist measures of state control in order to bring "Freedom and Security" to the nation-state, but with further deterioration of Your society, economy, and environment to hold the state together, You will have to implement further and further Draconian measures to sequester the voices of democracy in Your society, so that they do not threaten Your ability to administer top-down state control and continue the necessary climate of fear.

Society - Nuclear War

Watch out for the danger of "nuking"[334] away pressing foreign policy issues-- using nuclear weapons on "terrorist" or "rogue states" that You do not feel like going into long drawn asymmetric war with. These are states that develop because of Your influence over its former government(s) that caused it (them) to betray its (their) people and in doing so sowed the seeds for fundamentalist or revolutionary movements; movements that gained popular support in the hope of retrieving the society from physical destruction or cultural/moral decay. Nuclear weapons should never be put into the conventional arsenal as "tactical weapons". If they are, they will be used in a tactical fashion in conflicts that are deemed by military officials as potentially too costly to place ground troops. These scenarios are essentially Nintendo wars using nuclear weapons, which, of course, will result in the mass-murder of thousands,

---

334.   Using nuclear weapons against an enemy state.

hundreds of thousands, possibly millions of people; environment disaster; and escalation of world conflict to that which sanctions the actual use of nuclear weapon in warfare, rather than using them simply as a deterrent against nuclear attack by Other nation-states.

WMDs (Weapons of Mass Destruction).

With this Individualistic value system, personal consumption becomes more important than the sustainability of one's own nation-state or to human survival in general - and enterprising persons, who are either antagonistic to You, or simply oblivious to the possible shared consequences of the proliferation of WMDs in the world, will sell those weapons, or the technologies to make them, to actors willing to engage in asymmetric warfare with You.

World War/Proliferation of WMDs

Using space systems and planning for pre-emptive attacks from space-based launch platforms can lead to a worldwide proliferation of WMDs to counter the threat that Other nation-states perceive from these moves. They can assume that they can be attacked without notice at anytime, so they will, as counteractive measure determine to also place weapons of mass-murder for potential use in Your nation-state or directed towards soft-targets in Other nation-states that serve or symbolize Your interests. The state of paranoia that You can place many governments in the world in can also provoke pre-emptive asymmetric attacks on You or Your interests as well. The entire level of war play can be elevated because this move--colonizing Space--can be viewed as excessively predatory and they can assume that the day of their end is imminent, so they would rather at least get the satisfaction of destroying some of You or Your interests. This is the same logic that existed in the Cold War: mutually assured destruction or parity. The danger that exists is You not realizing how much a threat this can be viewed as: unprovoked attacks from the sky, "satellite-killing" satellites destroying their communications, financial, and telecom-based defense systems instantly through the destruction of their communications satellites, etc. This is enough to make some defense personnel "crazy" with suicidal-homicidal tendencies. If You are to be viewed as a non-linear thinker through Your policies and methods of warfare, this scenario is not as frightening, because the Others can feel assured that You make actions based on the contemplation of potential consequences and a realization of interconnectedness as inhabitants of the Earth.

If, through Your unbalanced administration of Cultural Warfare, there is lot of collateral societal, economic, and environmental damage due to actions taken, with no regard to the consequences, especially with statements of surprise from You when things do go array; it is only logical that the Others should deduce that You could possibly undertake rash military action on a whim, using these space-based systems. They could see You causing a catastrophe and then actually being surprised when something goes too far with You having the resultant reaction of blaming the results on some symptom, rather than on the root cause--Your inadequately thought out plans.

Military (Space and Environment)
Do not amplify the chaos in a world that has an expanding black market proliferation of arms and a sizable "legitimate" arms market combined with the growing popularity of private security firms (private mercenary armies) by justifying further WMD development and militarization of space, because there is an almost certainty because of the nature of linear science that major accident and/or false alarm or even sabotage could occur leading to environmental disaster of a magnitude not yet contemplated.

Narcissism.
In regard to the policies of Your nation-state's government, You should be aware that Your nation-state is operating in a reality of out-of-control narcissism when the need for hegemony weighs higher than the human survival of Your nation-state--social cohesiveness, economic vitality, cultural integrity, individual self-fulfillment,and environmental sustainability.

> - If trade comes before survival and
> -Image comes before health,
> then narcissism is out of control.

Social Decline.
Be observant of social decline in Your own nation-state and also in Your subject nation-state to gauge when it would be advantageous to allow increased immigration of workers from Your subject nation-state into Your own nation-state. You can use immigrant labor as a means of mitigating an increasingly bad labor situation in Your own nation-state. They will enthusiastically do work in conditions and for wages that have grown to be unacceptable/non-livable by workers of Your own nation-state; and serve as scapegoats for the worsening labor situation as well. Out-of-work laborers will take out their frustrations on the immigrants instead of on the decisions of Your government or business community.

Societal Breakdown

Externalizing domestic social problems instead of dealing with the root causes can lead to realities such as the following:

1. 'Law and Order' used as a solution to social problems, i.e. incarceration and the building of more and more prisons as a major social control measure;

2. The poor enlisting in the military as a means of escaping poverty and the lack of educational opportunities;

3. The fighting of external wars to utilize this swollen military of the poor and disenfranchised, in order to externalize domestic social problems.

Exporting Revolutions and Social Breakdown.

There was one distinguishing feature common to many of the 103 charred bodies of the victims of a fire that swept through a wing of an overcrowded prison in San Pero Sula, in northern Honduras, on May 17th. Most of the bodies were heavily tattooed. The dead were all members of youth gangs, most imprisoned for the mere act of belonging.

Youth gangs and the crime and violence they engender have become one of the most serious problems facing the five small and poor countries of Central America...

... The gangs' origins lie in the wars that engulfed Central America in the 1970s and 1980s. To escape them, many Central Americans migrated to the United States, and particularly to Los Angeles. Their children imitated that city's gang culture. In 1992, as the wars were dying down, the United States decided to start deporting jailed gang members when their sentences were over.

Back in countries that were almost foreign to them, with no jobs, the deportees set up their own gangs. According to government estimates, 36,000 people are said to belong to gangs in Honduras, 14,000 in Guatemala, 10,500 in El Salvador, 1,100 in Nicaragua and 2,600 in Costa Rica. The true figure is almost certainly much higher. The most notorious of hundreds of gangs or *maras*, is the Mara Salvatrucha, named for its Salvadorean founder who claimed to be as wise as a trout. Its initials appear in graffiti across the region. Many of the prison dead were MS members.

To see why young men – and women – flock to the gangs, just go to one of the poorer neighbourhoods of a city such as Managua, Nicaragua's capital. Each barrio has its own gang. In llario Sanchez, for example, one youth in three belongs to El Cartel, the local gang, according, according to "Jean Paul", one of its members who says he takes his *nom de guerre* from a rap singer. Most have their own weapons, usually machetes; some even make their own pistols. With jobs scarce, he argues that there is little else to do than join a gang. Crime becomes the only route to respect, power and money. Some of the money goes on drugs, which are dealt and consumed openly on the streets.[335]

As the need for quantifying human worth increases in populations that do not have the resources to do so (at least on a level at which they can afford to consume Your cultural icons), frustration will grow, especially among the youth. People that were not formerly 'poor', will become presently 'poor' because they do not have the ability to possess Your symbols of worth. Though they may have intact families, strong communities, a sense of worth,

---

335.   "Bringing It All Back Home". The Economist May 22-28th, 2004. p.31

and adequate necessities (or a number of these, if not at all), they will become 'poor' and how they are pre-judged and treated in society will further confirm their place in terms of 'human worth'.

Though the aforementioned quote may refer to an 'exported problem', it is an internal problem'. If the opportunities within Your nation-state do not exist for either the youth to embark on a path towards self-fulfillment/self-actualization, or if they are 'affected' by the Consumerist Culture that You have projected on Your subject nation-state, they do not have the means to legitimately consume Your externally-projected (and therefore internally-projected) icons of 'worth'. You will have the development of a dynamic similar to that described in the above quote. The problem in Your case is that there is no place to deport them to except to prison, which is not necessarily a bad thing. But if this is the course of action that You wish to take (in allowing this scenario to play itself out), You will need to do a cost-benefits analysis of the cost of sustaining living costs of prison labor versus the profits gained from the products and services that they produce and consume.

As in the case of decentralized slavery--that of many private owners--slaves must be fed, housed, and kept marginally, mentally stable as to ensure productivity and lessen the potential for collective revolts. Slaves are not "free" labor. In this era of moving production to the lowest cost centers, Your prison labor will have to profitably compete against low-cost wage centers such as in Your subject nation-state, or in the subject nation-states of Other Princes.[336] You will have to ascertain whether or not it is worth the financial and other support costs of maintaining, essentially, a prison-based labor pool in a 'Global Economy', rather than proactively addressing the social disintegration of Your own nation-state, facilitated and exacerbated by the externalization of Your national interests.

Inconsistency in National Image and Projected Image.

One thing that You always must be aware of is the multiplication of social, economic, and environmental problems in Your own nation-state and the percentage of the population that becomes consciously aware of their disadvantageous status in their society in comparison with the idealized lifestyle that You project onto Your subject nation-state. As time goes on, movements will likely arise calling for the rectification of social, economic, and environmental ills and for legislative change in Your own nation-state's governmental system.

Foreign Policy and Your Populace.

A people with greater consumer potential (in a quantitative-based value system) believe that, because they are "rich" and "Developed", they have a say in the affairs of "poor" and "underdeveloped" nation-states.

Watch out! A linear thinking consumerist populace can dictate the foreign policy of Your nation-state through democratic means. To avert this possibility, You may have to implement more and more fascist-type security measures to assure control over policy and use fear to distract the public. But the price for this is possible social dissolution due to criminal justice 'solutions' to major social problems and/or rapid democratic nationalism (fascism) that leads You to have to attack Other nation-states to create a war to drive Your economy[337], preserve social cohesiveness, and provide a "wartime" excuse for popular repression.

The Cost of War.

One cost of asymmetric warfare is the loss of national morale: losing soldiers to endless conflicts outside. A weakened national morale coupled with a national culture of Individualistic Materialism is an unattractive population. Because of the level of insecurity that people in Your nation-state will be living with, the population can react in one of two ways: 1. overcompensating for this national insecurity (remember the population will feel "attacked" - they will

---

336.   An illustration of the emergence of this dynamic can be seen in the years leading up to the U.S. Civil War, during the 19th century. The Northern half of the U.S. was the industrial sector, The Prince; while the Southern half was the producer of raw materials, the subject. The North sourced its raw materials from the South, whose production was based on a slave labor force necessitated by the TransAtlantic Triangle Trade that began during the beginning of the Colonial Period. By the mid-1800's the cost of maintaining slaves had become too high for the sustainability of the Southern economy and the North was not going to change its relationship or pricing structure with the South. So, Southerners as a move to facilitate the continued sustainability of their economy and standard of living (way of life), reestablished ties with the former Colonial master, England. By creating a direct relationship with England, the South could then renegotiate its position in the Colonial/global hierarchy. It may not have been able to liberate itself and recreate itself enough to become its own Prince, but it was thought that under the trade umbrella of England, that it would fare better than it presently did under the control of the North.

The South desired to remain a 'nation-state' based on slave labor, with the lifestyle that a plantation economy grants its elites, but the actual 'cost' of slavery exceeded its economic sustainability, and as a result it lost its 'freedom' as a Confederacy of 'sovereign states' within the Union of the post-Civil War United States of America. It is my opinion that it is better, both socially and financially, to enable the poor to be consumers/self-sufficient rather than a social liability to be dealt with in the present and in the future. But this attitude requires emotional independence and maturity in a Prince. He cannot be involved in a codependent relationship with the poor of His subject nation-state(s), and especially not of His own nation-state, in which he derives emotional fulfillment from the worship and idolization of Him by his 'poor'. Because of their low savings rate and high levels of consumerism and consumption; and at least for the short to medium term, His poor are to be a source of perpetual income generation, not a source of worry and the cause of his eventual downfall.

337.   i.e. Military Keynesianism

432

not see the connection between Your conquests and the resulting asymmetric warfare) in a rabid sense of patriotism further supporting the government but this time in a more xenophobic, more ethnocentrically reactionary fashion and; 2. the more conservative and ethnocentric elements of Your nation-state will feel that Your government is destroying the government's stature abroad and weakening its foundations at home leading to xenophobia and ethnocentric racism directed internally, essentially "reclaiming the country" for its true heirs. In this climate, the non-dominant groups, ethic, racial, and religious minorities will also become more reactionary because of the perceived need to protect themselves from any negative actions by the dominant group. In this tense social environment, any number of reactionary laws can be passed in order to placate the population's sense of anxiety and lack of "control" of their lives.

The problem is that no matter how well You co-opt the media into projecting Your desired message and picture of the conflict to the population, eventually the number of casualties will build up to a point in which the dead and wounded become "real people"--the casualties and bodies of persons that people know, such as family members, neighbors, and community members. And this is only talking about a foreign asymmetric war.

A domestically-carried out asymmetric attack or war (on Your own soil) could force fascist-type policies to be implemented in order to keep social control, because as a reaction people within the society could perceive Other sectors of the society as complicit in the attacks and merit internal dissension and violence against fellow countrypeople.

Misdirected Foreign Policy.

On the following page, let us revisit the two roads that I described in the introduction: the Road of Interconnectedness and Harmony; and the Road of Separation and Control. I am presenting You with two illustrations of the internal road that I gave You in the introduction to re-articulate the purpose of Your conquest: Sustainable Exploitation, not the loss of Your own focus, which, through the loss of a clearly defined point of reference and point of departure, can lead to self-destructive domestic and foreign policy.

From George Washington's Farewell Address[338]

"It is our true policy to steer clear of permanent alliances with any portion of the foreign world, so far, I mean, as we are now liberty to do it; for let me not be understood as capable of

---

338.   Ibid, Commager

patronizing infidelity to existing engagements. I hold the maxim no less applicable to public than to private affairs that honesty is always the best policy. I repeat, therefore, let those engagements be observed in their genuine sense. But in my opinion it is unnecessary and would be unwise to extend them.

Taking care always to keep ourselves by suitable establishments on a respectable defensive posture, we may safely trust to temporary alliances for extraordinary emergencies."

John Q. Adams[339]

"The true American goes not abroad in search of monsters to destroy… [America] well knows that by once enlisting under other banners than her own, were they even the banners of foreign independence, she would involve herself, beyond the power of extrication, in all the wars of interest and intrigue, of individual avarice, envy, and ambition. She might become the dictatress of the world; she would no longer be the ruler of her own spirit."

July 4, 1821

---

339.   Ibid, Williams

III. The World

Chapter 42:
The World - Economic Collapse

In the debt-ridden Third World, the state is the main target of the 'structural adjustment' packages imposed by the creditor countries. The planning role of the state has been jeopardized, and its capacity to design economic, commercial and educational policies has been severely curtailed. The only role left for the central government is the administration of economic plans made elsewhere and the exercise of social repression. [339]

Economy - Introduction.

This is an illustration of why it is advisable to have some apprehension in depending on corporate governance for sustainable environmental policies and practices:

As human societies have been increasingly urbanized the separation between human societies and nature seems to be increasingly spinning out of control.

Given the global and regional urban environmental scenarios, our intention... is to demonstrate why it is necessary for governments to address urgently their urban environmental problems. We advocate here the need to go back to an understanding of basic human and urban ecological principles. Because of the complexity of the urban ecosystem, we contend that there can be no solutions to the problems of urban ecosystems unless the issues are adopted by national governments and urban administrations. Enlightened elites and decision makers and firm government are the only ways to ensure the successful management and sustenance of viable urban ecosystems.

Victor R. Savage and Lily Kong
Department of Geography
The National University of Singapore[340]

---

339.   Bravo, p.180 from Goldstein D. Third World Biotechnology and the Foreign Debt Problem (1991), monograph, p.9
340.   "Urban Constraints, Political Imperatives: Environmental "Design" In Singapore." Victor R. Savage and Lily Kong. Paper Submitted to the Symposium on Environment and Culture with Emphasis on Urban Issues, The Siam Society Under Royal Patronage, Bangkok, 1993. p.58

Economic Breakdown of Society

Two economic dynamics in a non-sustainable 'Global Economy':

1. Free trade agreements that erode social economies andenvironments; as well as the cultural flood gates that have prevented the development of a Culture of Selfishness;

2. The exacerbation of North vs. South dynamic and resulting regional and world conflicts over resources – more 'rich' people than ever before, but many more 'poor' people than ever before. The will of the mob will prevail. If it has been converted to the same value system as its ruler(s), social disintegration, economic chaos, and environmental misuse are certain, because there are not enough resources to sustain a planet of 'Individuals'.

Economic Collapse

Financial collapse in a Rational world: if confidence in any one of the major currencies that are based on faith and abstraction (currencies not based on tangible resources: precious metals, commodities, etc.) were to collapse there would be a total crash, because all of the electronic and paper money that does not actually exist--it is based on nothing but hope that the majority of the world will agree to be content with their place in the hierarchy. If this "money" (or even worse, debt) was to be called for, it could not come from anywhere--it could only be printed--and if it were known to just be printed there would be massive deflation because this paper would become worthless and other tangible wealth would be worth something. However, this entire system of foreign exchange and capital markets is an abstraction based in a non-reality of a presupposed "Natural Order of Humanity" but is also based in error in a non-reality of infinite resources.

Economic Breakdown & Technology

The process through which labor is deskilled is through the wholesale universal application of new technologies worldwide acts as a catalyst for creating social and economic dislocation and the elimination of the concept of 'family wage' labor. This will lead to a lowering of wages worldwide. The "race to the bottom" by TNCs will lead to the convergence of the cost of labor and will even affect industrialized nation-states. The cost of goods will remain the same (because in the Global Economy, profit maximization is paramount), but the cost of living of the "unskilled" will become higher and higher eventually leading the realization that "Life was easier, before the Modern Age". The additional danger to the industrialized nation-states is that labor costs will also converge for "skilled" labor as well as for "professionals" (i.e. physicians, scientists, engineers, etc.) as well. At some point the cost of foregoing

'Development and Modernity' will be assumed to be very little as compared to the cost of a deteriorated society and economy, and problems will ensue for the governments that place their citizenry in harm's way.

In both North and South, besides the effects of wage convergence, another assault on the stability of the labor force is the effect that new technologies have on eliminating many professions - efficiency becomes the most important factor of the production process regardless of the human cost. When people and technologies are put into the same equation when determining the costs of production, people compete with technology as quantitative values to be measured against each other. The 'Free Market' automatically re-assesses the relational value of people to that of a quantitative monetary value when calculating the efficiency equation.

Economic Collapse & Global Health

Private financial capital can also play a positive role in creating favourable conditions for population curtailment. As opposed to investments in plant and equipment, purchases of stocks and bonds are fully liquid and can be withdrawn instantly. When the Mexican meltdown occurred in late 1994, the resulting peso crisis precipitated widespread business failures, skyrocketing interest rates, mass bankruptcies and dismissals of personnel. As a result, food consumption was cut by a quarter, suicide rates reached new highs and violent crimes became far more prevalent. A similar scenario already exists in Russia and is now taking hold in Thailand, Korea, Indonesia and elsewhere in South-East Asia as well. Markets discipline instantly; they hold, as it were, permanent elections.[341]

If the disintegration or war (civil and/or international war) of Your subject's nation-state causes panic in World Financial Markets (especially if, through its demise; other conflict develops in the region) because of threatened supplies of resources, finished goods and services; and the threat of restricted access to consumer markets in the region from the products of Other Princes, this could cause a massive devaluing of the financial markets which will have devastating consequences worldwide. This is especially if this type of financial crisis causes Other nation-states to go into 'cardiac arrest', including You, unwisely embracing these rationalizing principles of governance and applying them to Your own society.

The more interdependent that You make the world, i.e. transferring the subject nation-state's government's sovereignty to You and the World Markets, the more You put Yourself at risk for societal and economic collapse if You, too, base Your "value" outside of the relational sphere and into the quantitative sphere centered in a 'Global Free Market'.

Global Markets are the engines of the destruction for domestic social

---

341.   George, p.78

markets of relative peace between neighboring nation-states.

Haves and Have-Nots

Globalization brings about an even greater division between 'haves' and 'have-nots', but the patience and tolerance of the 'have-nots' is waning; especially because of the advent of the Internet and its ability to broadcast Your projections almost anywhere in the world in this 'new' valuation of humanity in quantitative terms, they will realize "how poor" they are as compared to their wealthier compatriots and as compared to those outsiders who they view as benefiting from their demise. Only the extremes of hunger and disease can supplant these thoughts through their shear threat to their immediate mortality. Other than this, You have the potential time-bomb of social revolt within Your subject-nation as well as in Other nation-states due to coalitions made because those of similar circumstances, communicating through these new means of communications.

Signs of the Times.

1. The global poor can lose patience in being perpetual losers in Your capitalist game. 'Commodified' people, being that they are now 'commodified' have less of an option to do things slowly; they have to participate in this 'dog-eat-dog' quantitative value reality. They do not have the luxury to be losers in Your game. They might have their land sold from under them, go hungry, go jobless, become sick, or even become sold to a human trafficker, because "poor people" have no value in this value framework. They can be sold and traded just like rice, corn, crude oil; or even worse sold in pieces, i.e. as involuntary and voluntary organ donors, and as surrogate mothers.

2. In this climate the development of narco-capitalist states is likely if the resources of their nation-state are owned either through a colonial legacy or through FDI, they have no choice but to still desire to be winners in Your world, but using the only resources available to them (to be trafficked as sex or non-sex labor), narcotics, arms, or blackmarket sales of commodities that only You are supposed to control (such as "conflict diamonds" coming from sources outside of Your control threatening Your price controls and market share); and "pirated goods" made from Your 'intellectual property'.

3. There will be an increase in piracy: ships, stealing oil tankers, shipping lanes attacked - corporations will have to hire their own mercenary navies to protect their ships. Private armies to protect train and truck shipments, private air forces to protect cargo flights.

4.   The legitimacy of narco-capitalist and bandit-capitalist states: criminal gangs can become the governments of 'rogue nation-states'. If a 'crime syndicate' government "takes care" of the "right people" it has legitimacy. The question is: When does a non-state organization gain the international recognition of being the legitimate government of the nation-state? – i.e. what determines whether "peacekeepers" are sent in to "save" a "legitimate" government, even if the "rebels"/new regime actually has the mandate. They may not always have "elections" – but one can recognize in a nation-state whether or not there is consensus and a mandate given to rule.

World Economy.

The World Economy (being that it is intertwined through Global Capital Markets) in its present state, can only bear so many 'failed', 'failing', or 'rogue' states that do not "play by the rules of Your 'Free-Market'" game If too many fall to the wayside, especially if they are the causalities cf "structural adjustment" measures, Other subject nation-states will realize that there is no 'Free-Market' - that in actuality, the 'Free Market' is operated from particular Princes' locales. They will come to the conclusion that they have done "everything right" and all they get is more and more of their nation-state controlled their FDI (Foreign Direct Investment) without the gains that they believe that investment brings and more and more of their sovereignty lost through transnational organizations like the WTO (World Trade Organization) that operate in a manner that makes and keeps rich countries rich-- maintaining a perpetual source of cheap labor and resources and perpetual market for their excess production. While they themselves lose more and more of their domestic economies everyday until they simply become a marketplace of foreign goods, and with a population in which only those who are well-placed in the foreign conglomerates and associated service firms to be able to purchase these items and the low-end surpluses consumed by the masses.

Endless Consumption

The world cannot sustain "everybody" desiring the consumption level of industrialized nation-states. All that this Ideology of Individualistic Materialism and the 'Free-Market' will provide is one large implosion: this can be summed up in two points: 1. an ecological footprint far larger than what the planet can sustain; and 2. a morally defunct world - a world of Legal Moralism, a desirous "do what You can get away with" mindset, without any internal sense of right and wrong , eating away at the social cohesion.

Hyperinflation and the scarcity of resources will result when too many subject nation-states embrace Individualistic Materialism as their primary value system, because it will become a matter of national esteem to consume and possess at the rate that You and other Princes do. They will desire to possess what You have, not only local versions of what You promote: a world driven by unlimited gluttony but with finite resources. Moreover, with a crazed desire to 'Modernize' and consume in Your image, all of the "problems" of "Now" will be overlooked for a linear-based life in the future. Consequences to the actions of now will be an afterthought. The inconvenience of counterbalancing results of unsustainable actions will be met with reactionary responses, based in the paranoid fantasy that those that do not share in their delusion of progress and/or oppose it are actually jealous of the progress-oriented non-sustainable lifestyles and value systems that they possess. Any person not enraptured by the quest towards 'Modernity', 'Progress', and Conspicuous Consumption will be an enemy of all Civilized Persons and all that is Good.

The Business of Poverty.

The "Aid Business" may appear to be advantageous to You and Your transnational corporations and NGOs because the monies donated are then filtered back into the hands of Your "helpers" who use these funds to do the "Development Work" and have access to inexpensively priced resources, but You cannot forget that You provide "aid" in order to avoid rectifying any root problems by barely staving off disaster and nurturing dependency on this help. At some point, if You are not astutely observant of the dynamics of the subject nation-states that You are manipulating, You could miscalculate the cycle of necessary "life saving and relief" and there can be catastrophic failure, resulting in extreme hardship and death for the population. Some in these subject nation-states may realize that You are using this "aid business" as a means of continuing the Colonial Period under the auspices of Humanism and desire to be totally independent of Your influence so that they can again control their resources, environment, society, economy, culture, education in a self-determined manner, rather than in compliance with 'International Standards'.

Graham Hancock in *Lord of Poverty* gives some good descriptions on how "aid money" perpetuates its existence while avoiding directly addressing the root causes of hardship and lack among the 'subject' populations:

There are an estimated 150,000 foreign experts working on development projects are. Of these **80,000** are in Africa, more expatriates than in the colonial period." This, according to him comes "to 15 billion US$", at the rate of US$100,000 per expert per year, a figure equal to one-third of all official "aid". Then, "the US gets $0.82 back in purchase orders for every dollar it puts into the World Bank. So it is with EEC and more particularly, French Aid, for which there is a high recirculatory flow.

- A "fish farm built by FAO in Malawi, next to a bird sanctuary," was a great success for the birds, who happily ate the fish...
- The notorious Polonoroeste project in Brazil to 'develop' the North by burning down the Amazon-jungle (the world's largest tropical rainforest with very wide genetic diversity) has triggered one of the greatest ecocatastrophes of our time...[342]

Conclusion - Economic Collapse.

... the current fiat money is created out of nothing and is mostly introduced into the economy in the form of debt, providing a tremendous advantage to those who create it. Moreover, interest charges on fiat money make the entire system not only unjust but unsustainable too. The easy creation of fiat money has brought about too much liquidity globally while interest charges force the additional creation of money that demands a constant growth in the real economy, just to maintain living standards. This is the reason why in almost all countries, including the developed nations, money and debt grow together. Growth in debt, in turn, has implications for financial management that makes the whole system unsustainable. All this has serious repercussions for the real economy. Major world economies, i.e. the United States, Europe, and Japan, are in financial and economic distress simultaneously, as never before.[343]

The question that existed during the Cold War exists now - we have Mutually Assured Destruction based on the situation in which whoever launches the first strike everybody loses.

In the world at this time there is a situation in which the World Economy is based on a fiat currency system. In the past, the word "world" was nothing more than a Universalistic Expression to describe one's particular geographic region in a grander context, i.e. the "Roman World"; but in this Age of Globalization and all of the forced connections made through and based in this fiat currency system, the "World" actually is the "world", not just a nationalistic expression based in Universalism. This fiat system is based on the supposition of perpetual growth, endless supply of resources, and limitless markets. This supposition is both flawed and borders on insanity. Being that we live and operate within a finite plane, naturally there are limits. The human mind can transform that which is into something else, but like the

---

342.   Excerpted from Hancock, Graham (1989) *Lords of Poverty*. London : Macmillan, 1989, reviewed AMPO Quarterly, Vol. 22 Nos 2-3, 1991 in *Descent of Man*.

343.   Meera, pp.117-8

First Law of Thermodynamics states, energy is neither created nor destroyed, it changes form. The world has a finite limitation on consumption. A World Economic System based on a false premise of "production" which is actually consumption created to accelerate further consumption. This will burn out, because consumption requires destruction and destruction requires creation so that it has materials to destroy in order to utilize, and vice versa.

If You are serious about 'ruling the world', strongly encouraging acceptance of the practice of the privatization of public goods[344], the transnational ownership of the modes of production, and the growing use of private security forces to protect these 'Free Market' assets should be a precursor to a deliberate collapse of the fiat currency system in order to finally disinherit the populations of subject nation-states of their last holdings. These subject nation-states, being based in a fiat system still possess residual connections to a world of tangible trade and tangible concepts of ownership, even though ownership has been abstracted and based on Your projected models. Their currencies are based on relationships with Yours and they will buy Your currency, to hold in reserve, in order to "empower" their own currencies, because their own currencies have little value in Your fiat world-- this is unless they, the currencies, are pegged to or linked somehow to Your "Global Trading Currencies".

If You (Your transnational corporations) take possession of the modes of production and public goods, You can in a sense, bankrupt Your subject nation-state(s) by simply allowing Your fiat currency to collapse, leaving their currencies and stock markets helpless to Your whims, as was practiced in the Asian currency crash in 1997. Your subject nation-states will be so desirous of Your approval and affirmation of participating in your fiat currency game that You can do a similar attack through the following: affirm X nation-state as a growing market by putting tremendous amounts of money into its markets, allow this investment by You to create confidence in its market so that its companies will list themselves on these markets and the population will invest its money into these markets, sell it Your holdings in its nation-state at record high prices (but based on stock trades for hard currency), sell all of Your shares on its markets and take all of Your money out of its banks – the result will be that the local "Market" assumes that a crash a happening due to flaws in its financial market place, and not because You simply took Your money out of its markets. As a response to Your liquidation, the entire nation-state will try to liquidate its assets in the "Market" in order to save themselves financially, driving the fall, faster and harder. The financial system will be reduced to

---

344.   Read the Magna Carta, it was the basis of English Common Law, the legal structure on which many current systems of governance are assumed to be based on. It was written to protect and stress the importance of public goods to the sustainability of a nation.

nothing within this nation-state, and being that You control the actual public goods and modes of production and have private armies to protect them, if You implement this massive collapse and promotion of local liquidation around the world in many subject nation-states simultaneously, You will actually control the world, because You will hold the means to eat, drink, travel, and operate.

It would be smarter to simply temporarily invest large amounts of capital into a single subject nation-state, liquidate, collapse it, and buy it wholesale for a fraction of what it cost before Your "interest" in its economy, but with a linear mind, You cannot stop with a single destroyed economy, it (a linear mind) needs to be in many economies, so that You can liberate the wealth from them and actually control them. Because, after all, if You do engage excessively in a linear approach, then Sustainable Exploitation is not really what You desire. It is actually the feeling of being a "living god" that You seek. And by collapsing the entire financial system, You will be that "living god" because You will hold the means of living in Your hands.

Now, on the flip side: 1. if You do decide to the take the world by collapsing the economy approach, it may not go as You plan and things may become hysterical and anarchy will break out in each of these nation-states. And in anarchic settings, organizing security forces and national defense forces will be of no use against the force of mob rule; 2. The scarier outcome: if Your subject nation-state(s) are not lost in the world of emulating You - in that they studied the Paper Economy/IPO boom in the 1980s and Asian currency crash of 1997 and are aware of the creative and destructive potential of directed behaviors in the "Marketplace", they will allow You to believe that they are buying into Your fiat system and the Culture of Individualistic Materialism by heavily increasing the consumption of raw materials in order to produce products to compete against You. They will generate more and more sales of these products and store Your nation-state's securities in their treasuries, and when the time is right, they will demand payment on Your nation-state's tender notes, and of course, because Your system is a fiat system based on an abstracted, intangible market You will default because You do not have the "money" to cover the recalling of Your own debt. Your system will collapse, and theirs' may collapse also because of the close relationship with Yours, but with certainty, Your days as Prince will be over; and a final less dramatic approach 3. If Your subject nation-states are aware as I said before about the power of market manipulation, they can work together to eliminate the power of Your fiat currency in the market. If there is another Prince with whom they prefer to deal with as a master, rather than

You, they can work to make its fiat currency (a)/(the) primary international trading currency. The power of Your fiat currency can come from being the currency by which major commodities such as crude oil, gold, silver, grain, sugar, etc. are traded in. If Your subject nation state(s) or a confederation (collaboration) of subject nation-states affiliated with a competing Prince decides to pay for these commodities (pricing in) with an alternative fiat currency (one comparable in having the ability to be used an international trading currency) they can unseat Your currency as a/the predominate fiat currency used in Global Trade. If this happens, You will have to consolidate the economic power of Your nation-state and of Your subject-nation states as a formal economic empire or "community", or Your own nation-state will be subject to the same destructive forces of the 'Global Market' that You have created for Your subject nation-states.

This is not a game. At some point, You will have to decide whether or not You are an Empire or not. If You have taken the Road of Conquest to this point and You do not make this decision, it is likely that the days of Your reluctant Empire are short. If You simply react in a linear fashion of short-medium term gain, You will probably bring about the economic collapse of the entire "World" that is integrated into this 'Global Economy'. If You force more powerful subject nation-states to the point where they realize their permanent place in Your hierarchy and/or become desirous of Your position of Prince (because of all of the projections that You have bombarded them with), they can either work to destroy You invasively by attacking Your fiat currency directly, leading to unknown and possibly disastrous consequences for both You and themselves--this is even scarier because the motive behind attacking You is You regain their honor from having been Your subject, meaning that loss is acceptable if it means that they regain their "face"--or collaborate against You with another Prince to depose You as the leading Prince. And lastly if these events do not come to fruition, though likely, it will be only due to the other alternative scenario: subject nation-states decide to deal in the world of tangible trade and begin to use tangible commodities such gold for balance-of-trade transactions and local currencies for domestic transactions to reestablish a hierarchy of nation-states more to their benefit. This is a less likely possibility mainly because if You have followed my advice, the populations of these nation-states will be solid believers in the fiat currency system, but if one the aforementioned scenarios were to proceed, there would be enough a disruption in the world economic system that You will have to put all of Your attention into maintaining the stability of the fiat system and Your own economic hegemony, taking Your attention off of the activities of the subject nation-states, leaving them to their own devices. Additionally, these "devices" will be ones that lessen Your hold over them. The only way that they can do this is to deny the importance of Your abstracted world and participate in the tangible world in which the sustainability of their nation-states once again becomes important.

This is a tremendous number of variables to contemplate and without an omniscient mind, making the "prefect" decision is impossible. You have started this game, and it (the Game) will find equilibrium. But this equilibrium will not be Adam Smith's equilibrium of the Market; it will be a tangible equilibrium based in the sustainability of humankind and Nature. The question is whether You are actually desirous of the responsibility of being a Prince, or whether You simply want to feel like a "living god". Tangible equilibrium is inevitable, the choice is whether You approach it voluntarily or involuntarily. Remember that I told You being a Prince is not for the faint-hearted or the weak; it is for the deliberate, and sometimes the price of power is death.

Economy
Tables and Charts

Characteristics of Fiat Money and Problems Caused

Fiat Money is Created Out of Nothing
1. Amplifies business cycles.
2. Causes inflation and asset price bubbles.
3. Debt bubbles and financial collapses of firms and governments.
4. Trade-off between inflation and unemployment.
5. Agriculture sector disadvantaged due to price controls in this sector.
6. Along with interest rates, it places the burden of a continuous growth requirement, promotes competition and accumulates wealth in the hands of a minority by taxing the majority.
7. Widening inequality in distribution of income that creates poverty with a host of social problems...

The Existence of Many Different Fiat Currencies
1. The many fiat national currencies currently existing provide a fertile ground for currency speculation, manipulation and arbitrage.
2. Makes it possible for huge amounts of short-term funds to move in and out of nations within seconds. This fact is very destabilizing, sometimes behaving as a shadow government that apparently disciplines 'misbehaving' governments!
3. Through the seigniorage of fiat money some nations gain substantially when other nations use their currency for international trade and dealings or in domestic transactions.
4. Provides an easy tool for domestic and international financial institutions to gain control over the money, wealth, the political structure (i.e. sovereignty) of nations, etc.

Gets Destroyed in Certain Circumstances
1. Causes a shrink in money supply and aggregate demand, and thereby recession.
2. Business failures and unemployment during financial collapses.
3. Bank failures and crises.
4. Leaves governments in debt.
5. Possible political turmoil.

Source: Table 2, p.76. Meera, Ahamed Kameel Mydin (2004) *The Theft of Nations: Returning to Gold.* Selangor Darul Ehsan, Malaysia: Pelanduk Publications (M) Sdn Bhd.

Protecting Against the "Theft" of Nations

Means of "Theft" | **Protection**

1. Savings of Nations — Use savings for domestic development as much as possible. Evaluate carefully when buying financial assets like bonds issued by another country or depositing savings there. Buying foreign financial assets can entail the outflow of domestic real goods and services.

2. Seigniorage — Prevent foreign commercial banks from operating in the nation since a fiat money interest-based system allows them to create the money of the nation.
Do not price and sell goods and services in foreign currencies.
Insist on national currency or even better, insist on real money rather than fiat money.
Use a common currency or gold to legal tender or usable domestically.
The gold dinar, other commodity monies and complementary currencies are some means of protecting against loss through seigniorage.

3. Lending Money at Interest — Do not borrow money at interest, particularly in the currency of another country. By borrowing in a foreign currency you effectively pass your "life-line" into the hands of that currency or the institution that lends the money.

4. War — Prepare yourself with the best of weapons so as to command wholesome respect rather than inviting oppression and aggression from potential enemies and predators.

Source: Table 1, p.48, Meera, Ahamed Kameel Mydin (2004) The Theft of Nations: Returning to Gold. Selangor Darul Ehsan, Malaysia: Pelanduk Publications (M) Sdn Bhd.

Chapter 43:
The World –
Environmental Collapse

In our world, human progress has largely been the result of increasing technological ability to interfere constructively in natural ecological processes. However, this interference has unforeseen consequences affecting environmental quality. These consequences were unimportant when men were few and only partly able to disturb the surroundings, but they become of real urgency when people are abundant. The gains to man from various types of environmental modification tend to obscure the fact that each carries the seed of trouble.

HRH Princess Galyani Vadhana[345]

Some numbers to ponder in regard to "sustainability" of the trend of "Progress":

• "Carbon dioxide levels today are 18 percent higher than in 1960 and an estimated 31 percent higher than they were at the onset of the Industrial Revolution in 1750.
• Half the world's original forest cover is gone and another 30 percent is degraded or fragmented.
• Industrial fleets have fished out at least 90 percent of all large ocean predators – tuna, marlin, sword fish, cod, halibut, skate, and flounder – in just the past 50 years, according to a study in *Nature* in 2003.
• An estimated 10-20 percent of the world's cropland, and more than 70 percent of the world's rangelands, are degraded."[346]

---

345.   Inaugural Address to the Symposium on Environment and Culture with Emphasis on Urban Issues, The Siam Society Under Royal Patronage, Bangkok, 1993, p. ix.
346.   "Population and Its Discontents" by Danielle Nierenburg and Mia MacDonald, September/October 2004 World Watch Institute, pp.14-15

Environment – Introduction

In this section, I will share with You a number of possible scenarios out of an innumerable number of possible outcomes of a global decision to take the 'Road of Separation and Control'.

I go into some discussion on oceans, groundwater, deforestation, flooding, climate change, natural and unnatural disasters, and biodiversity.

There are a multitude of other topics such as air pollution or even total unknowns such as the effects of the massive extraction of gold from the earth on the planet's spin; the extraction of underground radioactive material such as uranium and its effects on the development of nutrient-rich soil; the massive extraction of petroleum from the earth and its long-term effects on the environment; the seeding of clouds to change weather patterns and the seeding of the ocean to promote specific changes in the chemistry of ocean; and the non-biodegradability of new toxic chemical compounds and new molecules created through nanotechnology, etc.

Environment & Growth

And Bangkok is just one if dozens of mega-cities that are springing up all over the global South. They form the destination for the greatest mass migration in human history: the urbanization of the developing world. Half a century ago, two-thirds of the earth's population lived in the countryside, and only greater New York had a population larger than 10 million. Now there are twenty such cities, and in thirty years, two-third of the world's population is expected to be urban. Essentially, that means a new Bangkok (at its official population) is being created every two months. The environmental woes of these new mega-cities are legion, and their infrastructure demands enormous. So much so that the problems posed by the lack of a civil society are usually overlooked.[347]

As the *World Disasters Report* puts in, "growing cities concentrate risk." Urban areas are dense concentrations not only of people but also buildings, roads, rail lines, pipelines, communications systems, and water and sanitary services. The concentration of these "lifelines" means that a disruption in service can affect a very large share of a region's population and economic activity. The earthquake that rocked Kobe, Japan, in 1995 killed 6,350 people and cost over $100 billion, making it the most expensive natural disaster in history. It disrupted the region's economic activity for months, including vital shipping and railway lines.[348]

The question is 'whose growth and for what reason?'. The purpose of cities to provide centralized coordination of the supply of goods and their distribution. A well-designed city will perform this task while also promoting

---

347.   Fahn, James David (2004) *A Land on Fire: The Environmental Consequences of the Southeast Asian Boom*. Bangkok: Silkworm Books. p.15
348.   "Unnatural Disasters", p.24

the development of a largely decentralized citywide economy, so that resources and capital are well distributed as to prevent the development of slums and areas of neglect.

Allowing the development of slums is like allowing the development of a tumor; it may stay benign, but it could also turn malignant and become nothing more than a representation of sickness in the body of a city.

With the formation of slums comes an easy point of migration for rural dwellers who are either deceived by false allure of opportunities in 'the city' or due to need to consume 'Modern' cultural icons of rural dwellers dispossessed from their land by city dwellers who require their resources either to "feed to city" or for export to other markets.

A badly-designed city, or a city that develops simply as a common point for more rural migration, will never develop its consciousness as a city and will only serve to be a place devoted to an export economy, in the same way that You have manipulated Your subject nation-state(s) to neglect their domestic development in order to focus on the development of an export economy.

If the world's new cities are all the 'badly designed'-type, resource allocation will certainly occur in an unsustainable manner, and these cities will eventually eat themselves from within in order to survive. There is a finite amount of resources and there is a finite limit as to how much of a body can be a tumor, even if it is benign. If too much of the body is focused solely on consumption, or if the part of the body's presence negatively affects the operation of function even it is not actually consuming an inordinate amount of resources, but is just there is a neutral, purposeless presence, homeostasis will be lost. This is because even a benign tumor, if it reaches a certain size, can become an impediment to the overall function of the body; and if it is malignant, it will actually compete for resources from the body as a whole for the purpose of 'Growth and Consumption'. A large unproductive group of people would be 'malignant' if they consume, create nothing, and are convinced that their worth is based on possession of icons defined by You. They are 'malignant' because they only take (consume), do not produce anything creative, and increase in number.

Do not make the mistake of viewing "production" in economic terms. Defining human "production" in economic terms, people work only to consume and not also to contribute positively to their own development and to society at large.[349] Having a higher factory input by workers who operate in this

---

349.　　Positive contributions are ones in which more is given than is required in resources to produce it, meaning that human intellectual, physical, spiritual 'capital' is added to create a higher value-added item, with the least amount of destruction/consumption required to produce it.

manner, who do not actualize their individual potential, but instead to purchase Your cultural icons are not 'productive'. They are only 'consumptive' – they simply use resources; their true value as people with individual gifts and potential is not utilized. Consumptive societies are not 'productive societies' when one does the equation as to how much has put into the equation versus what is taken out of it.

"Growth" is an intellectual, spiritual, and cultural term, not an economic term. When 'Growth' is used as an economic term, it is a misnomer, because true trade operates in an environment of relative valuing: "I give you X because I need Y at an equivalent rate of exchange".

Again, the redefinition of reality that You use to control Your subject nation-state is just that: a means of control so that You can dominate it; but You can never buy into these false definitions that You project. You should only disrupt and destroy to a point at which it is still advantageous for You to do so. Promoting 'Economic Growth' to the point where irreparable environmental destruction and assured social collapse is imminent, because of an unsustainable level of consumption and badly coordinated resource allocation, is not in Your interests, nor is it in the interest of maintaining a planet that You can continue to exploit. The danger in the Ideology of 'Perpetual Growth' that You have promoted is that if You are successful in convincing Your subject nation-state that it exists in a world defined by You, and in that world it has no value unless it emulates You in consumptive patterns, values, governance, etc.. And it will do whatever is required to achieve Your approval, even if this means emulating the highly destructive processes that have brought You to preeminence in the world. Once this cycle starts, there will be no stopping it unless it (Your subject nation-state(s)) decides that it wants to define its own reality, otherwise it will copy You in its embrace of environmentally destructive practices to create maximum economic growth and a high level of consumerism needed to achieve the highest possible 'Growth Rates' and lowest possible savings rates. In this perspective, 'Maximum Consumption' equals 'Highest Civilization'.

Conservationism & Environmentalism

Legitimate environmental criticisms can be easily viewed as neocolonialist because of the long history of 'conservationist' policies being used to appropriate land and resources from the subject nation-states and their indigenous communities by Colonial Powers.

'Advice' on how lands and resources 'should be used' can easily be viewed as being based in the 'advisor's' vested interest, especially if the person or group giving the advice is living a high standard of living, supported by a high rate of consumption. A "Green"[350] provider of advice that lives an unsustainable standard of living can easily be dismissed, as well as any legitimate criticism or observation.[351]

Remember that before Your encouragement (Your projections) to adopt a quantitative system for valuing everything from people to environment to economy, they (the subject nation-states) would have been more apt to sacrifice 'Rapid Growth' for shared global environmental sustainability; but because they are being pushed into a consumerist worldview, any calls for moderation and sustainability will simply be viewed as You attempting to deny them the right to consume as much as You do and live at the same standard of living. Any thoughts of environmental, social, and economic sustainability go "out the window" when discussing these issues with a Consumerist.

Oceans.

Unmonitored and unregulated 'Growth' will lead to the following threats to the sustainability of the ocean: coral reef degradation (including coral mining); chemical pollution, such as heavy metals, oil spills, agrochemical runoff, etc.; nutrient pollution leading to algae-induced hypoxia and toxic algae blooms; mangrove depletion; overfishing; fishing of marine young; shellfish poisoning; non-sustainable aquaculture; biological pollution, such as the carrying of invasive species to other locales in ship ballast tanks; excessive ultraviolet radiation due to thinned absent ozone layer over areas of the ocean; higher ocean water temperatures and climate change leading to coral bleaching and ice cap melting leading to the disruption of the biological and hydrological cycles (cycle of air and sea currents and the nutrients that are carried within this cycle).

Oceans & Temperate Zones

Those oblivious to the potential effects of climate change will likely be some of the hardest hit by its ill effects. Of course, subject nation-states will suffer the most because many are island nation-states and/or have high population density in coastal cities, but those in temperate zones, the locales of most Princes, will likely lose the 'temperate-ness' of these zones with higher temperature increases, eliminating the ease in producing food that these regions have become accustomed to.

---

350.   'Environmentalist'/Environmentally Conscious
351.   See Grove, Richard H. (1988) *Ecology, Climate and Empire: The Indian Legacy in Global Environmental History, 1400-1940*. Delhi: Oxford University Press, for more background of how the 'environmentalist' movement grew out of colonial resource management policy; and how some of these attitudes and rhetoric are perpetuated by the post-Colonial elites.

The following quote is a prediction by meteorologists concerning the change in weather that could affect temperate zones:

Arctic Ice Cap Will Melt Completely in 100 Years
AEP Wed. Aug. 13, 2003

The Arctic ice cap will melt completely within the next century if carbon dioxide emissions continue to earth's atmosphere at current rates, according to an international study.
"Since 1978, the ice cap has shrunk by nearly three or four percent per decade. At the 21st century there will be no more ice at the North Pole in summer," one of the study's authors... Johannesson told AFP on Wednesday.
"If the CO2 emissions continue to accelerate, that may occur sooner."
According to Johannesson, the total melting of the ice cap would set free a massive flow (of water,) which would strongly reduce warm surface ocean currents such as the Gulf Stream. The Gulf Stream is the reason behind Europe's temperate climate and a reduction in it would have serious consequences for climate and the ecosystem in the continent...[352]

In truth, this has already began to happen, and there are free passages across the North Pole that ships can travel through, but on the bright side, with no Arctic ice cap, the shipping time between Northern Europe and Japan will be reduced by 5-10 days, allowing for more trade and increasing 'Economic Growth'.

Oceans & Tropical Zones

On the other hand, this global warming, like I mentioned before, will probably wash away island-states such as Tuvalu, Tokelau, and the Maldives; and cause major problems in more tropical subject nation-states. The following denotes tangible effect on the environment in a tropical locale:

Scientists are blaming global warming for falling fish harvest in Africa's Lake Tanganyike, threatening the diets of several poor nations.

Warming air and water and decreasing wind have reduced the amount of mixing between the lake's surface water and deeper, nutrient-rich layers. The changes have reduced algae growth, reducing food for several important fish species, the researchers found...

... Many scientists believe that climate change is caused by large volumes of carbon dioxide and other heat-trapping gases that industrialized nations release into the atmosphere...

... The lake yields 2,000,000 tons of fish a year, an important source of food and revenue for the poor shoreline countries of Burundi, Tanzania, Zimbabwe and the Democratic Republic of Congo.

---

352.   "Arctic Ice Cap Will Melt Completely in 100 Years", AEP Wed. Aug. 13, 2003

However, the harvest of sardines, the lake's main commercial fish, has declined as much as 50 percent since the 1970s...[353]

Aquaculture & Threatening Oceans

Years of relentless exploitation in the oceans have taken their toll: 11 of the world's 15 most important fishing areas, and 70 percent of the major fish species, are either fully, or overexploited, according to the U.N. Food and Agriculture (FAO)... Landings of the most commercially valuable species, including cod, tuna, and haddock, have dropped by one forth since 1970...

In addition to the people already suffering from malnutrition, more than 1 billion poor consumers who depend on fish to fulfill their protein needs may become malnourished if per capita fish supplies fail to keep pace with growing human appetites.[354]

Do not fail to realize that the growth of aquaculture is taking the slack for lessening open ocean supplies of seafood. The problem with this is that it will leave biologically-dead areas of ocean in its wake[355] if too intensively farmed; and substantial land-based resources (i.e. grains, etc.) or other harvested marine life (for feed) are needed to feed to the fish. In the case of farmed shrimp, mangrove forests must be destroyed, eliminating natural habitat for fishes and shrimp, leading to shore erosion and eventual biological death of the area.

Loss of Marine Mammals.

Like in the case of the excessive loss of large land-based vertebrates--land mammals--to the catastrophic multiple consequences because of the loss of their natural habitat due to unsustainable logging, land clearing, and land development as well as pollution, the excessive disruption of the lives and habitat of sea mammals can also have disastrous consequences....

Depleting fisheries can send shockwaves through the marine food chain. In Alaska, for example, Pollock catches have nearly tripled since 1986. Since the late 1960s, populations of Steller sea lions, which feed on Pollock, have dropped 80-90 percent in the Gulf of Alaska. In 1990, the National Marine Fisheries Service (NMFS) designated the sea lion as threatened under the Endangered Species Act. And in May 1997, the species reclassified as endangered. In turn, the loss of sea lions has deprived killer whales of their primary source of food. The whales are now eating sea otters, a leaner and bonier mammal than sea lions. As

353.   "African Fish Harvest Blamed on Warming", AP Africa, Aug. 13, 2003.
354.   "Safeguarding the Health of Oceans." Anne Platt McGinn.World Watch.
355.   This is similar to how over-farmed land can become nutrient poor, leading to soil erosion, and in the worst cases eventual desertification.

a result, sea otter populations have declined by 90 percent since 1990, triggered a surge in their prey, sea urchins.[356]

Many anti-environmentalists, drunk with the 'hubris' that afflicts scientists, will glibly tell us that whatever changes have been wrought by technology, a new equilibrium will appear. That is absolutely true; but who can assure us that the human animal will survive within the new balance?[357]

I only mentioned this and have used these examples because these invasive sustained disruption on the cycle life are easily identifiable consequences of such immoderate actions, but the impact on the entire system both land and marine-based will probably not be "easily identified" until it is too late to correct; with the consequences for humanity being undesirable to say the least.

Loss of Marine Mammals & Technology
The need for more and more an invasive or pervasive military presence has driven the race for development to the ocean. The use of high-power sonar to monitor the oceans of the Earth for 'enemy vessels' will cause the deaths of countless marine mammals whose hearing range is in the sub-sonic range, i.e. whales and dolphins. This will cause the disruption of the entire marine ecosystem because the domino effect of the loss of these numbers of marine mammals, and because of the unknown physical effects on other marine life due to the exposure to these super-amplified sub-sonic frequencies.

Unsustainable Fishing Practices & the Global Culture of the 'Individual'.
Dynamite fishing and the use of sodium cyanide is increasingly becoming more popular because of the increased incomes that fisherman can gain from these larger, more quickly obtained catches. Using sodium cyanide is even a greater boon because fish are only stunned, so that they can be caught alive, which brings a fisherman several times more than a dead catch. The problem is that the dynamite fishing and sodium cyanide kill the coral reefs which sustain the local marine environment. In the past, being of a different worldview and value system (one of sustainable living), it is likely that a fisherman would have been more considerate to the environment, but being new converts[358] to the consumerist value system of Individualistic Materialism they too desire to accumulate and consume as much as possible,

---

356.   "Safeguarding the Health of Oceans". Worldwatch Paper 145, March 1999. p.32
357.   Mendis, p.31. This quote is also noted in Chapter 33, "Progress at all Costs".

no matter the cost to themselves, their environments, or the sustainability of they and their families' futures.

A value system is that, a value system. Value systems determine how one views the world and how to assess situations, make decisions, and act accordingly. A person of a quantitative value system whose means of generating an income comes from the natural environment will cease to view the environment relationally; he or she will view it quantitatively. If they have been quantified, and converted into one with a quantitative value system, no amount of 'environmental' or 'conservationist' reasoning will convince them that they should be moderate today so that they can have something for tomorrow, especially if they are being bombarded with projections of icons that they must acquire to be a person of 'worth'. If today's resources dry up, they will act accordingly and take them from somebody else.

In a quantified world, the only crime is 'not having'. 'Poverty'[359] is a pathological state in a quantified world. If a transgression against another brings one greater 'worth', it was truly not a crime, it was simply that the one was shrewder than the Other. The crime is not participating in the game of the quantified world and insisting on being a 'relational' being. For this they will be eliminated, because a virus can leave no cell unharmed, for it may be the one that produces antibodies and elicits a collective response from other cells to combat the virus.

If You are effective in Your projecting of this 'new'/Modern new system on Your subject nation-state(s)' and it become either necessary or simply more initially attractive to embrace by the multitudes of the world's population You will have amplified the 'Consumerist' response to a level in which humanity will consume itself, because there are not enough resources in the natural environment to fulfill the inexhaustible hunger of a planet of quantified, consumeristic Individuals.

Deforestation.

Though the razing of forests to make way for commercial livestock grazing, pulp for paper products, provide lumber for furniture, housing, etc, might be profitable; these activities are done in a manner in which the forests do not have time to begin the process of regenerating themselves will leave the planet with less oxygen, less carbon dioxide absorption, less wetlands (less

---

358.   You will find that the vigor which with Your subject converts to the Ideology of Individualistic Materialism and the other "Modern" ideals will resemble that of a new religious convert - hungry and willing to devour anything that their new "life" will teach them. This is in fact what You are giving them - a new religion, a new relationship with humanity, the natural environmeant and the Universe.
359.   As defined by You in Your projections.

groundwater), less stable hillsides, less habitat for animals and plants, less trees for future exploitation, less plants and animals from which many of the 'Modern' pharmaceutical "wonder drugs" created for a system of non-preventative Managed-Care Individualized Medicine (and also of which lower-dose traditional medicines are made).

There will be more flooding, more landslides, more desertification, more exposure to superpathogens unknown to those in the 'Modern Age'.[360]

Biological Diversity & Genetic Modification.

...The introduction of crops lased with genes that produce everything from herbicide tolerance to antibodies for genital herpes to drugs to treat cystic fibrosis and Alzheimer's Disease raises serious environmental questions. And we don't know what happens to insects, birds and animals that ingest plant materials containing exotic new gene traits mixing with non-GM food crops and native weeds creating a new kind of bioengineered pollution.[361]

You should be concerned about the new combinations of genetically modified materials in the environment, but from the standpoint of biodiversity; this is not only what You should be concerned about. What You should be concerned with is the development of monocultures in Your and the world's food supply.

The natural genetic diversity that exists in Nature is a natural protection for the sustainability of organisms. It is the genetic diversity of crops that prevents them from all falling susceptible to the same diseases and encourages the development of optimum traits for particular environments. The monocultures that are G-M crops may possess traits that make them very marketable, but in reality, it is their very genetic singularity that makes them so unattractive to use. Monocultures are highly susceptable to crop failures. Examples of this can be found in tragedies such as the Irish Potato Famine.

Besides the deliberate planting of these monocrops to create a monoculture with particular phenotypical traits, the organisms themselves take over fields and often time become the only crop present. Again, from the standpoint of "production" and profitability they do seem to beneficial initially, but what if this monocrop does not have resistance to a particular pathogen? It can totally die-off, and worse than that is, if this new monoculture is what makes up the stable food supply of a nation-state, and there is a failure, there

---

360.   Indigenous people know/have known the existence of these superpathogens, i.e. "new" hemorrhagic viruses, etc., or at the least known of life forms that should be left undisturbed, and left those areas unsettled and ungrazed, but in the 'race to the bottom' and the 'race to consume' any and all possible resources are being utilized to create capital to consume, Universal icons of human worth as defined by the Global Consumerist Culture.
361.   "Bioengineered Food Can't Be Forced Down European's Throats". St. Paul Pioneer Press

could be massive starvation; and there would be no alternative of the same or similar species that could possibly overcome the disease. Those affected would be sentenced to death, because they chose to eliminate Nature's gift of genetic diversity in their environment.

Biological Diversity & Genetic Modification - Dangers

The additional downside to the venturing into and eliminating forests that have never been touched is that contact is also sometimes made with life forms that have not yet been introduced to the human species--human, animal, or plant pathogens to which humans have not yet been exposed to. Some of these, because of the unfamiliarity between species and/or the virulent nature of these life forms, can pose an unimaginable threat or benefit to humankind --- a more likely threat in the case of microbes. But to add insult to injury, with the proliferation of genetically-engineered organisms and the free plasmid rings that give them their "special traits", we are at a stage in which two "harmless" life forms could exchange genetic material and emerge as something that we cannot yet conceive with unforeseen consequences. With 'Rational' science, Progress is often all that matters, but being in the reality that we are not omniscient, and therefore cannot be aware of all variables, it is better to limit experiments to ones that can be conceived of having lesser collateral damage. And, in these cases of the rapid "discovery" and elimination of the planet's biodiversity, You could possibly be creating monsters while simultaneously destroying the cures in Your zeal to consume all that is consumable.With the trend to deforest the earth in the name of profit and in "providing consumers with the most choices at the greatest value" one point beyond the obvious point of forests acting as the lungs of the planet by respirating; absorbing carbon dioxide and excreting oxygen, and acting as anchors that hold together the land and offer the necessary environment for wetlands and flood control, is that they are also the home of an immense diversity of life forms. These life forms make up a large part of the genetic diversity of the planet and with the loss of these forests, also goes the habitat for these plants, animals, microbes, and fungi.

I do not say this to You in an alarmist fashion. Monsters in the microbe world are a tangible reality, i.e. Nepa, Ebola, Zancomycin-resistant staph, HIV, Multiple-drug resistant Tuberculosis, Marburg virus, SARS, Avian influenza, etc.

Biological Diversity and Genetic Modification -
Scarcity of Resources & The Age of Resource Wars
As the world's population grows and the ratio of resource consumption to product output increases, the ability for the natural environment to provide enough resources for human survival, i.e. food and water will decrease. The future wars will be over resources. They may initially be conflicts over sources of energy, but they will increasingly be over water rights, fishing grounds, and arable land. If You are successful in creating a worldwide Culture of Consumerism, You will be able to initiate the Age of Resource Wars.

Environment, Health, & Poor Communities.

The environmental health consequences of inadequate water and sanitation are devastating. The UN attributes 2.2 million deaths annually to poor water and sanitation. Specific effects on human health are broad: 4 billion cases of diarrhea annually (causing 15 percent of all child mortality under age five in developing countries); a 10 percent rate of injection by intestinal worms in developing countries; 6 million people blind from trachoma; 200 million infected with schistosomiasis; and heightened incidence of diseases including cholera, typhoid, and viral hepatitis A, just to name a few. It is hard to imagine a more pressing environmental health problem or one that more strongly diminished the length and quality of life and human productivity in the developing world.[362]

Looking at this initially, it does not look like it should be of any concern to You, but in truth it does affect You and the world-at-large.

In terms of affecting You, if You have any industrial capacity in a subject nation-state that is negatively affected by the problems caused by an inadequate clean water supply, the productivity of Your activities will not be sustainable because of sickness and absenteeism, also sick people's immune systems are weak and therefore better vectors for the spread of disease, in general. In this Globalized world of high speed trade, and rapid transportation, the spread of pathogens is already much easier; but the maintenance of "areas of sickness" in the world only provides for the best of breeding grounds for disease that could lead to regional and worldwide epidemics.

Groundwater.

Throughout history, civilizations have used the subterranean world as a receptacle for waste – a place to bury the dead, or to landfill trash, for instance. But prior to the twentieth century, these practices did not usually result in serious damage to groundwater. As water percolated down through soil and rocks, bacteria, fungi, and other such biological pollutants were naturally filtered out, or diluted. But in recent years, groundwater's natural defense systems

---

362.   "Water Supply and Poor Communities: What's Price Got to Do With It?", Environmental Magazine Dec. 2003, p.24

have been vastly overextended. The sheer volume of pollutants sent underground has escalated – and at the same time, scientists have introduced thousands of new substances not found in nature. Globally, the production of synthetic chemicals has vaulted from under 150,000 tons in 1935 to more than 150 millions tons in 1995. Many of these substances not only endure far longer in the environment, they are often more toxic than their predecessors. Pesticide formulations available today, for instance, are between 10 and 100 times more potent than those sold in 1975.[363]

...Earth is a closed ecological system in which nothing permanently disappears. The methods normally used to conceal garbage and other waste – landfills, septic tanks, and sewers – become the major conduits of chemical pollution of groundwater.[364]

Playing with the planet's groundwater is a serious game, mainly because it is a large component of the greater hydrological system made by groundwater, the earth, surface water, and the ocean. The amount of the quality of groundwater is becoming more and more important as aquifers are being drained and surface water (lakes and rivers) are being used to their limits--drained, dammed, and polluted past usability. Also being that the water in wetlands originates in the groundwater, the loss of this resource also means the loss of the water source for wetlands, destroying the natural habitat for many types of wildlife.

One largely unknown factor concerning the overuse of groundwater is that the sediment which usually holds the groundwater, if not utilized in a sustainable fashion, can compact, shrinking the actual storage capacity of the underlying aquifer. If this happens, the damage to the aquifer is irreversible.[365]

An additional negative to the shrinking aquifers is their role in absorbing excess water from surface water such as rivers and lakes. In the case of the aforementioned unnatural disaster and/or regular heavy rains, lakes and rivers that would normally stay within certain bounds will flood.

Sustainable Farming.

Even more radical gains may be within reach by overhauling the polluting systems themselves. In China, for example, by planting more diverse varieties of rice instead of monocultures, thousands of rice farmers have completely eliminated their pesticide use – and at the same time, have doubled their yields. Field based training has helped farmers in Indonesia, Peru, and Cuba to control pests through non-polluting biological, rather than chemical, means. Some pioneering water utilities and governments have found that it costs

---

363.   "Deep Trouble: The Hidden Threat of Groundwater Pollution" by Payal Sampat, Worldwatch Paper 154 December 2000 World Watch Institute, p.7
364.   Ibid, p.31
365.   See Renner, p.13

less to support such sustainable farming practices. Some pioneering water utilities and governments have found that it costs less to support such sustainable farming practices than to strip chemicals out of polluted water. And by reusing discarded materials and spent chemicals, some firms are finding ways to shrink their waste stream – thereby protecting groundwater from chemical that lack out of landfills and septic systems.[366]

Pesticides are designed to kill. Yet it took several years after the first synthetic pesticides were introduced in the 1940s before it became apparent that these chemicals were also injuring organisms other than pests – including humans. Even after the health threats of some of these poisons were widely recognized in the 1960s, scientists believed that the real dangers lay in their dispersal among animals and plants – not deep underground. It was generally assumed that very little pesticide would leach below the upper layers of soil, and that if it did, it would be degraded before it could get any deeper. Soil, after all, is known to be a natural filter, purifying water as it trickles through. Industrial or agricultural chemicals, like such natural contaminants as bacteria or leaf mold, would be filtered out as the water percolated through the soil, or so it was thought.[367]

Central American farmers who used agroecological (sustainable) farming methods fared far better during that hurricane than conventional farmers. According to a post-disaster survey of able practices (which emphasize soil and water conservation) experienced very little erosion and retained far more precious topsoil than conventional farms. When an entire hillside or watershed uses agroecological practices, the movement of soils and water that causes landslides at lower elevations can be prevented.[368]

Though this may be true, and it sounds responsible to promote 'alternative' or sustainable farming methods to diminish some of environmental impact that comes as a consequence of conventional farming, You most likely have done a good job in convincing Your subject nation-state(s) that both conventional agriculture and the promotion of G-M crops is to its advantage. If You are successful with these agriculture campaigns there will not only be continued chemical pollution in the groundwater, but also genetic pollution in the environment, for which we have yet to see the long-term effects of the existence of free genetically-engineered plasmid rings in the natural environment.

An additional impact on the environment by unsustainable farming is the massive amount of water needed for irrigation, by far the largest consumer of groundwater, followed by industrial use. The actual water consumption by humans and for sustainable farming comes after these commercial uses, with even commercial farming being more and more displaced by industrial use, because the industrial use of water creates more income than commercial agricultural use.

---

366.   "Deep Trouble", p.9
367.   Ibid, p.24
368.   "Unnatural Disasters", p.2

One more aspect to 'sustainable farming' is the impact on commercial livestock farming on local water sources. The commercialization of chicken and pig farming is creating massive amounts of excrement that no water source in any condition, except for possibly the deep ocean, can handle. This fecal waste is put directly into local sewage systems and is killing whole rivers, lakes, and bays. The centralization of livestock farming is doing away with the ability to distribute waste products over a very large geographical area that could have absorbed animal waste in the past. And with the avoidance of abative technologies such as bioenergy, i.e. turning the methane in the waste into energy, to insist on using petroleum products at any and all costs, no other solution is left in dealing with this waste except for attempting to integrate it back into the environment.

Flooding.

Likewise, common response to floods is to try to prevent them by controlling rivers. But contrary to popular belief, containing a river in embankments, dams, channels, reservoirs, and other structures does not reduce flooding. Instead, it dramatically increases the rate of flow, and causes even worse flooding downstream.[369]

The 1993 Mississippi flood's human and economic costs, combined with its benefits to the ecosystem's functions, inspired a rethinking of the way large rivers are managed. After the flood, a federal task force recommended ending the nation's over-reliance on engineering and structural means of flood control in favor of floodplain restoration and management. It emphasized managing the river as a whole ecosystem rather than as short segment.[370]

This is because the source water is still coming out at the same rate. The only way to truly mitigate this is to disproportionately use the groundwater source (including aquifer). If the groundwater sources are depleted, the surface water will cease to exist. Of course, this is not a desirable solution to the problem of flooding, but if this trend of groundwater depletion continues, except for the unforeseen superstorms that may come in the future, and the hypersensitivity to flooding that deforested flood plains and hillsides will have, flooding due to overabundance of surface water because of the inability of groundwater and aquifers to absorb these excesses will disappear. The only water that will be present is that which comes from the sky and the ocean, and the hydrological system will be disrupted for affected land areas because there will not be the evaporation required with increased temperatures due to climate change combined with loss of forests and wetlands - this will be the

369.   "Unnatural Disasters." Janet Abramovitz. Worldwatch Paper 158. October 2001. Worldwatch Institute, p.19
370.   Ibid, p.21

scenario for desertification. Those areas that do not go the way of the desert will go the opposite direction with the onslaught of climate change - more intense storm activity, mudslides, floods, landslides, avalanches, storm surges, and rising sea levels.

Climate Change.

"Experts New Data Show Global Warming" AP News April 28, 2005
Climate scientists armed with new data from deep in the ocean and far into space have found that Earth is absorbing much more heat than it is giving off, a conclusion they say validates projections of global warming.

Lead scientist James Hansen, a prominent NASA climatologist, described the findings on the planet's out-of-balance energy exchange as a "smoking gun" that should dispel doubts about forecasts of climate change...

...Hansen's team, reporting Thursday in the journal Science, said they also determined that global temperatures will rise 1 degree Fahrenheit this century even if greenhouse gases are capped tomorrow.

If carbon dioxide and other heat-trapping emissions instead continue to grow, as expected, things could spin "out of our control," especially as ocean levels rise from melting Greenland and Antarctic ice sheets, the researchers said. International experts predict a 10-degree leap in Fahrenheit readings in such a worst-case scenario.

The NASA-led researchers were able to measure Earth's energy imbalance because of more precise ocean readings collected by 1,800 technology-packed floats deployed in seas worldwide beginning in 2000,

in an international monitoring effort called Argo...

...With this data, the scientists calculated the oceans' heat content and the global energy imbalance. They found that for every square meter of surface area, the planet is absorbing almost one watt more of the sun's energy than it is radiating back to space as heat — a historically large imbalance. Such absorbed energy will steadily warm the atmosphere.

The 0.85-watt figure corresponds well with the energy imbalance predicted by the researchers' supercomputer simulations of climate change, the report said.

Those computer models factor in greenhouse gases in the atmosphere, including carbon dioxide, methane and other gases - produced by everything from automobiles to pig farms. Those gases keep heat from escaping into space. Significantly, greenhouse emissions have increased at a rate consistent with the detected energy imbalance, the researchers said."

"There can no longer be genuine doubt that human-made gases are the dominant cause of observed warming," said Hansen, director of NASA's Goddard Institute for Space Studies at Columbia University's Earth Institute. "This energy imbalance is the `smoking gun' that we have been looking for."...

...In February, scientists at San Diego's Scripps Institution of Oceanography said their research - not yet published - also showed a close correlation between climate models and the observed temperatures of oceans, further defusing skeptics' past criticism of uncertainties in modeling...

... Besides raising ocean levels, global warming is expected to intensify storms, spread disease to new areas, and shift climate zones, possibly making farmlands drier and deserts wetter.[371]

---

371.   "Experts New Data Show Global Warming" by Charles J. Hanley, AP News, April 28, 2005

The concentration of people and infrastructure in cities and along coats, as well as growing pressure on ecosystems. The looming prospect of climate change and sea level can only exacerbate these troubling trends.

Scientists project that in the future the weather is likely to become more erratic and extreme as a result of climate change. The Intergovernmental Panel on Climate Change (IPCC) reports that the globally averaged surface air temperature is projected to increase 1.4 – 5.8 degrees Celsius by 2100 relative to 1990. New IPCC studies highlight the projected disaster-related impacts of climate change during the twentieth century. These include increased coastal flooding and infrastructure damage due to sea level rise; higher maximum temperatures with more droughts, heat waves, and fires in many areas; more intense tropical storms; more intense tropical storms; more intense precipitation events over most regions that will increase floods, landslides, avalanches, and mudslides; and intensified droughts and floods associated with El Nino events. The IPCC projects that "the most widespread risk to settlements from climate change is flooding and landslides driven by projected increase in rainfall intensity and, in coastal areas, sea level rise." In Asia, projections of sea level rise, increased floods and droughts in both temperate and tropical areas, and heavier monsoon rains will worsen the problems of this densely populated and disaster-prone region.

It is already clear that sea levels are rising. During the twentieth century, global average sea level rose by 10-20 centimeters, according to the IPCC, and it is projected to rise another 9-88 centimeters by 2100. But some areas will likely experience sea level increases of twice the global average, notes the British Meteorological Office.[372]

Disasters, whether they are man-made or natural does not matter – You must be prepared for them. Do not get lost in the debate over whether 'greenhouse emissions' are the cause, or not. You should aim for sustainable industry – period: meaning lessening emissions simply because it should be obvious that smoke stacks and exhaust pipes are not "naturally-occurring" and therefore Nature has to adjust to accommodate them; saving forests not just because they look pretty and colorful birds live there, but because they serve a tangible use in providing for flood control, water supply, genetic biodiversity, and carbon dioxide absorption and oxygen production.

There is ample opportunity for actions to reduce disaster risks within the Framework Convention on Climate Change, as there is language that obliges signatories to cooperate in adapting to the impacts of climate change, including land use and water resource planning as well as disaster mitigation and adaptation to climate change into efforts to achieve sustainable[373] and equitable development is highlighted in the latest IPCC reports. The "win-win" solutions are summed up: "Policies that lessen pressures on resources, improve management of environmental risks, and increase the welfare of the poorest members of society can simultaneously advance sustainable development and equity,

---

372.   "Unnatural Disasters", p.38
373.   Ibid, p.40

enhance adaptive capacity, and reduce vulnerability to climate and other stresses.[374]

To the extent possible, people and structures should be located out of harm's way. When hazards are unavoidable, development can be made to withstand them – for example, buildings in earthquake zones should be designed to weather earthquakes. Disaster preparedness, too, is an integral part of saving lives and lowering the economic tool.[375]

A critical part of good land use planning is maintaining or restoring healthy ecosystems so they can provide valuable services. China, for example, now recognizes that forests are 10 times more valuable for flood control and water supply than they are for timber. Since the logging ban was introduced, the government has been paying former loggers to plant trees in the upper watershed. The resiliency of agroecological farming in the face of Hurricane Mitch, noted earlier, provides a model for better land use.[376]

Instead of relying on structural engineering, the time has come to tap nature's engineering techniques – using the services provided by healthy and resilient ecosystems. Dunes, barrier islands, mangrove forests, and coastal wetlands are natural shock absorbers that protect against coastal storms. Wetlands, floodplain, and forest are spongers that absorb flood waters. Nature provides these valuable services for free, and we should take advantage of them rather than undermining them.[377]

Disasters.

In much of the developing world, urbanization has additional dangers. A good deal of the growth is unplanned, unregulated, and unregistered... Up to half the people in the largest cities of the developing world live in unplanned squatter colonies, which are often sited in vulnerable areas such as floodplains and hillsides or even garbage dumps. The poorer communities are far less likely to have public services such as water, sanitation, storm drains, and health and emergency services. As a result, when disasters strike, the residents are even worse off. After disasters they have few, in any, resources to fall back on to survive and rebuild.

As Kunda Dixit and Inam Ahmed put it, when writing about floods in the vast Himalayan watershed: "Complete flood control... is impossible. Even partial control is ... problematic.... So the question arises: Should we try to prevent floods at all? Or should we be looking at what is it we do that makes floods worse? Is it better to try to live with them, and to minimize the danger to infrastructure while maximizing the advantages that annual floods bring to farmers?" The same questions must be asked about natural hazards everywhere.[378]

An additional aspect of urbanization that I did not mention in the narrative

---

374.   Ibid, p.39
375.   Ibid, p.41
376.   Ibid, p.41
377.   Ibid, p.43
378.   Ibid, p.49

entitled "Environment - Introduction", in this chapter, is that all cities, either well-planned or unplanned, concentrate risk of the nation-state's assets, human, economic, and social. Cities hold the largest number of people as well as the economic center, the modes of production, and are usually the heart of the nation-state's infrastructure, utilities, communications, healthcare, and transportation. Large-scale destructive events that hit cities adversely affect everyone in the nation-state except for possibly rural people who do not rely on the services of the government and/or infrastructure.

Natural disasters come as they do as a part of the natural cycle of environmental events, but with the massive rate of consumption of resources and the often deliberate destruction and misuse of the environment for commercial reasons, or even for survival for those affected by the forces of Globalization such as those dispossessed of their land and having to clear important forests in order to make charcoal to cook with, or "poaching" to have food to eat, etc. Through these assaults on the environment, whether malevolent, neglectful, or reactionary, You will have set the stage for unnatural environmental events, and when these do occur, the more urbanized nation-states become, the greater the effect on the population will be in terms of survivability and resilience.

From the standpoint of maintaining order after such an event, cities with high wealth-to-poverty ratios and the slums that accompany these ratios will be harder to bring back to stability, because the poor are more susceptible to disasters, and if their plight cannot be mitigated in a reasonable amount of time, You--more likely You subject nation-state(s)--will have to deal with the possibility of major looting, riots, rebellion, disorder and may have to resort to very Draconian or counterinsurgency measures to maintain order and bring the city or nation-state back under the control of the government, while still having to deal with problems of getting the city functional again, if the disaster is not too destructive to do so.

Environment - Danger.

The 'Developed World' may come to its senses and begin to convert some of its industrial processes to those that are sustainable – to the extent that it does not too radically change their "way of life". The big danger is that the 'developing world', the overwhelming majority of the world's population, will adopt the unsustainable methods that granted the 'Developed World' its hegemony. The more they internalize linear thought processes and a life Ideology of Individualism/Individualistic Materialism it will be hard to convince them to not engage in the same processes that gave You power over them. At a different time, they might have been satisfied with their own reality and developing their own national potential according to their own success models, but now You have brought them into the world of 'Comparison' and 'Competition' based on the acquisition of Your cultural ideals and icons, in which success is defined very simply: resembling Your ideal as closely as possible.

Conclusion – Environmental Collapse.

In Nature's cycle of life, 'taking' requires 'giving' (or being 'taken') as a natural counterbalance. Those cognitively outside of this reality are not given (because of their 'unsustainable' value systems) reprieves for their ignorance. They, like all other 'life' are simply subject to balancing of the 'Equation'. Nature does not 'punish' or 'seek retribution' for acts of unbalance, it simply sets the stage for rectifying these aberrations. For, in truth, there are no aberrations in a perfect equation, only intensified balancing measures. There is no 'battle' between humanity and Nature for hegemony. Any 'separationist' thoughts of this sort are only illusions in the mind of a Rationalist. It is impossible to escape the causality of the Natural Universe. Within this causality there is only one 'life', one 'equation'; and it is always balanced. There is no 'too far' or 'too much' for the equation; these extremes can only be experienced by the actors through which it actualizes itself. No form of 'life' within the 'equation' is any more significant than a single separate grain of sand is to an entire beach. To truly believe that being one separate grain of sand or a group of grains of sand within the multitudes of Creation truly impacts on this 'equation' is nothing more than arrogance. In truth, this talk of 'sustainability' and 'unsustainability' is more a question of voluntary choices and involuntary choices. Any 'life' that proves to maximize its allotted creative or destructive qualities out of moderation will be accordingly balanced or re-integrated into the Source of the equation. Human beings who get too caught up in their own delusions of importance, acting too immoderately, can prove to outlive (or accelerate) their usefulness within this equation. Every 'grain of sand' on the beach is an interconnected piece of life. This 'life' expands and contracts based on the collective status of the equation. The 'expansion' and 'contraction' is the equation experiencing Itself.[379]

Those who call for sustainability are those that desire to both acknowledge their connectedness to a balanced system while simultaneously being aware of their individual aspects within and as a part of this system.

---

379.   These last two sentences presuppose an even greater presumption. These are simply part of the thought process of this narrative and make up a hypothesis that supports this Conclusion.

Those who desire single-minded expression as individual aspects can do so, without any worries. But this 'separate' self-identity will be short-lived because though it may only see itself as a separate individual aspect, it still has an innate responsibility to play some 'involuntary' role in this system. It may believe that its predatory or destructive nature is an individualized expression of Self separate from the equation, but its intense desire to seek its path is nothing more than blind submission to its role in this system of life rather than 'sighted' submission to this system of life that one who acknowledges the causal reality is aware of.

We are the sum of ourselves. However, as much as we take, we must give. If we take to create, then we must give what is created back to the equation. Whoever takes less has to give less within the cycle of creation and destruction. But if a philosophy of 'taking'/'consumption' under the misnomer of 'creating something','Growth', or 'Progress' is effectively disseminated and embraced by a large percentage of humanity, though in the minds of these involved, they may believe that they are 'building something'/'progressing'/ 'achieving' the highest human potential, they are actually collectively 'taking'/ 'consuming' on a monumental scale. This level of 'taking' requires 'giving' on the same level. If humanity takes so much from Nature to only feed on insatiable desire to perpetually consume while creating 'nothing' from it, the same vacuum that they are creating will consume them.

In the same way that a black hole, before it collapses in on itself, was a bloated mass consuming seemingly endless quantities of matter to create its 'grand structure' as a 'super-giant star', humanity can achieve the grandeur of nothingness – it can expand so greatly and create unsustainable societies that appear to be the grandest ever, in all time, all the while consuming everything in its wake, and then one day it explodes: all of the 'binding energy' that held all of the cultures of the world together releases itself in exchange for the predominate one of 'nothing' (the one that You have projected onto the world); and with this 'binding energy's' release, the whole of humanity explodes, in the same manner that a super-giant star turns into a supernova and then after the release of all that which held humanity 'together', it falls in onto itself with the ultimate of intensity, taking all that was 'of created structure' and pulls it totally apart, leaving only the raw density of a body seeking 'stability' because it has strayed so far from its 'creative' purpose. It will instead (like a vampire in the Universe) become a vacuum whose energy has now been inverted and serves only to pull other creative things apart. It told the equation that it did not desire its role as a creative force in the Universe; the Equation allowed it to consume to the point that it itself became the vacuum that it could not fill by choosing 'consuming'/destruction instead of 'creating'.

Humanity is at its crossroads – it can continue to be a creative force in the Universe or it can serve the material world that it consumes. If it chooses 'life'/moderated creation and destruction, it will tell the Equation that it does not need to be counterbalanced and does not need to have its 'creative' purpose substituted by Others. If humanity continues to 'serve' what it consumes, it will inform the Universe that it desires not to get what it needs to create from the Source of the 'equation', but rather it would only like to grow more powerful from consuming of the equation instead. In this case, humanity will lose its purpose as a creative force in the Universe and will assume its new role as the perpetual consumer/predator that it now desires to be.

Humanity must make a choice. Those who call for unsustainable life choices are not 'bad' for humanity. They are what they are, destructive actors. Destructive actors are needed to take apart created things so that there are resources to continue to create with. Problems come when humanity fails to recognize 'destructive actors' and instead views them as 'creative actors'. In the same way that viruses kill just enough animal and plant life to keep equilibrium, humanity must do the same. Viruses perform their role as facilitators of destruction needed to keep the equation in equilibrium; but those affected by the viruses are not to take on the behavior of the viruses simply because the virus convinces them that it is superior because it is not restricted by the 'limitations' of being a 'cell' in a collective body. What it fails to tell them, and may not even realize (linear thinking), is that it requires hosts to multiply. It is like a vampire, the 'living dead'.

Many classify 'life' as that which is able to reproduce by itself.[380] Viruses fall outside of this definition because they cannot reproduce without a host body. Without a host it lays dormant until a weakened body (cell) is present and it takes advantage of this weakness. It may be proud of its efficient killing abilities, but it like all created matter, simply follows its innate purpose: it regulates populations of life so that they do not overconsume their resources, resulting in the death of the entire body/population. If those affected by viruses adopt the Ideology of Viruses, the result will be the death of the entire body/population facilitated under the banner of 'superiority' because of the viruses' lack of awareness/conscious denial of the limitations required by interconnected systems.

---

380.   In the field of biology, 'life' is classified as that which is able to reproduce by itself within its own species, which technically excludes viruses, because they require the resources of another species to reproduce, i.e. "create".

Environment Tables and Charts

Classical Agricultural Model

(originating fundamentally in developed countries)

External dependence
- of the country on other countries
- of the provinces on the country
- of localities on the province and the country

Cutting edge technology
- imported raw materials for animals feed
- widespread utilization of chemical pesticides and fertilizers
- consumption of fuel & lubricants

Tight relationship between bank credit and production; high interest rates

Priority given to mechanization as a production technology

Introduction of new crops at the expense of autochthonous crops and production systems

Search for efficiency through intensification and mechanization

Real possibility of investing in production and commercialization

Accelerated rural exodus

Satisfying ever-increasing needs has more ecological or environmental consequences, such as soil erosion, salinization, waterlogging, etc.

Alternative Agricultural Model

Maximum advantage taken of:
- the land
- human resources of the zone or locality
- broad community participation
- cutting edge technology, but appropriate to zone where used
- organic fertilizers & crop rotation
- biological control of pests
- biological cycles and seasonality of crops and animals
- natural energy sources (hydro, wind, solar, slopes, biomass etc.)
- animal traction
- rational use of pastures and forage for both grazing and feedlots, search for locally supplied animal nutrition

Diversification of crops and autochthonous production systems based on accumulated knowledge

Introduction of scientific practices that correspond to the particulars of each zone; new varieties of crops and animals, planting densities, seed treatments, post-harvest storage, etc.

Preservation of the environment and the ecosystem

Need for systemic training (management, nutritional, technical)

Systemic technical assistance

Promote cooperation among producers, within and between communities

Obstacles to overcome:
- difficulties in the commercialization of agricultural products because of the number of intermediaries
- control over the market
- poverty among the peasantry
- distances to markets and urban centers (lack of sufficient roads and means of transport)
- illiteracy

Source: Strategy for the development of specific projects: most relevant considerations to keep in mind. (Cuban Ministry of Agriculture chart circulated to planning staff)[379]

---

379.   From pp.30-31 *The Greening of the Revolution: Cuba's Experiment With Organic Agriculture*. Medes Benjamin & Peter Rossett, Melbourne, Australia: Ocean Press 1999.

Classical Model: Prime for Your exploitation

Alternative Model: Lessens (eliminates) Your control over the subject society and environmental (land/resources). If this is implemented it can lead to a systematically eradication of Your influence over its society and economy. If Your subject nation-state can feed itself without 'Your "help", it will be going a long way in fulfilling its mandate to its population. The control of the food economy is a substantial step in independence from the dependent relationship that You have created onto Your subject's nation-state. Its dependency on You to meet its food supply needs is a powerful psychological deterrent to it being too assertive in demanding 'parity' in its relationship with You. You cannot at any cost allow Your subject to adjust its agricultural policy to a sustainable/organic model.

Estimated Annual Investment Required to Meet Urgent Social and Environmental Needs Worldwide

Social/Environmental Need	Annual Cost (billion dollars)
Enhance energy efficiency	33
Prevent soil erosion	24
Provide adequate shelter	21
Eliminate malnourishment and starvation	19
Promote renewable energy sources	17
Stabilize population(family planning and reproductive health)	17
Provide safe, clean drinking water	15
Provide primary healthcare for all	15
Counter desertification	12
Manage forest sustainably	6
Preserve biodiversity	5
Cut illiteracy in half over 10 years	6
Enhance child survival, development, and protection	3
Phase out chlorofluorocarbons (to 2008)	
Immunize children worldwide to prevent 1 million deaths annually	1.5
Total	196.3

Source: Worldwatch Institute based on Economists Allied for Arms Reduction, "What the World Wants – and How to Pay for It," undated fact sheet, on U.N. Development Programme (UNDP), *Human Development Report 1994* (New York: Oxford University Press, 1994), on United Nations, "UN Financial Crisis Affecting Operational Activities for Development, Says Secretary-General at Development Pledging Conference," press release, New York, November 1, 1995, on Patti L. Petesch, *North-South Environmental Strategies, Costs, and Bargains*, Policy Essay No.5 (Washington, D.C.: Overseas Development Council, 1992), on Norman Myers, *Ultimate Security: The Environmental Basis of Political Stability* (New York: W.W. Norton & Company, 1993), on Andrew Jordan, "Financing the UNCED Agenda: The Controversy over Additionality," *Environment*, April 1994, and on Dragojub Najman and Hans d'Orville, *Towards a New Multilateralism: Funding Global Priorities* (New York: Independent Commission on Population and Quality of Life, May 1995)

Commentary:

You should realize that these are only temporary solutions – band-aid solutions. The near future of the earth and humanity is not sustainable with the global proliferation of this quantitative value system of Individualistic Materialism. It must be contained within Your subject nation-state; and within Your subject nation-state they cannot be allowed to amass enough capital to consume at the rate of Your own nation-state. It is to be exploited, not join in the race to fully exploit the planet and consume all of its resources. As long as human beings' value is assessed quantitatively in this world of mass transportation, high-speed communications, and globalization of trade, this value system will continue to spread like a virus. The good-intentioned efforts of some citizens in "rich" countries will amount to nothing if people in the "poor" countries aspire for and work towards an ethic of frantic conspicuous consumption in a crazed desire to emulate the "rich" way of life, because it is the "Modern" or "Developed" way of human life. These "fixes" are not sustainable at the rates of consumption in the industrialized world. Therefore, if the "rest" were to be co-opted into this equation, unless ALL consume in a more sustainable manner, this only serves to be a short-time solution and will only accelerate the exhaustion of the finite resources of the planet. Living standards can be raised, but the excessive, environmentally wasteful and destructive patterns of consumption must also be phased out, i.e. organic agriculture; alternative sustainable power sources; mass transportation; sustainable architecture; minimalization of pollution; recycling of waste materials into either energy sources or raw materials for production; preventative medicine; de-populating of cities back into rural areas; the reestablishment of the extended family (i.e. eliminating the need of a mobile labor force); returning industry to the home-community; business based in the trade of items of value rather than on abstract currencies not based in any standard of value; preservation of local cultures – this diversity in the origin of innovation, not mimicry; early childhood education geared toward recognizing natural gifts and tendencies towards an art or profession, education based on the development of critical thinking, development of individual potential and contribution to community; re-affirming of oral and literary traditions, with limitations on the exposure of youth to interactive electronic media, i.e. television, video games; communication as opposed to litigation; an acknowledgement that it is unacceptable to allow any person to live without nourishing food, clean water, shelter, education, healthcare, safety, and love (love defined as being valued as a member of a community), and the opportunity to develop their individual creative potential, and the freedom to travel.

International Water Disputes of Varying Intensity, Eighties and Nineties

Body of Water	Countries Involved	Subject of Dispute
Nile	Egypt, Ethiopia, Sudan	Water diversion, flooding, siltation
Euphrates	Iraq, Syria, Turkey	Reduced, water flow, salinization
Jordan, Yarmuk,	Israel, Jordan, Syria,	Water flow, diversion
Litani	Lebanon	
West Bank	Israel, Palestinians	Water allocation and aquifer water rights
Indus, Sutlei	India, Pakistan	Irrigation
Brahmaputra, Ganges	Bangladesh, India	Water flow, siltation, flooding
Salween/ Nu Jiang	Burma, China	Siltation, flooding
Mekong	Cambodia, Laos, Thailand, Vietnam, China	Water flow, flooding
Aral Sea	Kazakstan, Uzbekistan, Turkmenistan	Repercussions of shrinking sea, water scarcity, salinization
Paraná	Argentina, Brazil	Dam, land inundation
Lauca	Bolivia, Chile	Dam, salinization
Rio Grande/Colorado	Mexico, United States	Water flow, salinization, pollution
Rhine	France, Germany, Netherlands, Switzerland	Industrial pollution
Szamos	Hungary, Romania	Industrial pollution
Danube	Hungary, Slovokia	Dam, flooding

This table is based on Table 3.1 in Michael Renner's, *National Security: The Economic and Environmental Dimensions*, Worldwatch Paper 89 (Washington, D.C.): Worldwatch Institute, May 1989), on Gleck, op.cit. in this note, on Günther Bächler, "The Anthropogenic Transformation of the Environment: A Source of War?" in Kurt R. Spillmann and Günther Bächler, eds., "Environmental Crisis: Regional conflicts and Ways of Cooperation," Occasional Paper No. 14, ENCOP, Bern, Switzerland, September 1995, and on Andrew Nette, "Sharing the Mekong Creates Problems," Third World Network Features, Malaysia, on the APC electronic conference igc:twn.features on March 27, 1996.

Dimensions and Magnitude of Human Insecurity, Early Nineties

Source of Insecurity	Observation
Income	1.3 billion people in developing countries live in poverty; 600 million are considered extremely poor; in industrial countries, 200 million people live below the poverty line.
Clean Water	1.3 billion people in developing countries lack access to safe water.
Literacy	900 million adults worldwide are illiterate.
Jobs	820 million people worldwide are unemployed or underemployed.
Food	800 million people in developing countries have inadequate food supplies; 500 million of them are chronically malnourished, and 175 million are children under the age of five.
Housing	500 million urban dwellers worldwide (out of 2.4 billion) are homeless or live in inadequate housing; 100 million young people are homeless ("street children")
Preventable Death	15-20 million people die each year due to starvation and disease aggravated by malnutrition; 10 million people die annually due to substandard housing, unsafe water, and poor sanitation in densely populated cities.

This table is based on various editions of the *Human Development Report*, on U.N. Department of Public Information (UNDPI) factsheets: "The Faces of Poverty" (March 1996), "The Geography of Poverty" (March 1996), and "Poverty: Casting Long Shadows" (February 1996), on U.N. Research Institute for Social Development (UNRISD), *States of Disarray: The Social Effects of Globalization* (Geneva: 195), and on United Nations, "Backgrounder – Global Report on Human Settlements Reveals: 50 Million Homeless or Poorly Housed in Cities Worldwide," in the APC electronic conference igc:unic.news on February 9, 1996. from Renner, Michael (1996) *Fighting for Survival: Environmental Decline, Social Conflict, and the New Age of Insecurity*. New York: W.W. Norton & Company.

Globalization has exacerbated this problem over the last 10 years through the 'commodification' of society, social economy, and environment.

Chapter 44:
The World – Social Collapse

Global Culture of Individualistic Materialism
and Unsustainable Security Policy - Introduction.

There is a kind of monkey trap used in Asia. A coconut is hollowed out and attached by a rope to a tree or stake in the ground. At the bottom of the coconut a small slit is made and some sweet food is placed inside. The hole on the bottom of the coconut is just big enough for the monkey to slide in his open hand, but does not allow for a closed fist to pass out. The monkey smells the sweets, reaches in with his hand to grasp the food and is then unable to withdraw it.

The clenched fist won't pass through the opening. When the hunters come, the monkey becomes frantic but cannot get away. There is no one keeping that monkey captive, except the force if its own attachment. All that it has to do is to open the hand. But so strong is the force of greed in the mind that it is a rare monkey which can let go.[380]

… many sources of conflict are simply not amenable to any military "solution". Poverty, unequal distribution of land, and the degradation of ecosystems are amongst the most real and pressing issues undermining people's security. Soldiers, tanks, or warplanes are at best irrelevant in this context, and more likely an obstacle. The military absorbs substantial resources that could help reduce the potential for violent conflict if invested in health, housing, education, poverty eradication, and environmental sustainability.[381]

Due to the spread of a Global Culture of Individualistic Materialism and the lack of attention paid to the sustainability of human security, the Age of the Nation-State may be coming to a close. Peoples will resort to depending on themselves and redefining relationships in order to survive and to achieve the necessary self-esteem for peace of mind instead of looking to government as an extension of their family and community security network.

---

380.   From Joseph Goldstein, The Experience of Insight – on the back cover of Goldstein, Joseph (2003) *Settling Back Into the Moment: A Meditator's Guide*. Dehiwala: Buddhist Cultural Centre.
381.   Renner p.29

Global Health - Introduction

"Nature is never truly conquered. The human retroviruses and their intricate relationship with the human cell are but one example of the fact. Indeed, perhaps conquest is the wrong metaphor to describe our relationship to nature, which not only surrounds but in the deepest sense also constitutes our being."

Robert Gallo, discoverer of the first human retrovirus[382]

Asymmetric Warfare

The Mice That Roared:
From the earliest time, small forces have found ways of wounding superpowers...
Heavily armored and drilled to advance as one giant machine, Roman legionary troops would cut to pieces any enemy not wise enough to flee. They were unstoppable in one group even if greatly outnumbered and no cavalry charge could break their unbroken wall of shields. Yet even in the best days of the empire, the Romans suffered defeats at the hands of much less accomplished enemies who lacked their costly equipment and elaborate training. Some relied on hit-and-run raids against Roman outposts, rear guards and stragglers, or the patient art of the ambush. Others lured legionary troops into forests where the trees broke up their wall of shields, leaving each heavily loaded man vulnerable to more agile enemies – that is how three entire legions, some 18,000 men, were massacred in a German forest in A.D. 9. Others would stab individual Roman soldiers in markets or alleys, even when capture and execution were inevitable – for there is nothing new about suicide attackers. What they all had in common was the avoidance of symmetrical combat, for to confront the legions in set-piece battle in open ground would guarantee defeat...
The Romans faced many such enemies, most of them now obliterated in historical memory, all of them handily defeated. Having to fight ordinary wars from time to time with the Parthians and Persians, their only worthy antagonists, they knew both kinds of war, and greatly preferred the much less bloody, costly, and dangerous asymmetrical kind. For us, too asymmetric is terrible with its sudden terrorist attacks, but the mass destruction and nuclear danger of symmetrical war would be far worse."[383]

"The more uncomfortable the guerilla fighter is, and the more he is initiated into the rigors of nature, the more he feels himself at home; his morale is higher; his sense of security, greater. At the same time he has learned to risk his life in every circumstance that might arise, to trust it to luck like a tossed coin. In general, as a result of this kind of combat, it matters little to the individual guerilla whether or not he survives."[384]

Ernesto "Che" Guevara

"One man's terrorist is another man's revolutionary".

V. Zapata, Mexican Educator

---

382.   Grmek, Mirko D. trans. Manlitz, Russell C. and Duffin, Jacalyn (1990) *History of AIDS: Emergence and Origin of a Modern Pandemic.* Princeton, NJ: Princeton University Press.
383.   Issues 2003, Newsweek International Dec. 2002-Feb. 2003. "Asymmetric War; How the Weak Fight".
384.   Gerassi ed., p.188

Individualistic Materialism can be a catalyst for social and moral dissolution. Reactionary movements to oppose the spread of these trends can arise. Asymmetric warfare can be viewed as a viable option in protecting the cultural, territorial, and economic integrity of economically and militarily weaker nation-states. The concept of 'terrorism' becomes relative to the reality of one's life experience. Depending on what side of the fence one stands on, the action of a government can be viewed as justified or mandated Rule of Law, or instead as state terrorism; while opposition to said government can be viewed as a struggle for freedom or fight against repression, or instead as non-state terrorism or insurrection. Whether resistance to Your influence in the world or that of Your compliant subject government is viewed as a 'terror group' or terrorist movement or a resistance group is a matter of perspective.

Fundamentalists, Revolutionaries, and Asymmetric Warfare.

One thing that You always must be aware of is the multiplication of social, economic, or environmental problems in Your subject nation-state and the percentage of the population that becomes consciously aware of disadvantageous status in their society and compared with the idealized lifestyle that You project onto Your subject nation-state. As time goes on, movements will likely arise calling for the rectification of social, economic, and environmental ills and calls for legislative change through their governmental system. If these calls are not heeded for a long period of time and the subject nation-state's government is viewed as a "puppet" to Your interests it may lose its legitimacy as the center of the valid "system" in the minds of some of the population. If some of its politicians, intellectuals, religious leaders, and students--active critical thinkers--view "working with the system for positive social change" as a naïve waste of time, because they are cognizant of the intent to which Your influence has infiltrated the nation psyche, they may move to change it from without.

In this case, You have to decide whether or not You wish to make Your involvement more invasive. These uncooperative leaders can prove to be detrimental to Your control over Your subject nation-state, so You can assassinate them or have friendly parties within Your subject government to assassinate them, but You must beware of the possibility that the persons that You assassinate have great popularity with population and this may cause problems for the sustainability of the mandate of Your puppet government. But on this same note, You could orchestrate a true coup d'tat or regime change' and do it quickly enough that the population is not impacted by a disruption of services; and that You have informed the Other Princes of Your plan and You can trust that they will not "react" economically or diplomatically against the interests of Your new subject government, and keep diplomatic and trade relations status quo (including regulating the responses of financial markets due to the news of the coup). But again, this is all a gamble. You already cannot control the variables of a "non-invasive" campaign; an invasive campaign amplifies the numbers of these variables even more.

You should also be aware that 'violence' is not limited to physical attacks. Oppression manifested as the lack of basic human needs--lack of housing, clean water, nutritious food, healthcare, education, obstacles of using potential, etc.--is violence. The awareness of this 'oppression' becomes more with every projection. With every realization of comparative 'poverty' Your subject's population will "realize" its position in the hierarchy of an idealized "Modern society".

If this is allowed to fester too long and You do not advise Your subject nation-state's government to implement fascist security measures based on "security needs" a more and more 'violent' solution to the nation-state's problems will emerge. If hope for change is lost amongst the majority of the population, either one of two scenarios will emerge – a virulent internal group of revolutionaries and fundamentalists will emerge as a last chance effort to "re-claim the soul" of its nation-state or a simply organized internal group will enlist the help of external groups with similar interests (especially those who see the root of their oppression being the value system that You espouse) to attack their nation-state's government to "re-claim" it for its people.

I am mentioning this to You because You should be aware of the corollary that "violence begets violence". The more 'violence' that Your subject nation-state's population is subjected to, the more 'violent' the reconciliation or rectification of the "problem" will be. The less hope that a population has for alleviating oppression, the more radical the 'solution' that will arise. If it seems that their government's participation in Your plan is the cementing (solidification and integration) of their society into a static hierarchical world order, a very violent group will likely arise. This is actually a very hard choice for the population to make because although they acknowledge that the focus of these groups is to expel the "outside aggressor", that the base philosophy(s) of this/these group(s) are likely more radical than people in the society would like to live under. So, if the "violence" experienced by Your subject nation-state's population reaches a boiling point, they will allow the emergence and movement of a very radical but effective group to displace You or Your influence from its society; and then the plan is that once You are expelled that it can work internally to expel this group so that it can once again govern itself based on cultural center-oriented principles and point of reference.[385]

It is not in Your interest for the population to come to the conclusion that in order to address its human security needs and halt the solidification of its society into a global hierarchical order that You define, that it makes the decision to risk a possible fifty or more years of fundamentalist or radical rule as the price for eliminating Your influence over its society. The danger in this is that once this type of radical group receives some sanction from its host population(s) it may view the "world" as its battleground for asymmetric warfare against You and may attack targets inside its host nation(s), Your interests in Other nation-states, and possibly target in Your own nation-state.

As hopeless as this may seem, the presence of this type of group can make Your ability to maneuver within Your subject's nation-state and in the world–at-large more difficult; but in Your case, even if this situation arises there is still hope. If You were to utilize a few specific "terrorist attacks" (either actual or orchestrated by You) as symbols of a threat to "Human Civilization at-large", You can turn this seemingly difficult situation into a boon for Your objectives to rule the world. If You convince the Other Princes and Other subject nation-states to also assume the need for "increased vigilance and security" even though the root cause of this "security concern" emanates from Your involvement and influence over Your subject subject-nation(s), You can facilitate a worldwide conversion to security-oriented 'fascist-styled' governance which will lead to You to being the center point of reference for "maintaining security". You will have access to multitudes of national databases, access to financial, personnel, and military data of all the countries that join You in Your "war against the radicals, terrorists,

---

385.　　　　Governments of post-Colonial nation-states, though they may seem to embody "Modern ideals" because of their economic status and/or free elections, many times exist solely to perpetuate a Colonial legacy. Meaning that political "freedom" i.e. voting may have been achieved but the social and economic inequalities that were established during the Colonial period are perpetuated. These adverse social, economic, and environmental conditions may be termed "oppression" or "the necessary cost of a Free Market Economy", but to those experiencing these conditions – they are living in a system of "violence". Under the Colonial system, because the oppressor represented an external force, therefore psychologically the people were in better state, because under colonialism there was hope for victory over and the expulsion of this Colonial power. But in a post-Colonial "politically independent" reality, to continue to experience Colonial subjugation, the psychological impact is far worse, because now there is no hope for change. Their own government has become an instrument in the perpetuation of colonization. The result is "violence". It may manifest as self-destructive behaviors and a rise of violent crimes in the society and/or it may manifest into a revolutionary/fundamentalist movements desiring to return their nation-state to a perceived state of reality that existed before the Colonial period. An irony of these movements is that though they may appear to be based on traditional values they well be infused with the "Modern" predatory value system that You have projected on their nation-state and may actual work to create a "new old state" that is actually based on Your projected value system.

fundamentalists, and haters of peace, the war-mongers, anti-democrats, and threats to civilization". You will be able to dictate the flow of trade, interest rates, inflation, and people (immigration) all in the name of security. If You "play Your cards right", You can solidify Your global control through a series of "justified" military expeditions. Once You become the "Savior of Humanity" by pulling the world together under an umbrella of "Peace", You will have greater influence over the transnational organization and will be able to initiate "internationally sanctioned" military "peacekeeping" expeditions during which You can take control of the target nation-states' resources under the guise of "responsible stewardship"[386] and fan the flames of resistance against You by doing acts that infuriate the very group(s) whose actions You utilized to justify the creation of a global security state.

I give this advice with enthusiasm because it will work, but again I must bring You back to perspective: 1. asymmetric warfare is unpredictable, and if You are unaware of all underground arms trading You are not privy to the location of a numbers of wandering Weapons of Mass Destruction, especially after the end of the Cold War; and 2. some nation-states, more likely subjects than Princes, will not wish to make their states into this newly-defined "security-oriented" model and grow tired of their status in the global hierarchy and may lend quiet support to groups such as the one(s) that You used to initiate this new world order and/or allow the movement or quietly sanction the emergence of internal; or regional non-state actors that call for separation from this new world order. In this case You have a true division between aligned--with Your new world design--and non-aligned--those now aware that the goal of 'Modernity' is the establishment of a static world order centered on You and Other Princes that support Your vision--; and You will have created a more serious situation that, if You desire to remain conqueror and builder of the 'Modern' Empire, will require more invasive action to create so much internal and external disruption that all nation-states will beg for peace. This can be successfully carried-off in a series of invasive measures such as training security forces of aligned nations in counterinsurgency methods to ensure internal security, lending support to opposition groups in non-aligned states to cause coups d'tat, and toppling unfriendly governments followed by the training of the new "friendly" governments' security forces in counterinsurgency tactics. These invasive measures should inspire non-state resistance groups to act, but in this new "security reality" of a world in turmoil,

---

386.   Like the Berlin Conference 1884-5 during which Africa when divided evenly by its stewards, the builders of the Schools of Democracy, and were the responsible trusteeship over each colonies' resources.

You will be able to use any means necessary to deal with them.

Again, I must keep You in perspective. The aforementioned plan will work if You conduct Your actions within the proper parameters, but be aware that asymmetric warfare and the manipulation of nation-states is not an exact science unless You are omniscient. Being that You are not, I will also share with You some issues concerning asymmetric warfare and radical groups (revolutionaries, terrorists and radicals) that You should be aware of.

I will start with a speech by Chief Hurao of Guahan (Guam), 1671. His speech articulates some of the sentiment of those who in the present-day wish to battle with You asymmetrically.

A Call to Arms

The entrancing effects of Your projections can cause Your own nation-state's population to believe in the superiority that You project over the subject nation and it can become easy to take for granted the sophistication of the subject – having disastrous consequences…

Speech by Chief Hurao
Hagatna, Guahan (Agana, Guam) 1671

The Europeans would have done better to remain in their own country. We have no need of their help to live happily. Satisfied with what our islands furnish us, we desire nothing else. The knowledge which they have given us has only increased our needs and stimulated our desires. They find it evil that we do not dress. If that were necessary nature would have provided. They treat us as gross people and regard us as barbarians. But do we have to believe them? Under the pretext of instructing us they are corrupting us. They take away from us the primitive simplicity in which we live.

They treat our history as fables and fictions. Haven't we the same right concerning that which they teach us as uncontestable truths? They abuse our simplicity and good faith. All their skill is directed towards tricking us; all their knowledge tends to make us unhappy. If we are ignorant and blind, as they would have us believe, is because we have learned their evil plans too late and have allowed them to settle here. Let us not lose courage in the presence of our misfortune. They are only a handful. We can easily defeat them. Even though we don't have their deadly weapons which spread destruction all over, we can overcome them by our number. We are stronger than we think and we can quickly free ourselves from these foreigners and regain our former freedom. They dare to take away our liberty which should be dearer to us than life itself. They try to persuade us that we will be happier and some of us have been blinded into believing their words. But can we have such sentiments if we reflect that we have been covered with misery and maladies ever since these foreigners have come to disturb our peace? Before they arrived on the island we did not know insects. Did we know rats, flies, mosquitoes and all the other little animals which constantly torment us? These are the beautiful presents they have made to us. And what have their floating machines brought us? Formerly we did not have rheumatism and inflammations. If we had sicknesses we had remedies for them. But they have brought us their diseases but do not teach us the remedies. Is it necessary that our cupidity and evil desires make us want to have iron and other bagatelles which only render us unhappy? The Spaniards reproach us because of our poverty, ignorance and lack of industry. But if we are poor, as they claim, then what do they search for here? If they didn't need us, they would not expose themselves to so many perils and make such great efforts to establish themselves in our midst. For what purpose do they teach us except to make us adopt their customs and subject ourselves to their laws and lose our precious liberty left to us by our ancestors? In a word they try to make us unhappy in the hope of an ephemereal happiness can only be enjoyed after death.

Chief Hurao and his allies were defeated by the Spanish due to disease and superior fire power, and the assumption that warfare also consisted of a preceding verbal battle (to avoid excessive human loss of life); but the chances of militarily weaker power succeeding (or at the very least inflicting sufficient heavy causalities) in today's asymmetric warfare scenarios is much higher, because the proliferation of war technologies and inexpensively manufactured chemical and biological weapons.

Remember: "… the acts of empire are seldom forgotten by those who have suffered them."[387]

War.

It (the "enemy") cannot fight You on Your terms – if it tries it will lose.[388]

If You provoke--effectively influence--Your subject nation-state, but not concurrently weaken its actual control over its resources and modes of production, and if a fascist government conversion is necessary to maintain Sustainable Exploitation, Your subject government may possibly have the very means (or at least the belief that if can) of circumventing Your control by attempting to simultaneously strengthening itself and operating within Your

---

387.   Johnson, p.58
388.   The U.S. waited until the U.K. was severely weakened by WWII to take control of the world stage; in particular, economic hegemony.

rule structure. The following are two illustrations of means in which a nation-state was only aggravated and not totally subjugated; leaving it to believe that it could possibly equal or exceed You. In these cases the subject nation-state did not internalize the notion that its Prince was actually the universal default and natural point of reference for the governance of its society.

According to political scientist Andrew Janos, "peripheral societies" can achieve economic and political independence through the two following measures:

1.The first was for dependent or "late developing" countries to attempt through war and revolution to reconstruct their environments. This strategy required a militarization of society and the use of a mobilized people to attack and transform the environment...This strategy required a militarization of society and the use of a mobilized people to attack and transform the environment. The execution of this strategy has taken the forms of aggression and conquest (Nazi Germany, Japan from 1931 to 1945), support for world revolution (Lenin's and Stalin's Russia), fomenting "people's wars" (China and Cuba), aggressive neutralism (India), and other projects aimed at altering an environment in which "advanced" countries exploit "developing" ones.

2.The second is a "drive to imitate the technological innovations of the advanced countries". "This strategy has generally been internally oriented. It is best illustrated by Japan's state-guided industrialization from 1868 to approximately the Great Depression and again from 1949 to the present. It may only involve the state's use of tariffs to shelter its own economy from the penetrative power of stronger national economies. This was the strategy of the United States during the ninetieth and early twentieth centuries, in accordance with the ideas of Alexander Hamilton and Fredrich List. A version of this strategy also became policy in West Germany after its defeat in World War II. But such a strategy involving state guidance of the economy, cartelization, and the strategic allocation of industrial finance may come to dominate a social system that development itself becomes the main legitimating and organizing principle of society, replacing or displacing democratic representation, tradition, or any other set of political or cultural principles."[389]

Unsustainable Security Policy.

Conditioned by a worldview that largely equates security with military strength, traditional analysts tend to regard emerging issues simply as new "threats" to be deterred. By subsuming these new issues under the old thinking of national military security, efforts to address them in effect become militarized. Hence, weapons proliferation is countered by developing new weapons for preemptive raids on foreign arms facilities instead of by promoting disarmament; refugees are seen as menacing hordes to be intercepted on the high seas instead of as people forced from their homes by poverty; environmental degradation is seen as simply another item in which national interests are to be protected against those of other nations instead of acknowledging the common challenge; and the proliferation of drugs is tackled through the military eradicating cocaine crops instead of through efforts to provide alternative livelihoods for desperate peasants.[390]

389.   Johnson, pp.145-5
390.   Renner, p.29

These reactionary Global Security Policies are a practice of 'Global Governance' based on knee-jerk, simple, soundbytes (easily converted into digestible bits for non-critically thinking domestic electoral constituents), not on sustainable security policy.

Health

The following are a number of possible scenarios out of an innumerable number of possibilities for the future of Global Public Health and the sustainability of "life".

Global Public Health.

The rise of health epidemics is due to inconsistent health delivery practices (over treating the rich and under treating the poor):

Some examples of worldwide Public Health and environmental disasters promoted by mass transportation - with global shipping there will be reoccurrence of epidemics of the past, i.e. influenza, TB, measles, etc, but with new resistance genes combined with the coming of the Post-Antibiotic Age due to the improper overuse of antibiotics and "saving for future ailments" underuse amongst the poor. The proliferation of "antibiotic" products in the commercial sector such as triclosan to appeal to consumer healthcare trends based on scientific ignorance which accelerates the development of other resistance strains, etc.

The Creation of Life.

The question took me by surprise. I was sitting in a noisy Boston café with two biochemists who were having a straight-faced conversation about putting together a budget to create synthetic life-forms. Next to me was Jack Szostak of Harvard Medical School, and across the table was Steven Benner, who had flown up from the University of Florida to pay Szostak a visit. The conversation was thrumming along, touching on the efficiencies of chemical reactions and the like, when Benner abruptly turned to me and asked, "How much do you think it would cost to create a self-replicating organism capable of Darwinian evolution...

...Szostak hopes to transform chemicals into a single-celled organism that will grow, divide, and evolve – and soon...

... Our ultimate goal is to create life... [391]

Energy is life. Energy is vibration. Every element has a particular vibration, i.e. sound, color, harmonic "structure". Variations of matter come from different configurations of different patterns and their collective (sum) vibration. Created life can not create life--human scientists can only arrange "life" into different configurations.

Problems can arise when linear-oriented scientists desire to indulge in the science of "creating life" because of their linear thought processes are

---

391.   "What Came Before DNA." By Carl Zimmer. Discover.June 2004 pp.34-37

ignorant to the continuous nature of energy. To them there is a beginning and an end, therefore Progress and a scientific learning curve arises from more and more invasive scientific mistakes in experimentation. These "creators", being ignorant of 'vibrational science'[392] in their rush to become 'gods' may arrange assemblages of matter that have sum vibrations that can be extremely adverse to Other life. In particular the "new" sciences genetic engineering and nanotechnology operate mostly in perspective of separation from the vibrational reality of the Universe that they exist in. Scientists believe that they can "create" events--particles, organisms outside of the realm of consequences. This "separate" approach is dangerous enough, but combined with ability to "create" new assemblages of matter, to operate without consideration of potential consequences is quite careless.

Another degree of ignorance that these scientists operate under is ignorance of the Law of Vibrational Attraction[393]. 'Like sum vibrations' attract 'like sum vibrations'. 'Sum vibrations' also include the sum vibrations of people, communities, nation-states, and the world-as-a-whole. Periods in human life attract sum vibrations of that period of time. A good example of this is the fascism that arose in the first half of 20th century Europe that took European tribal wars and made them into world conflicts. The barbarism inflicted onto the world by these same nation-states (and/or their precursors) during their period of exploration, conquest, and colonization created a sum vibration of these actions and children were "born" of these time; and because they lived in a time and place in which these behaviors and thought processes were sanctioned and encouraged (even if the intent was to only use these traits on "Others") they were able to reach their full destructive potential as representations of these societies' sum vibrations.

I make this point, because in this age of genetic manipulation; if organisms, molecular assemblage, plant, animal, or humanoid are "created" with a particular sum vibrational configuration that matches the particular sum vibratory patterns in this time period, especially if Your efforts lead the proliferation of a Global Consciousness of Individualistic Materialism and predatory external-based life philosophies, these can be very horrific outcomes in these scientific attempts at "creating life".

Remember, the Universe is a balanced equation. It is perpetual; there is no end to "life". "Life" balances its own equation. "Life" gives birth to similar "life", but this is in the (ordered) quest towards "0" (zero): stability. No-

---

392.   Notice the dichotomy in contemporary physics between adherents of particle theory-based physics and wave theory-based physics.
393.   I coined the term "Law of Vibrational Attraction" for this narrative.

thingness is the goal – unlimited potential energy that arises from total submission to the Source. All life desires to be "0" unconsciously; i.e. radioactive decay, the actualization of personal potential – full surrender to the innate purpose. This desire (knowledge of purpose) arises even if its conscious and subconscious minds desire individuality, hence all of humanity[394] (even those more acclimated towards a solely physical plane temporal consciousness) desires submission, i.e. harmonious living: meaning that those who deny their "true" desire to be "at harmony with" to unconsciously desire to "destroy" themselves in order to return to "0".

The Proliferation of Livestock Antibiotics and the Spread of Antibiotic-Resistant Strains of Human Pathogens.

By the mid 1990s antibiotic production and use in the United States, and globally, was largely about livestock management: human medicinal and public health use of the "magic bullets" accounted for just 0.01 to 10 percent of some antibiotic uses…

Barely were new drugs on the market when their counterparts went into use in livestock. Soon resistant microbes emerged in the animals and spread to people…

The fundamental problem: whether the drug was called an antibiotic or a growth promoter: it was a member of a finite group of some 250 antibacterial agents that attacked their targets in just six different ways. If a bacterium developed resistance to one particular agent, it was actually insensitive to all of the antibiotics that relied on the same attack mechanism. Worse yet, the ability to resist one or more of those six (and only six) ways that antibiotics targeted bacteria could be carried from one microbe to another aboard genetic rings, called transposons. These pieces of genetic information were apart of a vast DNA and RNA lending library from which microbes readily borrowed and shared information as they swam through their soupy environs. An animal microbe that was harmless to humans could acquire resistance as a result of growth promoter use in, say, chickens, and then share its resistance transposons with human pathogens it encountered in the gut of a person dining on undercooked chicken or runny eggs.[395]

This is an illustration of the reality of the coming of a Post-Antibiotic Age, due to the cumulative global misuse of antibiotics. Do not allow the focus of the aforementioned quote to cause You to miss the point that I am making. Because of the logistical "connectedness" of the planet now due to rapid modes of transportation, weaknesses in the 'antibiotic shield', wherever they may occur in the world, have the potential to affect the whole of humanity. If through Your influence, effective, traditional, non-industrially synthesized

---

394.   In the case of a non-protein based "life" form such as an inorganic configuration of atoms, it may be manipulated by external forces, but there is an ingrained "consciousness of purpose": desiring to be used to its full potential and in line with the goal of "stability".

395.   Garrett, p.468

antibiotic therapies have been disqualified as valid by sweeping generalizations about alternative medicine by Your science; combined with the spread of pathogens to nation-states that have never been exposed to them, therefore lacking the traditional means of combating them; combined with an individualized healthcare ethic that essentially says that medical care should only go to those with the means to pay for it; combined with the spread of a wide array of pathogens due to rapid global transportation and shipping; combined with the migrations of economic and political refugees displaced and adversely effected by the effects of Your influence or their nation-state's governments seeking peace, success, piece-of-mind in Your own nation-state, and in the nation-states of other Princes; combined by the increase of 'unnatural disasters' and destructiveness of 'natural disasters' due to excessive logging, forest clearing, and wetlands abatement contributing to landslides and flooding which make effective waterbourne disease vectors; combined with the intrusion into wilderness areas that have never experienced human contact, containing a plethora of "unknown" plant and animal pathogens; combined with the expansion of xenotransplantation technologies by scientists with linear thought processes; combined with the expansion of genetic engineering and cloning technologies by scientists with linear thought processes; combined with the development of genetic modification technologies for agribusiness to make "better plants", "better livestock", and "organic pharmaceutical production" by scientists with linear thought processes; combined with the injection of antibiotics, growth hormones, gene therapy agents into animals raised for human consumption, as well as well as the use of animal that made from genetically-modified crops and that made from animals of the same species in feeding livestock and seafood that is produced for human consumption; combined with the collective weakening of communities' immune system due to the inhalation, consumption, and absorption of thousands of industrial chemicals and their increasing 'chemical combinations' in the environment.

With all of these 'combinations', possibly the coming of the Post-Antibiotic Age might possibly be the lesser of Your worries, if You have successfully indoctrinated Your subject nation-state into adopting public health and environmental policies that are crafted to only benefit those of quantitative worth. Regardless of how people are quantified, humanity is interconnected.

"Typhoid Mary" did not impact only the poor and disenfranchised, nor did the 1918 Influenza epidemic, nor does HIV, nor will the offspring of these 'combinations' limit their spread to those not of 'means'.

Linear-Thinking and the Development of Biotechnology.

In the quest for greater gains in biotechnology, either for greater profit potential, the key of the "fountain of youth" and eternal physical life; or even to improve the quality of life of human beings in general, more attention must be paid to potential catastrophic dangers in experimentation and application of these technologies. To the linear-minded scientist, no consequence is too great for the "advancement of science," for they believe that "only through mistakes is Progress made". For scientists enamored with their own self-image of being omniscient and infallible, fears concerning their lack of concern for the consequences of their scientific endeavors fall on deaf ears. But in today's extremely invasive world of scientific experimentation especially in the fields on biotechnology, nanotechnology, and even artificial intelligence, the domino effect of major mistakes or even small miscalculations, or even data overlooked, because it was not a known variable at the time of the initiation of the experimentation, can be disastrous on a global level.

I will give an example through the words of a group concerned with the potentialities of xenotransplantation:

The alleged chronic shortage of human organs has led some researchers and federal health officials in the US and elsewhere to consider using organs from animals such as pigs and nonhuman primates. Xenotransplatation, attempted since 1905, is marred by a history of failures and intense human and animal suffering. But the prospect of commercializing the technology has created huger financial incentives for biotechnology and pharmaceutical companies who have invested hundreds of millions of dollars into xenotransplantation...

...many animals viruses have the ability to jump species barriers and kill humans. Viruses that are harmless to their animal hosts can be deadly when transmitted to humans. For example, Macaque herpes is harmless to Macaque monkeys, but lethal to humans...

...Pigs, genetically altered to carry human genes, are being considered as the source animals of choice for xenotransplants, despite the existence of over 25 diseases in pigs that can infect humans. The influenza virus of 1918, which resembled a common swine flu, killed more people in modern history than any other epidemic including AIDS and the Black Plague. New mutations of swine influenza are being seen around the globe, and novel pig viruses keep surfacing. In October 1997, medical journals reported that Porcine Endogenous Retroviruses (PERVs), present throughout the pig genome, infected human cells in test tubes. That same year, the Australian "paramyxovirus"[396] infected piggery

---

396.   Paramyxoviruses make up a large family of viruses that cause human diseases such as mumps, measles, parainfluenza, and childhood croup. They also cause a number of diseases in animals such as pigs, horses, lions, bats, and seals. Paramyxoviruses are rapidly growing group of "newly discovered" viruses; the latest "discovery" being the Nepa/Nipah virus. These "new" viruses can find their way into becoming "new" human pathogens by meeting (both animal and human viruses) inside of a shared host such as a pig, infecting the pig at the same time. In Chinese history, there are records of epidemics, in which what would be termed now as an "offending virus", started an epidemic, spreading first in the bird population, and then continuing on to areas where duck and pig farmers were in close quarters.

workers with flu-like symptoms. And, most recently, the "Nipah" virus, killing 100+ and leading to the mass slaughter of some one million pigs, as well as several dogs and horses...

...There is no way to screen for viruses that are not yet known. Proceeding with xenotransplantation could expose patients and nonpatients to a host of new animal viruses which could remain dormant for months or years before being detected...

...In all areas of human activity, particularly when money is involved, the potential for fraud, error, and negligence exists. In the past, such behavior has placed human health at considerable risk. Witness the HIV-contaminated blood scandals in France, China, Japan and the US, for example, in which employees and/or medical authorities knowingly allowed HIV-contaminated blood to be used for hemophiliacs...

...Biotechnology companies are breeding pigs with human genes in the hopes of fooling the human immune system into accepting a foreign organ from another species. This disturbing genetic reconstruction of life (the creation of animals that are, in essence, part animal and part human) is advancing on a commercial scale with almost no informed public discussion or effective oversight...[397]

In 2002, 103 people died in an outbreak of Nepa virus. Nearly 300 people in Singapore and Malaysia were infected. All lived around pigs. In Australia, a virus in horses killed two trainers who worked with them. Today, at least 10 people are dead and 350 others infected with a virus world health workers are calling Severe Acute Respiratory Syndrome. Researchers think they may have a handle on the culprit behind SARS. It appears to be of the same family that killed seals and lions, and moved from pigs and horses to humans: the paramyxoviruses.

These stories of paramyxovirus epidemics are frightening. But perhaps more disquieting is this: These are close relations of our childhood companions – chickenpox, measles, and mumps...

... This flexibility stems, in a large part, from the nature of viruses. Viruses are little genetic instruction sets waiting to be carried out. What is critical here is that paramyxoviruses, such as influenza viruses, are poor copiers. There is no spellchecking and no repair. Their offspring are often full of errors, say Dr. David Mindell, a professor of ecology and evolutionary biology at the University of Michigan...

... What contributes to the mutability of paramyxoviruses and influenza may be the hosts in which they land. In influenza, the pattern is well known. The virus lives in waterfowl without causing disease. But when waterfowl mix with domestic animals, the virus can jump species. In China, where poultry, pigs, and people live in close proximity, its an easy set up steps. Pigs make ideal cauldrons for virus brewing. The animal's cells carry receptors for both bird and human viruses. Which viruses from both species meet inside a pig cell, they may swap genes. The result is a new viral form fit for humans.

Such species mixing may have played a role in the SARS virus...

... "The more worldwide movement of people you have, the more population density you have, the easier it is for the disease to move" say Dr. Susan McLellan, a tropical disease specialist at Tulane University in New Orleans.[398]

---

397.   "What's Wrong With Xenotransplantation?" Campaign for Responsible Transplantation, http://www.crt-online.org/wrong.html

An additional danger to think about is that those either under Your hire, the hire of Other Princes, or under the hire of those that may oppose You can utilize these cross-species disease transference pathways and exploit their potential for spreading pathogens as a means of biological warfare. This topic of xenotransplantation and discussion of cross-species spreading of disease is a serious one. With a percentage of the factors in play that You have initiated, You need to be prepared for many combinations of consequences or responses to these. Putting direct effort into scientific work that is in the realm of the cross-species transference of organisms and/or genetic material is not something to be taken lightly. Because it is an unknown area of scientific knowledge and because we have already witnessed (experienced) a very, very small "taste" of the negative potentialities of experimentation gone awry simply through the deaths that have occurred through closer human contact with animals as a result of migration of rural populations to cities and the over-encroachment of land traditionally occupied by wildlife as a response to development, logging, grazing, etc...; be prepared for the possibility of unimaginable disease spread scenarios due to the disturbance of the natural balance that prevents the excessive sharing of diseases between different species in nature.

Global Public Health Breakdown.

Concentrating national health budgets on clinical medicine and hospital 'cures' rather than on prevention will produce a similar effect. Most Third World governments need little urging in this direction and have for years targeted health spending to the more prosperous classes of their own societies. The rich have access to modern hospital facilities while elsewhere in rundown rural and neighborhood clinics, hypodermic needles are reused and simple lab tests cannot be run. Public hospitals may themselves be the most efficient disease vectors one could imagine.[399]

The lack of adequate Public Health infrastructure allows for the rapid silent transmission of epidemics and exposure to chemical, biological, and nuclear agents.

---

398.   "Animal to Human Mutation of Virus Often a Simple Step" by Jenni Laidman, Blade Science Writer. Sunday, March 23, 2003. Toledo Blade.
399.   George, Susan (1999) *Lugano Report: On Preserving Capitalism in the Twenty-first Century.* London: Pluto Press. p.130

Free Trade, Urbanization, and the Spread of Disease[400].

New exotic and cross-species diseases can make an easy entry into Your nation-state because of the global economic 'race to the bottom' that forces those in low-cost locales to quickly urbanize leading to three major Public Health stressors. Due to Your nation-state's participation in this 'Free Trade' with the present-day rapid modes of transportation and enormous volume of shipping, it will be susceptible to whatever public health dangers that brew in the locales from which You and Your nation-state's businesses extract resources, products, and services from. These stressors are:

1. High population density in small cramped unsanitary urban spaces - spread of communicable diseases, and if antibiotics are being misused also as a breading ground from resistant strains;

2. High population density in areas susceptible to disasters[401] such as flooding, mudslides, etc. a breeding ground for water-bourne human diseases.

3. The aforementioned (Number 2) is likely to occur more and more because of the need to acquire land to build new urban dwellings; i.e. clearing land, hills, forests make very unstable environmental and ecological systems that will still have to contend with the normal cycle of natural disasters are possibly a lot more, because of an increase in erratic weather that stems from natural and human-induced climate change;

4. The close dwellings of rural people in urban settings allows for the spread of disease that would not normally (or at least frequently) occur in rural environments, i.e. the raising of many species of animals in close quarters and in contact with each other leading to cross-species disease outbreaks due to natural vectors such as pigs that can host both, for example, avian and human disease and the contact of such disease within this host vector can lead to genetic exchanges with disastrous outcomes for human and animal populations;

---

400.   This is a portion of a narrative from Chapter 40, Your Own Nation-States' Social Sphere.
401.   I did not use the term 'natural disasters' because a number of contemporary 'natural disasters' as the direct result of past environmentally-invasive actions such as excessive cutting and clearing of wetlands followed by the settlement of adjacent hillsides. The resulting mudslides and flooding are not 'natural disasters'.

Health and the Urban Poor.

The re-emergence of epidemics of communicable disease among urban poor who embrace a 'separationist' value system, i.e. become 'alone' in a predatory consumerist social environment, whereas, as communal rural people, they were never 'alone'. Physical poverty (lack of basic needs such a proper nutrition and healthcare) in a urban environment, combined with the social 'isolation' that comes with an Individualistic Materialistic value system can lead to the psychosomatic exacerbation of many health ailments. The following is an illustration of this possibility:

"One particular health problem, tuberculosis, deserves special mention. It is suspected to be a major cause of death among the Batak. Many may probably believe that tuberculosis is a straightforward infectious disease, with the appropriate medicine and professional supervision being the keys to cure. But both contraction and recovery from the disease are known to be powerfully influenced by factors in one's social environment. Jackson (1954), for example, showed that alcoholics who tried to stop drinking on their own were many times more likely to develop tuberculosis symptoms than those alcoholics who attempted to stop drinking with the support of an organized program, such as Alcoholics Anonymous. Holmes (1956) showed that the incidence of tuberculosis in Seattle was highest among people who were "socially marginal"; those living alone in one room those single or divorced; those of minority status in their neighborhoods; and those who experienced the death of a parent, or divorce of their parents, before age 18. Reviewing a variety of such studies, Chen and Cobb (1960) conclude that tuberculosis is a disease of social isolation, that is, a disease of the failure of social support systems. This circumstance helps to explain, for example, why Bantu working in South African cities suffer one of the highest tuberculosis rates in the world, while Bantu who remain behind in their native villages are largely resistant to infection, despite exposure to their severely ill, city-working kin, many of whom return to their kraals to die (Dubos and Dubos 1952: 194). Thus, more than changes in diet, working conditions, or exposure to the bacilli explain outbreaks of tuberculosis in a society, for such outbreaks reflect as well "the complex of disturbances brought about in the community as a whole by most forms of social upheavals, be they abrupt changes in ancestral habits, rapid industrialization, or wars"(ibid.:195-196).[402]

Population.

In nation-states where the arable land-people ratio is truly strained and food pressures are not actually from the disproportionate or misallocation of land, the affected governments may not heed Your advice or the advice of Other Princes and Your NGOs in regard to working to decrease the population because of their realization that the 'population problem' is not merely a question of number, but also a problem of consumption.

---

402.   Eder, James F. (1993) *On the Road to Tribal Extinction: Depopulation, Deculturation, and Adaptive Well-Being Among the Batak of the Philippines.* Quezon City (MM); New Day Publishers. p.204

"... the problem isn't just gross numbers, it's consumption too: a newborn in the U.S. or Europe will put greater pressure on the Earth's carrying capacity than a whole family of newborns in India."[403]

These calls for "family planning" for the greater good and sustainability of humanity will be laughed off in the same manner as conservation initiatives for raw materials and animals that were overconsumed for the use of Your nation-state and the nation-state's of Other Princes. It will be seen as a continued trend of hypocrisy in which the burden of moderated consumption and sustainable practices has to be borne by the subject nation-states while the Princes are allowed to consume at the same rates. And any wholesale prohibitions are viewed as only coming about when the consumer desire or profitability of these commodities wanes in the Prince's nation-states. I do not mean to go into a tangent within the environmental realm, but of course society, environment, and economy are interconnected. If the subject nation-states come to the realization that Your calls for Global Population Control are only a means of decreasing pressure on the finite resources of the Earth so that You and Your counterparts can continue to live at the same levels of consumption, the result will not be good. The likelihood is that the impetus for national 'Development' in subject nation-state's will become even more reactionary – desirous of the consumption rates and standard of living that You have, they will proceed with the same tunnel-vision growth policies that You used that leave environmental management as a concern for the distant future. And in regard to population control, if they do try to mirror You/Your nation-state in the quest to consume like You, they will see that it is because of Your large population that production on a massive scale was possible.

Once this reactionary 'Growth' policy becomes a part of a nation-state collective psyche, the value system of Individualistic Materialism/ Consumerism that You have projected onto it will be fully "charged". In this 'reactionary state', a subject nation-state will not see the wisdom in any calls for moderated consumption and the implementation of sustainable policies, because it will be seen as only 'another attempt' to keep them 'underdeveloped' for the purposes of exploitation and to deny them the opportunity to enjoy the standard of living that You and Other Princes enjoy.

Remember that while all of these discussions of national 'Growth' policies, etc. are going on in the government circles, the populations of these subject nation-states are being inundated by the consumerist messages that You are projecting on them in the global and local mass media. At the very

---

403.   Ibid, "Population and Its Discontents", p.13

time of these discussions amongst the people of these nation-states, a reactionary attitude towards 'Development' and 'Growth' will already be growing because they are experiencing the re-invention of their society, economy, and environment due to the internalization of this consumerist value system.

Remember unless a government's mandate is that of only 'maintaining physical security/'law and order', a government's mandate is to support and maintain the cultural viability and human security needs of the population, and therefore will have to, at least on some level, reflect the common consensus of the people. In the case of a people turned into reactionaries by the quantitative re-valuing of their society, economy, and environment by You; their government will also reflect this attitude, and will work to 'sustain' this new consumerist re-ordering of its nation-state.

The Danger of Population Growth
Rapid population growth due to people's reactions to lack of resources and the new re-definition of "poverty", coupled with the loss of indigenous methods of contraception due to 'Modern' acculturation in 'developing' nation-states and widespread public health initiatives in 'developed' nation-states has led to massive worldwide population-growth. This trend is slowing in the 'Developed' nation-states due to changing social attitudes that come about because of economic prosperity and the quantitative revaluing of the society; but the 'developing' world population growth is increasing because of the greater and greater anxiety of meeting basic needs and the hope that some offspring will be 'saviors' who bring their families wealth in the new ('Modern') paradigm of 'Poverty'.

In these 'developing' nation-states disparities in wealth promote having large families as a means of coping with economic uncertainty and a more material-based existence. Remember, before this recent trend of urbanization, most of the world's population were rural people. Before, enough children were needed to continue the family name, help out economically, and take care of elders in old age; now more children are needed, almost on a 'lottery' sense in hoping that one child will hopefully "do well" and bring the family out of poverty and into the ranks of "consumers".

Estimates of future numbers are based on the latest United Nations population projections, using their medium-level figures. Under this scenario, world population will grow from 6.1 billion in 2000 to 9.4 billion in 2050 – a gain of 3.3 billion. The other two U.N. projections put global population in 2050 as high as 11.2 billion or as low as 7.7 billion.[404]

There are 16 areas that, if this trend of massive growth continues, will be seriously negatively affected by this: "grain production, fresh water, biodiversity, climate change, oceanic fish catch, jobs, cropland, forests, housing, energy, urbanization, natural recreation areas, education, waste, meat production, and income"[405].

Conclusion - Social Collapse

Again, if You insist on using linear-thinking to govern, with its inability to contemplate multiple, concurrent, and resulting variables and causalities, You should like I mentioned before in terms of being a conqueror, be deliberate. Do not get Your objectives confused - Your objective is Sustainable Exploitation not a co-dependent emotional relationship with Your nation-state and its inevitable failure as a 'state'. In the way of thinking You should go 'full throttle' in Your linear thinking. The results will still be an inevitable human catastrophe because 'Scientific Progress' will supercede any reasonable and obviously apparent observations concerning the breakdown of societies, economies, and the environment; but at least you can feel that You have put Your best effort forward. With 'Scientific Progress' You may even get to a point in which You feel that You are omnipotent; but remember omnipotence without omniscience is nothing more than arrogant ignorance.

I will conclude this section with a discussion of what You will have created if You have followed my advise in using the methodology of Cultural Warfare. You will have promoted, essentially, an Ideology of Externalization - external consumption, external fulfilment, external control as a means of temporarily placating the internal need for actualization and stability. Through maintaining an external environment of fear and anxiety, You will have been able to perpetuate a climate of reactionary decisions and the submission of identity and fulfilment to Others. Hopefully You have done this with some degree of non-linear contemplation. Within the realm of technology--which humanity is exporting its decisions and sense of "Progress" to--there are two roads: the more likely sustainable and the certainly unsustainable. I will term this dichotomy as Robotics vs. Artificial Intelligence.

Without omniscience, one, regardless of intent, runs the risk when using too invasive a technology, of doing more harm that one could have ever imagined. This is because the consequences of such transgressions can not

---

404.   "Beyond Malthus: Sixteen Dimensions of the Population Problem". Lester R. Brown, Gary Gardner, and Brian Halwell. Worldwatch Paper 143. September 1998. p.7
405.   Ibid.

be contemplated until the "unthinkable" occurs. This is why science should embark down roads in which humanity can most likely survive the worst case scenario. Nanotechnology, genetic engineering, and artificial intelligence (I will group these three all under the topic, Artificial Intelligence (AI), because of the high degree of positive assumptions that must be made to contemplate possible variable outcomes of too invasive a development or "discovery" within each discipline) are roads that You truly know nothing about You and should tread very carefully and intuitively down, and in many cases, if at all.

Though it may be cumbersome and require a great deal of rethinking what You think You know of science, it might be advisable to give some degree of attention to wave-based physics instead of basing everything that You know on particle physics. Particle physics is far simpler to understand and You can continue Your science at the rapid rate at which You are now, but because You do not acknowledge the multitudes of variables that multidimensional quantum physics brings into question, it does not mean that these variables and interrelationships are not there. Just because You live in the mountains and cannot see the ocean; it does not mean that the ocean does not exist (and does not have some impact on Your life, in some way or another, i.e. the hydrological cycle). A side-effect of internalized Platonic thinking is that the user assumes that they know much more than they actually do; while wise and "intelligent" thinkers, through learning and experience, realize how little they do know more and more everyday. I am telling You to look a bit more at this type of physics as a base of Your scientific thinking more closely, because it is less invasive, and with some understanding of how interrelated all things are, You can make better decisions as to how to continue Your development of technology to support Your goal of Sustainable Exploitation.

True scientific advances come with the development of the full human potential and building upon this human potential as well as utilizing nature's systems and structures as models to build upon. The blueprint already exists. There is no need to play some mental game in which You believe You are "creating" something new. All that You can do is assemble and disassemble what already exists. It is better to maximize the potential of systems that already work. One thing to remember is that human beings are at the center of human technology. You cannot export the responsibility of maintaining balance upon an external construction. There is no man vs. machine dichotomy. Believing that machines can replace human beings is lunacy; this is the same projection of universality that You are to put onto Your subjects. Any machine that exists is at its essence, its "creator". The dreams and the personality of the "creator" are embedded in the assemblage of materials that they call their "creation". On this same note, "Artificial Intelligence" is not an "independent" intelligent machine, it is the dream of its "creator" actualized. It embodies the "creator's" desire to be God and to have "created life". But within this "artificial intelligence" lies the flawed linear thinking of its master. It can only learn from whatever cognitions it is given or has access to and interprets them from the perspective and value system of its "creator"; therefore it is not omniscient, consequently unable to contemplate every variable, and is disconnected from its "creator's" intuition or sense of interconnection and humanity. It can carry out its "creator's" linear-oriented dream of "creating a perfect world" in the image of its master. There is no objectivity, this is why all must be responsible to themselves and in balance with those around them. These human 'gods' can presuppose all knowledge, and then neglect responsibility for their actions, after which justifying their actions as doing "what they thought was best for Humanity".

A lot of what is called "technology" is actually nothing more than a lazy escape from having to develop one's self and/or is an embodiment of the Platonic antagonism towards Nature by "creating" externally as a means of avoiding looking inward and possibly having to submit to a Natural Law or predestined purpose (i.e. being given certain gifts and talents to actualize), or being influenced by feelings. Human beings on average only use 5% of their brain capacity. The other 95% is neglected in external attempts at manipulating Nature instead of developing one's full created potential. Essentially, a lot of "Modern" technology is like taking LSD instead of working to have an actual transcendental spiritual experience. This "experience" can be bought and "consumed" without having to put effort into "creating" from one's own ability. Modern telecommunications, instead of building on expanding and intensifying human beings' natural intuitive and telepathic abilities, instead totally disembodies this experience and at this time is actually leading to a serious decline in actual human social relationships and personal communications.

When people buy into the superiority of the "illusion" of the externalized world over the reality of the limitlessness of human potential, they essentially turn the world into an idol. All of their personal power is exported to this "illusion" that is supposed to give them an identity and take responsibility for all of their actions. At this point, they give away their personal power for the satisfaction of their egos. This externalization of personal power is what You want to achieve with Your projections, but again You must remember that You are not to be subject to Your own projections and that You must manage this new world of perpetual children that You are creating, otherwise it will all fall apart, threatening the existence and solvency of Your subject nation-state(s),

Your own nation-state, the world-at-large; and most of all--Your goal of Sustainable Exploitation.

For example, You want Your subjects to submit themselves to You so that You can perpetually exploit them. They submit themselves to You because You give them an identify and sense of hope amidst a world of fear, anxiety, and instability. Whatever You "create" they will embrace and consume because it is of You, and through consuming it they can feel as if they are progressing towards the 'Modernity' and 'Civility' that You embody. Therefore, You should create technologies that will not threaten the survivability of humanity.

Machines (technology) are to be used to supplement human abilities in those lacking a particular competency within their own body. I say this in support with my statement at the beginning of this narrative on robotics vs. artificial intelligence. In terms of technology development, I would support the development of robotics and discourage the development of artificial intelligence, because the former is designed based on efficient physiological designs from Nature (or in cybernetics, directly connected to a life form that directs its activities) and acknowledges that it (the robot) plays a supplemental role in life. The latter is based on the supposition that man can "create life" and that he has the "intelligence" to design a life free of unknown variables. The former has a "future", while the latter is highly likely to be the next installment in a continuing history of good-intentioned scientific failures by the next generation of Dr. Frankenstein. But this time, it is not a small rural town that is threatened by his creation, but the entire of humanity. Your scientists must have some sense of interconnectedness of life and an understanding that actions have consequences, unlike the Rationalist "Mad Scientist" whose egotistical desire to "create a Perfect World" threatens the existence of all on the planet, despite the "Rational" criticism that he receives from those around him who know that by the very nature of him being a 'Rational' scientist that views himself immune from the limitations of being a "minuscule part of an enormous singularity". He is a grain of sand who believes that he can name, define, and control the entire beach.

Do not worry - do not be afraid to use less invasive technologies. You want to be around to enjoy Your conquest; You do not want to bring an early demise upon Yourself because You let a group of delusional, narcissistic megalomaniacs have too much influence on Your world. Even if Your subjects were to try to use these technologies to gain independence from You, it will be to no avail. Technological solutions to problems of value systems are nothing but band-aid "solutions" for symptoms of the problems, and will only further delay and intensify the pain of trying to achieve balance, because the root problem is not being addressed. They can only be free of You if they rid themselves of the predatory value system that You are placing upon them. This value system is turning them from a creative force into a Virus.

But for You to note as well--if You have not managed Your level of exploitation and consumption at a sustainable level--trying to maintain the same levels of consumption through "new and innovative technologies" is the same as a full-on embrace of the Viral Culture. If they do not realize that if they take, they must give. And if they do not give (create) at the same ratio as they take, it will be taken back from them involuntarily. Though the Viral Culture does not recognize or is not cognizant of the interconnectedness of all things, Nature does. It will collaborate on all levels to destroy what is destroying it and to take back what is necessary to continue the operation of a balanced system.

If You have brought humanity to the brink of destruction through Your mismanaged conquest, You cannot continue to play band-aid games with the survival of the species. You have to truly introspect and realize what it is that has brought humanity to the brink - Your influence, Your value system, and Your invasive disregard for the natural environment.

What will You do if You if You have brought humanity to this point and wish to survive?

What will Your subjects' do if they wish to survive?

IV. The Three Roads

Chapter 45:
The Three Roads That
Today's Interdependent World
Can Take

Modern civilization, then, will reach its higher stage of development only if and when it perceives the full impact of its relations with the global environment. The "culture of environment" needs to be developed as the quintessence of our civilization and has to enter deeply into our consciousness.

The culture of the environment will in the course of time dislodge the debased conceptions of the environment that have hitherto satisfied the urban ego. The vulgar, unbridled activities of the men obsessed with the cult of raping nature, who stop at nothing for quick and more and more money, will be restraining and more in the direction of cooperating with nature.

The culture of environment requires decision-makers to accord respect to nature and to adapt an attitude of prudence. To decide on an action, they should exercise caution regarding all of its possible environmental ramifications, and must be prepared to give nature the benefit of the doubt. We should all err on the side of protecting our environment.

Unless modes in civilization, which is now universal, is integrated with the inchoate culture of environment, ultimately the world's civilization is likely to perish, and together with it man himself.

Professor Adul Wichiencharoen
Member, The National Environmental Board,
Thailand

Three Choices.

I say, therefore that all these kinds of government are harmful in consequences of the short life of three good ones and the viciousness of three bad ones. Having noted these failings, prudent lawgivers rejected each of these forms individually and chose instead to combine, them into one that would be firmer and more stable than any, since each form would serve as a check upon the others in a state having monarchy, aristocracy, and democracy at one and the same time.

The Prince

Advice to a Wise Prince.

This is Rational thinking with an element of social responsibility added - not just taking the money and resources (an allusion to Platonic forms of government all based different monetary needs expected for the aristocracy of philosopher Machiavelli: Monarchy, Tyranny, Aristocracy, Oligarchy, Democracy, Anarchy) But realize the resources must be shared at least to some extent. Not everyone needs to be materially rich, but everyone must have their basic security, psychological, and cultural needs met.

The "new" civilization cannot be ruled under the 'Rule of Law' if it is to be successful – it must be based on mutual respect, harmony, and shared responsibility. Otherwise the Rule of Law will have to take care of the world. How will resources be allocated without conflict? Equally or unequally? Even if one area lacks in resources, it may have a far greater level of consumption that than a place of "actual wealth". How will this be reconciled?[406] [407] [408]

---

406.   Like I mentioned before, earlier in this discourse, according to William Rees, Professor and Community Planning at the University of British Columbia defines 'ecological footprint' as the "corresponding area of productive land and aquatic ecosystems required to produce the resources used, and to assimilate the wastes produced, by a defined population at a specified material standard of living, wherever on Earth that land may be located." He estimates that the footprint of the Netherlands - for food production alone - appropriates between 100,000 and 140,000 square kilometers of agricultural land, mostly in the 'developing' world. He says further: "This 'imported land' is five to seven times larger than the area of Holland's domestic arable land... It is worth remembering that Holland, like Japan, is often held up as an economic success story and an example for the developing world to follow. Despite small size, few natural resources, and a relatively high population... Holland... enjoy(s) high material standards and positive current accounts and trade balances as measured in monetary terms. However, our analysis of physical flows shows that these and most other so-called 'advanced' economies are running massive, unaccounted for ecological deficits with the rest of the planet... Even if their land area were twice as productive as world averages, many European countries would still run a deficit more than three times larger than domestic natural income. These data emphasize that (most developed countries) are over-populated in ecological terms - they could not maintain themselves at current material standards if forced by changing circumstances to live on their remaining endowments of domestic natural capital...
          ...Ecological deficits are a measure of the entropic load and resultant 'disordering' being imposed on the ecosphere by so-called advanced countries as the unaccounted cost of maintaining and further expanding their wealthy consumer economies. This massive entropic imbalance invokes what might be called the axiom of ecological footprint analysis: On a finite planet, not all countries or regions can be net importers of carrying capacity. This, in turn, has serious implications for global development trends. --- Continued on next footnote.

"Civilization" and War.

"We live in what is the most violent time in human history: the twentieth century accounts for 75 percent of all war deaths inflicted since the rise of the Roman Empire."[409]

3 Roads.

1. *Exploitative World Government*: i.e. its creators create a worldwide financial collapse leaving "money" as worthless. A worldwide underclass is immediately created, with only those who physically own and control the modes and production and raw resources and have cooperative relationships with each other with "power". They can create a world hierarchy to their liking because they control the food supply, the water supply, the energy supply, industrial capability, the pharmaceutical supply, and the raw materials it needs to produce. The privatization of public goods (utilities), Free Markets (unimpeded Foreign Direct Investment) to possess lands containing raw materials, i.e. oil, uranium, metal ores, etc.; the possession of the world's germ culture, the advent of genetically modified foods, and chemical

---

407.   Last footnote continued --- The current objective of international development is to raise the developing world to present first world material standard. To achieve this objective, the Brundtland Commission argued for more rapid economic growth in both industrial and developing countries and suggested that 'a five to ten-fold increase in world industrial output can be anticipated by the time world population stabilizes some time in the next century.'(WCED, 1987).

Let us examine this prospect using ecological footprint analysis. If just the present [January 1996] world population of 5.8 billion people were to live at current North American ecological standards (say 4.5 ha/person), a reasonable first approximation of the total productive land requirement would be 26 billion hectares (assuming present technologies). However, there are only just over 13 billion hectares of land on Earth, of which only 8.8 billion are ecologically productive cropland, pasture, or forest (1.5ha/person). In short, we would need an additional two planet Earths to accommodate the increased ecological load of people alive today. If the population were to stabilize at between 10 and 11 billion sometime in the next century [the 21st century], five additional Earths would be needed, all else being equal - and this just to maintain the present rate of ecological decline (Rees and Weinburger, 1994).

While this may seem to be an astonishing result, empirical evidence suggests that five phantom planets is, in fact, a considerable underestimate... Global and regional-scale ecological change in the form of atmospheric change, ozone depletion, deforestation, fisheries collapse, loss of biodiversity, etc., is accelerating. This is direct evidence that aggregate consumption exceeds natural income in certain critical categories and that the carrying capacity of this one Earth is being steadily eroded. In short, the ecological footprint of the present world population/economy already exceeds the total productive land area (or ecological space) available on Earth.

This situation is, of course, largely attributable to consumption by that wealthy quarter of the world's population who use 75% of global resources. The WCED's five to ten-fold increase in industrial output' was deemed necessary to address this obvious inequity while accommodating a much larger population. However, since the world is already ecologically full, sustainable growth on this scale using present technology would require **five to ten additional planets**" --- From "Sustainability: Positioning the Concept As a Global Goal", Global Vision's NGO Position Paper for the International Conference on Environment and Society: Education and Public Awareness for Sustainability, Organised by UNESCO and the Government of Greece, Thessalonki, Greece, 8-12 December 1997. By Michael O'Callaghan. pp. 5-6. Re-published in "Sustainable Development: Education, The Force for Change", Transdisciplinary Project "Educating for a Sustainable Future", (EDP) UNESCO, 1999, Paris.

synthesis of natural biology, and the ownership of the human genome will grant this group the control over life and death on the planet.

Additionally nuclear-armed space-based launch platforms and "satellite-killer" anti-satellite ballistic systems can be used to expedite the transformation from "old world order" to "new world order".

2. *Seemingly Humanistic World Government*: this is also a linear culture-based configuration, i.e. Enlightenment Project. The "best" organization and distribution of lands and resources will be decided by a small number of people. This will eventually break down into region blocs due to issues of resource allocation, cultural preservation, and ecological responsibility. The "Tower of Babel": paved with good intentions and doomed to failure.

3. *Division of the world into tribes, regions, confederations with the possible re-assessing of boundaries back to more fluid boundaries that existed before the creation of abstracted modern nation-states*--states formed for the purpose of resource allocation ruled by an external colonial power. This would come about by a strong Non-Aligned Movement that originates from powerful subject nation-states that tire of their participation in a non-sustainable game that threatens their existence and the existence of the planet as a whole.

3 Roads - Regionalism.

Regionalism does not necessarily contradict the universalistic position of the United Nations. It may be considered, rather, as an attempt to "channel" globalization at an optimal policy level. Global governance structures may not operate so readily to reflect the interest of individual countries, while nation-level and UN-level (global) responses may be ineffective. But if the answer is regionalism, then a mechanism needs to be found that enables small countries – developing countries as well as "superpowers" – to exercise equal weight in decision-making processes. Belgian Prime Minister Verhofstadt recently formulated a proposal for such a mechanism: his idea is to convert the G8 into a "network of the big regional continental organizations." In that framework, Verhofstadt is thinking about a club of regional groupings. Such as the European Union, Mercosur, ASEAN, etc. in such a club, the African Union could have the same weight as, for example NAFTA. And each regional grouping should act as a forum to balance small and big countries' interests. As one can imagine, there are lots of critical and practical objections to such a proposal, such as: Who is going to stipulate who can become member of what club? Will the small countries within these groupings have enough say? Will any alliances be created that again contain the

---

408.   For example, in the future how will "Developed" countries reconcile the use of lands and resources of the "developing" countries that make-up their ecological footprint with increasing scarcity of resources due to increasing consumption and the continous rise of global population. (Conclusion to the two prior footnotes).
409.   Renner, p.30 from William Eckhardt, "War-Related Deaths Since 3000 B.C.," Bulletin of Peace Proposals, Vol. 22, No. 4, 1991.

classical North-South contradictions?[410]

This type of system still is more than likely controlled by major powers (Princes) unless these regional organizations passed legislation that favors local ownership and control over resources, i.e. high export tariffs for foreign-owned interests (extra-regional interests), a regional currency, barter-currency trading with other regions based on relative value of items to each party, etc. If this type of system is actually an attempt at Sustainable Exploitation and a continuation of the global hierarchy desired by the most powerful Princes, it will likely go through a very violent turnover, because this would be the failure of "hope" for a better future for the majority of the world[411], which would probably lead to internal strife and expressed tribalism and/or aggressive nationalization of resources within each region away from the Princes which could lead to military action by the Princes against the regions in order to "protect their interests".

3 Roads – Regionalism - One World
Regional Economic cooperation may arise in response to a universalizing "one-world" transnational governing apparatus.

3 Roads - Tribalism
(Reassess Governance Style - Tribalism)

> The social, economic, and environmental trends that are key to human security are increasingly being shaped not only by the fragmentation implied in the rise of "tribalism," but also by globalization. Trade, investment, travel, and communications tie countries and communities more closely together. Although the nation-state is far from being eclipsed, countries and national governments have less and less ability to shape their own destinies. The meaning of borders, community, and sovereignty is in flux, and that in turn makes national (as opposed to global) security a tenuous concept.[412]

> In the absence of strong rules and norms, globalization could turn into a free-for-all, an intensifying competition among communities worldwide over jobs, income, and economic well-being. By generating deep apprehension and feelings of insecurity, the very unevenness and uncertainty of the globalization process is in itself becoming a source of conflict.[413]

---

410.   "Regional Integration and Global Governance". UNUnexions. August 2003. p.4
411.   In Ch.15 in the section on "Reconciliation Committees" (p.235) I discussed the consequences of creating conditions in which hope disappears. The death of "Hope" can result in disastrous consequences at a nation-state level; this can result in internal strife or in the formation of grouping of like-minded nation-states that feel that they do not fare well in a statistically-ordered "Hopeless' hierarchical order.
412.   Renner, p.27
413.   Ibid, p.28

A society weakened by Market Forces and external influence over its system of governance will not last long if it promotes small government and the Free Market.

After suffering from the effects of Applied Rationalism, nation-states have to start from scratch--how to allocate resources, how to educate, how to govern, how to trade, etc.[414]

3 Roads - World Fascism

Fascism is the result of internal moral decay and addiction to the belief of superiority caused by amoral external methods of control to exploit the resources of the Other. If You are successful in Your quest - You will be the head of a new global order. You have to maneuver past all of the potential pitfalls and have, at least for the present, have created an environment resembling Sustainable Exploitation.

2 Roads.

One can discern two trajectories in current history: one aiming toward hegemony, acting rationally within a lunatic doctrinal framework as if it threatened survival; the other dedicated to the belief that "another world is possible," in the words that animate the World Social Forum, challenging the reigning ideological system and seeking to create constructive alternatives of thought, action, and institutions. Which trajectory will dominate, no one can foretell. The pattern is familiar throughout history; a crucial difference today is that the stakes are far higher.

Noam Chomsky[415]

---

414. For example, "criminal justice" in the Micronesian state of Chuuk, until the recent advent of incarceration, was primarily based on healing the community, not on punishing individuals. In the case of murder, forgiveness, not holding hate was viewed as in the interest of the community. If you took the life of another person, your family would have to give foodstuffs as a peace offering and lose you to the affected family as a replacement for the family member that you killed. Your family suffers from your actions, but because the debt was paid, hard feelings between families do not fester. And the affected family adopts you as a replacement for the son or daughter that you killed; and they accept you into the family to replace the lost loved one and to heal and forgive you by loving you as a member of their family.
415. Chomsky, p.236

3 Roads - Two Choices.

There are 2 actual Roads:

Both roads – 1. 'Interconnectedness and Harmony' and 2. 'Separation and Control' lead to the same place.

Progression of Time (Circle)

The Road of Interconnectedness and Harmony

Involuntary compliance to Nature

Voluntary compliance with Nature

The Road of Separation and Control

Involuntary compliance to Nature

Purposeful irresponsible non-compliance with Nature

Involuntary compliance with Nature

A Happy Ending.

This is a reassuring thought amidst all of this "impeding doom" talk - Regardless of what I have said in this section, You still have the "Rationalist Hope" – The successful overpowering and circumvention of Nature.

The Great Hope: The goal is to destroy enough and hopefully develop (and stay just ahead of the annihilation of the human race) through 'Progress' and make enough 'Progress' in space travel and atmospheric manipulation; doing this right before the earth throws humanity off of it, so that the eugenically correct group of Your choosing can travel to Mars to continue to progress again and at a much faster rate, upon its destruction, on to Europa, and on and on, and on as so is the Rational Hope: a galactic virus – inserting its genetic material into a planet's nucleus using its resources to replicate itself in order to consume enough to feel like its master then leave it destroyed but escaping in time to make it to the next host planet.

The key is making the planet believe that this "Viral" form of life is actually in its best interests, because through it may be painful, it too is part of the Universe and part of the cycle of life, only that is role in creation is to bring death and subsequent transformation and re-birth, rather than life. *It is the destroyer of worlds – that which brings involuntary compliance to a harmonious relationship with the Universe. It can be called the Prince of Peace… He who evokes life through the celebration of Death.*

Afterword:

I wrote this book with the assumption that all human actions emanate from two value systems and variations between the two: 1. one based on a realization of interconnectedness and a need to promote harmony through a healthy respect of diversity and the cultivation of individual potential (in order to fill the void that would be replaced by a need for continuous consumption as possession); and 2. exploitation based on a ideology of Separation and Control, utilizing the "freedom" of linear thought process to "Progress" without the burden of responsibility or consequences; replacing the "need" in the target to self-actualize with an addiction (the vice) to Conspicuous Consumption as a means of amassing power, control, and comparative recognition in an oppositional relationship with Nature and all Others. I analyzed current world trends in governance and wrote from the perspective of an advisor to a modern leader who wishes to attain global hegemony at any cost. I have tried my best to do this in as short a time as possible, by writing conclusions to several years of observations of living, working, traveling, and researching in a number of different countries, and through extensive travel over the last few years to gain inspiration and keep the content of the book as up to date and relevant as possible. This is my gift to the Prince who desires of it; and to the subject who wishes to understand its place in the global hierarchy.

Afterword-Conclusion

At this time, the world is falling apart due to the fact that there is an increasing trend worldwide to embrace ideologies and methods of governance that are obviously destructive to the cohesiveness of their society, economy, and environment.

They embrace these because they are masked in universalistic rhetoric. My true opinion is that the future of humanity is threatened because policy-makers are blind to consequences of their actions in their quest to achieve utopian goals without a grounding in the concrete world.

Using 'The Prince' is only a device that I thought of after organizing and writing a large amount of the book. I wanted to use a first-person writing style to create a participatory dialogue between the reader and the book in the same way that the medium of television creates an active dialogue between the viewer and the program; the viewers 'watches', not 'looks'. I would like the reader to have a conversation with the book. This use of language is used to take the reader through the same process that I am describing in the book: to cause the reader to analyze themselves as to how their (their country's) situation reality compared with perceived reality. If they are initiaters of conflict, the reader will realize it, read further which explains who applied rationalism (linear thinking) and Universal Humanism work a state the "+"s (positives) and "-"s (negatives) of each and state the possible consequences of non-grounded policy-making.

By the end of reading the book, the reader will contemplate whether they are active participants, unwitting collaborators, or victims of this methodology of conquest and will act accordingly.

The relationship between this book's 'Prince' and The Prince's 'Prince' is that both Niccolo Machiavelli and I desired to write a satirical work to raise the consciousness of those in power. He wrote to Medici and I am writing to the 'modern Princes'--leaders of modern nation-states, and to their subjects.

It is a good work [The Prince], but even Machiavelli himself, being a lover of ancient Rome, "missed the boat". He wrote the Prince in order to get himself back into politics. The Prince is a purposeful perversion of the Roman government ideals that He embraced. He, himself, did not contemplate the fact that Rome contributed to its own destruction through the application of universalism to its sphere of influence. The physical destruction of the cultures that it encountered destroyed the 'states' that were the floodgates that held back the 'barbarian hordes' that eventually conquered a Rome that was being eroded from the inside from its own conflicts and decline of values.

A 'wise' conqueror is aware and appreciates the differences between itself and its target. An 'unwise' conqueror believes that "its way" is the best way; and because of this will be blind to any problems that its influence may cause to the society.

A 'wise' conqueror who decides to use these methods of eliminating the culture of the target is aware of the dis-locative influence that it may have on the conquered and assumes the responsibility for managing it, while exploiting it. In this way it lessens the chance that any negative affects of its influence spill over into areas not under its control and of the corruption of its values at home due to the perpetuation of hypocrisies that differ from stated national ideas and social mores.

Preface to Author's Note

This book began as a series of thoughts, some organized as essays, some as short narratives detailing a theory of Cultural Warfare based on creating cognitive dissonance in a subject nation-state. After which, I had a thought to read *The Prince* for ideas on the style in which these essays should be presented. Upon review it seemed to be a natural fit, for this work to be written in the spirit and style of Niccolo Machiavelli. Machiavelli desired an ideal society and was saddened by the state of affairs in his day. He wrote to the Prince of Florence, Lorenzo de' Medici, to illustrate the means of achieving the objectives of gaining and sustaining hegemony and posterity of his powerful nation-state. After writing the Prince, Machiavelli wrote the Discourses; a more 'ideal' means of governance; written with nostalgia of what he observed in history as the better aspects of the Roman state. The author follows in the spirit of Machiavelli's *The Prince,* by describing present-day strategies for the total domination of a nation-state over another; its root ideology and methodology, as well as the consequences of such actions.

Author's Note:

I had been writing a book on life purpose, took a break and went to Japan for the World Cup festivities. During my time in Tokyo and met with the principles of a development consulting company about some possible future collaboration on projects. During our meeting, we had a conversation about cultural preservation and development and how, as development professionals, even something that may seem of "universal" concern such as a cultural preservation component can be a imposition on the client state, and discussed the importance of providing only the services that the client state requests.

After returning from this trip, the thesis for this book came to me all at once. I had put a little thought into a book that I was thinking of writing jointly with someone on the significance of cultural center in ethnic communities and sovereign nations. So, I sat down for about a week and wrote extemporaneously about Cultural Warfare. It started off like a combination between *The Prince* and the *Art of War*, discussing the methodology of conducting effective Cultural Warfare. Cognitive dissonance has always intrigued me as a method of behavior modification and I realized that a variation on the theory of cognitive dissonance could illustrate the process that is being used. Then I delved into the resulting consequences of Cultural Warfare and the resulting instability. After which I put more into what I term *Cultural Cognitive Dissonance*, projection, codependency, the pros and cons of using this methodology, and whom would be the most likely to use it. Next came more in depth thought on linear thinking, which roots lie in rational thought, which of course goes back to Plato, Newton, Leibniz, Descartes, Darwin, etc. After this I explored into how linear thinking can manifest in terms of cultural chauvinism/universalism – i.e. Cultural Imperialism and Universal Humanism. Then I looked at avenues through which Cultural Warfare could be applied, i.e. applications. I looked at the experiences of nations of peoples that were colonial powers and those subjected to colonial rule sometime during the last five-hundred years from the Americas to Africa, to Asia, to Europe, to Oceania; and the present day manifestations of these 'nations'.

This book emerges from two concepts that I have embraced as important in my life: the theory of cognitive dissonance and the concept of the point of reference/point of departure and its relation to Modernity. I conducted research to support my arguments, but decided to let this work stand as a theory, with the exception of quotes and a few notes that add color to my observations. This book is written to create dialogue with the reader. The reader can fill in his or her own support or rebuttal to my arguments. This book is written to provoke discussion about a very important topic – the significance of culture in institutions of governance in an increasingly integrated global web, with the potential implications of the erosion of cultures to be replaced by one or a few primary cultures justified by economic arguments of the merits of surrendering culture for 'Modernity'. Responsibility or lack there of - the choice is here. Are we so technologically advanced (approaching omnipotence) that we no longer need to operate with discretion and in balance with our environment (social and physical), chasing blindly after Progress, not really knowing where that is, or even acknowledging that that question is not an objective one, that it too is grounded in culture?

As a child, I learned about behavioral psychology in my home, and there was a library of psychology books that I had access to. Initially during grade school, I was intrigued by Pavlov's and Skinner's work in Classical and Operant Conditioning, but as a teenager I became more impressed by Cognitive Dissonance as a method of behavior modification.

During my second year of college, I attended a foreign study program in Japan. During that time I took a course on Japanese Modernism and post-Modernism. The concepts of point of reference and point of departure stuck to me. These concepts articulated what I had been trying to formulate in terms of the creation of a national mythology to promote a re-definition of self when faced with Cultural Imperialism. In this course, my professor illustrated how essential the formulation of national mythology and the creation of a cultural point of reference was to Meiji Period Japan. Japan, under the threat of involuntarily "westernizing" due to forced "Free Trade" after the arrival of Commodore Perry, was alarmed by the prospect of its citizenry exchanging Japanese values, behavior ideals, fashion, and other essential points of reference for that of the West. The intellectuals in the Meiji Government decided to "re-create" Japanese-ness, emphasizing desired cultural forms, religion, and social mores to establish a national cultural center, a "center" from which a national purpose could be derived and promoted. This center was fundamental to the rapid and focused industrialization of Japan; but as a result of having to re-define itself (adding associative cognitions to neutralize the effect of the dissociative ones) a stronger sense of nationalism that led to imperialism developed. This reaction was not one anticipated by those powers forcing Japan to "open" its society and markets to their cultural imperialism. The linear approach of this "attack" prevented the initiators from looking forward to try to predict what would happen if its efforts (Cultural Imperialism) were not successful. The need to feel superior discounted any voices in the West that may have warned of the potential for nationalistic tendencies among the Japanese government and populace, because the initiators could not imagine why anyone would not want to be like them (this was an addiction, a codependent (narcissistic) relationship in which the initiator required acceptance and affirmation by its target subject). The Japanese victory over Russia at Port Arthur in 1905 must have been a terrible day for those who had underestimated Japan. In the quest for world domination, because of an incomplete assault and underestimating the target, the Western cultural imperialists of the time had actually promoted the development of (in only forty years) an economic and cultural rival that is still a major power to this day. There are no isolated acts.

But the danger for 'Modern' (or contemporarily titled 'post-Modern') Japan concerns that same question of center: in its reactionary response to the Cultural Imperialism and threat of physical domination by the West, did it betray its sense of "cultural center" in this response? Was its imperialist period, pre-war development, and post-war "success" only the filler in the delayed response to a re-definition of self that may not have been in consequence of its "true cultural center". The Japanese experience provides a contemporary example of a nation-state that at different times during the last one-hundred years embodied some of both aspects of both a Prince and a subject, and its present-day struggles and successes reflect this reality.

On the same note, the reactionary means through which Japan made this transformation had delayed negative effect. The decision to deny certain essential aspects of the Japanese cultural center was also made. The results of the true "decision" took one-hundred years to manifest, but in taking a reactionary move to imperialism rather than an attitude of defensive expansionism, the true center was betrayed. In this present day, the cultivation of Japanese-ness has been forsaken for the goal of "catching up with and beating the West", but in this goal, the hierarchy of the "West" as something to emulate and surpass became the goal--an externalization of Self. Japanese success has not been to actualize its innate potential and greatness, but rather prove to be greater than the master/Big Brother. The effect may be the same – self-fulfillment, comparatively fulfilled, but the attitude of a country varies with these two – Japan has reached its plateau within the parameters of a Western success model, but how does it fare in a Japanese success model? What constitutes Japanese Success and Modernity: the ability the consume Western cultural icons?; technological supremacy?; the sustainability of the Japanese family?; preservation and continuity of culture?; a happy, self-fulfilled population?, a "wired" (or more correctly "wireless') society with lessening interpersonal communication and true social interaction?

Author's Note - Conclusion

The point of this book is not to advocate or criticize of any specific policies or actors, but instead to illustrate problems that can occur when linear thinking is applied to a life point of view based in an assumption of separateness and the need for competition over harmony (balance of creative and destructive elements/motivations/actions) as a means for survival rather than actually "living", growing, and "progressing" intellectually and intuitively (spiritually).

I travel and work in several locations internationally as a development consultant and researcher. I work with governments, community organizations, and interact with people from all walks of life. During the time in which I was writing this book I did considerable travel - this book comes largely from extensive research and the many conversations that I was able to have on my research trips, projects, and at academic conferences.

Grammar Notes:

Participatory Writing

I wrote this book in the first-person to create a dialogue with the reader so the reader can talk back. Possibly in later books, I will leave space for the reader to record their initial response if they so desire. This is 'participatory writing'.

Many of the narratives are written in longer, almost run-on sentences. I believe that a writer should complete his or her thoughts before punctuating. Premature punctuation breaks thoughts up unnaturally. Simple thoughts can be expressed in standard punctuation, but layered thoughts must be allowed to extend themselves until they have fully stretched themselves up so that the reader can contemplate the entire thought as a whole entity.

Initially, I did not want to include any quotes because I thought that it would upset the balance of the neutrality and vagueness in reference to specific nations, but some quotes that I found were too good to exclude.

This is a 'subjective research' effort - conducting research to substantiate a prior formed conclusion, not hypothesis. Like working on an equation backwards- Answer first, then create proof. This is not making a hypothesis and then trying to prove it.

One thing to note about this work: this is a whole work, not a compilation of pieces. If one wishes to take portions, quotes, etc. out of the work, they should do so in the context in which they are placed in the book. Taking these out without context renders them irrelevant because this is a holistic work. It was written as a whole – I started with a skeleton (the entire structure of the book) ("center") from the beginning. After the "center" of the book was created then I filled in details such as the beginning and ending, quotes, additional narratives.

In the 'separationist' world that we live in now, it has become common practice to take things out of context to use them to our own devices. I did this myself in my method of research. I already knew what I wanted to say - I came to several conclusions based on one primary assumption derived from years of life, travel, and research. The research that I did for this book is a collection of sources that I found that support my arguments. I even took quotes out of context to serve my needs – arrangements of words that support my theory. I am sure that some of the authors that I listed in my "Suggested Reading" section do not appreciate being used as support for some of my arguments, but this is the point that I am making – all things emanate from a Source. The combination of components that make up the physical manifestation of the Source-thought are perfect in their structure, in reference to its "center", that which binds all of these components together. If you try to take these components away from their structure and utilize them in a way as to "name" and "define" them, this is nothing but an attempt to control through "re-definition". One who engages in this practice, must, as to not appear to be ignorant, acknowledge that he or she is in the act of "re-creating", using the elements of a prior "creation". Using the elements of another is what we are supposed to do, but to use these elements to push our own agendas should be acknowledged. The structure in which they were found fit that reality, but once you change anything you have begun a new process of creation. This new "Individualistic Culture of Consumption as a means of control" lacks in the acknowledgment of what it really is. A being that consumes for the purpose of controlling must realize that it is utilizing the elements that it is consuming. It may view this process as merely 'consumption' but the elements/components are still being used, and being that they are being utilized, an understanding of the consequences of taking the components of another creation and re-creating must be realized. Consumption is an active act, not a passive act. That which is consumed is not being utilized for another function. If one desires their reality to sustain itself, all of the elements needed to sustain it must be put into the equation. If one consumes in a fashion that denies the reality that they live in the elements necessary for its sustenance, it was change into a new reality – hence a causal reality. There are no independent actions. People must take responsibility for all that emanates from them, whether active or passive; and understand that they are "important" because their actions in some way or another affect the reality that they and those around them, and those not around them live in. It is said that love is merely being born into a community. I agree. Love is the child of creation, the plus and minus, creative and destructive, active and passive origin of creation. All persons are born as love and in love; and therefore as a responsibility of the gift of living in this plane should make love and give birth to love. It is our birthrate, we have no other [reason] to be here but to perpetuate and live in love.

Future Tense

A large portion of this book is written in the future tense; this is used when I am saying a continuous thought that is placed in the past tense. Writing words down on paper has one major disadvantage when it comes to articulating human ideas: the written word captures the "moment" - what the writer feels at a particular 'moment in time. The thought put to paper may be one of "now", a static reality; because it is written on paper it assumes perpetuity. But the reality is that a static thought is based on a temporary reality.

The use of the continuous tense allows you to view this work as a snapshot of a moment in time, i.e. observations of a chosen path. This future may or may not come about, but at the moment of conception, what was created was a view based on that "present reality". If you stay on this same path, the eventuality of this 'snapshot analysis of the present' increases.

This also allows for a better use of the first person point of view that I speak to you in, because I actually provide you with choices throughout this book. You can, through dialoguing with me through reading, see the direction that your decisions take you. This is written as a 'crystal ball' for the present. The future is not known, but we can affect our present reality through our thoughts and decisions (actions).

Research Method

Being that I spend a lot of my time in Western Pacific, access to written research materials is less and academic conference discussions are more infrequent, because of the lack of major literary-based research institutions in the Region, except for a few at the University of Guam. The vast depository of knowledge in Micronesia is still maintained in the oral tradition. Conversations with elders in the Region, and living in the communities over the years also provided me with an entirely different perspective on "human nature", "time", and "success" than one would derive from the predominate "literature" and from the global nass media. So after had developed my thesis, and wrote a large number of narratives extemporaneously, I decided to look for books whose authors had a strong grasp on each of the matters concerned. I wanted to have "conversations" with those whom I could discuss these matters and reflect on them. For example, for conversation on applied rationalism, I conversed with Marimba Ani; for free trade and global finance, I conversed with John Gray, for rule of law, Patrick H. Glenn; for modernity, Stephen Toulmin; for environmental conflict, Michael Renner; and public health, Ernesto Bravo; for agriculture, Rossett and Medea; aesthetics, W.E. Abraham; indigenous people's movements, Cultural Survival Quarterly; globalization, Saskia Sassen; for history of science, Lewis Mumford; for education, Carter G. Woodson; for satire, Niccolo Machiavelli; etc. From these and other "conversations", I wrote affirmations and rebuttals to their arguments and then wrote narratives from the perspectives of an advisor to a 'Modern Prince'.

This is a compilation of my thoughts and experiences working, living, researching, but to as to not be limited by my own experience, I wanted to discuss some theoretical perspectives with scholars of whom I feel are highly competent in their fields.

After constructing a theorical framework based on these "conversations", I took a number of trips to research libraries, bookstores, and academic conferences around the world to construct an adequate literature review. And, from this assemblage of research, from a truly international body of knowledge, I was able to extract the quotations that I needed to illustrate the theiry that I was putting forth.

The governing "worldview" of the thesis comes from the completion of many conversations that I had on my travels with elders, youth, governmental officials, businesspersons, activists, community leaders, religious leaders, security professionals, and scholars.

The world is in such a fragile state that this discussion must be had. If there is a universalizing power (state), let it reveal itself and its true intentions; other nations will acknowledge their subordinate status, and react accordingly.

The purpose of this book is to promote cognitive independence in the reader so that he or she can act as active protagonists in shaping our world[416].

---

416. "Cognitive independence to act as active protagonists in our history". I like this assertion. It was stated by Rose Maria Massón Cruz, Cuban educator of pedagogy.

References and Suggested Reading List:

I have tried to, in addition to sources that provided me with inspiration and quotations, create a useful bibliography of works that I have found that either support what I have written or go into more detail about some of the issues that I have covered.

Abbas, Lichtman, and Pober (1994) *Cellular and Molecular Immunology.* Philadelphia: W.B. Saunders Company.

Abraham, W.E. (1962) *The Mind of Africa.* The University of Chicago Press. London: Weidenfeld and Nicolson.

"Africa's Hunt for Investments." African Business. December 2003. pp. 1-14.

"African Fish Harvest Blamed on Warming", AP Africa, Aug. 13, 2003.

"Ainu Shamanism: A Forbidden Path to Universal Knowledge". Tanaka, Sakurako. Cultural Survival Quarterly: World Report on the Rights, Voices, and Visions of Indigenous People. Sumhbmer 2003. Vol. 27, Issue 2. pp. 44-47.

Akbar, Na'im, Ph.D. (1984) *Chains and Images of Psychological Slavery.* Jersey City: New Mind Productions.

American Indian Movement Resolution. Sovereign Dine' Nation, Window Rock, Arizona, May 11, 1984. Cultural Survival Quarterly: World Report on the Rights, Voices, and Visions of Indigenous People. Summer 2003. Vol. 27, Issue 2. p. 27.

"The Anatomy of Resource Wars", WorldWatch Paper 162, October 2002, Michael Renner, p.11 from International Crisis Group, *Dialogue or Destruction? Organizing Peace as the War in Sudan Escalates*, ICGF Africa Report No. 48, Nairobi and Brussels, 27 June 2002.

Ani, Marimba (1994) *Yurugu: An African-Centered Critique of European and Cultural Thought and Behavior.* Lawrenceville, NJ: Africa World Press.

"Animal to Human Mutation of Virus Often a Simple Step" by Jenni Laidman, Blade Science Writer. Sunday, March 23, 2003. Toledo Blade.

Armah, Ayi Kweh (1973) *Two Thousand Seasons*. London: Heinemann.

arogundade, ben (2000) *black beauty: a history and a celebration*. New York: Thunder's Mouth Press.

Andres, Tomas D. (1989) *Positive Filipino Values*. Quezon City: New Day Publishers.

Anderson, Benedict. (1983) *Imagined Communities*. London: Verso.

"Arctic Ice Cap Will Melt Completely in 100 Years", AEP Wed. Aug. 13, 2003.

Asao, Makoto and Amano Ikuo. (1972) *Education and Japan's Modernization (Kyoiku to Nihon no Kindaika)*. Tokyo: Ministry of Foreign Affairs.

"Asymmetric War: How the Weak Fight". Issues 2003, Newsweek International Dec. 2002- Feb. 2003.

Bakan, Joel (2004) *The Corporation*. New York: Free Press.

Battle, J.A. (1969) *Culture and Education for the Contemporary*. Columbus: Charles E. Merrill Publishing Company.

Ben-Dasan, Isaiah (1972) *The Japanese and the Jews*. New York: Weatherhill.

"Better Living in the Village: A Well-Balanced Development Policy in Benin". Gabriel Agbede. Cultural Survival Quarterly: World Report on the Rights, Voices, and Visions of Indigenous People. Summer 2003. Vol. 27, Issue 2. p. 68.

"Between Localization and Internationalization – Primary Education in Modern Taiwan." May 2003. Sinorama. pp. 20-29 Kwang Hua Publishing. Los Angeles.

"Beyond Malthus: Sixteen Dimensions of the Population Problem". Lester R. Brown, Gary Gardner, and Brian Halwell. Worldwatch Paper 143. September 1998. p.7.

Bireda, Martha R., Cummings, Jaha F., Pangelinan, Zita P. (2004) *Preserving Cultural Integrity in the Age of Globalization: An Educational Response.* Tokyo: ARI.

Bireda, Martha R. (1990) *Love Addiction: A Guide to Emotional Independence.* Oakland: New Harbinger Publications, Inc.

Boahen, A. Adu (1987) *African Perspectives of Colonialism.* Baltimore: Johns Hopkins University Press.

Booth, Eric (1999) *The Everyday Work of Art.* Naperville, Ill.: Scurcebooks, Inc.

Boris, Eileen and Prugl, Elisabeth eds. (1996) *Homeworkers in Global Perspective: Invisible No More.* New York: Routledge.

Bravo, Ernesto Mario (1998) *Development Within Underdevelopment?: New Trends in Cuban Medicine.* La Habana: Editorial Elfos Scientiae.

Buchanan, Patrick, J. (2002) *The Death of the West: How Dying Populations and Immigrant Invasions Imperil Our Country and Civilization.* New York: Thomas Dunne Books.

"Cash for Kava, But A What Cost?" Olivier Wortel. Pacific Magazine. April 2004. p.10.

Cesare, Aimee (translated by Joan Pinkham) (2000) *Discourse on Colonization.* New York: New York University Press.

"The Channeling of Negro Aggression by the Cultural Process." Hortense Powdermaker. p.325. The National Temper: Reading in American Culture and Society. Edited by Lawence W. Levine and Robert Middlekauff. Harcourt Brace Jovanovich, Inc. New York. 1972.

"Character Education: Promoting Community Responsibility" by Jaha F. Cummings presented at the X Semanario Cientifico Sobre la Calidad de la Educacion (10th Scientific Seminar on the Quality of Education), Havana, Cuba Oct. 27th – 31st, 2003.

Chomsky, Noam (2003) *Hegemony or Survival: America's Quest for Global Dominance*. New York: Metropolitan Books.

Chu, Chin-Ning (1994) *Thick-Face, Black Heart: The Path to Thriving, Winning, and Succeeding*. New York: Warner Books.

Coelho, Paulo (1995) *The Alchemist*. San Francisco: Harper San Francisco.

"Conservation Policy and Indigenous Peoples". Cultural Survival Quarterly: World Report on the Rights, Voices and Visions of Indigenous Peoples, Spring 2004. p.19

Confucius. trans. By D.C. Lau (1979) *The Analects*. London: Penguin Books.

"The Connected Earth". Professor David Rhind. Global Mapping Newsletter. No. 9. March 25, 1998. The Secretariat of the International Steering Committee for Global Mapping (ISCGM), Tsukuba-shi, Japan.

Constantino, Renato (1982) *The Miseducation of the Filipino*. Quezon City: Foundation for Nationalist Studies.

Constantino, Letizia, R. (1982) *World Bank Textbooks: Scenario for Deception*. Quezon City: Foundation for Nationalist Studies.

Convention on the Prevention and Punishment of the Crime of Genocide, General Assembly Resolution 260 A (III), 9 December 1948.

"Cosmetic Surgery For Better Looks in Vogue." by Sohn Suk-Joo, Korea Times, May 31, 2001.

"Cosmetic Surgery and Diet" by Lee Eun-Pyo, Korea Times, July 31, 2002.

"Culture of Corruption: A Problem of Definition and Perception". Robert A. Underwood, Professor University of Guam in "Government Ethics and Corruption on Guam" Judith Paulette Gutherz and Daljit Singh eds., College of Business and Public Administration, University of Guam, Mangilao, Guam 1986.

"Cyber Threat Trends and US Network Security". Statement of the Record for the Joint Economic Committee. Lawrence K. Gershwin, National Intelligence Officer for Science and Technology. June 21, 2001.

"Dartmouth Professor Brings Cultural Introspection to the Classroom", Vox of Dartmouth, April 7, 2003 by Tamara Steinart.

Darwin, Charles (1859) *Origin of Species by Means of Natural Selection or The Preservation of Favoured Races in the Struggle for Life.*

"Deep Trouble: The Hidden Threat of Groundwater Pollution" by Payal Sampat, Worldwatch Paper 154 December 2000 World Watch Institute, p.7.

Dewey, John (1916 - Macmillan) *Democracy and Education: An Introduction to the Philosophy of Education.* New York: The Free Press.

De Soto, Hernando (1989) *The Other Path: The Invisible Revolution in the Third World.* New York: Harper and Row.

"Defending REACH". Environmental Business. Margot Wallstro:m December 2003. Surrey, UK. p.18

Descartes, Rene' (1637) *Discourse on Method.*

"Dilemma For Fiji Media and the Constitution". Philip Cass. South Pacific Centre for Communication and Information in Development (SPCenCIID), University of Papua New Guinea Press. November 1995. pp. 69-72.

Dippattamenton I Kaotao Guinahan Chamorro (Department cf Chamorro Affairs). *Chamarro Heritage A Sense of Place: Guidelines, Procedures and Recommendations For Authenticating Chamorro Heritage.* Department of Chamorro Affairs, Research, Publications and Training Division. 2003.

Discussion with Anita P. DeFrantz, Ph.D., University of San Francisco - Emerita.

Discussion with Tomas Graman, Department of Language and Literature, Carrol College, Helena (Montana).

Discussion with Rosa Maria Massón Cruz, Cuban Educator of Pedagogy .

ERD Working Paper No.21, The Doha Agenda and Development: A View from the Uruguay Round. Economics and Research Department, Asian Development Bank. J. Michael Finger, September 2002, Manila. p.16.

"Downsizing Korea?: The Difficult Demise of Lifetime Employment and the Prospects for Further Reform". Law and Policy in International Business, Georgetown University Law Center, Winter 2003. Vol. 34, Number 2, Brett M. Kitt.

"'Ecology' and the Modernization of Fascism in the German Ultra-right", Janet Biehl, Introduction to Ecofascism, Lessons from the German Experience, by Janet Biehl and Peter Staudenmaier, AK Press, 1995, Scotland.

Eder, James F. (1993) On the Road to Tribal Extinction: Depopulation, Deculturation, and Adaptive Well-Being Among the Batak of the Philippines. Quezon City (MM): New Day Publishers.

Einstein, Albert (1950) Out of My Later Years. Philosophy Library

Epega, Afolabi A. and (trans.) Neimark, Philip John (1995). The Sacred Ifa Oracle. New York: HarperSanFrancisco.

"EU Ban on G-M Crops". Environment and Climate News: The Monthly Newspaper for Common-Sense Environmentalists. Vol. 6, No. 6 – July 2003. p.10

"EU Rejects Early Yuan Floating." Shanghai Daily. Monday, September 15, 2003. p.3.

"Europe's Endangered Liberal Order". Timothy Garton Ash. Foreign Affairs. March/April 1998. pp. 51- 65.

Evangelista, Oscar. L. (2002) *Building the National Community: Problems and Prospects and Other Historical Essays*. Quezon City: New Day Publishers.

"Evangelising the World". New Straits Times. Monday, July 21, 2003. New Straits Times Press. Kuala Lumpur. By Simon Romeo. p. 10.

"Experts: New Data Show Global Warming" by Charles J. Hanley. AP, April 28, 2005.

"Fading Green?" Environmental Politics in the Mercosur Free Trade Agreement". Kathryn Hochstetler. Latin American Politics and Society. University of Miami. 2003 Vol.45, Number 4, Winter 2003.

Fahn, James David (2004) *A Land on Fire: The Environmental Consequences of the Southeast Asian Boom*. Bangkok: Silkworm Books.

"Features of the Recent Improvement in the Propensity to Consume". Tokyo-Mitsubishi Review. Vol. 8, No.1, January 2003.

Festinger, Leon (1957) *A Theory of Cognitive Dissonance*. Stanford University Press. Stanford.

Fighting for Survival from Volker Boge, "Bougainville: A 'Classical' Environmental Conflict?" Occasional Paper No.3, Environment and Conflicts Project (ENCOP), Bern, Switzerland, October 1992, p.52.

"Forbes: 'Keep Yuan Stable'". China Daily. Wednesday 17, 2003, Vol. 23, No. 2318. by Zhang Yong and Liang Yu.

"Willie Lynch Speech" Freedman Institute, Gambrills, Maryland.

"Friends of the Kel Essuf: Perspectives on Shamanism in Taureg Mediumistic Healing". Susan J. Rasmussan. Cultural Survival Quarterly: World Report on the Rights, Voices, and Visions of Indigenous People. Summer 2003. Vol. 27, Issue 2. pp. 32-35.

Freire, Paulo (1993) *The Pedagogy of the Oppressed*. New York: Continuum: New York.

"From Cultural Differences to Differences in Cultural Frame of Reference" by John U. Ogbu in Patricia M. Greenfield and Rodney R. Cocking eds. (1994) *Cross-Cultural Roots of Minority Child Development*. Hillsdale, New Jersey: Lawrence Erlbaum Associates, Publishers. p. 367.

"The Future of African Gods: The Clash of Civilization". Molefi Kete Asante, PhD. Accra – W.E.B. DuBois Center July 10, 1998.

Galbraith, John Kenneth (1969) *Ambassador's Journal: A Personal Acount of the Kennedy Years*. New American Library.

Garrett, Laurie (2000) *Betrayal of Trust: The Collapse of Global Public Health*. New York: Hyperion.

George, Susan (1999) *Lugano Report: On Preserving Capitalism in the Twenty-first Century*. London: Pluto Press.

"George Washington's Farewell Address," in *Documents of American History*, ed. Henry Steele Commager. Appleton-Century-Crofts, Inc. 1958.

Gerassi, John ed. *Venceremos!: The Speeches and Writings of Che Guevara*. Panther Modern Society.

Glenn, Patrick H. (2000) *Legal Traditions of the World: Sustainable Diversity in Law*. Oxford: Oxford University Press.

"The Global Menace of Local Strife". The Economist. May 24, 2003. pp. 23-25.

Goldsmith E. (1992) *The Way: An Ecological World View. London: Rider.*

Goldstein, Joseph (2003) *Settling Back Into the Moment: A Meditator's Guide*. Dehiwala: Buddhist Cultural Centre.

Gould, Stephen Jay (1981) *The Mismeasure of Man*. New York: W.W. Norton.

Gray, John (1998) *False Dawn: The Delusions of Global Capitalism*. New York: The New Press.

Green, Jim ed. (2003) *Albert Einstein*. Melbourne: Ocean Press.

Greene, Robert (1998) *The 48 Laws of Power.* New York: Penguin Books.

Grove, Richard H. (1988) *Ecology, Climate and Empire: The Indian Legacy in Global Environmental History, 1400-1940.* Delhi: Oxford University Press.
Hagberg, Sten "Learning to Live or to Leave?: Education and Identity in Burkina Faso". A contribution to the POVERTY CONFERENCE, SIda, Stockholm, 18 October 2001.

Hall, Ronald. E. (2001) *Filipina Eurogamy: Skin Color as Vehicle of Psychological Colonization.* Quezon City: Giraffe Books.

Hass, Wiles, and Bondi (1970) *Reading in Curriculum.* Boston: Allyn and Bacon, Inc.

Havelock, Eric A. (1963) *Preface to Plato.* Cambridge: The Belknap of Harvard University Press.

"Healing Makes Our Hearts Happy: Ju'hoan Spirituality and the Struggle for Self-Determination". Richard Katz and Megan Bisele in conversation with =Oma Djo.
Cultural Survival Quarterly: World Report on the Rights, Voices, and Visions of Indigenous People. Summer 2003. Vol. 27, Issue 2. pp. 16-19.

Huntington, Samuel P. (1996) *The Clash of Civilizations: Remaking of World Order.* New York: Simon and Schuster.

Hezel, Francis X. S.J. (1983) *The First Taint of Civilization: A History of the Caroline and Marshall Islands in Pre-Colonial Days, 1521-1885.* Honolulu: University of Hawaii Press.

Hodges, Donald C. (1986) *Intellectual Foundations of the Nicaraguan Revolution.* Austin: University of Texas Press.

The Holy Bible, King James Version.

Speech by Chief Hurao, 1671, Hagatna, Guahan (Present-day Guam). Department of Chamorro Affairs, Guam.

"Human Rights Record of the United States in 2002" by the Information Office of the State Council of the People's Republic of China. April 3, 2003. from *Human Rights*, China Society for Human Rights Studies, Beijing. Vol.2, No.4, July 2003. pp.12-19.

Hurmence, Belinda ed. (1996) *My Folks Don't Want Me To Talk About Slavery.* Winston-Salem, N.C.: John F. Blair Publisher.

"The Hype of Hypermarkets." Malaysian Business. November 1, 1999. p.9.

"Ideology and the Archaeological Record in Africa: Interpreting Symbolism in Iron Smelting Technology." Peter Schmidt and Bertram Mapunda, Journal of Anthropological Archaeology, Vol. 16. 1997.

Iida, Fumihiko (1999) *Ikigai no souzou (The Real Aim of Our Life).* Tokyo: PHP Bunko, PHP Kenkyuujo.

"Improving Regional Healthcare in West Africa Using Current Space Systems Technology". By Dr. Mae Jemison. This paper was presented at the 1992 World Space Congress, Washington D.C.

"Indigenous Cultures of Globalization." Tuo Chinula. Islands Business. August 1999. p.28.

"Initiation: Remembering One's Purpose by Malidoma Some". In Context: A Quarterly of Humane Sustainable Development, Winter 1993, p. 30.

"Investigative Journalism in Melanesia: Is It Needed?" Walter Nalangu. Pacific Journalism Review. South Pacific Centre for Communication and Information in Development (SPCenCIID), University of Papua New Guinea Press. November 1995. pp. 16-22.

International Covenant on Economic, Social and Cultural Rights, G.A. res. 2200A (XXI), 21 U.N.GAOR Supp. (No. 16) at 49, U.N. Doc. A/6316 (1966).

Jacobs, Paul and Landau, Saul with Pell, Eve (1971) *To Serve to Devil: Volume 2: Colonials and Sojourners.* New York: Random House.

Jameson, Fredric and Masao Miyoshi ed. (1998) *The Cultures of Globalization.* Raleigh-Durham: Duke University Press.

"Japan's Economic Development." Hiromatsu, Takeshi and Kobayashi, Minoru. International Society for Educational Information, Inc. Tokyo. March 1997.

Jocano, Landa. F. (1997) *Filipino Value System: A Cultural Definition*. Metro Manila: PUNLAD Research House, Inc.

"John Quincy Adams. July 4,1821," in William Appleman Williams, *The Contours of American History*". New York: World Publishing Co., 1961.

Johnson, Chalmers (2000) *Blowback: The Costs and Consequences of American Empire*. New York: Owl (Henry Holt).

Journal of African Civilizations Vol. I, No. 2, November 1979.

Kaplan, Robert (2001) *Soldiers of God: With Islamic Warriors in Afghanistan and Pakistan*. New York: Vintage Books.

Katoh, Kenichi (2001) *Gurobarizumu e no chousen: karamojia undou no 20 nen (ue)*. Tokyo: Mainichi Shinbunsya.

Katoh, Kenichi (2001) *Gurobarizumu e no chousen: karamojia undou no 20 nen (sita)*. Tokyo: Mainichi Shinbunsya.

Katz, Daniel eds. (1954) *Public Opinion and Propaganda: A Book of Readings*. New York: Holt, Rinehart and Winston.

Kobayashi, Yoshinori (1998) *Sensou-ron (About War)*. Tokyo: Gentosha.

Kobayashi, Yoshinori (2001) *Sensou-ron (About War) 2*. Tokyo: Gentosha.

Koechler, Hans *Manila Lectures 2002: Terrorism and the Quest For a Just World Order*. Foundation For Social Justice. Quezon City, Philippines. July 2002.

Kotkin, Joel (1992) *Tribes: How Race, Religion, and Identity Determine Success in the New Global Economy*. New York: Random House.

Kyoto Protocol to the United Nations Framework Convention on Climate Change. Third Session Kyoto, 1-10 December 1997.

Lao Tsu (translated by Gia-Fu Feng and Jane English) (1997) *Tao Te Ching*. New York: Vintage Books.

"The Law of the Islands" Marshall Islands Journal. Francis X. Hezel. S. J. Friday March 8, 2002. pp. 18-19.

"Learn from Cuba, says World Bank by Jim Lobe" April 30, 2001 InterPress Third World News Agency (IPS), Rome.

Levine, Lawrence W. and Middlekauff, Robert (1972) *The National Temper: Readings in American Culture and Society*. New York: Harcourt Brace Jovanovich.

Linnekin, Jocelyn and Poyer, Lin (1990) *Cultural and Ethnicity in the Pacific*. Honolulu: University of Hawaii Press.

"Local Crops Help the Whole World" by Lewis W. Diuguid, The Kansas City Star, August 20, 2003.

Lopez, Zenaida Puig C. Dra. and Palmer, Elena Mateo Lic. Ma (1989) *Documents on the History of the United States, Part 2*. Havana: Editorial Pueblo y Educacion.

"Losing Strands in the Web of Life: Vertebrate Declines and the Conservation of Biological Diversity". John Tuxill. Worldwatch Paper 141. Worldwatch Institute. May 1998.

Lovejoy, Arthur O. (1936) *The Great Chain of Being*. Cambridge: Harvard University Press.

Lowen, Alexander, M.D. (1985) *Narcissism: Denial of True Self*. New York: Touchstone.

Lowry, Charles A. (1962) *Communism and Christ*. New York: Collier Books. 1962.

Lowry, Richard J. ed. (1973) *Dominance, Self-Esteem, Self-Actualization: Germinal Papers of A.H. Maslow*. Belmont: Wadsworth Publishing Company.

Mabubani, Kishore (2002) *Can Asians Think?: Understanding the Divide Between East and West.* South Royalton, Vermont: Steerforth Press.

Mabuhay Magazine Dec. 2002 (Philippine Airlines) Inside front cover.
Machiavelli, Niccolo (translated by Daniel Donno). (1966) *The Prince.* New York: Bantam Books. New York. First Published 1513.

"Manuscripts for Peace in Mali". Larry Childs and Issa Mohammed. Cultural Survival Quarterly: World Report on the Rights, Voices, and Visions of Indigenous People. Summer 2003. Vol. 27, Issue 2. pp. 7-8.

Mao Tse Tung. *Mao Zhuxi Yu Lu (Quotations from Chairman Mao) "precious red book".* May 1964. People's Liberation Army General Political Department. Beijing, China.

Maslog, Crispin C. (1994) *Communication, Values and Society.* Quezon City: New Day Publishers.

Maslow, Abraham (1970) *Motivation and Personality.* New York: HarperCollins Publishers.

Massoudy, Hassan (illus.) (2004) *Perfect Harmony: Sufi Poetry of Ibn 'Arabi.* Boston: Shambhala.

Meera, Ahamed Kameel Mydin (2004) *The Theft of Nations: Returning to Gold.* Selangor Darul Ehsan, Malaysia: Pelanduk Publications (M) Sdn Bhd.

Mendis, L.N.T. (2004) *Descent of Man.* Colombo: Vijitha Yapa Publications.

"Missionaries Under Cover." Time. Vol. 161, No.26. June 30, 2003. pp. 36-44.

Miyamoto, Musashi trans. by Harris, Victor (1974) *The Book of Five Rings.* Overlook Press.

Muhammad W.D. A Message of Concern to the American People Chicago: *American Muslim Journal,* Regular Feature, 1980-1983.

Mumford, Lewis (1934) *Technics and Civilization.* San Diego: Harcourt Brace & Company.

"The New Melting Pot: Changing Faces of International Migration and Policy Implications for Southern California". Georges Vernez. October 2003. Pacific Council on International Policy. Los Angeles, California.

1994 *Human Development Report*, UNDP, U.N. Department of Public Information (UNDPI). 1994.

Nishimoto, Mitoji (1969) *The Development of Educational Broadcasting in Japan*. Tokyo: Sophia University in Cooperation with Charles E. Tuttle Co.

"Now the Negative News From Paradise: Pacific countries are increasingly sensitive about media coverage. Singled out for special scrutiny and criticism are the Australian and New Zealand media, which specializes in the region. An Asian perspective."
Kunda Dixit. South Pacific Centre for Communication and Information in Development (SPCenCIID), University of Papua New Guinea Press. November 1995. pp. 116-118.

"Oil Boardrooms Echo Sounds of Sao Tome Coup". Monday, July 21, 2003. New Straits Times Press. Kuala Lumpur. p.10.

Ong, Walter J. (1988) *Orality and Literacy* (2003 Edition). London: Routledge.

"Open Source Information". Army Magazine, July 1997.

"Oppression, Assimilation, and the Preservation of Identity: A Comparative Study of the Korean Minority in Japan and African-Americans." Jaha F. Cummings. Paper Presentation. 1995 Pedagogy of the Oppressed Conference. University of Nebraska, Omaha.

Oral statement presented to United Nations Commission on Human Rights, Sub-Commission on the Prevention of Discrimination and Protection of Minorities, Fiftieth session, by Miloon Kothari, 12 August 1998, for the International NGO Committee on Human Rights in Trade and Investment.

Organizational Chart of the Bureau of Public Health, Ministry of Health, Republic of Palau presented at the Annual Primary Health Care Conference, November 29th - December 3rd, 2004.

Park, Joe. Ph.D. (1958) *Selected Readings in the Philosophy of Education.* New York: Macmillan.

Parrinder, Geoffrey (1949) *West African Religion: A Study of the Beliefs and Practices of Akan, Ewe, Yoruba, Ibo, and Kindred Peoples.* Epworth Press. London.

Parrin, Noel Perrin (1979) *Giving Up the Gun: Japan's Reversion to the Sword, 1543-1879.* Boston: Nonpareil Books.

Pieterse, Jan Nederveen (1992) *White and Black: Images of Africa and Blacks in Western Popular Culture.* Yale University Press. Cosmic Illusion Productions Foundation, Amsterdam.

"Plan Colombia". TRIcontinental. Year 36, Number, Number 151, 2002.

Plato. trans. Benjamin Jowett (2000) *The Republic.* Mineola, New York: Dover Publications, Inc.

"Population and Its Discontents" by Danielle Nierenburg and Mia MacDonald, September/October 2004, Worldwatch Institute.

Programa de trabajo del medico y enferma de la familia, el policlinico y el hospital (Havana: MINSAP, 1988) pp.4-5.

"The Quest for WTO Access". MEED (Middle East Economic Digest). 19 December 2003 – 1 January 2004. Vol.47, No.51. pp. 35-42.

Ra Un Nefer Amen (1994) *Metu Neter Vol.2 Anuk Ausar: The Kamitic Initiation System.* New York: Khamit Corp.

"Regional Integration and Global Governance". UNUnexions. August 2003. pp.1 and 4. United Nations University.

Renner, Michael (1996) *Fighting For Survival: Environmental Decline, Social Conflict, and the New Age of Insecurity.* New York: W.W. Norton & Company.

"Researchers Use Scientific Methods of the West to See How Ancient Remedies of the East Really Work". Associated Press – Hong Kong. January 22, 2003.

Resolution of the Fifth Annual Meeting of the Traditional Elders Circle. Northern Cheyenne Nation, Two Moons' Camp, Rosebud Creek, Montana, USA. October 1980. Cultural Survival Quarterly. Summer 2003. Vol. 27, Issue 2. p 24.

"Resolution No. 65/2003". Cuban Foreign Trade 3/2003. Havana. Chamber of Commerce of the Republic of Cuba. (Re: Use of convertible peso – pegging the US dollar 1:1)

Reynolds, David. K. Ph.D. (1979) *The Heart of the Japanese People*. Tokyo: Nichieisha Co. Ltd.

"Risking Corn, Risking Culture". Claire Hope Cummings. Worldwatch Magazine. November/December 2002.

Rittberger, Volker ed. (2001) *Global Governance and the United Nations System*. Tokyo:United Nations University Press.

Ritzer, George (2000) *The McDonaldization of Society.* Thousand Oaks, California: Pine Forge Press.

Ronan, Colin A. (1978) *The Shorter Science and Civilisation in China: An Abridgment of John Needhman's Original Text, Volume 1.* Cambridge: Cambridge University Press.

Rossett, Peter and Benjamin, Medea, eds. (1994) *The Greening of the Revolution: Cuba's Experiment With Organic Agriculture*. Melbourne: Ocean Press.

"The Rule of Law Revival". Thomas Carothers. Foreign Affairs. March/April 1998. pp. 95-106.

"Safeguarding the Health of Oceans." Anne Platt McGinn. Worldwatch Paper 145, March 1999. Worldwatch Institute. p.31.

Salley, Columbus and Behm, Ronald (1981) *What Color Is Your God? Black Consciousness & the Christian Faith.* InterVarsity Press (InterVarsity Christian Fellowship) Madison, WI.

Samson, G.B. (1950) *The Western World and Japan: A Study in the Interaction of European and Asiatic Cultures*. Alfred A. Knopf.

Sassen, Saskia (2001) *The Global City*. Princeton: Princeton University Press.

Sayers, Dorothy (1971) *Are Women Human?* Grand Rapids, Michigan: William B. Eerdmans Publishing Co.

Schmidt, P.R.(ed.)(1996) *The Culture and Technology of African Iron Production*. Gainsville: University Press of Florida.

Schmookler, Andrew Bard (1995) *Parable of Tribes: The Problem of Power in Social Evolution*. Albany: State University of New York Press.

"Science Finds Cure for Maize Disease." African Business. December 2003. p.25.

Sellmann, James. D. (2002) *Timing and Rulership in Master Lü's Spring and Autumn Annals (Lushi chunqiu)*. Albany: State University of New York Press.

Seto, Jun'ichi Background Information Material on Juvenile Crime, Foreign Press Center, Tokyo, Japan. June 1998.

Shaw, George Bernard (1951) *Seven Plays*. Mead, New York: Dodd.

Shore, D. "Steel-Making in Ancient Africa." *Blacks in Science, Ancient and Modern* (I. Van Sertima, ed.) New Brunswick: Transaction Books, 1983, pp.157-162.

"Sidelined on Human Rights: America Bows Out". Kenneth Roth. Foreign Affairs. March/April 1998. pp. 2-6.

"The Singapore Family in the 1990s: Implication for Counseling." Micronesian Educator: A Journal of Research and Practice on Education in Guam and Micronesia. Vol. 4, 1993. A Publication of the University of Guam Press.

Sittirak, Sinith (2000) *The Daughters of Development: Women and the Changing Environment*. London: Zed Books.

Social Process in Hawaii. Volume 36, 1994. Guest Editor Paul Spickard. Department of Sociology, University of Hawaii at Manoa. University of Hawaii Press.

"The Silent Return of Colonialism" Tricontinental, 2003. pp.51-2.

Soros, George (2002) *George Soros on Globalization*. New York: Public Affairs.

Spier, J. M. (1954) trans. by David Hugh Freeman (1973) *An Introduction to Christian Philosophy*. Nutley, New Jersey: Craig Press.

Spindler, George D. ed. (1974) *Education and Cultural Process: Toward An Anthropology of Education*. New York: Holt, Rinehart and Winston, Inc.

"Spiritual Hucksterism: The Rise of the Plastic Medicine Men". Ward Churchill. Cultural Survival Quarterly: World Report on the Rights, Voices, and Visions of Indigenous People. Summer 2003. Vol. 27, Issue 2. p. 26.

Sta. Maria, Felice Prudente (2001) *A Cultural Worker's Manual: Essays in Appreciating the Everyday*. Pasig City, Metro Manila: Anvil.

Soggard, Vigo (1975) *Everything You Need to Know For a Cassette Ministry*. Minneapolis: Bethany Fellowship Inc.

"Surgical Beauty Syndrome". Park Moo-jung. Korea Times. May 15, 2001.

Sustainability: Positioning the Concept as a Global Goal. Global Vision's NGO Position Paper for the International Conference on Environment and Society: Education and Public Awareness for Sustainability. Organized by UNESCO and the Government of Greece. Thessaloniki, Greece, 8-12 December 1997. Re-published in "Sustainable Development: Education, The Force of Change", Transdisciplinary Project "Educating for a Sustainable Future", (EDP) UNESCO, 1999, Paris.

"Terrorism and the Quest For a Just World Order". Hans Koechler: Manila Lectures 2002. Foundation for Social Justice. Quezon City. 2002.

"Third World Water Forum". Koji Uchikawa. Global Mapping Newsletter. No. 29. March 25, 2003. The Secretariat of the International Steering Committee for Global Mapping (ISCGM), Tsukuba-shi, Japan.

Tobin, Jack. A. (2002) *Stories From the Marshall Islands*. Honolulu: University of Hawaii Press.

Toulmin, Stephen (1992) *Cosmopolis: The Hidden Agenda of Modernity*. Chicago: The University of Chicago Press.

"Toward a Real Global Warming Treaty". Richard N. Cooper. Foreign Affairs. March/April 1998. pp. 66-79.

Turner, James E. (1986) *Atoms, Radiation, and Radiation Protection*. Elmsford, New York: Pergamon Press.

Vinacke, Harold M. (1950) *A History of the Far East in Modern Times*. New York: Appleton-Century-Crofts, Inc.

"Unnatural Disasters" by Janet Abramovitz. Worldwatch Paper 158, Worldwatch Institute. Oct. 2001.

UN Convention on the Prevention and Punishment of the Crime of Genocide (1945).

United States Constitution, Article 13, Section One. Declared ratified December 18, 1865.

Universal Declaration of Human Rights. Adopted and proclaimed by General Assembly Resolution 217 A (III) of 10 December 1948.

"Unnatural Disasters." Janet Abramovitz. Worldwatch Paper 158. October 2001. Worldwatch Institute.

Van Sertima, Ivan ed. (1990) *Blacks in Science: Ancient and Modern (Incorporating the Journal of African Civilizations April and November 1983 – Issues Vol.5, Nos. 1 &2)*. New Brunswick, New Jersey: Transaction Books.

Warren, James Francis (2000) *The Global Economy and the Sulu Zone: Connections, Commodities, and Culture*. Quezon City: New Day Publishers.

Washburn, Dennis C. (1995) *The Dilemma of the Modern*. New Haven: Yale University Press.

"Water Supply and Poor Communities: What's Price Got to Do With It?", Environmental Magazine Dec. 2003, p.24.

"Weapons of Mass Destruction". Richard K. Betts. Foreign Affairs. January/February 1998.

Weidenbaum, Murray and Hughes, Samuel. (1996) *Bamboo Network: How Expatriate Chinese Entrepreneurs Are Creating A New Economic Superpower in Asia*. New York: The Free Press.

Weiner, Norbert (1967) *The Human Use of Human Beings*. Avon Books.

"What Came Before DNA?" Carl Zimmer. Discover Magazine. June 2004. pp.34-7.

"What's Wrong With Xenotransplantation?" Campaign for Responsible Transplantation. http://www.crt-online.org/wrong.html

"Who Gave Mankind the Gift of WMD?" Pat Buchanan. WorldNetDaily August 28, 2002. Creator's Syndicate 2002.

"Wind Powering Native America". Winona LaDuke. Cultural Survival Quarterly: World Report on the Rights, Voices, and Visions of Indigenous People. Summer 2003. Vol. 27, Issue 2. pp. 73-74.

Wolff, Leon (1961) *Little Brown Brother*. Garden City, New York: Doubleday and Company, Inc.

Woodson, Carter. G. (1990) *The Miseducation of the Negro*. Lawrenceville, N.J.: Africa World Press.

Yoshida, Shigeru (1967) *Japan's Decisive Century 1867-1967*. New York: Frederic A. Praeger.

The Yurayaco Declaration of the Union de Medicos Indigenas Yageceros de la Amazonia Colombiana (UMIYAC). Yurayaco, Colombia, June 1999. Cultural Survival Quarterly. Summer 2003. p. 25.

Yun, Venerable Master Hsing trans. John Balcom, Ph.D. (2002) *On Buddhist Democracy, Freedom, and Equity.* Hacienda Heights, CA: Bucdha's Light Publishing.

Movies
Movie, Director, Studio, Subject Reference

12 Monkeys (1996), Director: Terry Gilliam, Studio: Universal
Science, Progress, Reactionary Politics

28 Days Later (2003) Danny Boyle, Studio: Twentieth Century Fox
Science and Progress

1984 (1984), Director: Michael Redford, Studio: MGM/UA
Security-based Governance Stalinism/Fascism

A.I. (2001), Director: Stephen Spielburg, Studio: Universal
Progress, Science and Technology

A Sound of Thunder (2004), Director: Peter Hyams, Studio: Warner
Linear Thinking, Science and Technology

Akira (1988), Director: Katsuhiro Otomo (Anime)
Science and Progress

Armageddon (1998), Director: Michael Bay, Studio: Touchstone
Linear Thinking, Oppositional Relationship with Nature, Man vs. Nature/God,
Progress, Science and Technology

Bicentennial Man (1999), Director: Chris Columbus, Studio: Touchstone
Progress, Technology (Robotics)

The Cat's Meow (2001), Director: Peter Bogdanovich, Studio: Lion's Gate
Mass Media

Contact (1997), Director: Robert Zemeckis, Studio: Warner
Linear Thinking, Oppositional Relationship with Nature, Man vs. Nature/God,
Progress, Science and Technology

The Core (2003), Director: Jon Amiel, Studio: Paramount
Linear Thinking, Oppositional Relationship with Nature, Man vs. Nature/God,
Progress, Science and Technology

Deep Impact (1998), Director: Mimi Leader, Studio: Paramount
Linear Thinking, Oppositional Relationship with Nature, Man vs. Nature/God,
Progress, Science and Technology

Frankenstein (1994), Director: Kenneth Branagh, Studio: Columbia/Tristar
Science/Progress

Gladiator (2000), Director: Ridley Scott, Studio: Umvd/Dreamworks - Rome
The Mob, Governance

Interview With A Vampire (1994), Director: Neil Jordan, Studio: Warner
Individualistic Materialism, Possession and Consumption Possession and
Control

The Island of Dr. Moreau (1977), Director: Don Taylor, Studio: MGM, UA
Science and Progress

Little Buddha (1994), Director: Bernardo Bertolucci, Studio: Miramax
Sustainability

Lord of the Rings - The Fellowship of the Ring (2001), Director: Peter
Jackson, Studio: New Line
Universalizing Human Nature

Matrix Revolutions (2003), Directors: Wachowski Brothers, Studio: Warner
Asymmetric Warfare

Minority Report (2002), Director: Steven Spielburg, Studio: Universal -
Science
Lack of Omniscience

Sky Captain and the World of Tomorrow (2004), Director: Kerry Conran,
Studio: Paramount
Progress, Universalizing Human Interest, Science and Technology

Stephen King's The Stand (1994), Director: Mick Garris, Studio: Lions Gate
Science and Technology/Progress

Star Wars II: Attack of the Clones (2002), Director: George Lucas, Studio: Twentieth Century Fox
Democratic Governance, Free Trade, Three Roads

Star Wars III: Revenge of the Sith (2005), Director: George Lucas
Democratic Governance

The Sum of All Fears (2002), Director: Phil Aiden Robinson, Studio: Paramount
Fascism

Terminator (1984), Director: James Cameron, Studio: MGM/UA
Universalizing Human Nature

To Live (1994), Director: Yimou Zhang, Studio: MGM/UA
Interconnectedness of Nature, Non-linear Thinking

The Year of Living Dangerously (1982), Director: Peter Weir, Studio: Metro-Goldwyn-Mayer
Free Press

Whale Rider (2003), Director: Niki Caro, Studio: New Line
Cultural Center

Index of Narrative Subject Headings by Chapter

CHAPTER 37 – YOUR SUBJECT NATION STATE'S ECONOMIC COLLAPSE

CHAPTER 38 – YOUR SUBJECT NATION STATE'S SOCIAL COLLAPSE

CHAPTER 45 – THE THREE ROADS THAT TODAY'S INTERDEPENDENT WORLD CAN TAKE

Glossary of Acronyms
(List of Acronyms)

AI	Artificial Intelligence
CCD	Cultural Cognitive Dissonance
CD	Cognitive Dissonance
CI	Cultural Imperialism
F-M	Free Market
FDI	Foreign Direct Investment
G-M	Genetically-Modified
IC	Individualized Care (Medicine)
IPM	Integrated Pest Management
IT	Information Technology
NGO	Non-government Organization
PSAC	Projection of Seemingly Associative Cognitions
PH	Public Health
SCA	Societal Conflict Agent
2nd CCD	Secondary (Cultural) Cognitive Dissonance
TNC	Transnational Corporation
UH	Universal Humanism
UN	United Nations
WHO	World Health Organization
WTO	World Trade Organization

ABOUT THE AUTHOR

J.F. Cummings is a researcher and consultant at a Tokyo think-tank that, through its collaborative research, consulting, and publishing efforts, works to support the full actualization of human potential and enhance the sustainability of families, communities, and nations. Clients are assisted by jointly developing culture-based national planning schemes, character education curricula, youth empowerment, entrepreneurship and business development, conflict resolution and reconciliation, anti-recidivism, and workforce development programs; resources for organizational development/ and capacity building, and providing advice on the application of sustainable technologies for healthcare, education, communications, utilities, and commerce.

Cummings' major research interests include Culture-based National Planning, Cultural Literacy and its Impact on the Sustainability of Communities and Nations; and The Role of Media and Education on Values Formation.

Some Recommended Titles by blue ocean press

**Parables of Milk and Might: Development Political Satire -
>>The Voices of the Affected<<**
By RAN (2008)
ISBN: 978-4-902837-21-8

Following over four decades of development politics, after the official end of colonialism in most countries in Africa, South America and Asia, it is difficult for the industrial countries to forego their economic interests in the developing countries, which are said to be independent. Their continued presence in these countries, controlling or dictating the trend of economic and political developments, is a proof of the protection of their interests.

Parables of Milk and Might is a satire on the international development sector, in particular, the relationship between the countries of the Global North and South. The book uses a wonderful combination of wordplay, metaphor, and humorous storytelling to get its message across.

From the author:
"The main purpose for writing this book is to use it to sensitize many people, both in the industrialized countries, as well as in the developing world, particularly in Africa and in Asia, the Caribbean and South American countries, about the negative effects of the global economic system, which is controlled by the powerful and wealthy countries, to the disadvantage of the developing countries. The sensitization will increase the awareness of people about the effects of this negative development, which is the cause of poverty, underdevelopment and conflicts in the world."

This book is translated from its original German.

What We Bury At Night:
Disposable Humanity
by Julian Aguon (2008)

ISBN: 978-4-902837-67-6

The fate of Micronesia is the fate of Sustainable Humanity. Micronesia is last domino in the quest to globalize the Earth into a singular monoculture. It is the region least "affected" by the increasingly global culture of conspicuous consumption and individualistic materialism. Micronesia is at a crossroads, as is the human race. If the last region on earth in which, among the majority of the population, communal living based on interconnectedness, extended families, shared resources, non-linear thinking, and a sustainable relationship with the natural environment is the norm is allowed to be destroyed, the future of humanity is truly in jeopardy. When imagination of indigenous youth and the viability of sustainable living are allowed to die, so does hope for the entire human race.

Micronesia is one of the last corners on earth where people, on the whole, still pattern life in humane and interdependent arrangements built on sustaining, life-supporting values, in short, where people still mostly function as people. This resilience, perhaps, is an offering of beauty - its contribution to the world.

This book is a series of essays describing the present day realities of the U.S.-Micronesia relationship through the eyes of the folk on the ground, being disappeared. Both elders and youth tell of the continuing harm of the U.S. colonial project in Micronesia, revealing how that project continues to starve the imaginations of entire peoples. Made up of more than 2,000 islands and atolls in three major archipelagos, the Carolines, the Marshalls, and the Marianas, Micronesia was known from the last World War until the 1970s as the Trust Territory of the Pacific Islands. All of it, the Republic of the Marshall Islands (RMI), the Federated States of Micronesia (FSM), the Republic of Palau (Belau), and the Commonwealth of the Northern Mariana Islands (CNMI), less Guam, which was cut from the rest after the Spanish-American war and lumped with the other 1898 Unfortunates: the Philippines, Puerto Rico, and Cuba. While the world looks away, this region of the planet is facing down death. Mostly losing. Current U.S. militarist and corporate plans for the region now threaten to destroy the life-affirming values that bind and sustain these ancient civilizations by deepening dispossession of the people.

Pathway to Change:
A Guide to Personal Transformation
by Martha R. Bireda, Ph.D.
ISBN: 978-4-902837-47-1 (2007)

Pathway To Change is a holistic approach to personal transformation that is based upon cognitive behavioral theory and emphasizes cognitive restructuring or belief system change. Participants in the process learn how to identify and modify erroneous and self-defeating beliefs and values that have led to poor choices and negative behaviors in the past. Correctional interventions that include a cognitive skills component have been found to have strong research support for their effectiveness.

Pathway to Change is a cognitive restructuring program that was created to break a cycle of self-destructive thoughts and behaviors in incarcerated populations. It has been implemented in prisons in the US for 10 years and has been highly effective in reducing the recidivism rates for the inmates who have gone through this process. Ideally, participants are taken through the *Pathway to Change* process by a certified PTC facilitator, but over the years we have found that this process is also effective on persons who seriously engage in the process in groups of their own making. This book is both a workbook for participants in a facilitated PTC workshop, as well as a tool for individual personal transformation for anyone who is "stuck".

In addition to its uses for self-therapy and anti-recidivism programs, PTC can also be used as a very effective tool in Workforce Development, Youth, Personal Empowerment, Employee Placement and Development, Career Counseling, Domestic Violence (for both perpetrators and victims), Substance Abuse, Delinquency Prevention, and Micro-enterprise/Entrepreneurship Programs.

Computing Reality

by Masudul Alam Choudhury & M. Shahadat Hossain

ISBN: 978-4-902837-13-7 (2007) - Hardcover
ISBN: 978-4-902837-01-3 (2008) - Softcover

Computing Reality is a rare and challenging research output in the area of cybernetic and system theory explaining the meaning behind the understanding, interpretation and application of scientific methodology for knowing scientific truth. The fundamental goal of Computing Reality is to explain how knowledge in scientific investigation can be derived, organized and deciphered in the light of unity of knowledge as the episteme. The book uses these foundational socio-scientific ideas in areas of philosophy of science, economics, society and science and computer modeling to explain specific socio-scientific problems in the light of the foundational conceptions and their application.

Computing Reality invites the reader into understanding a fresh new look at the nature of relations between reasoning, science, and society. Special reference is given to certain fundamental issues of economics and world-system in the context of liberalism, globalization and Islam. The technical along with a generalist treatment in the book presents a comprehensive originality of a phenomenological model whose origin lies in a systemic and cybernetic view of unity of knowledge.Some of the new ideas presented here can be of a substantively provocative nature to the serious student, academic and researcher in philosophy of science. The book is nonetheless written for the generalist informed reader as well, enabling the interface with today's increasing consciousness on the relationship between religion, morality, ethics, science and society. The book may be considered as a pioneering contributing to post-modernist criticism of foundational questions of science and society.

Ordering blue ocean press books

Books can be purchased and ordered from your local bookstore.

Books can also be purchased online from retailers such as:
Amazon sites (com, co.uk, co.jp, fr, ca, de), Barnes and Nobles (bn.com), Powells.com, Abebooks.com, Alibris.com, and other fine internet retailers.

Institutional Buyers, Booksellers, and Libraries can order books from the following wholesalers and distributors:

U.S. and Canada
Ingram Book Group (ipage, Ingram Library Services, Ingram Int'l):
Tel: (800) 937-0152 TOLL FREE
Ipage/Ingram: E-mail: ipage.ingrambook.com
Ingram Library Services Inc.: Tel: (800) 937-5300 TOLL FREE
E-mail: customer.requirements@ingrambook.com
Baker & Taylor:Tel.: (800) 775-1800 TOLL FREE
E-mail: btinfo@btol.com
NACSCORP (a wholly-owned, for-profit subsidiary of the National Association of College Stores): Tel: 800 321-3883
E-mail: orders@nacscorp.com

U.K. and Worldwide
Gardners Books: Tel: 0800 521777 FREEPHONE (UK)
Tel: +44 (0)1323 521777
UK Sales Enquires: sales@gardners.com
Export Sales Enquiries: export@gardners.com
Bertrams Freephone: Tel. 0800 333344 FREEPHONE (UK)
Tel: +44 871 803 6600
Email: orders@bertrams.com
Baker & Taylor: Tel. (800) 7750-1800 TOLL FREE (US)
Tel. (815) 802-2317
E-mail: btinfo@btol.com , keenj@btol.com
Ingram International: Tel.: (615) 793-5000
E-mail: ii.info@ingrambook.com